Adobe Photoshop
A Complete Course and Compendium of Features

Second Edition

Steve Laskevitch

Second Edition

Adobe Photoshop

A Complete

Course

and

Compendium

of Features

rockynook

Adobe Photoshop: A Complete Course and Compendium of Features
Second Edition

Steve Laskevitch
luminousworks.com

Editor: Jocelyn Howell
Project manager: Lisa Brazieal
Marketing coordinator: Katie Walker
Interior and cover design, layout, and type: Steve Laskevitch

ISBN: 979-8-88814-017-8
2nd Edition (1st printing, August 2023)

Rocky Nook Inc.
1010 B Street, Suite 350
San Rafael, CA 94901
USA

www.rockynook.com

Distributed in the UK and Europe by Publishers Group UK
Distributed in the U.S. and all other territories by Publishers Group West

Library of Congress Control Number: 2022950234

Printed in China

About the Author

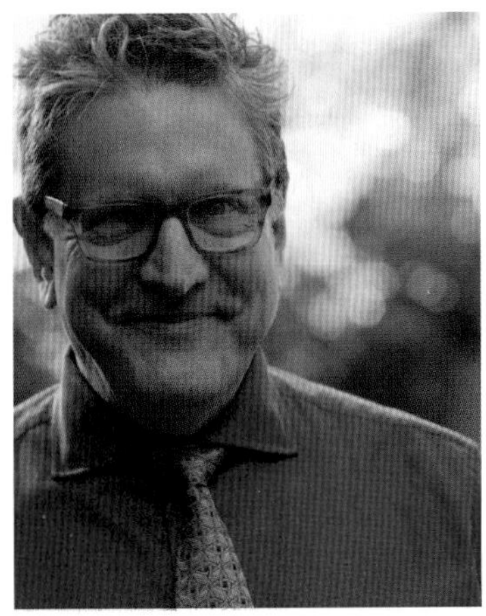

Steve Laskevitch is lead instructor and founder of Luminous Works, the only Adobe Authorized Training Center in the northwestern United States (https://luminousworks.com). He is an Adobe Certified Expert (and Adobe Certified Instructor) in Photoshop, Lightroom, Illustrator, and InDesign.

While studying as a physics undergraduate, Steve was invited to instruct a few courses and immediately fell in love with teaching. He discovered his creative passions while learning photography and designing posters and flyers for the organizations he led at university. The worlds of graphic design and photography led him merrily away from a career in physics.

Steve has spent the twenty-first century both teaching and doing desktop publishing and building production workflows for many companies and individuals. He's taught at Cornish College of the Arts (where he was awarded the Excellence in Teaching Award), University of Washington Professional & Continuing Education (nominated for their Excellence in Teaching Award), and Seattle Central College.

Steve has regularly helped Adobe Systems prepare expert- and instructor-certification exams, and for nearly five years he led the InDesign User Group in Seattle, InDesign's birthplace. Now he is Luminous Works' curriculum director and lead instructor, author of this volume and *Adobe InDesign: A Complete Course and Compendium of Features*, and speaker to user groups and at industry conferences.

Steve is obsessed with New Haven–style pizza. Don't tell, but the best of that is to be had in Portland, Oregon. Despite this fact, he and his wife teach and live in Seattle.

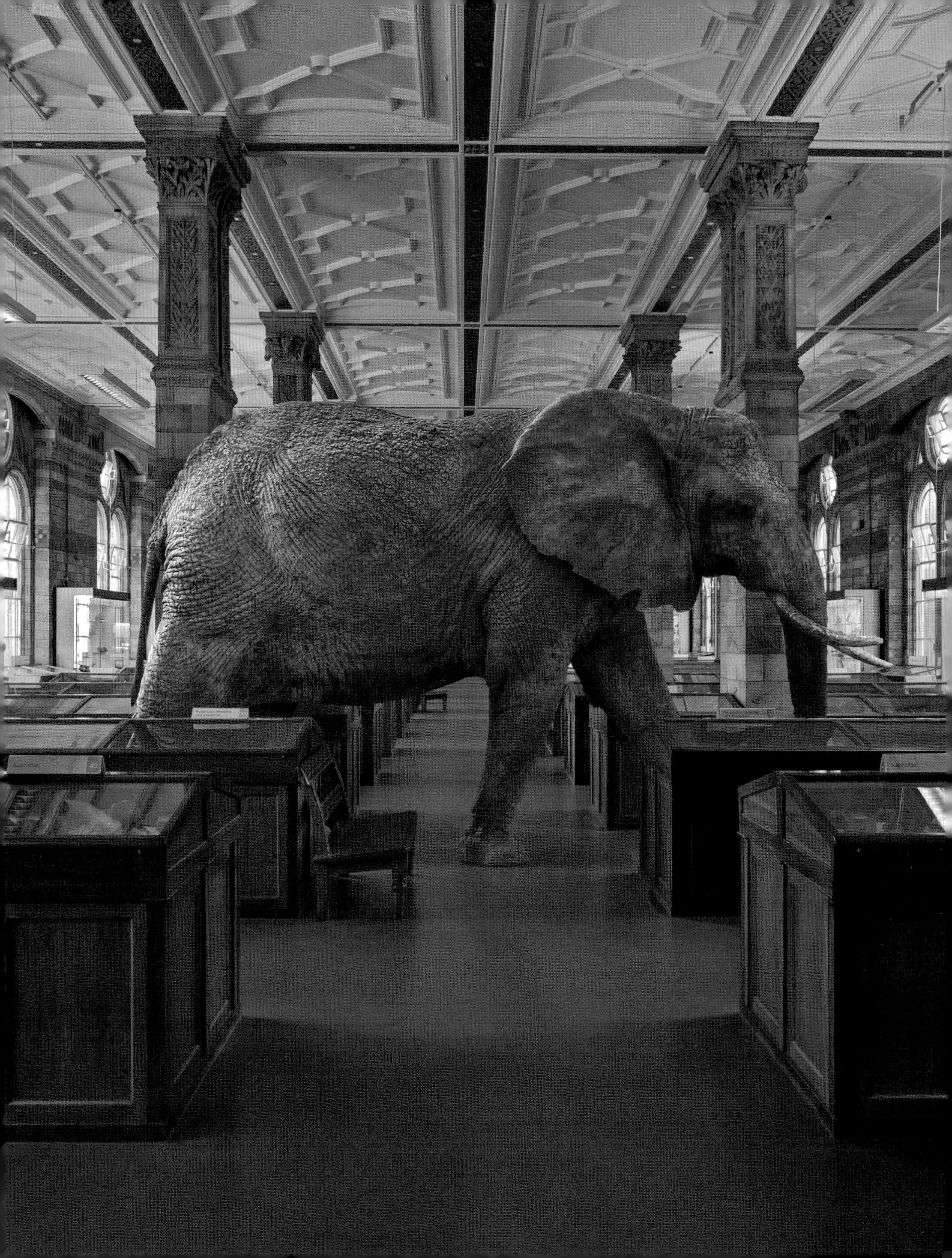

Acknowledgments

Let me address the obvious: no one gains any success entirely on their own. For me, there are too many people to thank, though all of them deserve my gratitude. But, for the sake of brevity, I will restrict myself to just a few.

Decades ago, while at university, several of my professors saw how much I enjoyed tutoring other students and noted that the tutoring appeared successful. It was then that I was given the opportunity to teach a few classes and discover the joy of the curriculum-building puzzle. I remember those mentors fondly.

Years later, Liz Atteberry, who ran one of the world's first Adobe Authorized Training Centers for which I worked, enabled and encouraged teaching the software I love to use. I'm forever grateful to her for giving me the chance to walk this happy path.

My Photoshop students over these decades have kept me inspired and, with their awesome questions, have allowed me to explore this application's deep secrets. To all of you, thanks.

To the Rocky Nook crew, especially my editor Jocelyn Howell, I thank you for being so fabulous to work with. It's a great partnership!

No greater inspiration is there than Carla Fraga, my wife. And no greater thanks are owed to anyone.

Steve Laskevitch
Seattle, March 2023

Contents

The Course

The Compendium

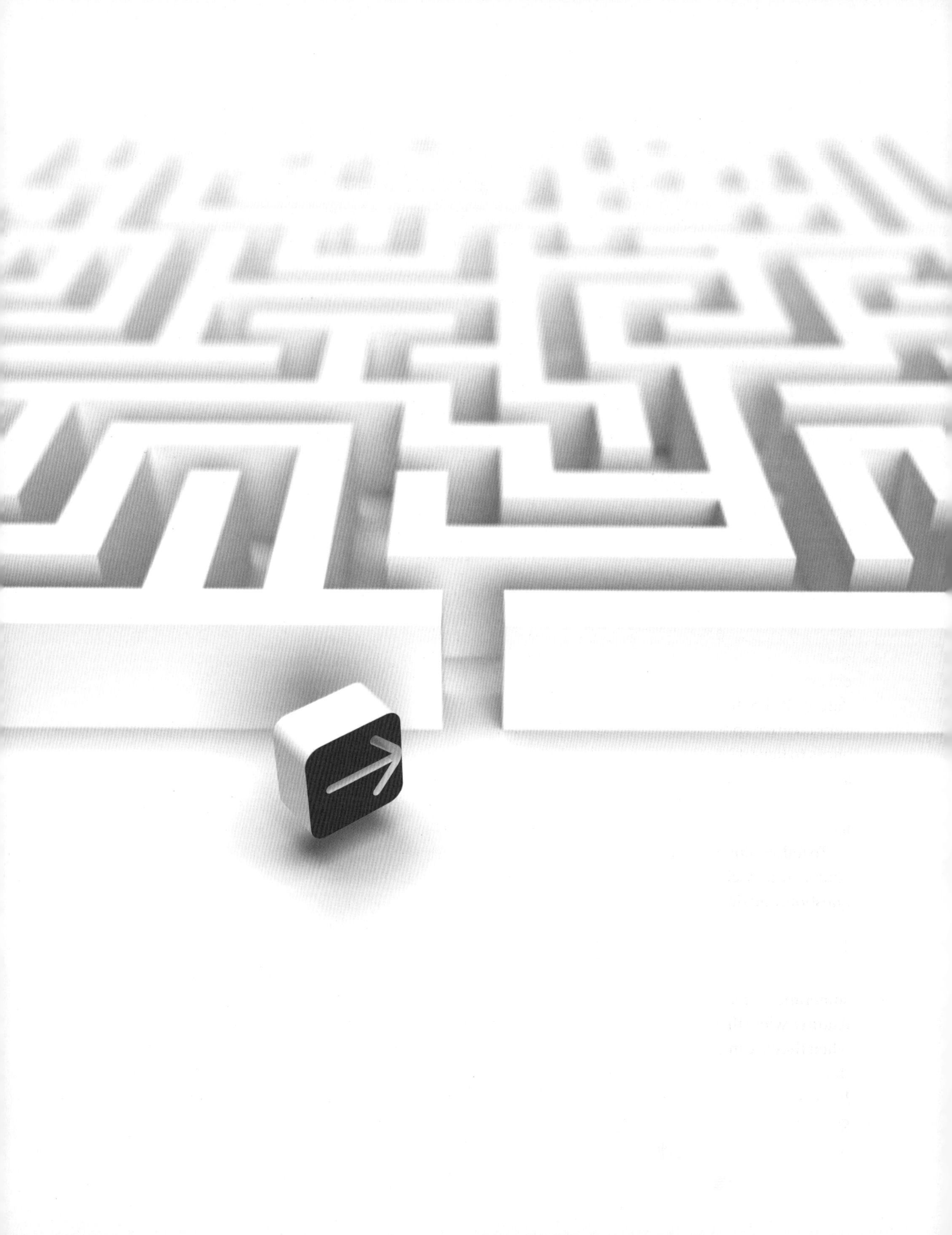

Start Here—An Introduction

Hi. I'm Steve, and I'll be your guide. In this book, you will be working your way through a full course curriculum that will expose you to all of the essential features and functions of Adobe Photoshop. Along the way, you'll learn the concepts and vocabulary of digital images. Between several larger projects are chapters of lessons. In those lessons, each action that I'd like you to try looks like this:

➡ This is what a lesson action looks like.

The paragraphs surrounding the action explain some of the why and how. For greater depth, the second section of this book is a Compendium of those features and functions, providing the "deep dive" needed for true mastery of this powerful application. Throughout the Course section, I will suggest readings in the Compendium section. Although you may be able to complete the entire course without them, I think if you do those readings you'll find yourself regularly nodding and muttering, "oh, that's why it works that way."

Software and Course Files

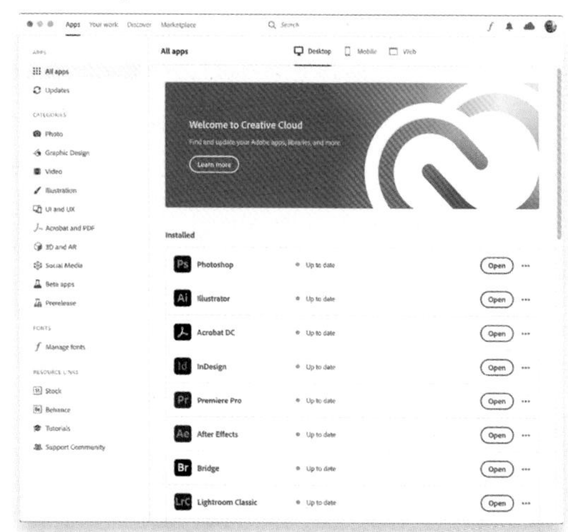

Have you installed Photoshop yet? If you work for a company with an enterprise license, it's likely your IT people have installed it for you. We will be using the Creative Cloud app as our hub for launching Adobe applications and accessing the services that come with a Creative Cloud (CC) license. This app also checks to make sure your software license is up to date, so it should remain running whenever you use your creative applications. I use the CC app's Preferences to have it launch on startup and auto-update software so I don't have to worry about it.

I most often launch Photoshop by clicking the Open button to the right of the Photoshop icon. If there's an update available, it'll be available in the Updates section.

To follow along with the projects and lessons in this book, you'll need the files. Launch your favorite web browser and go to rockynook.com/photoshopCandC2E, answer a simple question, and download the files. Put them somewhere convenient (and memorable).

Photoshop Versions

Beta To include the most up-to-date features in this book, I used Photoshop 2023, and sometimes a beta version of it (which you can access, too). That means I'm showing a few features while they're still in development, and they may look or behave slightly differently when they are in general release and this book is in your hands. To signal that a feature is in flux, I'll use the icon you see at the beginning of this paragraph. If you would like to try the Photoshop beta, look for Beta apps on the left-hand side of the CC app. You, too, can see and guide Photoshop's future.

Image File Formats

Raster and Vector

Digital image files fall into two major categories: *raster* images, those composed of pixels, and *vector* graphics, which use geometry. The majority of the files you will use in the course are raster images. We will also use a few vector graphics, made in both Adobe Illustrator and Photoshop. Since we'll be spending so much time with pixels, however, it's best to know just a little bit more about them before we start our lessons.

The word "pixel" stands for "picture element," and the idea to use many small elements to compose a picture is an ancient one.

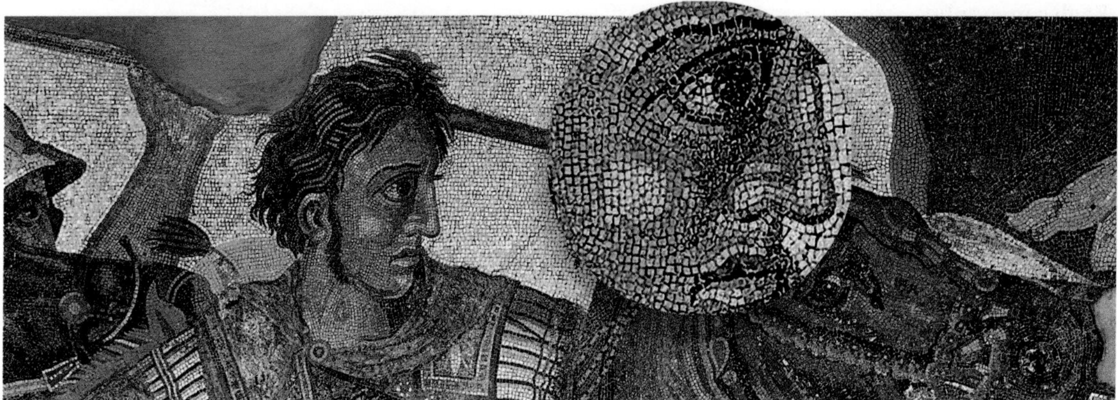

If we have enough pixels, packed together tightly enough, we can believe we see an image. Electronic displays use this principal and so does imaging software. The measure of the pixel density in an image is called its *resolution*, and it is measured either in pixels per inch (ppi) or pixels per centimeter (ppcm), depending on where you live. I apologize to my readers outside the United States, but I will most often use pixels per inch.

Some use the word "resolution" a little differently. When referring to video or displays, some will refer to the number of pixels across the width or height of the device. For example, "1080p" refers to images and devices that are 1,080 pixels tall, and "4K" refers to those that are approximately 4,000 pixels wide. I call this a measure of "pixel dimensions." If you stand too close to a 200-inch 4K display, the image may look more like the mosaic above than a pleasing image. That's because its resolution (its density) is only 20 ppi. But the 27-inch 4K display in front of me now has a resolution of almost 150 ppi, rendering this text very sharply.

Photoshop users may care about both definitions. Web and interface designers worry about the proportion of a screen an image will occupy, and thus pixel dimensions play a large role for them. Images intended for print require a high density of pixels to look pleasing.

If an image has too many or too few pixels, it can be *resampled*. Photoshop possesses several algorithms from which we can choose to achieve results with the highest fidelity. There are frequent updates and improvements to this process so beware of old advice. Don't tell anyone, but we can often reliably double the resolution of some images, or more. The results are not as good as starting with an image of that many pixels, of course, but if we're lucky, few will notice.

File Formats

There are many file formats to choose from when saving your work from Photoshop. The choice depends on the needs of your recipient and what kind of data needs to be preserved. Most of these formats hold only raster data, whereas SVG and PDF can hold both raster and vector data. Also, one can include data in these formats either by opening those files directly in Photoshop or by "placing" them, usually as something called a Smart Object, which is covered in both the Course and the Compendium sections of this book.

DNG & Raw Files

Many digital cameras can save their images as raw files. Raw data is not even pixels yet! Each sensor photosite has an electrical charge on it. When light hits it, the charge increases: more light, more charge. A raw "image" is really a record of all the changes in charge that occured in the mosaic of photosites.

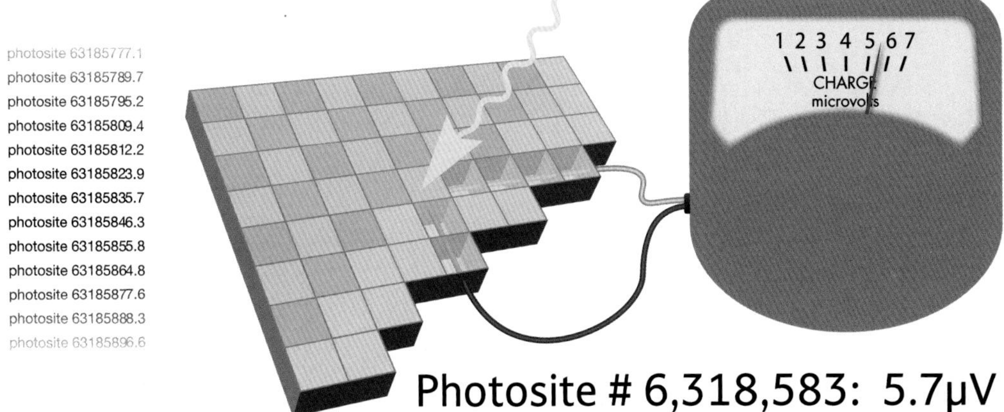

Every camera manufacturer has its own proprietary raw file format—one that contains all the data recorded by the sensors. These include NEF (Nikon) and CR2 (Canon), as well as many other formats. It takes software to interpret ("demosaic") that data as a raster image . Photoshop, through its plugin Adobe Camera Raw (ACR), is precisely that software. Unfortunately, that support does not extend to adding metadata (keywords, copyright) or saving ACR edits into these manufacturer-proprietary formats. For that, there is the Adobe Digital Negative (DNG) format. Unless you use DNG, metadata is saved in an accompanying "sidecar" file or a central database—indirect at best. Some of the files used in the course are raw files (DNGs, actually).

Photoshop (PSD) & Large Document Format (PSB)

Most of the files we will use in the course are Photoshop's "native" file format, Photoshop Document (PSD). After completing edits in Photoshop, it's important to save your image in a format that stores all the structure and information you have added so you can access it all when you open the file later. PSD stores all of that information, including Channels, Layers, and more. PSD files also provide powerful integration features when used with other Adobe products like InDesign and Illustrator.

Photoshop PSD files can support file sizes up to 2GB. For the majority of images, this is sufficient. But in the real world of digital imaging, it is possible to have much larger files. Photoshop supports these by using the Large Document Format (PSB). This format supports all of the features of PSD files, but also supports files of any size. It is also the format used for the content of a layer type called a Smart Object.

TIFF

Tagged Image File Format (TIFF) is an industry standard. In many ways, a basic TIFF is just a big array of pixels stored in a large file, although it can also preserve much of what the Photoshop format does. Also, depending on the options chosen when saving it, a TIFF may be accessible to someone who does not have Photoshop. Finally, TIFFs are typically saved *losslessly*. That is, no data is lost unless you specify that it is. That stands in stark contrast to the next format.

JPEG

JPEGs (Joint Photographic Experts Group) are ubiquitous because they can be viewed on any device by any user. They have file sizes that are much smaller than TIFFs, for example. Does that sound too good to be true? There is one issue: they achieve their small file sizes by discarding data. That may not be a problem for snapshots from a party, but may matter greatly for photos from a once-in-a-lifetime vacation or expensive location shoot.

We often receive JPEGs from others. So if we open and edit one, we'll need to save it in a lossless format to arrest any further degradation. PSD or TIFF will do nicely, as we'll see.

PNG

Unlike JPEGs, PNGs (Portable Network Graphics) can contain transparent or translucent pixels. Also unlike JPEGs, PNGs use lossless compression to make their file sizes smaller than a simple recording of the color (and opacity) of each pixel, but the result has exactly the same quality. This makes PNGs a good choice for graphics like logos that, for some reason, must use a raster format rather than vector.

SVG

Scalable Vector Graphics (SVG), whose name I find redundant, is the primary vector format that is used for web design. Although most designers create SVG files from Adobe Illustrator, you may create them from Photoshop as well. If you attempt to open an SVG directly in Photoshop (rather than place it as a Smart Object), Photoshop will ask you how it should be "rasterized," that is, turned into pixels.

PDF

Adobe's ubiquitous Portable Document Format (PDF) is a broadly supported way to provide your documents to someone who doesn't have Photoshop. It retains vector and raster (pixel) data. As with SVGs, opening a PDF often results in its being rasterized, becoming a simple image.

A Note Regarding Keyboard Shortcuts

To be efficient in Photoshop, or any application, we should take advantage of time-saving features like shortcuts. I will always share menu-driven ways to achieve our ends (when such exist), but I'll encourage faster ways too. A comprehensive list of shortcuts is in the Appendix of this book. Wherever shortcuts appear, the Mac shortcut precedes the shortcut for Windows: ⌘-Z/Ctrl-Z is the universal shortcut for the menu item Edit > Undo.

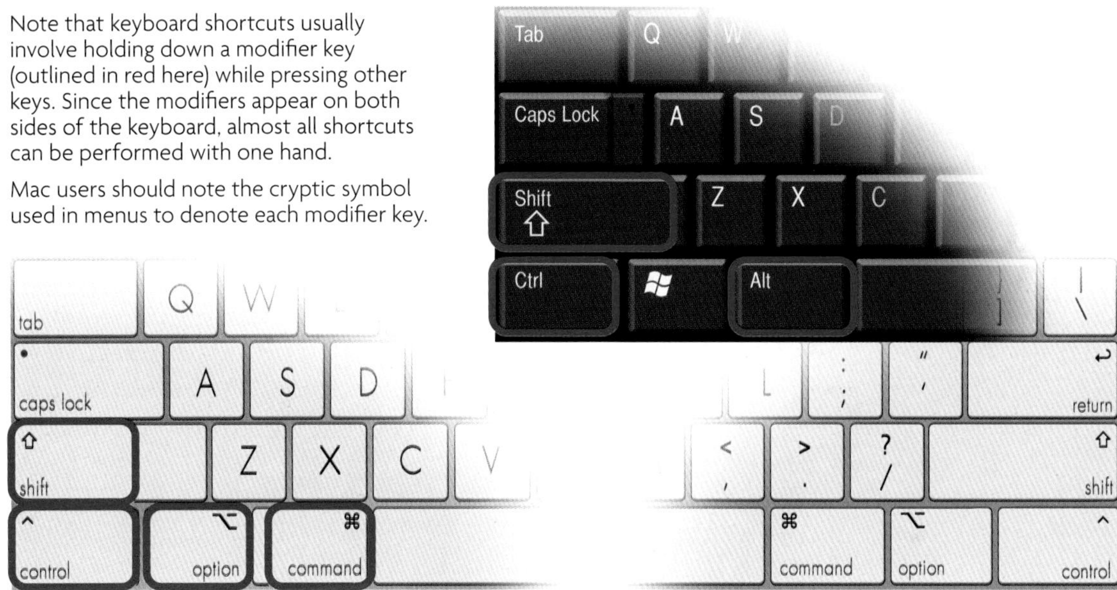

Note that keyboard shortcuts usually involve holding down a modifier key (outlined in red here) while pressing other keys. Since the modifiers appear on both sides of the keyboard, almost all shortcuts can be performed with one hand.

Mac users should note the cryptic symbol used in menus to denote each modifier key.

THE COURSE

1 Preliminary Tuning

In this brief chapter, we configure a few preferences and adjust the Photoshop workspace to make this daunting application more our own. In the process, we learn a little vocabulary too.

Then we'll be in position to really play this instrument.

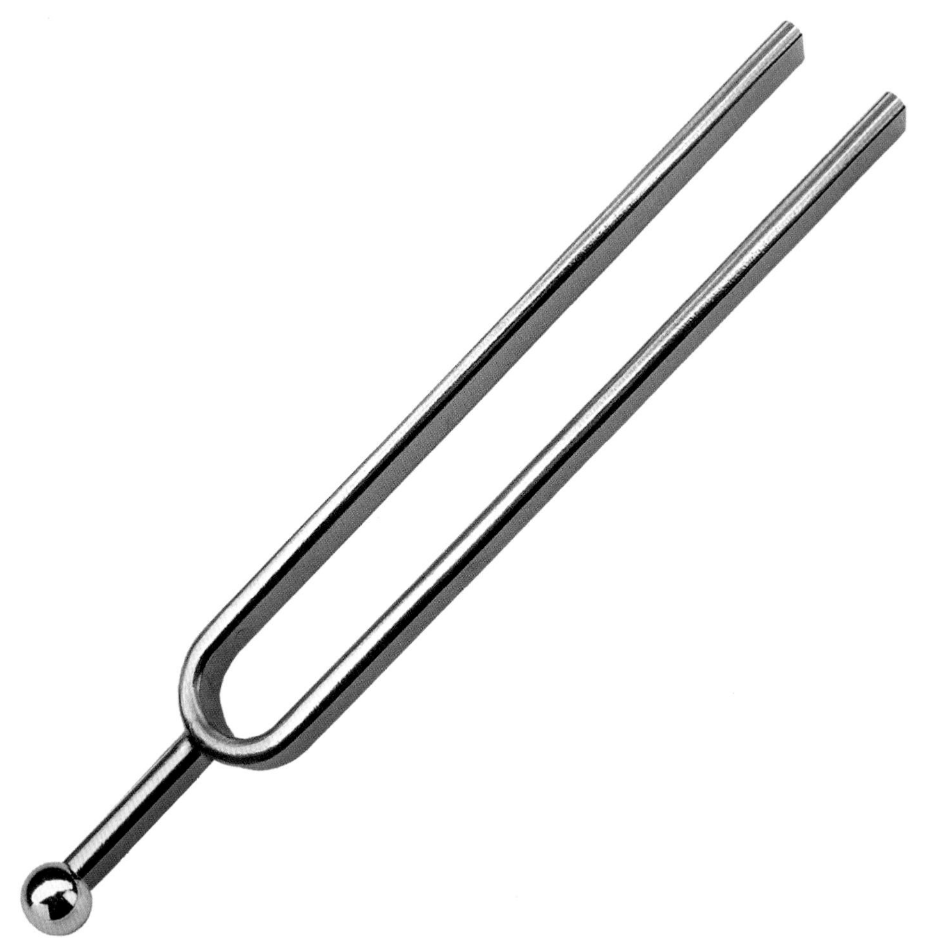

Preferences

For our first exercise, these few suggestions on how to configure Photoshop will do. More suggestions will be made throughout this course. To make our user experience as pleasant as possible, let's adjust our Preferences. In the future, you may use the included find field (in the upper-right of the Preferences dialog box) to locate harder-to-find Preferences.

- It's quick and easy to get to the Preferences: On a Mac, use the Photoshop menu > Settings (macOS Ventura or newer) or Photoshop > Preferences (older macOS versions); on Windows, go to the Edit menu > Preferences. Or use the shortcut ⌘-K/Ctrl-K.

Interface

This book makes extensive use of screenshots (pictures of my screen while using Photoshop). To make these as legible as possible, I'm going to make Photoshop's user interface a little less dark and murky. If you wish your screen to match these images, you may do the same.

- Click Interface on the left side of the Preferences dialog box. Choose whichever Color Theme you wish. I'm using the lightest one.
- In the Presentation section, you may change the font size of user interface ("UI") elements. I use Large, which is not very large at all. The entire user interface can be scaled to match. This is possibly useful on high-resolution displays.

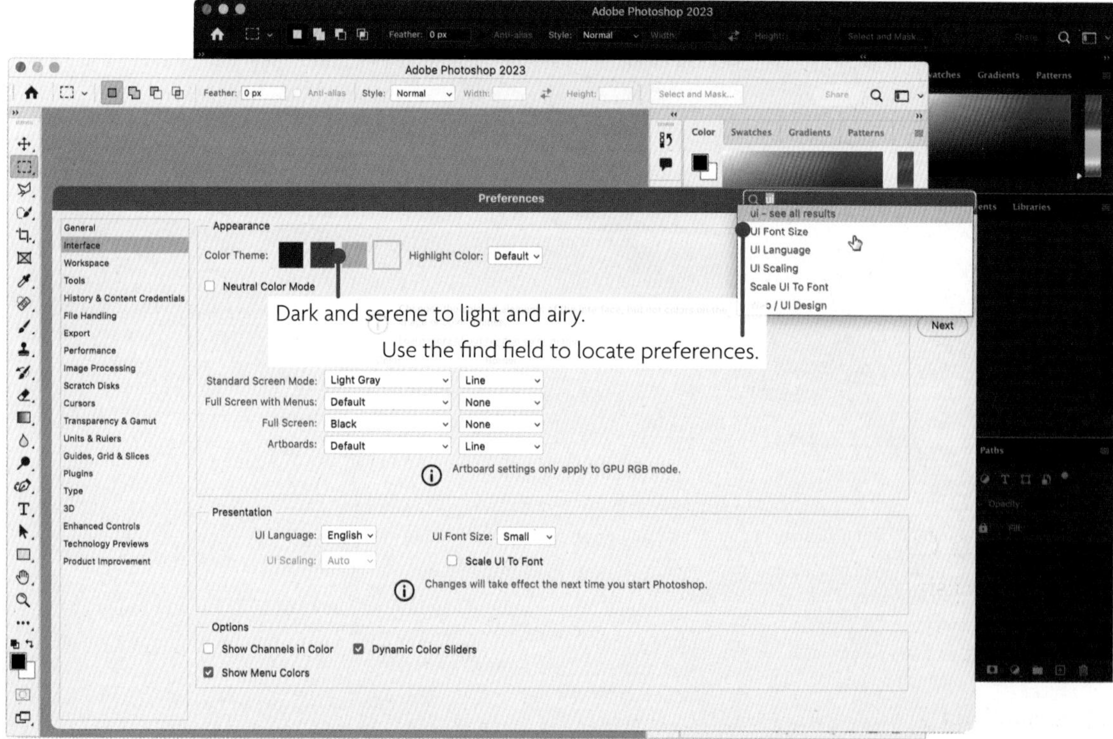

History & Content Credentials

If you work as a journalist or historian, or you simply want your audience to know that you've done nothing exceptional or devious with your images, you can attach data to your image that establishes provenance in accordance with the Coalition for Content Provenance and Authenticity (C2PA). At the bottom of the History & Content Credentials preferences is a link to learn more.

File Handling

There are several annoyances that I would like to prevent for both of us. Sometimes, when saving files of certain formats, Photoshop will interrupt the process with alerts and dialog boxes that are needless at best, and are often confusing to new users.

Also, crashes happen. So we've been taught to save often, which is good advice, including in Photoshop. Luckily, Photoshop saves recovery data in case we forget to save our files as frequently as we aspire to.

What follows are my suggestions (with explanations) for settings that will save time and minimize annoying messages.

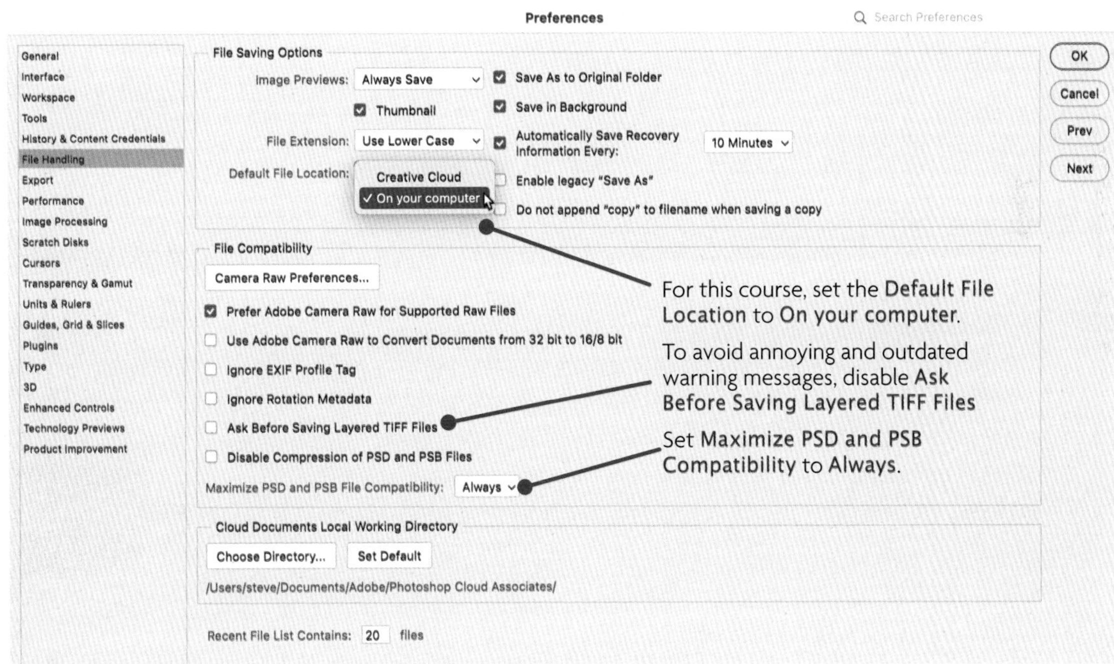

Save As to Original Folder

For those occasional instances when I save a copy of a file, I usually want it to be in the same folder as the original. Of course, it's easy to choose a different location. This preference checkbox makes the original file's folder the first suggestion.

- Ensure that the checkbox for this option is checked.

Default File Location

Adobe wants you to be able to access your files from any location, on any device, and offer others a chance to collaborate. These things are most easily done if files are saved to Adobe's cloud servers.

Of course, you can choose to save files to your computer instead. In every Save As dialog box is the option to switch. When you find you use one more than the other, set your preference here. For the purposes of the Course in this book, it's probably best to choose your computer.

➡ Set Default File Location to On your computer.

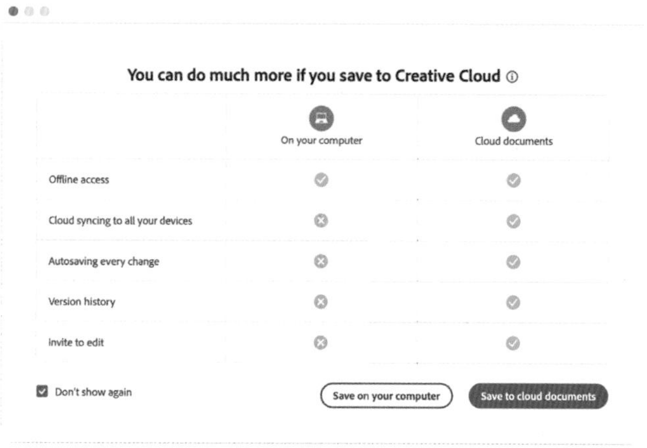

If you don't set this preference now, the default will be to Save to Creative Cloud. In a Save As dialog box, we click the On your computer button, which triggers yet another message that tells us how much better life would be saving to the cloud.

For now, insist on saving locally: tick the box to Don't show again, then click Save on your computer yet again. By all means, when the Course is completed, you may improve your life and work collaboratively and across devices by changing this preference to save to the cloud. See this chapter's next section for more on that.

You can do much more if you save to Creative Cloud ⓘ

	On your computer	Cloud documents
Offline access	✓	✓
Cloud syncing to all your devices	✗	✓
Autosaving every change	✗	✓
Version history	✗	✓
Invite to edit	✗	✓

☑ Don't show again — Save on your computer — Save to cloud documents

Automatically Save Recovery Information Every...

Although Photoshop isn't saving your actual file, this is still useful in the event of a crash. When you next restart the application, Photoshop will show you a likeness of the document you were working on. If this option is set to 10 Minutes, that is the maximum amount of work you will have lost. You should know that large, complex documents take longer to save, and so does their recovery information. During that time, Photoshop runs more slowly.

➡ Choose a frequency that reflects your level of caution.

Layered TIFF Files and Maximize PSD and PSB File Compatibility

Layers are the most important feature in Photoshop and there are several file formats that use them. When you save a document that contains layers and choose one of these formats, you are presented with odd warnings.

Saving to a TIFF format will prompt an obvious warning that adding layers increases file size. You can disable that warning here. Photoshop's native format, Photoshop Document (PSD), and its close cousin for documents larger than 2 gigabytes, Large Document format (PSB), also prompt you when first saving a document with layers. To better ensure that these files can be opened with other versions of the program, and to generate a usable preview inside other applications, we need to maximize the file's compatibility.

➡ Disable the option to Ask Before Saving Layered TIFF Files, and choose Always for the option to Maximize PSD and PSB File Compatibility.

Amusing fact: the letters of the extension for Photoshop's Large Document format, PSB, stand for "**P**hotoshop **B**ig!"

Image Processing

This is a new and growing page. As Adobe offers its cloud computing services for more Photoshop processes, look for more options to appear here. At the moment, we are able to choose whether the Select Subject algorithm is performed on our own devices or in the cloud. The former is faster, the latter is better. If you've got a good internet connection, take advantage of the cloud processing!

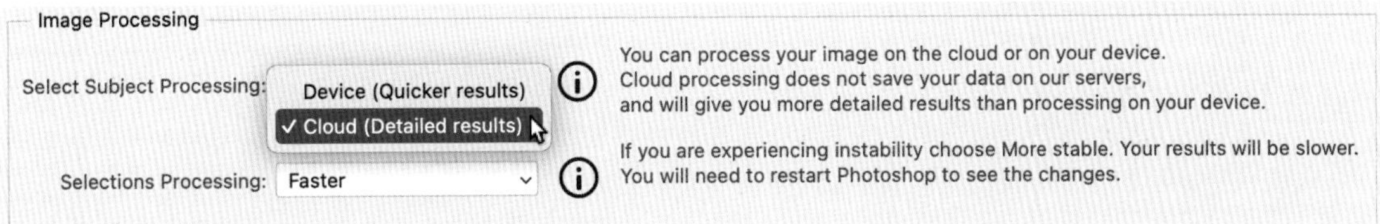

Performance

There is likely nothing you need to change in these preferences. But I'd like you to be aware of something. Many applications, Photoshop included, rely increasingly on a computer's graphics processor (its GPU) to do its work. If the one installed on your computer is supported, it will be listed here and the Use Graphics Processor box will be checked. Some troubleshooting steps require you to disable and/or enable that setting.

Technology Previews

This preference is where you can enable experimental features that vary with version. Often, these features ship with the application eventually. In the version that's current as I write this book, the previewed feature called Preserve Details 2.0 Upscale is available. It's an artificial intelligence–assisted way to "upsample" an image. That is, when pixels are added, this method keeps important details (like hair) sharp without damaging softer transitions (like skin). Check on this part of the Preferences after updating to see what's new.

Note: I'll let you know what other Preferences may need to be adjusted as we go forward.

➡ Click OK so we can adjust the interface a bit more.

Save to the Cloud or Computer?

As mentioned in the discussion of File Handling Preferences, we can choose to save documents to our computer or on Adobe's servers as cloud documents. The first time we choose Save As (or until we check the Don't show again box and change our preferences), we see this dialog box:

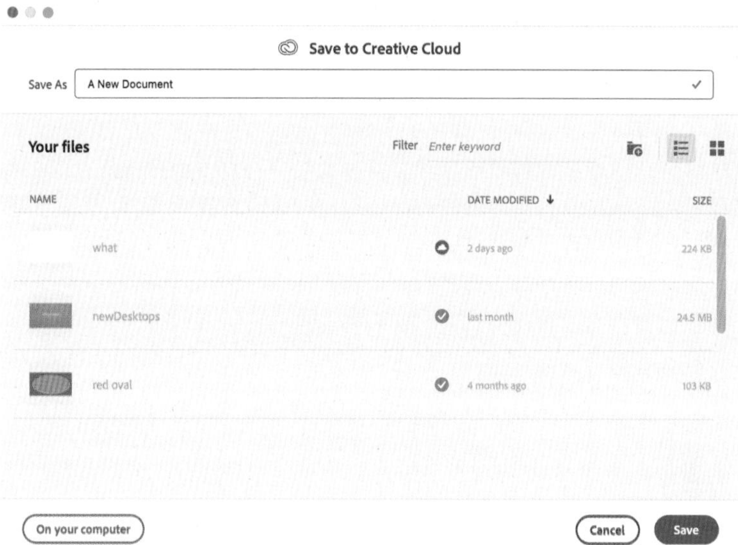

Even if we choose to not see this, we will still have the option to Save to cloud documents from the standard Save As dialog. We can see and open what we've saved there from the Creative Cloud desktop app, too. Reminder: the File Handling Preferences is another place to choose your preferred default.

Version History Panel

One of the advantages of saving to the cloud is having a version history for your documents. If you realize you liked the way an image was last week, you can revert to it, for example. Choose Window > Version History to access this new panel. You can access files you've saved to cloud documents by going to Files > Your files in the Creative Cloud desktop app. There, on the left, you can access your libraries as well. Click the Your files icon ( ). Once a cloud doc is open, you edit it as normal. However, some seconds after you save, a new version will appear in the Version History panel.

You likely will not care about every version—you might be hitting Save periodically just out of caution. But if a version appears that you wish to restore later, Mark it by clicking the bookmark icon to its right (see the figure that follows). You'll be given the option to name it. Do so in a way that will help identify it later.

The ellipsis icon (...) shows a menu with several options, including a way to rename the version (in case "final_14b" wasn't good enough).

You can choose Revert to this version if the current state of the document no longer pleases you. This is good if you've done so many edits that you've run out of entries in the History panel. Or if you've saved a faulty version more recently than a good one. Open the faulty document, then restore it to the superior version.

If you need a closer look at a version just to be sure it's better than what you've got, or you want to show a colleague next to you, choose Open in a new tab. Then you can deeply compare without risking a premature reversion.

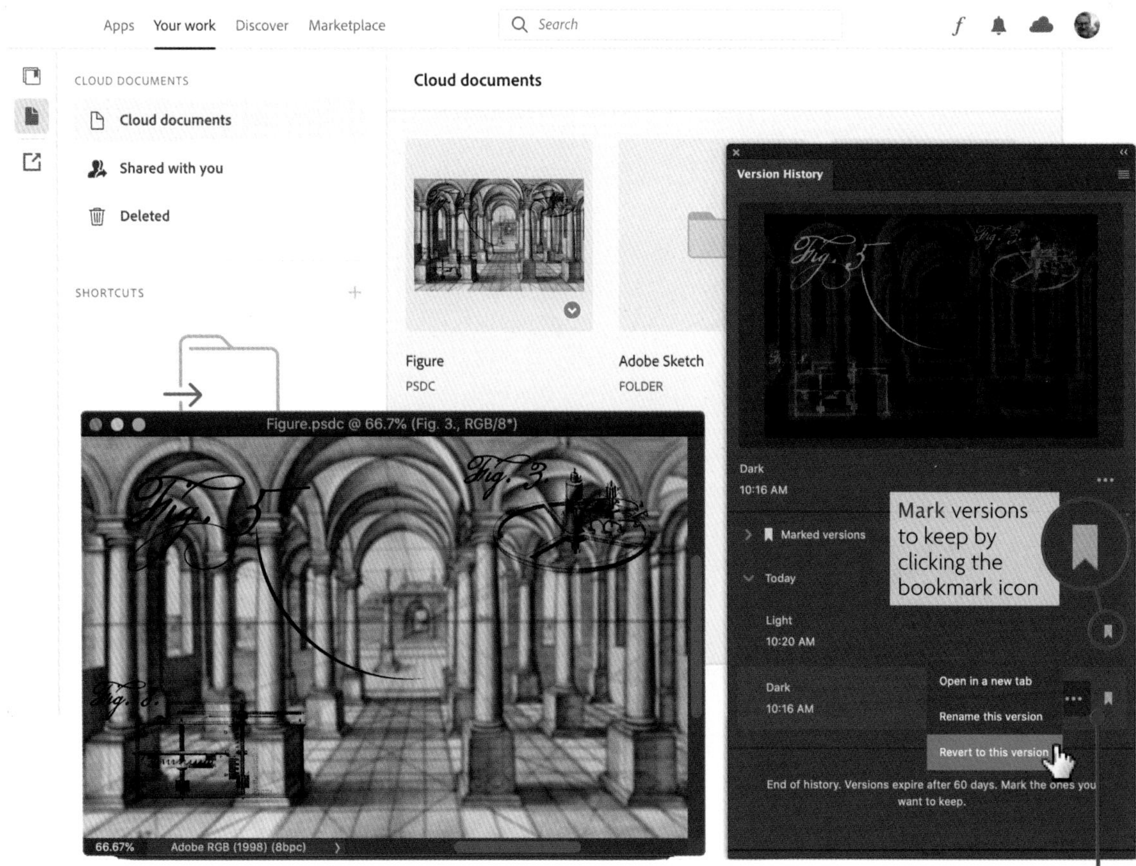

Each time you edit then save a cloud document, a new version appears in the Version History panel. It can take some time, be patient.

Versions will evaporate after one month. If you want one to linger, Mark it by clicking the bookmark icon to its right. You'll be given the option to name for easier identification, too. Use the ellipsis (...) for more options.

Collaboration

Via the Share button in Photoshop's Options Bar, you can invite others to safely edit your cloud files collaboratively. This is a new and developing feature in Photoshop, so expect more elaborate ways to share the workload.

Configuring the Workspace

When you first install Photoshop, some features that you'll need frequently are out of sight, and some that you'll need only infrequently are taking up lots of space. Let's fix this!

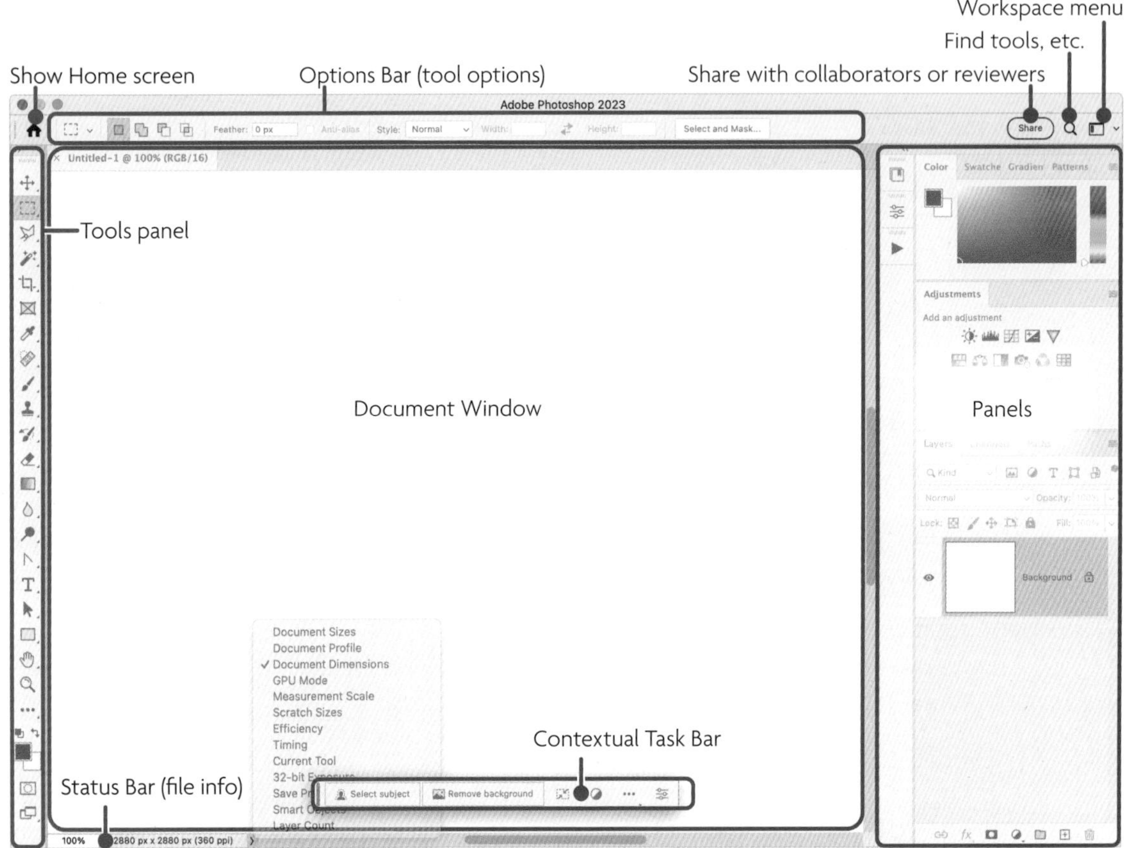

In the figure above, you can see Photoshop's basic geography. If you're using Microsoft Windows, you'll notice that it's extremely similar to the view on the Mac from which this image was made. The area where we work is called the document window. It is surrounded by panels. On the left is the Tools panel. You will soon learn that we switch tools very frequently. On the right are other panels—initially, some are expanded and at least one is collapsed to nothing more than an icon. Later you will find the right side populated by a great number of panels. Just above the document window is the Options Bar. Luckily, here you can find many options that each tool offers.

At the top of the stack of panels is small button with << or >> in it. When clicked, it collapses or expands the panels below it. Clicking it again reverses the process.

You can adjust each panel's height by grabbing the "bar" separating them—watch for the two-headed arrow, then click and drag to resize the panels above and below the bar.

Incidentally, while your attention is on the upper-right part of Photoshop's interface, note the several icons above the panels. The magnifier opens a search window that you use to search the help system, stock images, Photoshop's features, and your own images (if you use Lightroom). The Share button allows you to share images via various apps on your computer.

Most useful to us at the moment is the button between those two: the Workspace menu. It lists various kinds of tasks that require different panels and tools. Choosing a task like Painting will change both the panels on the right to allow elaborate brush control and the Tools panel to include all Photoshop tools that use a painting metaphor. Returning to the Essentials workspace shows us where we started. We will create our own workspace.

Example: The Painting workspace changes both the tools and panels.

Dock and Arrange Panels

We'll alter the Essentials workspace slightly to give us more room to move and to reveal the panels we need most often.

The panels we see on the right are currently "docked." That is, they form columns and can be docked next to other docks. Any panel can be docked by dragging it by its name to where you'd like to dock it. A blue highlight will reveal where it'll go.

- Choose Essentials from the Workspace menu.
- Move the Libraries panel and the Properties panel to the collapsed dock just to the left of the Color panel. (See the figure below.)

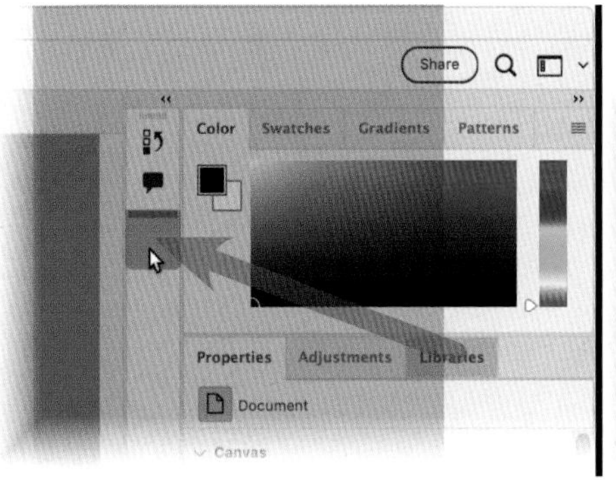

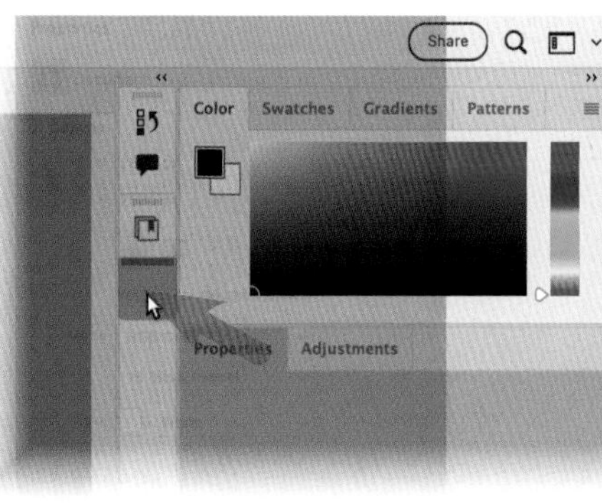

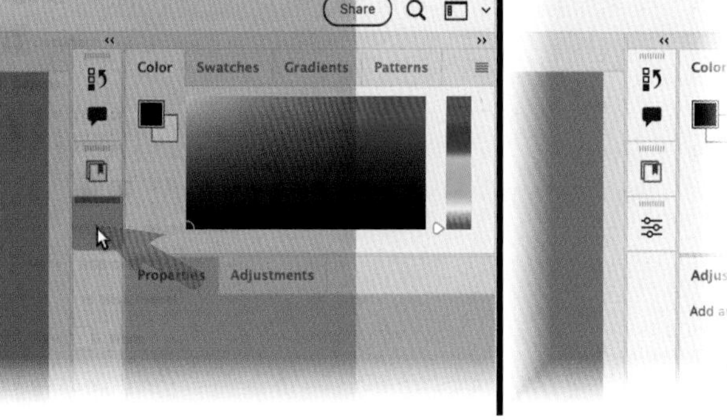

Drag the Libraries panel to the collapsed dock, just under the icon that's already there. Watch for the blue! Then do the same for the Properties panel.

Create a New Workspace

This new arrangement is pleasant! One click on the icons in the collapsed dock reveals them, and another click conceals them again.

- Since the panels appear to be just as we'd like them (for now), capture that arrangement by returning to the Workspace menu and choosing New Workspace…. Give it a name: I'm going with "A better start." Check the box for Toolbar too. If any of those panels go missing, or the expected tools aren't available in the Tools panel, or if the panels are simply messy, you can choose Reset A better start from the Workspace menu anytime.

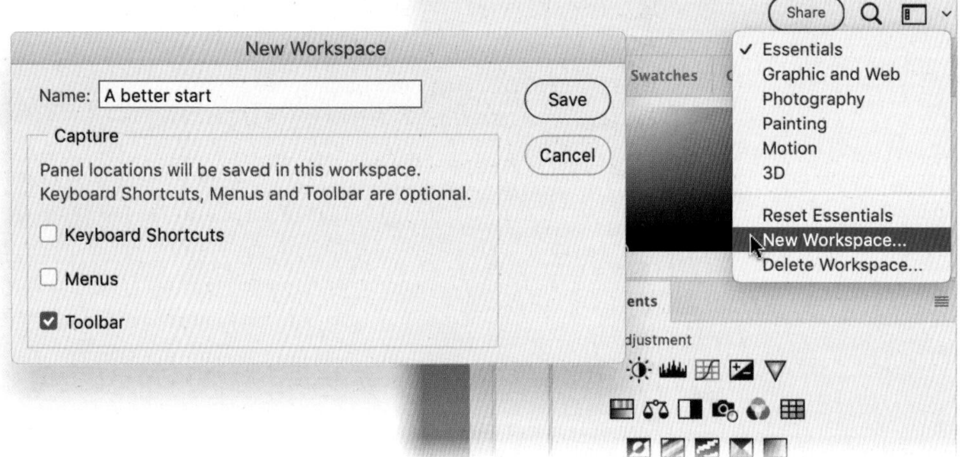

My friend John Cornicello, a wise Photoshop user, likes to keep the Tools panel on the right as well. He moves it by the texture at its top to the very right edge of the screen so that all his tools and panels are in the same place. For now, however, I will keep the tools in their original position.

It's very cool how much we can customize the interface! We can edit which tools are shown, the keyboard shortcuts, and even which menu items are visible. Consider the pranking possibilities!

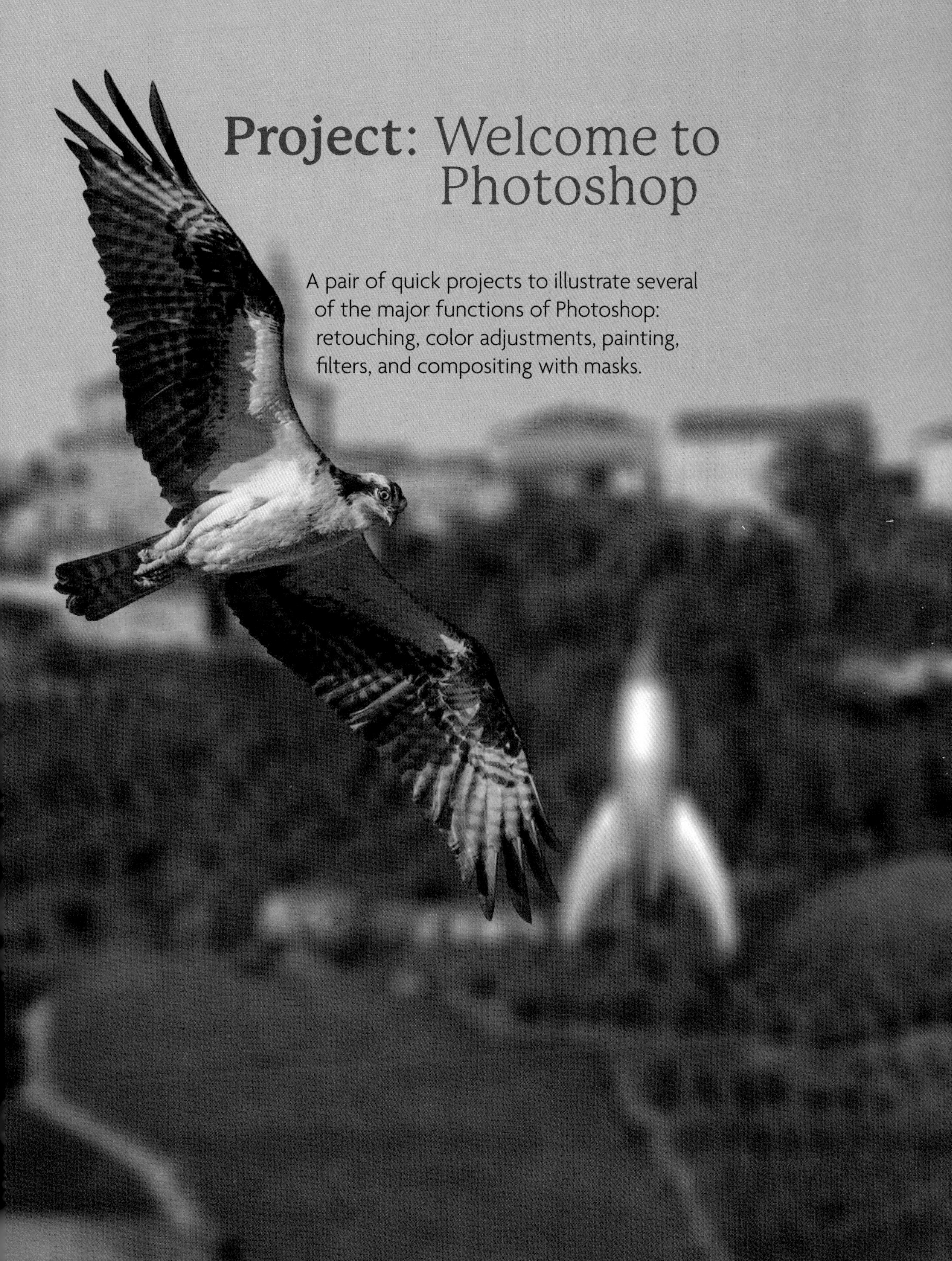

Project: Welcome to Photoshop

A pair of quick projects to illustrate several of the major functions of Photoshop: retouching, color adjustments, painting, filters, and compositing with masks.

Lesson A: Intro to Layers

Let's start with a short explanatory exercise. Do you remember where you put the files you downloaded? In the main folder there is a folder called "Project A- Welcome" with the files we need for this project.

From the "Project A- Welcome" folder, open the image called "trading_faces.psd."

Backgrounds vs Pixel Layers

The most important feature in Photoshop is the Layers panel and what it contains. The longest (and first) chapter in this book's Compendium is called "Layers & Smart Objects." I can promise it will likely be the one you refer to most.

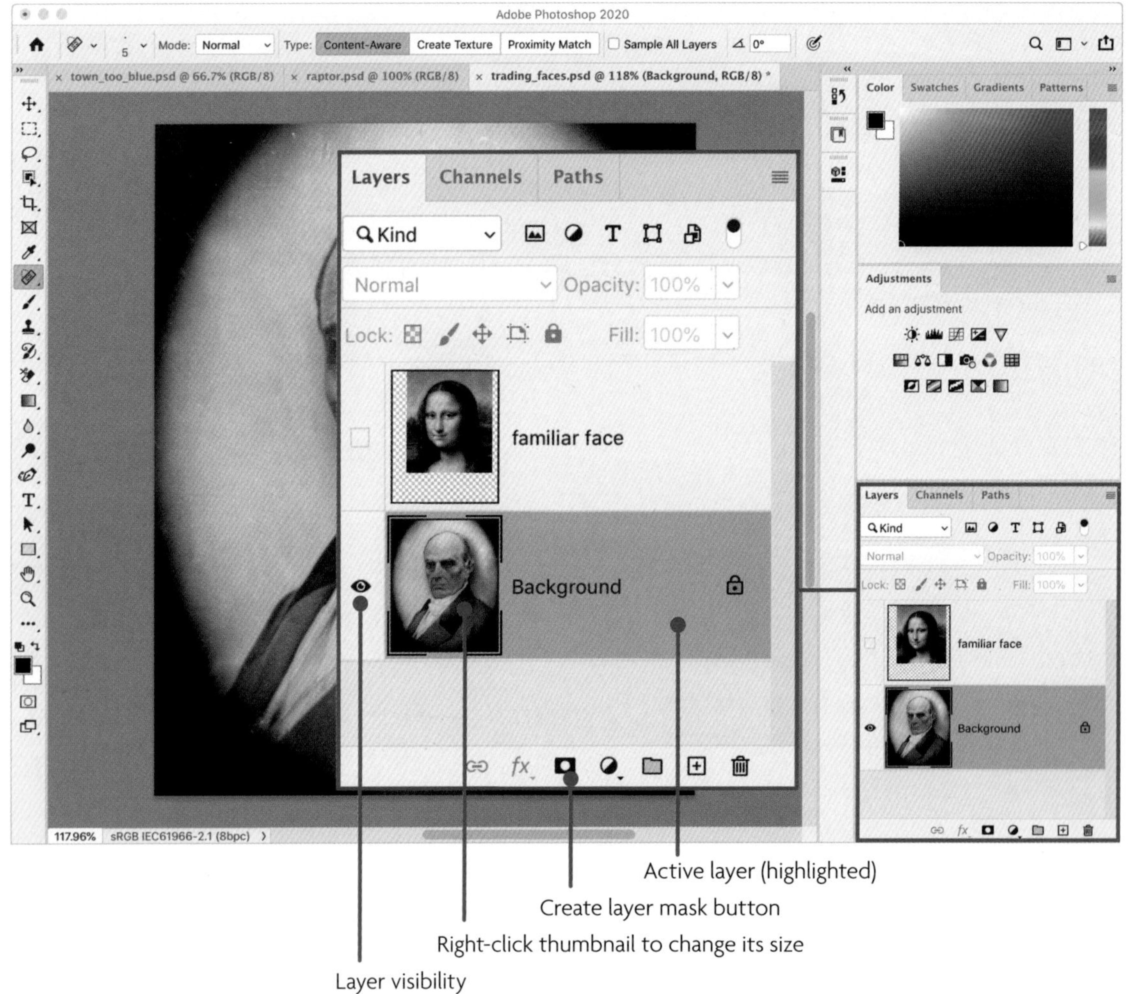

This document contains two layers, one of which is hidden. Look at the Layers panel in the lower-right corner of Photoshop's interface. Those layers are of two different kinds: a Background and a pixel (or image) layer. Backgrounds are very limited: they have to be the bottom layer and they cannot have transparency. Sometimes we need to change layer stacking order or achieve transparency, so we end up converting the Background into a pixel layer or something called a Smart Object. Let's explore a few of these things.

- Right-click on either layer thumbnail and choose Large Thumbnails. When layers proliferate, you'll want them small again, but this should be helpful for now.
- Click the small square to the left of the layer called "familiar face." It's now visible.
- Click once near the top layer's name. The layer is now highlighted, which means it's the active layer.

When a layer is active, anything you do happens to that layer alone. We could move, blur, or lighten or darken it, and all other layers will remain untouched. We are going to mask this layer, hiding the bits we don't want to see. When we're done, her face will be on his head! But that's a little later.

- Click the little padlock near the Background's name. As you can see, it isn't a hard lock to pick!

Now that layer is no longer a Background. It needs a better name.

- Double-click the current name and type something. I think "grumpy face" is appropriate.
- Drag that layer just above the other one. You'll see a blue line appear when you get to the right spot. Then drag it below again.

Layers higher in the stack are in front of and obscure those below.

- Highlight the top layer ("familiar face"). Note the Opacity control near the top of the Layers panel.

There are several ways to make the layer less opaque. Try this: hover the cursor over the word Opacity and notice how it looks like a pointing hand with tiny arrows pointing right and left. That's a "scrubby cursor." It is available whenever you hover over the name of a numeric field. To "scrub" the value of that field, press and drag left or right to lower or raise (respectively) the value.

- Scrub the Opacity to the left to lower it. Note that I've already positioned that layer over the face of Mr. Grumpy. We'll learn about how to do that soon. Scrub the Opacity back to 100%.

There's more to do, but you may wish to save before moving on. If you'd like to save the document, press ⌘-S/Ctrl-S or choose File > Save.

Lesson B: Selections & Masking

Selections are a big part of Photoshop. They're how we tell the application which pixels we want to affect. Masks are a means of hiding pixels, areas of an image we don't want to see. We *could* delete those pixels, but we might regret it. I make mistakes and change my mind sometimes, and so do my clients. You too? Hiding areas with a mask means we can reveal those pixels if minds change or errors are discovered. That's why masking is considered a best practice.

Masking Metaphor

Let's borrow a visual from the "Selections & Masks" chapter of the Compendium. You really should check out "A Metaphor and Example" (page 289) for the full story. But in brief, a mask acts like a kind of light-block that prevents the entire image from being visible. And it does this without damaging the image.

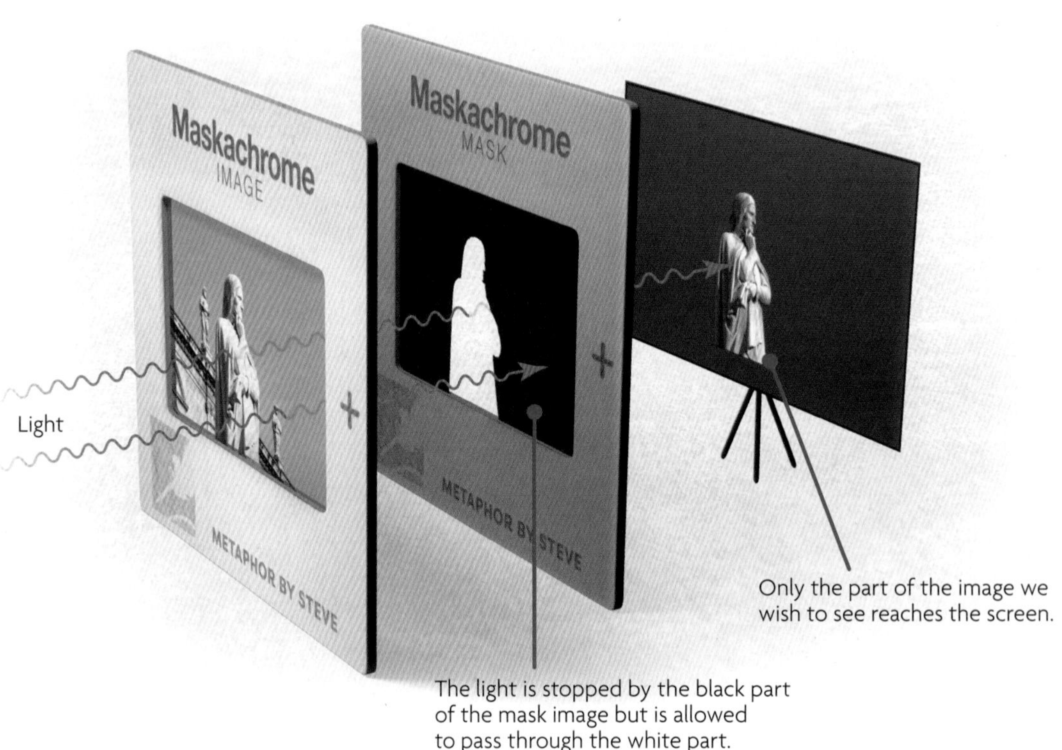
Maskachrome
IMAGE
METAPHOR BY STEVE
Maskachrome
MASK
METAPHOR BY STEVE
Light
Only the part of the image we wish to see reaches the screen.
The light is stopped by the black part of the mask image but is allowed to pass through the white part.

A Warm-Up

In the image called "trading_faces.psd" we've got two layers, and the top one needs to lose some content so it can blend in with what's below.

Basic Procedure to Make a Mask

The first thing to do is to indicate, at least approximately, which pixels should remain visible. For this image, those will be the pixels forming the central parts of Mona Lisa's face.

In this case, we don't need high precision, so we'll select that area with the Lasso tool (L).

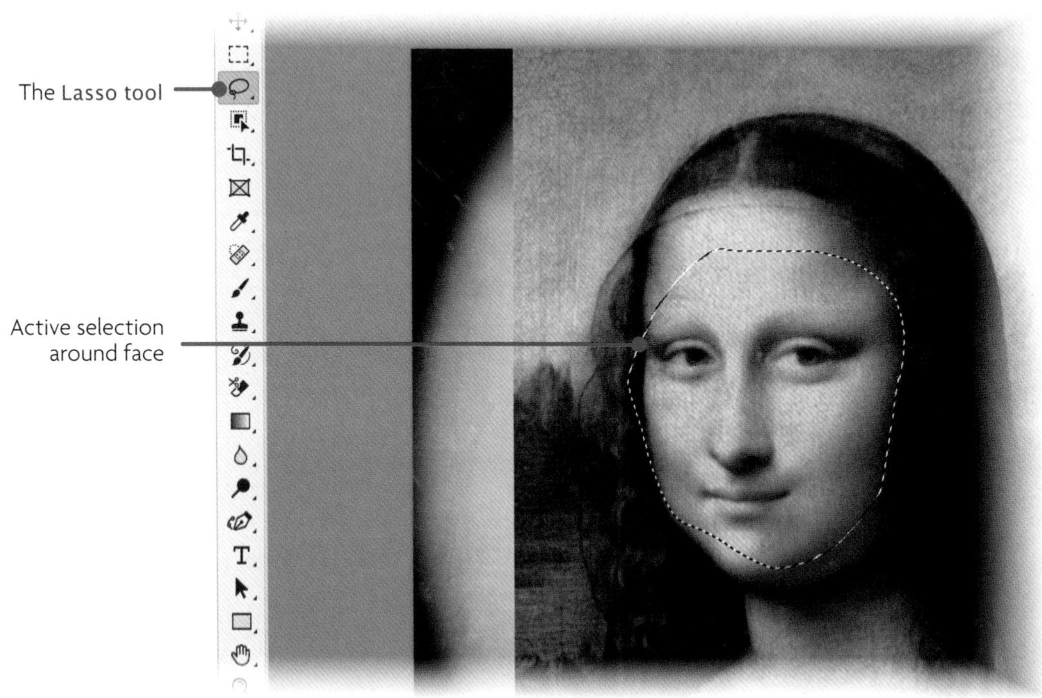

- Make sure the "familiar face" layer is highlighted.
- Tap the L key to activate the Lasso tool. Some tools have intuitive shortcuts like that; most don't. Look at the Tools panel and you'll see that the Lasso tool is now active.
- Press and drag to draw around the main parts of her face. You don't need to be too careful this time. But if you really are unhappy with the first attempt, click just once outside your current selection and then try again.
- You now have a selection marquee (nickname: "marching ants"). You're ready to make the mask.
- Click the Add layer mask button (◘) at the bottom of the Layers panel, or choose Layer > Layer Mask > Reveal Selection. I know it looks pretty bad so far.
- Open the Properties panel. Choose Window > Properties to do so. The Window menu is where all Photoshop's panels are listed.

Basic Mask Properties

Since you just created the mask, it is targeted, or active. If you look carefully at the Layers panel, you'll see little brackets around the mask thumbnail that has appeared on the "familiar face" layer. The Properties panel will also indicate that the mask is the active part of the active layer. If you click once on the image thumbnail, the Properties panel will say "Pixel Layer" at the top. Clicking on the mask thumbnail shows the mask's properties. We're going to blur (or feather) this mask.

- Drag the Feather slider (or scrub the word "Feather") until her face is blending in a bit with his head. I find that a value of about 20 pixels works well in this case.

The edges of the familiar face are now translucent, fading away to cause this blending. If you were to disable the visibility of the grumpy face layer, you'd see her face fading into a checkerboard pattern (Photoshop's way of indicating transparent areas).

When I adjusted Feather, the result was pretty good, except on the left side where some of her hair was still visible.

Take a good look at that mask thumbnail. Notice that it's black where pixels are hidden and white where they're shown. If we paint with black on that mask, we'll hide any last bits. Painting with white reveals pixels again; handy if we hid too much.

Painting on Masks

Again, be sure the mask thumbnail is active.

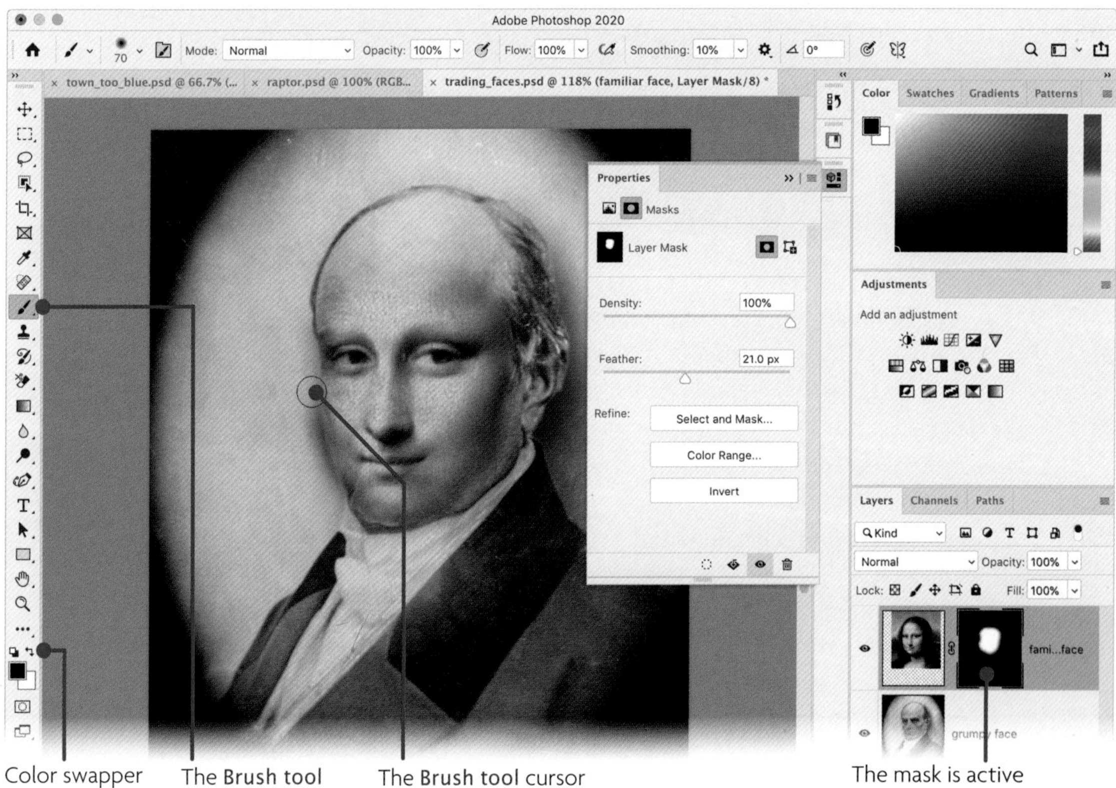

- Choose the Brush tool by tapping the B key.

Note near the bottom of the Tools panel that the Foreground and Background colors are white and black (the defaults). If not, tapping D for "default" makes it so. When you paint, it's the Foreground color that gets applied. We want that to be black so we can hide the last bits of the Mona Lisa image. If the colors are in the wrong position, click the two-headed arrow near those color chips to swap them, or tap the X key to do so. I told you some shortcuts are not intuitive.

- Ensure the Foreground color is black.

The brush is likely too small if it's still at its default size. Also, it's likely a Soft Round brush, which is perfect for our mask. If the brush is using a different preset (from previous experiments, perhaps), right-click on the image and choose Soft Round from the General Brushes presets.

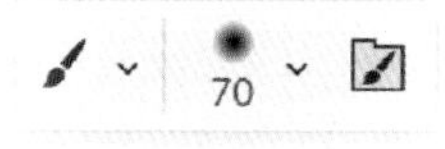

- Resize the brush by pressing the square bracket keys ([and]), using the right bracket to make the brush bigger. It appears I went with a brush that is 70 pixels across. You can check the size at the top of the screen in the Options Bar.
- Press and drag to paint along the left side of her face (I suppose it's *her* right side, but it's to *our* left).

As you paint, it looks like erasure, but the pixels are merely being hidden. If you were to paint with white, they would reappear. Try it!

- Tap X to swap black and white, and paint somewhere to hide pixels.

We can go back and forth like that quite a bit, often using smaller and smaller brushes to hide and show exactly what we like.

The grumpy face is now obscured by Mona Lisa's more pleasant, if mysterious, one.

- Choose File > Save, then either choose File > Close or click the small X in the image's tab.

Lesson C: Opening Multiple Images

Viewing Multiple Documents

➡ Open two of the files in the Project A folder: "town_too_blue.psd" and "raptor.psd."

You may not realize both are open in Photoshop until you look closely toward the upper left of the interface, where there's a tab for each document. Click each tab to go from one to the other.

You can see them side-by-side or one below the other if you wish:

➡ Choose Window > Arrange > Tile All Horizontally or Tile All Vertically.

That can be useful at times, but we'll find the space-saving aspect of tabs advantageous most of the time. So to get back to that:

➡ Choose Window > Arrange > Consolidate All to Tabs.

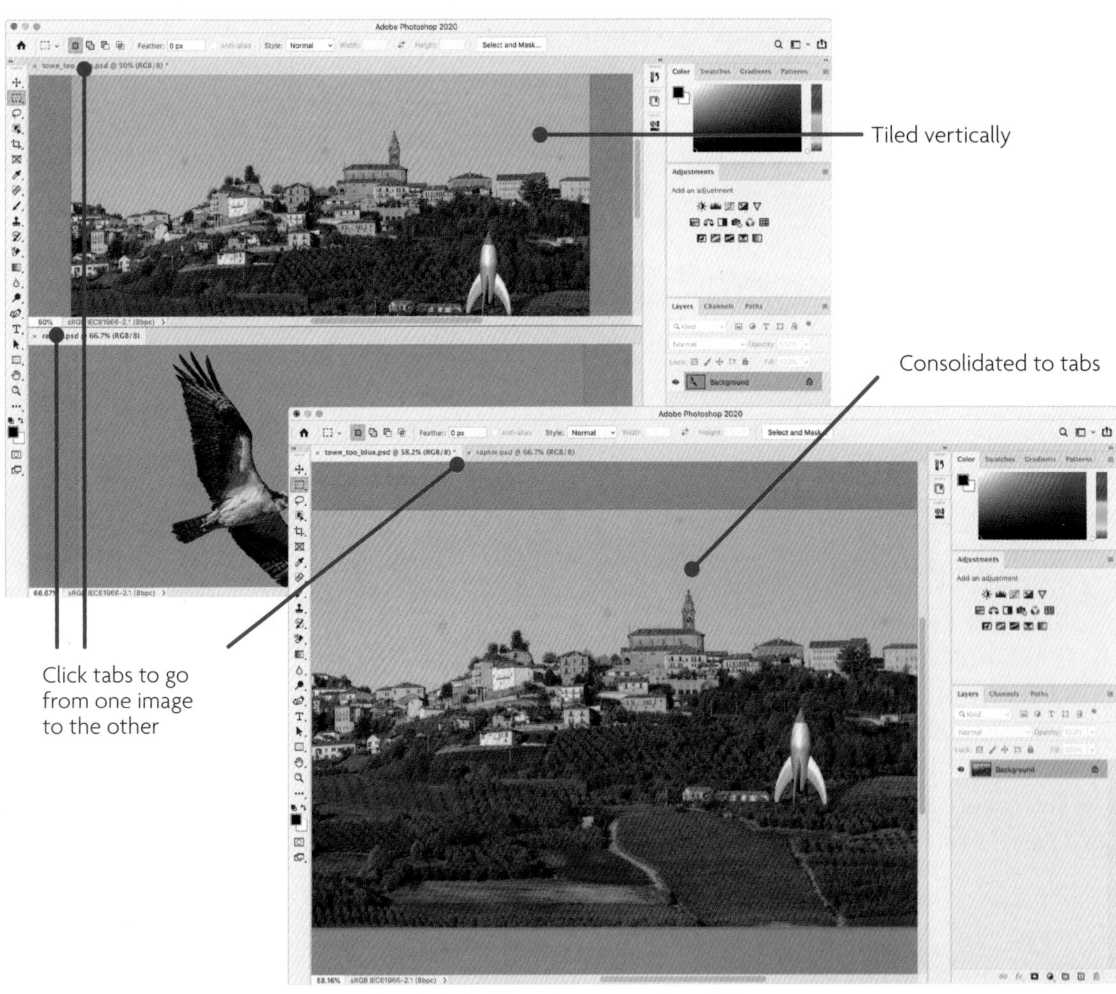

Lesson D: Basic Retouching

The photo of the Italian hill town ("town_too_blue.psd") has several problems. First, I realize that it's kind of boring. Yes, it looks like a nice town, but there's nothing notable or unusual about it. That's why we're going to put a bird on it. Also, although it was photographed near sunset, the golden light seems to be missing. It's too blue. We'll fix that in Lesson E, shortly.

First, let's deal with those ugly blemishes in the sky and field. These appear to be bits of dust on my camera's sensor and so are likely in the photos I made shortly after this one too. To deal with these, we're going to use a powerful (but simple-to-use) tool and a professional workflow. See the "Retouching & Reworking" chapter in the Compendium for much more.

Nondestructive Retouching

Retouching is almost always obscuring flaws or blemishes with more acceptable material. That is, we take good bits from one part of an image (or another one) and put those over the bad bits. Because I make mistakes or change my mind, I use layers when I do this. I put the good bits on their own layer. If I later realize I made an error, I simply erase that bit.

- In the image "town_too_blue.psd," create a new layer. Either use the Layers panel menu (the small lines in that panel's upper-right corner) to choose New Layer... or go to Layer > New > Layer.... This will open a dialog box that prompts for a name. Let's use "Retouch."

That is now the active (highlighted) layer in the Layers panel. Of the many tools Photoshop has for retouching, let's just go with the one that's used most often. It brilliantly finds good material in the image to hide blemishes we identify by painting on them.

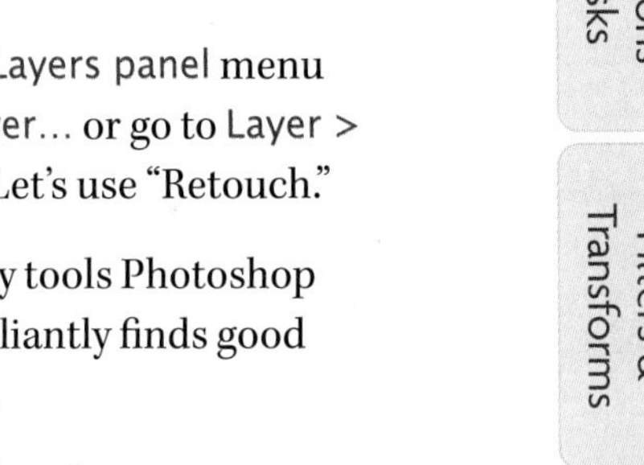

- In the Tools panel, select the Spot Healing Brush tool (it resembles a bandage next to a dotted oval). Like many tools, this one needs its options adjusted before it's as good as we'd like it to be. In this case, to create repairs (good bits) on your new layer, you have more to do.
- In the Options Bar along the top of the screen, check the box that reads Sample All Layers. Otherwise, this tool won't even see the good pixels on the layer below, let alone sample them (pick them up).
- This tool uses a brush cursor to "paint" over blemishes. Use the bracket keys on your keyboard ([or]) to shrink or enlarge the brush so it's a little bigger than those sensor-dust spots. The size is noted near the left end of the Options Bar. I chose a size of about 80 pixels.
- "Paint" over a spot, *completely* covering it. This identifies the problem. Release the mouse, and Photoshop fixes it!

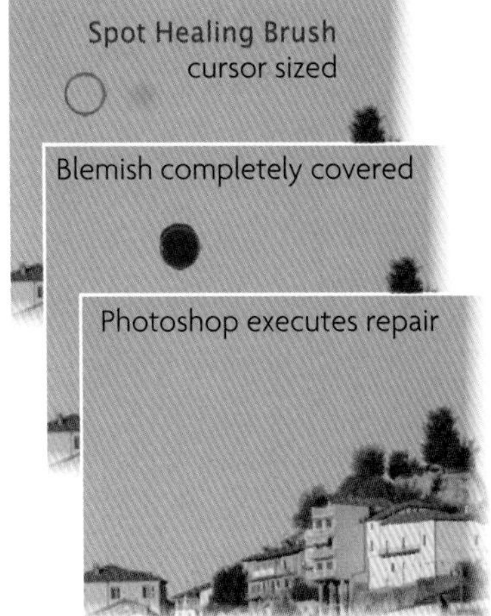

Even the spot on the roof of the church is fixed easily. If you make a mistake, undo is a quick ⌘-Z/Ctrl-Z.

Lesson E: An Adjustment

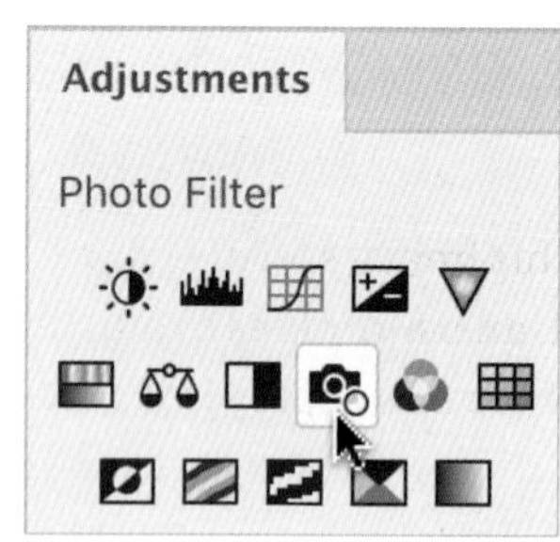

At this point, the town image is composed of two layers. If you disable either layer's visibility, you'll see only the other. By toggling the visibility of the retouch layer, you'll enjoy a before and after. We can now perform an adjustment to get the color to its evening glory.

To adjust both layers simultaneously, we will use something called an adjustment layer. If it's above both the layers that make up our image, it will affect both. Adjustment layers affect only (and usually all) the layers below them.

What's the Problem Here?

In this image's case, the issue is with color only, I believe. The image is neither too light nor too dark. That is, there is no *tonal* problem. Of course, this is Photoshop, so there are several adjustments from which to choose that affect color without affecting tone. We'll use a wonderfully effective and intuitive one called Photo Filter.

This adjustment simulates putting a colored piece of glass in front of a camera's lens. Photographers use such filters to colorize the scene in front of them to "warm" or "cool" the scene, for example.

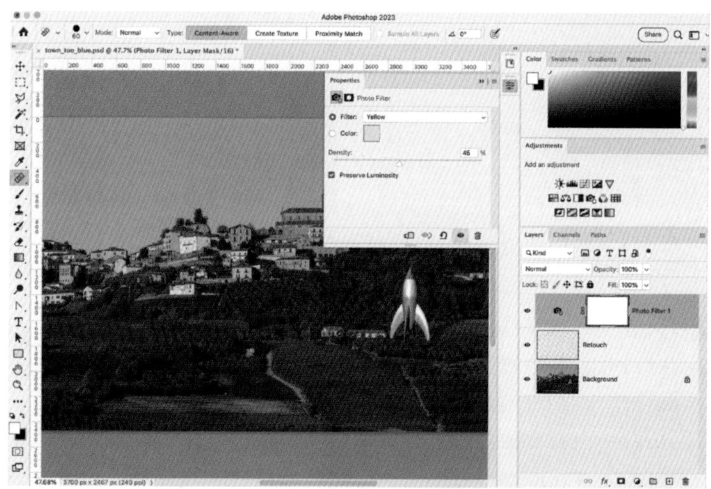

- In the Adjustments panel, click on the icon near that resembles a camera. This creates a Photo Filter adjustment layer. Look at the Layers panel. If this new layer isn't at the top, above the others, drag it there.

The Properties panel should be showing the options available for this adjustment. It also defaults to a classic Warming Filter (85), which simulates a standard 85 filter photographers may carry in their bags. This is a step in approximately the right direction. The blueness is too cold, so warming is right. But this choice is more orange than the yellow we need.

- In the Properties panel, choose Yellow from the Filter menu. To enhance the effect, increase the Density by dragging its slider or scrubbing the word "Density" to about the halfway point. The image now resembles my recollection.

Lesson F: Layers on the Move

This image still needs something to liven it up. Take a look at the image called "raptor.psd." In it, an osprey flies against a blue sky near sunset: a lovely addition to the Italian countryside. Once this osprey image is added, we'll go about removing the blue sky to leave only the bird.

Drag, Keep Dragging, and Drop

It's slightly tricky to use a "drag-and-drop" method of copying a layer to another document, but its speed makes it worth the trouble.

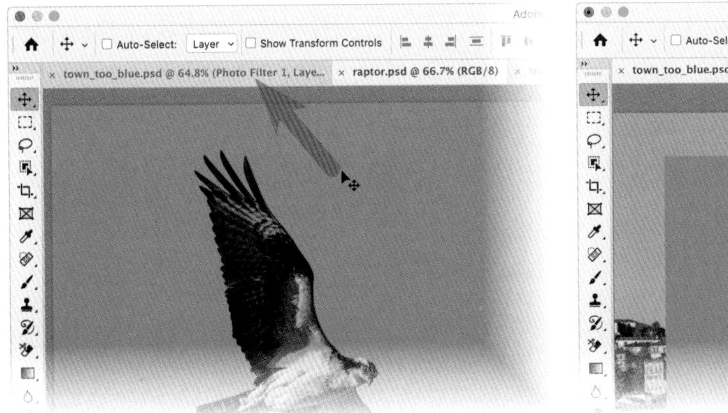

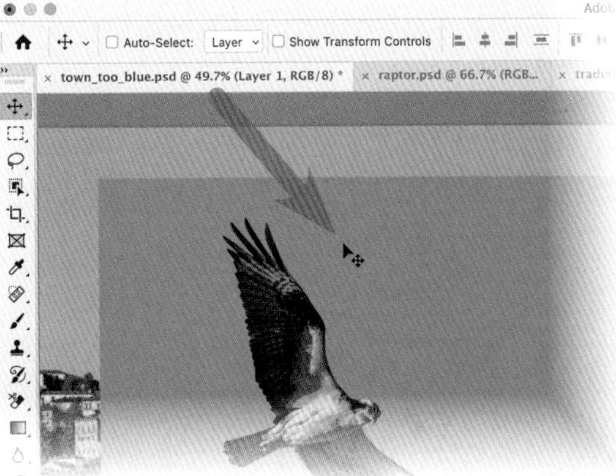

In one continuous action, using the Move tool, drag the layer you want to copy to the tab of the document to which you want to copy it, pausing when that destination image appears, then continuing to drag down onto the destination's canvas.

- Choose the Move tool (V) from the Tools panel (it's at the top).
- Position the cursor somewhere within the image, then, *in one go*, drag the image to the tab with the name of our destination image (town_too_blue.psd), ***do not release the mouse when that image appears***, continue to drag down onto the destination image, and then release. To repeat: drag the image up to the other tab, pause (without releasing) until the other image appears, drag down into the other image's document window, and release.
- Double-click the layer's name to rename it "osprey."

Or you can use old-fashioned copy and paste if the layer you're copying isn't a Background:

- In the Layers panel of raptor.psd, click the padlock on the Background to convert it to a pixel layer. Double-click the layer's name to rename it "osprey."
- With that layer highlighted, choose Edit > Copy or use the shortcut ⌘-C/Ctrl-C.
- Go to the destination image, town_too_blue.psd. Highlight the top layer so the pasted one appears above it. Then choose Edit > Paste or use ⌘-V/Ctrl-V to paste.

To remove the sky and leave only the osprey, we'll have to create a mask. Read on!

A Few Selection Methods

Now back to our osprey and quaint Italian hill town in town_too_blue.psd. We need to select the osprey; then, when we add the mask, the sky will be hidden. There are several tools that allow us to select subjects against homogeneous backgrounds like that blue sky around the raptor. For much, much more on the following selection methods, set aside time to study the "Selections & Masks" chapter of this book's Compendium.

Object Selection Tool Intro

- Highlight the osprey layer, then select the Object Selection tool (W; or fourth from the top). This tool is nested with others so you may have to right-click and choose the Object Selection tool.

In the Options Bar, a refresh icon will start to spin. It may not spin long because this tool looks for objects within an image and this image has few of them.

- Slowly move the cursor into the image. When you hover the cursor over the osprey, the bird is highlighted in magenta to indicate that it's been discovered. Click on the osprey and a very good selection is made.

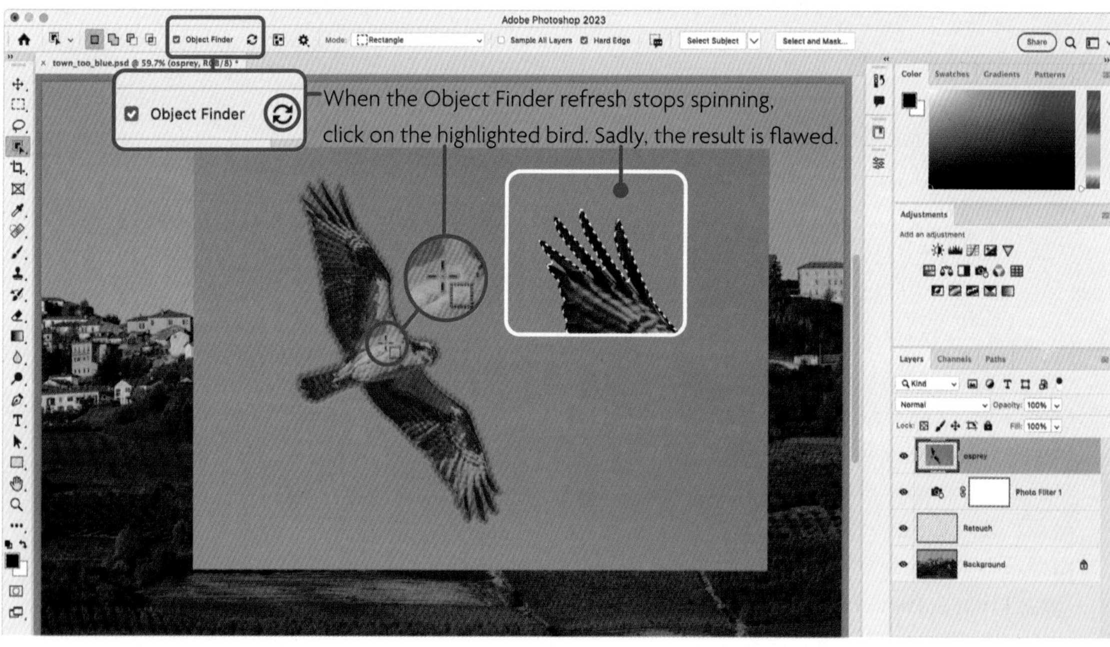

Good, but not quite good enough. Unless a Photoshop update has improved this tool since I wrote these words (quite possible!), there will be some sky-blue pixels selected between the wingtip feathers.

- Since this isn't quite right, and we wish to try something else, choose Select > Deselect or use the shortcut ⌘-D/Ctrl-D.

Quick Selection Tool Intro

This tool is a little more work. With it, we "paint" over material we want selected and it learns about the colors, textures, and perimeter we're after. I find that if you paint a little, release, paint a little more, release, etc., it does better than if you try to paint over an entire object at once. This is true, at any rate, for subjects more entangled in their environments than a bird of prey alone in the sky. With this image, you may do well enough by painting carefully over most of the osprey.

- Right-click on the Object Selection tool to reveal the tools hidden behind it. One is called the Quick Selection tool—choose it. The cursor will be a smallish brush (a circle).
- Keeping the cursor within the bird's perimeter, paint over its length. *Avoid getting too close to the edge of the bird.* If the brush touches blue sky, stop, undo, and try again more carefully.

If we were to zoom in and use progressively tinier brush sizes, we would be able to select the osprey very well. However, we should note that the bird is in front of a backdrop that's very different than it is in color and tone. And just as moviemakers use blue and green screens to isolate subjects and put them in different circumstances, so can we.

- There's an easier way for this image, so choose Select > Deselect or use ⌘-D/Ctrl-D.

Magic Wand

Since this is the oldest of these selection tools, I sometimes call it the Elder Wand. To use this tool advantageously, we have to know there exists a command that inverts a selection . We note this because the blue pixels and the transparent ones surrounding the bird are very easy to select. We can then invert that selection to have a very precise selection of our subject.

- Right-click on the Quick Selection tool to reveal the Magic Wand tool—choose it. The cursor will resemble the tool icon, a magic wand.
- Click once on the transparent pixels surrounding the entire osprey layer. The selection stops at the blue, opaque pixels.
- Then, to add the blue pixels to that selection, hold down the Shift key and click on part of the blue sky around the osprey. You now have a great selection of everything *except* the bird. This is because this tool selects pixels similar to what's clicked, stopping at something sufficiently different.
- Choose Select > Inverse. Awesome!
- Click the Add layer mask button (◘) at the bottom of the Layers panel, or choose Layer > Layer Mask > Reveal Selection.

We could call it done here. But rarely are our subjects so neatly isolated in a scene. So let's look at one more method that works well even in more complex images.

- Choose Edit > Undo or use ⌘-Z/Ctrl-Z then Select > Deselect or use ⌘-D/Ctrl-D.

Select Subject

This tool is under ongoing development, so if it doesn't work as you expect on an image, try it again when there's an update to Photoshop. When you have any of the previous three tools selected in the Tools panel, there will be a button available in the Options Bar.

It can perform its calculations either on your computer or tablet ("Device") or on Adobe's computers ("Cloud"). The former is quicker, the latter better.

- Make sure to highlight your choice of the Object Selection tool, the Quick Selection tool, or the Magic Wand tool. This will cause the Select Subject button to appear in the Options Bar.
- Click the small arrow to the right of the words "Select Subject" and choose Cloud (Detailed results). Consider setting this as the default in the preferences for "Image Processing" (page 11).

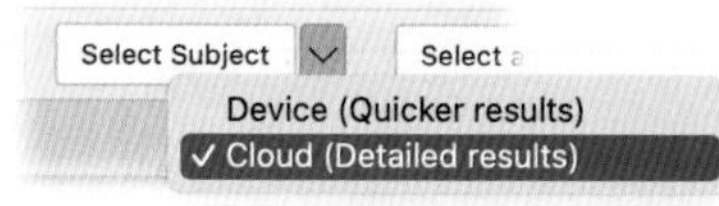

- Now click Select Subject. It will take a few seconds before returning a really nice selection of the osprey.
- Click the Add layer mask button (◘) at the bottom of the Layers panel, or choose Layer > Layer Mask > Reveal Selection.

Lesson G: Intro to Smart Objects and Filters

Now, just one last thing bothers me. If a bird like that was photographed with a long focal length lens, the backdrop would be somewhat out of focus. If we don't arrange that, the town in the background competes with the osprey visually. Let's get eyes to focus on the bird, since it's the most interesting thing in the photo.

Nondestructive Alteration

- Highlight the Background in the Layers panel by clicking near its name.
- Holding down the Shift key, click near the *name* of the Photo Filter layer so it and the Retouch layer are highlighted too.

We're going to put all three layers into a Smart Object, a kind of container layer that can hold many different kinds of data. The biggest benefit to us is that a Smart Object can have many different kinds of effects applied to it that can be edited or removed later if we wish. In this case, we're gong to apply one of Photoshop's many blur filters. Smart Objects and all the various layer types are covered in, you guessed it, the Compendium. Filters too.

- With those layers highlighted, right-click near the name of any of them, then choose Convert to Smart Object. Those layers are now safely inside the Smart Object.
- Rename the Smart Object "the scene."
- Choose Filter > Blur Gallery > Field Blur. Don't be startled as the whole interface becomes dedicated to this function.

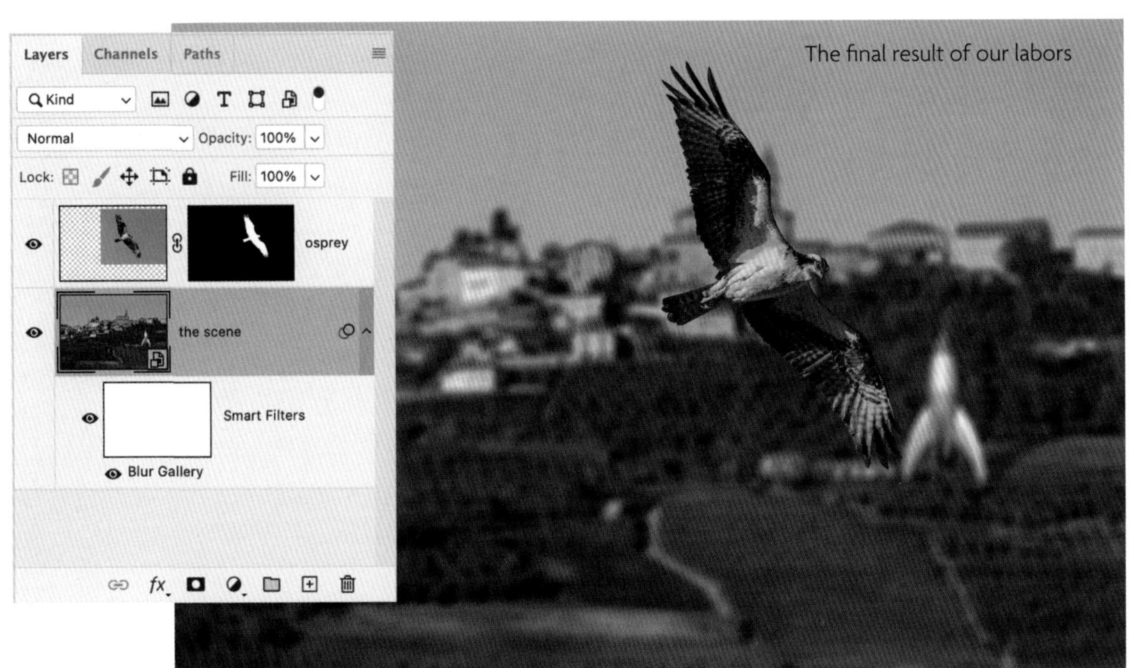

The final result of our labors

In the upper right of the interface, you'll see a slider for the amount of Blur. Along the top of the interface are a few options, including the OK button we'll use to commit this filter.

- Use the Blur slider or scrub the word "Blur" to get the amount that is pleasing to you. I like it at about 20 pixels for this image.
- Since any noise in the image has been blurred away, giving a too-smooth look, use the lower-right Noise panel to add some grain: about 10% will do for an Amount to match the noise on the osprey. This is really only visible at high magnifications.
- Enable the High Quality checkbox at the top of the interface then click OK. When the filter is finished applying, you'll see it listed under the layer's entry in the Layers panel, as in the illustration on the previous page.

A Note Regarding Navigation

There will be times when you'd like to zoom in or pan across an image in which you have zoomed. This seems a fine time to cover that.

Most tools have a letter that accesses them: B for the Brush tool or J for the Spot Healing Brush tool are examples. Z for Zoom tool is another. However, we rarely want to use those tools for more than a moment, and then only to better see what we're doing with other tools. So here's what I recommend:

- Choose a generic tool. A safe one is the Rectangular Marquee tool; tap M to select it. We're not going to use it, but it doesn't hurt anything if you accidentally use it.
- Hold down (don't tap) the Z key and keep holding it! Look at the cursor when it's over the image. It should resemble a magnifier.
- Keep holding down that Z! With the cursor over the osprey, use your mouse to press-and-drag rightward. You're zooming in. Leftward is zooming out. Zoom in a good bit. Release the mouse, then (finally) release the Z key.

When you're done, you should be zoomed on the bird and the active tool should still be the Rectangular Marquee tool. Yes, this does take a little practice. The beauty of this trick is that it works with any tool that has a letter shortcut and that you need only momentarily. Try one more. Since you're zoomed in, let's trying panning. Although H does access the Hand tool, it does a disorienting zoom out/zoom in thing as it's used. I prefer using the Spacebar—not intuitive, but easier on the eyes.

- Hold down the Spacebar. Drag in the image to explore other parts of it. You're panning with the Hand tool.
- When done, release the Spacebar.
- To see the entire image, use the shortcut ⌘-0/Ctrl-0 (that's a zero!).
- Save your hard work (⌘-S/Ctrl-S).

Well done.

2 A Few Adjustments

A look at several of the many types of adjustments on offer—others will follow later. Your companion for this chapter's exercises will be the "Adjustments & Color" chapter of the Compendium. Everything discussed on the next several pages is more fully examined there. Here, we'll get your hands dirty exploring these ideas and features.

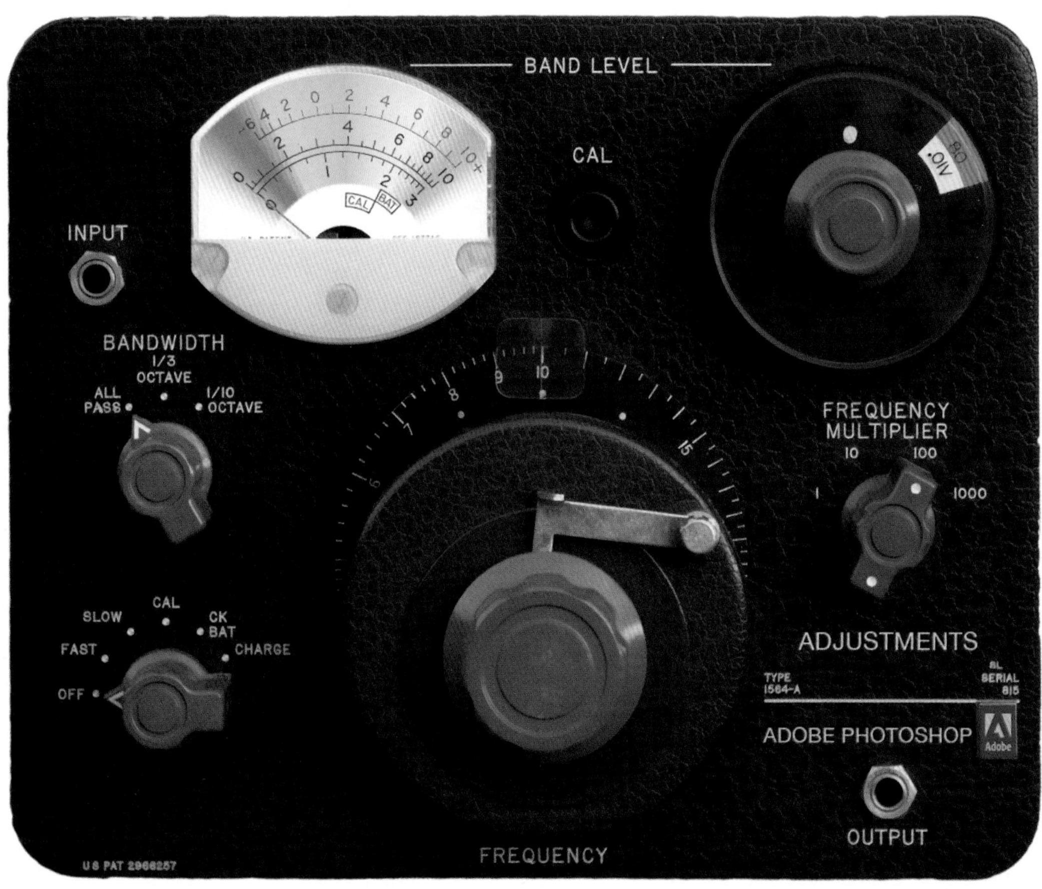

Lesson A: The Color Wheel

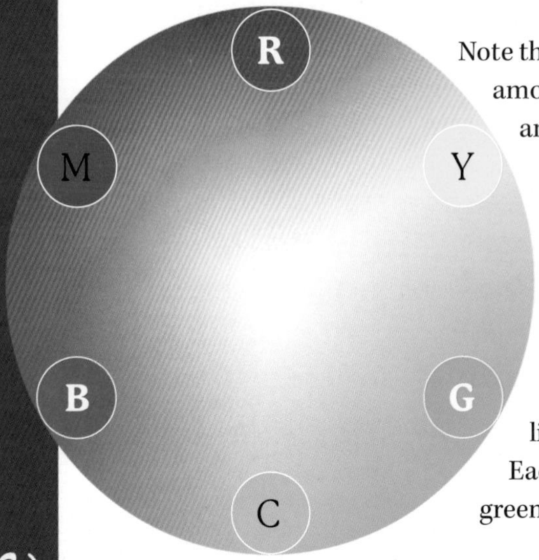

Note the brightly colored figure here. Knowing the relationships among these *primary* colors will allow you to evaluate images and make whatever adjustments you need to.

Additive Primaries

I've featured the big three, the additive primaries, with white letters in the figure: R, G, and B, for red, green, and blue. Any color can be made from these three colors of light. Yellow, for example, is the combination of red and green light: their sum. Add all three together and you get white. Each image you open has three color channels holding its red, green, and blue data.

Complementary Colors

Photoshop's color adjustments always operate on these three color channels, sometimes directly, sometimes indirectly. So, for example, it's useful to think of an image that's too magenta as lacking green. Things look a bit yellow? Add blue! They're too red? Remove some, but not too much or you'll get cyan, red's opposite. That is, if you add those three colors of light unequally, then you see that deficient color's opposite (complement).

See"RGB and Photo History" (page 215) for some visuals.

Fixing Only What's Wrong

Color Casts in Images

To spot color casts, try to find anything in the image that *should be* neutral (a shade of gray). Visually, try to isolate that element so you're not overly influenced by the colors around it, although light does have a way of bouncing around in a scene. Is that element too "cold" (blue or cyan, maybe) or too "warm" (ruddy or orange, perhaps)?

Correcting Color, Tone, or Both

If the problem is just color, there are certain adjustments that specialize in that. Is the image too light or dark? Is the contrast wrong? Maybe all of these? Knowing the problem dictates the treatment.

For example, if we use an adjustment to add red, green, or blue, we're adding light and so lightening the image. Or to remove a green cast from an image, you'd remove green and, depending on the tool used, darken the image. Let's look at some problems and fixes.

Lesson B: Photo Filter Adjustment

Have a look in the Course Files folder and locate the folder "02 A Few Adjustments." Open the file within called "B Photo Filter.psd."

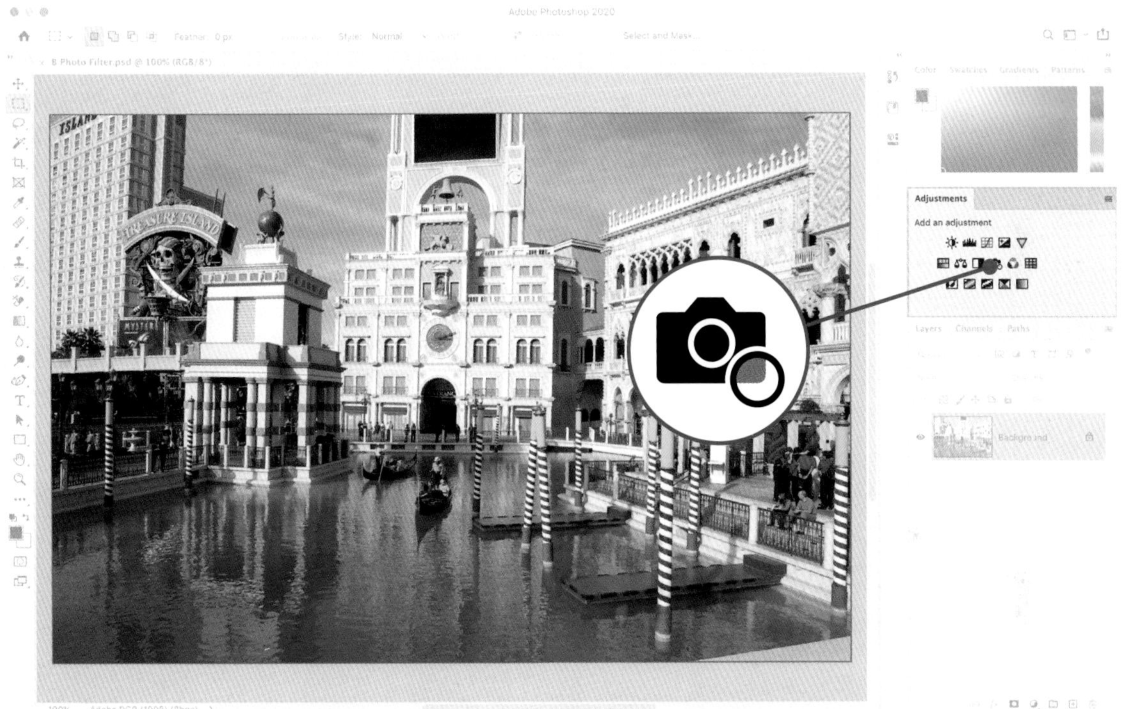

To my eye, based on the time of day and time of year (winter), the image looks too cool—bluish. The time of day can be discerned by the lengths of shadows, image metadata, or, as in this case, a big clock in the middle of the frame.

The image looks neither too light nor too dark. Thus, the only issue is the cool color cast pervading the whole image. So we need to perform an adjustment that doesn't necessarily affect tone but does affect color.

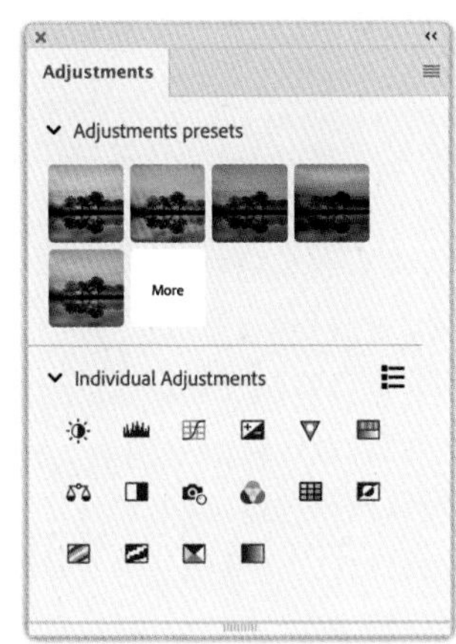

Beta As I write, this panel is undergoing a redesign and has this arrangement in the beta version. The top section creates groups of adjustments to achieve an overall visual effect.

The lower section can display individual adjustments as icons or as a list including their names.

In the Adjustments panel, click the icon for Photo Filter (it looks like a camera with a small round thing in front of it). This creates an adjustment layer above the Background and opens the Properties panel, which shows this adjustment's properties.

Adjustment as Diagnostic and Cure

If you're not convinced the image needs warming, we can use the Photo Filter adjustment to puzzle that out. As soon as the adjustment appears, it uses the first choice in its Filter menu, Warming Filter (85). Frankly, I think that is a marked improvement.

But don't take my word for it. We can try other settings to see if moving the image's color in other directions is more helpful.

- Choose one of the cooling filters from the Filter drop-down menu.
- Toggle the visibility of the adjustment layer by clicking the eye icon next to the layer name in the Layers panel or at the bottom of the Properties panel.

Does the image look better or worse? This is the bottom line: we want an improvement. The cooling filters make the image more blue, accentuating the problem it already had.

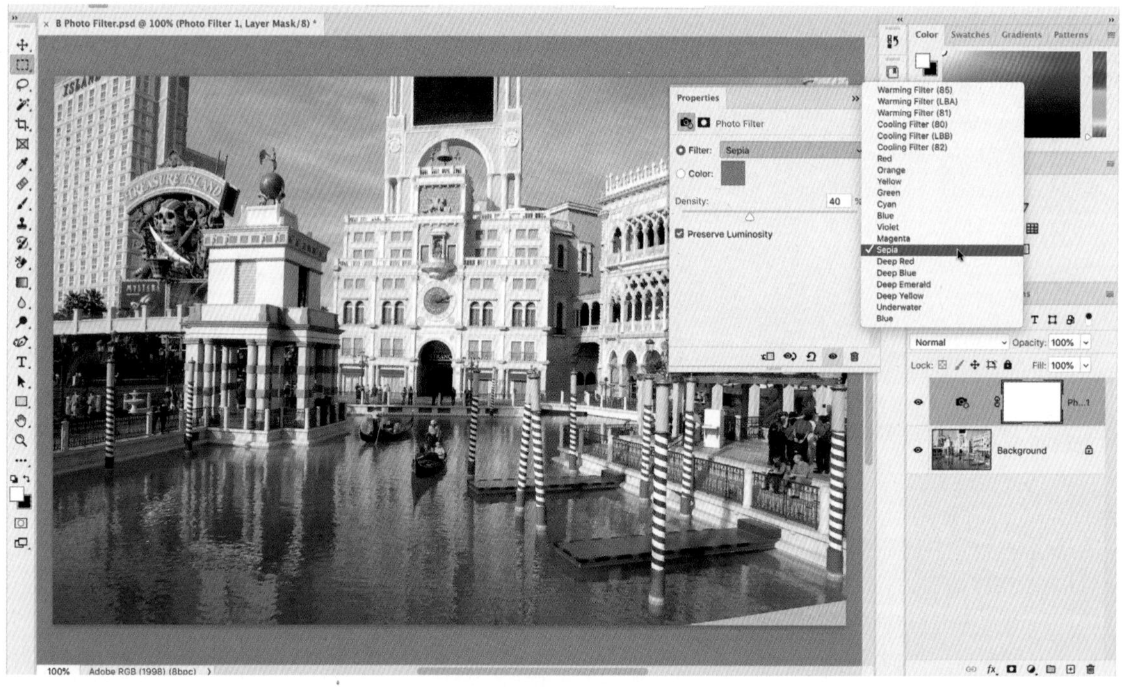

- Choose the Red filter and the Yellow filter. It seems like the correct choice would be somewhere in between, like perhaps the Orange filter. Most of the warming filters are a version of orange, as is the Sepia filter (its brown is just a darker orange). I like its result best if one more refinement is made.
- Choose the Sepia filter, then adjust the Density slider. This is essentially the strength of the adjustment. I've set mine to 40%, which is a bit high, but is noticeable in this book. The effect is like holding an orange/brown-tinted piece of glass in front of the lens when making a photo.

If we really did affix a physical tinted-glass filter in front of our lens, we would have had to adjust the exposure to compensate, as such a filter would diminish the light impacting the sensor. By default, this adjustment makes that compensation for us. That's the job of the Preserve Luminosity checkbox. If this is unchecked, the image will be darker, noticeable especially in the highlights. Since it's sometimes a favorable effect, you should try it when applying this adjustment to see if it helps.

In this case, the high Density setting causes the image to become far too dark and muddy if Preserve Luminosity is unchecked.

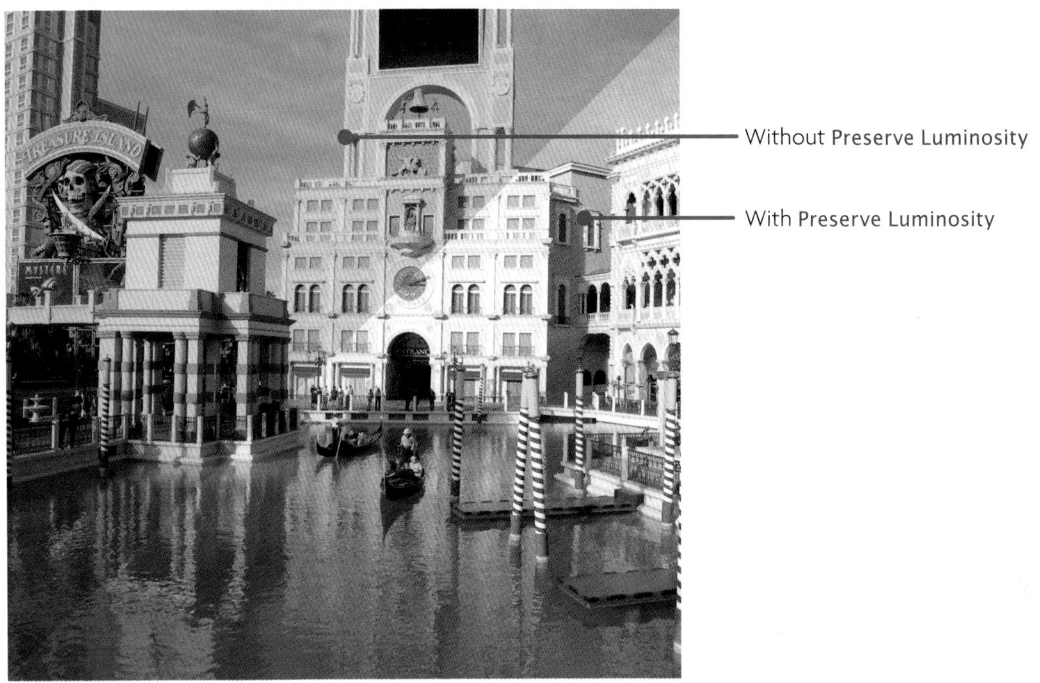

➡ Save (⌘-S/Ctrl-S) and close the document. You've made it better!

Lesson C: Curves

Possibly the most powerful adjustment, Curves is used primarily when we have tonal issues, and it can correct color issues as well.

- Open the file called “C Curves.psd” from the “02 A Few Adjustments” folder. Hopefully, you will agree that it looks terrible.
- Click the Curves adjustment icon in the Adjustments panel to create an adjustment layer.

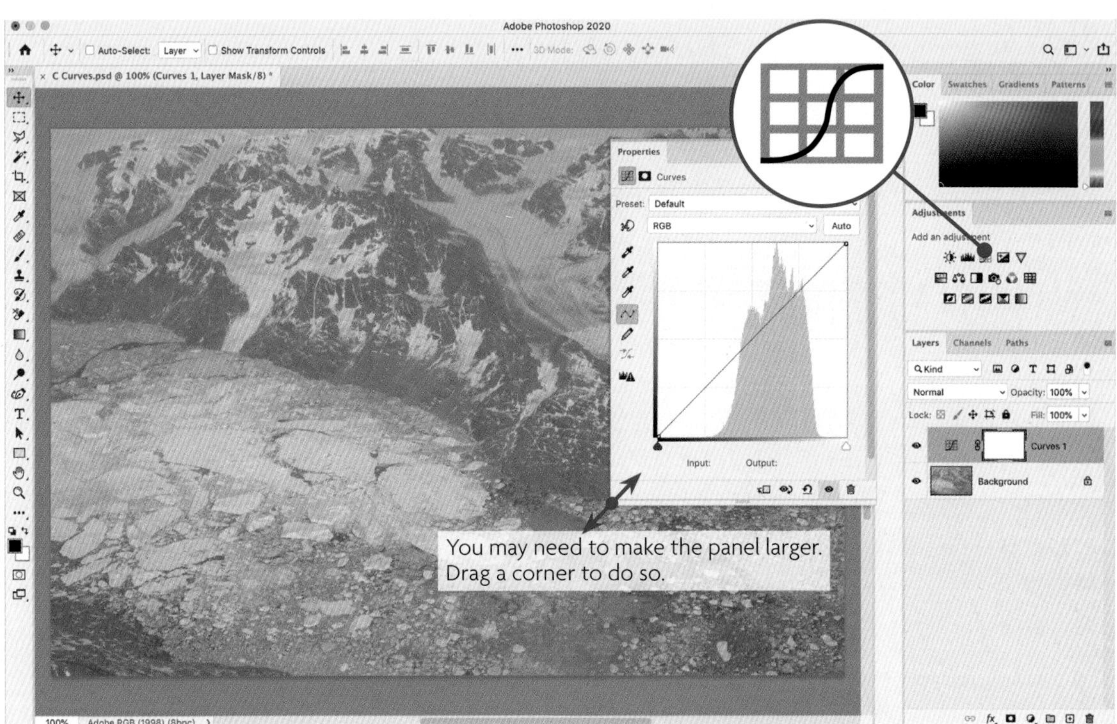

Tone Plus Color

Curves can lighten or darken all color channels at once or individually. If we darken only the red channel, for example, less red light is allowed to our eyes and the image looks darker and more cyan. If we darken the red, green, and blue channels together, the image will be darker but won’t develop a color cast.

Note that the Properties panel displays a histogram in a square with a 4x4 grid. Running diagonally from the lower left to the upper right is the eponymous curve. Yes, it’s a straight line for the moment.

- Experiment with the curve: press and drag the center of the curve upward a little. Note the point you’ve created on the curve (which is now a curved line). The image is now lighter too. Drag that point downward to darken the image.

If you're careful to position that point in the horizontal center, then you're predominantly affecting midtones, with highlights and shadows experiencing less effect. How do you know this? The horizontal axis is "input." Note the grayscale running along the bottom of the grid from black to white. There's one running vertically on the left side, too, for "output." When you drag a point upward from the center, you should read the curve like a graph: that midtone input is now output as a lighter color, with black and white, if present, not affected at all.

In this image, there are no fully white or black pixels. The histogram's peaks and valleys stop well short of either end. The image's pixels possess fewer tones than they might. The ice and snow should contain some pure white pixels, and there likely should be some totally black pixels too. Thus, this image lacks contrast. It also has a pronounced blue cast. We'll be fixing both, eventually. You might want to read a little bit about "Histograms" (page 231).

➡ Before we continue, reset the adjustment: click the Reset button (↺) at the bottom of the Properties panel.

Monochromatic Contrast Enhancement

Note the sliders along the bottom of the histogram grid in the Properties panel. These make it easier to grab the curve's endpoints, which control black and white in the image.

➡ Drag the black-point slider to the right until it reaches where the histogram begins to ascend. Do the same with the white-point slider, only dragging left. Notice the improvement to the image's contrast (but certainly not its color).

Clipping and Avoiding It

➡ Hold down the option/Alt key and drag the white-point slider left. Don't be startled!

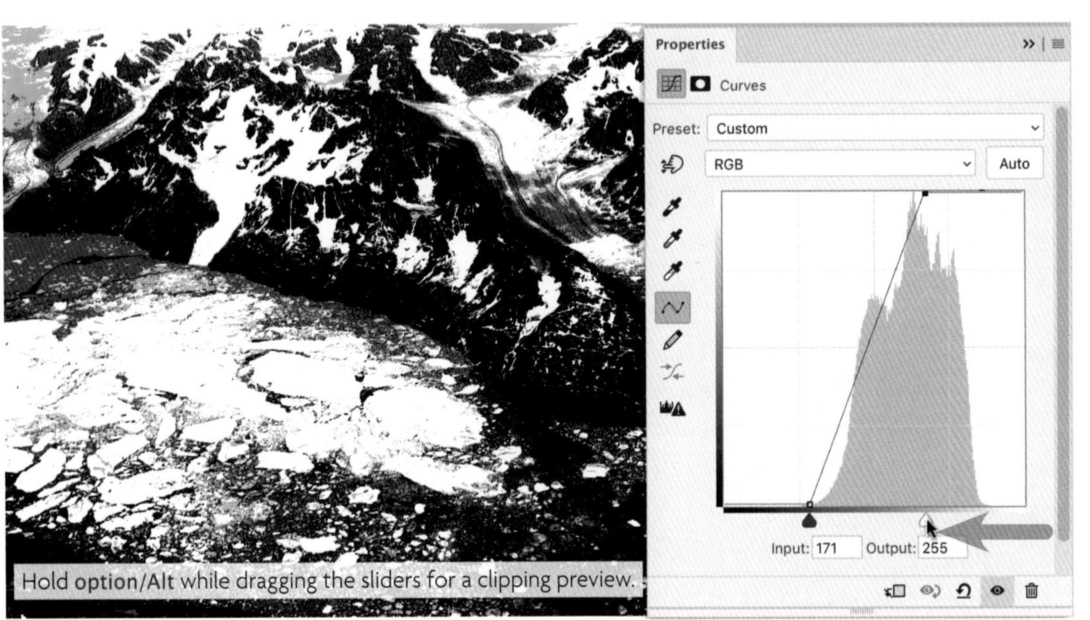

Hold option/Alt while dragging the sliders for a clipping preview.

This time, Photoshop is trying to help you notice if you are losing detail at either end of the tonal range. This is called "clipping," and we usually try to avoid it. If you did what's shown in the figure, option/Alt-dragging the white-point slider quite far to the left, you will clip the highlights severely. That is, any pixels that turn white are getting clipped to white.

➡ Look at the numbers below the slider in the Input and Output fields.

When you option/Alt-drag the white-point slider inward, the Output reads 255 (the level or tone for white; 0 is the level for black). In my example illustration, the Input reads 171, a tone just a bit brighter than midtones. This means that any pixel with a level or tone of 171 or higher is being clipped to white. All those pixels in the histogram at and to the right of the white-point slider will lose all detail.

We want *some* pixels to glisten white, but not that many! So we'd back off until only a few pixels were clipped. If you see colors other than white, that means the clipping is occurring on only one or two channels and not all three. Blue would indicate that only the blue channel is getting clipped, and cyan that both the blue and green are. Since this image has a blue problem, we see blue when we "back off" on the white slider adjustment.

If this image were more neutral, we could option/Alt-drag the black- and white-point sliders inward until a few pixels were clipped: a few white pixels showing on a black field if we're dragging the black slider, and black on white for the white slider. This act is called a "monochromatic contrast enhancement" since it doesn't affect color that much. In this case, the image isn't neutral but rather strongly blue. So this is not the answer here.

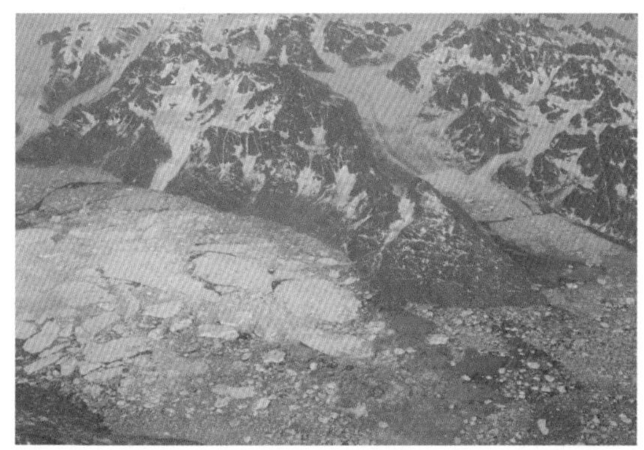

The original image: flat and blue.

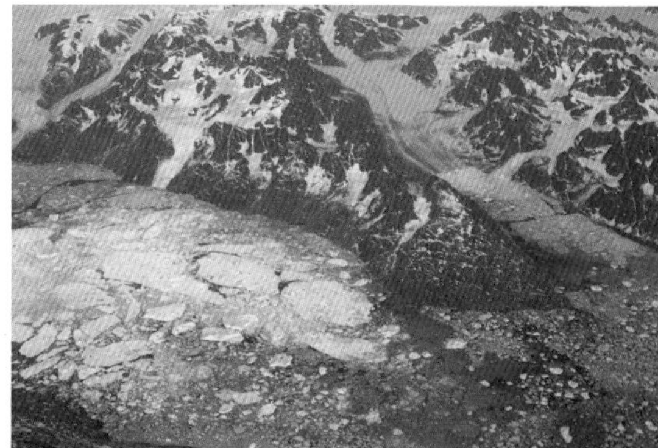

After a monochromatic contrast enhancement.

Per-Channel Contrast Enhancement

Since the steps above didn't help us cure all that ills this image, reset (↺) the adjustment again. We will do similar steps, but for each color channel. If we improve the contrast on each channel consistently (the same amount of clipping), we should have a color-corrected result.

➡ At the top of the Curves Properties panel, click on the menu that currently reads RGB and choose Red instead. You'll see a reddish histogram and a reddish curve so you know what you're adjusting. The same is true of the Green and Blue channels.

- Option/Alt-drag the black-point slider inward, and the entire image turns red until you start to clip pixels, which will show as black. You'll see the opposite when you option/Alt-drag the white-point slider inward, with red specks appearing on a black field when highlights are clipped. Be sure to clip only a few pixels at each end.
- Repeat this on the green channel (shown below) and the blue channel. Try to clip about the same amount of pixels on each channel, even though you'll have to drag the sliders different distances on each channel's curve.

Hold option/Alt while dragging the sliders for a clipping preview.

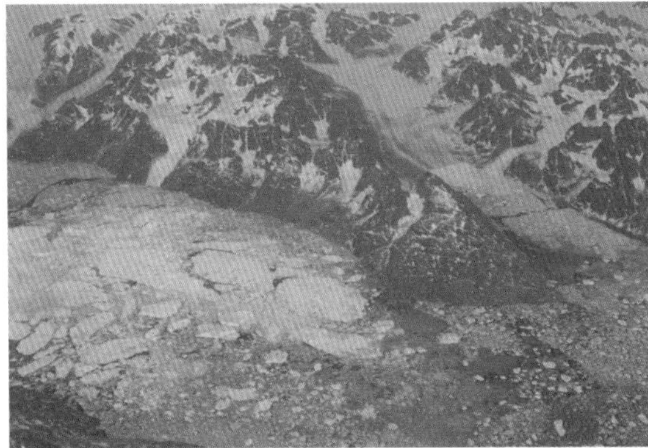

The original image: flat and blue.

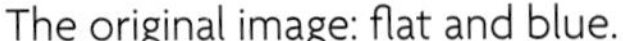

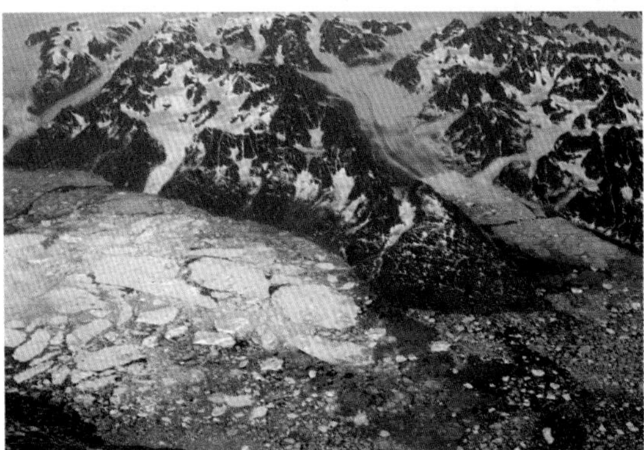

After a per-channel contrast enhancement. Yay!

This process can help an enormous number of images, at least if they lack contrast. If you return to the RGB curve in the Properties panel, you'll see each channel's curve and the black monochromatic curve too. You can use the latter to add or remove a bit of light by dragging up or down in the middle, while still benefiting from your previous labor.

We have actually stretched each channel's histogram to reach black and white. The Curves interface is a touch misleading about that. To see the actual resulting histogram for the image, choose Window > Histogram to open the Histogram panel.

Auto and Semi-Auto Curves

You may have noticed the little Auto button to the right of the Channel menu in the Properties panel. Photoshop's default behavior for that button uses a sophisticated but monochromatic algorithm to improve the image's brightness and contrast. Sadly, it does nothing good for this image's color cast.

You're not going to like this next step, but here goes:

- Reset (⟲) the adjustment one last time. Try not to be demoralized.
- Click the Auto button and try to keep the disappointment at bay. That's a fancy curve Photoshop has made that does *not* fix our image! (Actually, if the image didn't have that blue color cast, the result would have looked nice.)
- Now, option/Alt-click the Auto button. Choices appear. I call this "semi-auto."
- The available Algorithms may remind you of the task we performed earlier. Try each, but settle on Enhance Per Channel Contrast. We're not shown which pixels are clipped, but we can adjust the amount of clipping by scrubbing the words Clip. I set highlight clipping to 0.01% to keep it minimal. I set black clipping higher for more contrast. Click OK.
- Save (⌘-S/Ctrl-S) and close.

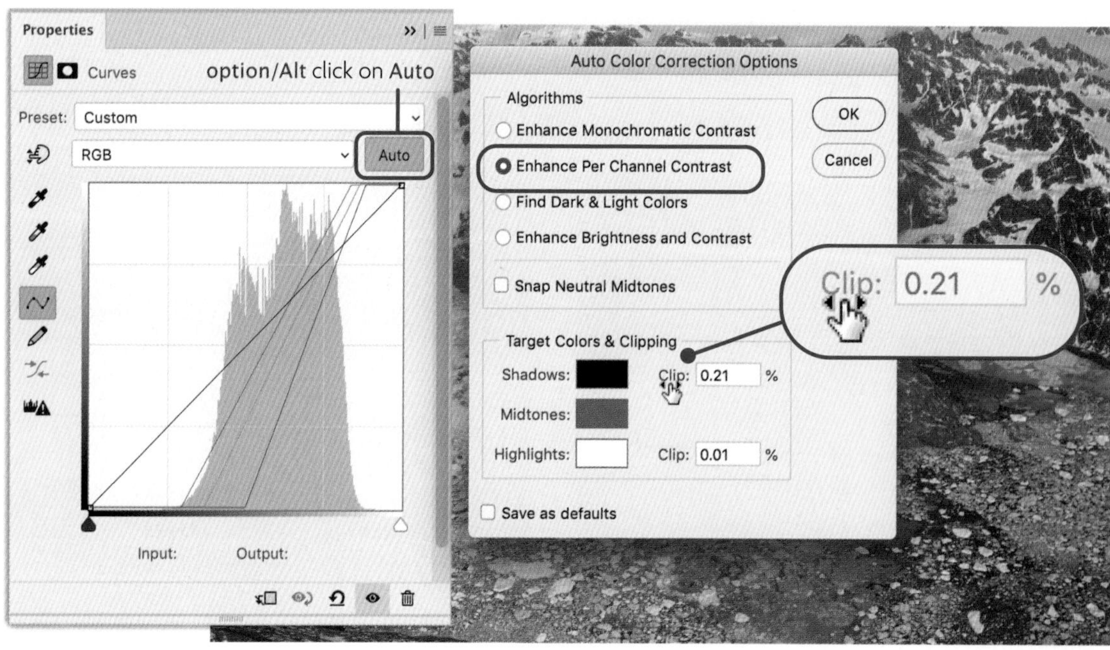

Lesson D: Vibrance & Hue/Saturation

There are several adjustments that affect the saturation of an image, and in this lesson we'll discuss two. As always in this book, you'll learn the foundations and rationale here and then you can deepen your knowledge in the Compendium. For this lesson, the good parts to reference are "Vibrance" (page 242) and "Hue/Saturation" (page 243).

Definition of Saturation

Saturation is a measure of the purity of a hue. Think of the light from a laser. It's impressively intense and vibrant—its color is *purely* of one wavelength, the ultimate saturated color. The color of an old incandescent bulb is a mix of yellows, reds, and oranges. Since it's not as pure a hue as the laser, we'd say it's less saturated. Full-spectrum lights produce a color that is pretty much completely unsaturated: all the visible hues are blended together as white light.

Color Clipping

An image with no saturation is grayscale. Each hue in a heavily saturated image is pure but without gradation of color. We call this "color clipping," and it's generally avoided. It can also occur when outputting an image: depending on the settings used, colors that didn't clip on-screen may clip in print, or colors that aren't clipped on one display may clip on another.

The Vibrance adjustment has two sliders: Vibrance and Saturation. The Hue/Saturation adjustment also has a Saturation slider, but it behaves (I'd say misbehaves) very differently from the identically named one in the Vibrance adjustment. Let's try them both. We'll use the same image so you can compare.

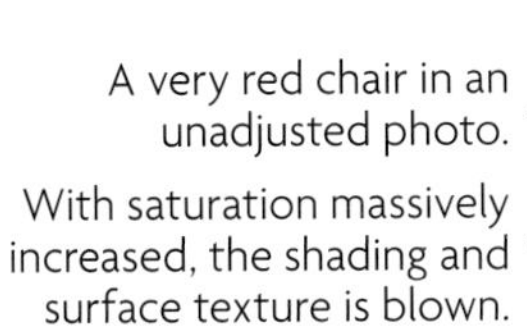

A very red chair in an unadjusted photo.

With saturation massively increased, the shading and surface texture is blown.

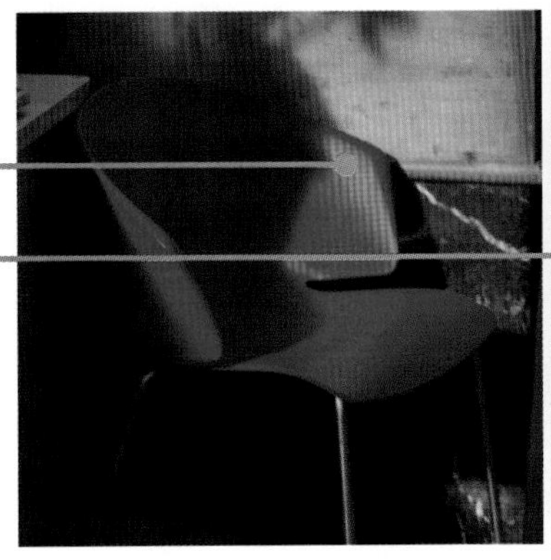

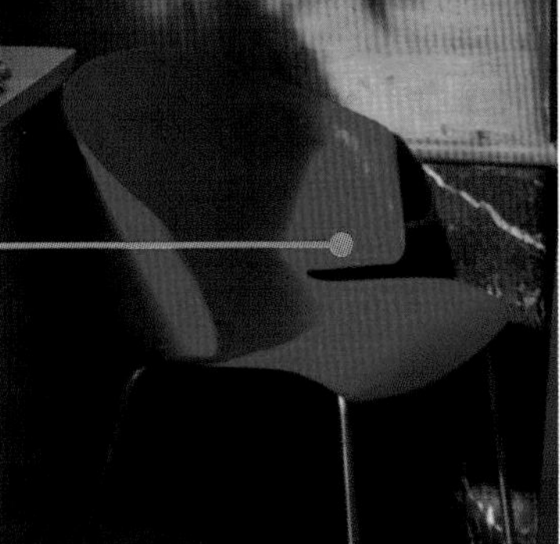

Vibrance

➡ Open the file called "D Vibrance Hue-Saturation.psd" from the "02 A Few Adjustments" folder. This image has both muted and gently saturated colors.

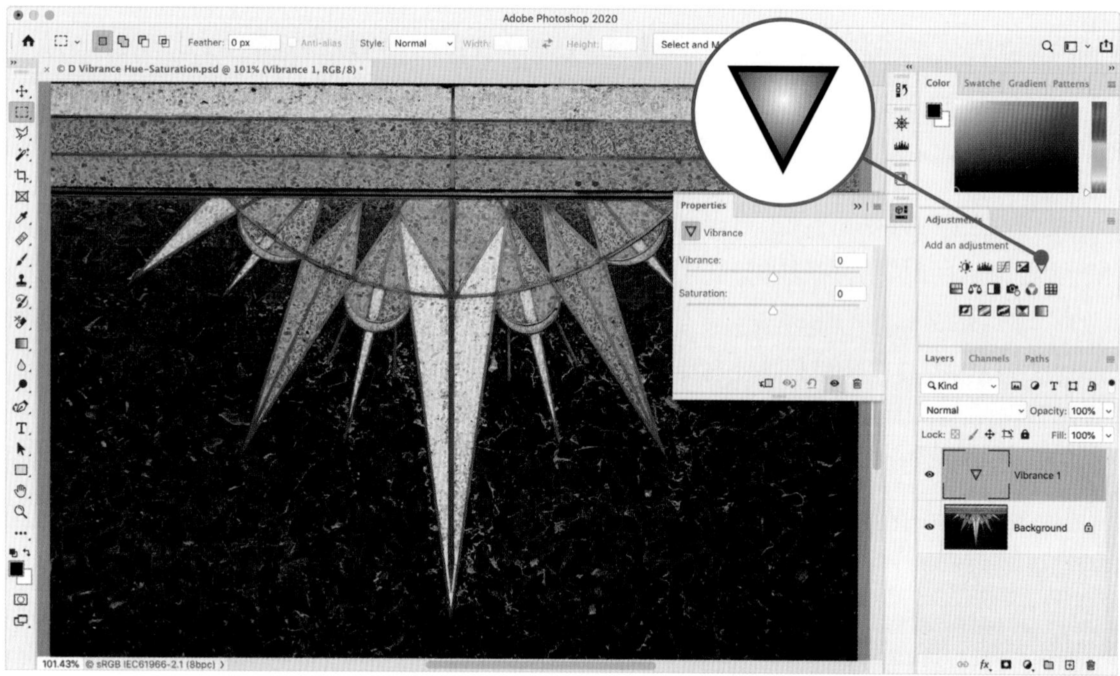

Create a Vibrance adjustment by clicking its icon in the Adjustments panel. Compare the sliders in the Properties panel.

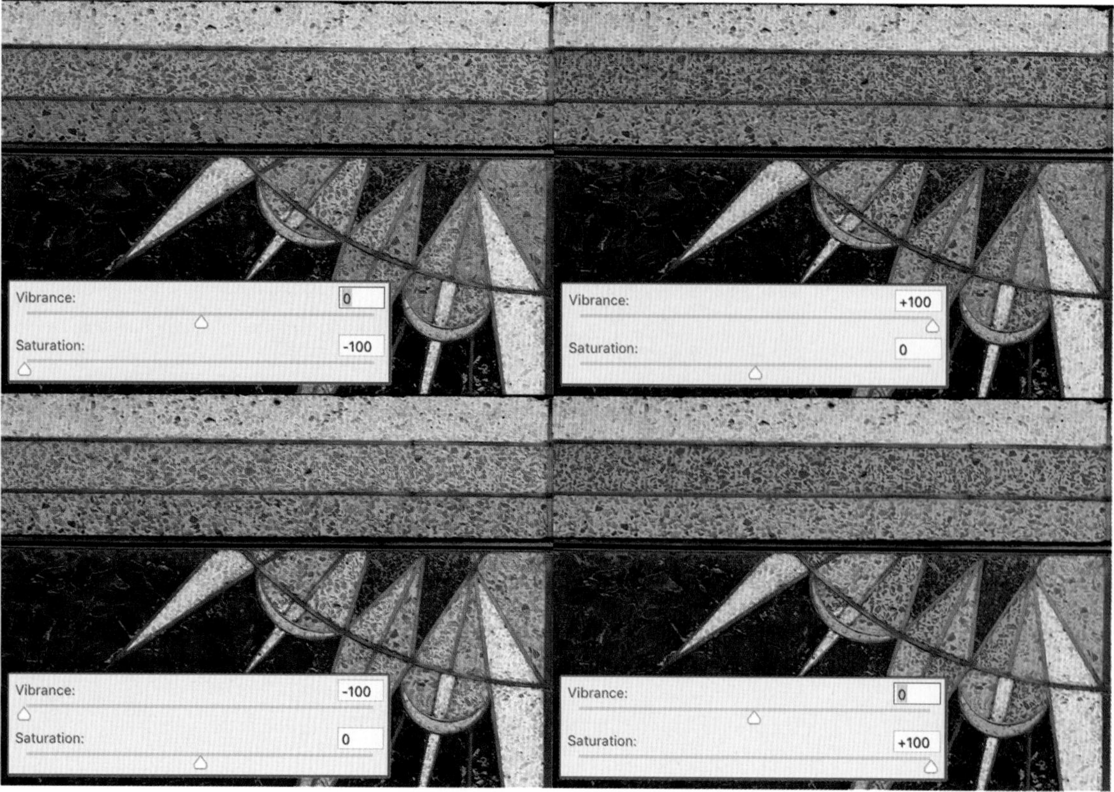

The Vibrance slider more strongly affects the least-saturated colors so it avoids clipping colors that started out more intense. It also avoids oversaturating skin tones. The Saturation slider is much stronger but shows some restraint. When lowered, it can remove all color from the image. This is also true with the Hue/Saturation adjustment with which users used to customize grayscale conversions.

Double-clicking the name (label) of a slider resets that control to 0.

By increasing the Saturation and reducing the Vibrance, you can remove color from nearly neutral areas. Note here how the yellowed white stone is made to look cleaner while the red and blue areas mostly retain their color.

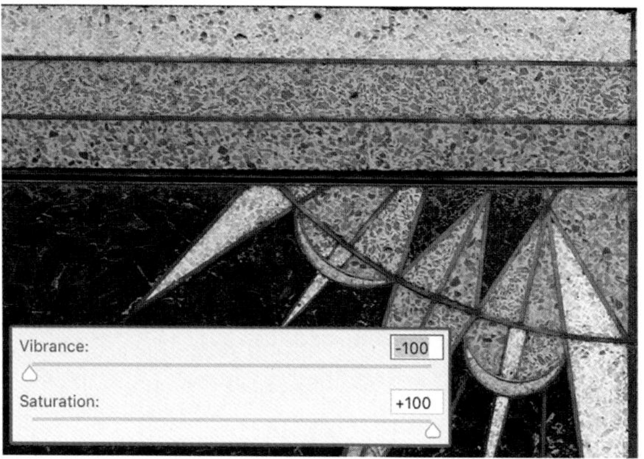

➡ Click the eye icon to the left of the Vibrance adjustment layer in the Layers panel to disable it for now. Don't delete it, as you may wish to compare it with our next adjustment.

Hue/Saturation

➡ If you closed it, reopen the file called "D Vibrance Hue-Saturation.psd."

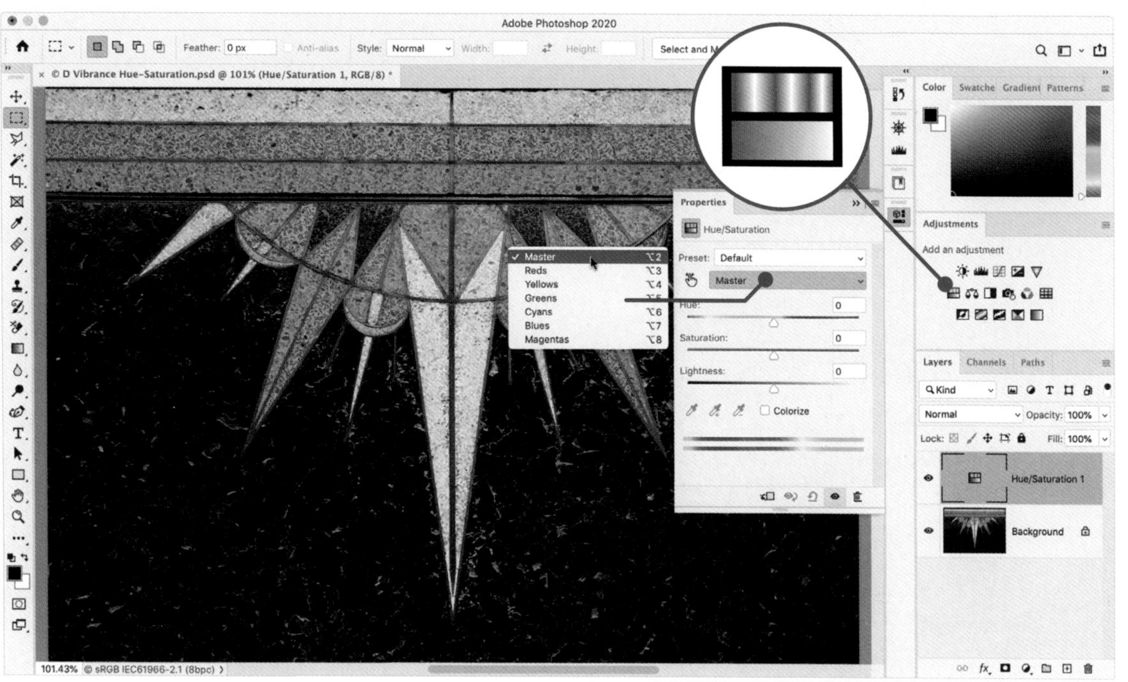

This adjustment can affect saturation, as you would guess, but it can also shift hue and affect lightness (tone) in an image. Remember the color wheel we saw earlier? Shifting hue means turning that wheel—either slightly or drastically. Let's experiment a bit, then we'll do something practical.

- Create the adjustment by clicking its icon in the Adjustments panel. Resize the Properties panel if necessary to see all its controls.
- First, let's try out the Saturation slider, moving it all the way to the right. Note how merciless it is compared to the sliders in the Vibrance adjustment. Now you know why those were invented! However, if used modestly, this one can do some good too.
- Double-click the name (label) of the Saturation slider to reset it to 0.
- Try the Hue slider.

Please note that dragging it either way to the end gets you to the same place: the other side of the color wheel! The numbers are a hint too: 180 or -180, as in 180°. Watching the color strips at the bottom of the panel is helpful to see how the current hues (top strip) become shifted to the hues directly below them. Each strip is essentially a color wheel snipped and flattened.

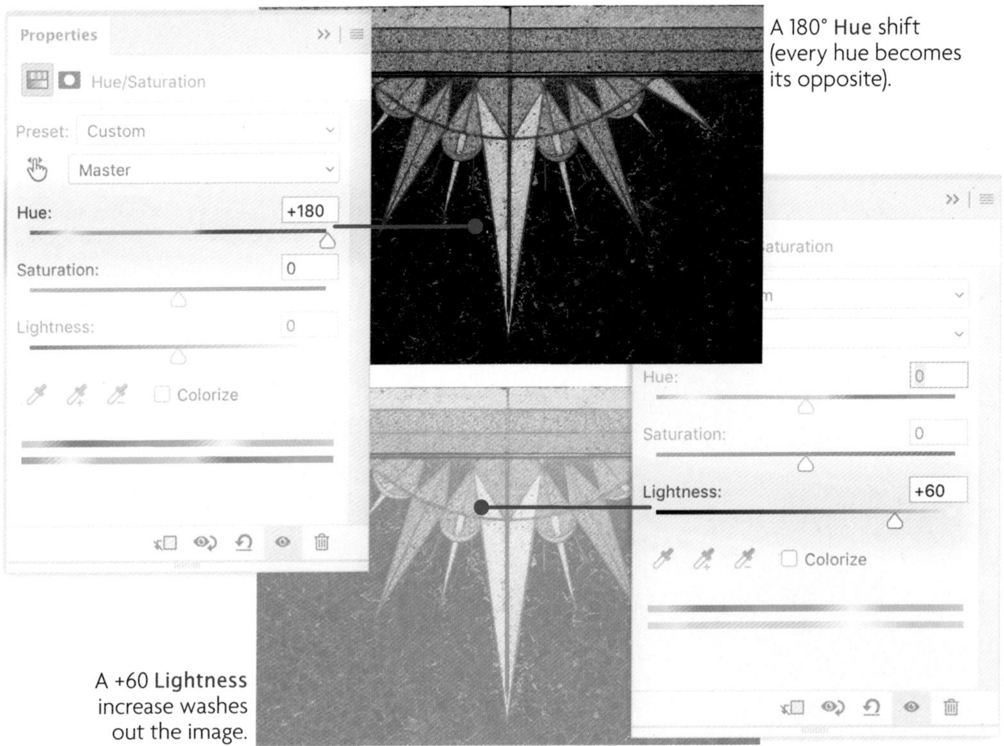

A 180° Hue shift (every hue becomes its opposite).

A +60 Lightness increase washes out the image.

- Try the Lightness slider. A bit blunt, isn't it? It will behave more nicely in the next context.

If you aren't impressed yet, that's alright. There's a really cool feature that you may find more exciting. You can adjust these attributes for each hue. That is, you can adjust the hue, saturation, and/or lightness of just blues, for example. Let's do that.

The Course

- Click the Reset button (↺) for a fresh start.

Note the menu with the word Master chosen and the small pointing hand to its left. These are two ways of choosing the hue you want to adjust. The menu seems fairly straightforward: if you want to adjust blues, you choose Blues from the menu.

That little hand resembles a scrubby cursor, the one you see when you hover over a field's label. Just hover the cursor over the word "Hue" or "Saturation" to see what I mean. Well, this tool can be used like that.

- Click the pointy finger icon (an on-image adjustment tool) to make it active. When you hover over the image, however, it looks like an eyedropper. That's OK.
- Click on a blue pixel with the tip of the eyedropper (its lower-left end). Unless you missed, the hue menu now reads Blues and a small interface has appeared between the hue strips at the bottom of the Properties panel (it's also called the Hue slider). It's *terrible* to have two things with the same name, but there it is. I'll call it the "Adjusted Hue Indicator."

The blues in the image don't exactly correspond to Photoshop's definition of blue. (On Photoshop's color wheel, blue is at the angle of 240°. That will be useful knowledge soon.) But let's continue for a moment as if our blues are their blues.

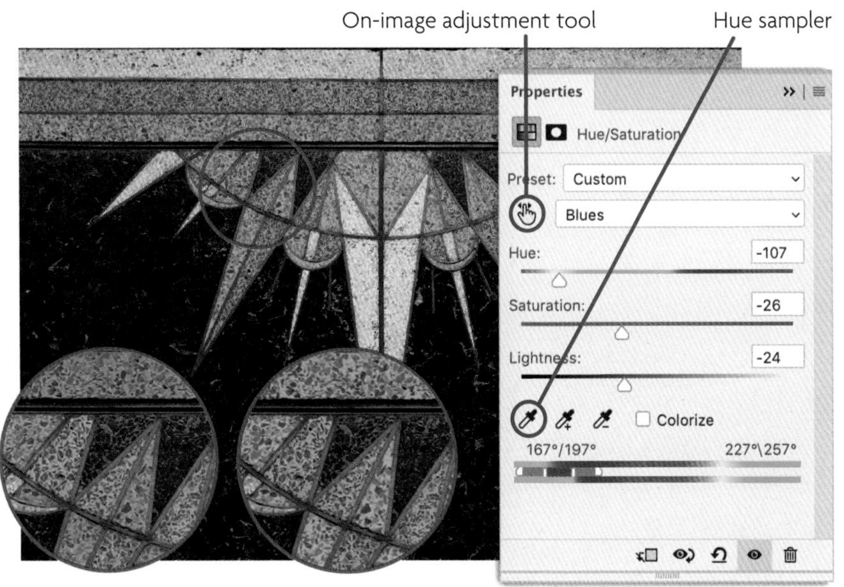

- Continue to use the on-image adjustment tool (☝) dragging on a blue part of the image. You're adjusting the saturation of that hue (note that the Saturation slider is moving when you do this).
- Drag on blue pixels while holding down option/Alt. The Saturation slider moves more slowly and carefully.
- Drag on blue pixels while holding down ⌘/Ctrl to move the Hue slider. Hold down ⌘-option/Ctrl-Alt to move the Hue slider more slowly.

As long as you press and drag on pixels that are within Photoshop's defined range for that hue, this will work. Dragging on a reddish pixel will change which hue you're adjusting entirely.

To precisely target the right range of hues for the image, there's another tool to enlist: the Hue sampler. It's the first eyedropper near the bottom of the Properties panel.

- Activate the Hue sampler by clicking its eyedropper icon. Click on a distinctly blue pixel in the image. If that is difficult to do, turn on your keyboard's caps lock for a precise cursor. Try to remember to turn off caps lock later!

The Adjusted Hue Indicator (officially, another thing called the Hue slider) has shifted to the left, closer to cyan. If it's wrapping around to the other end, ⌘/Ctrl-drag the hue strips to offset them. The central part of that indicator is under the hues that will be fully adjusted, the outer parts are under those hues that will be partially adjusted. The numbers above the hue strips show the exact hue angles on the color wheel that are being affected. Check out the diagram below.

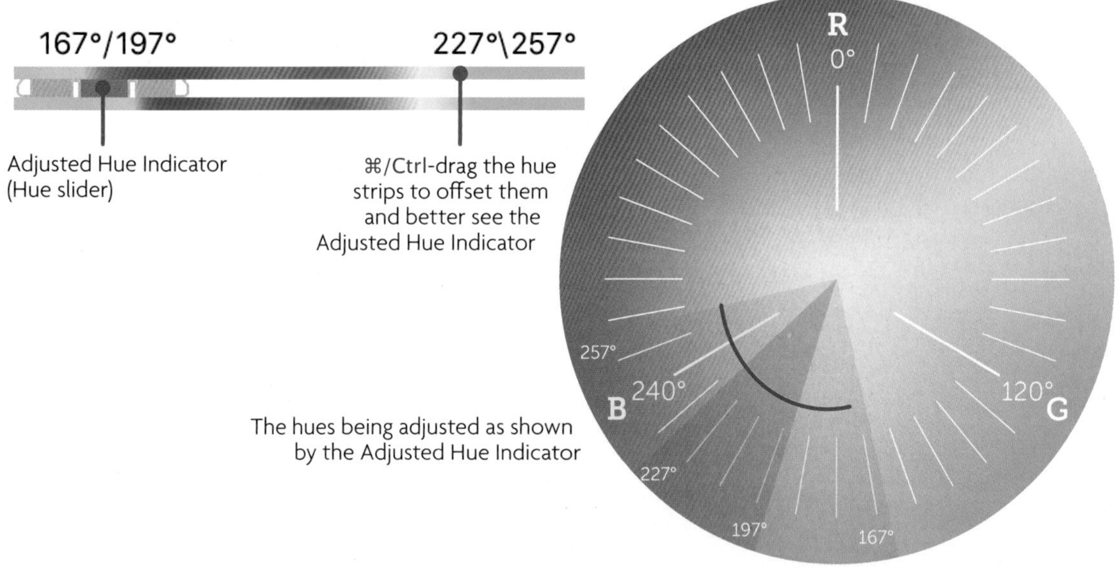

- Save your work (⌘-S/Ctrl-S) and close the document.

If you'd like to learn even more about this adjustment, see "Hue/Saturation" (page 243). Yes, there's more! In fact, now that you understand the approach to using adjustment layers, you can explore the other adjustments too. Use the "Adjustments & Color" chapter of the Compendium as your guide.

Limiting Adjustments

To affect only some areas of an image and not others requires us to make selections and masks. So you won't be surprised when you turn the page and see what's up next.

3 Selections & Masking

In this chapter, we'll learn to use a few selection tools and apply them to adjustments and the separation of subjects from their backgrounds. For each of these lessons, you'll need the files in the downloaded course folder "03 Selections and Masking."

You will find that the "Selections & Masks" chapter of the Compendium is a fine companion to these lessons.

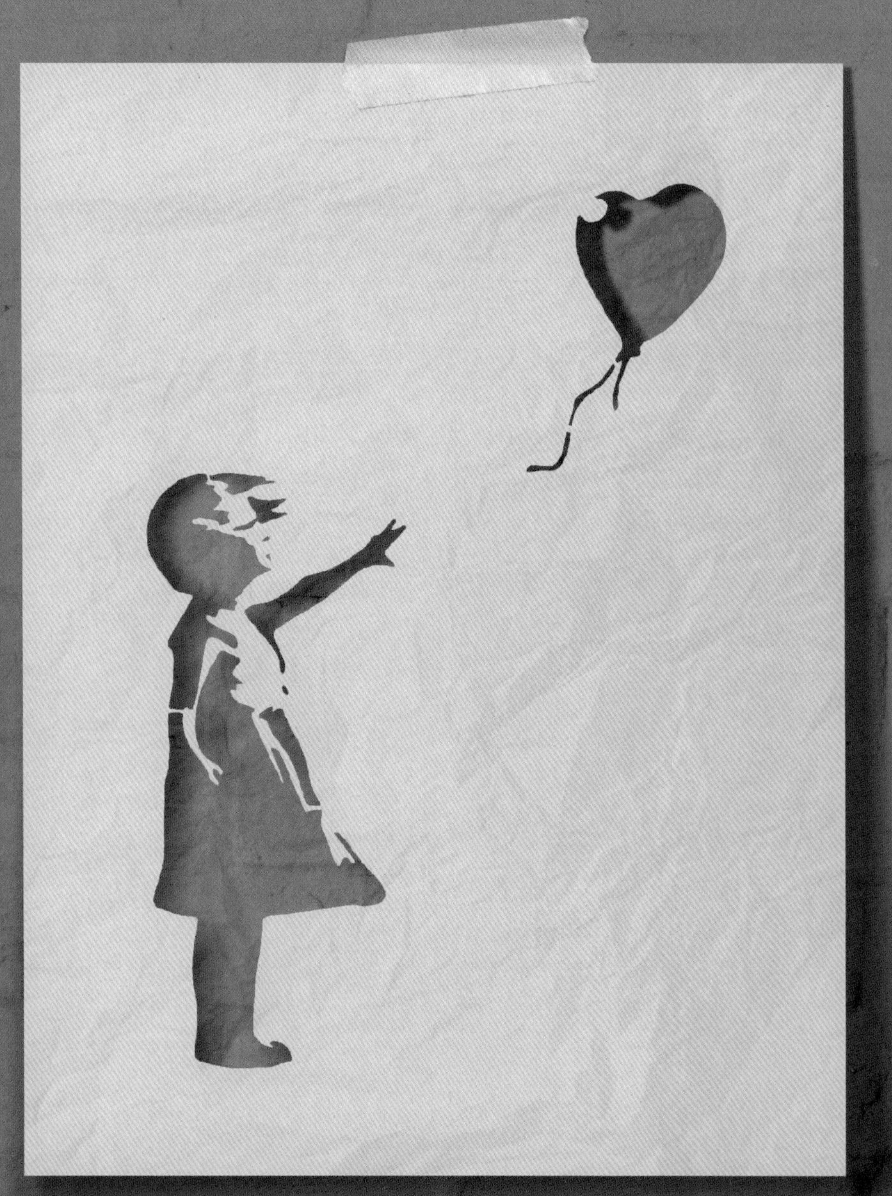

Warm-Up

In the Welcome Project, we created a mask to isolate a bird so we could put it into another photo. If you need a review, see "Lesson B: Selections & Masking" (page 20). In this chapter, the lessons will be a little more abstract, so I think a warm-up exercise would be helpful.

- Open a document from chapter 2: "B Photo Filter.psd."

If you saved it with its adjustment layer in place, I'd like you to look at that adjustment layer's thumbnails. (If you didn't save your work from chapter 2, simply click on the Photo Filter icon in the Adjustments panel to add an adjustment layer now.) The adjustment layer has two thumbnails. If you haven't done so yet, right-click on the first of those thumbnails and choose Large Thumbnails so you can see what you're doing. An additional benefit of larger thumbnails is that you can tell what kind of adjustment layer you've got in front of you.

- Click on the adjustment layer's second thumbnail, the one for its mask.

That's right, adjustment layers are born with masks so that you can quickly hide the adjustment where you may not wish to see it. Well, it's quick when you know how.

- Once the mask is targeted (it'll have a small frame around its thumbnail in the Layers panel), press the D key (as in "default") on your keyboard to ensure you've got the default colors of white for the Foreground color and black for the Background color (note their chips near the bottom of the Tools panel). Keep looking at those chips as you…
- Press the X key (as in "eXchange") to swap those colors, making black the Foreground color, the one with which you're about to paint. You also could have clicked the small two-headed arrow near those color chips.
- One more letter: press the B key (as in "Brush") to quickly select the Brush tool. Note that it's selected in the Tools panel now.

I wrote "One more letter," but I didn't mean you were done with the keyboard just yet. Move your cursor over the image—the sky would be best. Can you see that the cursor is a circle? That's the size of the brush. Its size can be seen and changed in the Options Bar (near the left end). It's faster, however, to use the left and right bracket keys ([and], next to P) on your keyboard to change the size: the left bracket for smaller, the right bracket for larger.

- Make the brush about 150 pixels across (about the size of the skull on the left side of the image). You're finally ready.
- Drag a paint stroke across the sky. You're painting with black, but it's on the mask. This means you're hiding that part of the active layer—in this case, an adjustment. The original, vibrant sky color becomes apparent again.

You can paint with smaller brushes to get into crevices to hide the adjustment *exactly* where you want to. Pressing X again and painting with white shows the adjustment layer again. In the following lessons, we're going to create adjustment layers that will be masked to specific areas as we create them. Some brush work may be useful, but it's not always necessary.

Lesson A: Rectangular Marquee

Much of what we'll see with this tool applies very well to the other tools, so please don't skip this lesson! I will assume you've done it later.

- Open the image "A rectangular marquee.psd" from the folder "03 Selections and Masking."
- Choose the Rectangular Marquee tool in the Tools panel by clicking it or tapping the M key (as in "Marquee") on your keyboard. That's right, more letters to learn!

Our objective is to select the central part of this image where the dog carving is and then lighten that area, leaving the outer parts of the image dark.

Basic Use

Before we attempt the final selection, let's see what this tool is about.

- Press and drag diagonally with the Rectangular Marquee tool. It doesn't matter whether you're dragging up or down, left or right, as long as you drag diagonally.
- Once you have the "marching ants," note how the cursor's appearance changes when it moves into and out of the perimeter of your selection. With the cursor inside, press and drag to move your selection.
- Click outside the marquee (selection) and you deselect.
- Make a new selection.
- Drag outside that selection to begin a new selection.

Note: Some selection tools can't be used to deselect by clicking outside the current selection, but instead will always make a new selection. I'll let you know when we get to one of those.

- This time, to deselect I want you to use a shortcut: ⌘-D/Ctrl-D (as in "Deselect"). No matter which tool made the selection or which tool you're wielding, this will work.

Modifier Keys

When arbitrary rectangles aren't sufficient, we can use modifier keys (option or shift on macOS; Alt or Shift on Windows).

- With no active selection, draw a new marquee, being sure to hold down the shift key, especially as you finish the selection. You now have a *perfectly* square selection. Interesting, right? You can start dragging before the shift key is held, but finish with it.
- Deselect (⌘-D/Ctrl-D).
- Starting in the center of the image (or perhaps at the dog's nose?), drag outward with the option/Alt key held down, especially as you finish the selection. It will have grown outward, centered on the point from which you started. Also cool.

But what happens when there is an active selection when using those modifiers? It is different! If you use a text-editing program, you may know that if you have a word selected, then shift-click later in the text, you've grown your selection (added to it). That's the case here too.

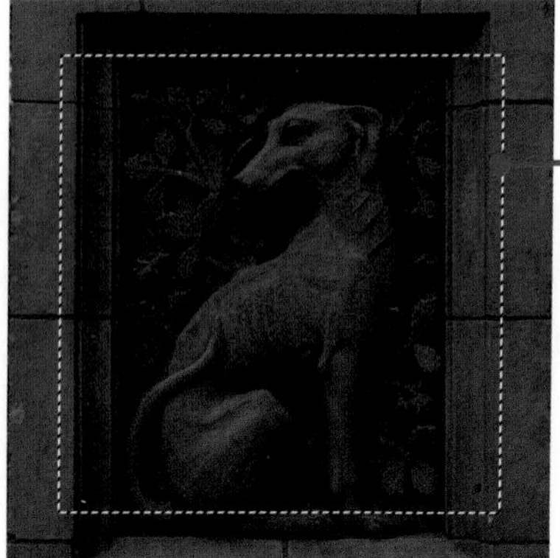

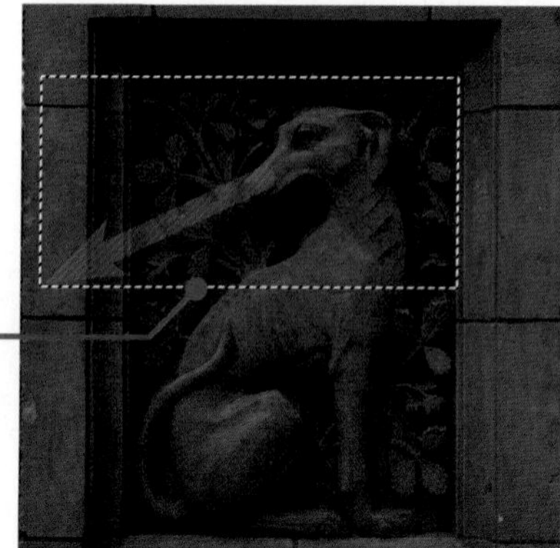

Starting with no selection:

Holding down the shift key as the marquee is ***finished*** constrains it to a square (left).

Holding down the option/Alt key as the marquee is ***finished*** causes it to grow outward, centered on the starting point (right).

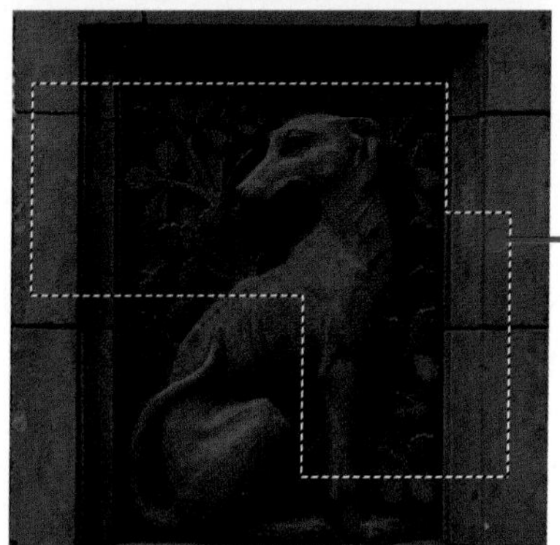

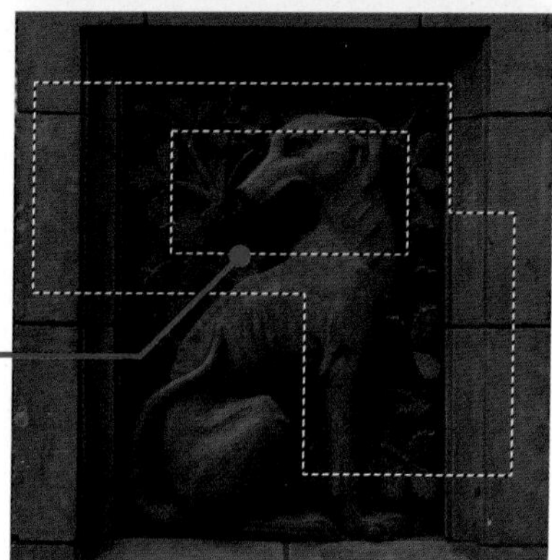

With an active selection:

Holding down shift as a second marquee is ***started*** adds the new area to the selection (left).

Holding down option/Alt as a second marquee is ***started*** removes that area from the selection (right).

- With an active selection, hold down shift and then start a new marquee, adding more area to the existing selection. Even if you release that key partway through, it will work.

The added area does not need to be contiguous with the actively selected area. It would still be a single selection in the same way a stencil is one stencil even if it has multiple holes in it.

- Use option/Alt to remove an area from the selection. If a stencil could have a cardboard (or plastic, etc.) island floating in the middle of a hole, that would be a good metaphor.

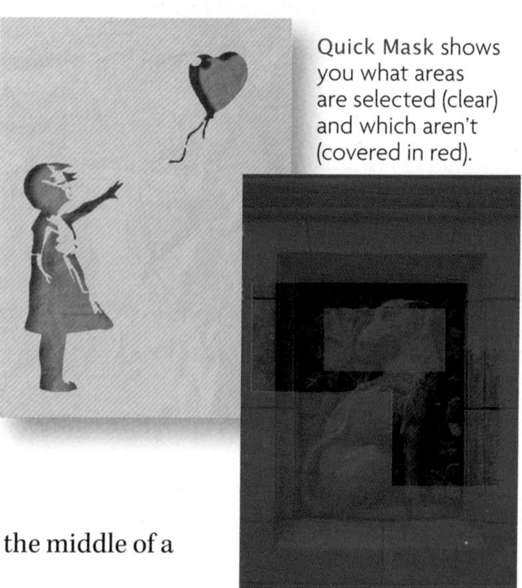

Quick Mask shows you what areas are selected (clear) and which aren't (covered in red).

- Tap the letter Q (as in "Quick Mask"). This shows you the virtual stencil that a selection actually is. For now, don't do anything in that mode. To exit that mode and see those marching ants again, tap Q a second time.

There is one more modifier key I'd like you to learn, and it will be surprising. It won't be useful in this lesson, but will definitely help in the next one. Be warned that you'll be holding the mouse button down a while.

- Be sure you're not in Quick Mask mode, then deselect (⌘-D/Ctrl-D).
- Start a new selection but don't release the mouse!
- Partway through, pause and hold down the spacebar (!). With that mouse button still held down, move your mouse hand. While the spacebar is held down and with the marquee unfinished, your mouse movements move the marquee-in-progress. Release only the spacebar and you can resize and reshape the marquee you're drawing.
- Release the mouse to complete the marquee. Yes, this does take practice!

When you feel that you've got that, at least for now, let's lighten up that lovely puppy.

- Deselect (⌘-D/Ctrl-D).
- Draw a marquee around the recess where the dog relief is.

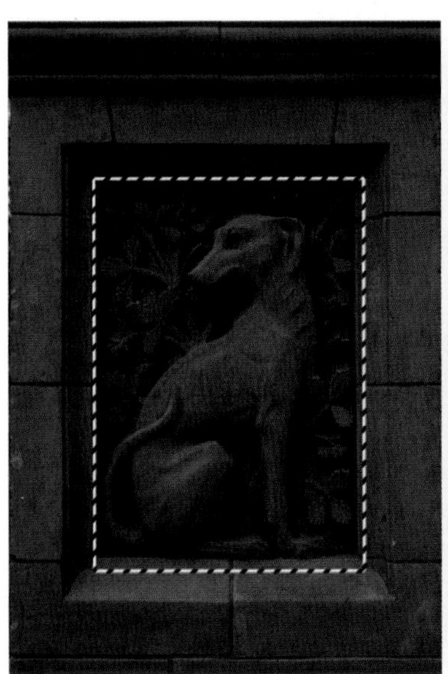

The **Rectangular Marquee**

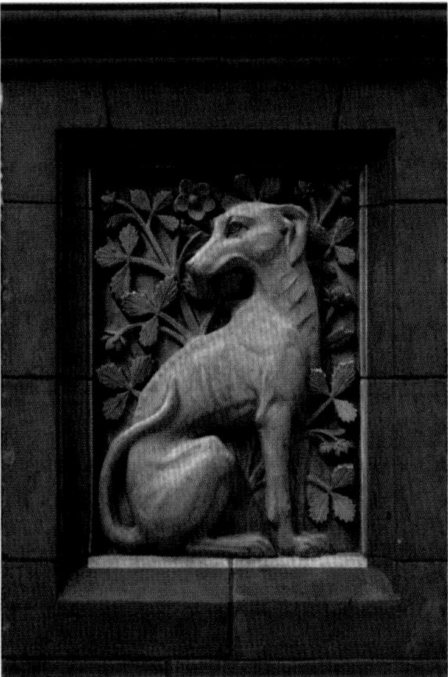

The **Curves** adjustment layer is automatically masked to the selected area

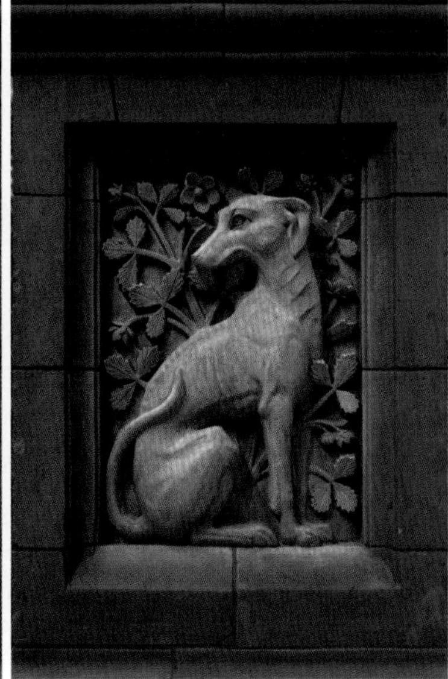

Applying **Feather** to the mask in the **Properties panel** to only partially affect pixels at mask's edges

- Make a Curves adjustment layer by clicking the Curves icon in the Adjustments panel.

The histogram will reveal that no pixel in that region is even as bright as a midtone. This image is dark! We need a substantial change:

- Drag the white-point slider to the left. Not necessarily all the way to the lightest pixels in the histogram, but almost. We can see the color of the sandstone now. But that sharp cutoff between adjusted and unadjusted areas…

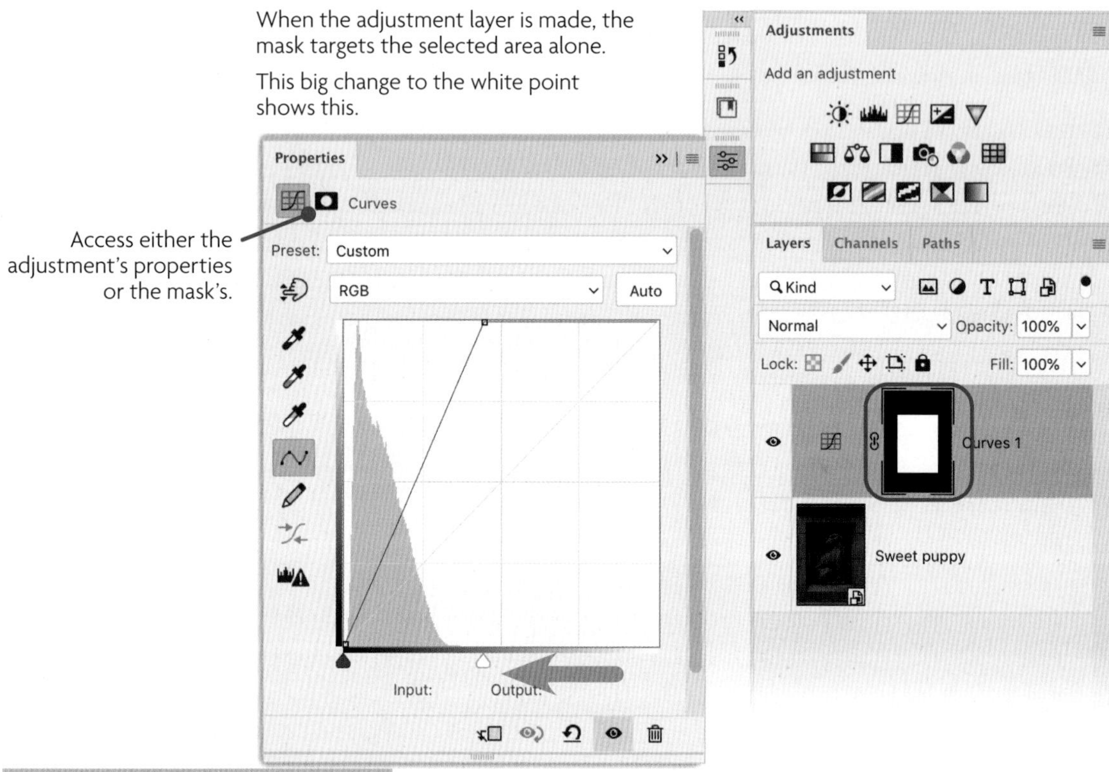

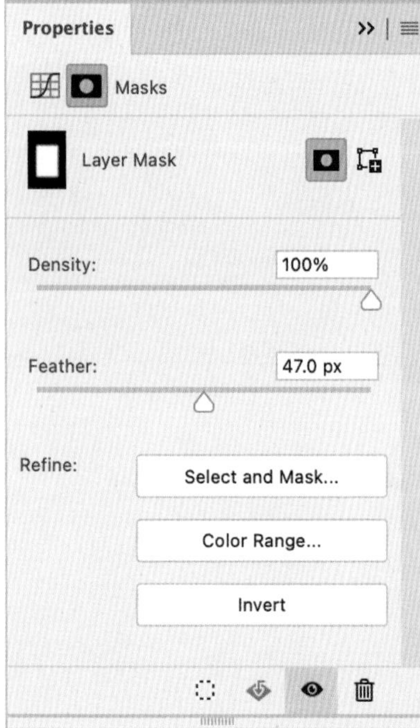

- Click on the mask thumbnail to show its properties in the Properties panel. You can also access the mask's properties (or the layer's) at the top of the Properties panel.
- In the Properties panel, drag the Feather slider to the right to nondestructively blur the mask. I found a value of 40–50 pixels looks good, like a light gently shining on that sculpted element.

Lesson B: Elliptical Marquee

- Open the file "B elliptical marquee.psd."
- Get to this tool by right-clicking on the Rectangular Marquee tool and choosing the Elliptical Marquee tool.

All the modifications of the Rectangular Marquee tool discussed on the previous pages are applicable to the Elliptical Marquee tool. The trick of using the spacebar to move the marquee while it's being drawn is especially useful here. The goal is to select the old well cover, then increase its saturation.

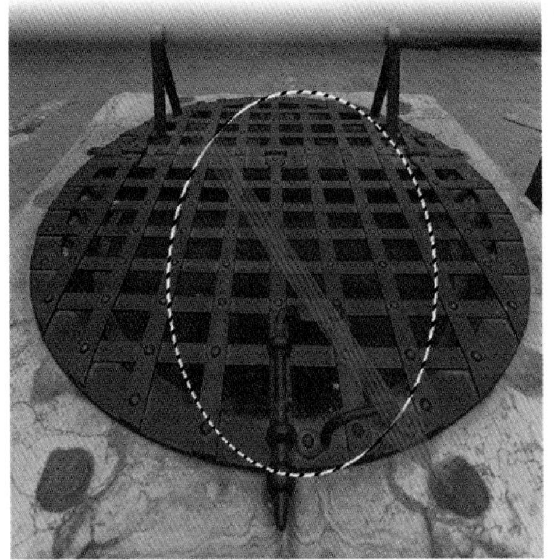

Dragging an Elliptical Marquee

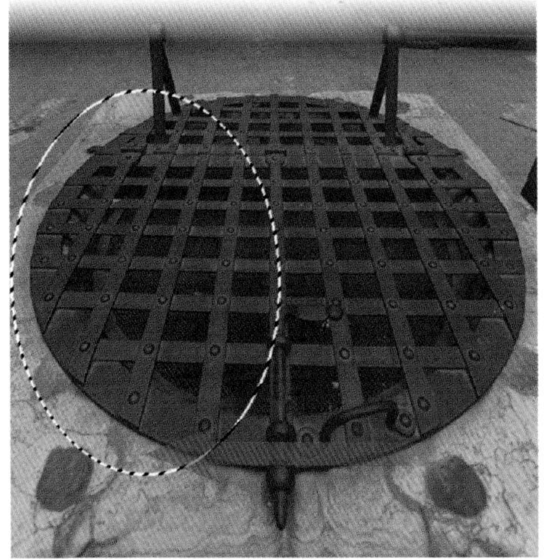

Dragging while holding down the spacebar

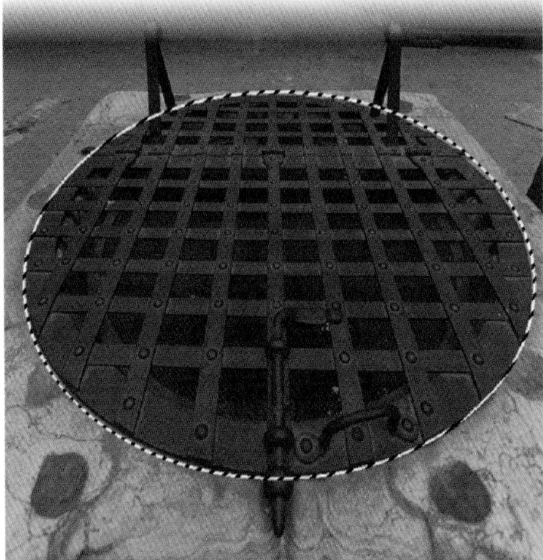

Result after using the spacebar occasionally while making the marquee

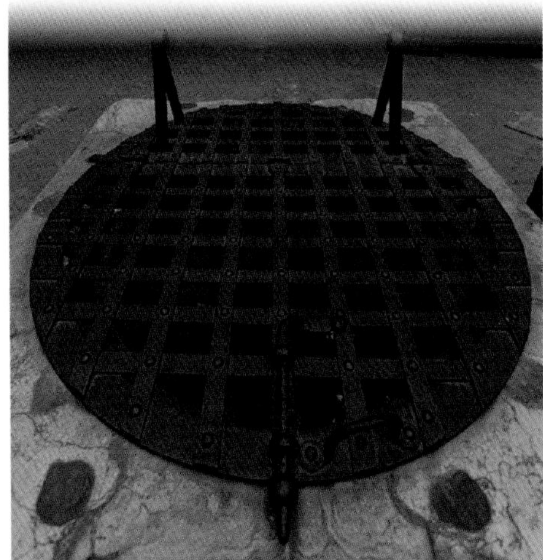

After creating a Vibrance adjustment layer, significantly increasing Saturation, and refining the mask

- As you drag with this tool, the marquee seems to slide a bit, making it difficult to position it precisely. Without releasing the mouse, press the spacebar to move the marquee, then release only the spacebar to resize and reshape. Release the mouse only when the marquee is sized correctly and positioned over the well cover. So, hold down the spacebar occasionally while creating the selection to move the marquee-in-progress.

Vibrance Adjustment

Now let's pump up the latent color in that metal grating.

- With the marquee in place, create a Vibrance adjustment layer by clicking its icon in the Adjustments panel.
- Since the color is so subtle, use the Saturation slider (and the Vibrance slider too, perhaps) to make a significant adjustment.

To extend the adjustment to the foreground bolt and background supports, we'll need to paint on this adjustment layer's mask.

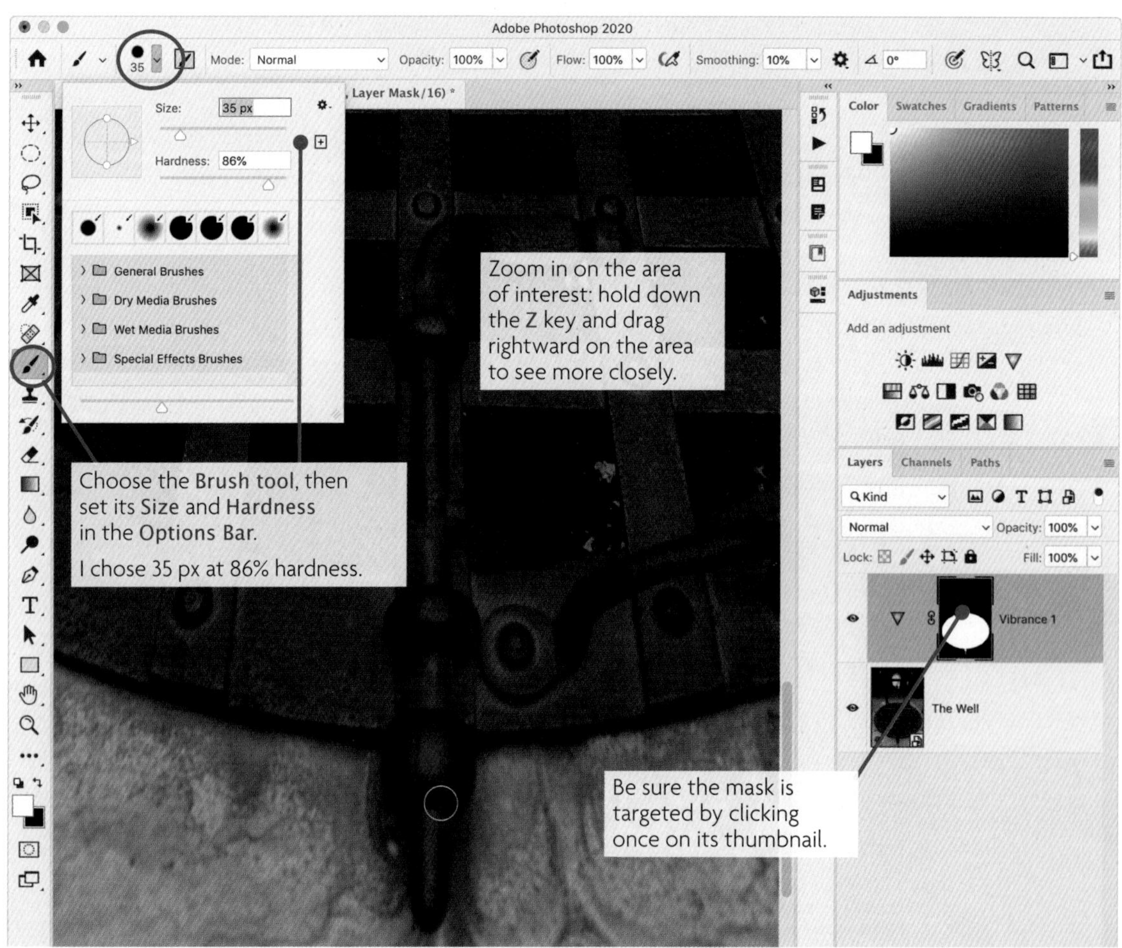
Adobe Photoshop 2020
Zoom in on the area of interest: hold down the Z key and drag rightward on the area to see more closely.
Choose the Brush tool, then set its Size and Hardness in the Options Bar.
I chose 35 px at 86% hardness.
Be sure the mask is targeted by clicking once on its thumbnail.
Size: 35 px
Hardness: 86%
General Brushes
Dry Media Brushes
Wet Media Brushes
Special Effects Brushes
Adjustments
Add an adjustment
Layers
Vibrance 1
The Well

- Hold down the Z key (don't just tap it). With the cursor over that bolt, press and drag rightward to zoom in on it. If it ends up a bit off-center, hold down the spacebar to pan with the Hand tool.
- Activate the Brush tool (tap the B key). To extend or limit where the adjustment is visible, we're gong to paint with white or black on the adjustment layer's mask.
- To be sure that the mask is targeted for painting, click just once on its thumbnail. It should have a small border around its corners.

To extend the adjustment over the bolt, we'll need white as our Foreground color so we can paint with white. Look near the bottom of the Tools panel to see the Foreground and Background color chips.

- Tap the D key to ensure those chips are the default colors of white and black. Get it? "D" for "Default." If the colors should become reversed, or you want them to be, you can tap the X key to "eXchange" them again.

Since the bolt is small and hard-edged, our brush should share those characteristics.

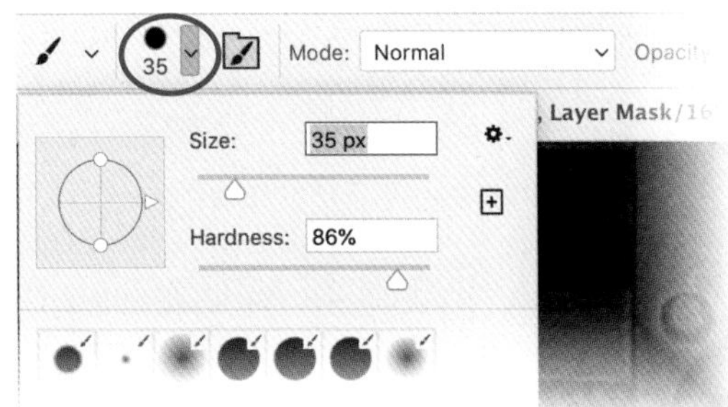

- In the Options Bar, click the small menu button next to the brush preview. A size of around 35 pixels and a high hardness value near 90% should be good here.
- Now paint on the bolt and you should see it getting a bit of color like the rest of the metalwork nearby. If there are areas that have been affected by the adjustment but should not have been, tap the X key to paint those areas of the mask with black.
- Pan up to the vertical supports of the well cover with the Hand tool (by holding down the spacebar and dragging).
- Paint on the vertical supports to enhance them, too.

Yes, I'm exposing you to a lot of shortcuts and I'm doing so early and often. Like any task, muscle memory gets built with repetition, and these shortcuts make you a fast and efficient Photoshop user. Stay with me!

- Save your work and choose File > Close.

Lesson C: Lasso & Polygonal Lasso

Now let's open an arresting image of a stop sign: "C polygonal lasso.psd." (The bad puns are free.) We'll be changing the color in the stop sign from red to green. First, we'll experiment with the tools under discussion.

The Lasso Tool

If you tap the L key, you find yourself wielding the Lasso tool—or one of them. There are two worth looking at: the regular Lasso tool and the Polygonal Lasso tool. Both are very easy to use. The first is *not* meant for creating precise, intricate selections, but rather loose, approximate ones.

- Activate the Lasso tool (tap the L key).
- Press and drag a loop around a part of the image (it doesn't matter where, as we won't use this tool in the end).
- When you release the mouse, you've got a selection in that shape.
- Deselect by either choosing Select > Deselect or using the shortcut ⌘-D/Ctrl-D.
- Now, make a U-shape with the Lasso tool, releasing the mouse some distance from where you started dragging. Photoshop will close the shape for you with a straight line.
- Deselect by either choosing Select > Deselect or using the shortcut ⌘-D/Ctrl-D.

The Polygonal Lasso Tool

Now let's try a more interesting tool. We'll do one or two practice rounds, then we'll make the selection we need.

- Activate the Polygonal Lasso tool by right-clicking the Lasso tool and choosing the second tool in that slot. You may also use shift-L to cycle through the lasso tools.
- This time, don't drag, but click repeatedly around an area of the image. Each click tacks down a vertex of the polygon you're creating. Click where you want each vertex to be.
- Work your way around a part of the image, then click on the spot where you started.

While you're creating a selection, there is no selection yet. So if you start this process unintentionally, the Deselect command will not help you. You have to tap the escape key to stop this tool. Or you can complete the selection-making task, after which Deselect will work.

There are three ways to finish a selection with the Polygonal Lasso tool:

- Work your way back to the starting point and make your last click there.
- Double-click the last vertex you set. This sets that vertex and closes the selection, and is the most efficient method. See the illustration that follows.
- From the position of the last vertex, press the Enter key instead of clicking. This creates that vertex and closes the selection. No one does this.

- Hold down the Z key to zoom in to the stop sign so you can more easily create the selection.
- For each click with the Polygonal Lasso tool, place the tip of the cursor in the white band between the edge of the sign and the red part of it. I started in the upper right and proceeded counterclockwise.
- Rather than click at what would be the last vertex, double-click (position 8 in the illustration below). This closes the shape and gives you marching ants.
- If you made a significant mistake, use it as an opportunity to practice: deselect by choosing Select > Deselect or using the shortcut ⌘-D/Ctrl-D, then try again.

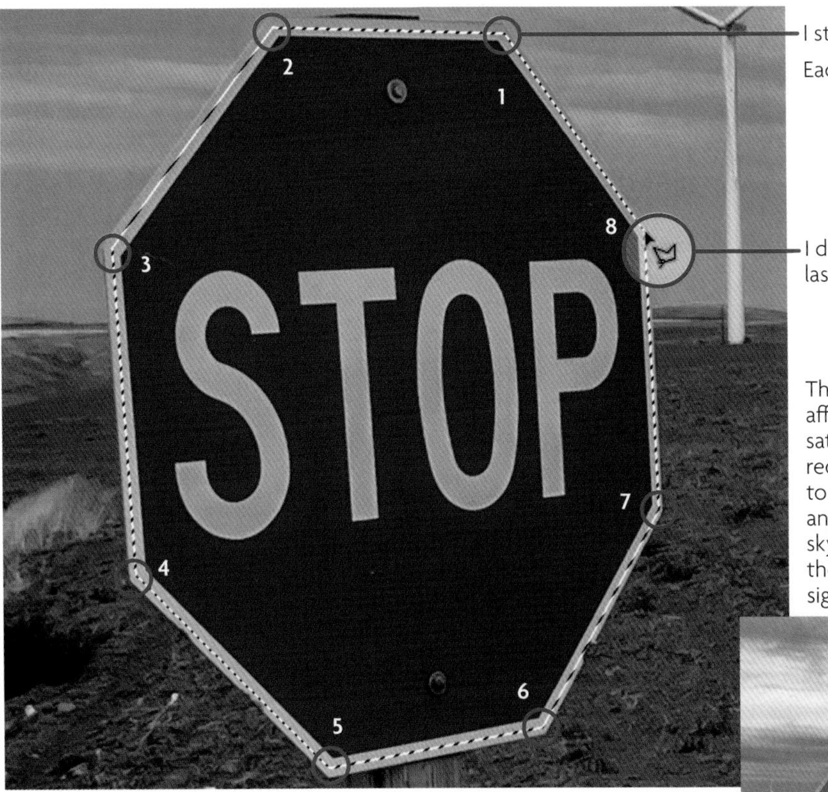

I started here with one click. Each ◯ is a subsequent click.

I double-clicked here to set the last vertex and close the shape.

The Hue adjustment doesn't affect tone or pixels with no saturation. To affect only the red of the stop sign, we have to surround it but exclude anything else with color (the sky or ground). So we click in the white gap between the sign's edge and the red.

With the completed selection, let's make that adjustment.

- With the marquee in place, create a Hue/Saturation adjustment layer by clicking its icon in the Adjustments panel.
- Move the Hue slider to the right until the stop sign's color is green.
- Admire your work for a while, then save the file and close it.

Lesson D: Object Selection

We used a number of tools in the Welcome project to select the osprey that we moved to the photo of the Italian town. You may wish to review that exercise. Let's take a look at how those tools work here. This time, we'll end with the Quick Selection tool. The first two methods (Select Subject and the Object Selection tool) are under very active development at Adobe, so we're all looking forward to how they grow into their potential.

- Open the document "D E Object Selection.psd." Our objective will be to mask the image so that only Peachy the Peach is visible, with neither the black velvet background nor the juggling balls.

Object Selection Tool

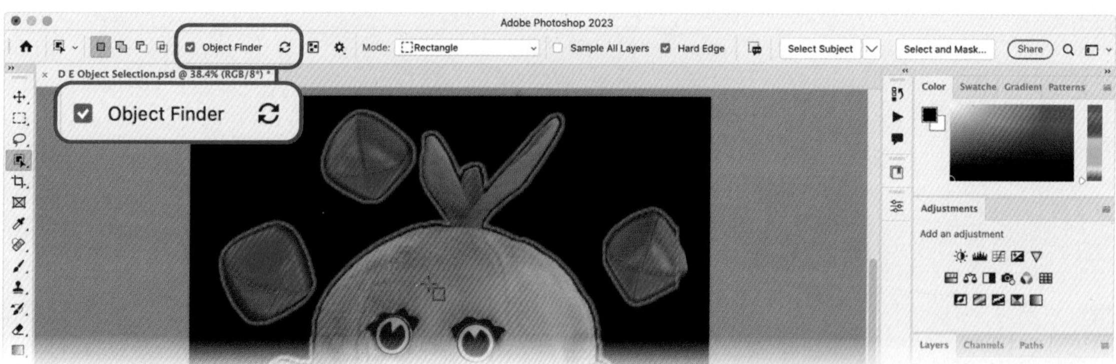

- In the Tools panel, choose the Object Selection tool (or tap the W key).
- Wait for the Object Finder Refresh in the Options Bar to stop spinning.
- Hover the cursor over Peachy and note that both she and the juggling balls are considered one object (at least, as of this writing).

You'd have to subsequently remove the juggling balls from the selection. That's not hard, as you'll see in the next section.

- Switch the Mode to Lasso, then make a loop around Peachy with a little care. A good selection results even with minor flubs!

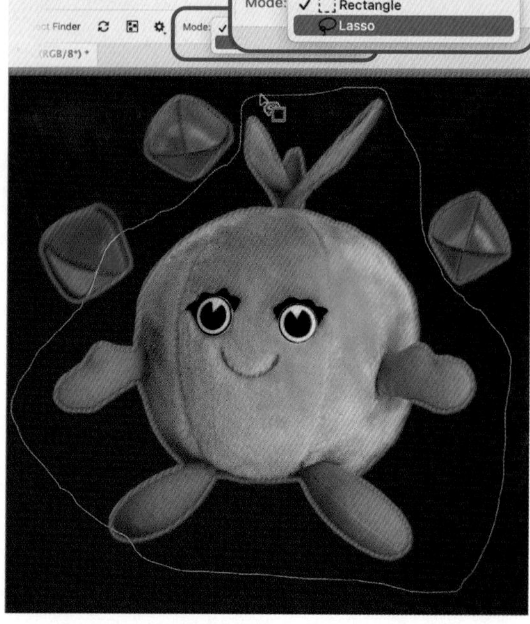

Magic Wand Tool

- Deselect then right-click on the Object Selection tool to choose the Magic Wand tool.
- Test its function by clicking with it in the middle of one of Peachy's eyes.

It selects the black of the eye, but the selection edge stops at the white area surrounding it. That's because this tool reads the color you click on and then grows a selection from that point outward until it reaches something different enough. That "different enough" value is set in the Options Bar with a control called Tolerance. Most often, the Tolerance value is a range of levels or tones on each color channel above and below that of the pixel you click on. But it can be different than that if the pixel you click on is very light or dark. So just know that high values will select larger areas than low values, and you should usually change Tolerance a little at a time.

Your keyboard's caps lock enables precise cursors to better know where you're clicking.

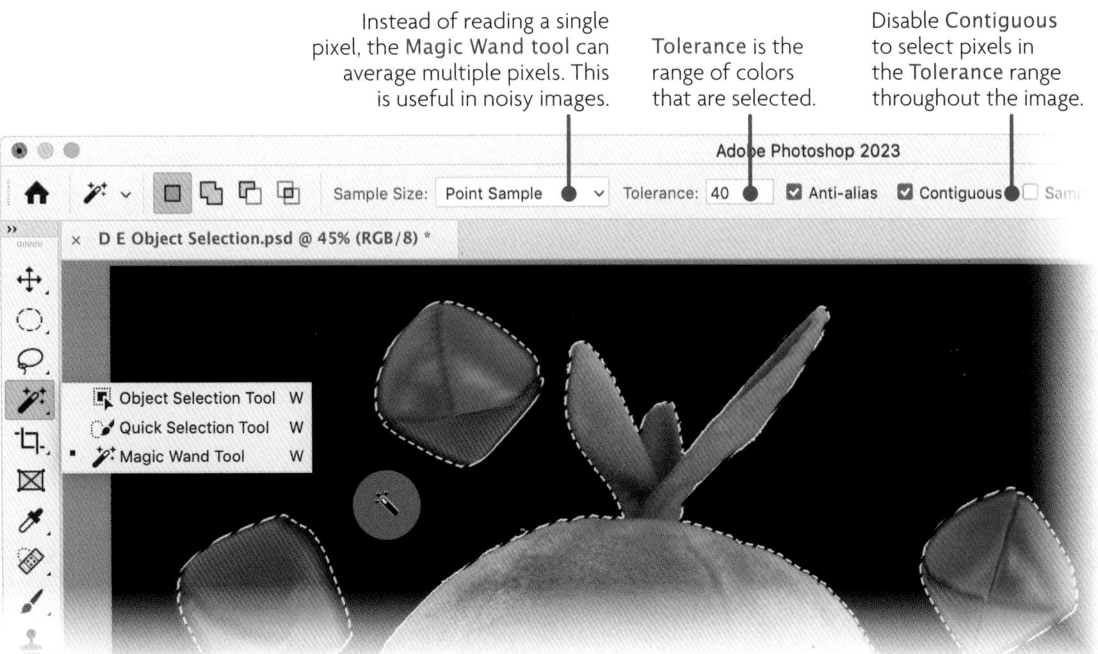

- Set the Tolerance to its default of 32. Click on one of Peachy's hands and note how well or poorly it was selected. Deselect.
- Set Tolerance to about 100 and try again. It's quite different. Then click on the surrounding black velvet. At such a high setting, the selection extends well into Peachy and much else.
- Deselect, set the Tolerance to 40 or 50, then click on the black velvet again. Now you've got a pretty nice selection of everything *except* Peachy and the juggling balls.
- Choose Select > Inverse to select Peachy and the balls.
- Switch to the Lasso tool. Hold down the option/Alt key so you can remove each juggling ball from the active selection by drawing a loop around it.

Quick Selection Tool

- Deselect if you haven't yet. Also, turn off caps lock if that's enabled.
- Right-click on the Magic Wand tool to access and activate the Quick Selection tool.

Like the Magic Wand tool, this tool reads what you click on (or drag over). It uses a circular, brushlike cursor to approximate the wand's Tolerance and Sampling Size: the larger this tool's brush, the more aggressive it becomes. The amount you sample in one stroke also affects how aggressively this tool selects. So I advise using smallish brushes and numerous strokes rather than one or a few strokes with a large brush size. For this image, that would mean a brush about 100 pixels across.

- Use the square bracket keys ([or]) to adjust the Quick Selection tool's brush size (look in the Options Bar to monitor its numeric size). A width of 100 pixels should be good, as that's a little narrower than Peachy's stem.

Warning: As you "paint" your selection with this tool, keep the cursor's edge within Peachy's perimeter. Each brush stroke tells Photoshop what textures and colors you want selected. Going over the lines confuses that. If you do so, undo (⌘-Z/Ctrl-Z) and try again more carefully.

- Drag across Peachy's forehead (as it were). The resulting marquee will extend to Peachy's edges without your having to get too close to them.
- With separate strokes, drag across her eyes, on each hand, on each foot, and between the feet. You may need to get close to the edges so be careful! Finally, include her leaves too.

You may notice that you didn't have to cover everything. It's likely Photoshop selected one of her hands for you. In other images, Photoshop's guesses could be wrong. When that's the case, hold down option/Alt and paint over the areas that shouldn't be selected. This helps the program know what you want and what you don't.

Rule of Thumb: When you make a mistake, undo. When Photoshop makes a mistake, gently correct it by option/Alt-painting with this tool.

Quick Mask Mode

Did you miss anything? Are you sure? Quick Mask is a cool and fast way to show you which areas are selected and which areas aren't.

- With an active selection, tap the Q key to toggle into and out of Quick Mask mode. While in it, a red translucent overlay covers what isn't selected. If you missed anything that should be selected, make a mental note of it. Then leave Quick Mask mode and add those areas.

Warning: Don't do any selection-making while in Quick Mask mode. Toggle back to regular mode first. The document tab says "Quick Mask" when in that mode. Tap Q to get out.

Select Subject

Available from Select > Subject or a button in the Options Bar when the Magic Wand, Quick Selection, or Object Selection tool is active, this function uses AI to analyze the image for a likely subject and selects it!

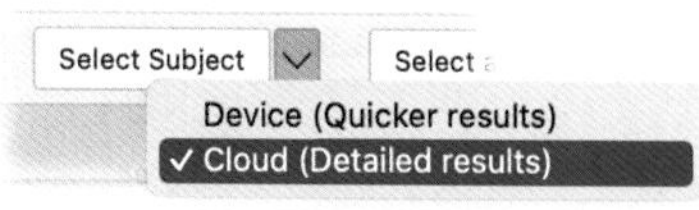

It presents a choice to use your computer or iPad ("Device") to process the selection or Adobe's computers ("Cloud"). Although uploading and downloading large images takes time on slower internet connections, the cloud result is noticeably better. To choose a processing default, visit the Image Processing preferences.

- Set the processing to Cloud (Detailed results) then click Select Subject.
- Do not deselect! We're going places with that selection.

Select and Mask Workspace

To perfect a selection, Photoshop offers an environment formerly called "Refine Edge" (still a great description) but now called Select and Mask. Note its button in the Options Bar when any selection tool is active. Although we can make selections as well as refine them there, let's use it to do only a refinement of the Peachy selection.

- With your Peachy selection intact, click the Select and Mask button or choose Select > Select and Mask. You're now in an entirely new workspace with its own tools and panels.

Before proceeding, you have a reading assignment. You'll recognize our protagonist, so it will be very relevant to this exercise.

- Read the section "Select and Mask" (page 278). You'll want to play along with this image as you do. When finished experimenting, remain in (or return to) Select and Mask and continue below.

Just Peachy

Now that you know the options available in Select and Mask, let's apply a few.

- Set the View to On White.
- In the Edge Detection section, try a Radius of about 8 pixels, with Smart Radius enabled.
- Because Peachy was surrounded by black pixels, some gray is contaminating her edge fuzz. So, in the Output Settings section, enable Decontaminate Colors at the full Amount.

The edges should look far better now!

- To be sure, enable High Quality Preview at the top of the workspace.
- When you click OK, you'll have a new Peachy layer that is masked to those perfectly fuzzy edges.
- Save this file. You'll need it in the next lesson, but you deserve a break!

Lesson E: Mini Project

Peachy In The Woods

You'll need two images for this little exercise: "D E Object Selection.psd" (the image of Peachy from the previous lesson) and "E Trains_and_Peachy.psd."

- Make the Peachy image active by clicking its tab.
- Activate the Move tool by clicking it in the Tools panel or by tapping the V key.

The next step, bringing Peachy to the scene in the woods, is slightly tricky. You must keep the mouse button depressed continuously while dragging up from the Peachy image to the other document's tab, waiting for the other image to appear, and then dragging downward into its document window before releasing. In class, I phrase it, "drag upward, pause, downward, release."

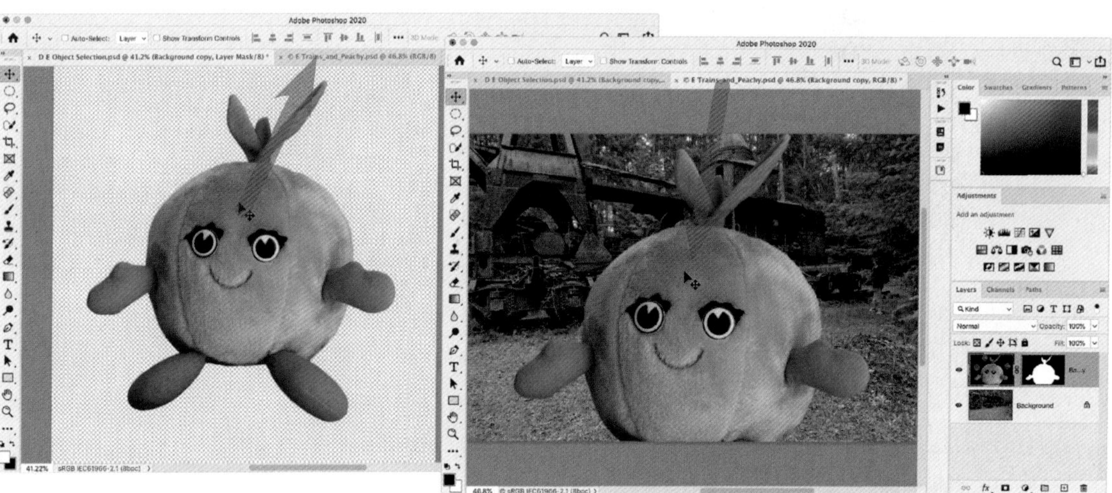

Drag the masked Peachy layer up to the other document's tab, pause for the other image to appear, then continue downward before releasing. If you release too soon, nothing happens!

- With the Move tool, drag Peachy up to the tab for "E Trains_and_Peachy.psd," positioning the cursor over that tab and keeping the mouse button pressed when that other image appears.
- When the destination image appears, continue dragging, but move downward onto the woodsy scene where you can release the mouse.

Although we used the "Move" tool, Peachy was actually copied from one document to the other. The Layers panel should show a new layer in the document to which we copied her.

- Rename that layer "Peachy" by double-clicking the current name.

We've reached a decision point. Although I think this photo-bomber Peachy is funny, we may wish to reduce her size so she appears to be on the ground nearer the rusted train. But if we changed our minds tomorrow and resized her again to her former large size, the result would be terrible. To reduce the size of an ordinary layer means we're eliminating a great many pixels. To enlarge a relative few pixels to cover a large area would make a very "pixelated" result.

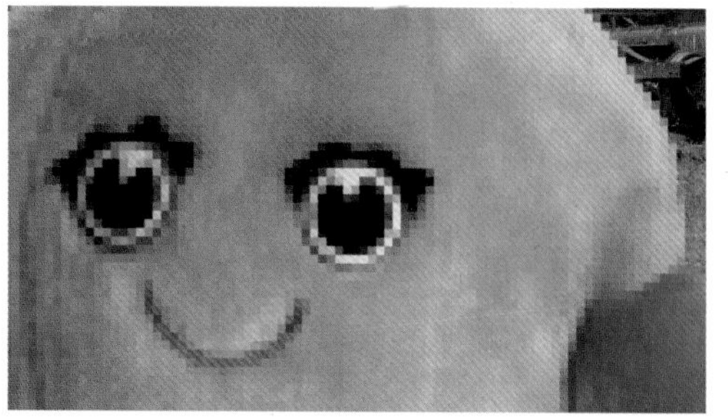

With a little forethought, we should convert the Peachy layer into a Smart Object. This protects and preserves the content. So if we one day reduce her size and then increase it the next, Photoshop really is using the full-resolution Peachy each time. This allows us to restore her to her full size with perfect fidelity. Here, you can see the result of reducing Peachy to 10% her initial size, then enlarging again to her original dimensions. Not good!

- Right-click near the name of the Peachy layer and choose Convert to Smart Object. Note the icon in the thumbnail to indicate this layer's new nature.

We can now apply filters and transformations repeatedly with no ill effect on the actual image data. Those filters and transformations can be removed at any time.

We have a couple of methods from which to choose for resizing her now. If the Move tool is active, note the checkbox in the Options Bar to Show Transform Controls. If enabled, you'll have quick access to transformations simply by activating the Move tool and highlighting the layer you want to transform.

But some people dislike this because they accidentally transform things. They prefer the more conscious decision to activate Free Transform. The shortcut to do so is somewhat intuitive (and fast): ⌘-T/Ctrl-T (as in "Transform"). This invokes the same transform controls but only when needed.

With either method, when the desired transformation is completed, we press Enter on the keyboard to commit it. Personally, I'm in the Free Transform camp. It's fast and I don't accidentally rotate layers like I sometimes do showing those controls all the time.

- With the Move tool active, be sure that Show Transform Controls is disabled (unchecked).
- With the Peachy Smart Object highlighted, use the shortcut ⌘-T/Ctrl-T or, slower, choose Edit > Free Transform. There is now a box surrounding Peachy with control handles on it.

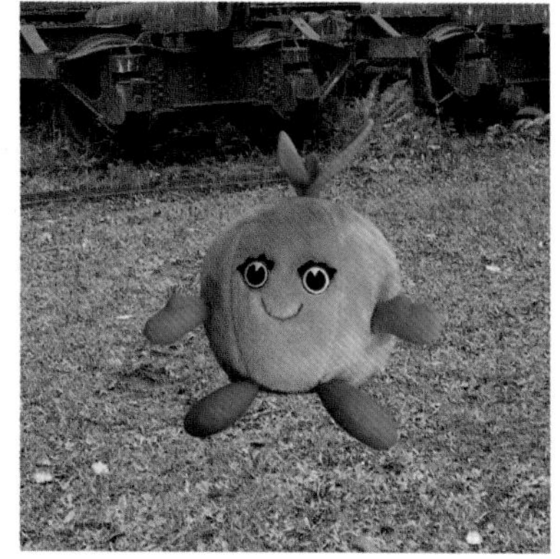

- *Resize* Peachy by dragging one of the control handles. *Move* Peachy by dragging with the cursor somewhere inside the box. *Rotate* Peachy by dragging with the cursor somewhere outside the box (but not too far outside). Resize her to about 20% of her original size (monitor the transformation specs in the Options Bar).
- Commit the transformation by pressing Enter, clicking the check mark (✓) in the Options Bar, or clicking well outside the transform box (wherever the cursor becomes a standard arrow).

A Quick Shadow

I located Peachy on the grass in the foreground. Right now it looks pretty fake because she isn't casting a shadow. But I've found that even a quick-and-dirty shadow will often do. We'll paint one below Peachy's, eh, bottom. That is, on a layer below Peachy but above the Background.

- Zoom in by holding down the Z key and then dragging rightward over Peachy. Not too much! You might also choose View > 100%, then pan to where you put Peachy.
- Highlight the Background layer, then use the Layers panel menu to choose New Layer….
- Type in a name like "shadow" or "cheesy shadow" and click OK.
- Activate the Brush tool. Set the Hardness to 0% for the soft shadow we need, and set the Size to about the width of Peachy's foot (for me, that was about 125 pixels).
- Set the colors to their defaults of black and white by tapping the D key. A quick glance at them should tell you that black is the Foreground color. Perfect.

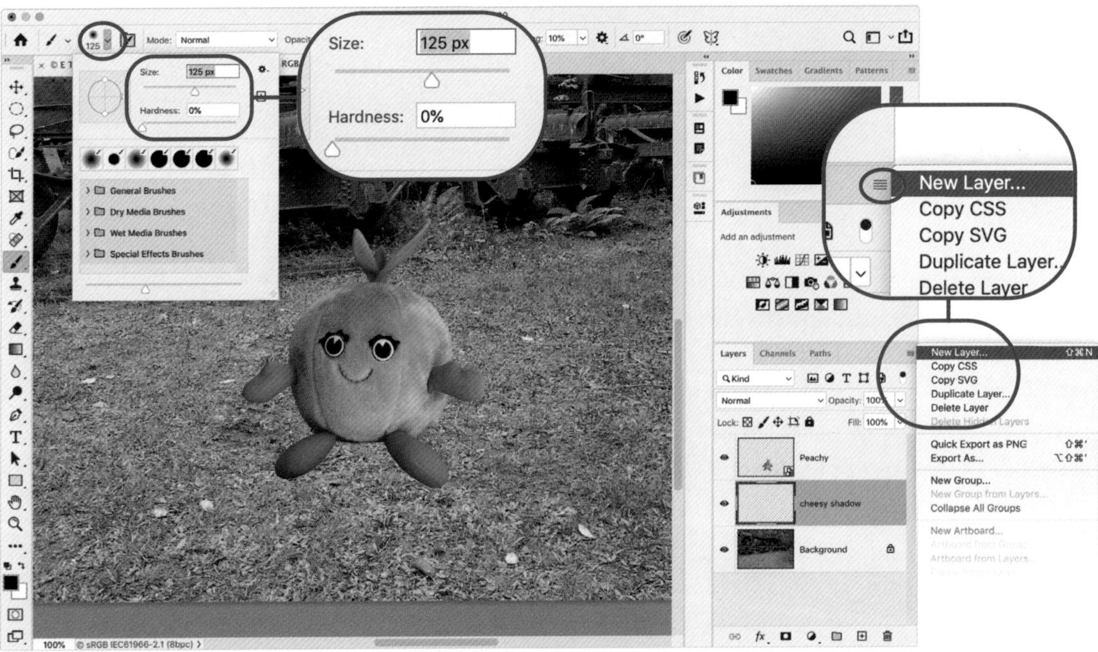

To paint in a quick "shadow," we slip a layer between the **Background** and the subject (here, Peachy). We simply paint on that layer with black, then lower the layer's opacity to taste.

Remember, you're about to paint behind Peachy, so don't worry that the brush looks like it's in front of her. *Just be sure that the shadow layer is highlighted.*

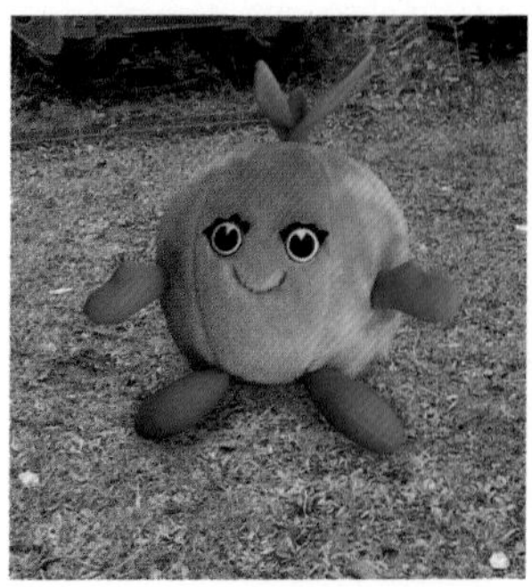

- Paint along the bottom of Peachy from toe to toe, perhaps going slightly below the centerline of her foot. Yes, the shadow looks way too dark.
- At the top of the Layers panel, lower the Opacity. I chose 45%.
- Unhappy with your painting? Press ⌘-Z/Ctrl-Z enough times to undo your work, then try again!

Lesson F: Color Range

- Open the document called "F G color range.psd."
- Press ⌘-0/Ctrl-0 to make the image as large as possible on the screen.

Our objective is to select the structures in the photo but to exclude the sky.

Photoshop can analyze an image to select nearly all the right pixels. Select > Subject is one that is getting better with each upgrade to the application. Select > Focus Area... can select the sharper elements in a photo, leaving blurred areas out. Neither is fully successful at selecting everything but the sky in this image. Even inverting the selection from Select > Sky misses the pixels entangled in the fence.

When Selecting Or Avoiding a Color

Once we select the structures in the photo, we can perform a color adjustment that affects only them. Those structures are detailed, vary in tone and color, and would be very hard to select with any of the tools we've seen so far. We noted earlier a command in the Select menu that could help us: Inverse. That means that if we can select everything *except* those structures (the blue sky in this photo), we can easily flip the selection around. Color Range selects pixels that fall into a range of color or, using its own selection-inverting function, all the pixels that don't. Select > Sky uses more than color and so is fooled by this image.

- Choose Select > Color Range.... Ignore the preview window in the dialog box for the moment. Do note that of the three eyedropper tools in the dialog, one is already active and ready to use.
- Look at the items in the Select menu at the top of the dialog box. It contains a list of generic hues and tones we can select. Rarely do they correspond to what we really want. The Skin Tones choice is better, when that's your target. It actually does a bit of face recognition. Stick to Sample Colors for now.
- Move the cursor into the image and click on something—anything. Now you can attend to the preview window! Try a few clicks here and there, but make the last click in the sky.
- Enable the Invert checkbox.

This inverts both the preview (white and black reverse) and what ends up selected in the end. This means we won't need the Inverse command later. Was your last click in the sky? Right now, if we committed the dialog (please don't), the color you clicked on and those very similar to it will *not* be selected, and everything else will be.

Right now, those few blues aren't as broad a range of color as we'd like it to be.

- Experiment with the Fuzziness slider. Higher values extend the color range, but not flexibly enough. If the value is high enough to target the entire sky, the buildings are targeted too. Perhaps just the windows that reflect a little sky can be allowed in that range, but not as large an area as a high Fuzziness value targets. It's close, but not precise enough.
- Lower the Fuzziness value again.

- Activate the second eyedropper in the dialog box (the one with the plus sign called the Add to Sample tool). We use this to add colors to the range, rather than relying on Fuzziness. Caps lock makes the cursor a crosshair, if that helps in tight spots.
- Click or even drag the cursor throughout the sky, avoiding buildings. Attempt a click between two post tops of the foreground fence.

It should be getting hard to tell which pixels are being targeted and which aren't. After all, that preview window is darn small. Note the menu at the bottom of the dialog: Selection Preview. This gives us several ways to use the Document Window to evaluate our progress.

- Choose Grayscale from the Selection Preview menu. Helpful, isn't it? Pressing the ⌘/Ctrl key shows the image in the preview window so you can recall it.
- Adjust the Fuzziness again, noting that we can much more easily control how much of the structures is targeted by our settings. A little bit in the windows of the building at left is fine, as is an edge of a clock face. They could be reflecting sky color a touch.
- Click OK to manifest the selection. Look at those busy marching ants! You've got a selection of the buildings and fence now. Considering the time of day, they could be warmed up a bit (the sun was low, as November was approaching).
- Use the Adjustments panel to create a Photo Filter adjustment to significantly warm up the buildings. It will be masked as precisely as you made your selection. Save your file!

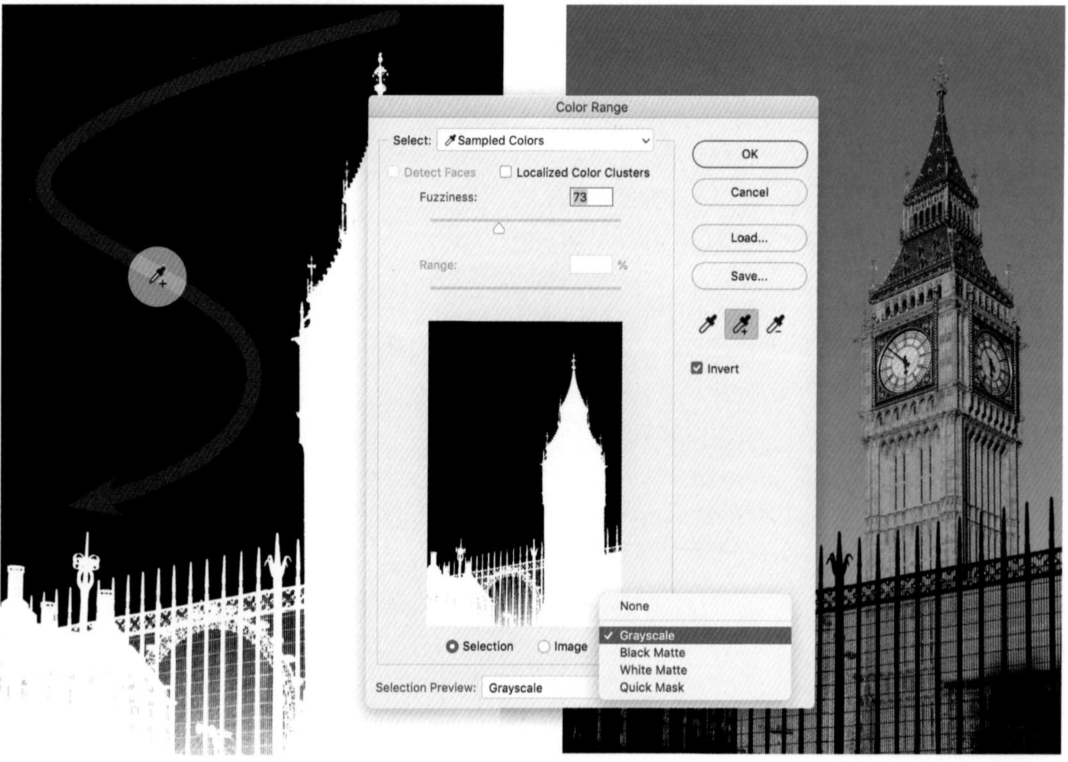

With Color Range, start sampling the targeted color with the eyedropper, then use the Add to Sample tool to add more. Fine-tune with Fuzziness. Here, we inverted to select non-blue pixels.

Lesson G: Saving & Loading Selections

Selections to Channels and Back

Some selections take a while to make, and sometimes we discover we need them again. Luckily there is a way to store them and bring them back to life.

- Reopen the document called "F G color range.psd."

In that document, we made a precise selection of everything except the sky pixels and used that selection to make a masked adjustment. That mask can get us that selection again!

- Hold down the ⌘/Ctrl key and click on the adjustment layer's mask. You've got marching ants again.

How? Photoshop covertly keeps track of mask pixels in the Channels panel. Let's have a look.

- Click on the mask again with no keys held down. We have to be sure its layer is highlighted and the mask is targeted.
- Look at the Channels panel. If it's not on-screen, choose Window > Channels.

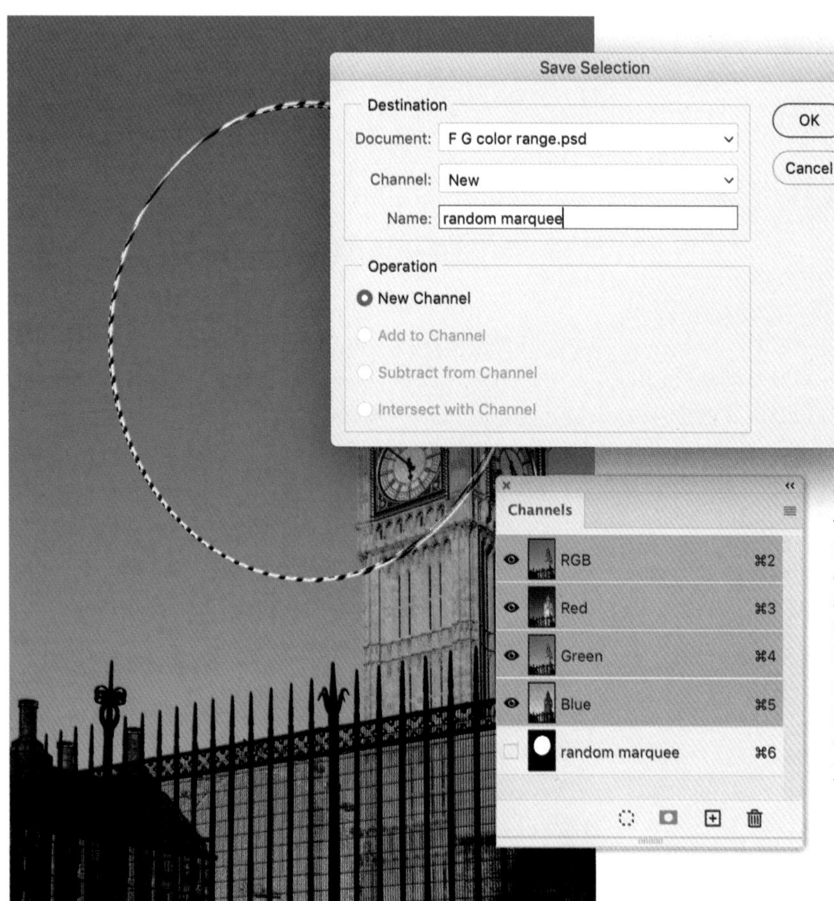

When you save a selection, the selected area is recorded as white on a channel. Unselected areas are black. Partially selected (feathered) areas are recorded in shades of gray.

Each shortcut shown will highlight and preview its channel. Here, ⌘-6 will show you the new alpha channel.

There's an extra channel there beyond the color channels. We call those non-color channels "alpha channels." When a mask is targeted, Photoshop uses a channel to manage it. If you click the layer thumbnail rather than the mask's, the RGB channel will be highlighted but the mask will be visible. Highlight a different layer and there's no more alpha channel (unless that layer has a mask too).

These mask alpha channels come and go as their layers are and aren't highlighted. You can also create your own more permanent alpha channels.

- View the Layers panel and highlight the Background. Draw a selection with a marquee tool or the Lasso tool.
- Choose Select > Save Selection.... Note that you're creating a new channel with a name of your choosing. Give it a name, then click OK.
- Deselect (⌘-D/Ctrl-D), then look at the Channels panel.

It doesn't matter what layer is highlighted, this channel will always be available. So if you ever need that selection again, you can ⌘/Ctrl-click on it. Go ahead, try it! If you make that channel visible (enabling the eye-con) while the RGB channel is visible, the alpha channel will look like a red translucent overlay. This helps you visually evaluate which areas of the image it covers.

- Before moving on, be sure to click (just one regular click) on the RGB channel so Photoshop's attention is on the image again.

Quick Mask Revealed

- Make another selection with whatever tool you like. Then tap the Q key to access Quick Mask.

If you look at the Channels panel, you'd think you saved the selection as a channel, then highlighted both it and the RGB channel. When that is done, the channel's black pixels are shown as a translucent color, usually red. The Quick Mask feature is like a fast, temporary version of this. Very fast (tapping a letter) and very temporary (tapping the letter again deletes the channel).

I usually use Quick Mask to view a complex selection and make sense of it. You could do other things. If you paint with white or black while in Quick Mask, you're adding to or taking away from the selection (respectively)! That is, you can hit Q, B (for "Brush"), D (for "Default" colors), and maybe X (to "eXchange" those colors), then paint areas into or out of the selection, and then hit Q to get back to the normal world again.

This is pretty esoteric stuff these days, but I wanted to be the one to tell you about it. I didn't want you hearing about this workflow on the street. We now "paint" selections in the Select and Mask workspace (there's a Brush tool there).

Luminosity Masks

I want to give you a final tip involving channels. The objective here is to brighten the darker areas without blowing out the light ones. More precisely, we're going to make an adjustment whose strength is inversely proportional to the image's luminosity.

- Open "G luminosity mask.psd."
- ⌘/Ctrl-click on each color channel, noticing that you get a selection each time.

That's right, getting a selection from a channel isn't limited to alpha channels. Where a channel is white, that area will be fully selected. Where it's black, it's not selected at all. Grays yield areas that are partially selected: the more that's selected, the lighter the gray. Phrased differently, the selection is proportional to the luminosity of the channel.

- ⌘/Ctrl-click on the RGB channel. You now have a selection that is proportional to the luminosity of the image. That is, the snow is the most selected thing. We want the opposite.
- Choose Select > Inverse. Now the snow is the least selected stuff.
- Create a Curves adjustment by clicking its icon in the Adjustments panel. Move the white-point slider in (leftward), noting that the highlights don't lose much at all. Push the middle of the curve up a bit, too, to give even more light to the metal fish, again without impacting the snowy parts of the image.
- Save, marvel a bit, then close the document.

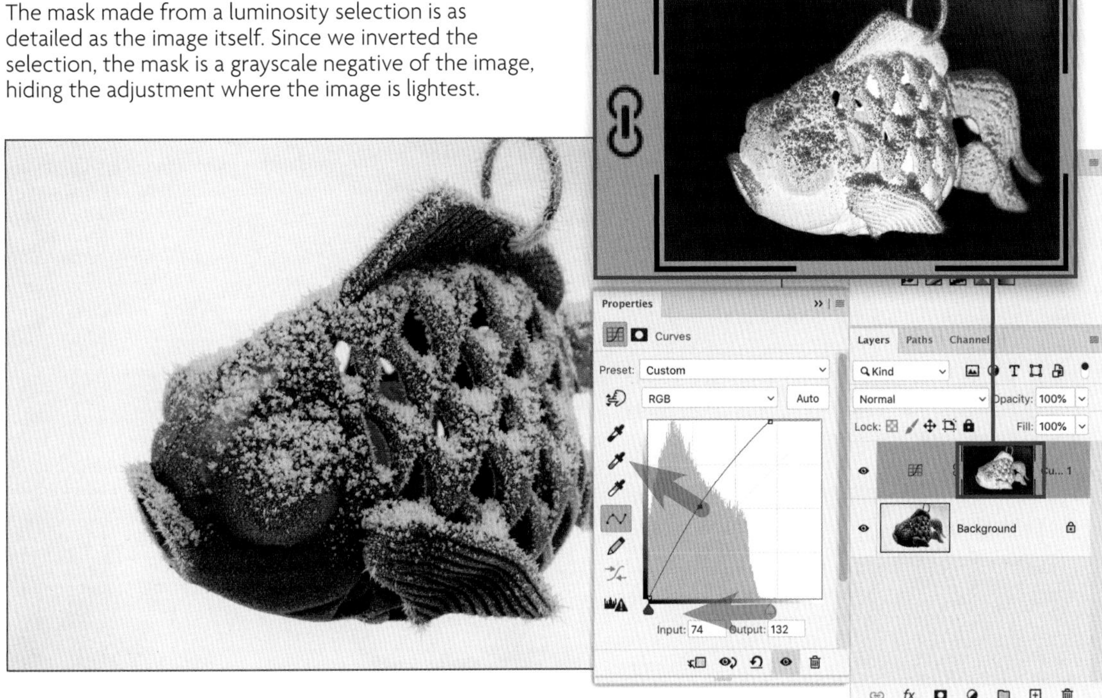

The mask made from a luminosity selection is as detailed as the image itself. Since we inverted the selection, the mask is a grayscale negative of the image, hiding the adjustment where the image is lightest.

4 Creative Features

Photoshop isn't just about photography: illustration and design happen here, too, with many features dedicated to those pursuits. Since I have found that every feature has aided my use of the application, often in unintended ways, photographers may want to work through this chapter too. We'll cover the basics in these lessons and the intricacies in the Compendium for those who want to go deeper.

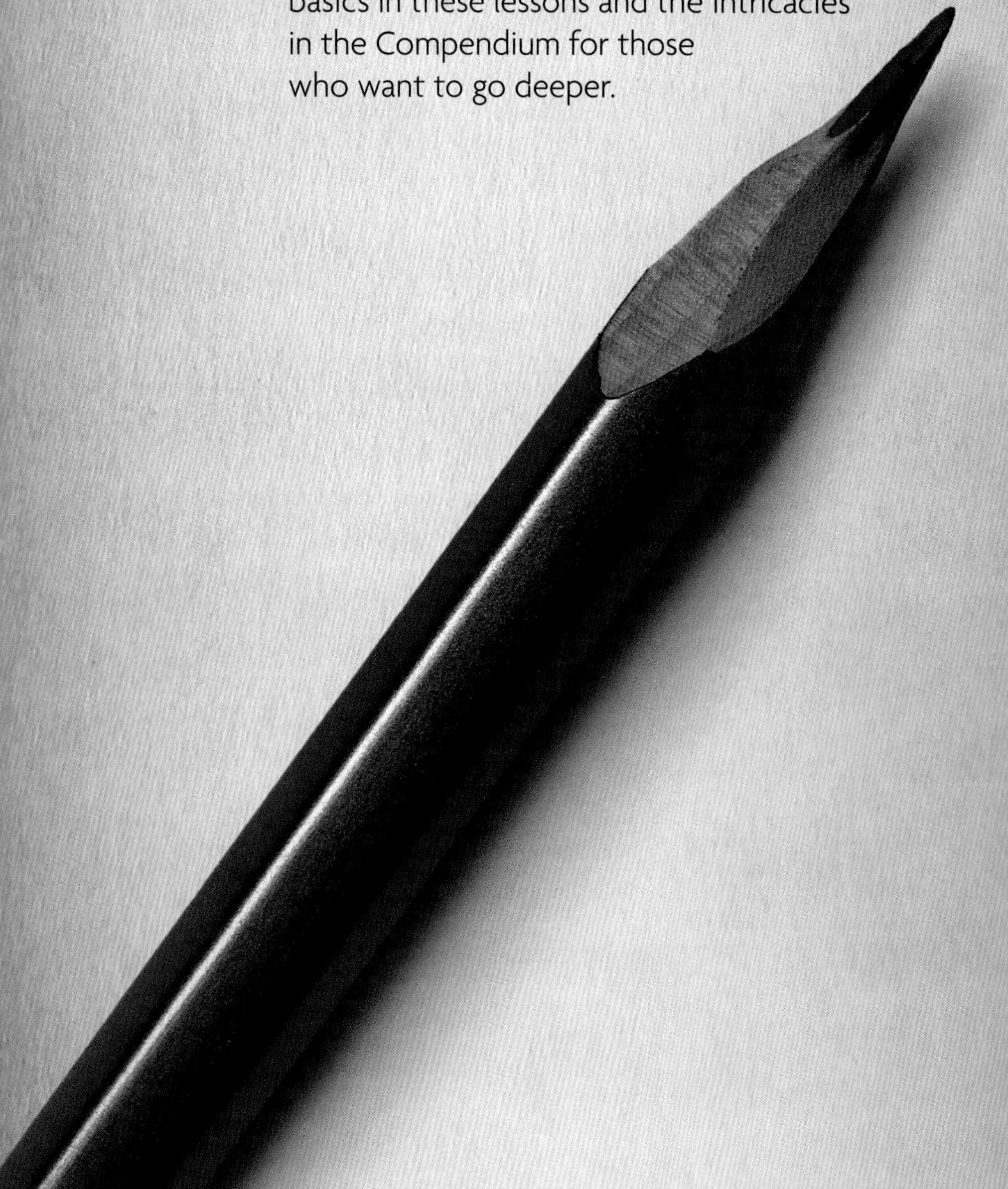

Lesson A: Creating Content

Something from nothing is the theme for this lesson. First, we'll fill the canvas with patterns, gradients, and colors. We'll complete a backdrop on top of which we'll create type.

Create a New Doc

We'll start by creating a new document.

- Launch Photoshop. If you are not shown the home screen, click the Home button at the left end of the Options Bar.
- Click the New file button. Many media choices are listed across the top of the resulting dialog box. I'd like you to choose Photo because it contains the reliable default settings we need for this lesson.
- Choose Default Photoshop Size. Interestingly, there's nothing particularly photo-centric about this preset. Click Create in the bottom-right corner of the dialog box.

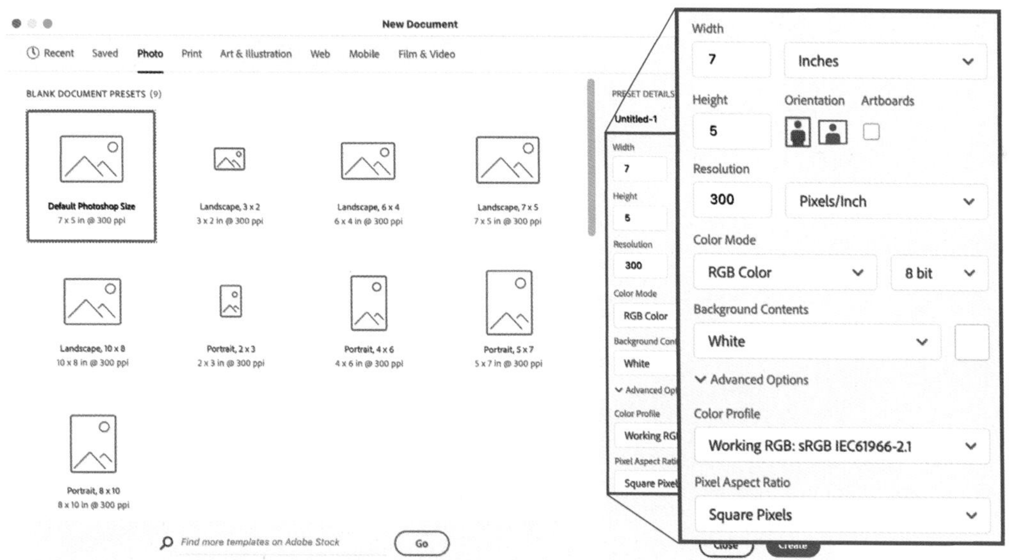

Creating a Pattern Fill Layer

Have a look at the Patterns panel in the upper right. In it is a list of folders, each of which has several patterns some nice folks at Adobe made for us. If you have an image that would make a nice pattern, choose Edit > Define Pattern..., and it will be added to this panel.

- To see them all, hold down ⌘/Ctrl and click on a small arrow to the left of a folder's name.

This exposes the contents of all the folders.

- Drag a pattern swatch onto the document "canvas."

Because the only layer present was a Background, the first pattern you drag creates a fill layer. Subsequently dragging or just clicking on a pattern replaces the pattern in that layer. Like any layer, its Opacity can be adjusted. Like adjustment layers, fill layers are born with a mask that can be painted with black to hide its content. Also, if there is an active selection when the pattern fill layer is made, it will be masked to the selected area. Recently applied patterns appear along the top of the Patterns panel.

- Apply a Water pattern last.
- Choose File > Save As..., choose to Save on your computer, and then choose where your other course files are stored. But we're not done. Atop that pattern, let's create a gradient fill layer.

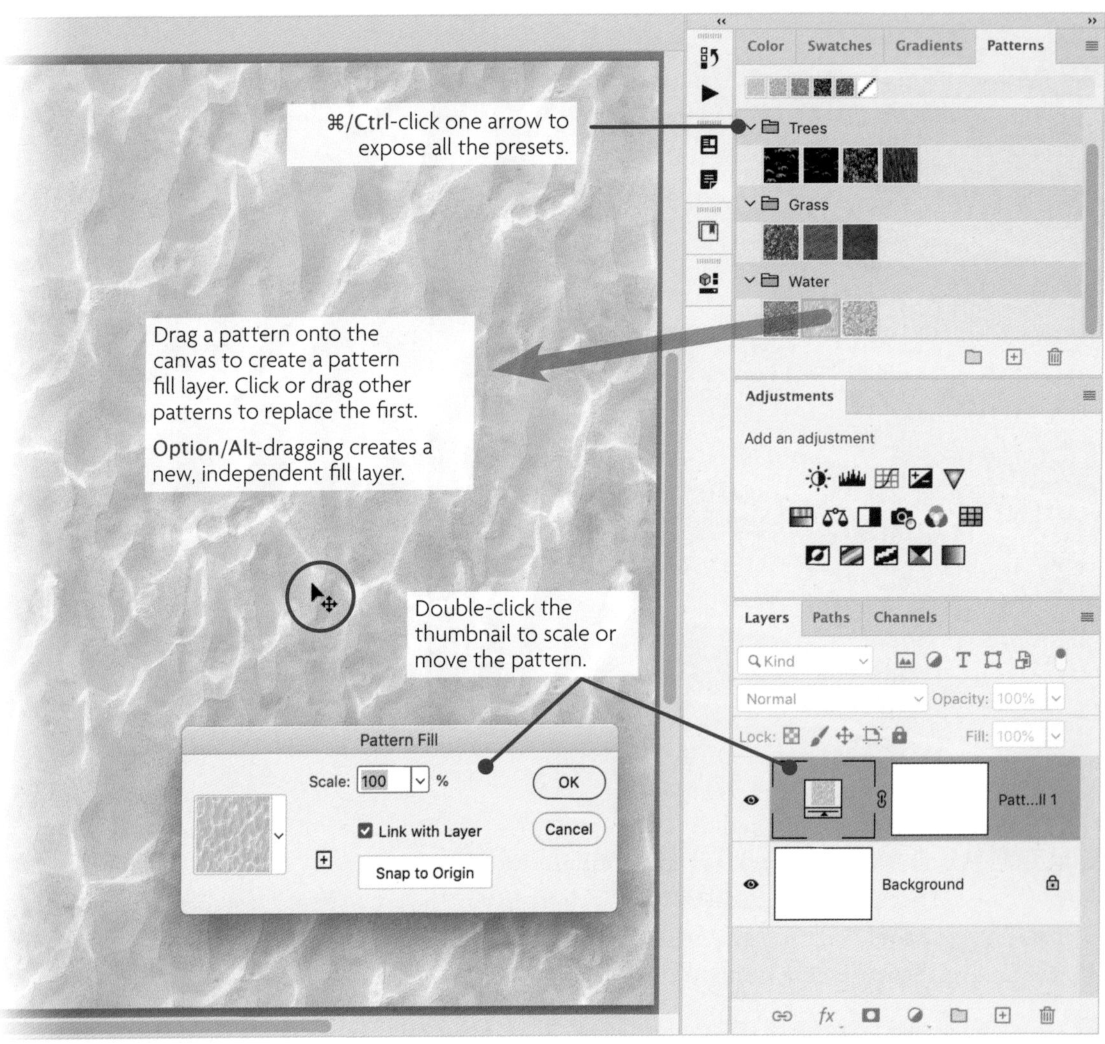

Creating a Gradient Fill Layer

Beta As I write, gradients are getting a major upgrade. If your version of Photoshop has the new live gradients, or you're willing to install the public beta version, continue with the exercise below and learn even more in "Gradient" (page 141).

- To determine if you have the upgrade, choose the Gradient tool. If there is a menu on the left end of the Options Bar offering Gradient or Classic gradient, you may work through the rest of this section. If not, open the document called "Classic Gradients.pdf" (in your Course files) and follow the excercise there.
- Expose the Gradients panel. To see them all, hold down ⌘/Ctrl and click on a small arrow to the left of a folder's name. This exposes the contents of all the folders.
- Choose the Gradient tool. Drag from the lower-left to the upper-right of the canvas.

Initially, this creates a whole new fill layer with a gradient in it. Choose a different gradient preset from the Gradients panel, the Properties panel, or the Options Bar!

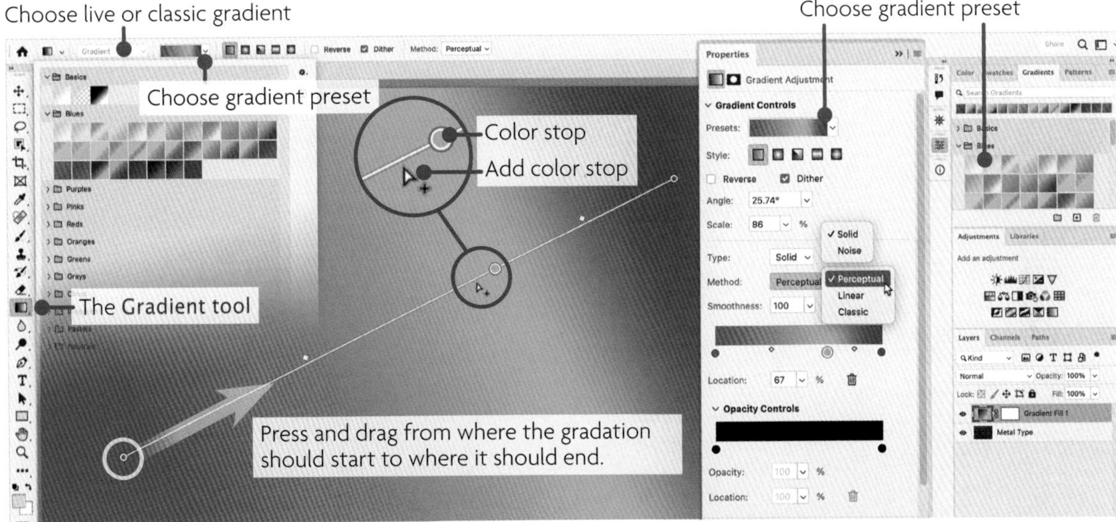

- Move one of the gradient's color stops (the small circles on the bar that appeared when you dragged with the Gradient tool). Moving an end point can change the gradient's angle and length.
- With the gradient fill layer highlighted, change its blend mode via the menu near the top of the Layers panel (it's currently set to Normal). You just have to hover over a mode's name to see it previewed. Choose Multiply.

It's a long list and each choice does something different. I put together a visual and technical reference of each one in (you guessed it) the Compendium: "Blend Modes" (page 176). Read it! The bottom line is that most of them will allow these layers to visually interact.

Creating a Color Fill Layer

We're going to replace that gradient with a solid color. It should inherit the gradient layer's Multiply blend mode.

- Expose the Swatches panel. To see them all, hold down ⌘/Ctrl and click on the small arrow to the left of a folder's name. This exposes the presets in all the folders.
- Drag a swatch onto the canvas, replacing the gradient we applied. To create a new, independent fill layer requires option/Alt-dragging the preset onto the canvas. This time, however, we're replacing the one type of fill layer with another.
- To make the overall texture quite subtle, highlight the pattern fill layer in the Layers panel and change its Opacity to a lower value, like 30% or so. Then highlight the top layer again.

Now we have an interesting, but not distracting texture over which we can put some text.

Type Layers

We now have a stage to do a little "type casting." You'll need the Type tool and a bit of restraint. There are several ways to approach this tool, but in Photoshop it's most common to need only a little bit of text, written large, for designs like book covers or fancy magazine article lead-ins. If you need lots of text, there are other applications (like InDesign) better suited for the task, and other books in this series to guide you through them.

But there are reasons to create type here in Photoshop. Let's examine one approach.

- Activate the Type tool by clicking it in the Tools panel or tapping the T key.
- With it, click in the center of the image. Very likely, the words "Lorem Ipsum" start where you clicked and go rightward from there.

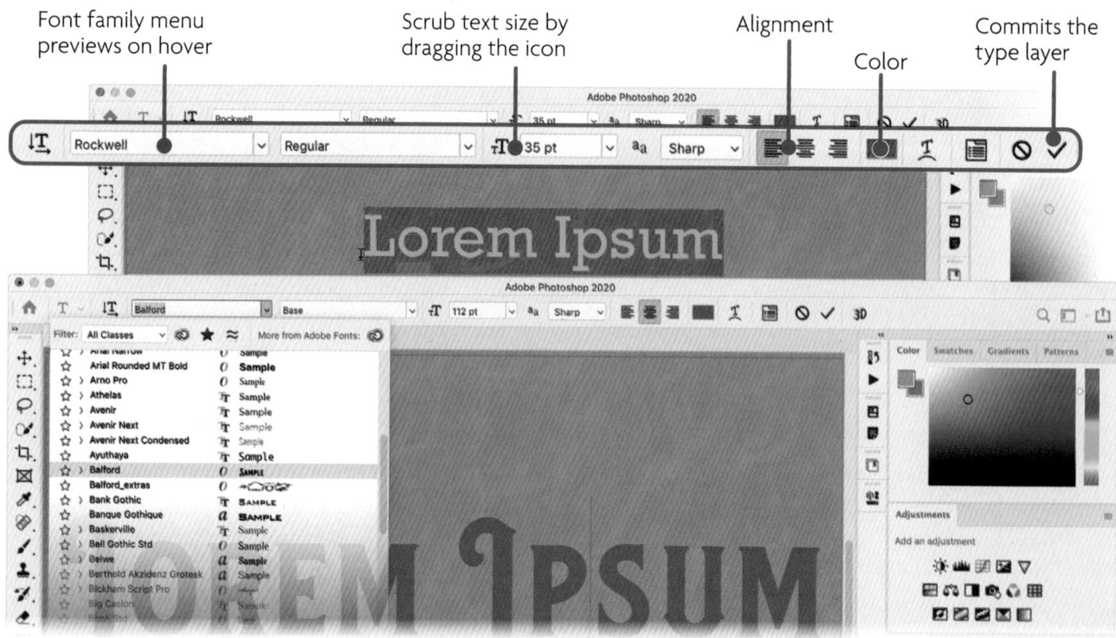

Until the type is committed, the type layer that holds it will have a generic name like "Layer 1." But before we commit this type, let's get it in better form. If the text becomes unselected at any point, just triple-click it with the Type tool.

- While the text is still highlighted, change its color by clicking on the color chip in the Options Bar (initially, it's probably set to black). This opens the color picker. See its how-to, "Color Picker" (page 225). While the color picker is open, the text's highlighting is disabled so you can see what you're doing. Choose a color that works well with your backdrop, then click OK.
- Set the alignment to centered by clicking on the Center text icon in the Options Bar. Since you set the type by clicking at a point in the image, the text is aligned to that point. So your text should be somewhat centered in the image. If not...
- Fine-tune the text's position. Watch the cursor as you move it slowly away from the text. When the cursor is not directly over the text but not too far away, it becomes the Move tool! When you see it, press and drag to move the text. Clicking when the cursor looks like a generic arrow commits the text—but not yet!
- Adjust the type size by scrubbing the size icon (just left of the current size). You may want to adjust the position of the text again afterward.
- Choose a different font from the font menu. Make sure the text is highlighted so that as you hover over font names, you'll see a preview in your document. Choose whatever you want except Papyrus, Comic Sans, Times New Roman, or Copperplate. Those will break your computer. Well, not really, but they ought to.

Does the spacing between any letters look odd? In mine, I dislike the space between the "P" and "S." If you have a similar complaint, you can kern those letters:

- Click once between two letters with the Type tool so a bar cursor blinks there. Hold down option/Alt, then use the left and right arrow keys (← or →) to change that spacing.
- Once you're happy with your text, commit it by clicking the check mark (✓) in the Options Bar.

Later, to quickly highlight the text, double-click the layer thumbnail. This switches to the Type tool too.

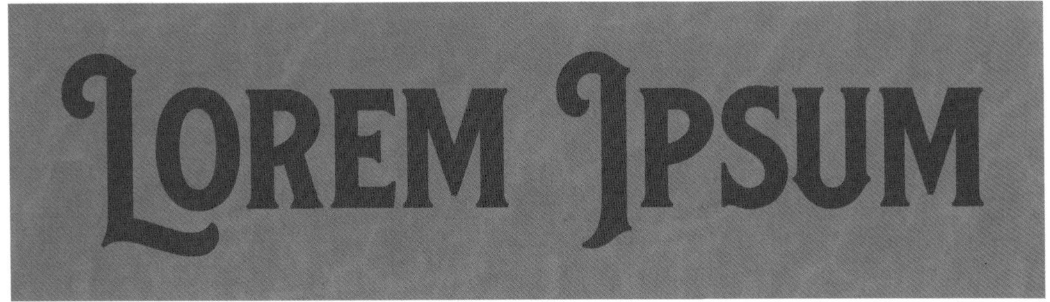

- Save.

Lesson B: Layer Styles

With layer styles, a layer can look dimensional, image-filled, or many other magical things. These pages will constitute your blind date with this feature. As always, you can develop a deeper relationship in the Compendium. In this case, "Layer Styles & Effects" (page 196).

- If necessary, reopen the document from the last lesson.

Drop Shadow and Bevel & Emboss

These are the core effects that constitute a layer style.

- Highlight the type layer.
- Click on the fx icon at the bottom of the Layers panel (Get it? "F-X" = "effects") and choose Drop Shadow. Note that it's highlighted at the bottom of the resulting dialog box.

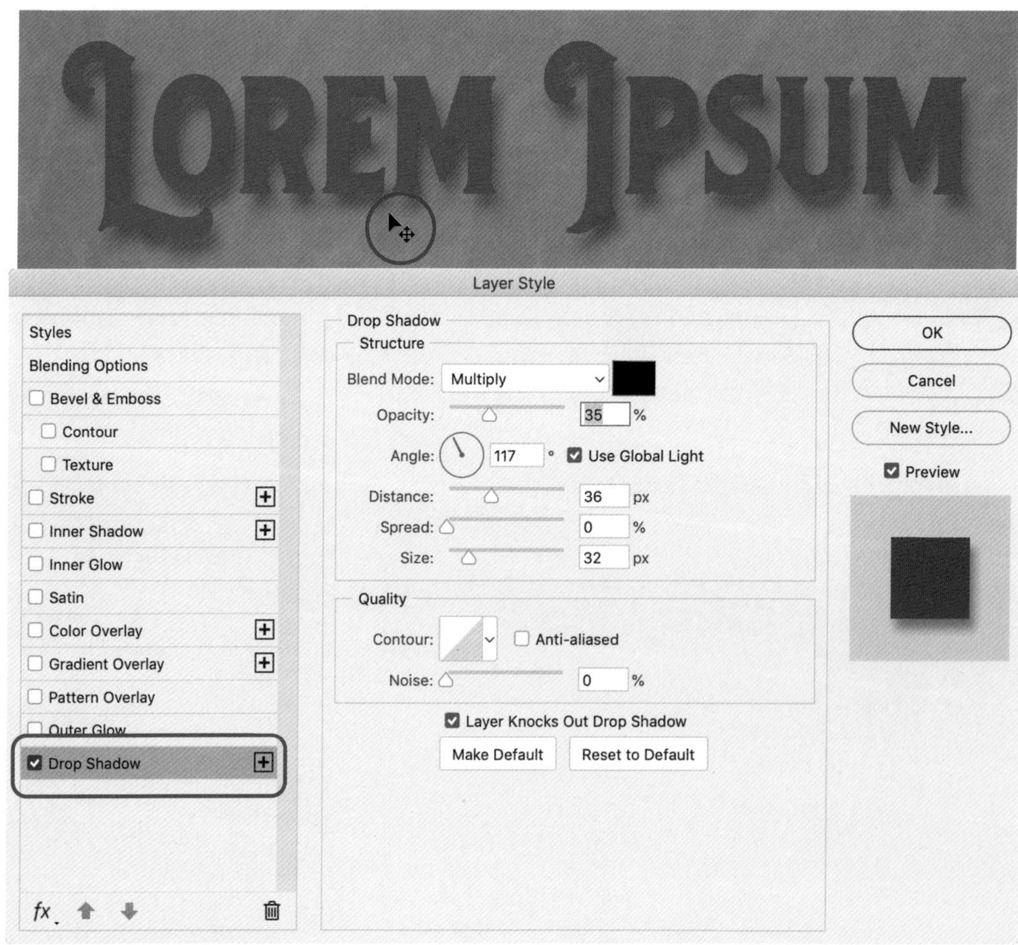

Of the many attributes of a shadow that can be edited, I'd like to focus on the four most important ones: Opacity, Angle, Distance, and so-called Size.

- Move your cursor into the image to discover it's the Move tool cursor. Press and drag on the shadow to move it where you'd like it. I moved mine down and right.

You just adjusted two of those four attributes! As you drag the shadow, the Distance and Angle change. The Distance is how far from the layer the shadow is, and the Angle is that of the light casting the shadow.

- Back in the Layer Style dialog box, adjust the Size. You'll see the shadow get more (or less) blurry.
- Finally, adjust the Opacity. I suggest starting at 0 and going up until it's subtle but useful.
- Click on Blending Options in the list on the left to see those controls. Our old friend the intuitive Opacity slider is here. But I'd like you to experiment with the Fill Opacity slider.
- Slide Fill Opacity to 0. The layer's actual content disappears, leaving our effects (actually, *effect*, the drop shadow) intact. A little bit of substance would be nice: set it to 20%.

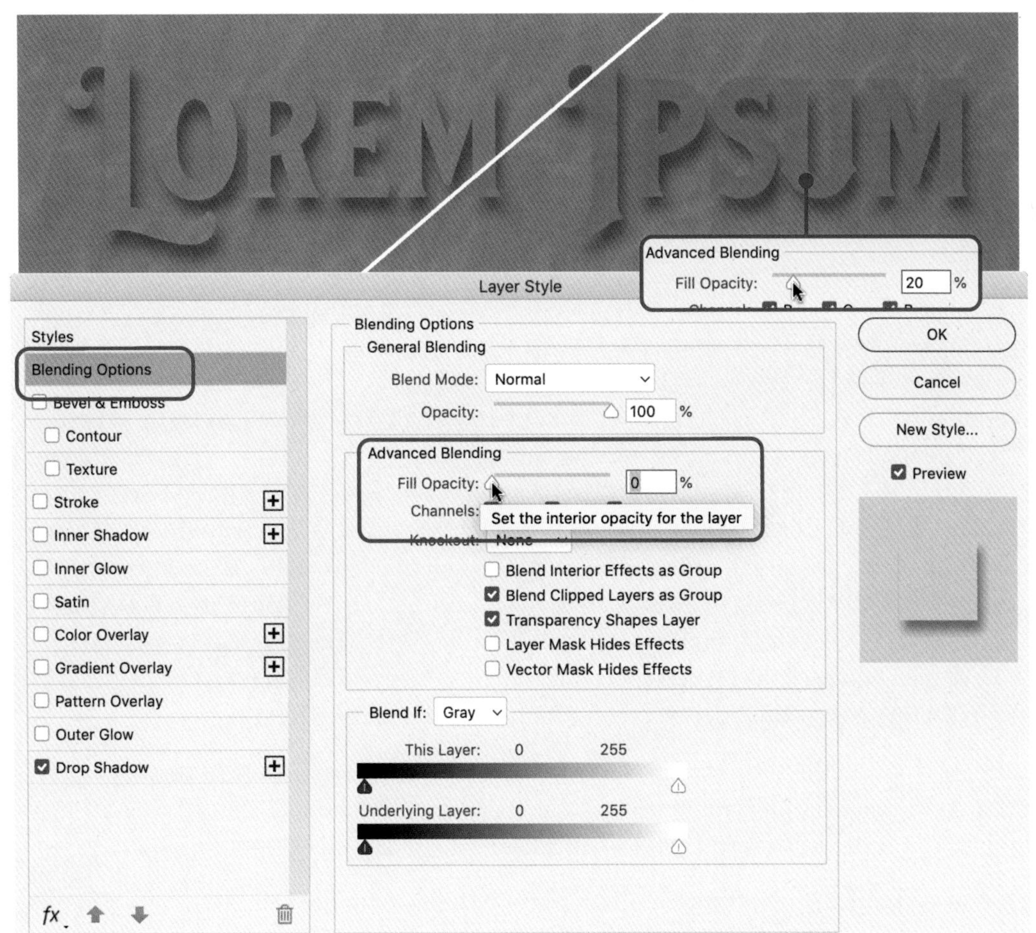

Now to give our ghostly text some depth.

- Click on Bevel & Emboss (the words, not just the checkbox). The settings we need are shown below, as well as generalities about the Layer Style dialog box.

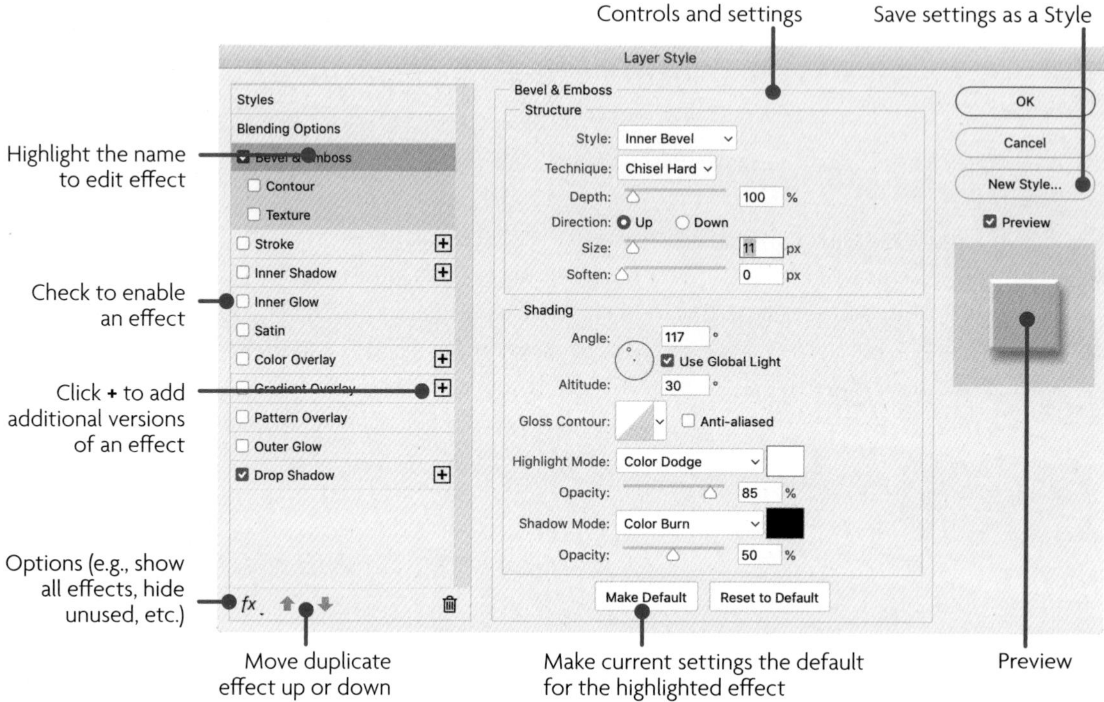

- At the top, set Technique to Chisel Hard. This looks crisp and not as blobby as it started.
- To really make the letters shine, set the Highlight Mode (near the bottom) to Color Dodge and about 85% Opacity.
- Similarly, set the Shadow Mode to Color Burn and about 50% Opacity. Now the letters are well-defined, despite remaining translucent in places.
- So that this look can be applied to other layers in the future, click the New Style… button.
- I chose the name "transparent aluminum." I disabled Add to my current library. You may leave that checked so you can access this style on any device on which you log in with your Adobe ID. Click OK in the New Style dialog and again in the Layer Style dialog box.
- Access the Styles panel (Window > Styles will summon it). Like the other preset panels we've seen, to see all the presets here, hold down ⌘/Ctrl and click on a small arrow to the left of a set's name. This exposes the contents of all the sets (folders).

Your new style is at the bottom of the list. Also, in the Layers panel, just under the type layer to which you applied your style, you'll find the "ingredients." Double-clicking those will let you edit their settings. The eye icons let you hide or show each effect.

- Choose a different style from the Styles panel. Note its ingredients in the Layers panel. You can edit those too. Clicking your style's thumbnail in the Styles panel restores it.

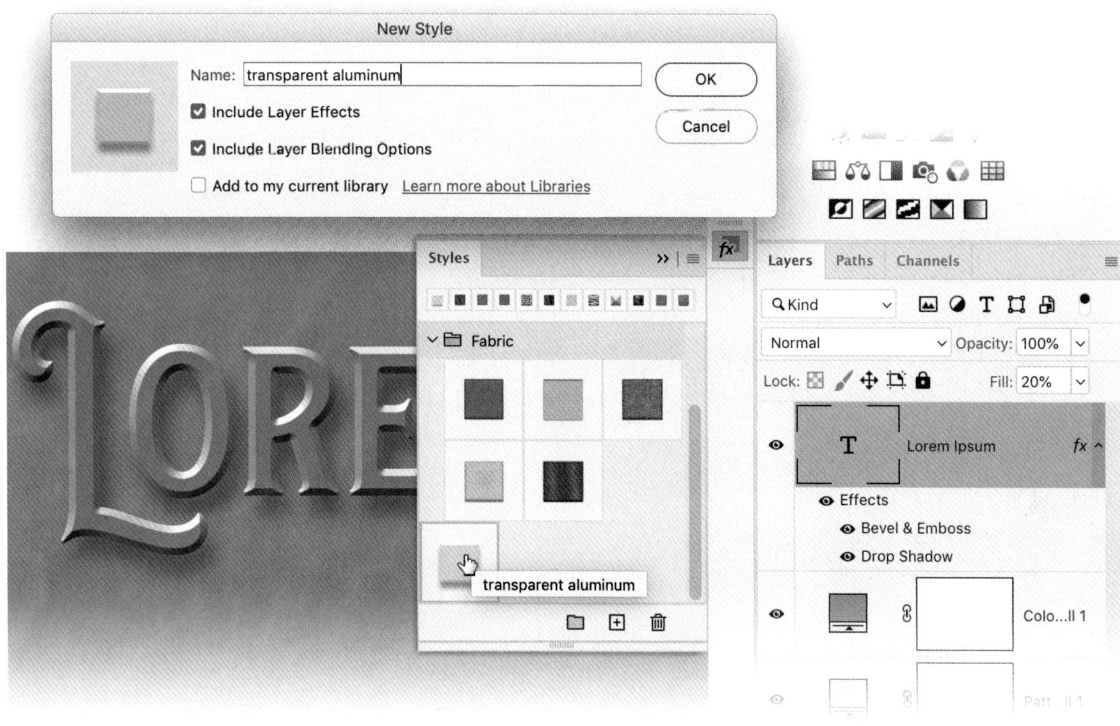
New Style
Name: transparent aluminum
OK
Cancel
Include Layer Effects
Include Layer Blending Options
Add to my current library
Learn more about Libraries
Styles
Fabric
transparent aluminum
Layers
Paths
Channels
Kind
Normal
Opacity: 100%
Lock:
Fill: 20%
Lorem Ipsum
Effects
Bevel & Emboss
Drop Shadow
Colo...ll 1

Lesson C: Smart Objects

In this lesson, we'll place an Adobe Illustrator file into a Photoshop document, establishing a link between the two. We'll see how easy it is to swap the file out for another and (if you have and are familiar with Illustrator) edit the Illustrator file and see the change in Photoshop.

- Open the file "C smart objects.psd." Check out each layer.

Smart Objects Are Smart Workflow

You'll see that the top layer called "crumpled" is just a gray piece of crumpled paper set to a blend mode that hides the gray, leaving only the crumply highlights and shadows imposed on the paper layer below it. This is just another attempt to intrigue you about blend modes.

- Make sure the top layer is highlighted before the next step.
- Choose File > Place Linked..., which will open a dialog box. In it, navigate to the same folder where the current file, "C smart objects.psd," is located. Open "C2 artist power.ai."
- That, in turn, opens yet another dialog box in which you can choose the crop, or how much of the file you want to see. The default, Bounding Box, is perfect. Click OK.
- One more task before the file is actually in this Photoshop document. Note the transform handles around the perimeter of the graphic. Scale it down a little by dragging a corner inward (if the shape distorts, hold down Shift); rotate it a little bit clockwise by dragging outside the box; and position it by dragging within the box. Press the Enter key or click the check mark in the Options Bar to commit.

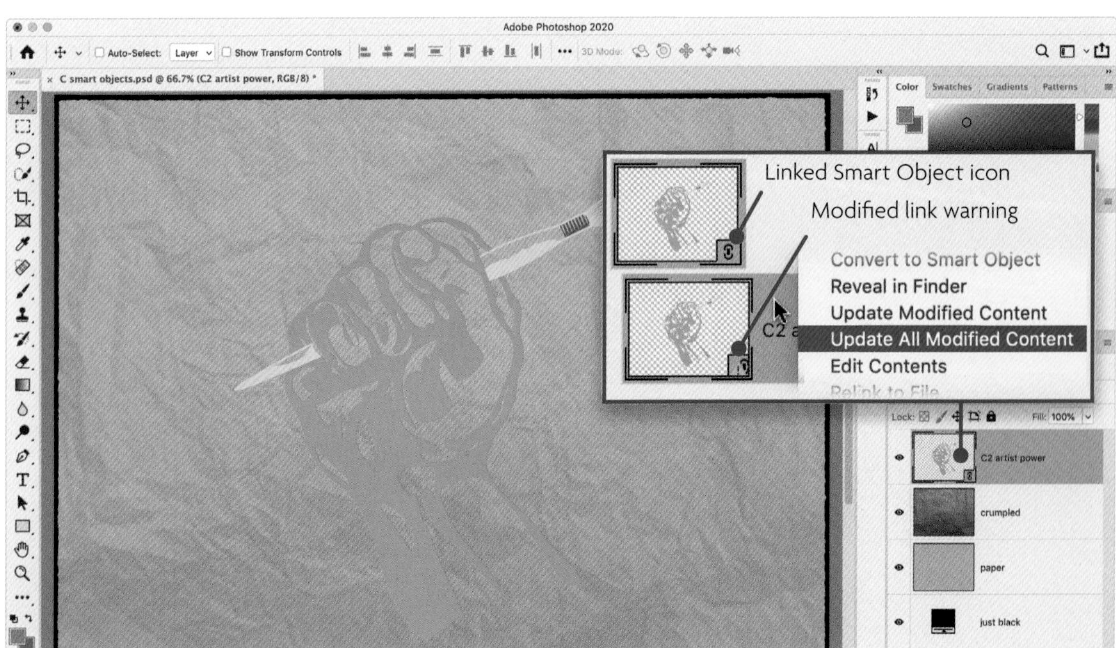

There should now be a new layer at the top of the stack with a chain-like icon in the lower-right corner of its thumbnail. This indicates that it's a linked Smart Object (SO). If that Illustrator file should be changed, so will that icon so you can update the SO to reflect that edit. Do so by right-clicking near the layer name choosing Update All Modified Content.

- Set the new layer's blend mode to Multiply so that it looks like it's printed on the paper.
- Since it's a Smart Object, we can apply filters fearlessly. Choose Filter > Blur > Gaussian Blur, setting the Radius quite high, like 25 pixels. Commit the blur by clicking OK, but don't worry: we won't leave it like that.

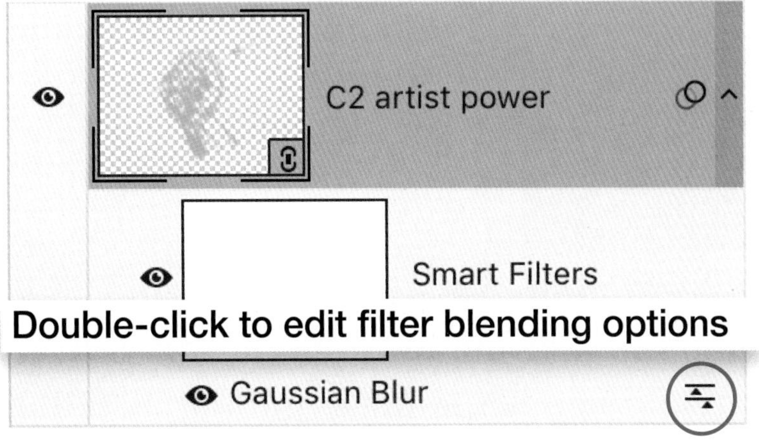

- Note the icon to the right of the filter entry in the Layers panel. Double-click it!
- Change the Mode to Hard Light and, perhaps, lower the Opacity a bit.

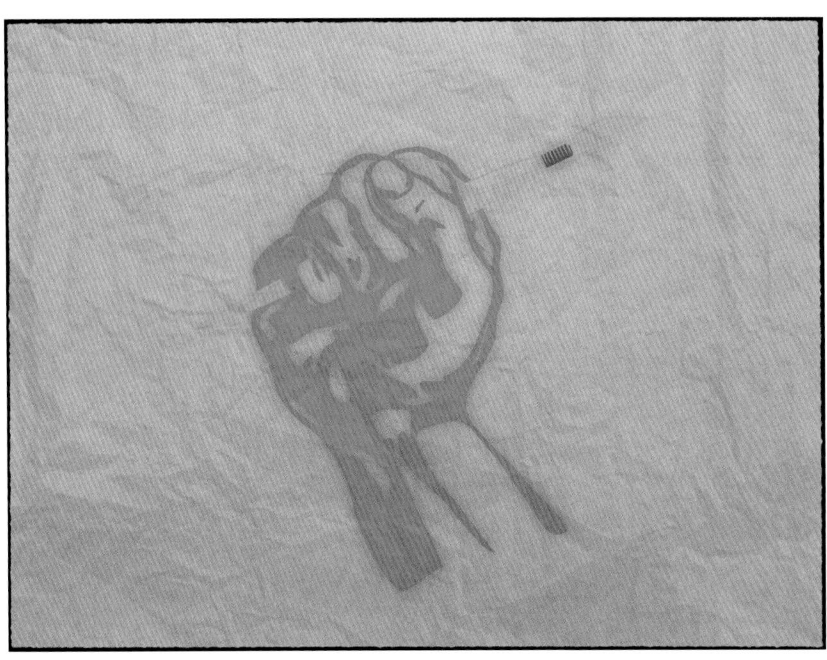

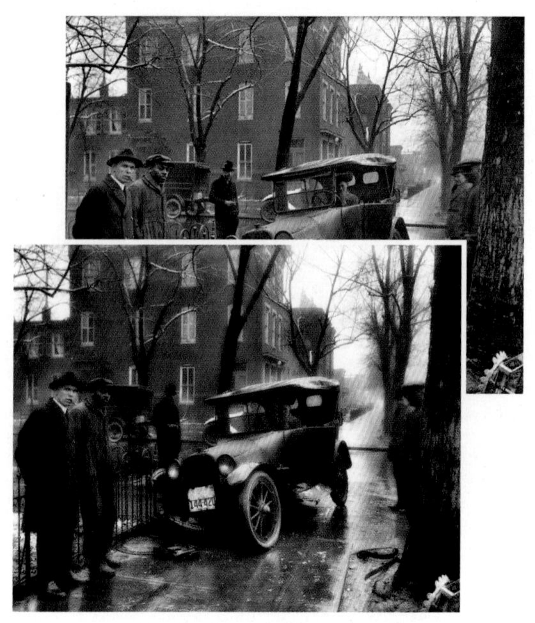

This is exactly like having two identical layers, the top one of which is blurred with that blend mode and opacity—without having to have two layers. In this case, it's like the ink bled into the paper. With photographs, especially vintage ones, this blended blur effect is nicely moody.

Now consider this scenario: the Illustrator artwork comes from a fickle collaborator. Just as you complete the effect we just enjoyed, you receive an updated file or a wholly new one. Must you start over? Would I be asking if the answer was yes?

- Right-click near the layer's name and choose Replace Contents…. Open the file called "C3 stem power.ai," again accepting Bounding Box for the crop.

The new art adopts all the edits you made to the former. This is ideal when multiple people have to collaborate to produce a finished product. If you have skills in and knowledge of Adobe Illustrator, there's one more thing you can do.

Right-clicking near the layer's name and choosing Edit Contents (or double-clicking the thumbnail) will launch Illustrator if it's installed. You can then edit the file, save it, and then return to Photoshop to see the result.

Lesson D: Blend If

This lesson has a couple of objectives. The first is to expose you to a cool but tricky masking technique. But the file's content is a nontrivial example of the last two lessons combining layer styles and filters applied to Smart Objects. If you experiment with those "Smart Filters" and styles, be sure to save a copy!

Now That's Shady

➡ Open the file "D Blend If.psd." Don't yet judge how silly it looks.

That lightning layer at the top is visible where it shouldn't be: where it's dark. I will admit that simply changing the blend mode from Normal to Screen or Color Dodge looks promising, and we may end up doing so, but for now leave the mode set to Normal.

➡ With the lightning layer highlighted, access the layer's Blending Options, either by using the fx menu at the bottom of the Layers panel or by double-clicking *near* (but not on) the layer's name.

Note the sliders at the bottom in the Blend If area. If we read that instead as "Visible If," then those sliders tell us that the lightning layer is visible where the shades of Gray on Current Layer are between 0 and 255, and where the Underlying Layer's grays are in that range too.

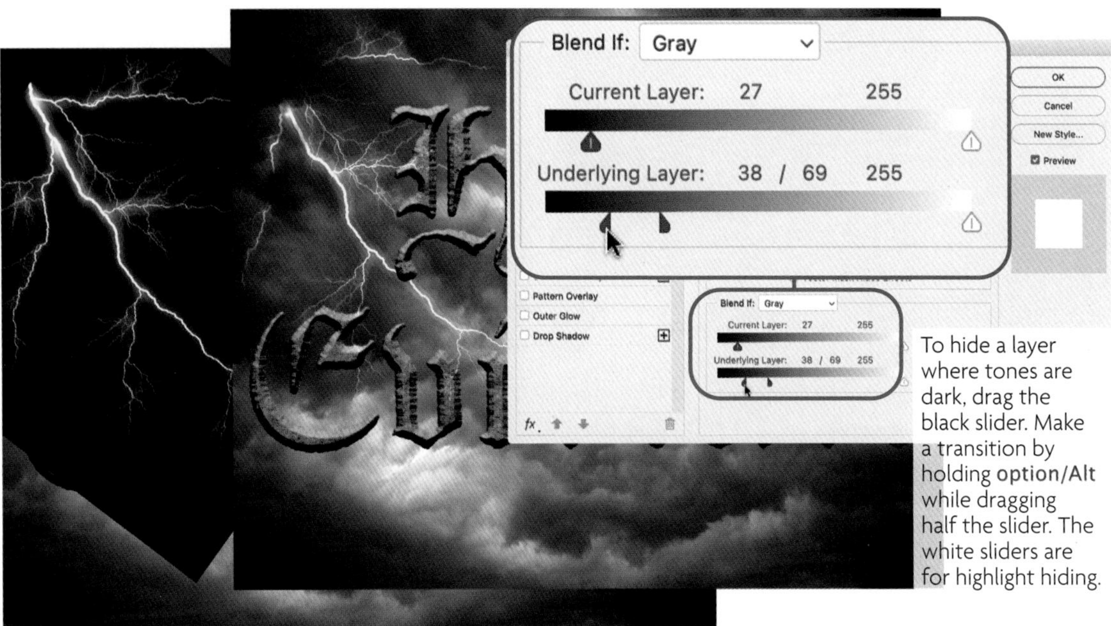

To hide a layer where tones are dark, drag the black slider. Make a transition by holding option/Alt while dragging half the slider. The white sliders are for highlight hiding.

➡ Drag the black Current Layer slider to the right a bit. Pretty nifty, eh?

Notice the numbers have changed. I dragged my black slider about a quarter of the way in to 60. This means that levels (shades) of 60 and lighter are visible, but those darker than 60 aren't.

- Drag that slider back to 0. This time, hold down option/Alt as you drag the slider's right half to the right just a little bit. The numbers now look something like "0/10 255."

This means that there is a range of tones over which pixels become invisible. This will be more useful for the next slider. So for now...

- Move both halves of that slider to the right, again to about 60. It's not critical that this one be "split."
- Now slowly move the Underlying Layer black slider to the right.

Where the clouds or type are very dark, the lightning vanishes, as if it's emanating from the clouds and zipping behind the letters in some spots. If those underlying layers ever got darker or lighter in places, our lightning would change where it's visible.

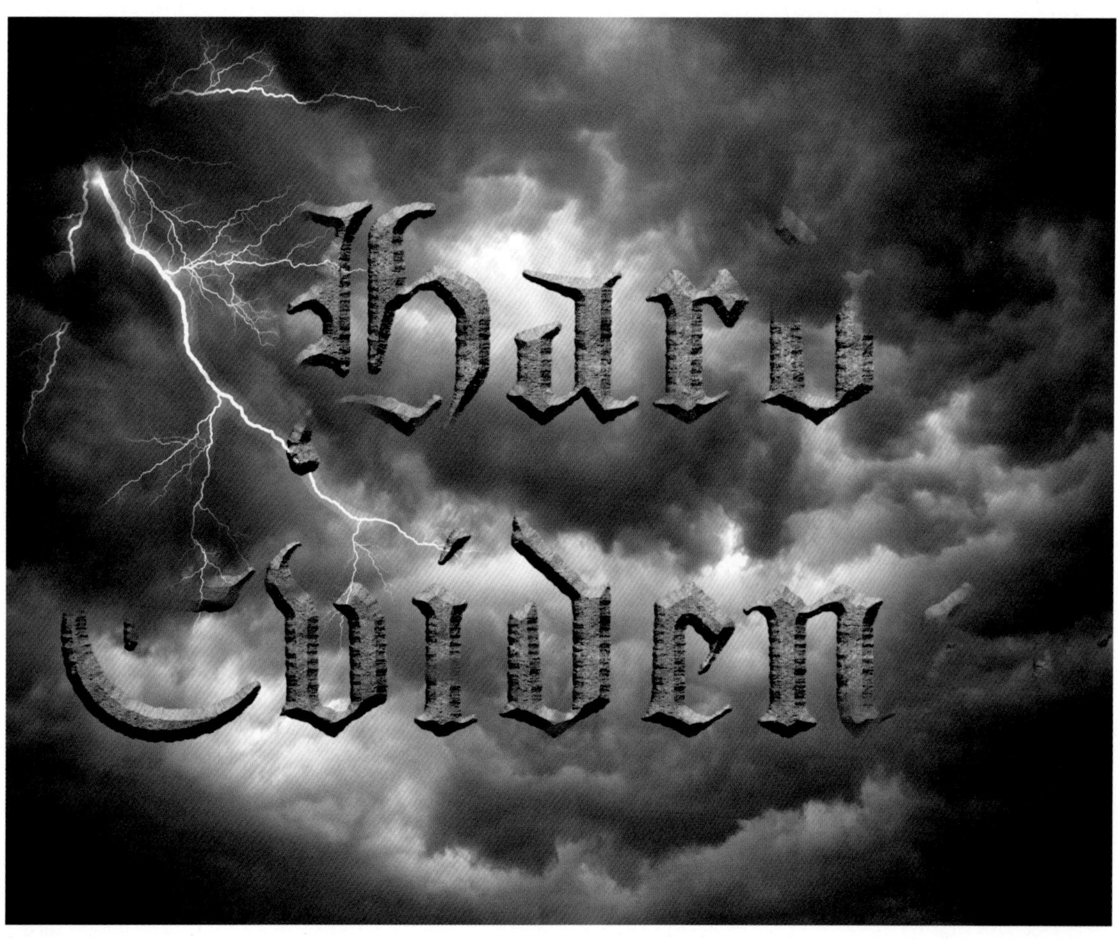

- Option/Alt-drag the left half of the Underlying Layer black slider left to see a transition.
- Finally, for this layer, set the Blend Mode to Color Dodge.
- Click OK. The icon on the right side of the layer means you've set Advanced Blending Options. That's helpful, otherwise later you'd wonder how you achieved that look.
- Highlight the stony type layer and access its Blending Options.
- To entangle the words in the clouds, we'll do something similar to what we just did: drag the Underlying Layer black slider to the right, maybe to about 100. Then option/Alt drag its left half leftward (to about 75, maybe).
- Click OK.
- Use the Move tool to drag that layer around the document a bit.

This layer is now very complex, so unless your computer is quite fast, there will be a noticeable lag. What's making it so complex? On the right side of the layer, past its indicator icons, is a disclosure arrow. Click it and you'll see that there are both Smart Filters and layer styles applied. Between those and our Blend If tweaks, Photoshop has a lot to calculate as you move the layer around.

You may click the little eyes to hide each effect or filter. The Smart Object's content is an actual type layer using a font you likely don't have. If you don't try to access the text, you can enjoy how it looks. However, if you attempt to edit the S.O.'s content, Photoshop will insist you get the font or live with a substitute from you computer. The good news is that I used a font from Adobe Fonts, so the font may auto-activate, or you can "Resolve Missing Fonts" if prompted.

Lesson E: Painting in Photoshop

Painters may find a more immersive experience in the dedicated painting app Adobe Fresco (adobe.com/products/fresco.html), but Photoshop has powerful painting features, too.

In this lesson, we'll dabble with those features. If you like the experience, there's the whole "Brushes & Painting" chapter in the Compendium! I'd suggest consulting it during the following experiments.

Prepare Your Canvas

- As you did in this chapter's first lesson, create a new, empty document: click the Home button at the left end of the Options Bar. Then click the New file button. Choose Photo to access the Default Photoshop Size. Click Create.

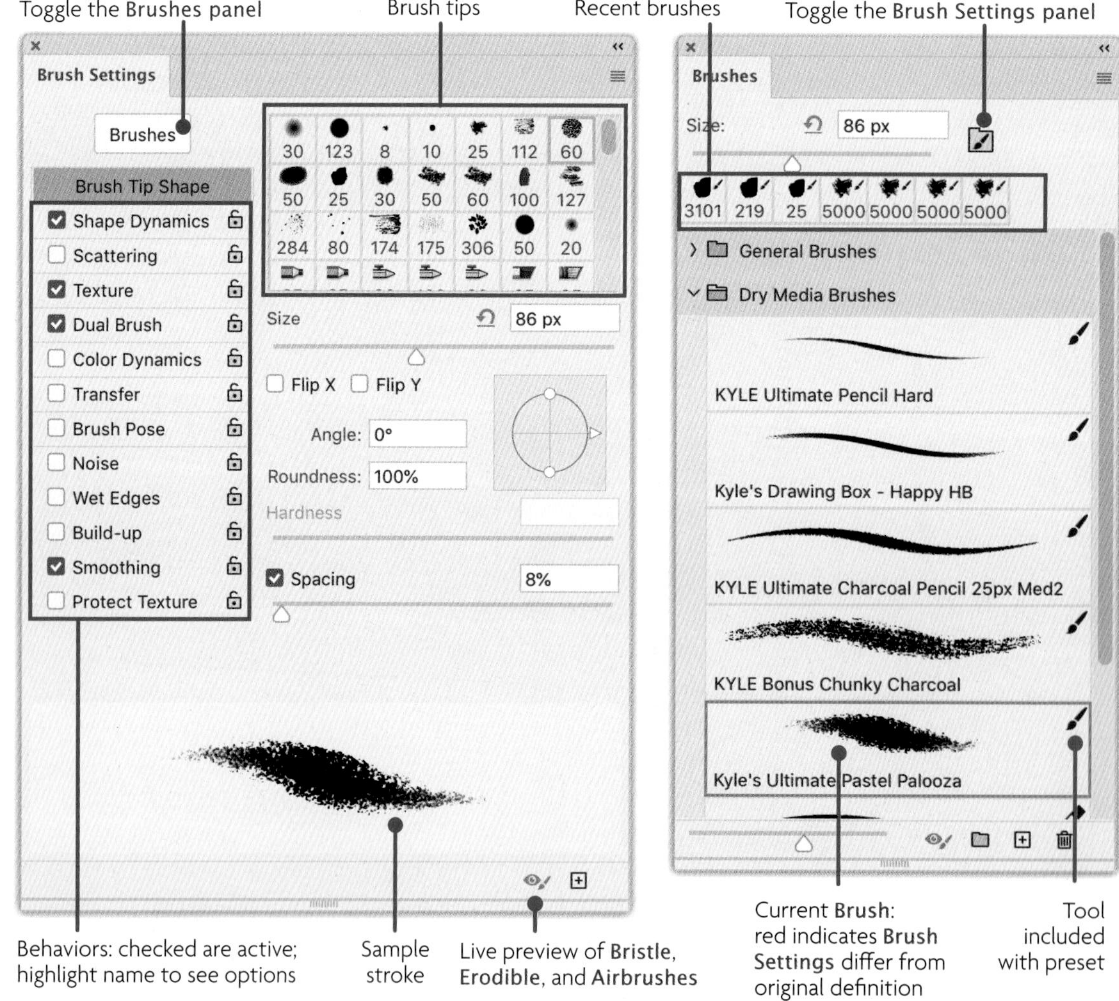

➡ Go to the Window menu, and open both the Brushes and Brush Settings panels.

Tools that use a brush cursor can be customized with the Brush Settings panel. Configurations made there can be saved to the Brushes panel. Configuring is choosing (or creating) a brush tip and adding behaviors to it. These can leverage stylus and pressure-sensitive tablets. Brushes (a.k.a. presets) can be tool-specific or used by any brush-using tool.

To facilitate your experimental doodling, let's make a layer structure that allows you to easily wipe the canvas clean without being too disruptive.

➡ From the Layers panel menu, choose New Layer.... Give it a name like "doodle," "masterpiece," or "artful," then click OK.

Now, here's the challenge when experimenting. If you simply press delete/backspace, that whole layer will be destroyed. If you wanted to protect the pristine Background, you'd have to create another. But when there's a selection active, delete/backspace removes only what's inside the marquee, not the layer it's on.

So, for quick erasure of my doodles but not my doodling layer, I marquee the whole layer with ⌘-A/Ctrl-A or by choosing Select > All. I simply choose not to notice those marching ants. When I want to wipe off the doodle layer, I hit delete/backspace and the layer is emptied but is still there, ready for more action.

Happy Little Dabs

➡ Select the whole layer with ⌘-A/Ctrl-.

➡ Activate the Brush tool by pressing the B key.

➡ Use the Color panel to choose a color with which to paint.

➡ In the Brush Settings panel, highlight Brush Tip Shape at the upper left. It is likely already highlighted. With the controls on the right, set both the brush's Hardness and Spacing to 100%. The sample brush stroke at the bottom is a hint of what you'll see in color when you paint a stroke.

➡ Drag across the canvas. Should look a bit like this: ●●●●●●●●●

That string of pearls indicates that a stroke isn't really continuous, but is a series of overlapping dabs. The spacing controls how tightly they overlap—if they do.

➡ Try different Spacing settings. After a bit, I bet you have a lot of strokes and no room to paint. Double-check that the marching ants are still there around the edges of the image. If so, press delete/backspace. Choose a low Spacing setting (a few percent).

➡ Change the Angle and Roundness with the interface illustrated here. With a strongly elliptical brush angled at roughly 45°, you now have a calligraphy brush. Try it. (Note: Just because you have a brush doesn't mean you'll be a fine calligrapher!)

In the top part of the Brush Settings panel, you'll see brush tips. They're used by the presets that are currently installed. Many are made from imagery. All the controls you've just been playing with can be used with those, too, except Hardness. Numbers in that window indicate the size of the tip in pixels.

- With your current settings, an interesting tip would be the one with a size of 174. Hovering over it shows the mysterious name "kyle drag mixed grays." Make a stroke with that tip.

The beginning and end of each stroke is rough like bristles were involved.

Setting Behavior and Qualities

This is where days are lost. On the left side of the Brush Settings panel you'll see the various categories of behaviors that a brush can enjoy. I'll mention a couple here and leave you to explore with the "Brushes & Painting" chapter in the Compendium as your guide.

- Assuming your marquee is still around the edges of the canvas, press delete/backspace.
- Increase the Spacing to a value like 25%. Make a reference brush stroke.
- On the left side of the Brush Settings panel, highlight the words Shape Dynamics.

If the checkbox wasn't checked, it is now. By highlighting the words, you can see the many controls on the right. You're going to crank up one of those controls at a time, making a stroke to see its effects.

- Set the Size Jitter to its maximum. Draw another stroke. "Jitter" means "randomizer." Each dab that comprises the stroke is a random size between 0 and the size you set in Brush Tip Shape.
- Set the Angle Jitter to its maximum. Make another stroke whose dabs are randomly rotated.

You get the idea! The other jitters are more subtle. Roundness Jitter randomizes each tip's roundness, of course. Flip X and Flip Y Jitter randomly flip each tip either horizontally or vertically. One more:

- Highlight Scattering so you can see its controls. Watch the stroke sample as you drag the Scatter slider.

The dabs move off perpendicular to the stroke direction. To make them also scatter along the stroke direction, check the Both Axes box. If the dabs get too spread out, you can multiply their number with the Count setting. Depending on the tip you choose, and other settings in this panel, this can provide interesting textures.

This has been just a taste. I hope you're intrigued and plan to explore more.

Project: Chalk Drawing

We will combine a picture of a blackboard with a black-on-white illustration to simulate fancy chalk art. The final layer structure will be fairly simple and minimal. The concepts and features to achieve this, however, will require focus.

Along the way, we'll do two explanatory exercises to clarify the concepts at work.

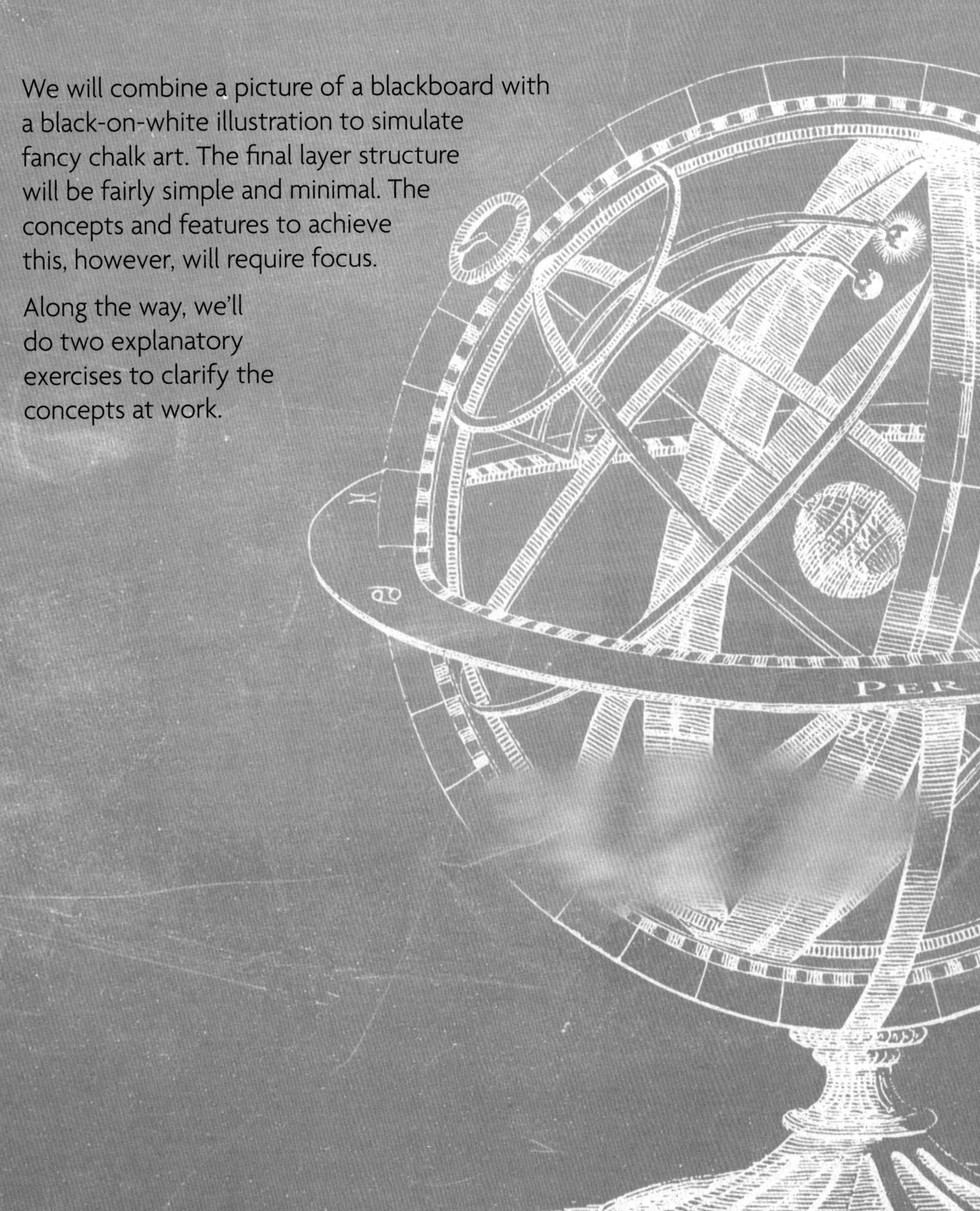

Lesson A: Placing the Art

As is so often the case in Photoshop, the first 90% of an effect is not too difficult. The last bit, the polish, is often the more difficult *and* satisfying aspect.

The files we need are all with the downloaded course files in a folder called "Project B-Chalk." Make that available. You'll see there's a finished version to reference if you'd like.

- Open the file "chalkboard BEFORE.psd." Unsurprisingly, it's a photo of a standard chalkboard. So, let's add more stuff!

Place and Finesse the Smart Object

- Choose File > Place Linked…, navigate to the "Project B- Chalk" folder, and open the file called "astro-illustration.ai." Click OK in the Open As Smart Object dialog box. The illustration appears in a transform box.
- Check that the constraint (chain icon) on the transform is enabled between the W and H scaling fields. Use the transform box to size and position the illustration on the board. Commit the transform when you think you like its size and position.

W: 100.00% H: 100.00% Constraint enabled
W: 100.00% H: 100.00% disabled

Eventually, we'll need a duplicate of this Smart Object. To keep things contained nicely, we should try to apply any needed effects as Smart Filters or layer styles.

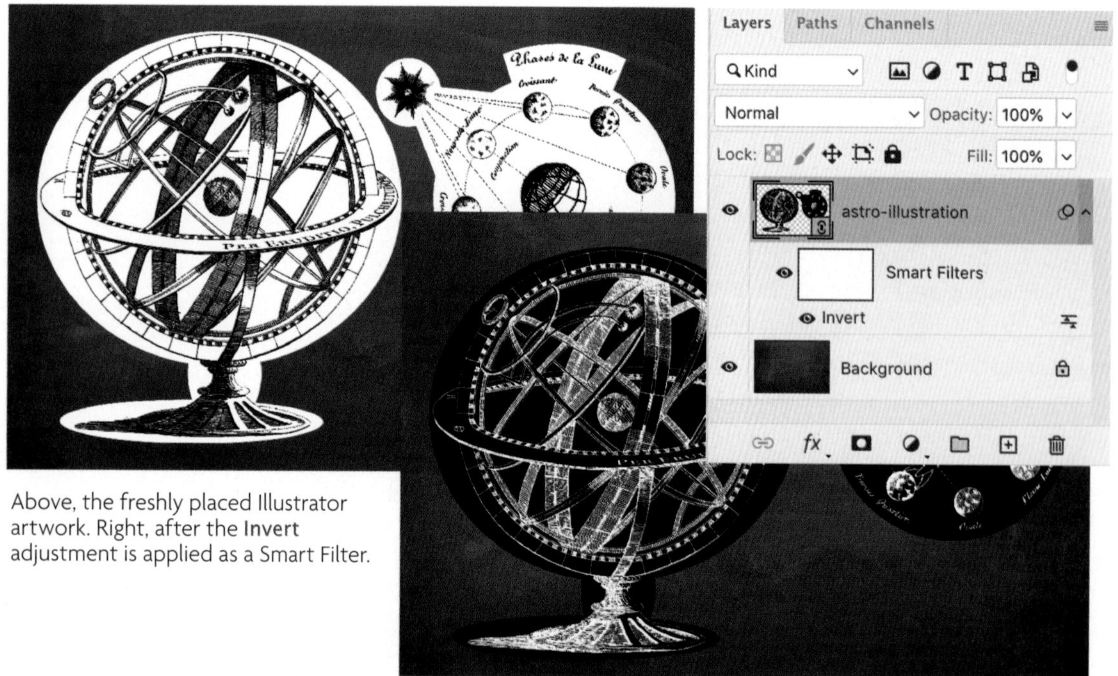

Above, the freshly placed Illustrator artwork. Right, after the **Invert** adjustment is applied as a Smart Filter.

- Choose Image > Adjustments > Invert. That adjustment shows up as a Smart Filter in the Layers panel. Now all that annoying opaque white is an equally annoying opaque black.
- Set the layer's blend mode to Screen, which makes black vanish. Yeah, this book has a lot to say about blend modes.

We seem to be almost done. Not so fast! Chalk is flaky and wouldn't be quite so sharp as what we have so far. If you zoom in to 200% or more (View > 200%), you'll see how it lacks those qualities. For the flaky part, we'll add a little noise.

- Choose Filter > Noise > Add Noise.... In the Add Noise dialog, check Monochromatic to prevent the noise from being colorful. For a slightly more natural Distribution, choose Gaussian. The amount is hard to decide because more of the image is getting noisy than we'd like. We'll take care of that soon. For now, set the Amount to about 30%, then click OK.

Notice that we have both white noise on dark, which we don't want, and black noise on the white "chalk lines," which we do. Now what made white disappear earlier? A blend mode (Screen). We need that one's opposite, Multiply, applied to this noise filter. You may recall we applied a blend mode to a Smart Filter in the last chapter too.

- Double-click the filter blending options icon to the right of Add Noise in the Layers panel. Set the Mode to Multiply to leave only the black noise, which is vanished by the layer's blend mode of Screen! So we end up causing little bits of chalk to flake off the board. Click OK.
- To soften the edges just a tiny bit, choose Filter > Blur > Gaussian Blur... and set it to just about .3 pixel—a subliminal value. No need for a blend mode here.

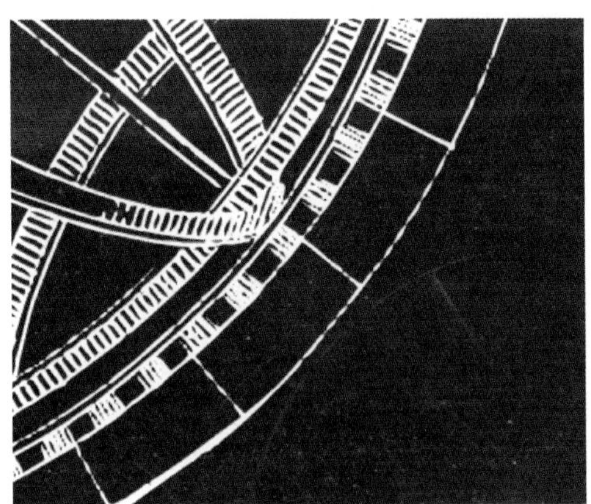

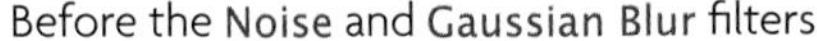

Before the Noise and Gaussian Blur filters

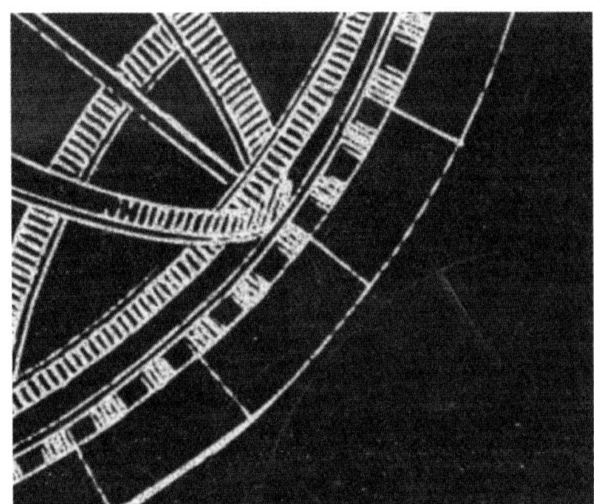

After the filters. Nicely chalky.

Now that would be a wonderful and educational project. It started as a question from a former student. I liked the question so much I added it to my classroom curriculum and this book. At this stage, he had a follow-up question. How could he add a bit of partial erasure?

That was both intriguing and a touch difficult to do in a way that would allow us to swap out the artwork at will, as he needed to do. So, I've prepared a couple explanatory exercises to get us there.

Lesson B: Knockout & Clip Mask Blending

Let's learn two features that will let us erase some chalk drawing and leave a bit of residue.

Knockout

Use a layer's content as a mask, a kind of layer drill.

- Open the file "concept- knockout.psd." Parts should look familiar.
- Double-click near the top layer's name ("scanner"). This opens the layer's Blending Options in the Layer Style dialog.
- Lower the Fill Opacity to about 33%. Of course, the green content of the layer diminishes, but as we saw before, it leaves the effects intact. That's why the stroke around the edges remains. Now here's the new thing…
- Choose each of the two items in the Knockout menu (a little lower in the dialog than the Fill Opacity). Right now, both Shallow and Deep yield the same result: a view of the Background layer. Shallow requires layer groups to exist in order to do something else. We're about to make one of those, so leave Knockout set to Shallow, then click OK.

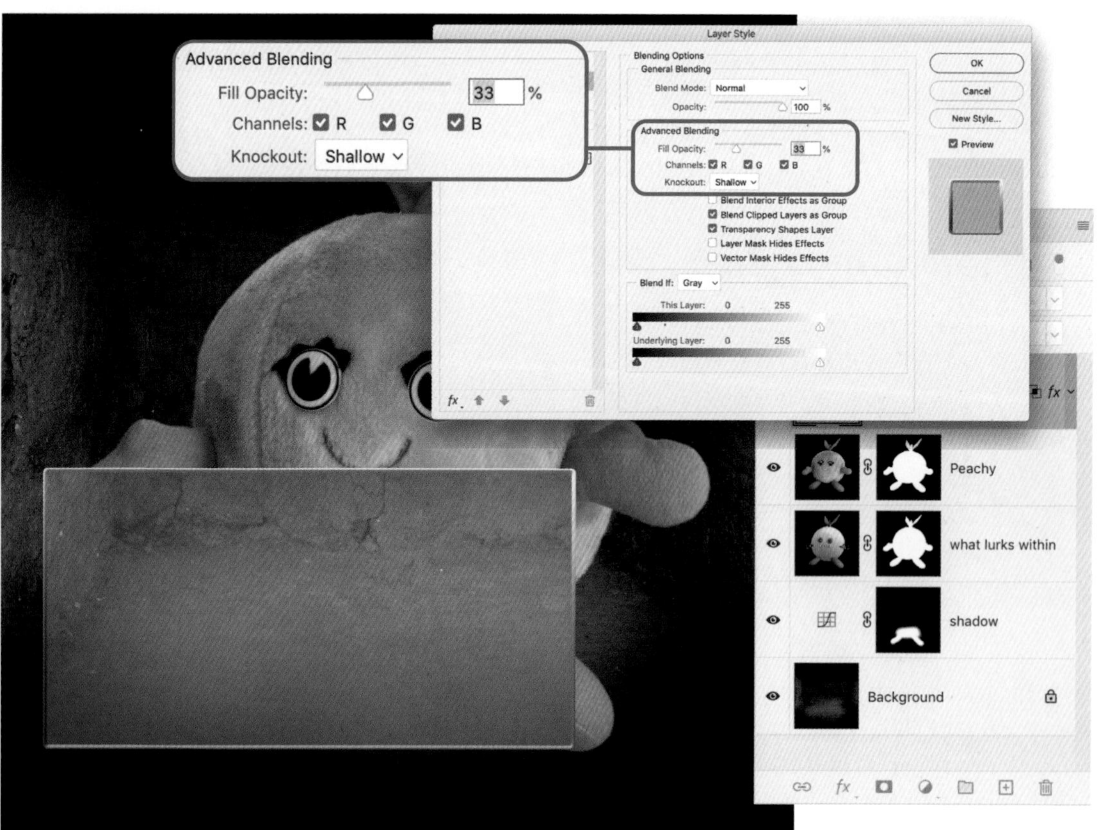

Knockout now uses the scanner layer to drill through all the layers below it, but it's unable to go through a Background, if one exists. Otherwise, it would go all the way through to transparency. We don't want to go that far. We want to drill through the Peachy layer only.

- To group layers and limit the Knockout, we need to highlight them. So click near the name of the Peachy layer, then shift-click near the name of the scanner layer. Choose Layer > Group Layers or use the shortcut ⌘-G/Ctrl-G. The two layers are now in a folder-like construction in the Layers panel called "Group 1." You'll see the view through the scanner layer is different too.
- Activate the Move tool and, in the Options Bar, set Auto-Select to Layer.
- Use the Move tool to drag the greenish "scanner" around the image. The group will expand and the scanner layer will be highlighted thanks to Auto-Select.

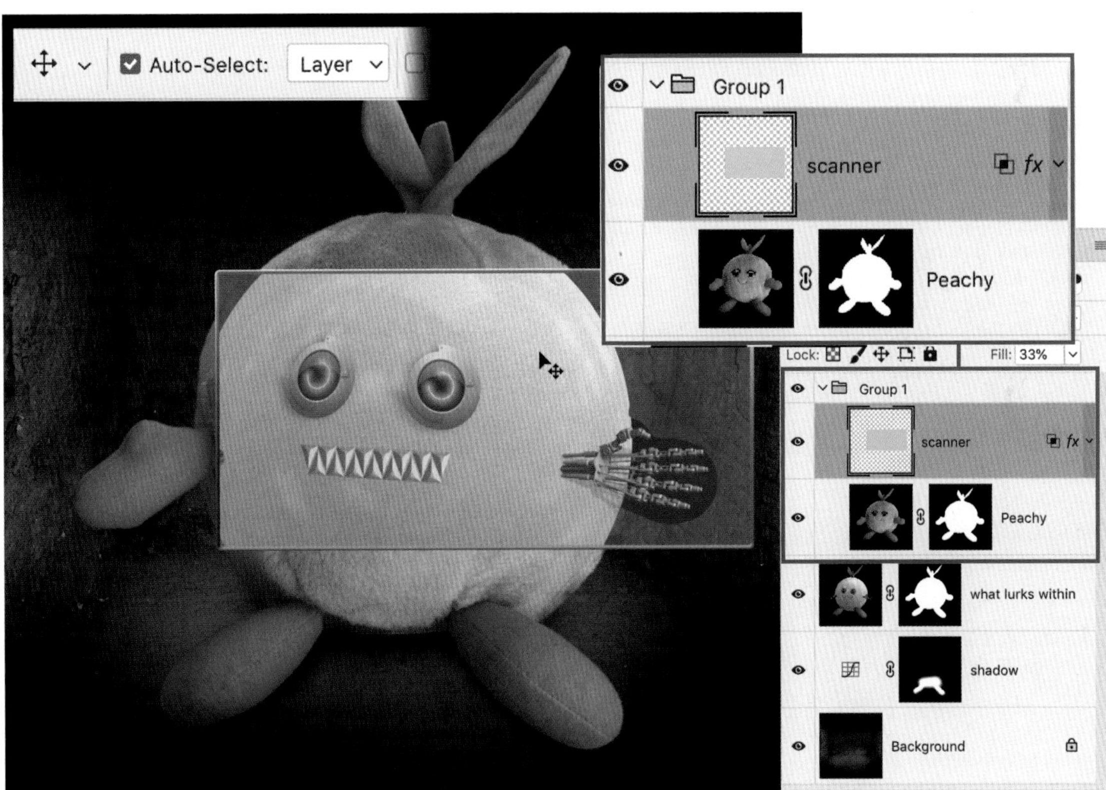

What you see are the layers below the group. That is, the scanner layer is now drilling through only the layer that is in its same group: Peachy. Elsewhere, Peachy continues to obscure those other, disturbing layers.

Soon, we'll use this to feature to have a chalk-erasure layer. Anything we paint on it will use Knockout to hide the fancy chalk drawing, revealing the blackboard below. When I shared that with my inquisitive student, he came back wanting some "residue" left from the erasure. Thus, we have a bit more to learn.

An interesting feature of groups is that they have their own opacity, blend modes, etc. They can have effects and be masked like layers. For more, see "Groups" (page 158).

Clip Mask with Blending Options

Clipping or clip masks use the visible extent of a layer, group, or Smart Object to control the visibility of other layers. So, if a photo is "clipped" to a type layer, the photo is visible only where the type is. It feels like the opposite of Knockout. The "base layer" of a clip mask is a support or foundation for other layers, where a layer used for Knockout is a hole punch.

- Open the file "concept- clip mask and blending.psd."
- With the layer called "clip" active, experiment with different Fill Opacity settings (note that it's called "Fill" at the top of the Layers panel). As it's lowered, the hot pink disappears, the bevel effect remains, and the cracks in the ground show through.
- Restore the Fill Opacity to 100% again and make the top layer ("tortoiseshell") visible. Since it uses the Multiply blend mode, we can see through it like we can tortoiseshell.

To make the word "clip" appear to be made of tortoiseshell, we will clip the top layer to the one below it. They'll mostly remain independent, but not entirely, as you'll see.

- Hold down the option/Alt key as you hover your cursor above the line between those two layers. You should see the icon illustrated below. When you do, click.

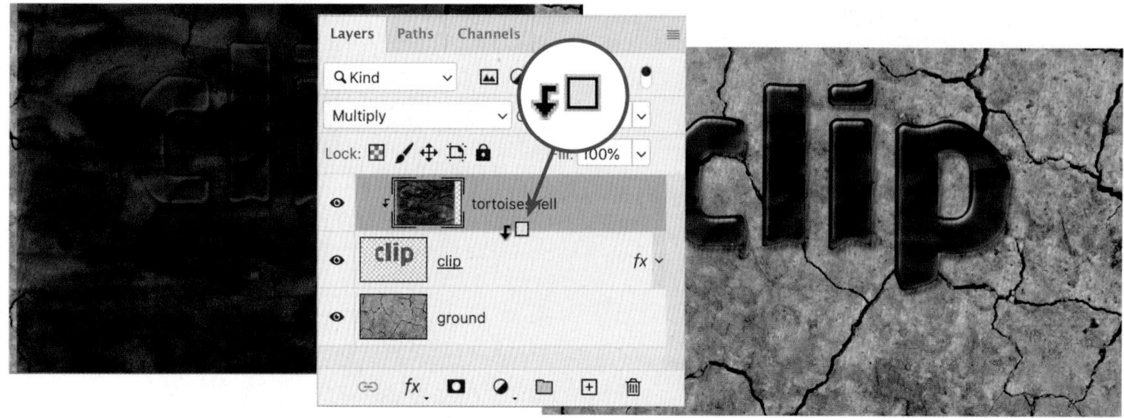

The word clip retains its effects and has adopted the tortoiseshell as its new content. We know that tortoiseshell is translucent and that we'd see the cracks in the ground through it. Now what feature did we use a little while ago to reveal those cracks? Fill Opacity, wasn't it?

- Lower the clip layer's Fill Opacity all the way to 0. Bummer, isn't it?

Recall two things: Fill Opacity lowers the opacity of a layer's content (but not the effects), and clipping renders the clipped layer as the content of the other. That's why the tortoiseshell disappears. But this is Photoshop, the program with a setting for everything.

- Double-click near the clip layer's name to open its Blending Options in the Layer Style dialog box.

Yes, the same place we found Knockout, Advanced Blending, is where we'll find the solution to this dilemma. Its phrasing is a bit opaque, but we'll work it out.

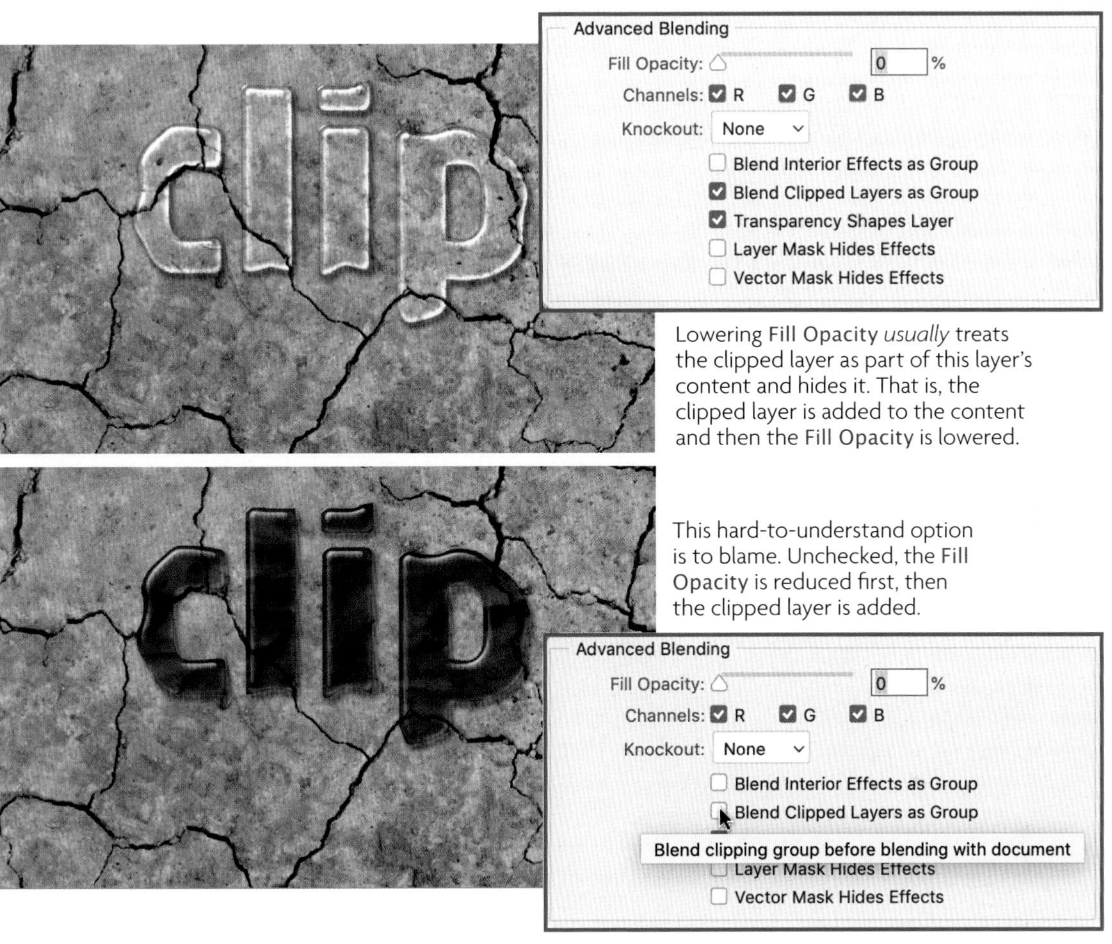

Lowering Fill Opacity *usually* treats the clipped layer as part of this layer's content and hides it. That is, the clipped layer is added to the content and then the Fill Opacity is lowered.

This hard-to-understand option is to blame. Unchecked, the Fill Opacity is reduced first, then the clipped layer is added.

Locate the Blend Clipped Layers as Group checkbox. Hovering over it reveals an "explanatory" tooltip. *Maybe* it helps. It includes the word "before." What they are trying to say is that the clipped layer is added to (blended with) the content and *then* the Fill Opacity is lowered, affecting everything. Unchecking that little box reduces the Fill Opacity first, hiding the hot pink, and then the tortoiseshell is added with its Multiply blend mode, allowing us to see all the way through to the cracks in the ground.

Combining the Two

I hope you're feeling more informed than abused by all this! If the latter, please blame me. If the former, thank my talented former student Thom Head for the inspiration.

The result is that we now know how to see the content of a layer that's been clipped to one with 0 Fill Opacity. That layer with 0 Fill Opacity can be used to Knockout one or more layers below it.

Our erasure layer will be the one with 0 Fill Opacity knocking out the chalk drawing while serving as the base layer to the mostly erased version. All we'll have to do is paint on that layer and it will look and act like actual chalk erasure with some residue left behind.

Lesson C: A Bit of Erasure

Layers with Options

- Back in "chalkboard BEFORE.psd," duplicate the astro-illustration layer. You can right-click and choose Duplicate Layer..., providing a name, if you like, or use the shortcut ⌘-J/Ctrl-J and accept the name given.
- Hide the original so we can focus on this one.
- With the duplicate highlighted, lower its opacity substantially (maybe to 40%).
- Hide it for a moment.

We'll use the existing eraser marks on the blackboard as guides. Now we can see streaks on the blackboard. Think about where you'd like the erasure to be. I see a strong eraser mark about one-third of the way up the left-hand side. That should be good to play with. It looks to be at between 10° and 15° from the horizontal. Why mention that? Well...

- Make that duped layer visible again. Choose Filter > Blur > Motion Blur.... Set its Angle to between 10° and 15°. Of course, you decide. You should also decide Distance. I'm going with 100 pixels. Click OK.
- Some of the lines in the art that happen to be at the same angle are still too sharp. Double-click on the name of the existing Gaussian Blur under the layer's name. It needs to be more than subliminal now. A Radius of 3 to 5 pixels should do.

That looks nicely, incompletely erased. But we don't want to see that layer everywhere. Let's create a new layer on which to paint an erasure area.

- Use the Layers panel menu to choose New Layer..., and give the layer a name like "erasure." Imaginative, I know.
- Activate the Brush tool (B). Choose any color at all from the Color panel. Choose a brush tip from the Brush Settings panel, just a soft round one will do.
- Disable any dynamics or scattering left over from former lessons. Adjust the size of the brush and paint along streaks on the board. This will not be the final attempt!

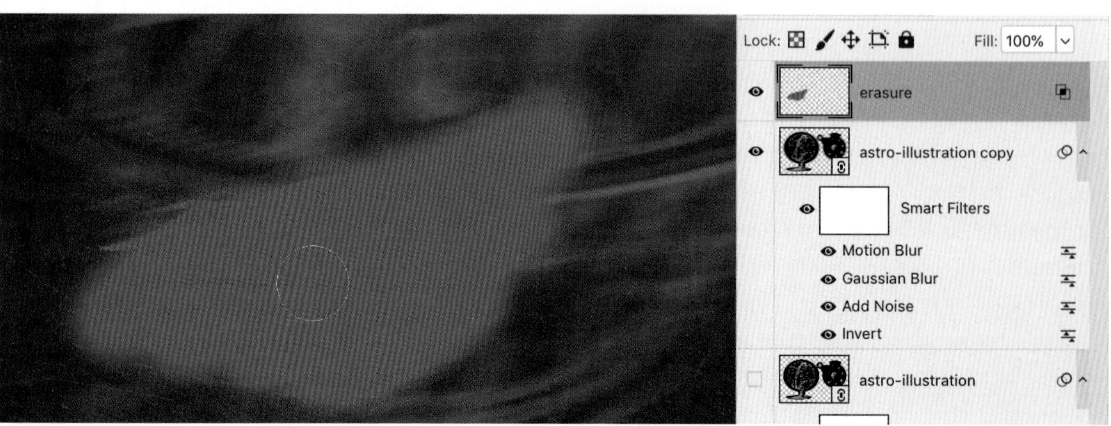

- In the Layers panel, drag the erasure layer below the blurred chalk art layer. Clip one to the other by option/Alt clicking the line between them. It doesn't look good yet.
- Double-click near the name of the erasure layer. Uncheck the Blend Clipped Layers as Group checkbox and lower the Fill Opacity to 0. Now you should see a bit of erasure and no more. Also, set Knockout to Deep. Click OK.

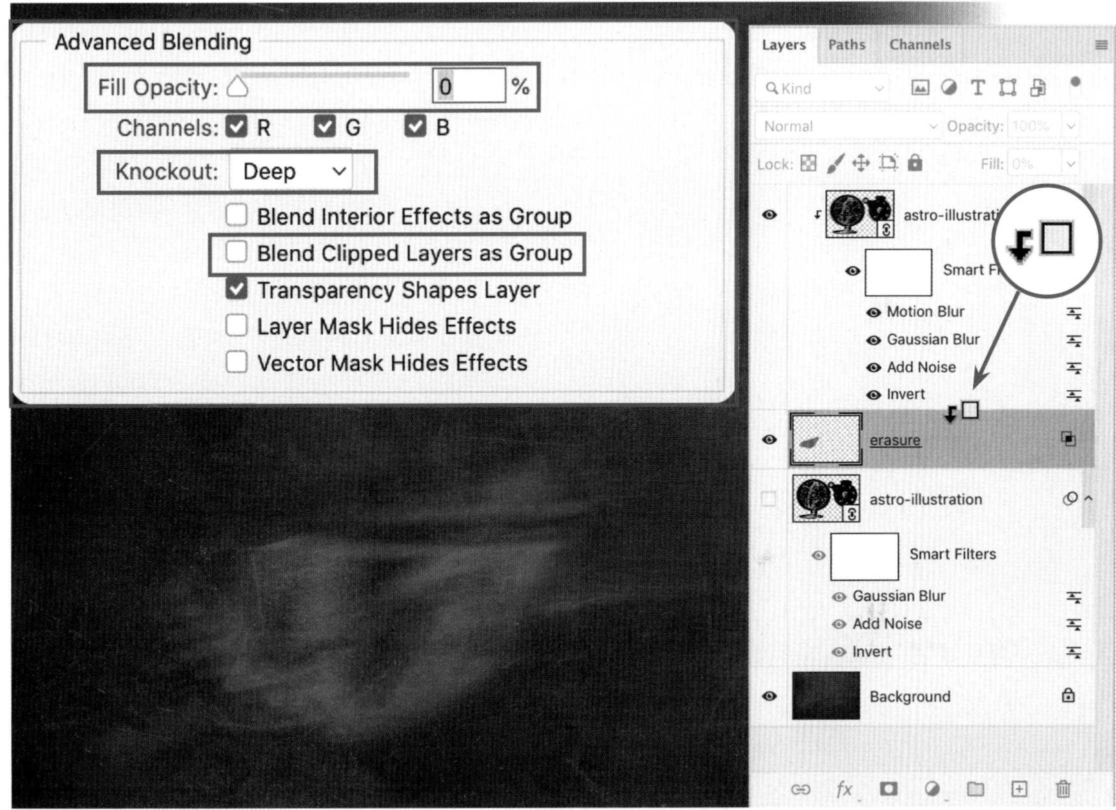

- Make the original astro-illustration layer visible. It should be hidden where you painted.
- Don't like your erasure? Select all (⌘-A/Ctrl-A), highlight the erasure layer, and press delete/backspace. Paint anywhere and it should look like you're erasing the art. Save!

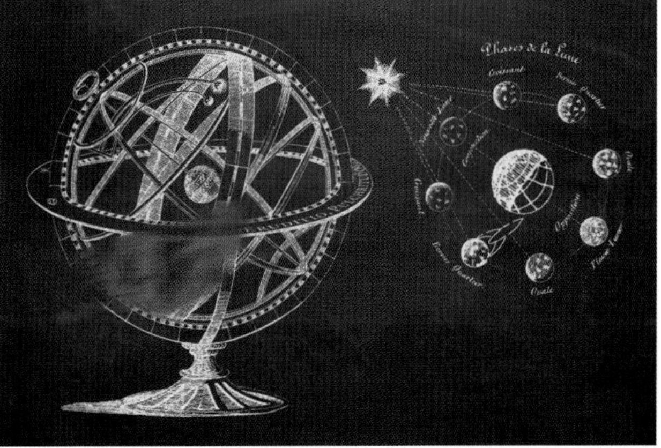

The result is one that can be endlessly altered as needed. The linked Smart Objects can be swapped out or edited, the filters can be tweaked, and the painting can be easily revisited. When we work for others (or do requests), this is valuable indeed.

5 Adobe Camera Raw & Software-Aided Photography

If you do a great deal of photography, you should look into Adobe Lightroom. With it, you can manage and "develop" your photos, adjusting them in ways that are similar to what we've seen here, and the edits are always nondestructive. From there, images can be passed to Photoshop for even more magic.

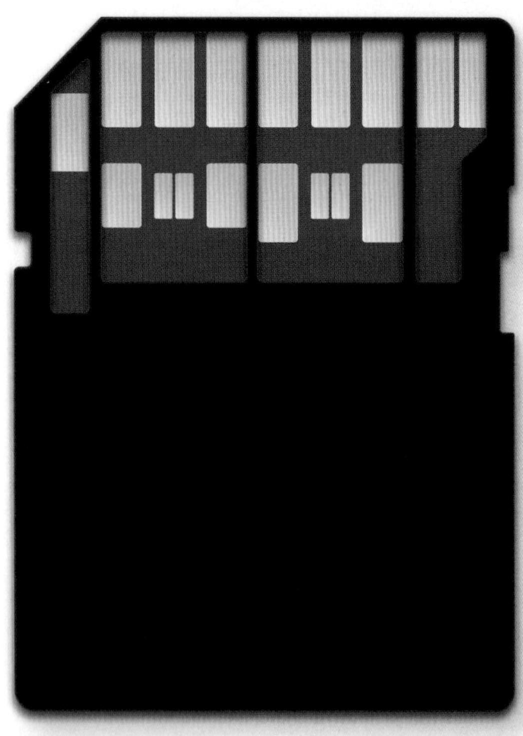

If you have a less severe photography habit, and you have access to a camera's "raw" captures, you may want to use Photoshop's companion applications: **Adobe Camera Raw (ACR)** and **Bridge**. ACR uses the same development engine as Lightroom, so you can make the same nondestructive edits. Bridge allows you to edit images' metadata and perform other organizational tasks. In this chapter, with an assist from Bridge, we'll look at the division of labor between ACR and Photoshop in the world of photographic capture. ACR has a lot to offer, so refer to the *Camera Raw & Lightroom* chapter in the Compendium for many more details.

Lesson A: From Bridge to ACR

Adobe Bridge can be used to download images from an attached camera (or camera card reader) and to navigate your computer's file system. We'll be doing the latter.

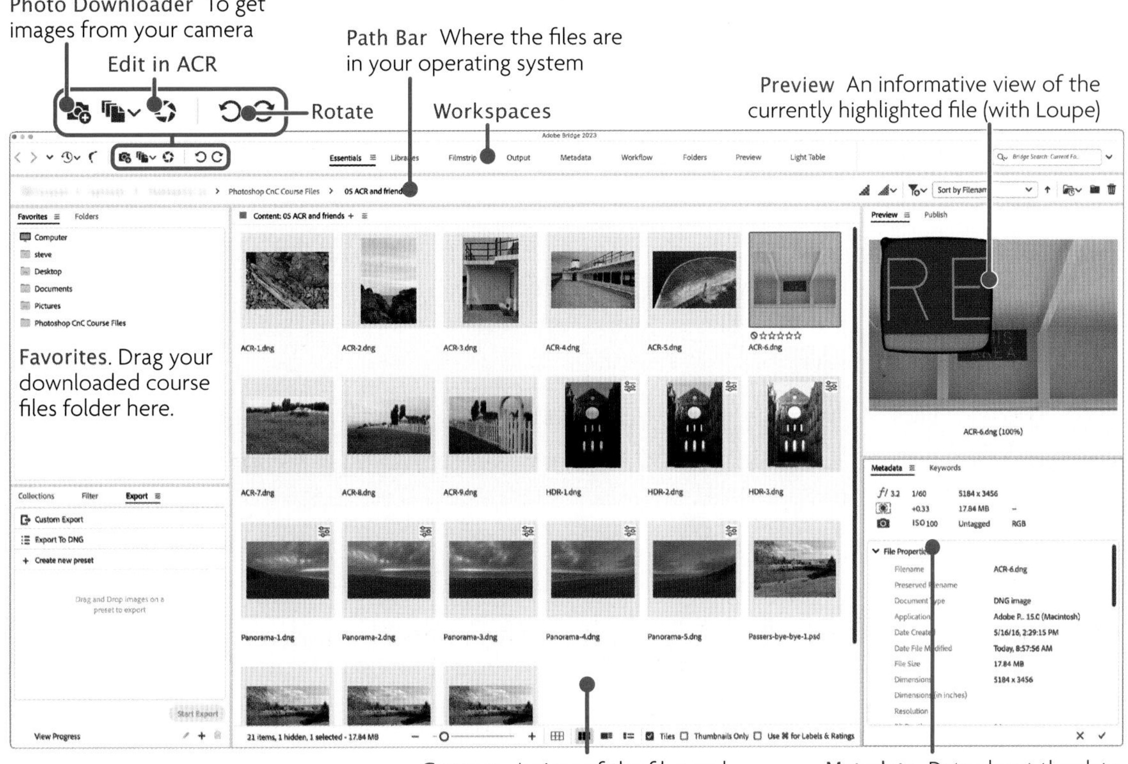

- To use Bridge, you need to have Bridge! If you haven't already, use the Creative Cloud app to install and launch it.
- There are preferences you may want to adjust, especially for the user interface. On a Mac, choose Adobe Bridge 2023 > Preferences…; on Windows, choose Edit > Preferences…; or press ⌘-K/Ctrl-K. Click on Interface in the column on the left, and choose a Color Theme (I chose the lightest) and Scaling (I chose one size up from small).
- To easily get to your course files, locate the downloaded course files folder in your operating system, then drag it into the Favorites panel and select it there. You'll see the folders it contains in the Content panel.
- Double-click the "05 ACR and friends" folder to see its contents. Highlight one of those image thumbnails.

When an image is highlighted, you can choose to view its Preview in the upper-right corner, its Metadata in the lower-right corner, and its location in your computer's file system along the top in the Path Bar. If one of these panels is hidden, you can choose it in the Window menu.

In the Metadata panel, you can enter keywords, contact info, and copyright info, and you can view the exposure and other image data that your camera provides.

You'll see an "adjusted" icon on the thumbnails of those raw images (in this case, DNG files) that have been edited in Adobe Camera Raw. The first set of images all begin with "ACR" and haven't yet been adjusted. That's what we're going to do.

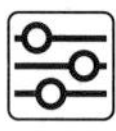

Processing Images with ACR

In ACR we can open multiple images at once. Then, in the ACR interface, we can edit all those images simultaneously or individually, just as in Lightroom. Although ACR is an application on our computers, it can't run unattended by either Bridge or Photoshop. It requires one of those as a "host" application.

Double-clicking images in Bridge pushes them off to Photoshop, which will launch and host ACR to edit them. Highlighting them and then using the shortcut ⌘-R/Ctrl-R (for "Raw") launches ACR immediately with Bridge hosting it. I'll do the latter when I've got Photoshop doing other things. We'll do it for the novelty.

- Select all nine "ACR" images by clicking the first one then shift-clicking the last.
- Use the shortcut ⌘-R/Ctrl-R. The ACR interface appears with a Filmstrip along the bottom containing those nine images.

In the upper right are numerous tools; along the right are various panels with lots of sliders; and there are a few buttons along the bottom too. All this is discussed in the "Camera Raw & Lightroom" chapter of the Compendium. Be aware that Adobe has a funny way of adding, renaming, or moving these once in a while.

There is exactly one kind of adjustment we can, and indeed should, perform to all of these images at once. It's a correction for the optics (lenses) used for these images.

- Click the name of the Optics panel to expose its options.
- Use the shortcut ⌘-A/Ctrl-A to select all the images in the Filmstrip.
- In the Optics panel, check the boxes for both Remove Chromatic Aberration and Use Profile Corrections.

Chromatic aberration is the inability to sharply focus sharp edges from the images' perimeters without fringing. You just fixed that. The optics used for each shot, embedded in its metadata, is used to apply a correction calculated by Adobe just for that lens. Every lens has some distortion and usually some vignetting (darkening around the edges). You just fixed that too. Imagine if you had hundreds of images selected right now. They'd all be thanking you.

Now we have to be a little more selective about the images we're editing and what we do.

- In the Filmstrip, click once on the first image ("ACR-1.dng") and return to the Basic panel (at the top of the stack). If you don't see the filenames, right-click on any thumbnail in the Filmstrip and click Show Filenames.

Basic Adjustments

For this and the following steps, you may want to keep the "Camera Raw & Lightroom" chapter of the Compendium bookmarked.

- At the top of the Basic panel, activate the White Balance tool (the eyedropper). Click on something that should be neutral (gray), like one of those stones. ACR *made* it neutral by adjusting color throughout the image. Essentially, you've told the image what color the light was.
- Click on the log with that tool, shamelessly lying to ACR that it should be neutral. Since it's so warm, the image becomes much cooler in an attempt to make the log gray. To recover from that deception, you better click on a stone again.
- Experiment with the Tone controls in the Basic panel (Exposure, Contrast, etc.). By working your way from the top down, you make increasingly surgical adjustments to the tone in the image. **Note:** Double-clicking any slider resets it.
- When you have pleasing contrast overall, mess with the Texture and Clarity sliders. These affect local contrast. Texture is smarter about not adding too much grain in skin tones.
- Dehaze won't do much good in this image, as there is no haze, but you should try it anyway. It's the software's version of a polarizing filter.
- The last two sliders are rather similar to Photoshop's Vibrance adjustment. As such, the Vibrance slider is the safer one.

Let's edit several images that need some of the same adjustments.

- Click on "ACR-3," then shift-click on "ACR-5." Now three images are targeted, though only the first is shown in the main window. Click in various areas with the White Balance tool and keep an eye on the three thumbnails. They all respond. That's good—the light was the same for all three.
- Try different adjustments and see if all three images benefit. If not, click on just one and give it special attention.

The best part? Everything you've done is just metadata. You're just interpreting the raw data for those images. That means if you return to ACR with them, you can reinterpret the raw data any way you like. If this isn't making sense, you haven't read the "Camera Raw & Lightroom" chapter of the Compendium. Maybe it's time to do that.

Workflow Options

To go beyond the nondestructive edits you can do in ACR, you can embed a copy of the raw data and edits inside a Photoshop Smart Object so you can do everything in this book to it.

- At the bottom of the ACR interface is a line of underlined text. Click it to edit ACR's Workflow Preferences.
- The only item we really need right now is the bottom checkbox: Open in Photoshop as Smart Object. Check it and click OK.
- Click Done in ACR, then watch the thumbnails in Bridge update. They'll also get the "adjusted" icon in their corners.

Lesson B: HDR

Manage Contrast with Multiple Images

High Dynamic Range is the term given to an image that contains a larger-than-usual tonal range from dark to light. Some cameras today natively capture very broad ranges without resorting to combining multiple exposures, as we're going to do here. Some cameras (including smartphones) can combine images to do this too.

In the folder we're looking at in Bridge, there are three images whose names begin with "HDR."

- Highlight one of those images at a time, looking at the Metadata panel to see their exposure data. Note the differences in the Preview panel too.

Each exposure is about two f-stops apart. In the lightest, the sky is blown out, but we can see details in the shadows. The darkest preserves the sky, but the shadows are black. We are going to blend them in two ways: once in ACR, and once using Photoshop's Merge to HDR Pro. You'll see that, although Photoshop's conversion can be superior, we can make an ACR HDR DNG ASAP IMHO. Sorry.

- Select HDR-1, HDR-2, and HDR-3, then use the shortcut ⌘-R/Ctrl-R to open them in ACR.
- Use the shortcut ⌘-A/Ctrl-A to select all three images in the Filmstrip.
- Right-click on one of them, then choose Merge to HDR.... There aren't many options via this route. Luckily ACR can Align Images and Apply Auto Settings to achieve a well-lit result. Both are almost always required and beautifully effective.

Deghost compensates for moving objects or shadows by choosing one of the exposures for such an item (like a bird flying through or a bush wiggling in a breeze). The Overlay shows you where deghosting is taking place. Here, the Low setting looks good.

- Click Merge.... You'll be asked where you would like your new DNG file to be saved. The same folder as the originals should be dandy.

But now what? That new DNG is added to the Filmstrip so you can apply adjustments to it. At the bottom of the dialog box, you can choose to Open Object (it will say Open Image if you didn't change the Workflow Preferences), which opens the image in Photoshop. You might also choose Save Image..., then choose a format and location. This is a great way to make a quick deliverable for someone who can't open raw files (which is almost everyone). But we have another experiment to run.

- In ACR, click Done.
- In Bridge, select the three original HDR DNGs again, but this time choose Tools > Photoshop > Merge to HDR Pro....

Photoshop launches or comes to the fore and performs some preparations before showing you a large dialog box. Though large, the preview is a low-resolution approximation. The final image will be better than what you see here.

As you can see, there are more options here. More than you need, luckily. Most will make a fringed monstrosity, if you're not careful. I usually restrict myself to a few adjustments. I enable Remove ghosts and Edge Smoothness to lessen edge-glow artifacts. I touch nothing in the Tone and Detail section because even small adjustments muddy the image. I do, however, adjust the Curve fairly often to put more light in the shadows, as I've done here.

What is Photoshop going to give you? Not a DNG. It will open an image that is in either 8-bit or 16-bit per channel (the latter affording you more latitude for additional adjustments). You can save that file in any format you prefer. I usually use PSD or TIFF.

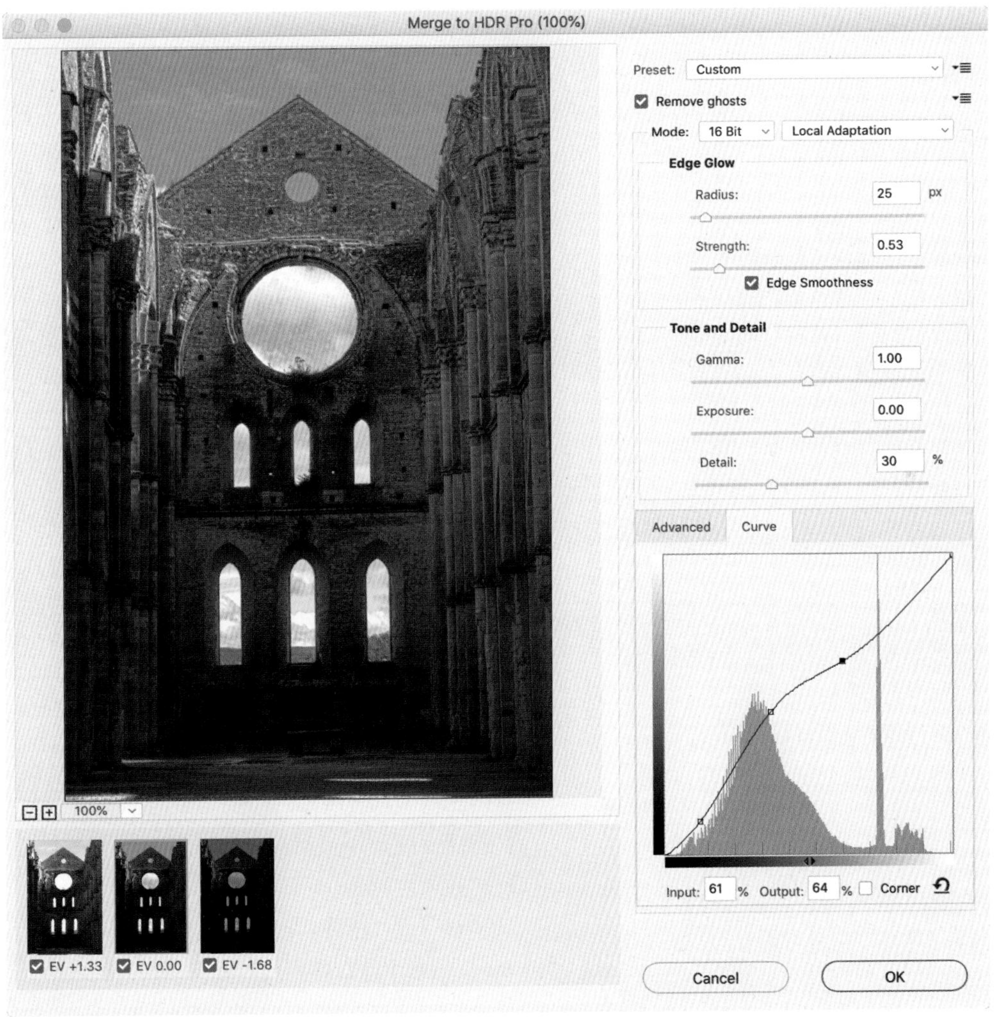

➡ Choose 16 Bit for Mode, then click OK to see the better, final result, saving the file as a PSD.

If you should ever choose 32 bit, all the tonal richness will be preserved, such that you can't see it all on screen. So the image looks dark. If you disable Complete Toning in Adobe Camera Raw, you can choose how the image *looks*, but all the tones collected from the three images will still be there. Few use 32 Bit, except for images called radiance maps for 3-D work.

Lesson C: Panorama

Let's construct a panoramic image. For this, we need appropriate source images. There are things that should be done when making the photos that will be combined like this.

Assemble Appropriately Captured Images

Each exposure should be the same so they can be blended together. This also implies that any adjustments done to an image after capture have to be done to all of the images in exactly the same way.

The images' field of view should overlap by about 30% so the software can recognize elements to align them well. In a perfect world (this is not it, by the way), each image would be shot on a perfectly level tripod with the lens rotated around its nodal point between each exposure.

I used to do that. Then one day I ran onto a beach moments before the sun set and squeezed off five frames. They were made with the same exposure settings, handheld, as I pivoted my body from left-to-right in the sand, hoping I was overlapping the images by enough. Then the sun was gone. I assumed Photoshop would punish me for my haste and laziness. I was very wrong!

Again, we'll compare ACR's merge with Photoshop's. They are similar but not the same. If you're displeased with one for your own work, by all means try the other.

- In Bridge, select the five images whose name begins with "Panorama." To try ACR's method first, use the shortcut ⌘-R/Ctrl-R to open the images in ACR.
- Use the shortcut ⌘-A/Ctrl-A to select all the images in the Filmstrip.
- Right-click on one, then choose Merge to Panorama.... A dialog box opens with ACR's initial offering.

Because I didn't use a level tripod and pivot around the lens's nodal point, the software warped each image to overlap and blend them like they're pasted inside a cylinder.

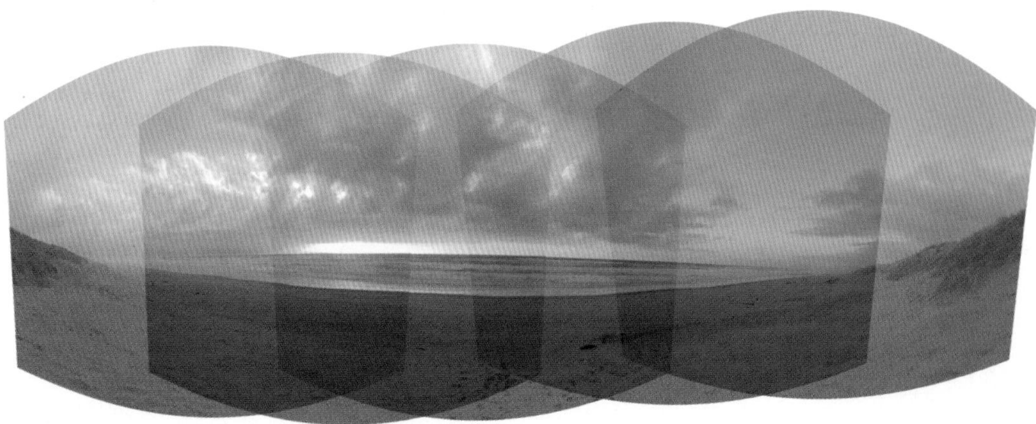

ACR figures out just how to cut each image to blend them nicely. Photoshop does that too. Since I panned around nearly 180° with a wide but not *very* wide lens, the choice of Cylindrical Projection (in the dialog box) is ideal. If there had been any sailboats in the shot, their masts would be nicely vertical in this projection too.

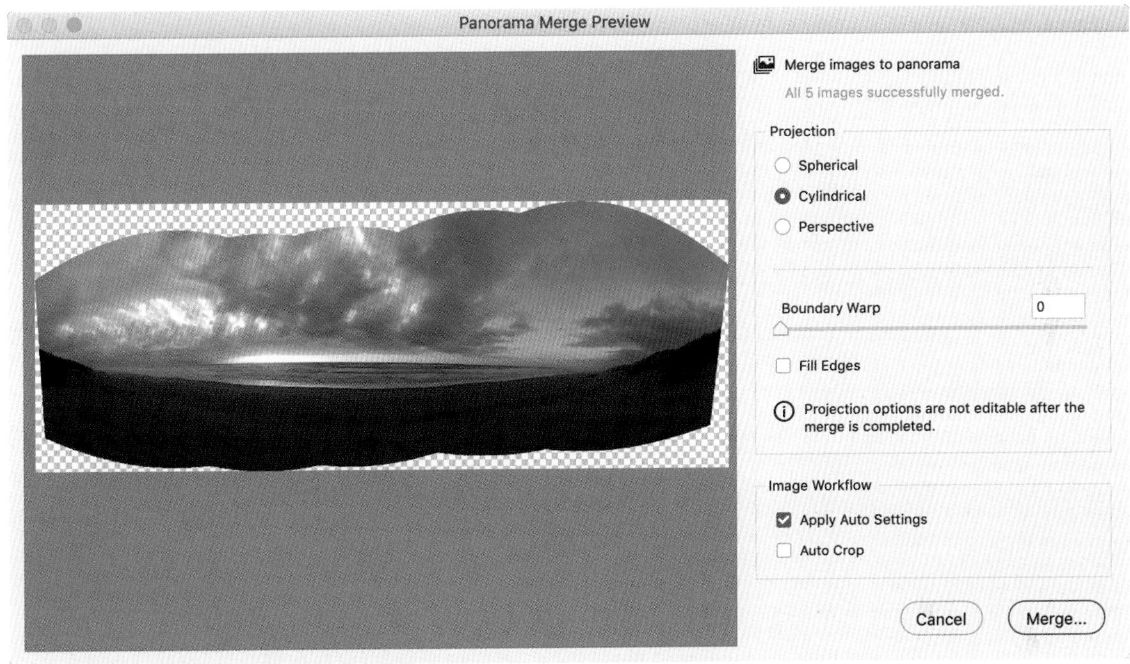

If I was using a fish-eye lens, Spherical would be more appropriate, as the images could be mapped to the inside of a sphere that way. But masts would bend oddly in that projection. If my shots covered less of an angle, and my subject had lots of straight lines like a building might, then I'd try Perspective Projection.

At the bottom, in the Image Workflow section, ACR is making an undesirable adjustment with its Apply Auto Settings. Sometimes it helps, but not this time.

- Disable Apply Auto Settings.

Now we have three ways to deal with the bulbous image boundaries.

- Try Auto Crop. Toggle it on then off so we can compare it to the other options. A lot gets chopped off. Uh-oh. Disable Auto Crop.

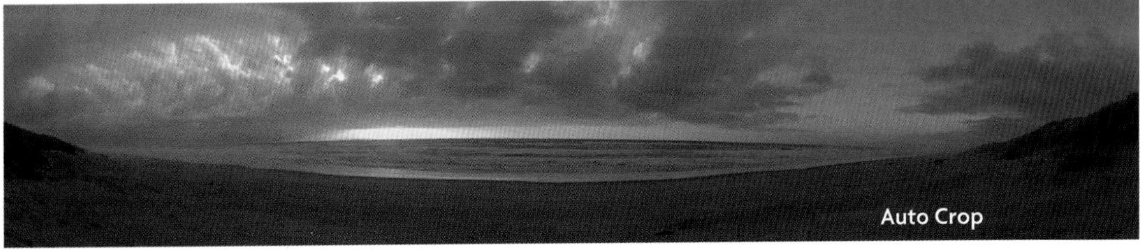

- Drag the Boundary Warp slider. Now *that* is interesting. But the horizon bows a bit. Still, we'll keep this in mind! Set Boundary Warp back to 0.

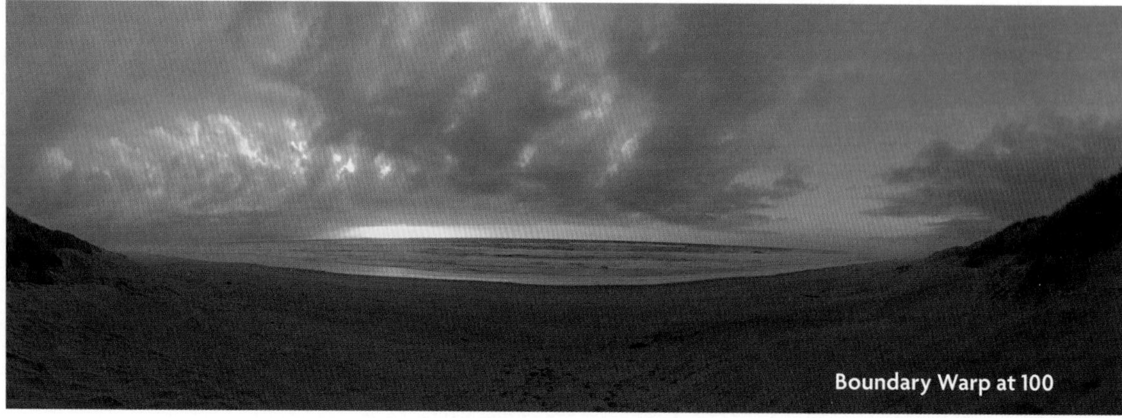
Boundary Warp at 100

- Enable Fill Edges. This uses an algorithm like Photoshop's Content-Aware Fill. Content is taken from elsewhere in the image to plausibly fill in those voids. That is pretty awesome!

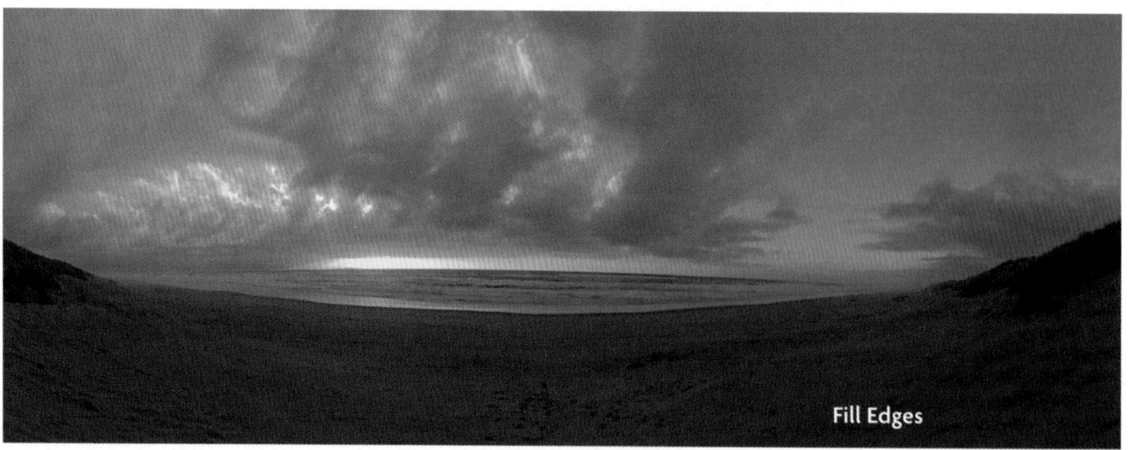
Fill Edges

- Clicking Merge... generates a new DNG that you can choose to edit in ACR.

You'll see it's added to the Filmstrip. Like with the HDR DNG, you can click Save Image... to create a deliverable, or Open Object to pass the pano to Photoshop for something fancy.

To compare with Photoshop's method, we have to change an ACR setting.

- Click line of underlined text at the bottom of the ACR interface to get to Workflow Preferences. Uncheck Open in Photoshop as Smart Object and click OK.
- Click Done in ACR and plan to return to the merged DNG later. Back to Bridge!
- With those original five images highlighted (they likely remained so), choose Tools > Photoshop > Photomerge....

Note that the images listed in the Photomerge dialog box are the ones you chose. Here, the projections are called Layout and there are two other choices: Collage (which rotates and scales to fit the pieces together, but won't make things bulbous) and Reposition (which will not transform the parts at all but will reposition them).

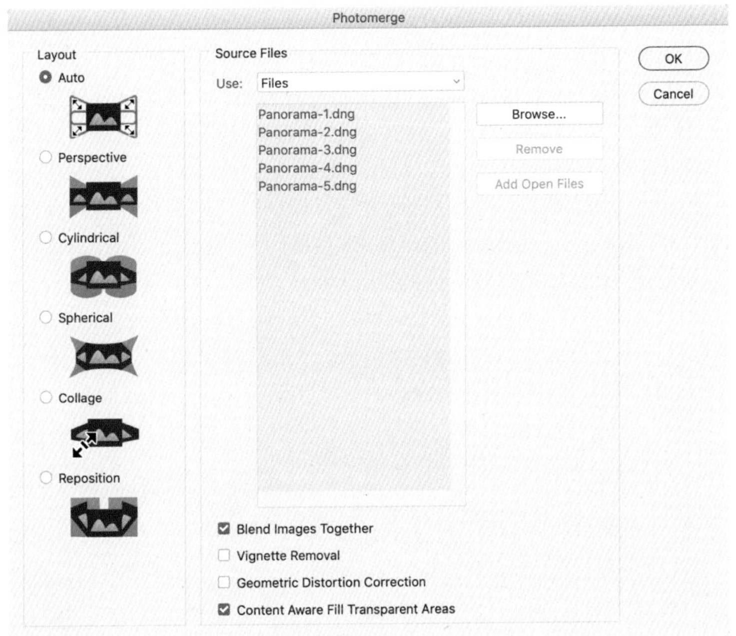

At the bottom of the dialog are checkboxes. Blend Images Together creates layer masks on the layers created for each image to stitch them together smoothly. Vignette Removal and Geometric Distortion Correction are there if we forgot to use those Lens Profile Corrections in ACR—but I didn't forget. Finally, Content Aware Fill Transparent Areas is the verbose equivalent of ACR's Fill Edges. We need only the first and last, and they're checked already. Auto Layout will be cylindrical because Photoshop is that smart. All you need to do is...

- Click OK and wait. If you don't like the way the edges were filled, remove the top layer! This is a rare time when I'd choose Layer > Flatten Image and then save the result.

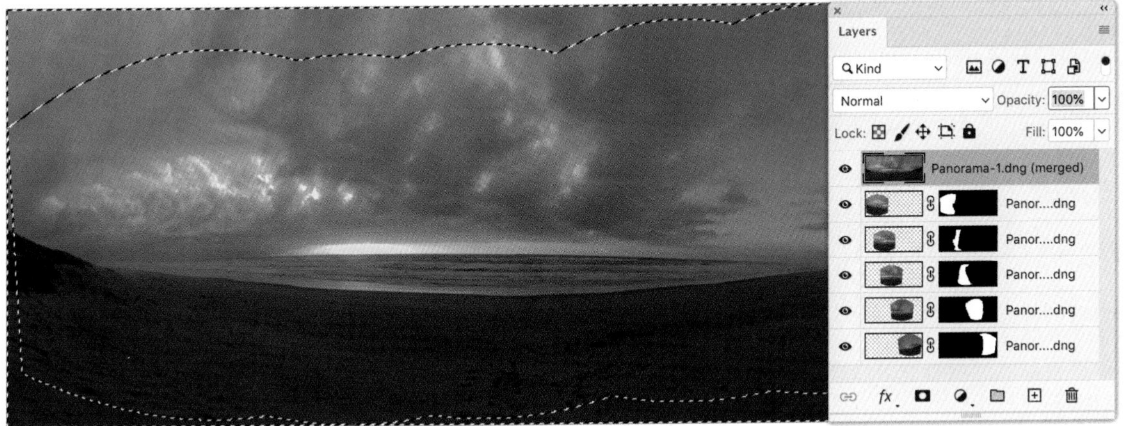

Lesson D: Passers-Bye-Bye

The last lesson in this chapter doesn't involve Adobe Camera Raw, nor does it need to include raw files. But it's a fun tip that uses software at its geekiest to help us achieve our desired image. Here's the background:

With film, photographers could make exposures as long as they wished. Some of the beautiful long-exposure photos made by Michael Kenna are hours long! But digital camera images get unusably noisy with really long exposures. So, instead of one long exposure, we can use many shorter ones *averaged* together! Astrophotographers have special software that can average thousands of images for a rich starscape. Here, we have just a few.

Photoshop has a Smart Object feature called Stack Modes. Imagine several similar images "stacked" as layers in a single document. Then you put all those layers into a single Smart Object and choose a Stack Mode that performs some mathematical analysis on those images. To save us the trouble of going through these steps, Photoshop's engineers made a script that does it for us!

- In Bridge, select the four PSDs with "Passers-bye-bye" in the name. Press the return/Enter key and they'll be opened in Photoshop. Be sure that no other images are open.

If you look at each, you'll see the photos are of the same scene and made a few seconds apart. Between images, the water flows and the people and pets move through the scene. I'd really like to be rid of those people.

Statistics Script

- Choose File > Scripts > Statistics…. This opens a dialog box.
- On the right-hand side, click Add Open Files, then those will be listed in the dialog.
- Choose Stack Mode should be set to Median.

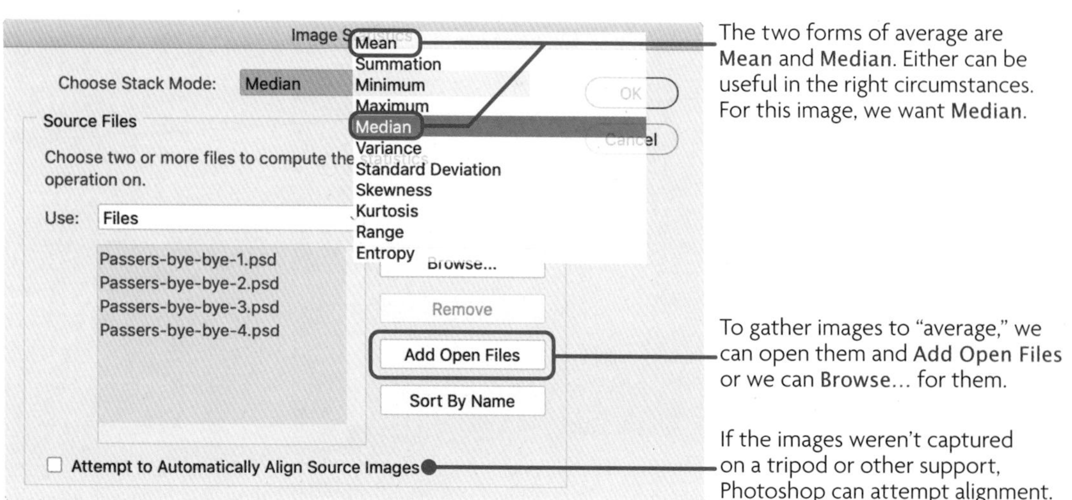

Both Mean and Median are averages. For content that changes from image to image, Mean would yield ghosts, whereas Median does better at removing that content. For Kenna-esque images, I'd likely choose Mean, but since I want the people and their dogs to disappear, we're going with Median. If you choose incorrectly, it's easy to change (and experiment) later.

- Click OK. The Layers panel will show a stack-rendering icon to remind you that you did this.

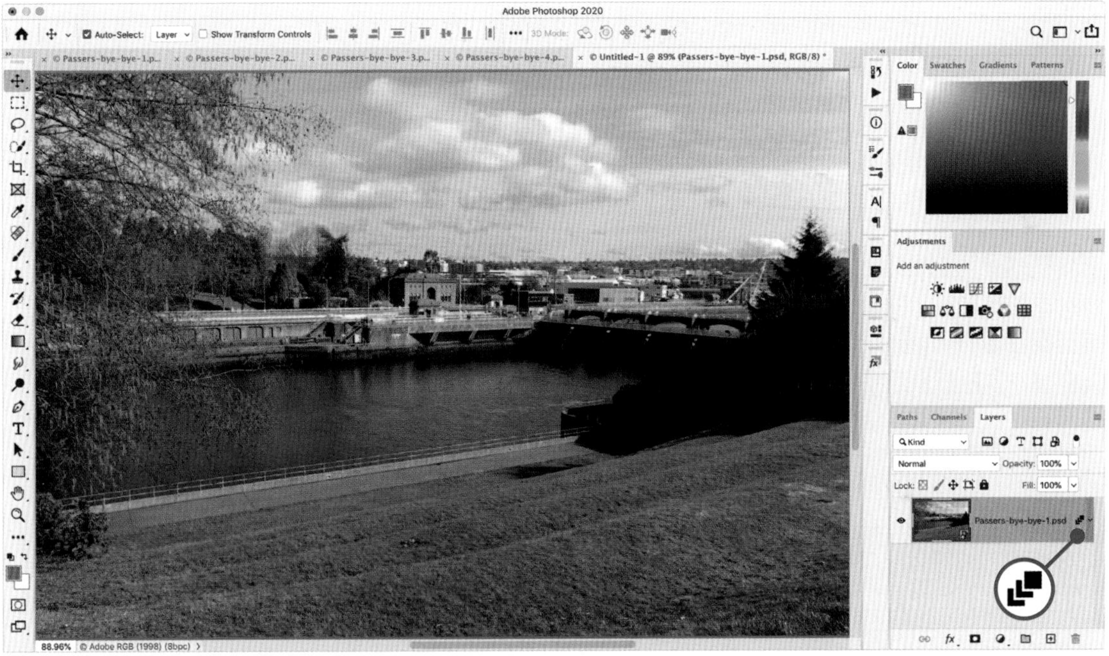

Stack Mode

After a few moments, we have the picture we wanted. Well, I admit, I can still see very faint people along the walkway. If I had the foresight to shoot a dozen images, we'd see no one at all! Are you curious what Mean would have done?

- Choose Layer > Smart Objects > Stack Mode > Mean (or any of the others to see just what they do).

I hope you enjoyed using science for art. In the next chapter, we try to leave the world better than we found it.

- Since this is a new document, choose File > Save As… if you'd like to keep this. Choose a location and commit.

6 Retouching & Transformation

Hiding blemishes is just the beginning. Photoshop has many tools for that task, as well as features for bending and twisting images to our liking. We'll see some here, and you can read about even more in the Compendium chapters "Retouching & Reworking" and "Filters & Transforms."

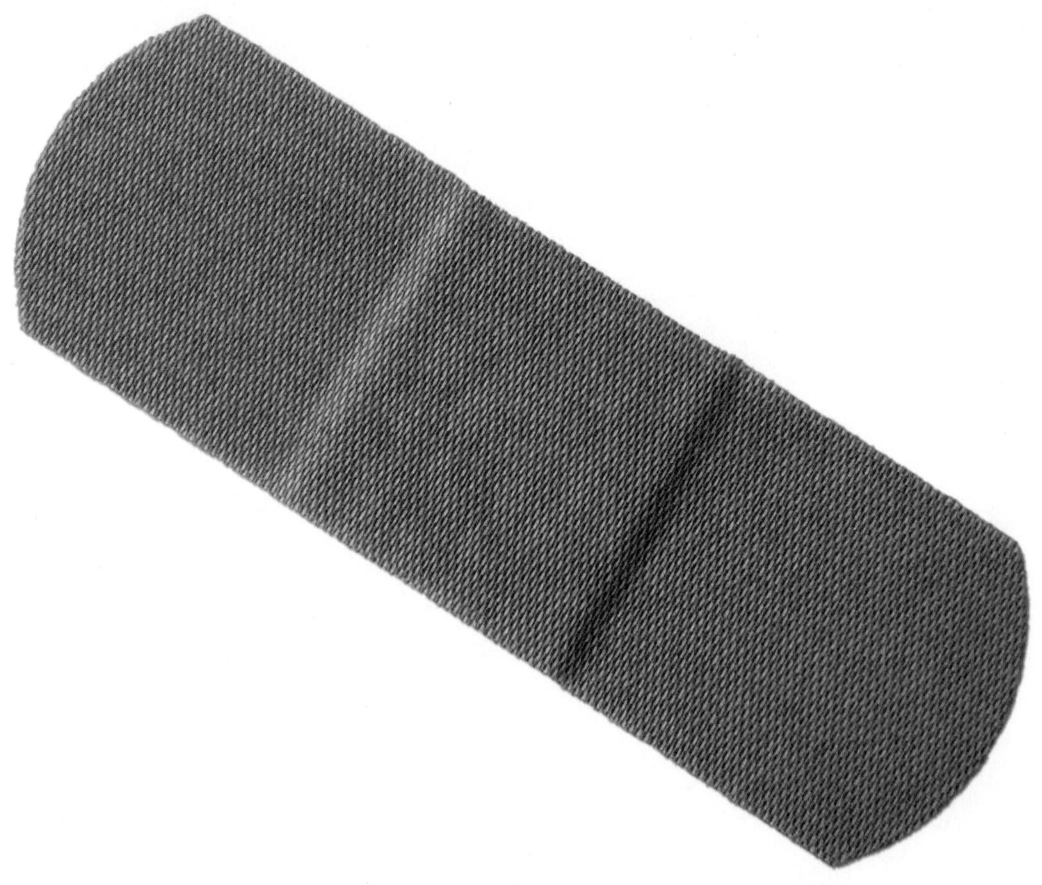

Lesson A: Clone, Heal, and Content-Aware Fill

There are many tools for removing blemishes from an image, but three are especially important. We'll use one image to discuss all three, from the eldest to the newest, and we'll include some workflow tips to keep in mind when images need adjustment as well as retouching.

➡ From the "06 Retouching" folder, open the image "A retouching tools.psd."

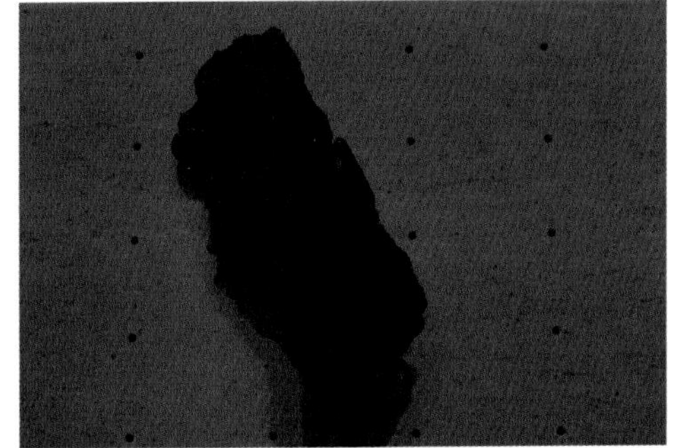

The image features a partial bronze face mounted on a marble surface pocked with distracting holes. If you look carefully, there is also a thin wedge in the upper left that shows the marble's edge. We're going to remove those holes and that wedge. Also, be aware that the marble is supposed to be white! This image is so discolored and dark we should deal with that first so we can see what we're doing.

➡ Create a Curves adjustment layer by clicking on the Curves icon in the Adjustments panel. While holding the option/Alt key, click the Auto button in the Properties panel so you can choose an algorithm and other options.

In the Curves Properties, option/Alt-click Auto and then choose Find Dark & Light Colors. Preserve dark areas by lowering the Shadows Clip to 0.01.

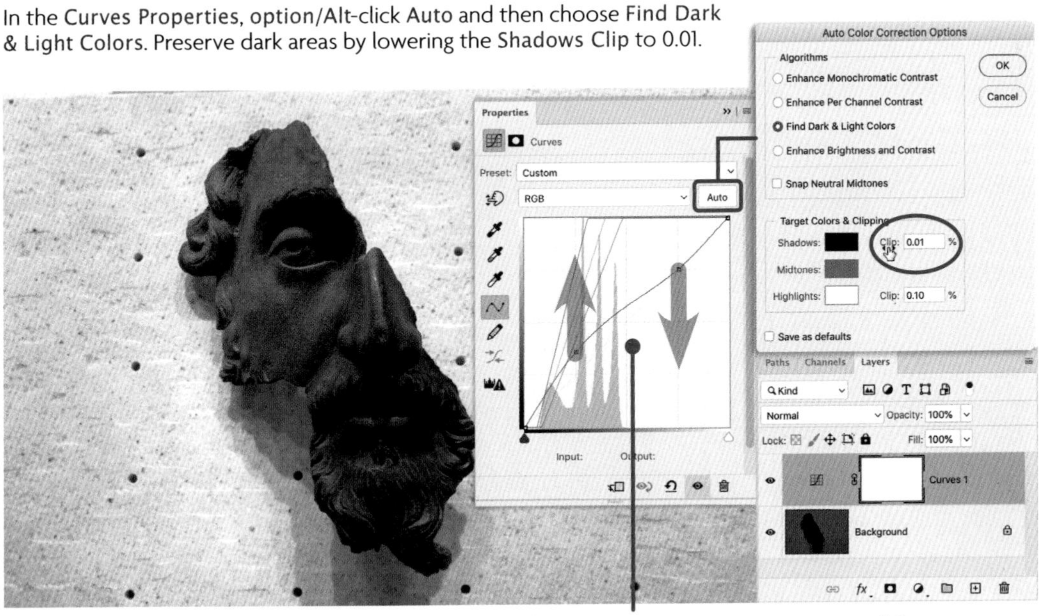

To enhance just the dark areas more after committing the Auto Color Correction Options dialog, push the RGB curve up a little in the dark end and pull it back down to restore the highlights.

➡ To restore the light and color to something more accurate, choose Find Dark & Light Colors. The shadow areas will still be quite dark so, while still in that dialog, lower the Shadow Clip to its lowest nonzero value. Click OK.

- In the Properties panel, adjust the RGB curve a little bit. Create points at the quarter and three-quarter tones, pushing up the point at the three-quarter tones (darker areas) to lighten the shadows a little.

The other point will keep the highlights intact. If you create a three-quarter-tones point and lift it in one go, you can drag the quarter-tones point down to the diagonal line to restore its position. Now we can see what's going on to do blemish removal.

Create a Retouch Layer

The big three retouching tools can all sample material from layers other than the one on which we use them. In this case, that means they will pick up unpunctured marble from the Background layer, depositing those nice pixels onto a layer above the Background to hide the holes. To do so, however, each tool will need its options set in the Options Bar.

- Highlight the Background layer, then create a new layer by opening the Layers panel menu and choosing New Layer…, or by pressing ⌘-shift-N/Ctrl-Shift-N. Name the new layer "retouching." ***This new layer should be between the Background and the adjustment layer!***

By putting this retouching layer below the adjustment, it is affected by the adjustment just as the Background is. As long as the new layer's content has the same dark, dingy look as the Background, the repairs will work perfectly. In other words, if we edit, remove, or replace the adjustment, we won't have to redo any retouching. For this to work, we will have to choose carefully when we set those options in the Options Bar.

Clone Stamp

We'll use this tool for the three holes just to the right of the bronze head. We will "sample" (pick up) some good marble to hide those holes.

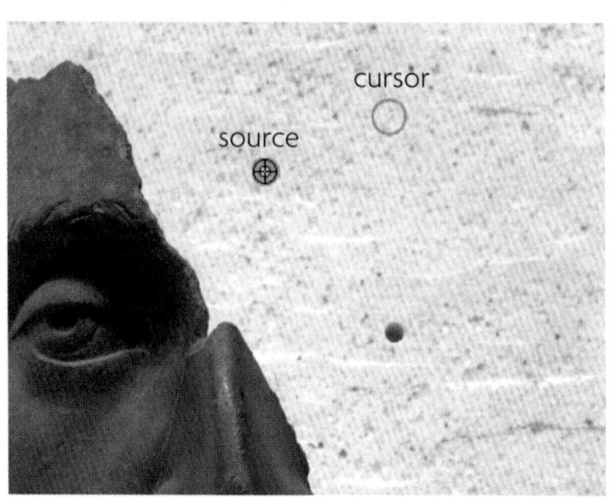

- Choose the Clone Stamp tool. In the Options Bar, set its Sample option to Current & Below so it can sample from anything you see, but without being influenced by the adjustment layer above.
- Use the bracket keys ([for smaller,] for larger) to set the size of the brush to be a little larger than one of the holes.
- Hold down option/Alt and click on a patch of intact marble below and to the left of the top centermost hole. If you move the cursor now, you will now see that material in it.
- With no keys held, paint over that hole with the Clone Stamp tool. Cover it over completely. Notice that while you're actively painting, a crosshair appears where you option/Alt-clicked. That's the source point. The source can be in a different open image!

There is now an alignment between source and cursor. Since your first source point was down and to the left of your first repair, the source will follow your cursor like a dog on a leash and will be below and to the left of anywhere you paint, until you set a new relationship by sampling a new source and applying it. The assumption is that desirable material will be near any blemish.

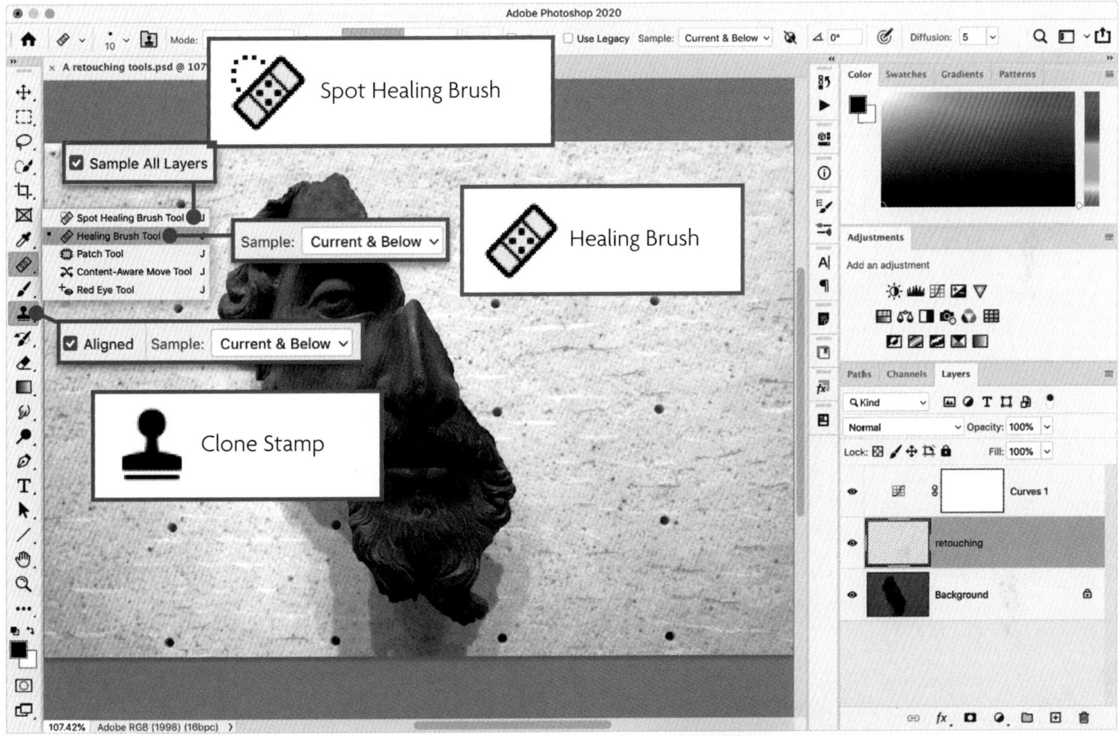

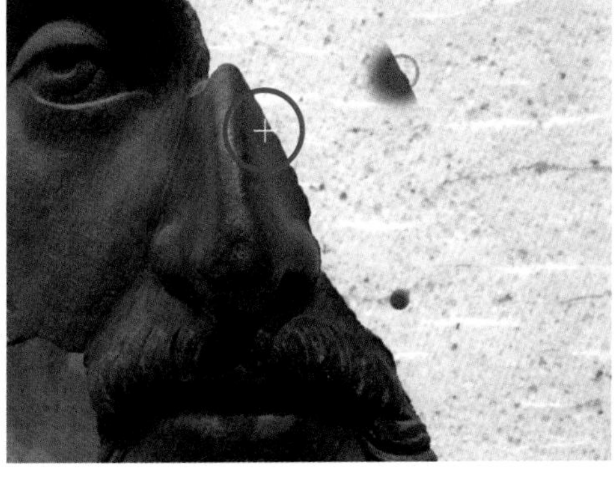

Now, I have intentionally sabotaged you for the sake of learning. Since the source is invisibly "aligned" to your cursor, as you attempt to remove the next hole, you'll see something unfortunate.

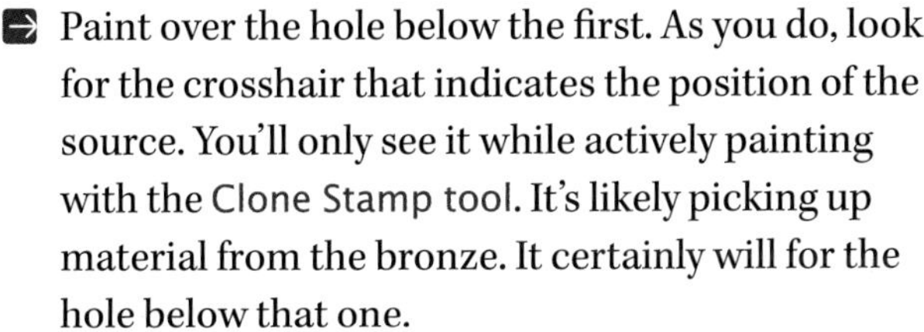

- Paint over the hole below the first. As you do, look for the crosshair that indicates the position of the source. You'll only see it while actively painting with the Clone Stamp tool. It's likely picking up material from the bronze. It certainly will for the hole below that one.
- When this occurs, undo (⌘-Z/Ctrl-Z). Then set a new source/cursor relationship by option/Alt-clicking to the right of that second hole and then painting over it. Just paint on the third hole and it should pick up from a source position to the right of it. Success! But prepare for another undo…

- As an experiment (and justification for switching tools shortly), sample (option/Alt-click) an area near the top of the image and attempt to remove a hole near the bottom.

The light patch you see is there because the top of the image is lighter than the bottom, and the Clone Stamp tool makes literal clones, or copies, of your source. Imagine the frustration if you had no appropriate source material to clone from.

A very common example is the occurrence of sensor dust in a portrait on the cheek of a person. If you sample from a less well-lit cheek, you'd have a larger blemish on your hands (on their face, actually). We need a tool that contextualizes our source so it blends in to its new surroundings. And we have such a tool.

Healing Brush

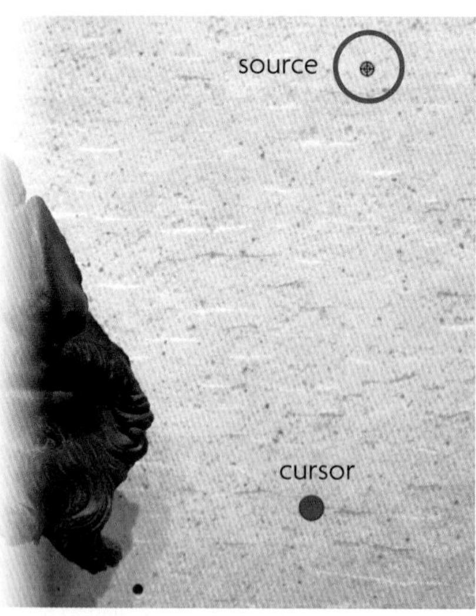

The Healing Brush tool applies the texture, rather than a literal "clone," of the source, but not the color or lightness of the source. It pulls in the color and tone from around the area where you paint to contextualize the repair. Also, the source doesn't follow the cursor around like the Clone Stamp's.

- Choose the Healing Brush tool. In the Options Bar, set its Sample option to Current & Below so it can sample without being influenced by the adjustment layer above.
- Use the bracket keys ([for smaller,] for larger) to set the size of the brush to be a little larger than one of the holes.
- Hold down option/Alt and click on a patch of intact marble near the top of the image. You will now see that material in the cursor.
- With no keys held down, paint over all the holes on the right side of the image (excluding the one on the edge of the shadow at the bottom). Be sure that you cover one *entire* hole with each brush stroke.
- To impress yourself, paint on the cheek of the bronze. Now it has marble texture where you painted but retains the color and luminosity of the patina!

It's a lovely innovation. Still, you need to specify a source. If only there were a way for Photoshop to do that on its own. (We call that a segue in the teaching biz.)

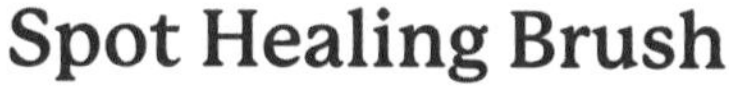

Spot Healing Brush

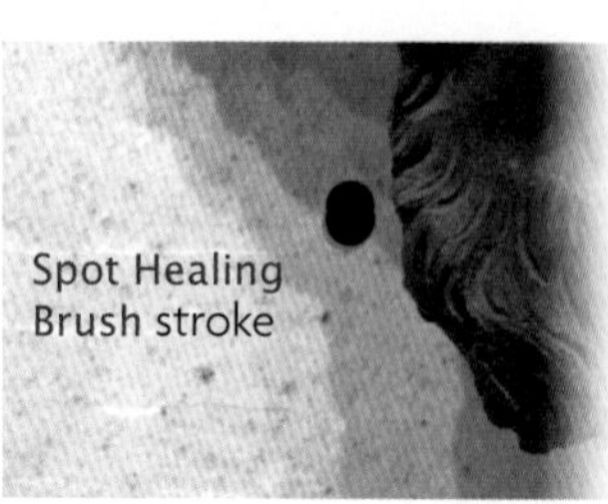

- Choose the Spot Healing Brush tool. In the Options Bar, check Sample All Layers. This tool is so smart, it knows how to deal with adjustments and much else.

- Use the bracket keys ([for smaller,] for larger) to set the size of the brush to be a little larger than one of the holes.
- There is no need to choose a source. Just paint over an entire hole in one stroke so Photoshop knows its extent. You'll see translucent black while you paint. When you release the mouse, material compatible with that area is found and applied.

Any brush-using tool can make a straight line in any direction with just two clicks:

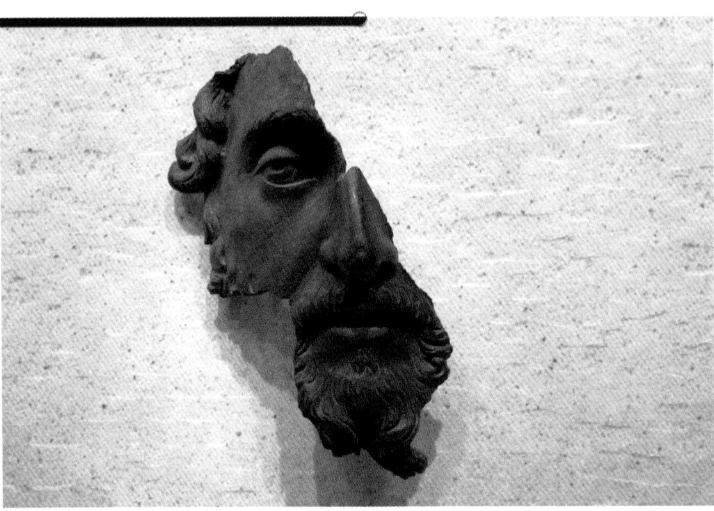

- For the little wedge in the image's upper-left corner, click at one end of it, then shift-click at the other. Photoshop will paint a full stroke from one clicked spot to the other.

You can imagine how helpful this will be for unsightly stray hairs or power lines (if they're reasonably straight).

- Save this image, but don't close it just yet.

Content-Aware Fill

The technology that the Spot Healing Brush tool uses by default is called Content-Aware Fill. This is also a stand-alone function that enjoys many options that let you refine its result. When blemishes are larger, this command is more useful than the Spot Healing Brush tool.

Content-Aware Fill's result can be output to a new layer, but it has to be the one to create it. Also, it can examine only one layer as it doesn't have a "sample all layers" option.

For this exercise, we'll choose the bronze head itself as the "flaw" that needs to be removed. In the end, we will have a photo of marble and nothing else.

- Highlight the top layer in the Layers panel (the adjustment layer).
- It's time to learn a new shortcut (actually, a few). Use this one: ⌘-option-shift-E/Ctrl-Alt-Shift-E. This creates a new layer that is a merged *copy* of all the visible layers.

Note: ⌘-E/Ctrl-E merges a highlighted layer into the one below it. ⌘-option-E/Ctrl-Alt-E merges a copy of the highlighted layer into the one below. (Recall that option/Alt-moving something makes a copy.) ⌘-shift-E/Ctrl-Shift-E merges all visible layers. Every combination involving the letter "E" does some kind of merging, and if option/Alt is involved, a copy is made.

Now we have a layer with content that needs to be replaced and that Content-Aware Fill

(CAF) can use as source material. We'll be able to delete it later after CAF creates yet another layer holding only the "repair." I guess you could say that this merged copy layer is a catalyst.

- To select the area to be filled, start with Select > Subject. Then use the Lasso tool while holding Shift to add the shadowed areas. If it's a touch tight, we'll be able to fix it shortly.
- Choose Edit > Content-Aware Fill….

You'll see a three-panel workspace. On the left is the image with its selection and an area in green around it. The Preview panel shows, after a delay, a first attempt at filling in the selected area. It has a zoom slider along its bottom. The third panel is the Content-Aware Fill panel. It has the controls needed to improve what we see in the preview.

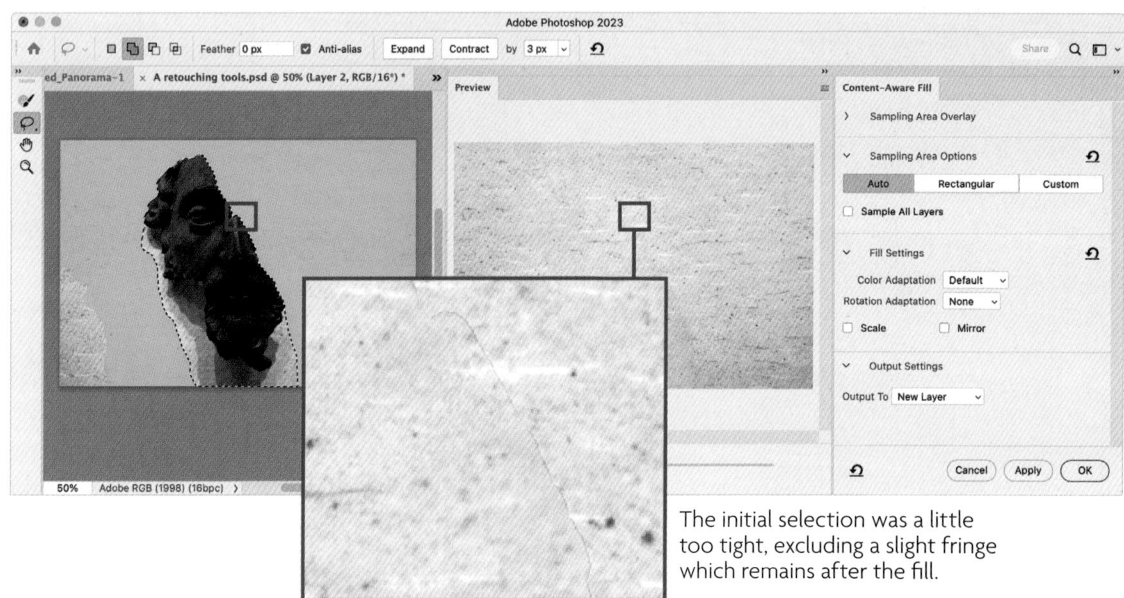

The initial selection was a little too tight, excluding a slight fringe which remains after the fill.

Sampling

The green overlay shows the region from which Photoshop is drawing material to fill the selected area. It will never include the selected area since that's the stuff we don't want. In the Content-Aware Fill panel, note the three buttons in the Sampling Area Options section: Auto, Rectangular, and Custom. Auto works an amazing amount of the time and will get better with every release of Photoshop, thanks to artificial intelligence. Rectangular will use a strictly rectangular area, as you would have guessed. That's useful in architectural imagery. Custom requires your intervention with the Sampling Brush tool (at the top of this workspace's tool panel) to indicate exactly which areas should be sampled from. You paint with it to show areas to use, and option/Alt-paint to remove areas. In this case, Auto works well.

However, the selection we made was likely a little too snug. Luckily, this workspace has tools and options to adjust it!

- Activate the Lasso tool. In the Options Bar at the top, note the Expand and Contract buttons with a value field to their right. Set that value to about 3 pixels, then hit the Expand button. The fill gets better!

If you need to add to or remove from the selection, note that the Lasso tool in this workspace is automatically in an "add" mode (it has a plus sign next to its cursor). Draw it around parts you need to add. Hold option/Alt to remove areas from the selection.

Fill Settings

In this portion of the Content-Aware Fill panel, we have means of making the sampled material better conform to its new home within our selection. Color Adaptation contextualizes the sampled stuff somewhat like the Healing Brush tool does. Rotation Adaptation twists and turns the sample material to better fit. Usually, I use this when I'm trying to fill a curved edge and I'm sampling from an area farther along that curve. In that case, the material needs to be turned to fit. Finally, the Scale and Mirror checkboxes give permission to resize and reflect some of the sampled material to fit. In some cases, we may need all of this help.

- Try different settings for the Adaptations as well as the transformation checkboxes. I found that I needed only to allow content to Mirror to make something I liked.
- Ensure that, in the Output Settings section, Output To is set to New Layer. Click OK.
- Your new content appears on a layer of its own. If you'd like, you might do a little touch up with the Spot Healing Brush tool.

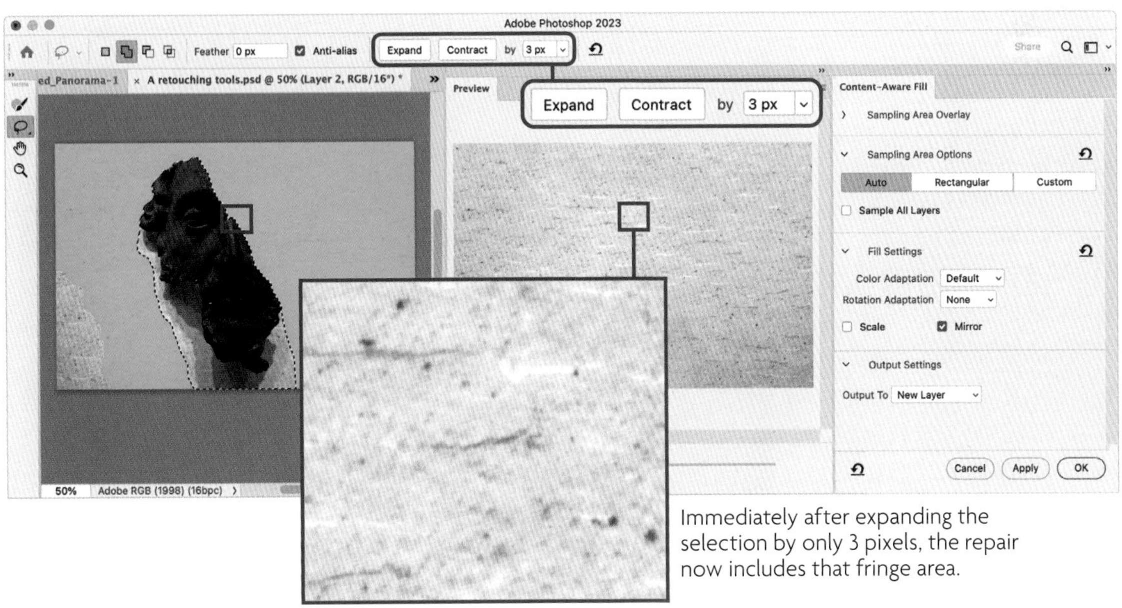

Immediately after expanding the selection by only 3 pixels, the repair now includes that fringe area.

- Save and close this document.

Lesson B: Transforms

Photoshop has a great many ways to bend and twist imagery. In this lesson, we'll look at two. In the Compendium, the chapter "Filters & Transforms" has much more to explore.

Free Transform

Free Transform is flexible and powerful. It can perform both precise geometric transformations as well as more sculptural warps.

- Open "B1 Free Transform.psd," a photo of a drinking glass.
- Right-click near the "glass" layer's name and select Convert to Smart Object. This will allow us to revisit the transformation any time to reverse or continue it.
- Choose Edit > Free Transform, or use the shortcut ⌘-T/Ctrl-T. You now have transform handles around the perimeter of the Smart Object and many options to use in the Options Bar. When we're done, we'll click the check mark or press the Enter key, but that's later.

Geometric

We'll start with simple alterations to shape.

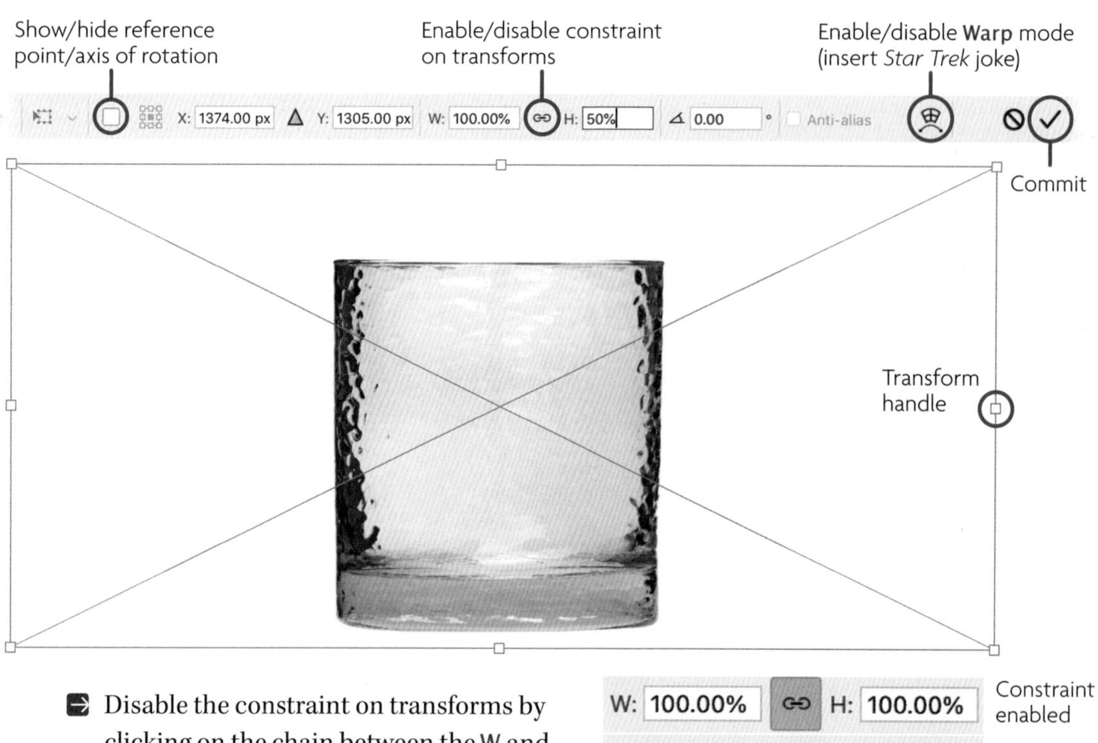

- Disable the constraint on transforms by clicking on the chain between the W and H scaling fields.

W: 100.00%	H: 100.00%	Constraint enabled
W: 100.00%	H: 100.00%	Disabled

- Drag either the top or bottom center transform handle to shorten the glass. Note the scaling in the H field. Try scrubbing the letter H itself. Then type a value in the field.
- With the cursor outside the transform box, drag to rotate, noting the value in the angle field. Reset the rotation by typing 0 in that field.
- Click the check mark to commit the transform.
- Now let's change our minds: Use the shortcut ⌘-T/Ctrl-T to get back to where you left off. Reset the H field to 100% to restore the glass's height. If necessary, drag the box itself to snap it back into the document boundaries.
- Click the Warp mode button. Engage!

Warp

This mode can be used in several different ways: freeform, with a grid, or using Warp presets.

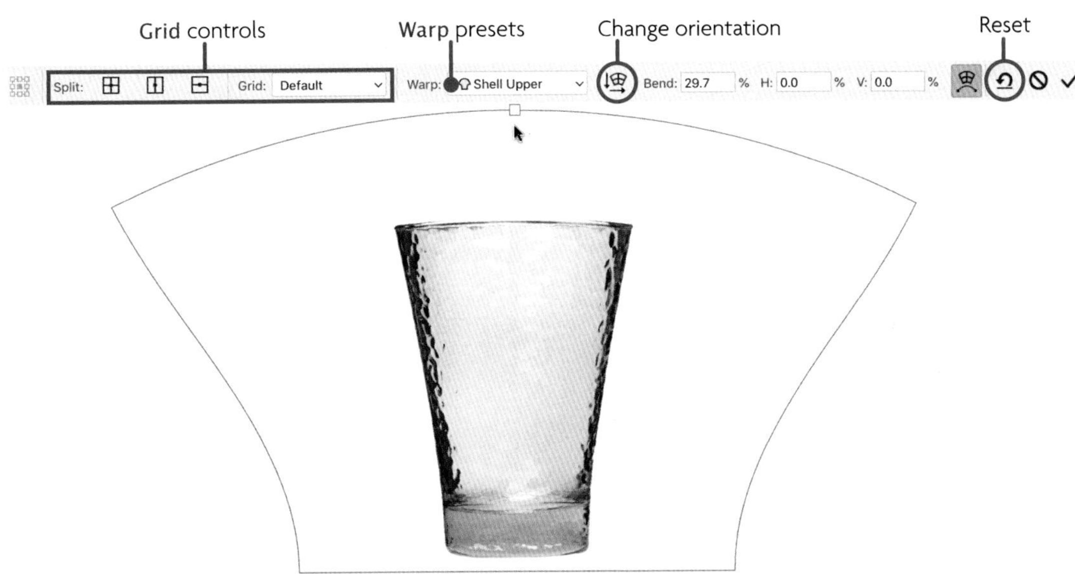

- Let's start with a preset. Use the Warp menu in the Options Bar and choose Shell Upper.
- You now have only one transform handle. To see it, you may have to zoom out a bit: ⌘--/Ctrl-- (that's "command minus" or "control minus").
- Drag that transform handle a bit to customize the flaring of the top of the glass.
- Try different presets in the Warp menu. Dragging the Wave preset's handle is entertaining—the glass is dancing. The button to the right of the Warp menu changes the orientation of the warp. So if you had been distorting vertically, you'll now be distorting horizontally.
- When you've had enough fun, click the Reset Warp button.
- Now let's warp in a freeform way: simply drag parts of the glass around like the image is made of something pliable.

This can be a powerful way to sculpt an image. Or it can make a mess of one.

- Reset again. Now to try a grid-based transformation.

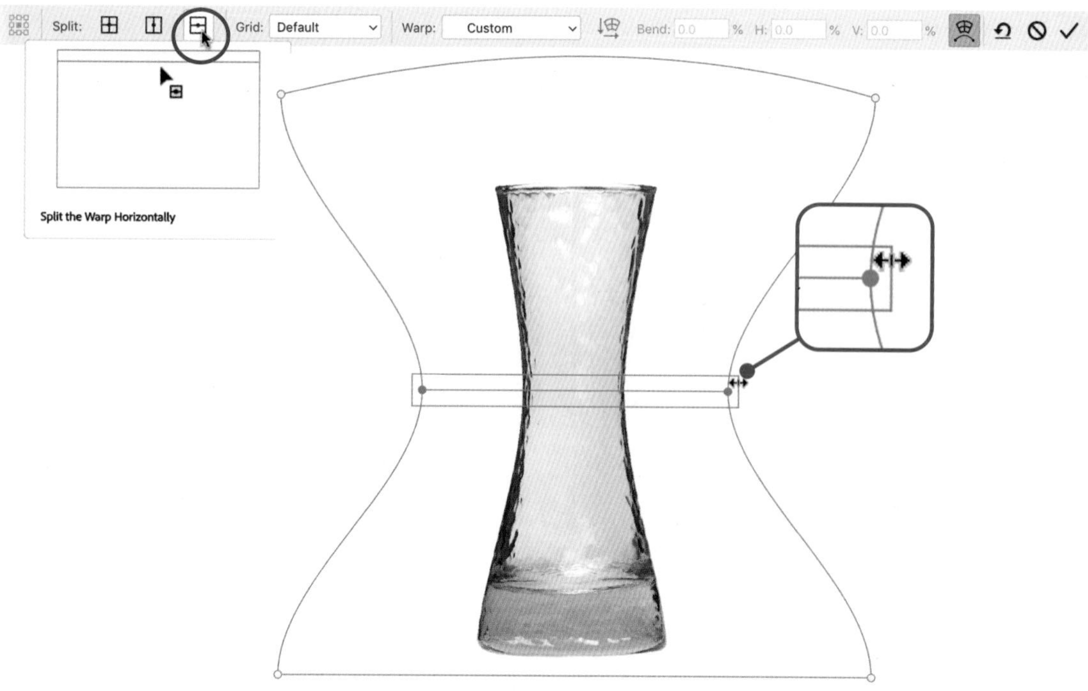

- We'll start with a very simple grid. Hover your cursor over the Split the Warp Horizontally button to see a small animation indicating what you're to do.
- Give the button a single click then move the cursor over the image. You'll find a line stuck to the cursor until you click to release it. Do so roughly in the center of the glass.

You may drag any one of the several handles to affect the warp. However, I want you to select two handles so we can alter them at once.

- Click a handle on one side of the line you just made, then shift-click the other end. A box appears around both. It's like a (limited) transform box for those two transform handles! Resize it to narrow the midsection of the glass.

If a particular transform would benefit from several grid lines, both horizontal and vertical, use the Grid menu to quickly generate a 3 x 3 to 5 x 5 grid.

- Warp the glass as you like, then click the check mark to commit it. Save and close the document.

Content-Aware Scale

I hope you noticed that when you initially shortened the glass, you distorted its details. There is a form of scaling that will alter the aspect ratio of an image but can have minimal impact on its content. Sadly, it cannot be applied to a Smart Object. When we're done, you'll choose File > Save As… to have a distorted version while retaining the original.

- Open "B2 CAS.psd." "CAS" stands for Content-Aware Scale.

The Course

- Choose Edit > Content-Aware Scale. Ensure that the constraint chain icon is disabled in the Options Bar.
- Drag a side handle inward and note how the round moon remains round. Or grab a corner and make the image resemble a panoramic image. Again, details remain less affected.

This tool carves away what the engineers call low-frequency areas, like the sky and water, respecting details ("high-frequency areas"). Unless you push too far, of course.

- Commit the transform and select File > Save As…, choosing a new name.

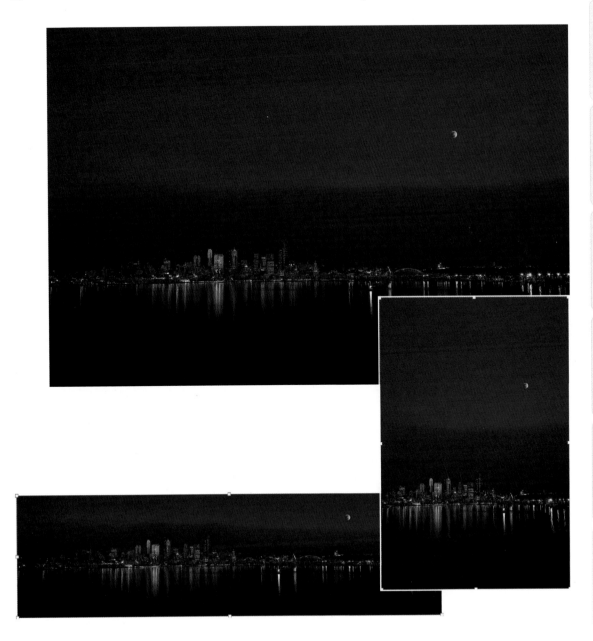

Project: A Surrealist Composite

Get ready to channel René Magritte and M. C. Escher. We're going to cook up this mind-bender with ingredients drawn from much of the course you're now completing. I'll be adding only very little new information so you can focus on applying what we've discussed.

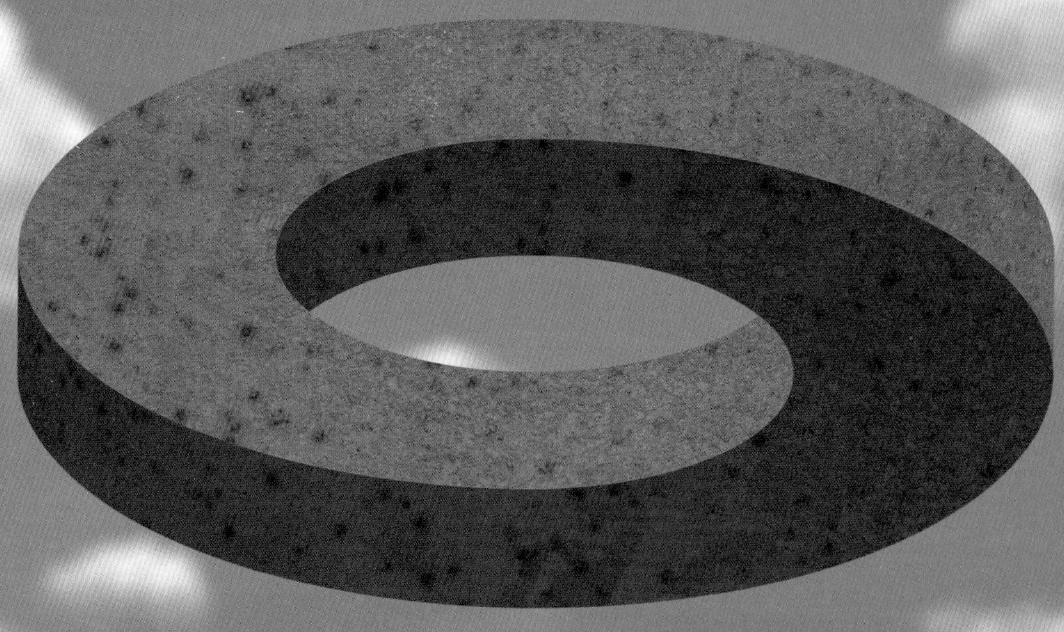

Lesson A: Where We're Going

Let's have a look at a finished version so you know the destination.

➡ Find the folder "Project C- Surreal" in your downloaded course files. Open the file "surreal result.psd." Let's pay special attention to the Layers panel. Of course, that's not unusual.

Tour the Finished Piece

The layer structure is not very intimidating, I think. Starting at the bottom, you'll see the sky image, the backdrop for our impossible, levitating ring. That sky layer has been converted to a Smart Object and blurred.

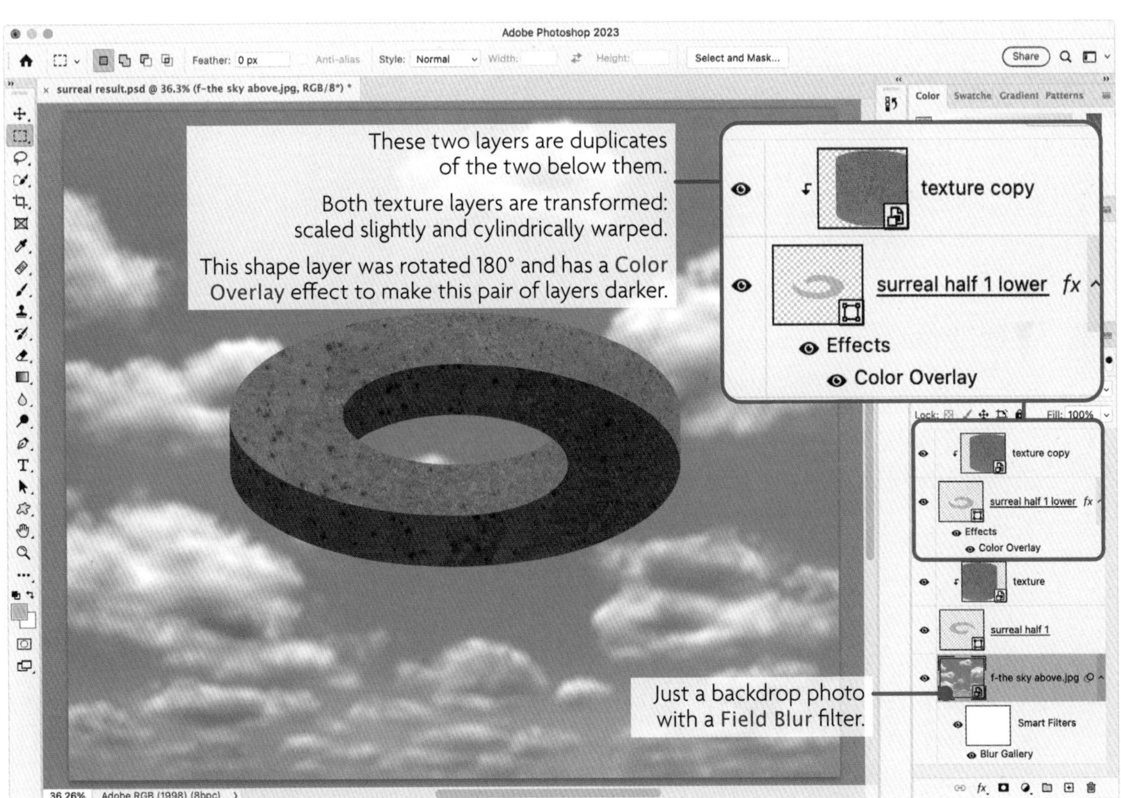

Above the sky, we find two pairs of layers. Each pair includes a vector shape layer and a Smart Object clipped to it. That is, we're using a "Clipping Mask" (page 295) to essentially mask each texture to the shape below it. The top shape layer is nothing more than a duplicate of the lower one rotated 180° and carefully positioned to abut the original. Both vector shapes are yellowish (the color hidden by the textures), but one has a Color Overlay effect to darken it.

Above each shape is a Smart Object that has been distorted with Free Transform's Cylinder Warp. This is to make the texture seem to bend around each shape's end.

- Toggle the visibility of the Color Overlay effect to see what you think.

Recall that Smart Objects are like documents within our document. These two Smart Objects are duplicates, so they use the same content. In this case, that content is five layers, each a photo of a texture.

- Double-click the thumbnail of one of the texture Smart Objects. Now you're looking at those five layers.

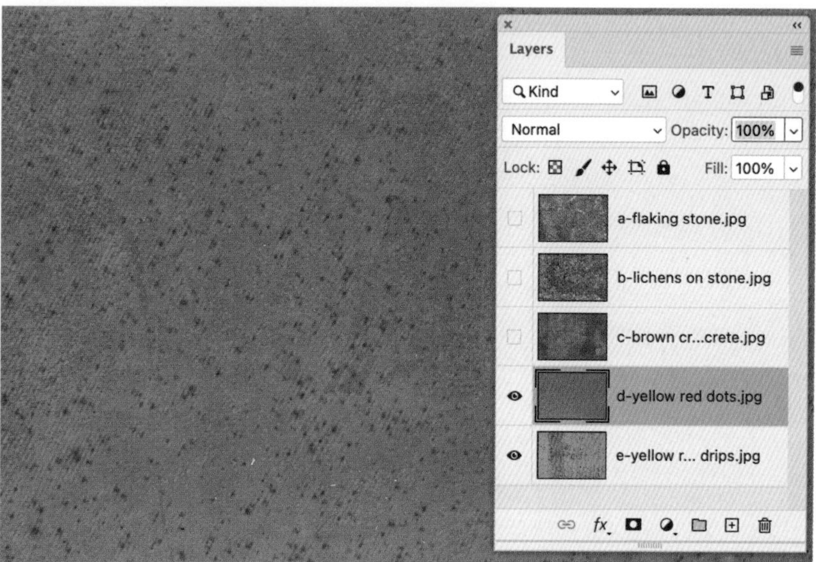

Each layer was initially a separate image document assembled as layers with a script in Adobe Bridge.

If you change which layers are visible in one Smart Object, you're changing both. Feel free to allow a different layer to show then save and close this temporary file.

- If you change which layers are visible in one Smart Object, you're changing both. Feel free to allow a different layer to show.
- Save and close this temporary file.

Let's have a look at the distortion on one of the Smart Objects.

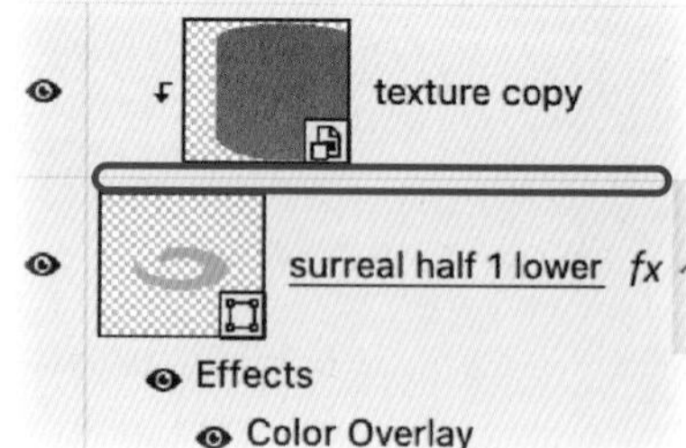

- option/Alt-click on the line between to the top two layers. This will unclip them.
- While they're unclipped, note how the texture appears to wrap around an unseen cylinder.
- Be sure the top layer (the texture copy) is highlighted. Activate Free Transform with the shortcut ⌘-T/Ctrl-T.
- Enter Warp mode by clicking the warp button in the Options Bar.

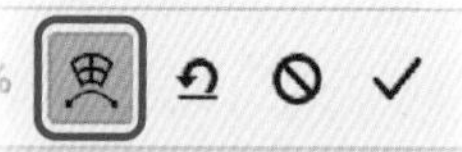

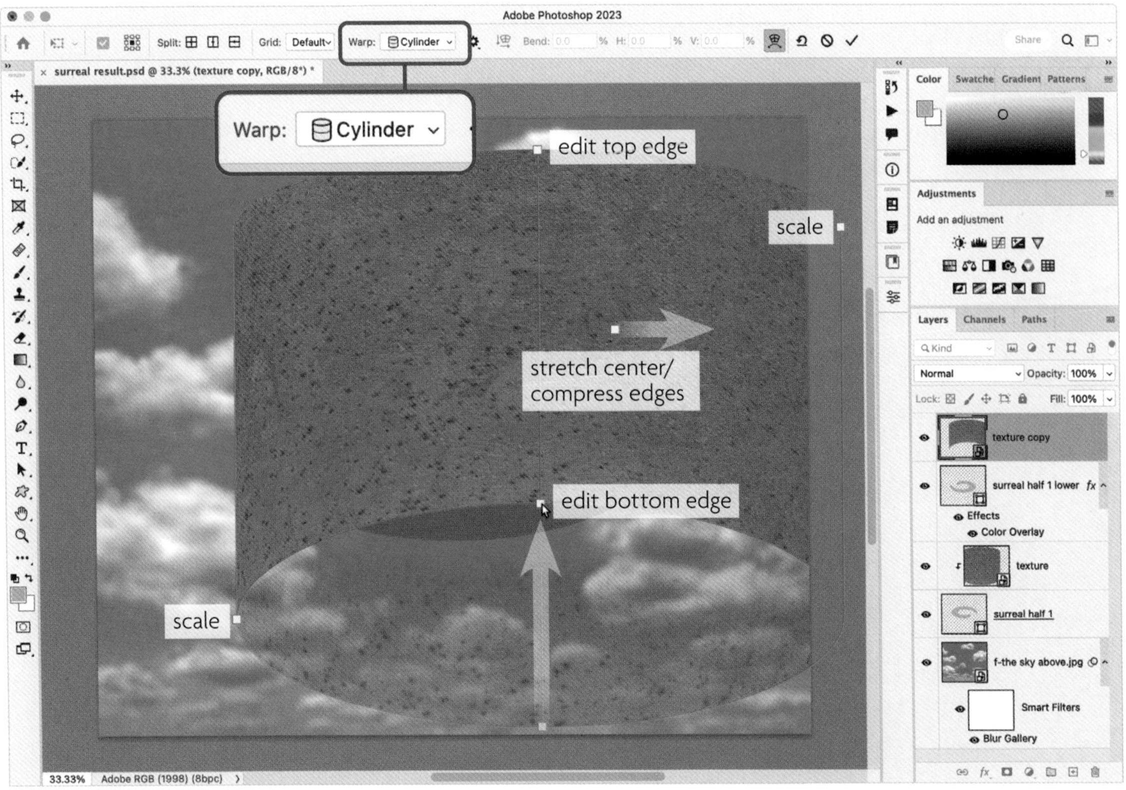

This is a new (for 2023) warp preset called Cylinder. Designers love to use this to "wrap" labels around bottles and cans. We'll use it to get a more natural wrap of our textures around the narrow ends of the shape layers.

- Drag the control point at the bottom upward and note how that affects the distortion. Why not experiment with the other control points, too (don't worry, we will leave the transform without accepting any changes).
- After you've messed around with the control points for a bit, press the escape key to leave the texture unscathed.
- option/Alt-click the line between the top two layers again to clip the texture to the shape layer.
- Close this document without saving so it can serve as a reference later if you need it.

Now, we're ready to build this from scratch!

Lesson B: Gathering the Ingredients

Let's leverage a Bridge script to gather nearly all our assets into one document. To make this project a little easier, we're going to use Adobe Bridge to grab the project assets.

- Launch Bridge. From Photoshop, you can do so by choosing File > Browse in Bridge… or using the shortcut ⌘-option-O/Ctrl-Alt-O.
- Use the Favorites panel or the Folders panel in Bridge to navigate to your course folder and, within it, the "Project C- Surreal" folder.

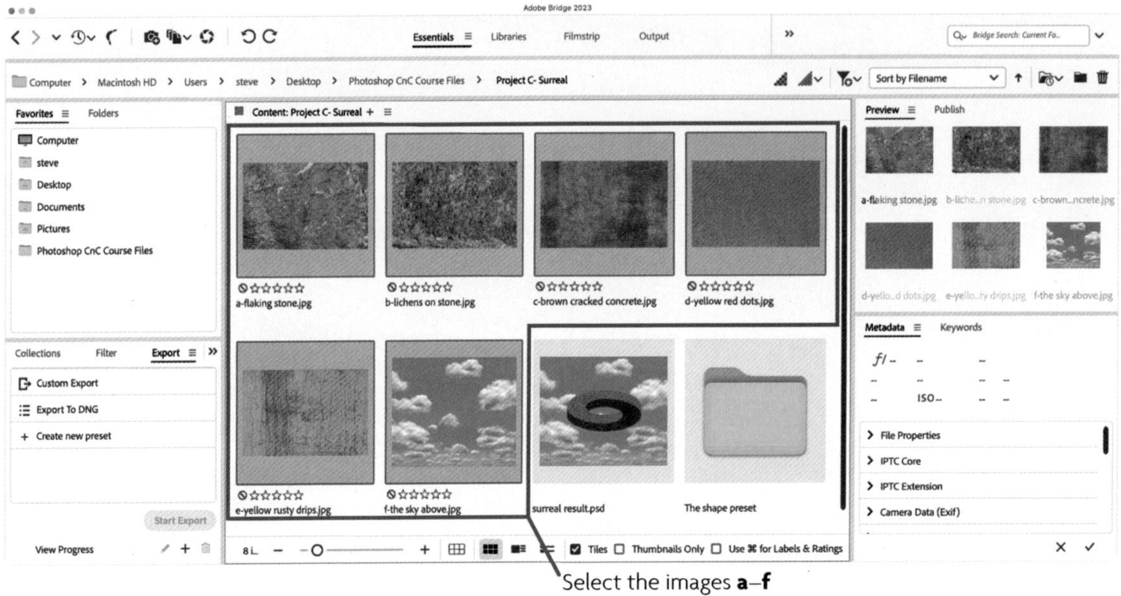

Select the images **a–f**

- Select images **a–f** by clicking on the first one and then shift-clicking on the last of those. Exclude the finished version and the shapes preset folder.
- Then use Bridge's Tools menu: choose Tools > Photoshop > Load Files into Photoshop Layers…. You'll soon have a document with six layers.
- Save it! Choose File > Save As…, then save it as a Photoshop document (psd) in your project folder. Give it a distinct name. I'll use "new surreal.psd."

Material Choices

Let's get our five materials tucked inside a Smart Object.

- Highlight the topmost layer then shift-click on the lowest non-sky layer. Right-click any one near its name and choose Convert to Smart Object.
- Rename it: "texture top" wouldn't be bad. We'll get back to this layer soon.

Custom Shape

The ring is composed of two identical shapes simply rotated 180º from one another. Such a shape exists for us to use in the project folder, but we need it to be in Photoshop.

- Choose Window > Shapes to get the Shapes panel.
- In the Shapes panel menu choose Import Shapes…. Navigate to the "Project C- Surreal" folder then into the "The shape preset" folder. Double click on the file called "Surreal Assist.csh." That unusual extension stands for "Custom SHape."

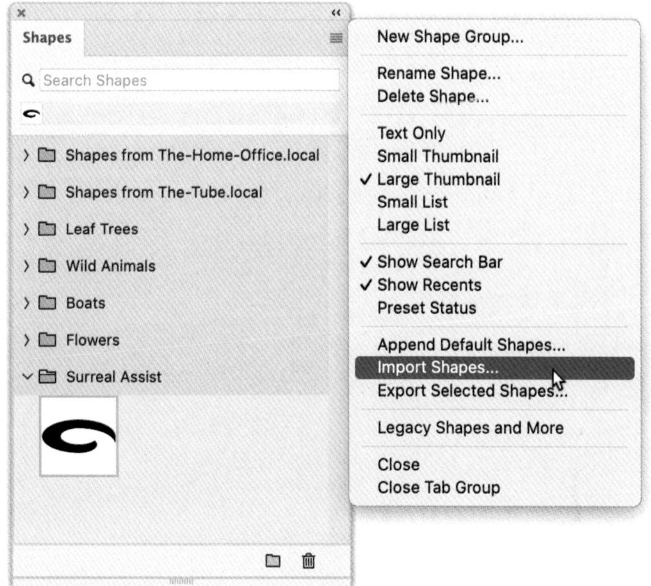

You'll now have the shape we need to complete this project. If you're curious, I made that shape in Adobe Illustrator.

- In the Tools panel, choose the Custom Shape tool (near the bottom, nested within the basic shapes). It looks like a blob.
- In the Shapes panel, choose the newest addition. At the bottom, unfurl the set to reveal the shape, then choose it.
- To keep it from distorting, hold down the shift key as you drag this tool across the image. Make it about 60%–70% the width of the image.
  This is not critical, I just think that looks good and we can change it shortly!

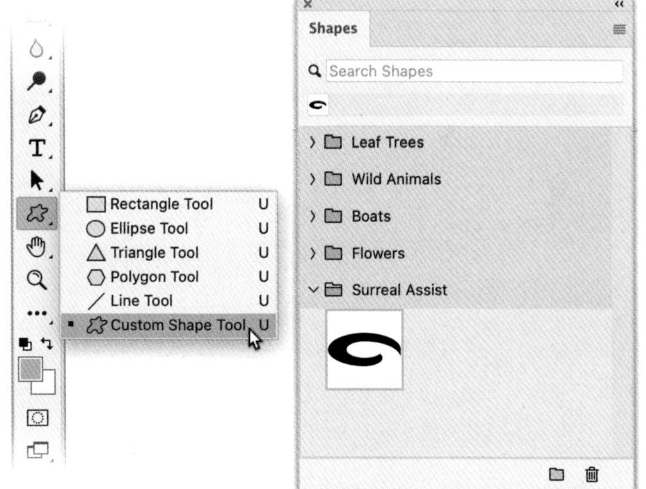

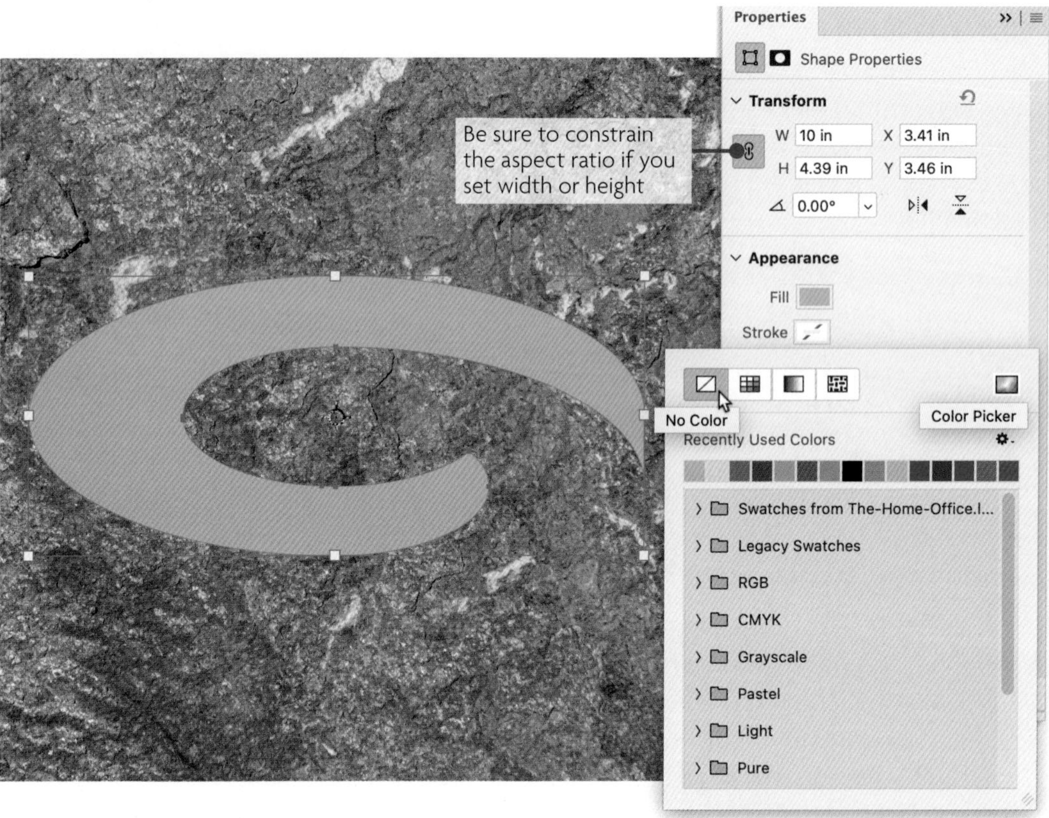

- In the Properties panel, click on the Stroke color to choose No Color. While there, set the size if you like (see screenshot above). I set the width of mine to "10 in." You may also change the fill color: Click Fill and then the Color Picker button to choose literally anything, or use a swatch if you see one you like.
- Use the Move tool to locate the object in the center of the texture.
- Set the shape layer's Opacity to a value like 50% so we can see the texture's details beneath it, but we still know where the shape is.

It's now time to warp that texture.

Lesson C: Bending & Warping

Free Transform

We don't need to be exacting in this step. Our objective is to give a hint that the texture is wrapping around a dimensional object.

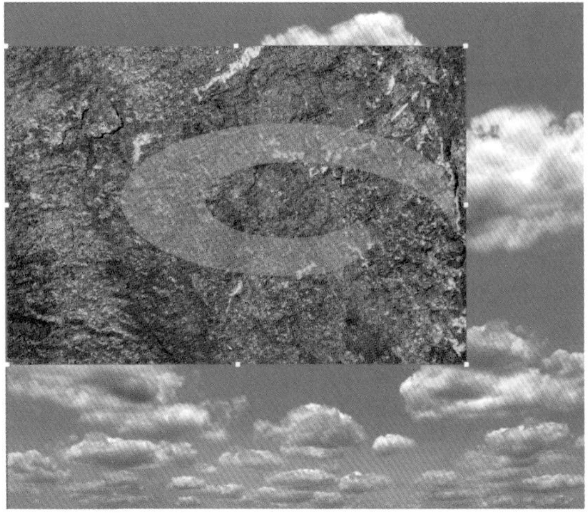

- Highlight the texture layer.
- Select Free Transform by using ⌘-T/Ctrl-T. Scale the texture so one edge is near the sharp "point" of the shape (its right) and the other edge is near the edge of the canvas.
- Then click the Warp mode button in the Options Bar. To review how warp works first, see "Warping and Sculpting" (page 337). However, this will be easier than most of what's discussed there.
- Choose the Cylinder preset from the Warp menu in the Options Bar. The texture might now be warped into a U-shape.
- Drag the top control point upward and the bottom one downward.

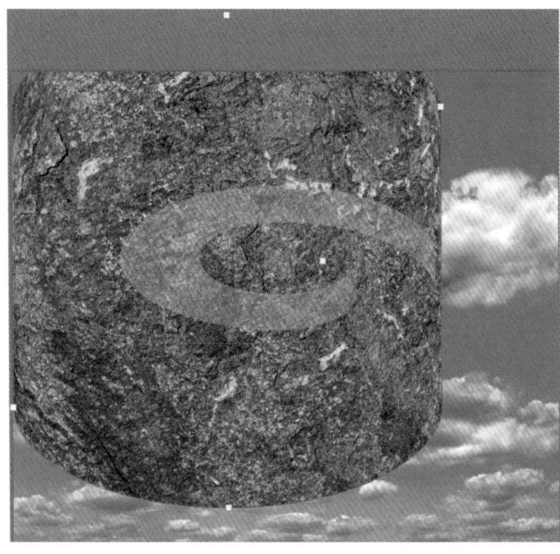

We're trying to get the most distortion near the point of the shape. Since the center of the texture is not very distorted and near the round edge of the shape (its left edge), the texture looks somewhat normal there.

- Drag the texture itself up or down to vertically center it on the shape, too.
- Commit the transform by clicking the check mark in the Options Bar or by pressing return/Enter.

Lesson D: Clipping & Fine-Tuning

We're already to the last few steps!

The Clipping Mask

- Move the texture layer to the top of the stack in the Layers panel.
- Highlight the shape layer and restore its Opacity to 100%.
- Holding down the option/Alt key, click the line between the texture layer and the shape layer to make a clipping mask.

Now the texture is visible only where the shape is.

The Other Half

The whole surreal ring is made of two nearly identical pieces. Now it's time to make the rest.

- Highlight both the shape and texture layers.
- Use the shortcut ⌘-J/Ctrl-J to very rapidly duplicate both. This will leave the duplicates highlighted, just as we need them to be.
- Select the duplicate shape layer alone.
- Use the fx menu at the bottom of the Layers panel and choose Color Overlay. Set that to 40% Opacity, the color to black, and the Blend Mode to either Normal or Multiply.

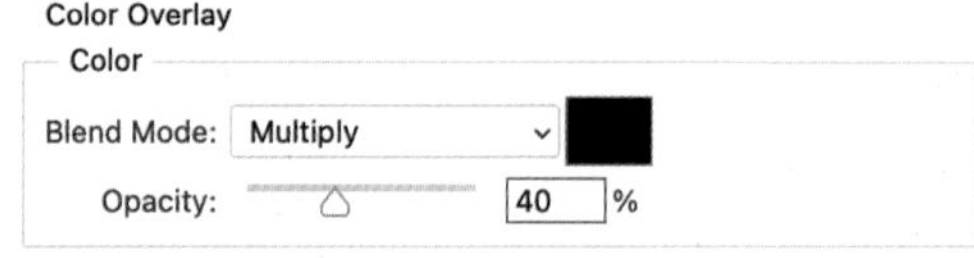

Now we can distinguish the two shape layers visually.

- Free Transform by using ⌘-T/Ctrl-T.
- Choices: You can rotate it 180° either by shift-dragging just outside the transform box or by typing "180" in the Rotate field in the Options Bar and pressing Enter.
- Press return/Enter to commit the transform.

True, this half is not yet where we need it to be.

- Highlight both that shape layer and its texture so you can move both.
- Likely holding the shift key to constrain motion to vertical, use the Move tool to get those layers in position. Zoom in close to see better. When the Move tool is active, pressing the keyboard's arrow keys nudges those layers a pixel at a time, so you can be as accurate as you wish.

Recall that the texture is in a Smart Object that contains four other texture layers.

Final Touches

Let's pick a different texture.

- Double-click on either texture layer's thumbnail. This generates a temporary file to show you the content of the Smart Object.
- Change which layers are visible and/or at the top of the layer stack.
- Close and save that temporary file and watch how the composite changes. Cool!

Let's add one last nuance.

- Convert the sky layer to a Smart Object.
- Apply Filter > Blur Gallery > Field Blur... choosing a noticeable amount of blur.

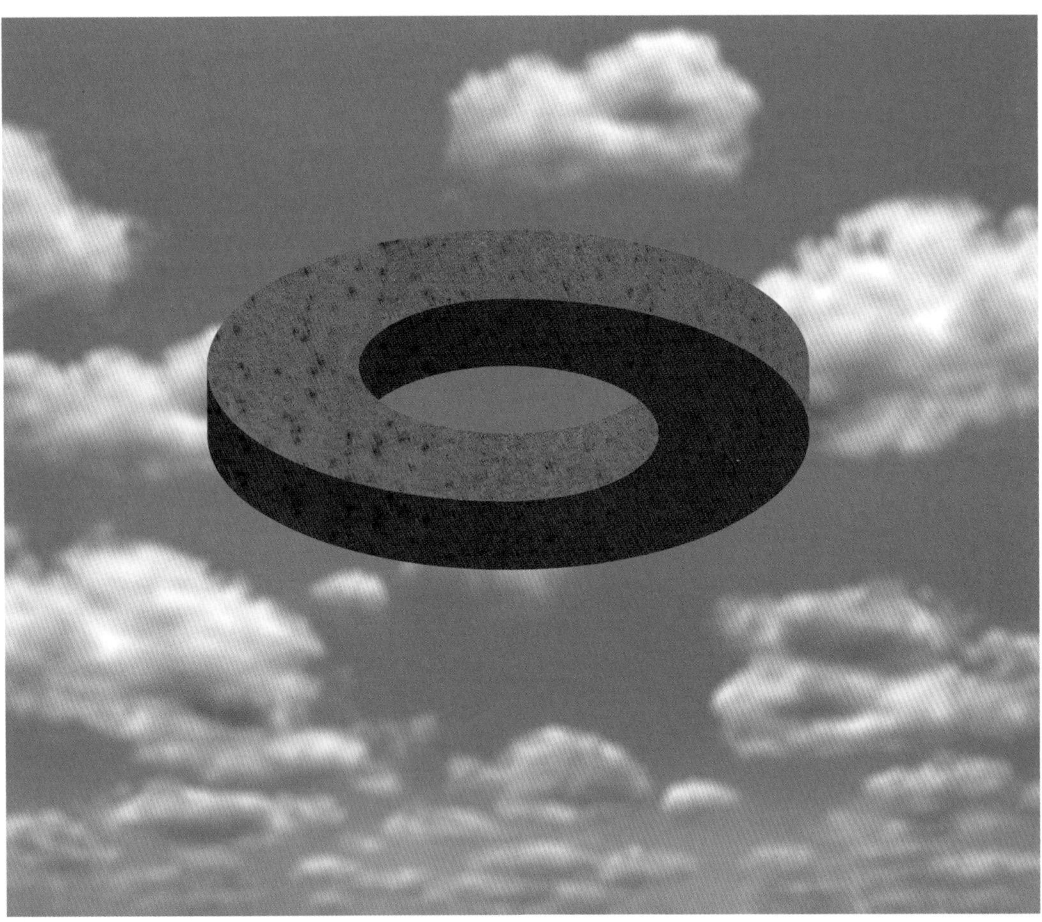

I hope you enjoyed this project as well as the others in this Course. As you can tell, there is much more to this book in the Compendium that follows. It's there to help you develop skills beyond those attained in the Course. Try to have fun as you learn more. Silly projects are at least as educational as serious ones!

THE COMPENDIUM

1 Layers & Smart Objects

The Layers feature is so integral to Photoshop that to ignore it is to essentially not use Photoshop. With the many kinds of layers offered, we can achieve our creative goals and do so nondestructively. That is, we can revisit a project many times and quickly make the changes we, or our clients, demand without having to start over.

Layers make Photoshop the ultimate palimpsest.

Layers

Layers serve many purposes and can contain many different kinds of content. Over the years, Photoshop has gained various kinds of layers to hold that content. Some, like text layers, are somewhat obvious. Others are more challenging to master. The most powerful—Smart Objects—have an entire section of this chapter dedicated to them.

The concept of layers is often compared to the process of making animated movies in the 1930s. A background image (a castle, for example) would be painted on glass. The characters to be animated (like Snow White) were drawn and painted on clear sheets of celluloid ("cels"), a number of which could be layered above the background to be photographed as a complete frame for the movie. Like those cels, layers can be transparent and/or blended visually.

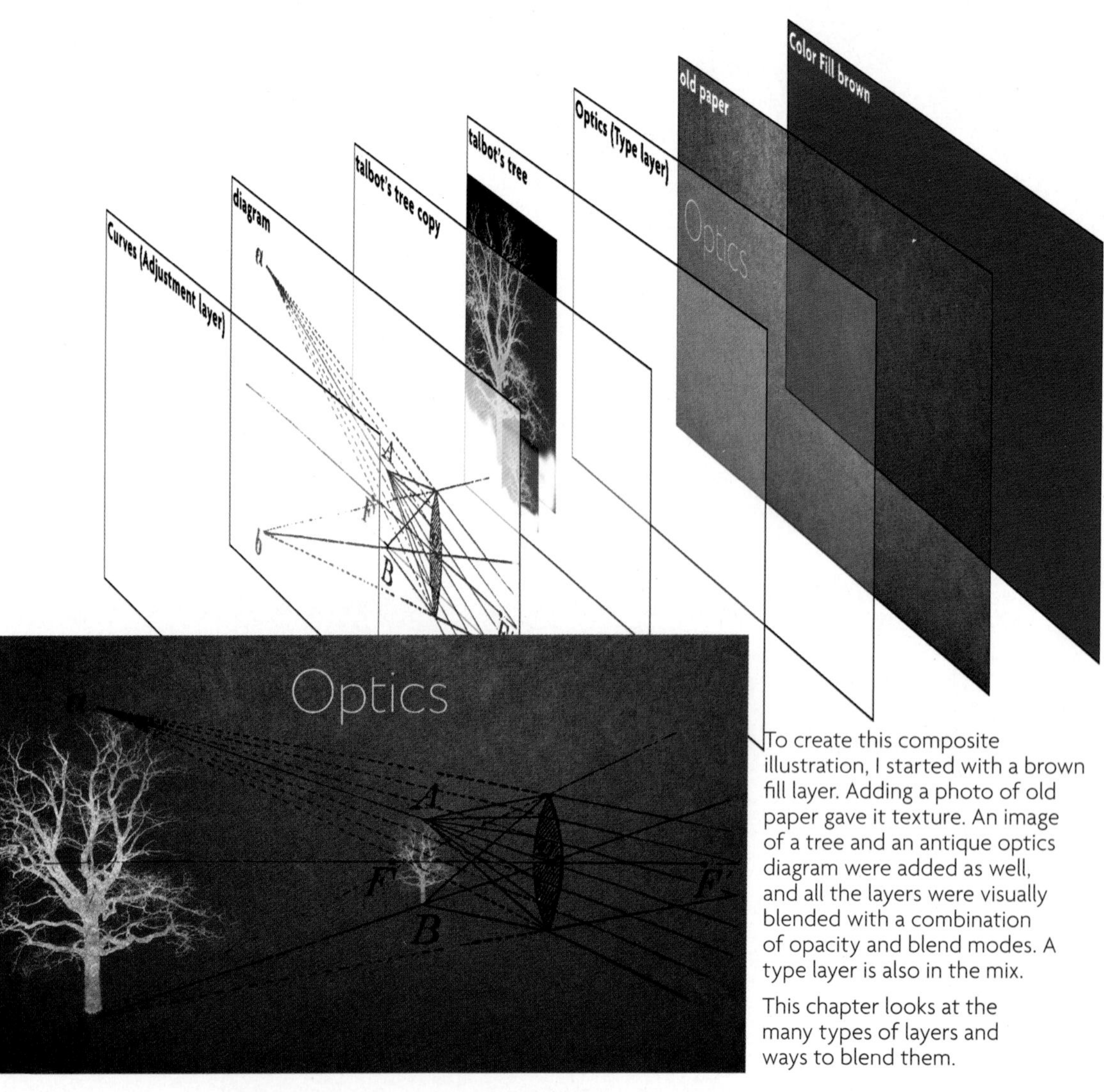

To create this composite illustration, I started with a brown fill layer. Adding a photo of old paper gave it texture. An image of a tree and an antique optics diagram were added as well, and all the layers were visually blended with a combination of opacity and blend modes. A type layer is also in the mix.

This chapter looks at the many types of layers and ways to blend them.

The Layers Panel

This panel is the most critical in Photoshop. Along with a visual list of a document's layers, it has a number of buttons and functions clustered at the top and bottom. Here is the Layers panel for the optics illustration on the previous page. It has examples of several layer types.

Note: Right-clicking is a powerful function. But where?

Right-clicking on each of these summons a different menu:

- Image thumbnail
- Mask thumbnail
- Near layer's name

Right-click on an image thumbnail to choose size: small, medium, large, or none.

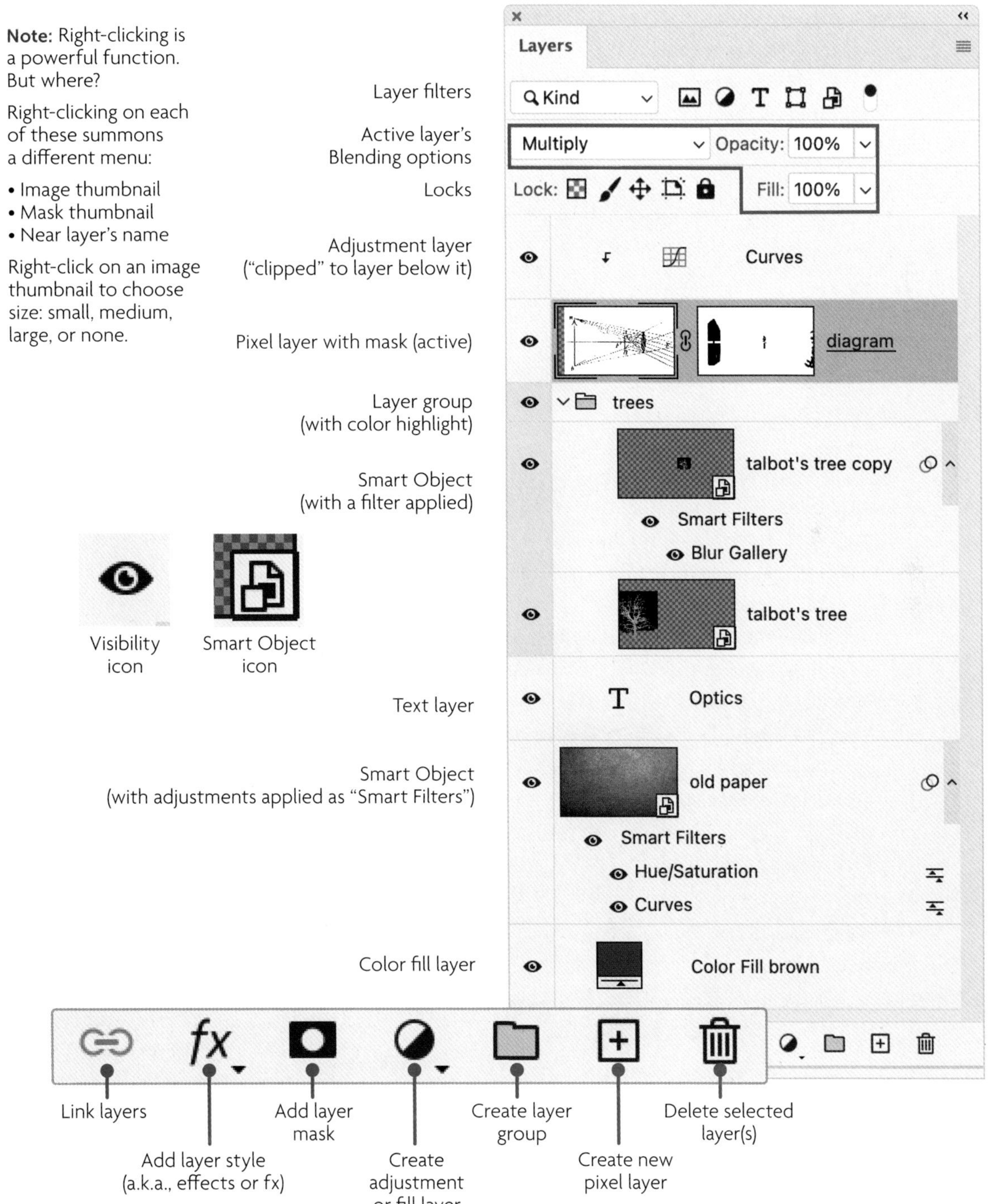

The Background

Not technically considered a layer at all, a Background is the only layer type supported by some file formats like JPEG. If you open a JPEG in Photoshop, a Background layer (and only that one) is exactly what you'll see. Backgrounds cannot have transparency (unlike the glass backgrounds of yesteryear). If you remove or hide the pixels that surround a subject, making them transparent, Photoshop will convert the Background to a pixel layer. However, if all one needs is an image in its original state, the Background has only half the digital overhead of a pixel layer of the same size, keeping the file size relatively small even if saved as a file format that compresses the image data less.

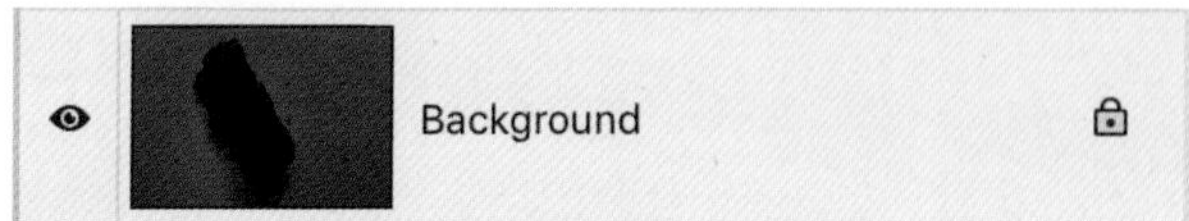

The small padlock to the right of a Background's name is there solely as a reminder of the limitations of Backgrounds. It does ***not*** indicate that the Background is protected in *any* way. Clicking the padlock converts the Background to a pixel layer, usually with the name "Layer 0." Incidentally, if you open a PNG file with transparent pixels, you may find it has a "Layer 0" already.

Converting a Background to a different kind of layer or adding a layer of any other kind to a document that contains only a Background will double that document's file size. That should never be a deterrent to doing those things! In fact, it's almost always necessary. I just don't want you to be surprised when it happens. Once a document has multiple layers (or no Background), there are some layer types that will add nothing further to the size at all!

Some recipients of your documents may request that you provide them with a "flattened" file. This means squishing all of a document's layers into a Background and nothing else. Since the intellectual property you build with Photoshop is primarily the layers you construct, you should never flatten your *original* files. If a flattened version is requested from you, use File > Save A Copy... then uncheck the Layers checkbox and/or choose a format that supports only Backgrounds. Photoshop will usually append the word "copy" to the name so you don't accidentally overwrite your original. You can disable this behavior in the File Handling preferences.

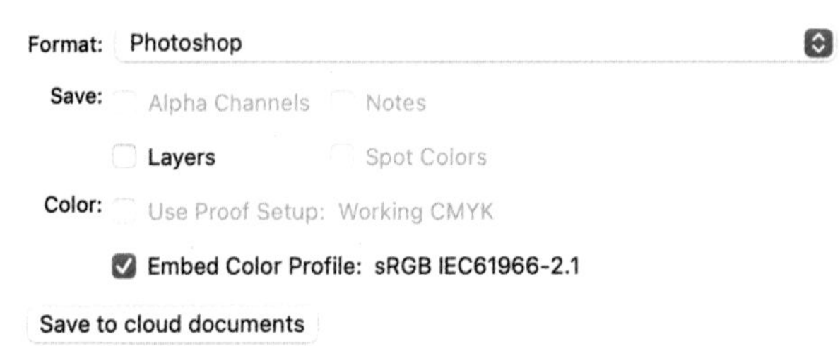

If you uncheck the Layers checkbox when saving a copy to a format that usually supports layers, or choose a format that does not support layers, Photoshop will automatically flatten all layers into a Background.

Pixel or Image Layer

For greater flexibility, a Background can be converted into a pixel layer. It can then be raised or lowered in the layer stack or its content can be dragged with the Move tool, leaving a transparent area in its wake. It has none of the restrictions of a Background, but lacks much of its simplicity. Converting a Background to a pixel layer increases data overhead and therefore file size. But since we're in Photoshop to get things done, this is often necessary. Pixel layers can be masked, transformed, and visually blended with layers below them.

When creating a new layer with the New Layer dialog box, you may give the layer a meaningful name (a very good practice), as well as choose whether it is fully opaque or not. The Mode refers to the blend mode, which is discussed at length later in this chapter: "General Blending Options" (page 176). What are clipping masks? That can be learned in "Clipping Mask" (page 295).

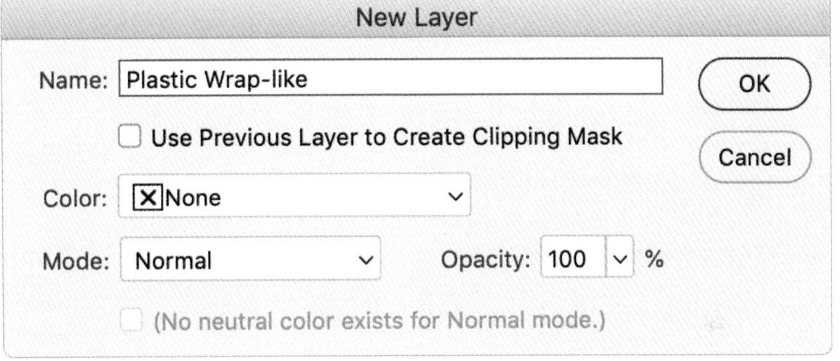

The new layer will be transparent (represented by a fine checkered pattern in its thumbnail).

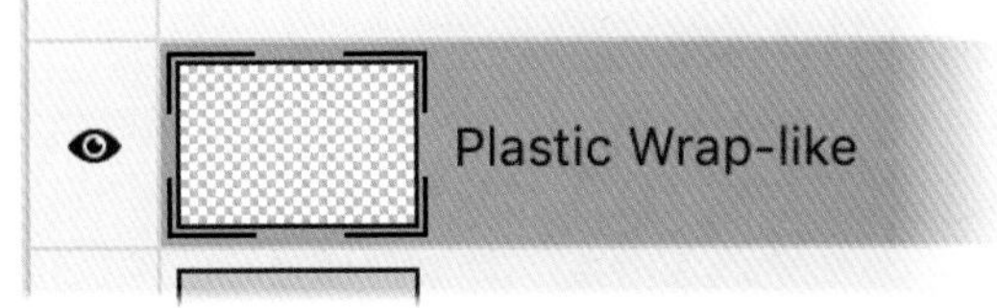

If you open a PNG file that has transparency, it often opens with a layer called "Layer 0." Also, if you wish to retouch or paint on an image nondestructively, you will create a new pixel layer above the other image layer(s). I compare this to wrapping something in plastic wrap and then painting on the plastic. If I regret my painting, I can simply delete that layer. There are so many ways to create layers! You may choose Layer > New > Layer..., which offers a chance to name the layer, as does the shortcut ⌘-shift-N/Ctrl-Shift-N. You may also use the Layers panel: click the small + button at the bottom (next to the trash can), or open the panel menu and choose New Layer....

Fill Layers

These come in three flavors: solid color, gradient, and pattern. They provide a way to fill the entire canvas with little or no increase in file size! The fastest way to create one of these is to drag a preset from one of the preset panels. You can create presets manually or with the well-hidden Capture panel. The Substance Materials panel can generate dynamic textures that can play the role of pattern fill layers. If you have an active selection, the fill layer will be masked to the selected area.

Solid Color

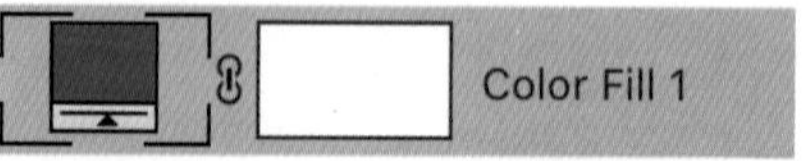

A solid color fill layer fills the canvas with a color you choose. If you have a selection active when the layer is created, the color will be masked to the selected area. Using the Layer > New Fill Layer menu or the New fill or adjustment layer button at the bottom of the Layers panel to select Solid Color brings up the Color Picker. Dragging a swatch from the Swatches panel onto the canvas also makes a fill layer in that color. You can edit a color fill layer by double-clicking its thumbnail or single-clicking a swatch.

If no layer exists other than a Background, then simply dragging a swatch onto the canvas creates an editable fill layer. If other layers exist, dragging may change a shape layer or clip the fill layer to another layer (see "Clipping Mask" on page 295). To prevent this, hold option/Alt as you drag a swatch onto the canvas.

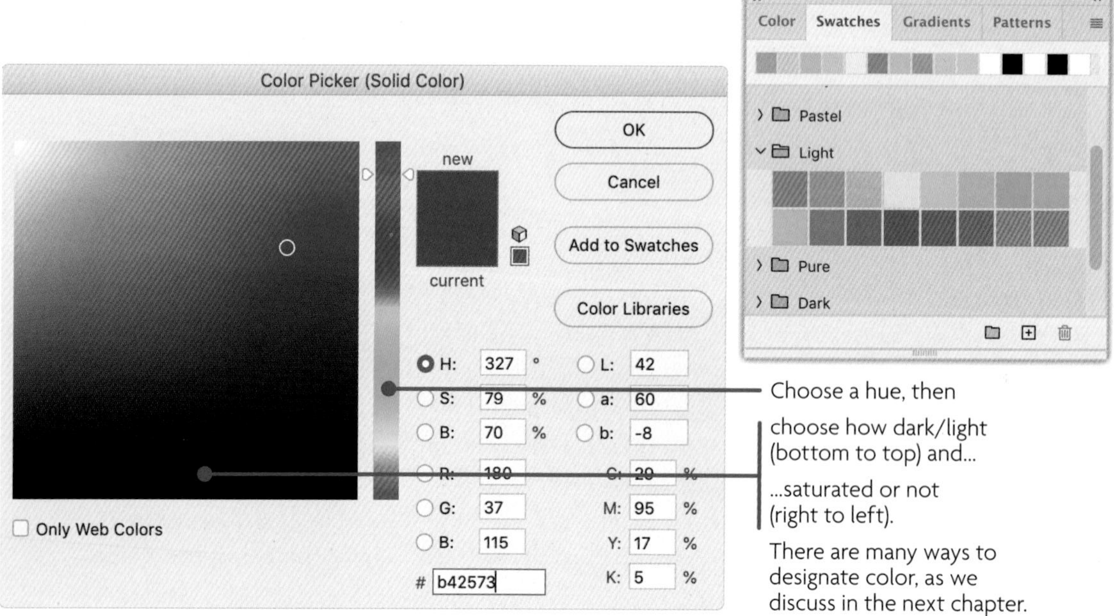

To reveal all presets in the Swatches panel, hold down ⌘/Ctrl as you click a disclosure arrow (>) to the left of a Swatch Group's name. Doing that again hides them. Use the Swatches panel menu to create new swatch presets or groups. Drag swatches into groups to organize them.

Gradient

A gradient fill layer fills the canvas with colors that transition however you like.

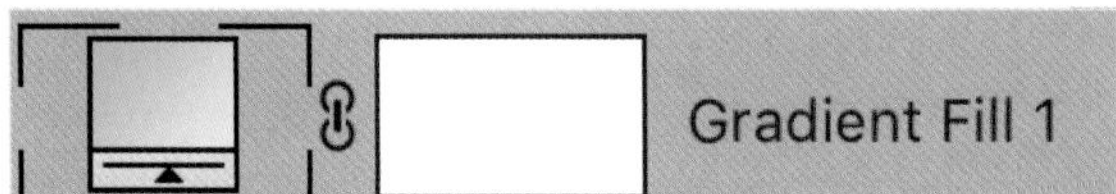

Beta As I write, gradients are getting a major upgrade. To show you how they work, I had to use the beta version of Photoshop in which the feature was still under development. So, gradients may change slightly when this book is in your hands.

The most efficient and intuitive way to create or edit a gradient is with the Gradient tool. This results in an easy-to-use on-canvas interface with additional options in the Properties panel. Choosing Gradient in the New Fill Layer menu or using the New fill or adjustment layer button to select Gradient brings up the Gradient Fill dialog, where you can choose the gradient from a collection of presets and customize it. Dragging a gradient preset onto the canvas makes a layer with that gradient. But regardless of how the layer is created, the Gradient tool (in cooperation with the Properties panel) is the easiest way to fine-tune the result!

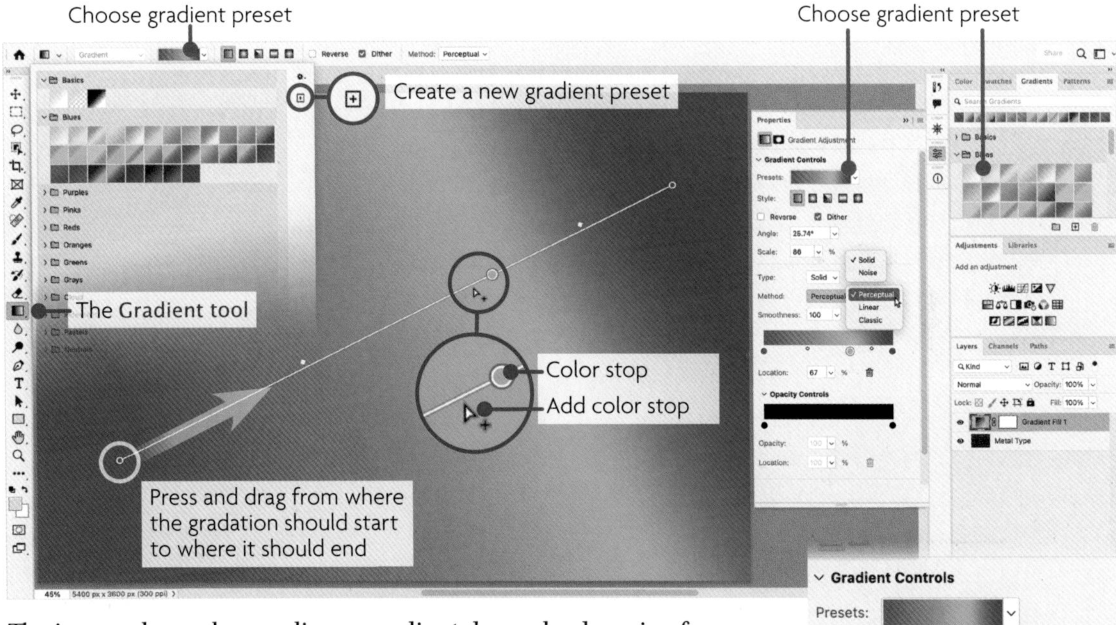

The image above shows a linear gradient drawn by dragging from the lower left to the upper right. I chose a preset from the Options Bar before dragging. Later, you can apply different presets from the Options Bar, the Gradients panel, or the Properties panel. Once the colors are chosen, there remain numerous properties to consider, but some need interpretation.

Dither allows each color in a gradient to slightly infiltrate adjacent colors to produce a result that seems smoother when the gradient would otherwise look posterized ("banded").

Color Stops define the main colors of a gradient and Photoshop interpolates between them. The Smoothness percentage controls how much the colors at color stops predominate over interpolated ones. So, ironically, 0% produces the most even transitions.

Method controls the color interpolation. Almost always, Perceptual yields the most visually intuitive result. Classic, formerly the only method, is very similar to what's used in Illustrator and InDesign but looks muddy compared to the others.

In the code, Linear is the simplest *mathematically*, but can appear very nonlinear. Bright, high luminance colors dominate darker ones. For example, a black-to-white gradient appears severely compressed at the dark end. But a Linear gradient with colors of equal luminance looks identical to a beautifully even Perceptual gradient. Due to this behavior, I tend to avoid Linear.

Once drawn, you can drag either end's color stop to visually adjust the angle or scale of the gradient. If you need exact values, look to the Properties panel. The Scale percentage listed there tells us how the length of the gradient compares to its maximum possible *visible* width. That is, the width of the canvas in the example above, or the width of a selection you may have had before drawing the gradient, which would now be its mask.

If you need a third (or thirtieth) color stop in your gradient, click just below the bar on the canvas or near the bottom of Gradient Controls in the Properties panel—watch for the cursor with the plus sign. Drag a stop to adjust its position, or set it precisely with the Location setting in the Properties panel. Double-click a stop to change its color with the Color Picker.

There are five choices for a gradient's Style. In the *Gradient Styles* figure at right, the angle for each gradient has been set to 45°, which matters least for the radial style. All offer on-canvas editing. Opacity within/along a gradient can be set with an independent set of Opacity Stops in the Properties panel.

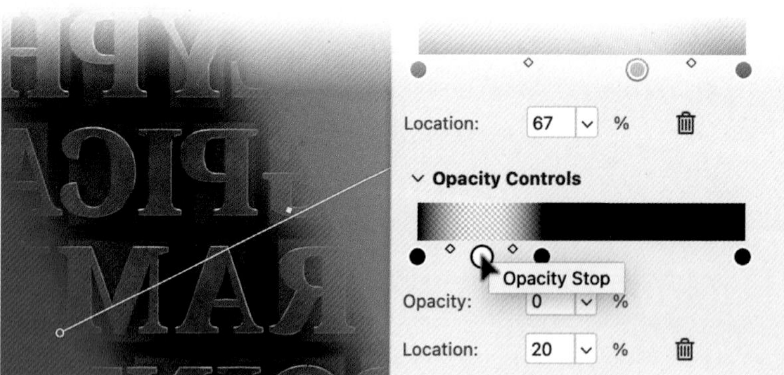

Changing the Type from Solid to Noise produces a dramatic change: colors are chosen randomly to produce colorful striations. Guide the randomizing algorithm primarily with the color sliders in the Properties panel. I typically change their Color Model to HSB to easily restrict colors to a range.

Oddly, the Restrict Colors checkbox only prevents the randomly generated colors from being too saturated. Finally, Roughness is a blur control. Low values are maximum blur.

Gradient Styles

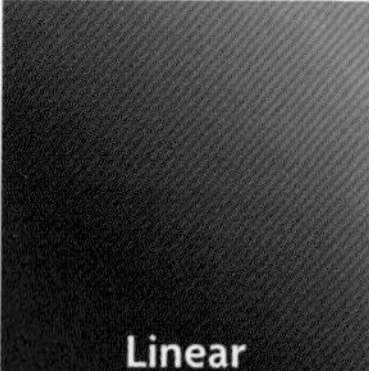

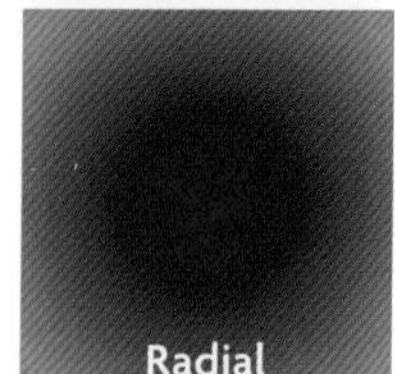

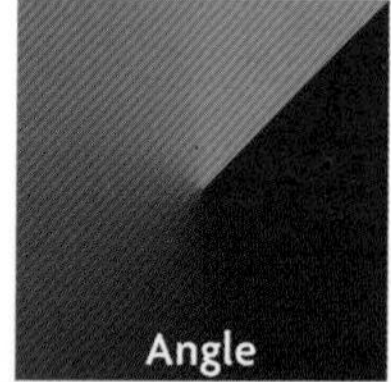

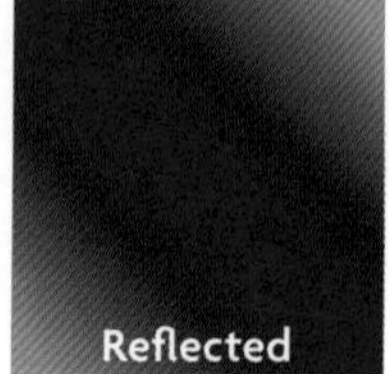

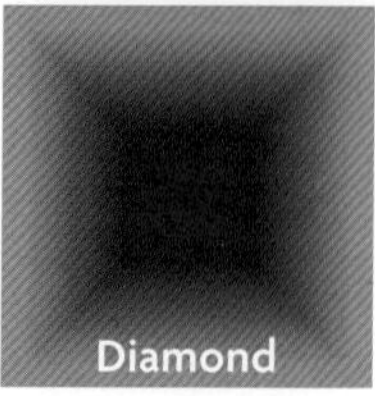

Drag and Drop

If no layer exists other than a Background, then simply dragging a gradient preset onto the canvas creates an editable fill layer. If other layers exist, dragging may change a shape layer or clip the fill layer to another layer (see "Clipping Mask" on page 295). To prevent this, hold option/Alt as you drag.

After a gradient fill layer exists, edit it with the Gradient tool as described above.

Pattern

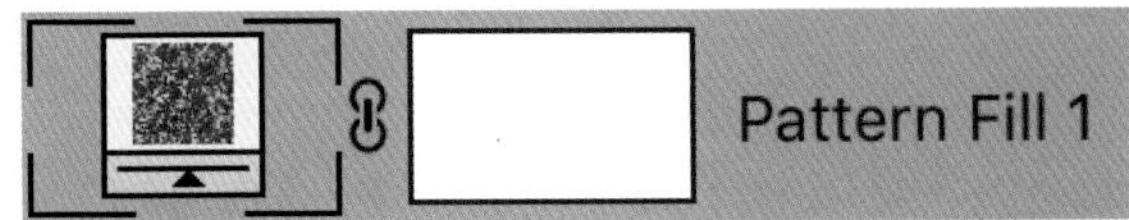

A pattern fill layer fills the canvas with a pattern you choose. If you have a selection active when the layer is created, the pattern will be masked to the selected area. Using the New Fill Layer menu or the New fill or adjustment layer button to select Pattern brings up the Pattern Fill dialog box, where you can choose a pattern from a collection of presets and customize it. Dragging a pattern preset onto the canvas makes a layer with that pattern. You can edit it by double-clicking the layer's thumbnail or single-clicking a different pattern preset. Creating patterns from scratch that appear even and don't possess obvious repeats is harder than most users expect.

If no layer exists other than a Background, then simply dragging a pattern preset onto the canvas creates an editable fill layer. If other layers exist, dragging may change a shape layer or clip the fill layer to another layer (see "Clipping Mask" on page 295). To prevent this, hold option/Alt as you drag.

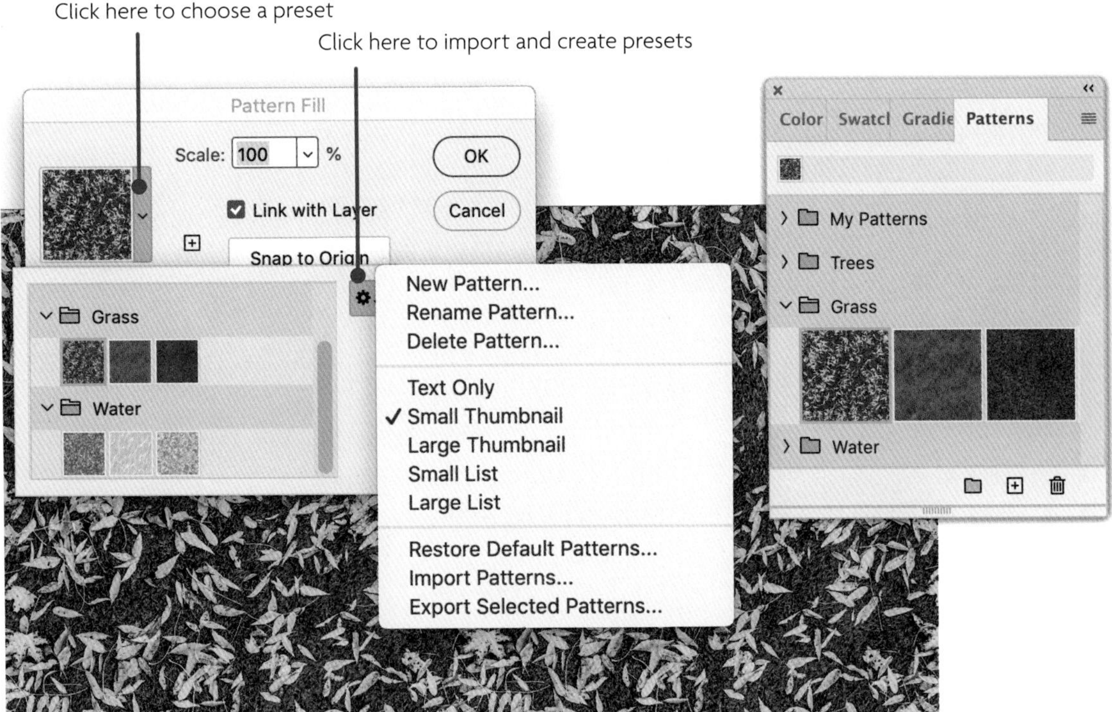

Rather than attempt to make a pattern, most users photograph textures (or obtain images of textures) to use as backdrops. If you'd like to try to make your own pattern, review the process explored in the Course: "Creating a Pattern Fill Layer" (page 73).

To show all presets in the Patterns panel, hold down ⌘/Ctrl as you click a disclosure arrow (>) to the left of a Pattern Group's name. Doing that again hides them. Use the Patterns panel menu to create new presets or groups. Drag presets into groups to organize them.

Capture Panel

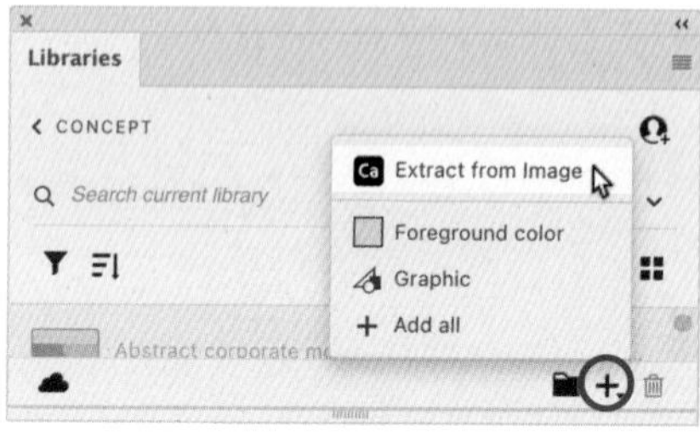

With this panel, you can generate patterns, color swatches, and gradients from open images, and even identify fonts in those images, each of which ends up in a Creative Cloud library. But don't look in the Window menu to find this panel! Well, not directly: Go to Window > Libraries to get the Libraries panel. At the bottom of it, you'll see a plus sign. Click it and choose Extract from Image. Pretty hidden, eh?

Substance Materials Panel

The Materials panel gives you access to editable 3D textures. The panel has dozens of materials built-in and can be loaded with more that you can make with the Adobe Substance applications or download from the Substance community. Although this panel generates a 2D layer like a pattern fill, the materials in it have texture with many adjustable parameters, across which you can cast virtual light to reveal the texture's depth.

To start, go to Window > Materials. Clicking on a material creates a Smart Object layer (masked, if there was an active selection) whose texture settings are applied as a Smart Filter. In the following example, that layer is below a type layer (the word "BRICKS") and uses the material called "Cartegena Wall Bricks."

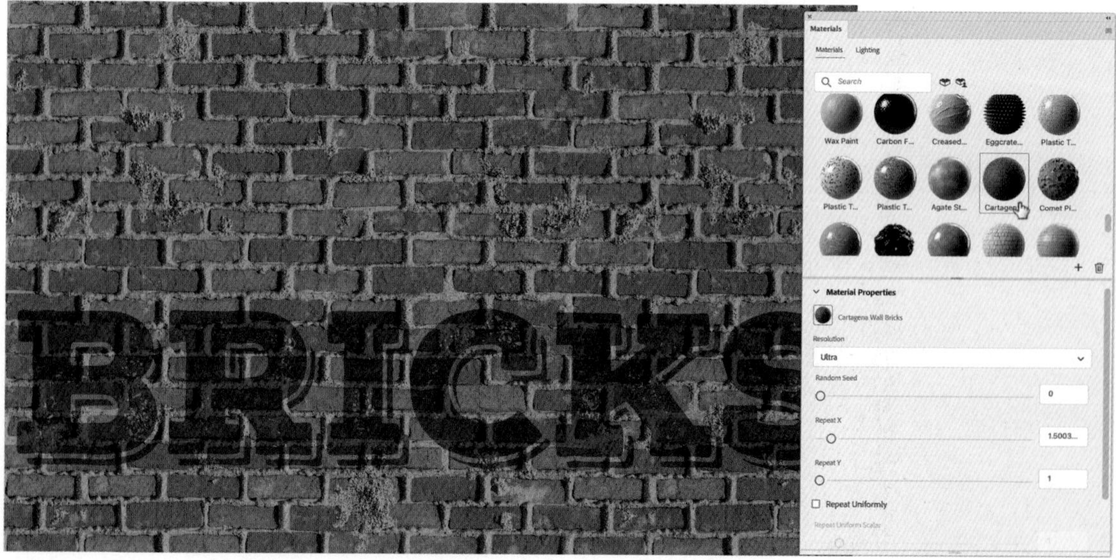

I wanted something that felt more big-city downtown. Since I don't enjoy a subscription to the Substance 3D applications, I chose to see what that user community was sharing for free by clicking the community assets button at the top of the Materials panel. This launches a web browser to show you the many assets (not just textures) you can use in the Substance programs, Photoshop, Illustrator, and more.

Subscriber assets (left, some free)
Free community assets (right)

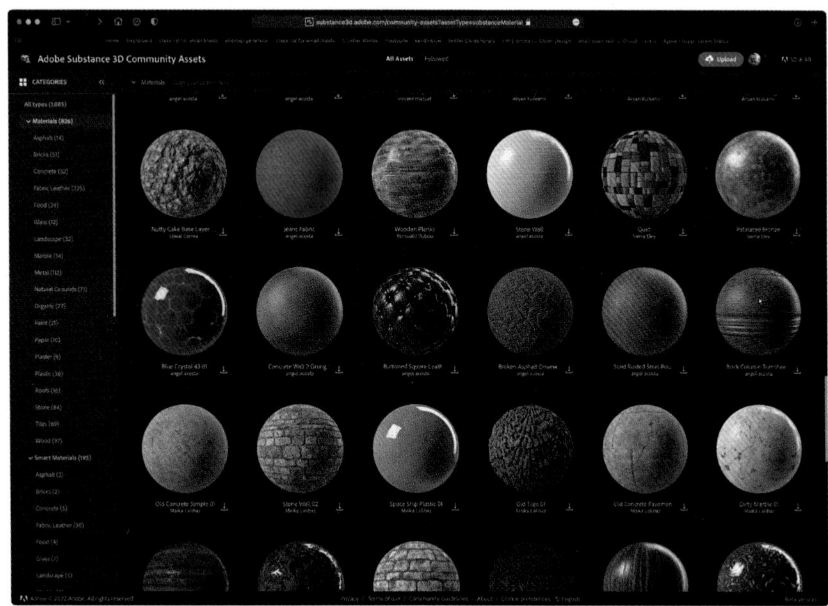

I chose a Photoshop-compatible material format (.sbsar) that had not only bricks, but other decorative architectural details as well.

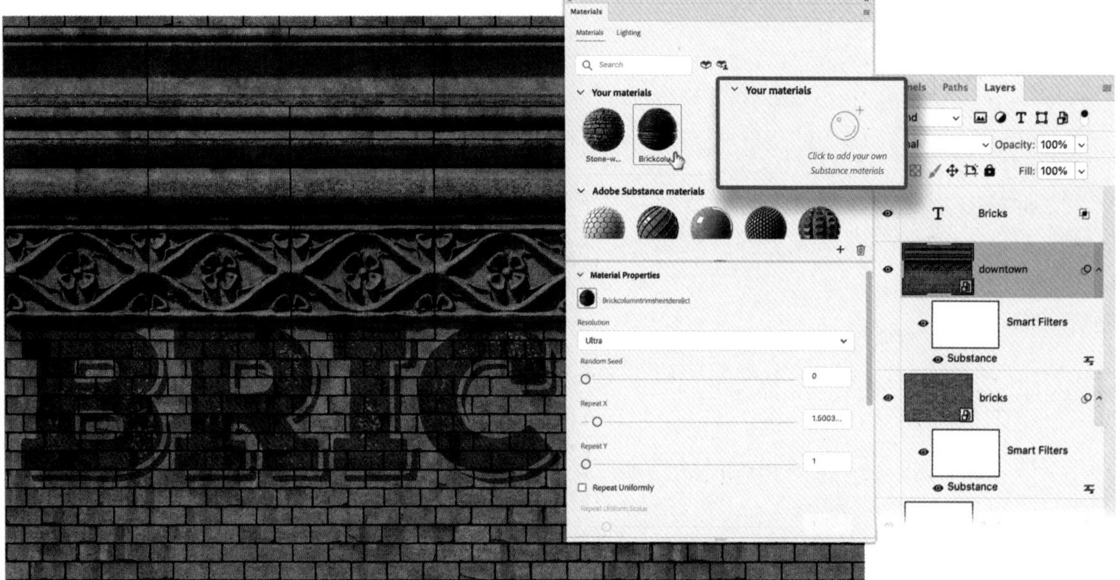

The Materials panel has a Lighting option (at the top). Its main controls are Rotation and Height. To best anticipate their effect, imagine the texture is on the ground in front of you. Height is the light's angle above the horizon (try starting at 45°). Changing the Rotation moves the light clockwise in the sky above you: Starting at 0° rotation, the light might start above and to the right, but 180° would be below and to the left.

Exposure is the light's intensity. Displacement controls how much the material protrudes from the surface. Below, I changed all of those settings as well as the color of the light for a early evening feel.

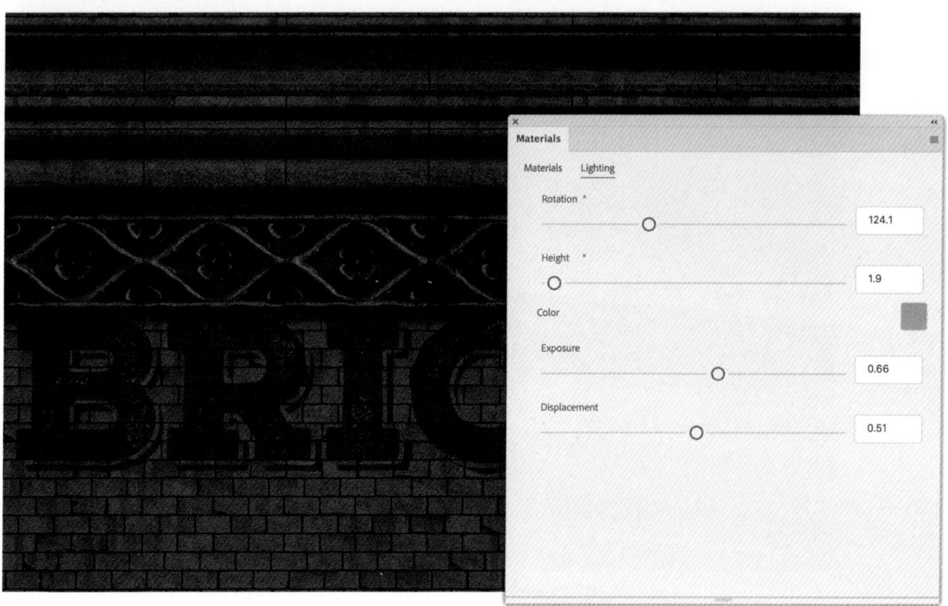

Vector Shape Layers

These layers contain vector shapes (like those created in Adobe Illustrator), whether they're a Pen tool creation, built-in shapes, or pasted Illustrator graphics. They can be edited with a small selection of tools provided for this purpose. Shape layers can be thought of as fill layers with vector masks. When one needs elaborate, logoesque shapes, however, it's still easiest to create them in Illustrator.

Apply a color swatch (or gradient or pattern) to a shape by highlighting the shape layer, then clicking a choice in the Swatches panel (or Gradients or Patterns panel).

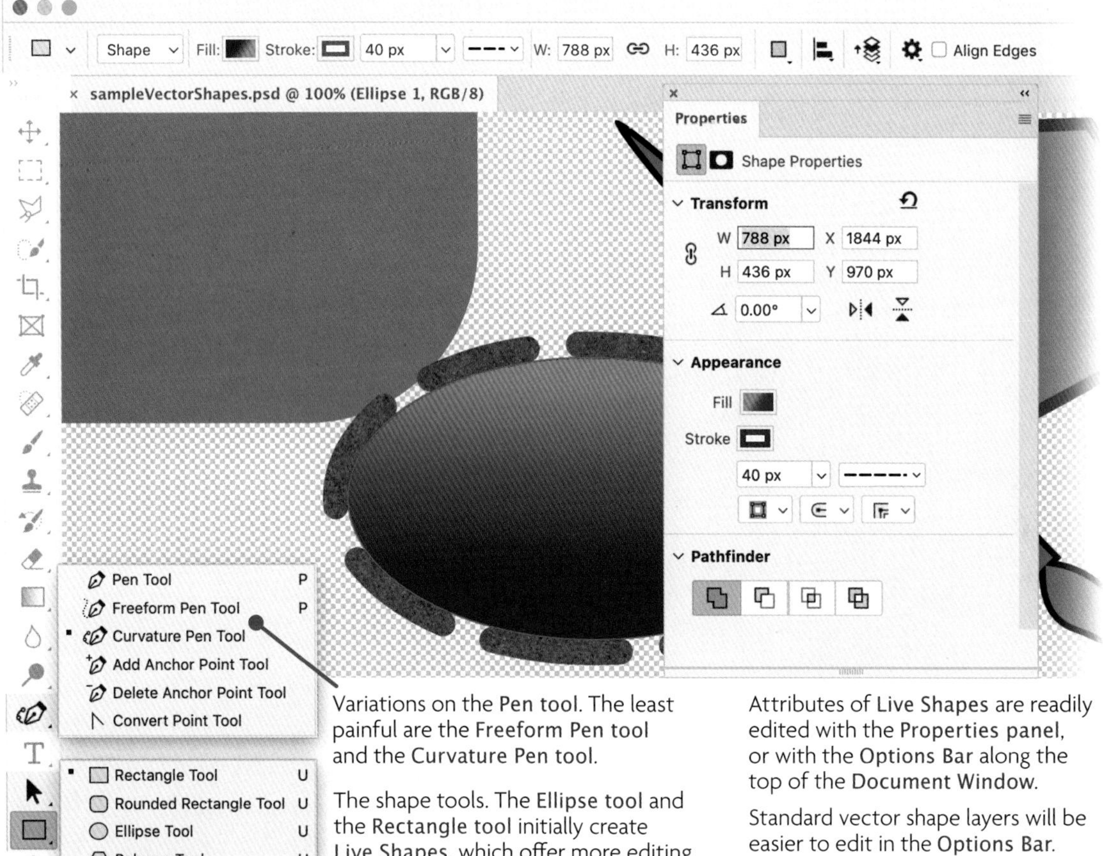

Variations on the Pen tool. The least painful are the Freeform Pen tool and the Curvature Pen tool.

The shape tools. The Ellipse tool and the Rectangle tool initially create Live Shapes, which offer more editing options than standard vector shapes.

Attributes of Live Shapes are readily edited with the Properties panel, or with the Options Bar along the top of the Document Window.

Standard vector shape layers will be easier to edit in the Options Bar.

Shape Tools

When you create a shape with any of the shape tools (by either dragging diagonally or just clicking and providing dimensions in a dialog box), a new vector shape layer appears in the Layers panel above the layer that was last highlighted. If you save the document as a Photoshop PDF, a recipient has little chance to learn that it was created in Photoshop rather than Illustrator, since the shapes will retain their vector scalability.

Most of the shape tools create arbitrary vector shapes, also called "paths," that can be manipulated with the Path Selection tool, or more surgically edited with the Direct Selection tool. The first resembles a black arrow and may seem to offer much the same as the Move tool. The latter allows you to select and move the individual anchor points that compose a path. If

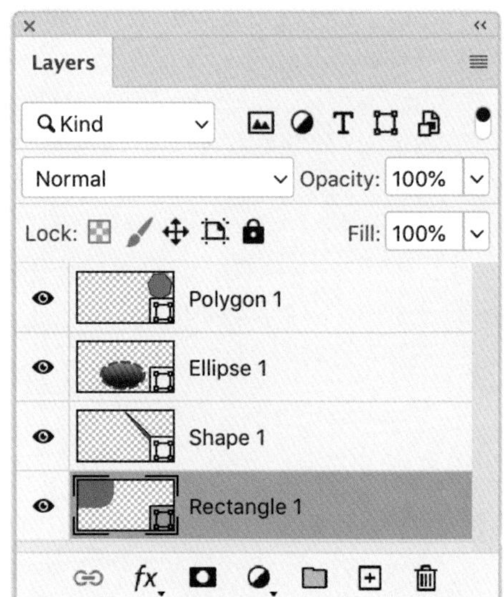

this is something that you will need to do frequently, you've discovered another reason to use Adobe Illustrator.

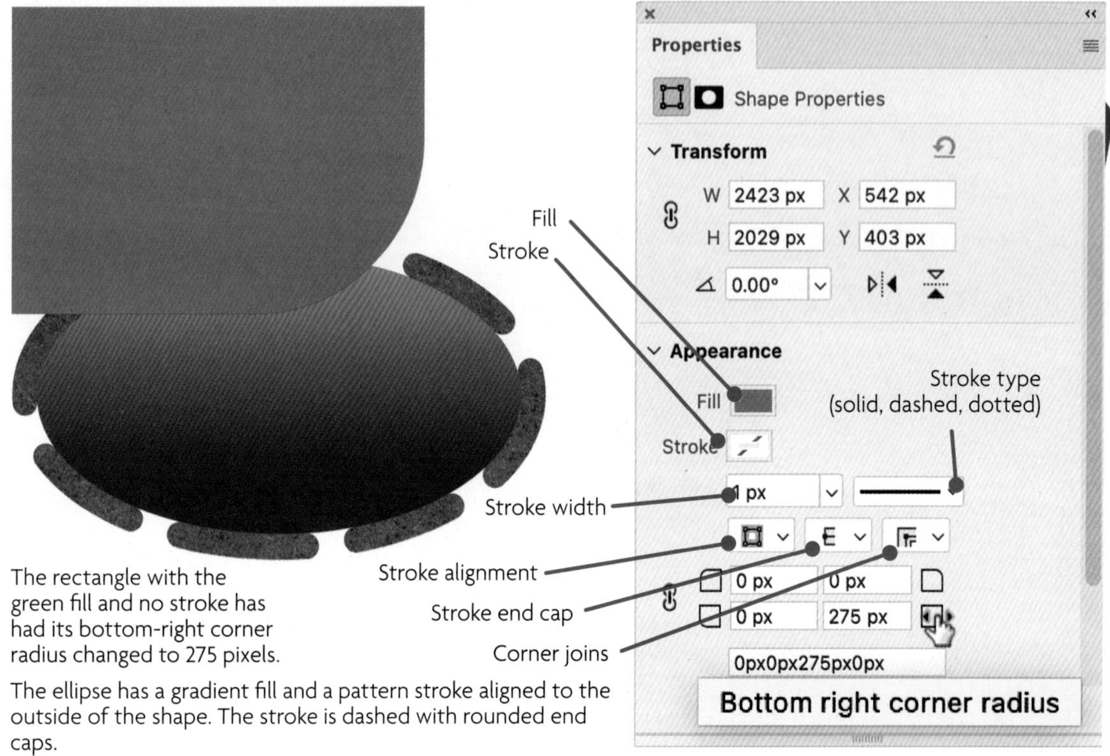

The rectangle with the green fill and no stroke has had its bottom-right corner radius changed to 275 pixels.

The ellipse has a gradient fill and a pattern stroke aligned to the outside of the shape. The stroke is dashed with rounded end caps.

Live Shapes

Edits like corner radius can be applied only to Live Shapes (created by the Rectangle tool and the Ellipse tool) whose edits can be revisited. Arbitrary shapes, like those made with any other tool, don't have such an option. If you attempt to use the Direct Selection tool to make a surgical edit to the corner of a rectangle, for example, you'll be warned that it will no longer be a Live Shape.

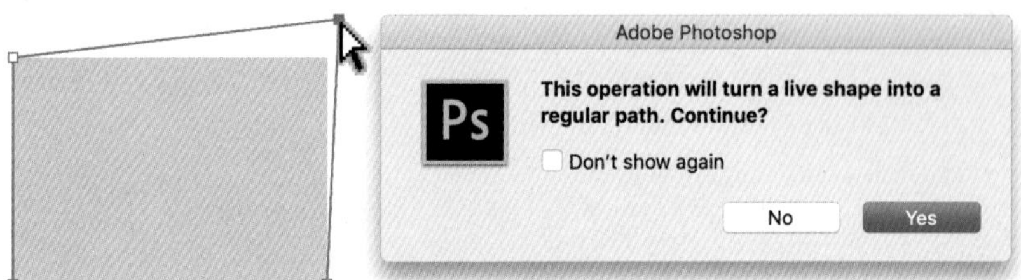

Before you worry about this, be aware that there's very little that is lost when this happens (besides the ability to change a rectangle's corner radius). If you were to click Yes to that warning, almost everything you were able to edit in the Properties panel is still editable in the Options Bar.

Shapes Panel and Tool

The Custom Shape tool and the Shapes panel offer many, many more options. Drag shapes onto the canvas from the panel or draw them to size with the tool after choosing a shape in the Options Bar.

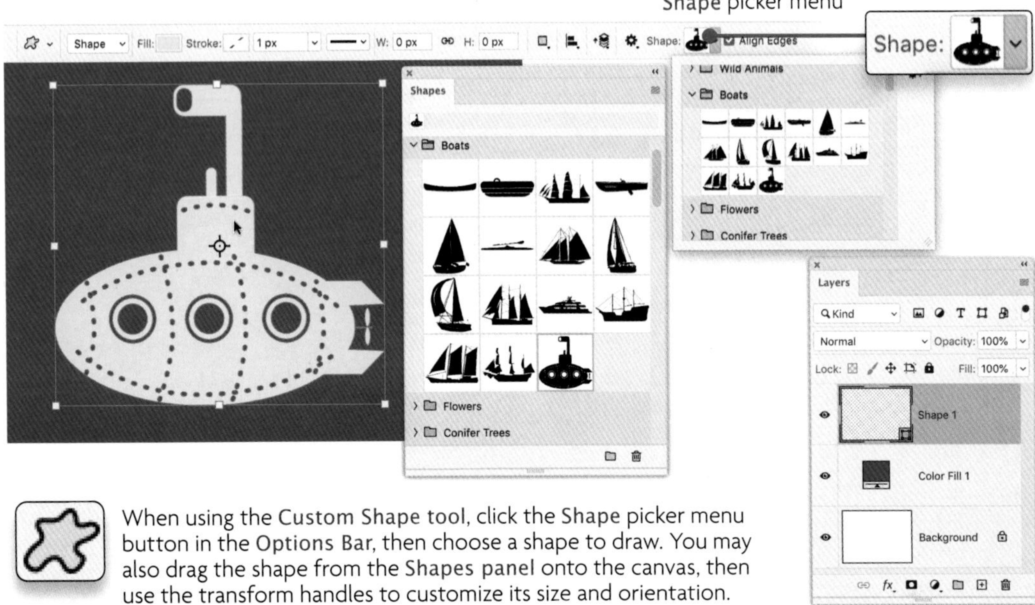

When using the Custom Shape tool, click the Shape picker menu button in the Options Bar, then choose a shape to draw. You may also drag the shape from the Shapes panel onto the canvas, then use the transform handles to customize its size and orientation.

If you have skill with editing or creating vector shapes, you can save your own to this list. At right is a shape I created in Illustrator and then pasted into Photoshop. When you do so, you are given several choices, of which I chose to paste as a shape layer.

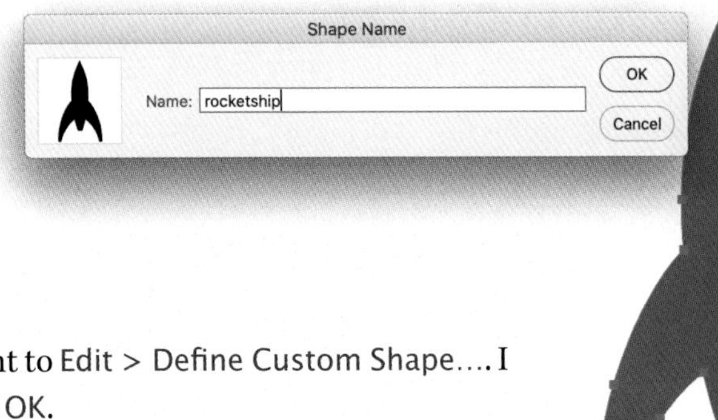

With that layer highlighted, I went to Edit > Define Custom Shape.... I gave it an obvious name and clicked OK.

Freeform Pen Tool

The Freeform Pen tool allows you to create vector shapes intuitively, simply by dragging.

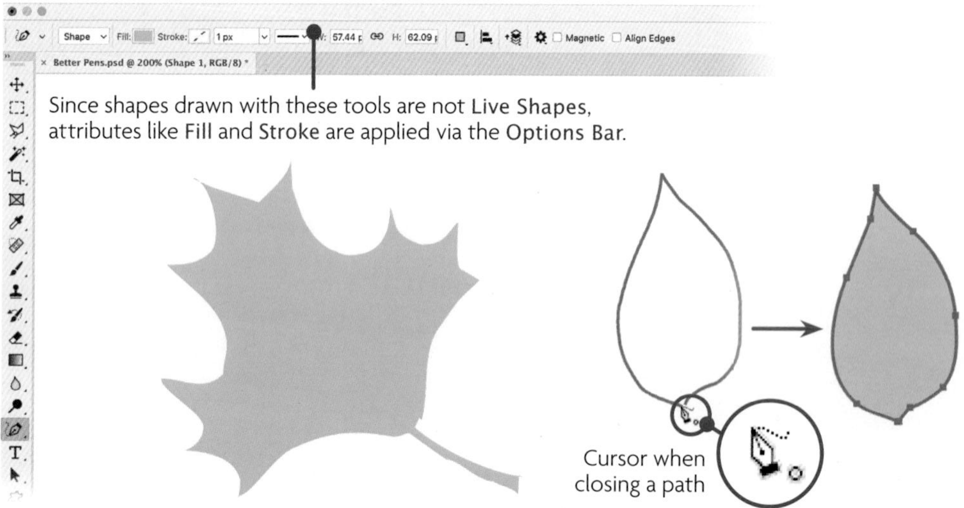

To choose the Freeform Pen tool from the Tools panel, you may have to right-click on the Pen tool to reveal its variants. Then, in the Options Bar, choose Shape from the Tool Mode menu. This will create a shape that will be filled with the Foreground color when you finish drawing. Later, you can change the fill's color or choose a gradient or pattern, or nothing at all, perhaps choosing a stroke instead. Even a stroke can be a gradient or pattern of whatever thickness. There are times when you would choose to create a colorless Path from the Tool Mode menu. One reason is to create a vector mask, as discussed in the "Selections & Masks" chapter: see "Vector Masks" (page 294). Another is in preparation to use a filter that requires a path, like the Flame filter. Lastly, but most likely with the Curvature Pen tool, you may be creating a selection of something with curvature, like the curvature that tool produces.

Using the Freeform Pen tool is easy. Simply drag with your mouse (or other input device)! If you want a closed shape, finish where you started. The cursor will even confirm that it will close the shape by displaying a small "O" next to it.

If you cannot make the shape you need with one stroke, that's okay. You can drag from the point where you left off. A slash ("/") appears to indicate that you will continue from a point.

As you can see from my example above, this tool is not intended for precision, technical drawing. The next one is!

The Curvature Pen Tool

Not as intuitive as the Freeform Pen tool, but still significantly easier than the brutal Pen tool, the Curvature Pen tool is used to create shapes that possess more precise geometry. Instead of dragging, you click to place points: a single click for points along a curve, a double click for corners.

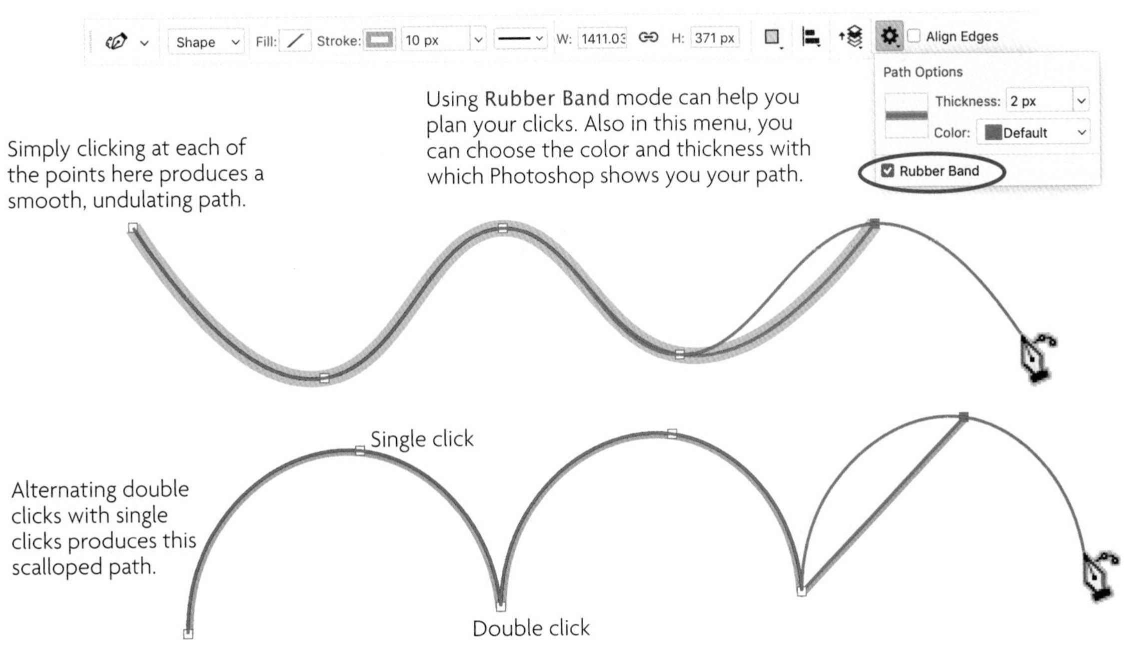

Using Rubber Band mode can help you plan your clicks. Also in this menu, you can choose the color and thickness with which Photoshop shows you your path.

Simply clicking at each of the points here produces a smooth, undulating path.

Alternating double clicks with single clicks produces this scalloped path.

To close a path to make a complete shape, just click on the point where you started. If you intended to create a corner, but forgot to double-click, you can just double-click on that last point (or any) to convert it. Indeed, the Curvature Pen tool is at least as useful for editing paths as it is for creating them.

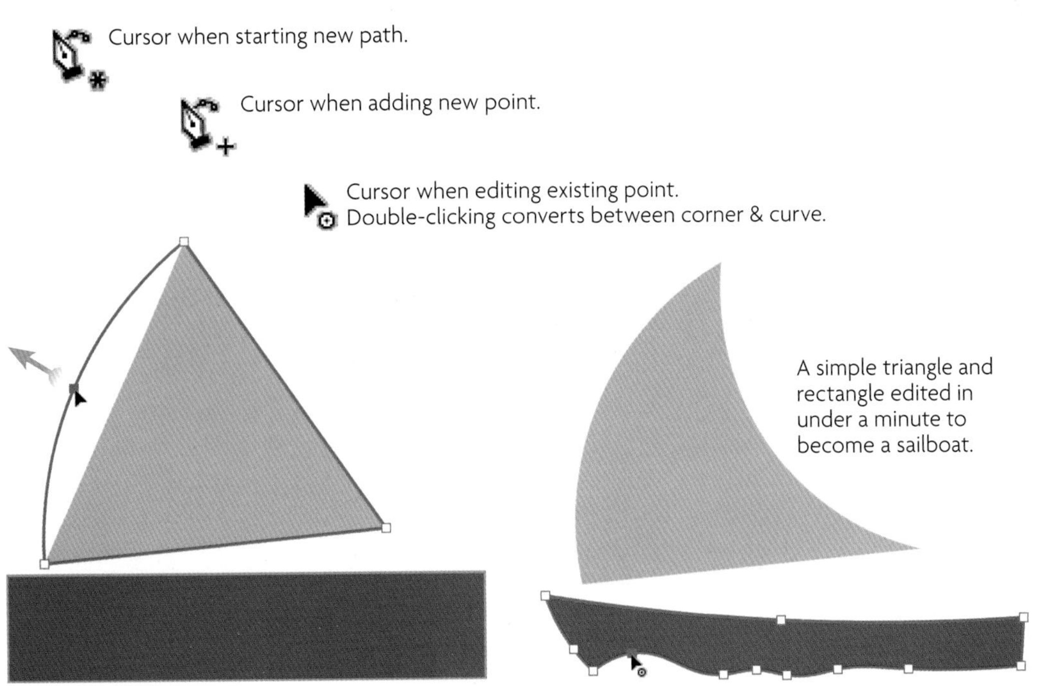

Cursor when starting new path.

Cursor when adding new point.

Cursor when editing existing point.
Double-clicking converts between corner & curve.

A simple triangle and rectangle edited in under a minute to become a sailboat.

To edit a shape, you must first select it with the Selection tool (it looks like a black arrow and is below the Type tool). Otherwise, Photoshop will assume you're trying to draw something new. In the example on the previous page, I had drawn a triangle as one shape layer (using the Polygon tool), and a rectangle as a second shape layer. I selected the triangle with the Selection tool, then switched to the Curvature Pen tool to push out one side and push in the opposite. Each act created a point I could readjust later. I added more points to the rectangle (after selecting it, of course).

Type Layers

These layers hold font data that can be [re]edited. Although Illustrator and especially InDesign handle text masterfully, we can do some work with type in Photoshop too. Most often, we do so to have the text interact with imagery in some way.

Working with text in Photoshop is both like and unlike working with text in other programs. My students often begin to think they've got the gist, then discover some odd Photoshop-specific quirk.

When you choose the Type tool in the Tools panel, the Options Bar immediately shows type-related attributes. So, if you happen to know before starting what font family, style, size, alignment, or color you'd like, you can choose them. If not, you can create a type layer and then choose. Ah, but there is one choice that needs to be made before you can start: Are you creating Point Text or Paragraph Text?

The first, Point Text, is most common in Photoshop. When you need only a few words, this is what's needed. Paragraph Text, as its name implies, is for when you feel more wordy, and is similar to an InDesign text frame.

If you ***click*** on a document canvas with the Type tool, you've created Point Text and the words "Lorem Ipsum" appear. If you ***drag*** diagonally to create a box with the Type tool, you create Paragraph Text and a great deal more Latin appears. This text is perfect if you are building a template and don't yet know what text will actually be used.

Once text is present, many type options appear in the Properties panel. Note the buttons resembling ellipses (**...**): These show even more options.

When either Point Text or Paragraph Text is first created, the placeholder text will be highlighted so you can edit it very quickly if you desire. If you choose a different size, for example, all the text will change. You may find it difficult to judge the color of the text while it is highlighted, but if you click the small rectangle in the Options Bar or Properties panel to choose a color, Photoshop will temporarily disable the highlighting so you can see what you're doing! Once you've chosen a color, the selection highlighting returns.

There are dedicated panels for type (Character and Paragraph), too, but all of their options are in the Properties panel.

One of my favorite type features is the ability to "scrub" the font size. If you hover the cursor over the font size icon, it will resemble a pointing hand with arrows to the left and right of the finger. Press your mouse button and drag left or right to decrease or increase the selected text's size *very* quickly.

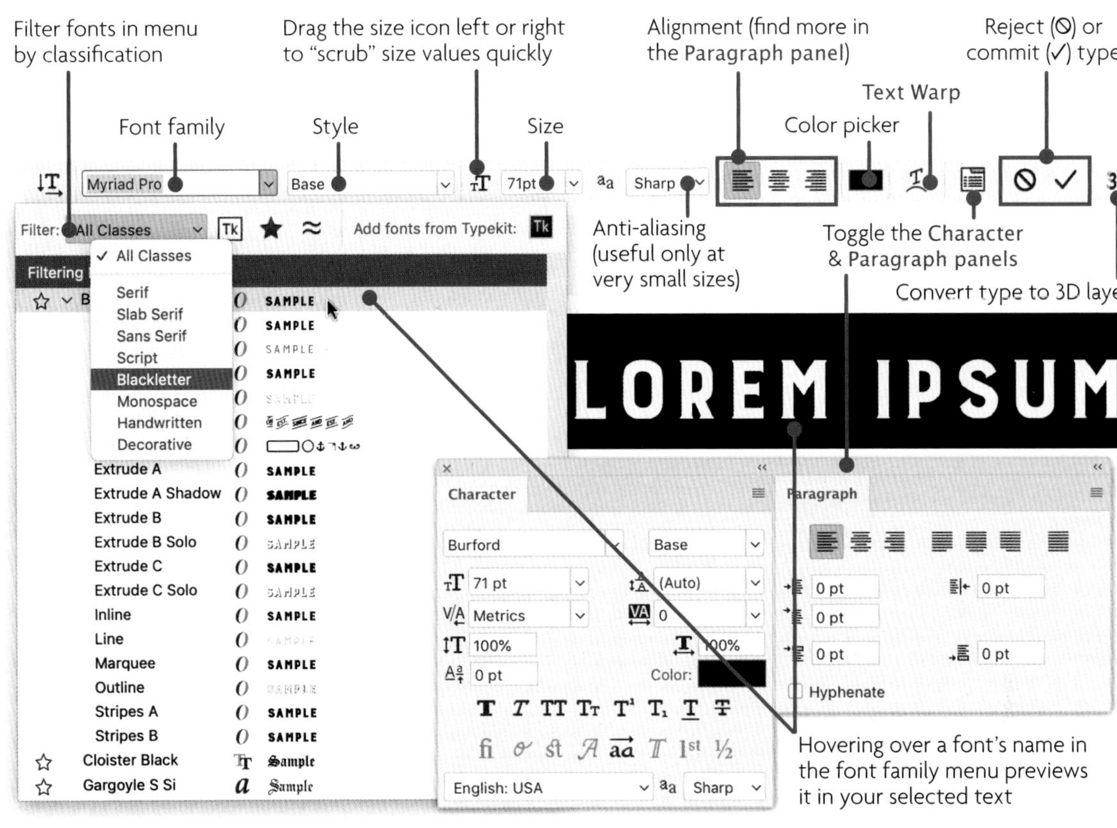

Notable Quirks

While text is highlighted, you're editing it, as you would expect. If you move the cursor slightly beyond the highlighting, however, it becomes the Move tool! Dragging then allows you to move the text that is still being edited. Move the cursor farther from the highlighted text, and the Move tool cursor becomes an arrow. Clicking then commits the edits to your text. By default, your text can also be committed by pressing return/Enter or Escape! If using the Escape key to commit text is odd to you, you can disable that behavior in the Preferences.

Paragraph Text is contained in a box. If you have more text than fits in that box, it will be "overset" and you won't see it. A small plus-sign appears in the lower-right corner of the text box to indicate this state. Just resize the text or the box and all should be well.

Speaking of resizing, the box's handles at each corner and in the middle of each side allow you to transform the box. However, if you hold down ⌘/Ctrl, resizing the Paragraph Text box resizes the text in it too. This works with Point Text as well. Holding that key produces transform handles around the perimeter of the text. In both cases, holding ⌘/Ctrl and dragging with the cursor anywhere outside the transform box will rotate the text. Paragraph Text allows rotation without holding down a key, but only when the cursor is very near to the corners of the text box.

Playful Type

If you wish to give your text a bit of a twist, literally, you may use the Text Warp button to access this nondestructive feature. That means you can revisit it as necessary.

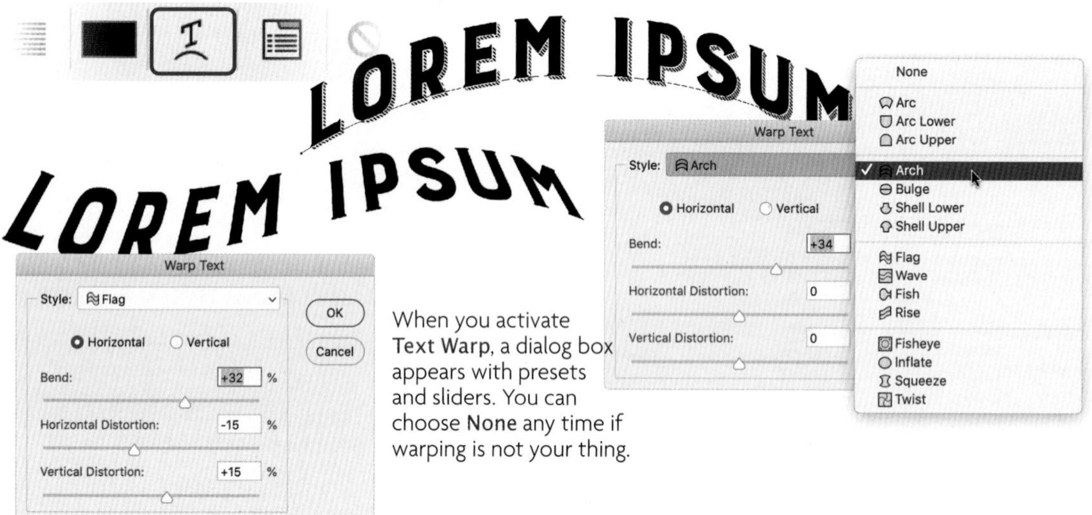

When you activate **Text Warp**, a dialog box appears with presets and sliders. You can choose **None** any time if warping is not your thing.

Adjustment Layers

Best created via the Adjustments panel, these give us nondestructive ways of adjusting the color and tone of layers below (behind) them. Most often, they do not increase file size. Since adjustments are covered extensively in the next chapter, I'm restricting this section to general concerns, and even many of these are covered in more depth elsewhere.

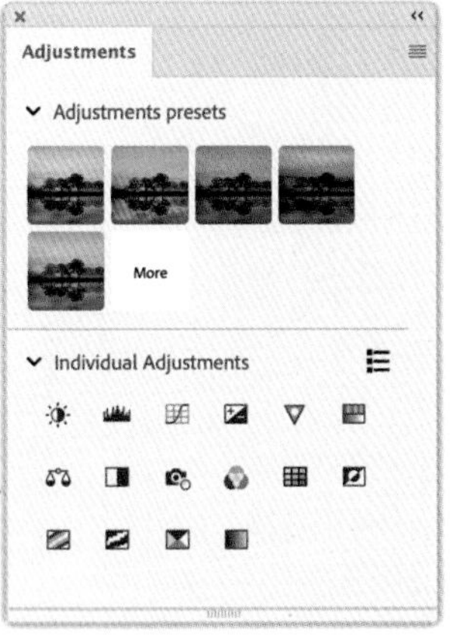

Beta As I write, this panel is undergoing a redesign and has this arrangement in the beta version. The top section creates groups of adjustments to achieve an overall visual effect.

The lower section can display individual adjustments as icons or as a list including their names.

The document in these illustrations has, at the start, two layers: one for the sky and another for the ring. With the top layer (the ring) highlighted, I clicked on an icon in the Adjustments panel (for a Curves adjustment this time, to lighten the image). The newly created adjustment layer appears above the ring layer and affects all the layers below it—in this case, just two layers.

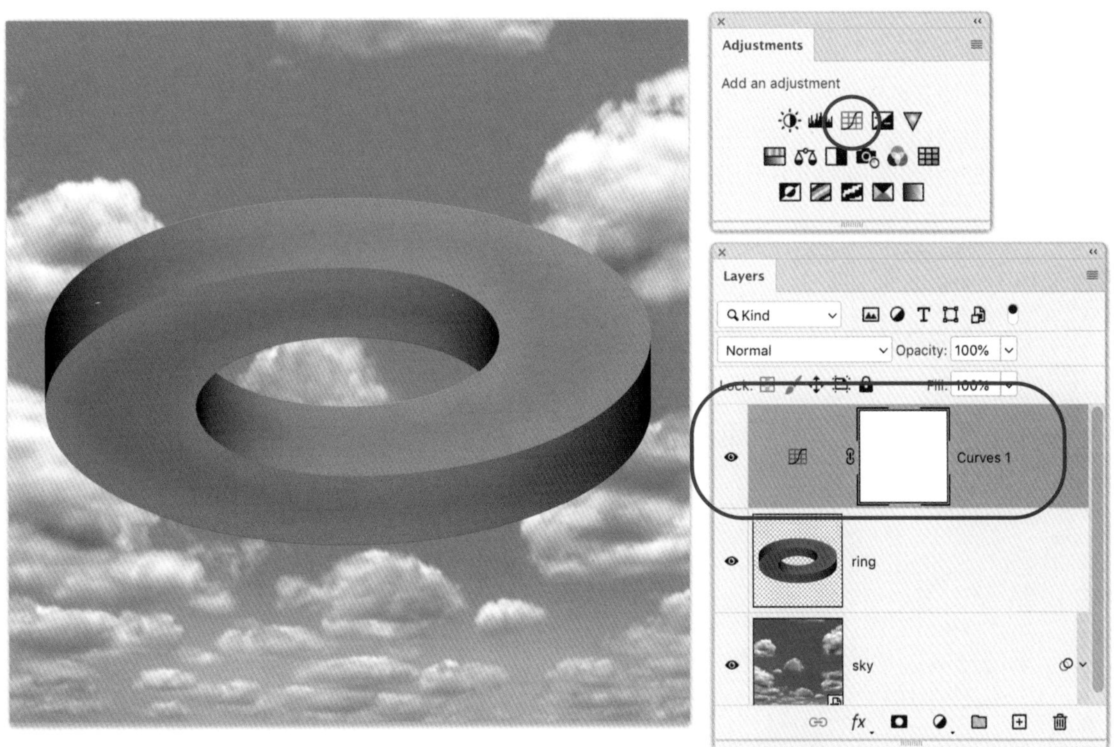

An adjustment layer needn't affect all layers, though. If it's moved lower in the stack, the layers above it remain unadjusted.

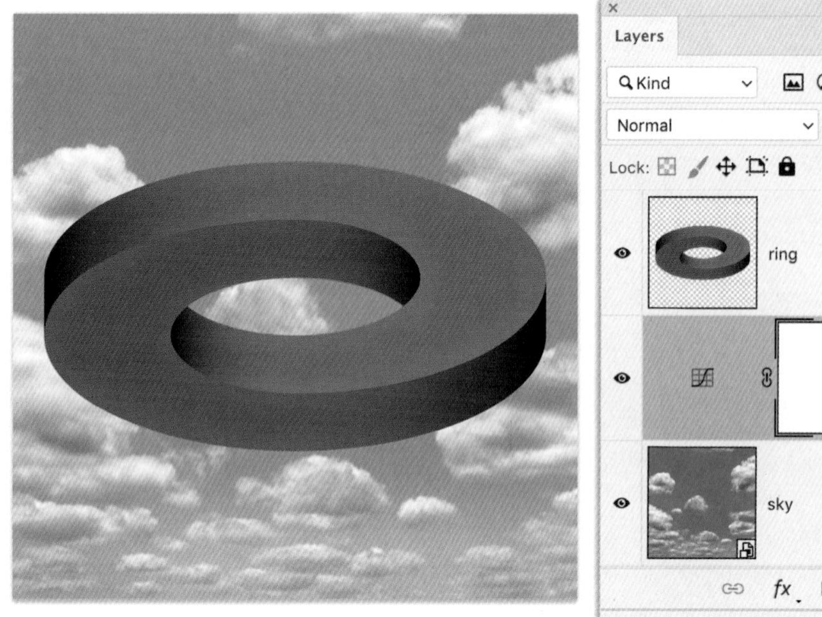

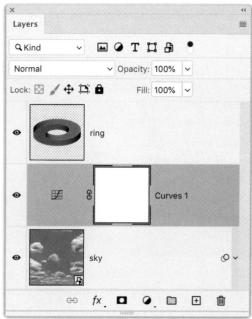

It's possible to limit the scope of an adjustment layer in other ways too. You can "clip" the adjustment to the layer below it by clicking the clip button in the Properties panel, or you can mask the adjustment layer. Note that the clipped adjustment layer is indented below, and has a small arrow pointing at the layer below it. Only the ring is lightened here.

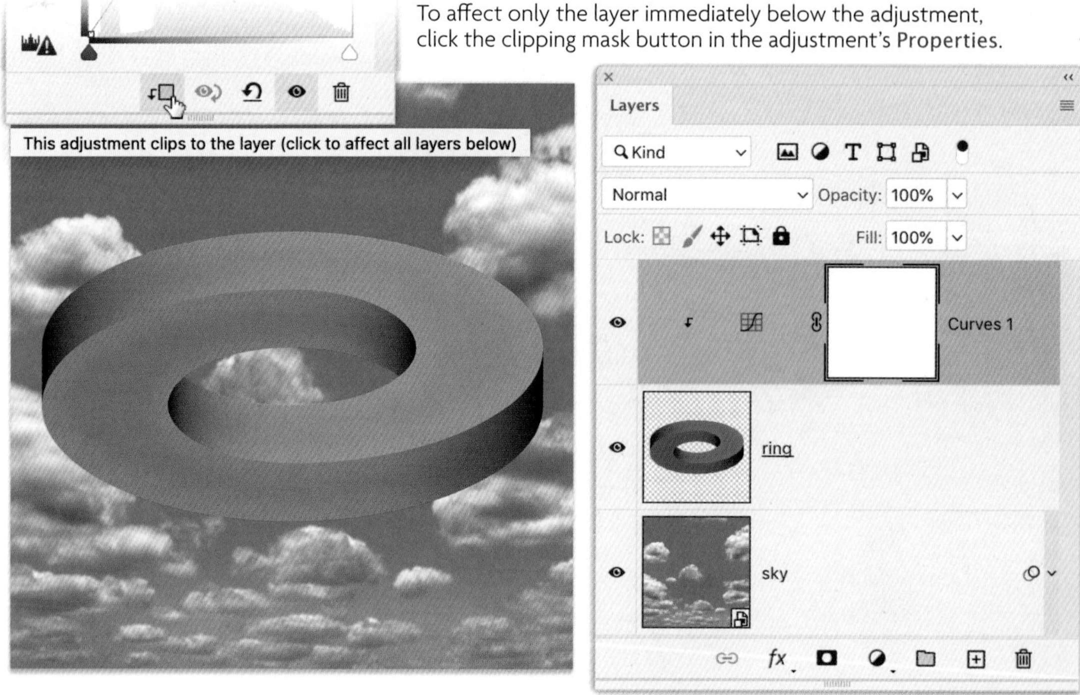

To affect only the layer immediately below the adjustment, click the clipping mask button in the adjustment's Properties.

Often, we can create a selection of the area we want to adjust. With that selection active (the "marching ants" in motion), we then create the adjustment. The adjustment layer will have a mask in the shape of our selection. Existing adjustment layers have masks, too, but are filled with white, hiding nothing. Painting with black on the mask will hide the adjustment.

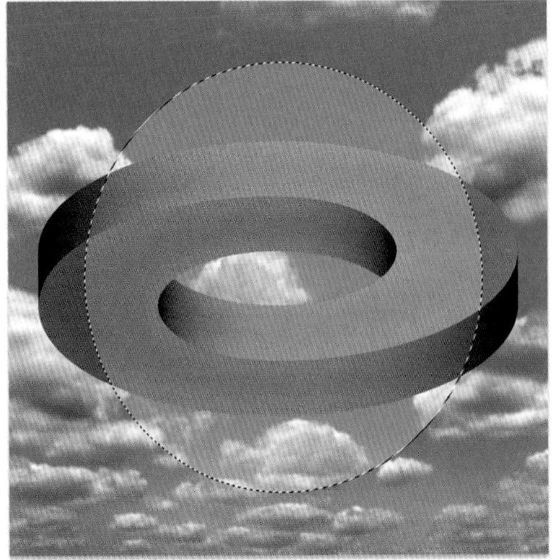

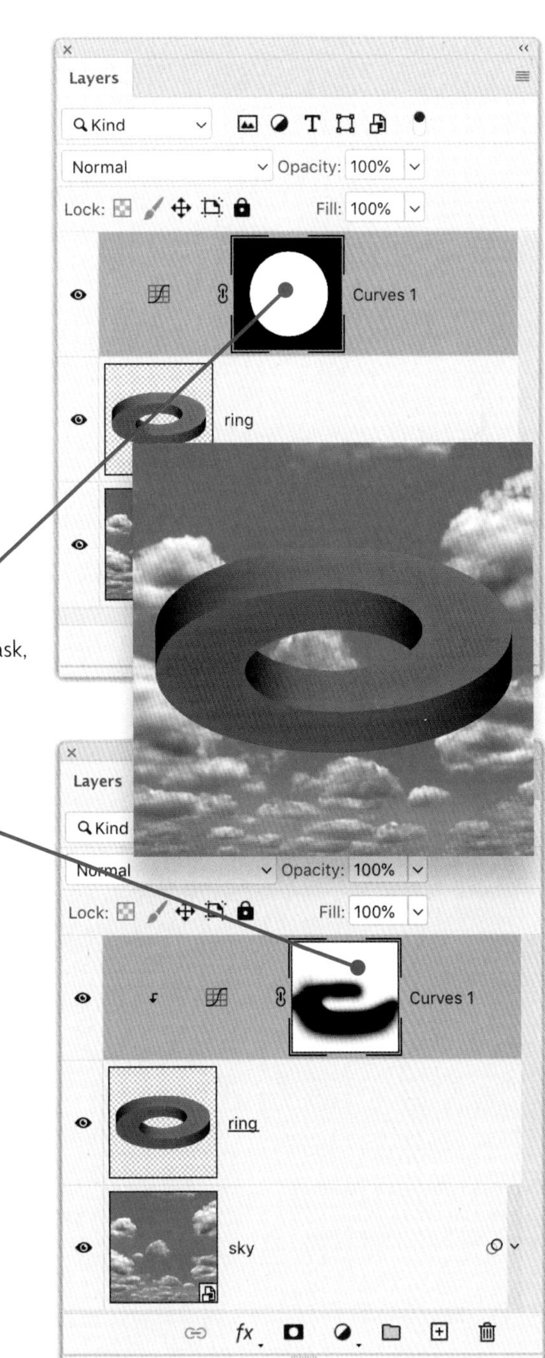

To the right, the original for reference.

Above, an elliptical marquee was made before the adjustment layer. When the adjustment is made, it's automatically masked to that elliptical area. In a layer mask, black represents the part of the layer that is hidden.

Below, an existing adjustment layer's mask was painted. All adjustment layers have a mask at their creation. This adjustment layer was clipped to the ring layer, then its mask was painted with black to hide even more of its lightening effect.

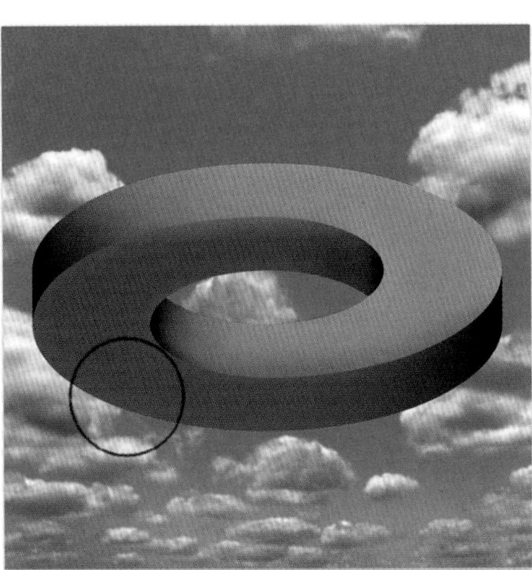

Groups

In darker, sadder times, when we wanted to apply some effect or filter to something composed of multiple layers, we had to merge those layers into one. Thus, to apply a drop shadow effect or blur filter, for example, we would either sacrifice the compositional freedom layers gives us, or merge those multiple layers into yet another layer, then hide the originals in case we needed to recompose. I still remember the shortcut to create a merged copy of multiple selected layers: ⌘-option-shift-E/Ctrl-Alt-Shift-E. It just rolls off the tongue.

Depending on the task, we now have more elegant nondestructive solutions that are easier to edit later. For filters and transformations that need to be applied to multiple layers, we should use Smart Objects, discussed later in this chapter. For multilayer effects, masks, and adjustments, as well for as organizing, we have groups. After both are discussed, we'll talk more about deciding when to use each.

Making a Group

The process is easy. You first highlight the layers to be grouped by clicking near the name of the first one, then, to select discontiguous layers, holding down ⌘/Ctrl while clicking near the names of the others. If the layers to be grouped are already contiguous, you may click the topmost or bottommost layer, then shift-click the one at the other end, highlighting the whole range of layers. Then, use ⌘-G/Ctrl-G or Layer > Group Layers.

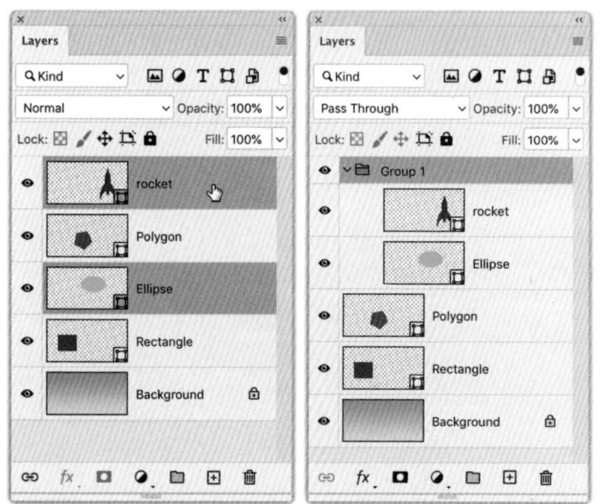

Two discontiguous layers highlighted, then grouped. Note that once grouped, they are contiguous with the group at the position of the higher layer.

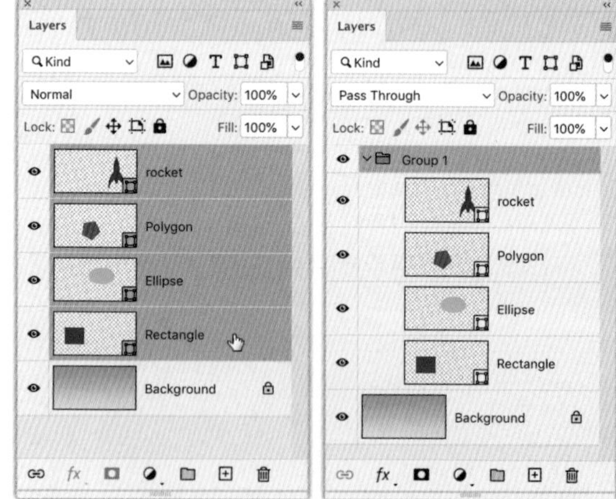

Four contiguous layers highlighted, then grouped.

If you change a blending option of the group, such as Opacity, the grouped objects don't blend with each other, but the group blends with the rest of the document as if the layers had been merged. We discuss how to leverage that in the last two chapters of this Compendium.

To easily select either the group or the layers within it, there are options for the Move tool that you'll need to adjust. Choose the Move tool and note the Auto-Select options on the left side of the Options Bar. There, you may select Group or Layer.

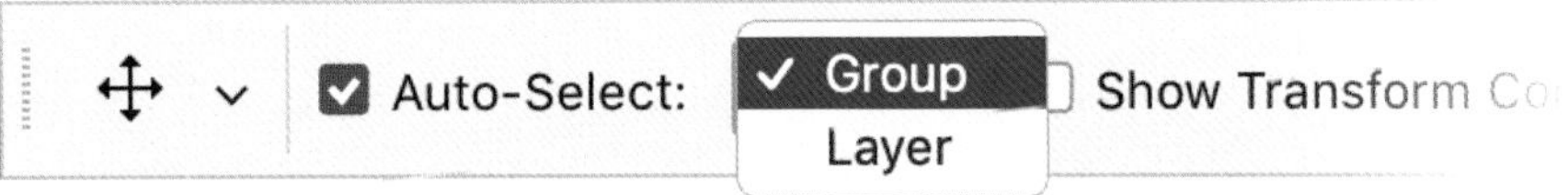

If Group is selected, clicking on or dragging any layer in the group selects or moves the whole group. This behavior is similar to other programs in which objects can be grouped, thus it is the default. If Layer is selected, clicking on or dragging any layer in a group selects or moves only that layer. With Auto-Select disabled, you must highlight the layer or group you want to move before using the Move tool. This is preferred when there is partial opacity: Although it looks like you're clicking on one layer's content, Auto-Select moves or selects a translucent layer above it instead. I change this setting *frequently*!

Both Like and Unlike Individual Layers

At first glance, groups appear to be no more than folders in which to stash our layers. They are! Like layers, groups can also have masks. So if you have several layers that need the same mask, you can first group them, then mask the group. Reminder: The process of masking is covered at length in chapter 4, "Selections & Masks" (page 269).

As mentioned above, groups can have blending modes or partial opacity, causing the group to look much like a merged layer. Groups may also have layer styles (effects like drop shadows) and may be used as the base "layer" of a clipping mask. See "Clipping Mask" (page 295) to know more about that feature.

In all those ways, groups act like single layers, but with the flexibility of having editable content. But they also allow us to corral layers with adjustments in an interesting way. As mentioned above, adjustment layers typically affect all the layers below them. This is true even if that adjustment layer is in a group, *unless* the blend mode of that group is changed.

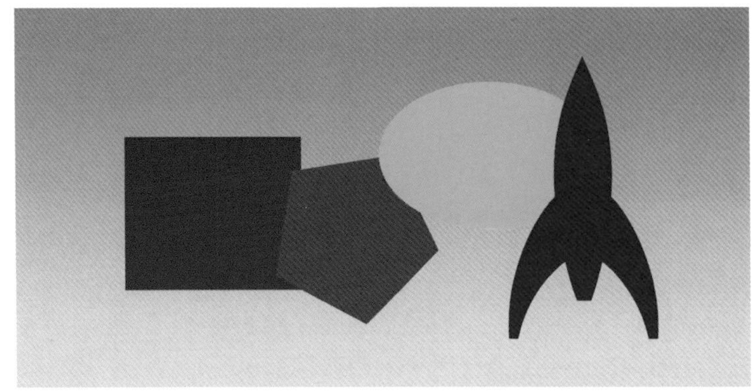

Here, we have a group of four objects above a Background containing a sky-like gradient. When a group is first made, its blend mode is one unique to groups, called Pass Through. As that name implies, each layer in the group will visually interact with layers below the group as they would had there been no group at all. So if an adjustment layer is inserted somewhere in the group, it will affect the Background as well. That is, its effect will "pass through" the group to other layers.

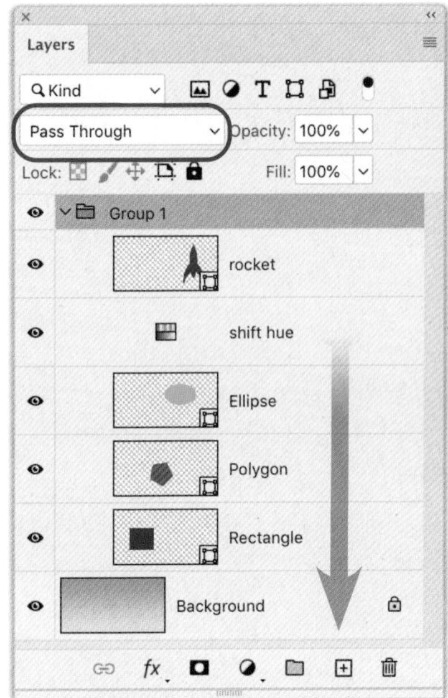

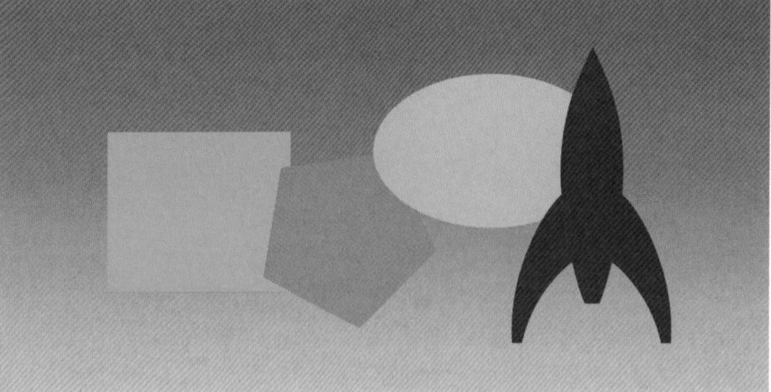

An adjustment layer has been introduced to the group just below its topmost layer. It is shifting the hues of everything below it, including the gradated blue background.

That is because the group's blend mode is still set to Pass Through.

When a group's blend mode is set to Normal, you may not notice any change at all—unless the group contains something that affected layers below the group, like this adjustment.

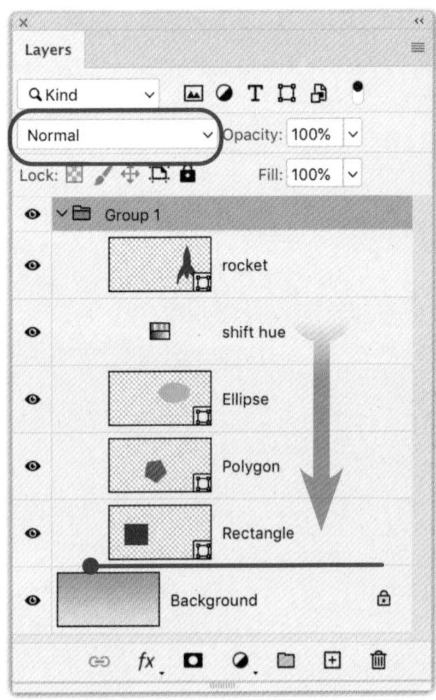

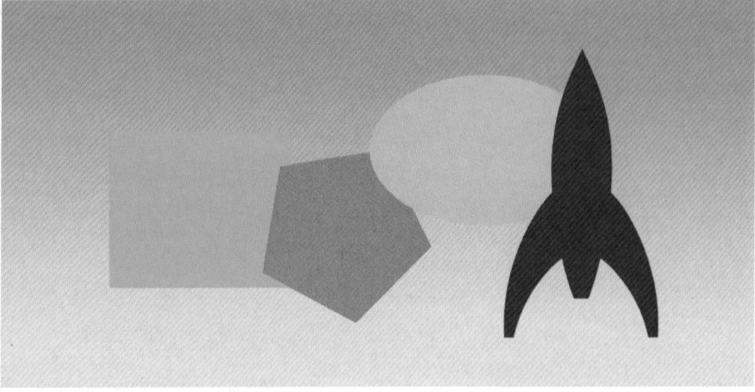

When the group's blend mode is set to Normal, the layers in the group are allowed to affect only each other. Thus, the adjustment's hue shifting stops at the rectangle.

This may seem unnecessarily complicated until you consider that we or someone we work for may want a change to the composition of this document. Had the layers been merged, we'd have to recreate all the pieces again. Groups give us most of the advantages of merging, but none of its adverse consequences.

Neat and Clean

Finally, let's not forget the most modest use of groups: neatening and organizing a complex and messy Layers panel. Even seemingly straightforward projects can get messier than anticipated.

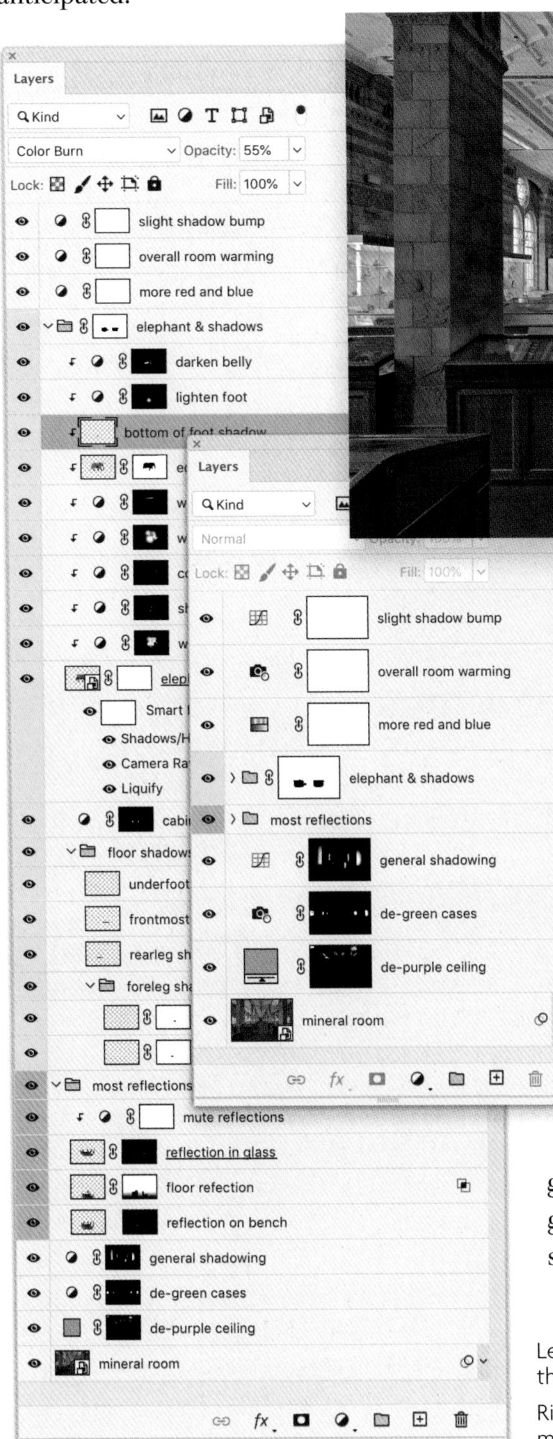

I love showing this project to students. Not because it's any great wonder, but because unlike so many demonstrations that make Photoshop users look like magicians, this one shows that even with the simple objective of putting an elephant in a room, there was real, messy work to be done.

When I dissect the piece for my students, groups help immensely. And, as a further aid, I right-clicked on two of the groups and chose a highlight color so I could better distinguish the contents of each group.

If you look at the full Layers panel, you may be able to see groups inside groups. I also named nearly every layer and group. I wish I could honestly say I always do so, because I thank myself later when I do.

Left: Layers panel with small thumbnails and groups expanded.

Right: Collapsed groups and medium-sized thumbnails.

Layers & Smart Objects

Artboards

Web and user interface (UI) designers often like to visualize how a design looks at different device sizes or, as illustrated here, how a site's pages flow. Artboards can help.

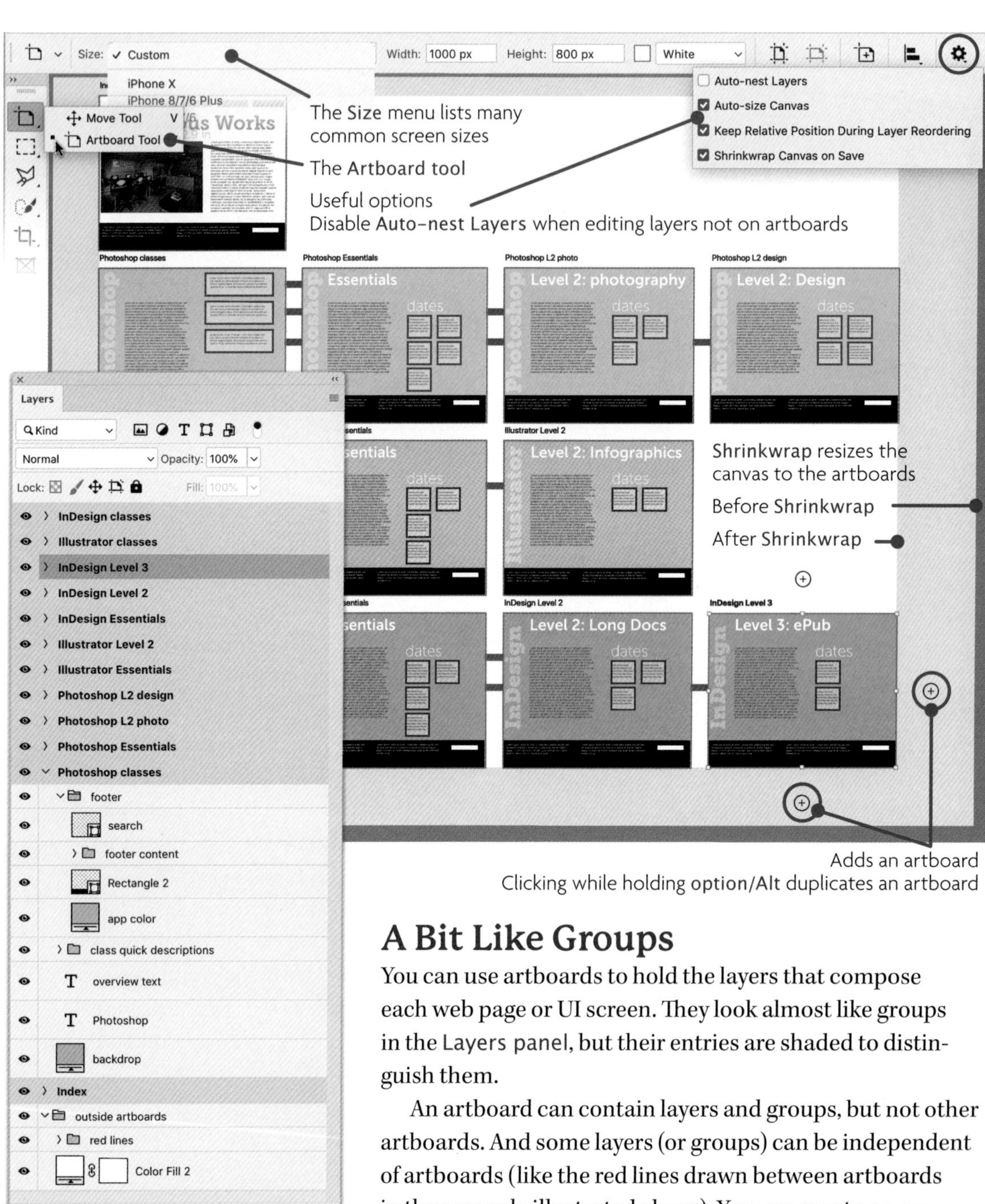
The Size menu lists many common screen sizes
The Artboard tool
Useful options
Disable Auto-nest Layers when editing layers not on artboards
Shrinkwrap resizes the canvas to the artboards
Before Shrinkwrap
After Shrinkwrap
Adds an artboard
Clicking while holding option/Alt duplicates an artboard

A Bit Like Groups

You can use artboards to hold the layers that compose each web page or UI screen. They look almost like groups in the Layers panel, but their entries are shaded to distinguish them.

An artboard can contain layers and groups, but not other artboards. And some layers (or groups) can be independent of artboards (like the red lines drawn between artboards in the example illustrated above). You can create a new document with artboards in mind or add them to an existing document. My preference in either case is to populate the first artboard and then duplicate it, especially if the content is similar in each. When you select an artboard with the Artboard tool, you'll see plus signs on each side. Clicking one makes a new, empty artboard, but option/Alt-clicking makes a duplicate.

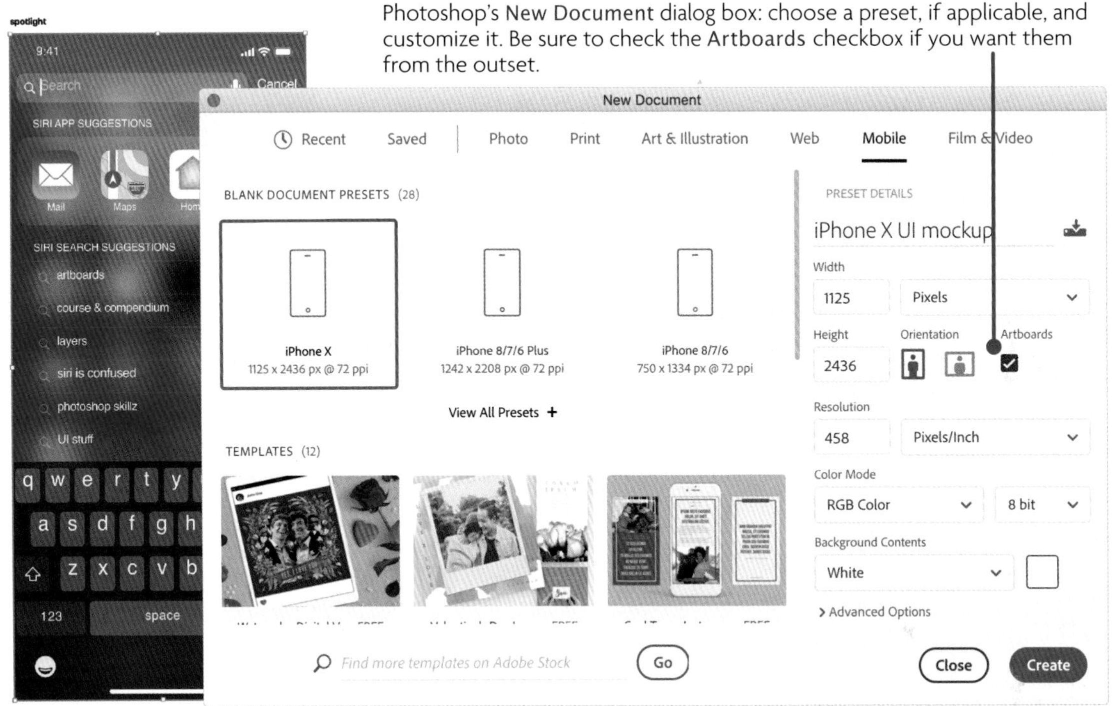

Photoshop's New Document dialog box: choose a preset, if applicable, and customize it. Be sure to check the Artboards checkbox if you want them from the outset.

If you have content that is repeated on each artboard, you will want to encase that content in a Smart Object, the next topic in this chapter. Copies of a Smart Object use the exact same assets. So editing one Smart Object's content changes the content of all of them, saving time and resources.

Smart Objects

Did I save the best for last? I believe I did. Smart Objects offer almost all of the advantages of groups and very few of their limitations. Like a group, Smart Objects (SOs) are containers that can hold all kinds of Photoshop layers, including groups. But they can also contain Illustrator graphics, raw image data, and other SOs. And *very* unlike layers or groups, you can nondestructively perform edits like applying filters and transformations that are destructive when performed on any other type of layer.

Creating Smart Objects

There are several ways to create a Smart Object: by converting one or more existing layers, or by inserting graphics from other documents (or even some other applications).

Converting

I wish this were called "encasing." Like Han Solo in carbonite or Tony Stark in his Iron Man suit, the contents of Smart Objects are protected from abuse. When I need to perform a potentially destructive action like using a filter (e.g., Gaussian Blur) or applying a transformation (like Puppet Warp or Free Transform), I usually do so after converting the subject to a Smart Object.

Simply right-click near the name of a layer and choose Convert to Smart Object. If you'd like to convert more than one layer, highlight each before right-clicking near the name of one of them. If the layers are stacked contiguously, click on the top one's name, then shift-click on the last one's name to highlight them all. You can do that in the other direction too. If the layers aren't contiguous, click the first, then ⌘/Ctrl click the others.

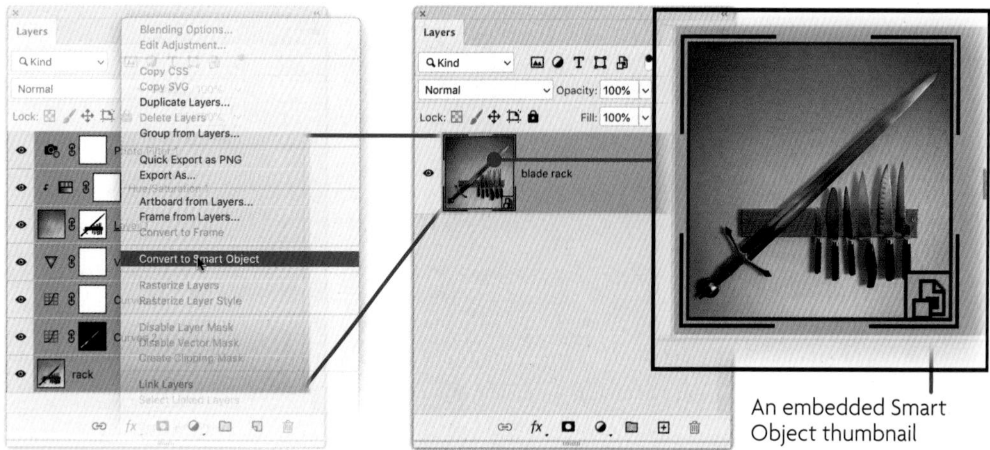

An embedded Smart Object thumbnail

The result startles the first time: it *looks like* you've merged the layers. There is a small but significant reassurance in the lower-right corner of the Smart Object's thumbnail. That icon lets you know that all those layers you had are safely inside their armor.

Any filter that's applied becomes a "Smart Filter" and can be edited or removed later. This is a powerful aid to building intricate visual effects. If you should transform the SO—for example, scaling it—you can reverse that easily when needed. These approaches are discussed at length chapter 5, "Filters & Transforms" (page 296).

Warning: If you attempt to retouch or paint on the SO, a potentially confusing warning message will appear. ***Clicking OK to Rasterize will destroy the contents of the Smart Object!*** The right answer is to choose Cancel, then create an empty layer above the Smart Object onto which to paint or put repairs.

The engineers are not dictators. The attitude is "well, if you *really* want to do this, we'll let you." For too many users, however, the term "rasterize" is rather opaque. It used to have a simple meaning: convert vector artwork into a raster (pixel-based) image. The term has been expanded beyond vector art to include *anything* that isn't simple pixels. So, if you clicked OK in that warning dialog, you would have a single pixel layer.

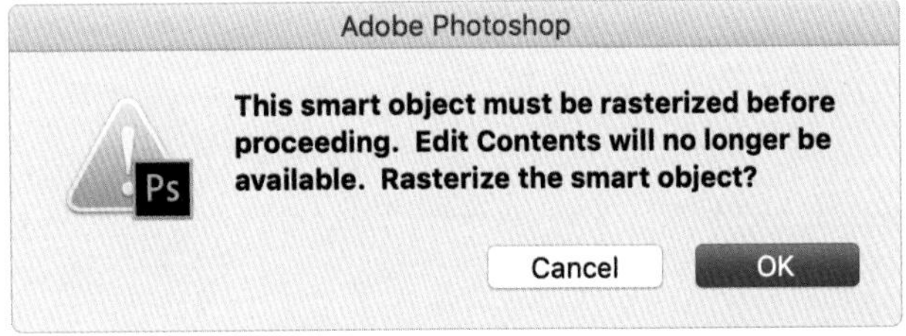

Placing

Sometimes I might have an entire file that I'd like to use as part of a Photoshop project. When that's the case, I choose to "place" it into the project's document.

To do this, go to File > Place Embedded... or Place Linked.... (The difference between the two is discussed below.) When you've chosen a file to place, it will appear on the canvas with transform handles so you can adjust its size immediately. If you look in the Options Bar, you'll see how much it's been scaled. You can choose to disallow any initial scaling in the General Preferences.

Placing other files allows us to perform Photoshop actions on Illustrator artwork, for example, while still retaining the ability to edit it in Illustrator. Even other Photoshop files can be used. For the sake of the space-time continuum, I've never tried to place a document into itself.

One of the more powerful options is placing raw files. There are several ways of doing this and many advantages. The methods and reasons are discussed both later in this Compendium (see chapter 7, "Camera Raw & Lightroom," page 354) and in the Course (in the chapter "Adobe Camera Raw & Software-Aided Photography," see "Processing Images with ACR" on page 102).

Pasting

When you paste content into a Photoshop file, it will become an embedded Smart Object. As is the case when placing, you are given transform handles to size it.

Linking vs Embedding

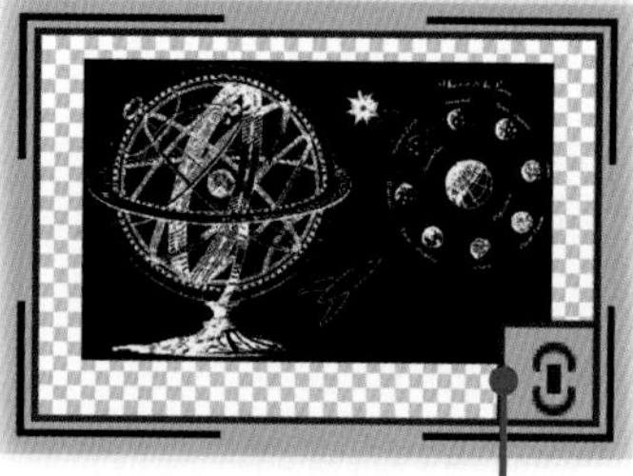

Linked Smart Object thumbnail

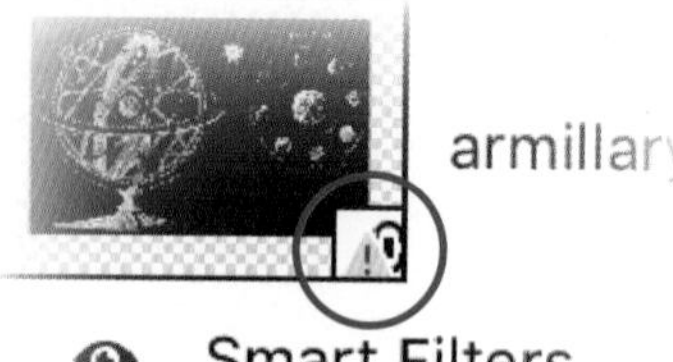

When the content of a linked Smart Object has changed, you should update it

Whether linking or embedding has the advantage depends on the circumstance. For example, if you need to use an infographic in several Photoshop projects, especially if that graphic may be edited later, then linking is the clear winner. When that infographic is edited in Illustrator (perhaps because the information it illustrates has changed), you should note a warning in the Smart Object thumbnail the next time you open any of the Photoshop documents that used it.

To update a Smart Object with modified content, right-click near its name in the Layers panel (*not* on the thumbnail), then choose Update Modified Content. Better, especially if there are several out-of-date Smart Objects, choose Update All Modified Content. In fact, I see no harm in choosing the latter every time.

When you need to provide your Photoshop project to someone else or move it to another computer, you will also need to supply any linked assets. This may sound like a time-consuming task, especially if you have many linked SOs, but there is a command to do this for you! The process is called "packaging," and the command is found at File > Package. This creates a folder whose name is based on the Photoshop file's, and in which you'll find a copy of that file and a folder called "Links" with copies of all the linked assets. InDesign and Illustrator both have this feature too.

An embedded Smart Object can be converted into a linked one. Right-click near its name and choose Convert to Linked…. You'll then be asked to choose where the new linked file should be. As with all linked Smart Objects, if the linked file is moved, the Smart Object's content can not be edited. Attempting to do so results in a dialog box requiring you to locate the file.

Workflows & Limitations

Lightroom and Raw Workflow

For those who use Adobe Lightroom, I recommend doing as much as possible with your raw images in Lightroom before turning to Photoshop. That's because *all* edits in Lightroom are nondestructive and can easily be revisited. Once an image is passed to Photoshop, a new TIFF file is generated that will be Photoshop's responsibility.

So when I need to edit in Photoshop a raw image that I manage in Lightroom, I right-click it in Lightroom and choose Edit In > Open as Smart Object in Photoshop…. When finished editing in Photoshop, simply Save, and a TIFF file is created with "-Edit" appended to the name, located in the same folder as the original, and managed by Lightroom. Subsequent edits to that TIFF should then be done in Photoshop, however. To do so, right-click its Lightroom thumbnail and choose Edit In > Adobe Photoshop. In the dialog that appears, choose Edit Original, meaning the TIFF, rather than generating yet another copy. This approach allows us to maximize the features of each of these two programs with the fewest number of files.

You may also set Adobe Camera Raw to supply Smart Objects to Photoshop (see "Workflow Options" on page 357). When you save the file that opens in Photoshop, you may choose any location for it.

In either case (Lightroom or ACR), the document you edit in Photoshop has a Smart Object whose content is raw data. Double-clicking its thumbnail will open Adobe Camera Raw to allow edits. You'll see all the edits you performed in ACR or Lightroom before pushing that data to Photoshop, which you can now alter.

Note: When editing the Smart Object's content, you aren't editing the original raw file, but rather a *copy* embedded in Photoshop. So the raw edits you make won't work their way back to the original capture. This is fine because other edits you've done to the Photoshop file (the SO's context) are likely the motivation to edit the SO.

Adobe Illustrator to Photoshop Workflow

You can File > Place Linked or Embedded or Edit > Paste Illustrator artwork into a Photoshop file. As discussed earlier, placing can either link or embed the original Illustrator document in its entirety. Pasting always embeds, but does allow you to be more selective about the exact content of the Smart Object that's created. In other words, you can copy just a small piece of a larger illustration to be pasted into Photoshop. Once embedded, the SO can be converted to a linked one.

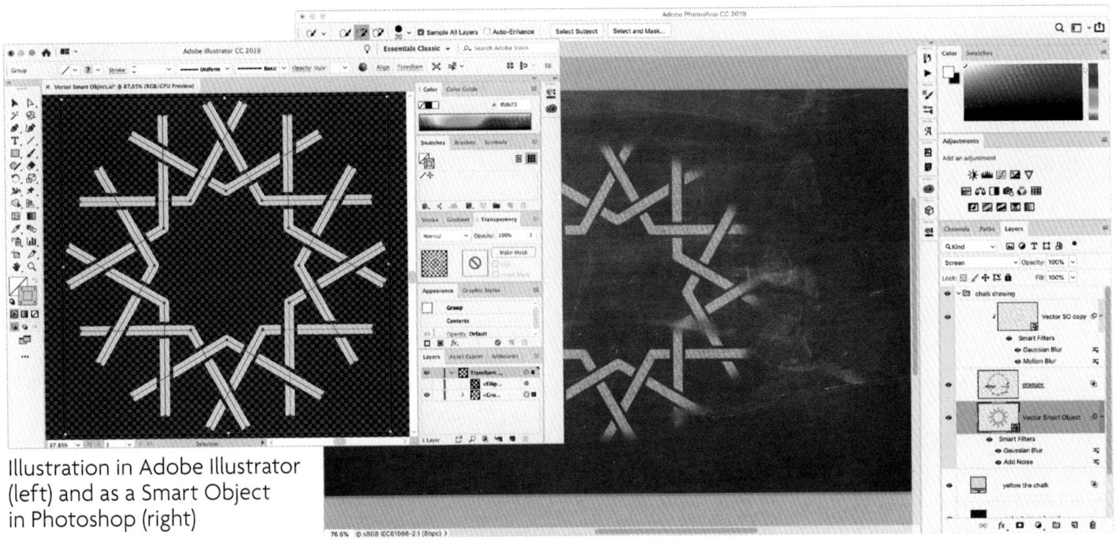

Illustration in Adobe Illustrator (left) and as a Smart Object in Photoshop (right)

When you double-click the Smart Object thumbnail, Adobe Illustrator will launch so you can edit its content. As always, simply save your edits, and the SO updates.

General Photoshop Use

In general Photoshop work, I convert one or more layers into Smart Objects if I need to apply a transformation or filter, since those are otherwise destructive processes. There are, however, a few transformations and filters that can't yet be applied to SOs. With each version of Photoshop, the list of those shrinks. If the filter or transform you need is grayed out when a Smart Object is highlighted, you've found one! In those rare cases, you will need to apply that function to an ordinary layer.

Likely the most general way to do so is to first apply allowed filters and transforms to the SO, if you need any. Then duplicate the Smart Object (⌘-J/Ctrl-J) and rasterize the copy (right-click near its name and choose Rasterize Layer). I also usually hide the SO by clicking its eye icon. I won't delete it because I may need it again, especially if I regret the actions I perform on its rasterized copy.

Frame Layers

No, I didn't forget to include this kind of layer. I include it here because it's extremely limited and use of the Frame tool creates Smart Objects. If a layer other than the Background layer is present, a frame drawn with the Frame tool will automatically contain (or "nest," in Photoshop parlance) the topmost layer, which is converted to a Smart Object. If you wish to frame a layer other than the top one, you will have to either lock all the layers above it (covered later in this chapter) or move the desired layer to the top. If you want to frame a Background, click its padlock to convert it to a pixel layer. If there was an empty frame when unlocking a Background, that frame will now contain the former Background.

As of this writing, I find the Frame tool frustrating and unwieldy in all but the very simplest (e.g., single layer) documents. Also, it is limited to rectangles and ellipses, although shapes drawn with the shape tools can be converted to frames. In that case, I'd prefer to use those shapes as vector masks, which are far more flexible and only slightly more difficult to manipulate. Read "Vector Masks" (page 294) to learn more about them.

Layer Comps

An Alternative to Multiple Files

The Layer Comps panel is a wonderful yet woefully underutilized feature. With it, we can capture "snapshots" of nearly the entire state of the Layers panel and then return to them later. This provides us with a way to experiment with different compositions and settings without having to make multiple documents. UI and web designers use this feature to show different states of an app. Authors of Photoshop books use this to illustrate stages of a process. Anyone can use this feature to show a client different versions of any project.

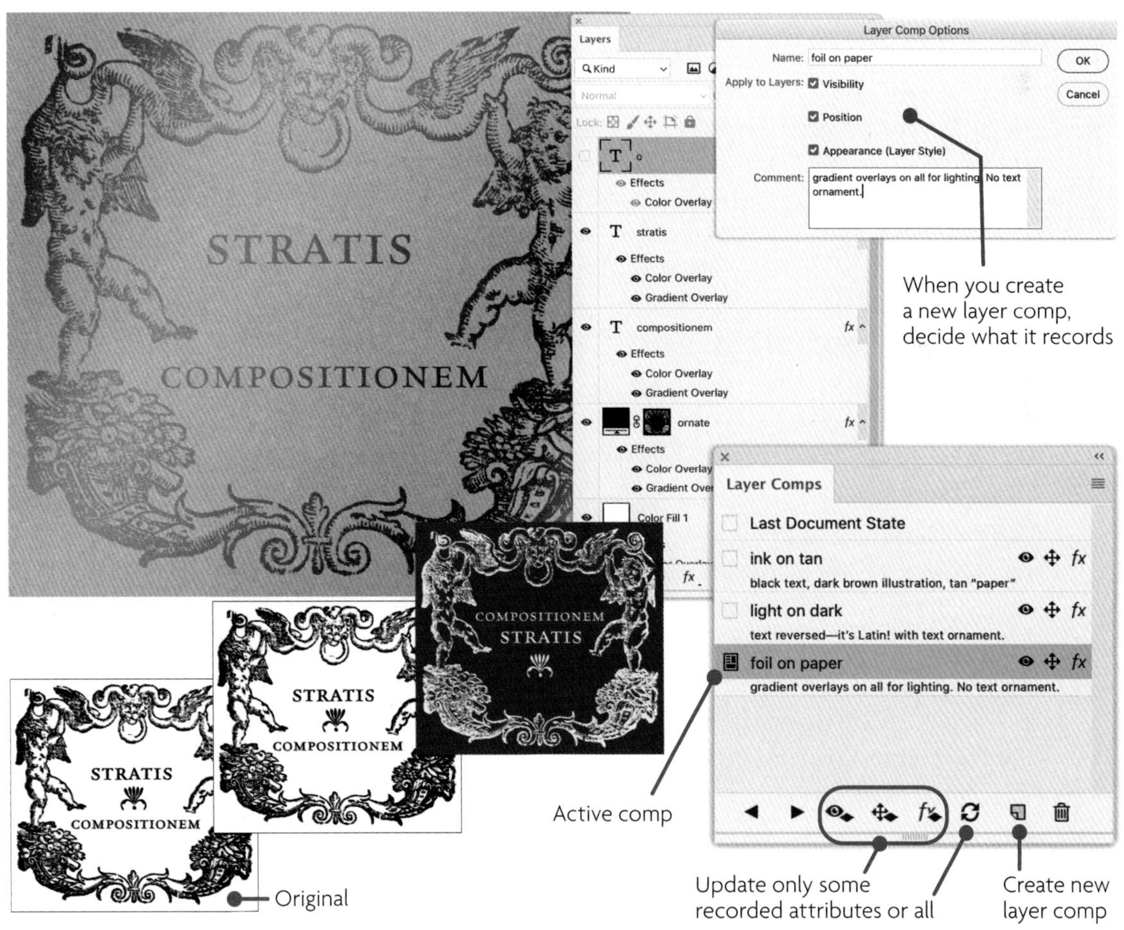

In this example, I started with three text layers and two color fill layers, one of which is masked to form an old-style printer's mark. That mark and the text were and remain black, while the bottommost layer is filled with white. I kept each word and a small text ornament on separate layers to make it easier to change the composition.

What Is Recorded?

When you create a new layer comp, you supply a name for it and add a comment that may help you or a colleague to know something about that comp. Users of Illustrator can choose a layer comp (and read its comment) when placing PSD files, for example.

You also decide which of three major attributes will be applied to layers when this layer comp is chosen later: *visibility* (whether the eye icon is on or off); *position* on the canvas of layer content; and *appearance*, which includes layer styles (including effects like drop shadows), opacity, blend modes, and other blending options.

A layer comp does ***not*** record or change a layer's content. Since I used color fill layers, I could easily change their color by double-clicking on their thumbnails. But that change of content isn't recorded by a layer comp: The color would remain constant no matter which comp I applied. So I used color, gradient, and pattern overlay effects, which a layer comp records and applies easily. For two of the comps I made, I hid the small text ornament layer, and for one I moved the words around. Since I wasn't sure how many attributes I may want to change in each comp, I checked the boxes for all three.

Since comps don't affect actual layer content, they don't capture changes to Smart Filters, nor do they note changes to adjustment layer settings. To accommodate the latter, I duplicate adjustment layers and change the settings on each duplicate, hiding or showing that adjustment layer and using layer comps to record whether it is visible or not. A layer comp can also record the Layer Comps within Smart Objects (page 171).

Applying, Editing, and Updating Layer Comps

Clicking the small space to the left of a layer comp's name applies it. When applied with no changes, an icon appears in that space. This confirms it's applied and that you haven't made any changes to the attributes it governs. For example, if the layer comp you apply doesn't affect position (that box was left unchecked when the layer comp was made), then you move a layer, that icon will remain. But if that layer comp controls appearance and you change the color of a drop shadow, the icon will vanish, since it's no longer in effect. The name will remain highlighted so you know which one has been altered.

To update a layer comp so it incorporates the change you made to the attribute it controls, click the update button while the comp is highlighted. In fact, any change to governed attributes to any layer will be incorporated. Let's say that you've applied a layer comp that controls all the attributes it can (visibility, position, and appearance), and you've changed each of those on some layers. If you wish to update only one of the attributes, one of the three buttons to the left of the overall update will serve.

You should notice that these have icons similar to those to the right of each layer comp's name. These indicate which attributes the layer comp changes when applied. If you wish to add or remove one, or to change the layer comp's name or comment, double-click to the right of the comp's name to open the Layer Comp Options dialog.

Often, I will want to export each comp as a file of its own. So I'll name (or rename) my layer comps concisely and remove the comment because their names and comments become the base names of the files that are generated.

Exporting Layer Comps

To supply your comps to someone who may not have Photoshop, it's usually best to generate a separate file for each one. If that's my goal, I will, as mentioned earlier, name the comps well and succinctly and forego comments. I'll also go through them a last time to be sure they each do what I hope they do! Choose File > Export > Layer Comps to Files….

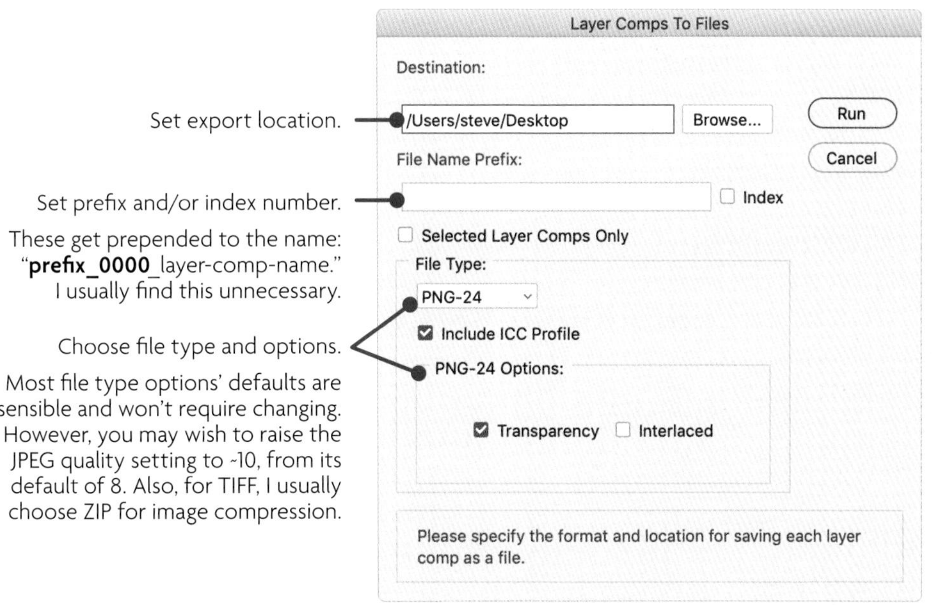
Layer Comps To Files
Destination:
/Users/steve/Desktop
Browse...
Run
Cancel
File Name Prefix:
Index
Selected Layer Comps Only
File Type:
PNG-24
Include ICC Profile
PNG-24 Options:
Transparency
Interlaced
Please specify the format and location for saving each layer comp as a file.
Set export location.
Set prefix and/or index number.
These get prepended to the name: "**prefix_0000**_layer-comp-name." I usually find this unnecessary.
Choose file type and options.
Most file type options' defaults are sensible and won't require changing. However, you may wish to raise the JPEG quality setting to ~10, from its default of 8. Also, for TIFF, I usually choose ZIP for image compression.

The choices are neither startling nor staggering. You choose a destination folder, what kind of files you want (TIFFs or JPEGs, for example), and (if needed) more text and/or a 4-digit index number, which is prepended to each layer comp's name when forming the exported file's name. If my comps are named uniquely, I don't bother with either prefixes or index numbers unless I need to sort them by name later.

Layer Comps within Smart Objects

If a Smart Object's content is a Photoshop document with layer comps, you may choose which comp is displayed via the Properties panel. Here, I used File > Place Linked… (embedded works too) and chose the document shown earlier.

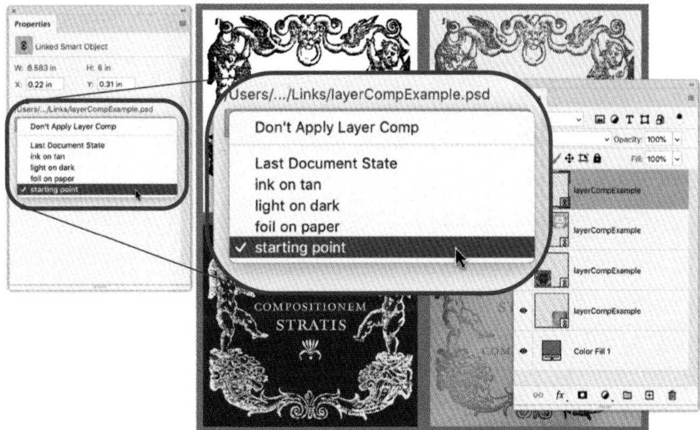
Users/…/Links/layerCompExample.psd
Don't Apply Layer Comp
Last Document State
ink on tan
light on dark
foil on paper
✓ starting point
COMPOSITIONEM
STRATIS

Layers & Smart Objects

Layer Locks & Filtering

At the top of Photoshop's Layers panel you will find two clusters of icons. The topmost cluster filters layers, allowing you to quickly hide layers, revealing only the ones you need to see. The other locks the active layer(s) in different ways.

Locks

These buttons provide a fast way to protect different aspects of layers. Some are more intuitive than others. Hover your cursor over each to see its name.

Lock Transparent Pixels

This lock protects the transparent parts of a layer. If you paint or apply a filter, only the nontransparent pixels are affected. Translucent pixels retain their level of transparency too. In the following illustration, I painted across this layer that contains opaque and translucent pixels.

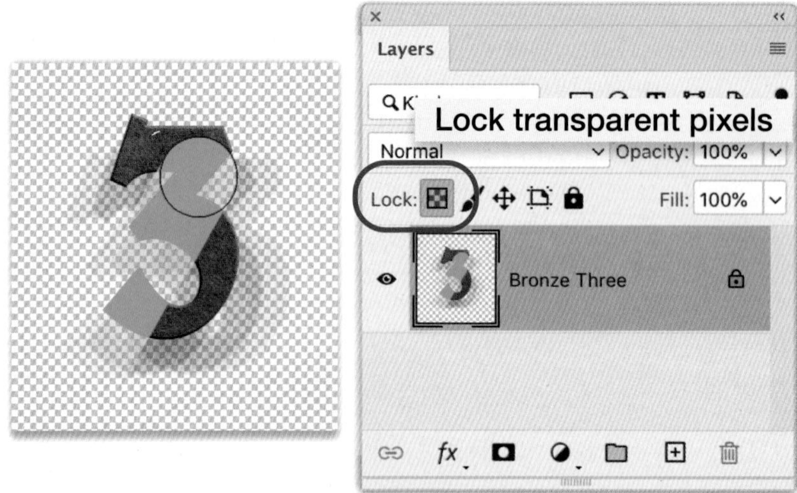

A filter, such as a blur, will affect only the "inside" details: the edge would not get blurry, for example, but the opaque details would. You may transform the layer (e.g., move or scale it).

Lock Image Pixels

This lock prohibits filters, painting, and anything that would alter the details of a layer, but like the previous lock, it does allow you to scale and do other transformations. Disallowed tools will show a forbidding cursor.

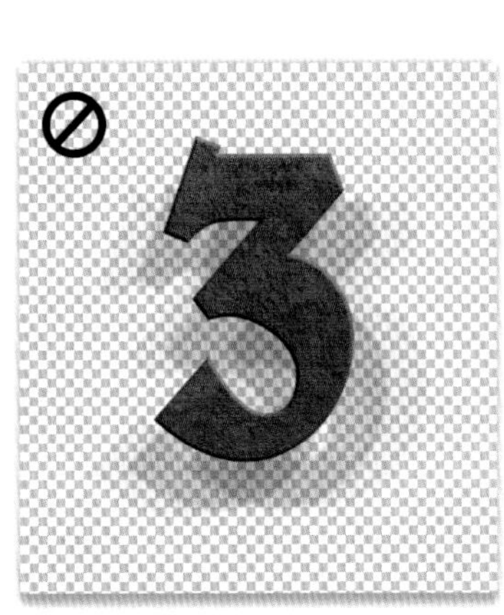

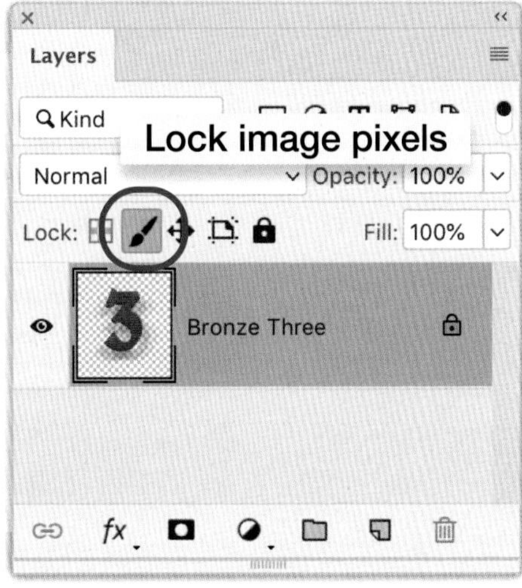

Lock Position

This prevents moving or transforming layers, but not filters or painting. This lock is the most similar to a Background's state.

Prevent Auto-Nesting

Sometimes when we create new artboards, and very often when we create frames with the Frame tool, one or more existing layers are affected.

Applying the fourth lock to layers prevents their automatic enclosure in frames and artboards. Luckily, we can apply locks to multiple layers simultaneously. In this example, the locked layer remains free after drawing with the Frame tool. If I unlock that layer, it would get captured by the frame.

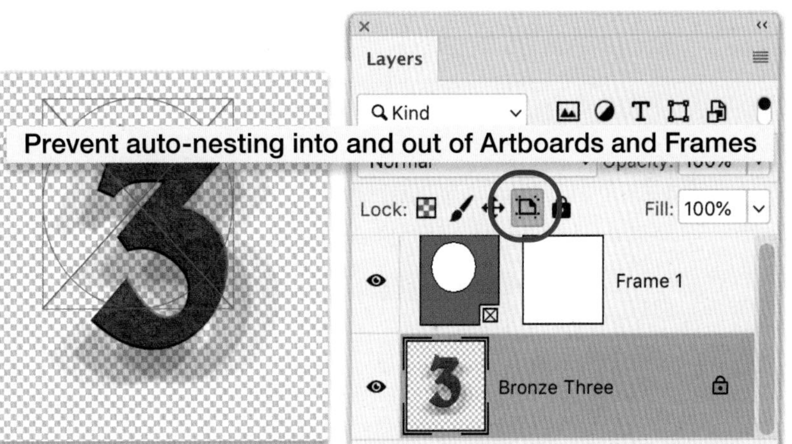

Lock All

This prevents all editing of a layer and is thus the most intuitive. You may still move the layer up and down in the layer stack, but its content is fully protected. Because it's the simplest to use and understand, it's the one I use the most.

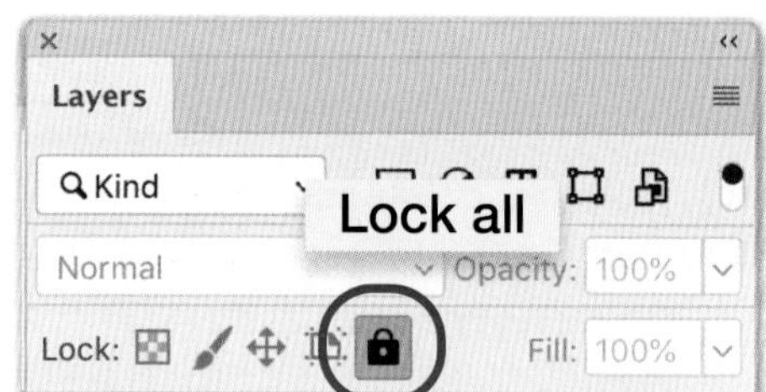

Layer Filters

When layers start to add up, it becomes harder to find the one you need to edit. Filters hide all but the layers you specify. Or you may wish to more easily edit all layers of a certain kind. For example, you may need to change the phrasing of all the text layers in a document. Filtering by Kind and then clicking the T icon will help ensure you're seeing all the text layers and nothing else. Below, I'm filtering to show only adjustment layers.

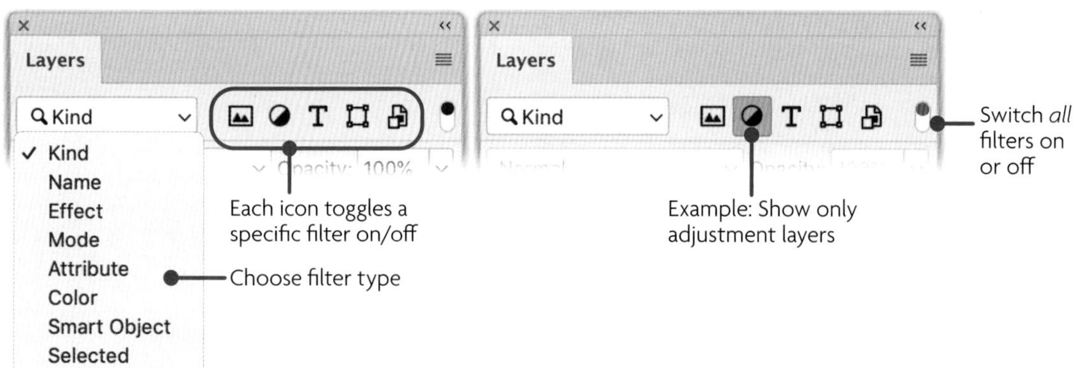

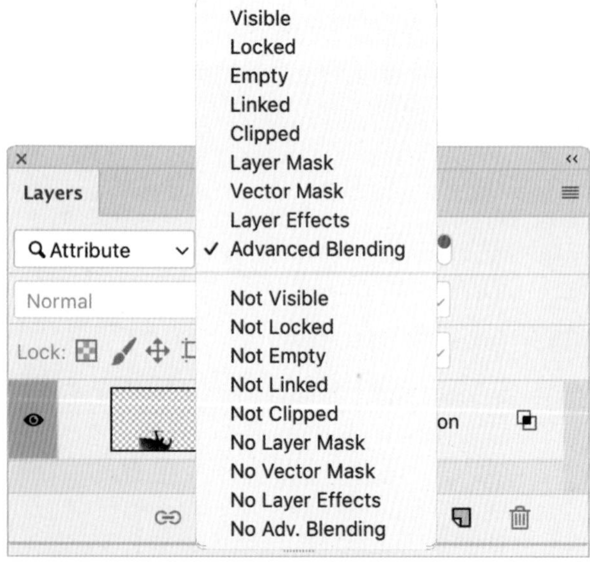

If a filter type offers more than one icon, you may combine them. Thus, I can filter to see both shape and adjustment layers. I cannot, however, filter to see pixel layers that have been clipped: I can filter to see pixel layers (filter type Kind) or clipped layers (Attribute), but since they're different types, I can't do both at once.

Attribute filters are powerful in that they can be both positive and negative. That is, I can choose to see all the locked layers or unlocked ones, or layers with or without layer masks. Here are a few more types:

Name Filters by text in the layers' names.

Effect Shows only those layers with a specific effect, like a drop shadow or bevel.

Mode Shows layers with a specific blend mode.

Color Useful if you've applied color labels to layers. This doesn't refer to color fill layers.

Smart Object Lets you filter by Smart Objects with specific criteria. Although you can filter by Smart Object with the Kind type of filter, this one lets you specify linked or embedded, or linked ones whose content needs updating or is missing.

Selected Shows layers you have highlighted, probably for the purpose of filtering to see them.

Artboard In a document with more than one artboard, this will restrict the view to the layers in only one at a time.

General Blending Options

Ordinarily, layers higher in the Layers panel obscure those below them. Likewise, painting in Photoshop deposits color that overwrites what was there previously. However, there are ways to cause layers and brush strokes to blend with what's below them.

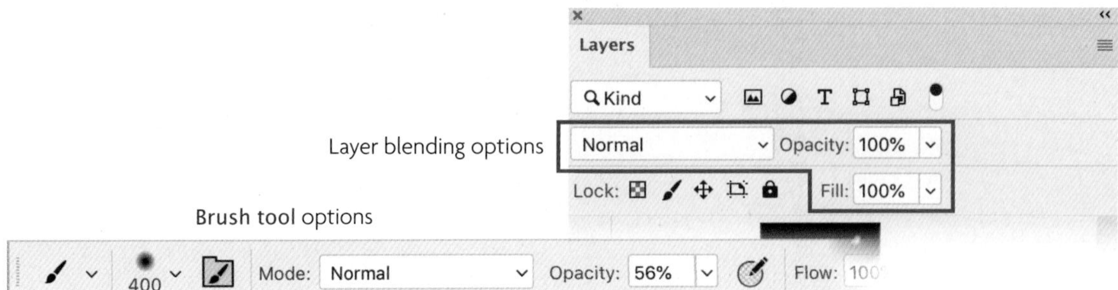

Opacity

If we lower a layer's Opacity, we can see through it. If the layer's Opacity is 50%, it is literally half as visible, and the layer(s) below makes up the other half. The same is true for any tool that uses a brush metaphor (the Brush tool is the most obvious, but others are painterly too). Both layers and tools that use brushes have other settings that *seem* to do the same thing as the Opacity setting. For layers, it's Fill, and for painterly tools, it's Flow. We'll discuss Flow in the "Brushes & Painting" chapter (see "Controlling Transfer: Opacity and Flow" on page 264). Fill *is* identical to Opacity unless Layer Styles or certain advanced blending options are used. More on that in the next section. There are several ways to adjust a layer's opacity:

- Click the word Opacity, type a value in the now-highlighted Opacity field, then press return/Enter. This is the least efficient way.
- Click the small arrow to the right of the field, then use the resulting slider. This, too, is rather slow.
- Rather than clicking the word Opacity, press and hold it, then drag left or right to "scrub" the value in the field. Release the mouse when you have the desired value.
- If the currently selected tool doesn't have its own Opacity setting, you may simply tap numbers on your keyboard: 3 produces 30% opacity, for example. Typing two numbers swiftly uses both for a more accurate result: 8 and 3 yield 83% opacity. If the active tool does have an Opacity setting (like the Brush tool), then typing numbers changes the opacity of the tool rather than that of the layer.

Blend Modes

Blend modes are another way to make layers visually interact. They are both wonderful and confusing. Names like Multiply and Difference may not be intuitive—unless you know what's meant by those terms. Even then, it is often profitable to try several blend modes to see which might yield the most pleasing result. In the table below, X indicates a general purpose for which a mode is used. A lighter X means that the mode may technically be in a category, but may not work as well as others in it. Note that some blend modes work only when painting or using the fill command. A mode's "neutral color" is one that vanishes when the mode is applied. If a mode has a neutral color, it will be black, white, or 50% gray.

Mode	Neutral Color	Darkening	Lightening	Contrast	Compare	Component
Pass Through		*Groups only, layers in group blend with all layers as if not grouped*				
Normal		*No blending*				
Dissolve		*Requires opacity adjustment to effect*				
Clear		*Painting/filling only: clear = erasure*				
Behind		*Painting/filling only: paints/fills behind current layer content*				
Darken		**X**			X	
Multiply		**X**				
Color Burn		**X**				
Linear Burn		**X**				
Darker Color		**X**			**X**	
Lighten			**X**		X	
Screen			**X**			
Color Dodge			**X**			
Linear Dodge (Add)			**X**			
Lighter Color			**X**		**X**	
Overlay				**X**	X	
Soft Light				**X**		
Hard Light				**X**		
Vivid Light				**X**		
Linear Light				**X**		
Pin Light				**X**		
Hard Mix				X		
Difference					**X**	
Exclusion					**X**	
Subtract		**X**			X	
Divide			**X**	X	X	
Hue						**X**
Saturation						**X**
Color						**X**
Luminosity						**X**

You'll notice that several have names derived from arithmetic (Subtract, Multiply, Divide). Indeed, most of the blend modes use a calculation involving each pixel in the layer to which the mode is applied and the pixels visible below it. Sometimes it's useful to know what that calculation is, but most often, a metaphor serves better. As I say to my students, "definitions may be necessary, but they're not necessarily definitive." Thus, I'm going to define most of the blend modes, showing examples of the most useful ones. Your projects and workflows will inevitably lead to your own favorites.

In the following groups of examples, I'll show a consistent pair of layers, one slightly offset from the other, so the blend modes can be compared. The top layer, a photo of a plush fruit named Peachy, is the one to which I've applied the blend modes. In some cases, I'll show additional, practical examples as well. In each grouping, I'll start with the most useful or definitive blend mode, then show the others that appear in the same section of the blend mode menu. As the table above shows, some modes can be put in multiple categories, but I'll show them with others nearby in the menu.

Advice: Experiment with blend modes as often as you can! In time, you'll have a visual memory of many of the main ones, and you'll know which one (or few) to try in a given circumstance.

Special Cases

These few (Normal, Pass Through, Dissolve, Clear, and Behind) don't really "blend" layers the way the others in this long list do. Let's get them out of the way first.

Normal

Every layer's default blend mode: Normal means no blending at all.

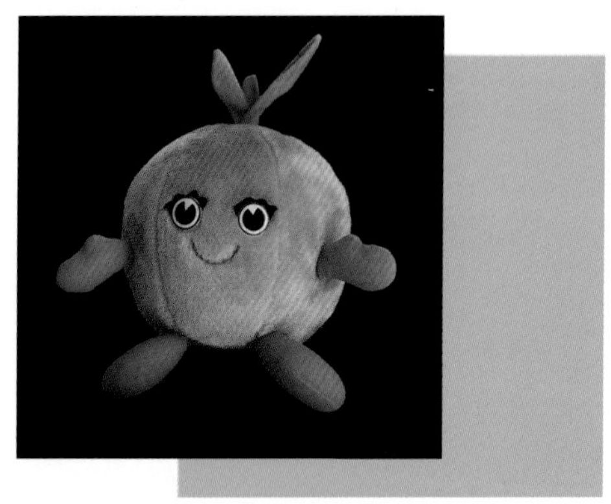

Pass Through

This is the default mode for groups of layers. The name means that the layers within the group blend with layers outside the group in exactly the way they would had they not been grouped at all. That is, each grouped layer blends with layers inside and outside the group equally.

Even changing a group's blend mode to Normal can make things look significantly different. This forces the layers in the group to blend only with each other. Think of this as a sub-composition within a larger document. In the past, we would have had to merge those layers together, losing the ability to edit them individually. A group with a blend mode other than Pass Through may be a substitute for a Smart Object in certain circumstances.

Dissolve

Dissolve is the only blend mode that requires another setting to be changed to see a result. With an Opacity of less than 100%, Dissolve causes a scattering of the layer's pixels (or those of a group or Smart Object) to disappear. If the Opacity is set to 70%, for example, 70% of the pixels remain fully opaque, and 30% completely vanish in a seemingly random scatter. In fact, most features that render partial opacity (erasure or layer masks) will give us Dissolve's effect, as seen in this example.

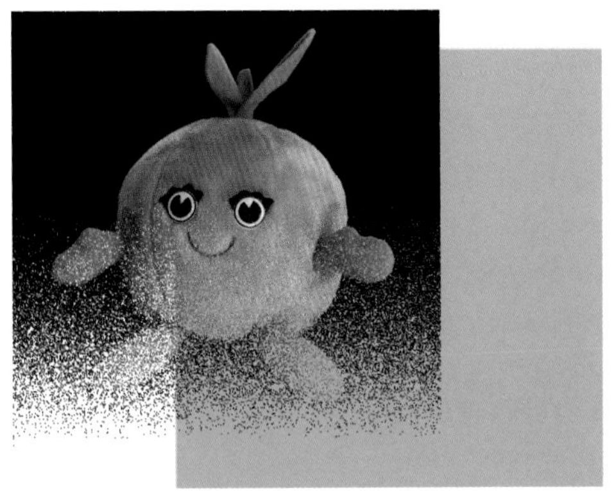

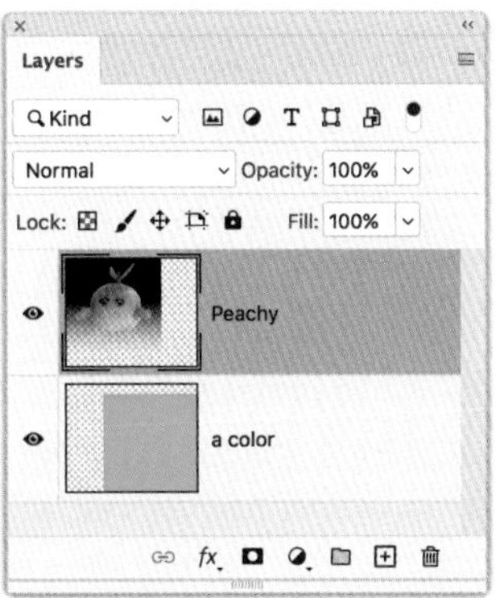

Clear

Clear is available only with the Brush tool, the Pencil tool, and the Fill command. It's essentially erasure. That's it: It deletes. Just use the Eraser tool!

Behind

Like Clear, Behind works only when painting or filling. In this example, I painted on the "back" of this fading version of the Peachy layer by setting the Brush tool blend mode to Behind.

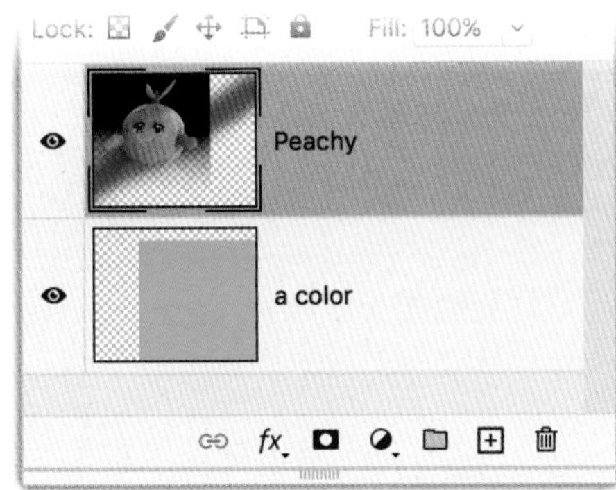

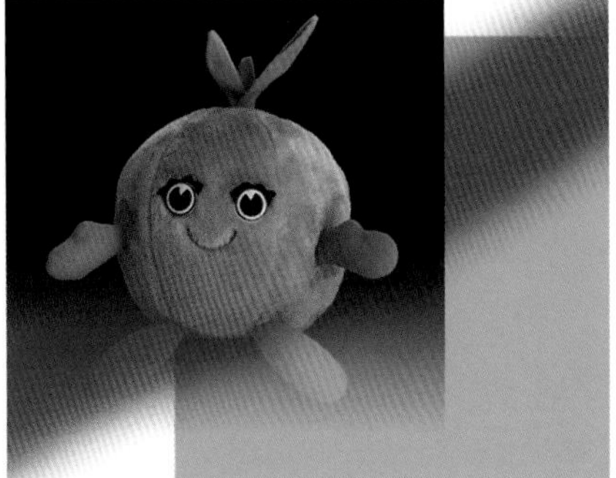

To Be Technical...

If you wish to have a deep understanding of what the rest of the blend modes actually do, you'll have to know a little bit about how Photoshop does math with color numbers when you apply a blend mode. For example, when we use the Multiply blend mode, just what numbers are being multiplied?

When blending RGB colors, instead of using the usual 256 values (0–255), the color numbers are "normalized" to a range of 0–1. When we use a blend mode called Subtract or

Multiply, it'll be numbers between 0 and 1 that are subtracted or multiplied. As fascinating as that is, the arithmetic doesn't necessarily bring an image to mind. So I rely more on visual metaphors to explain the blend modes whenever possible. For a few modes, I'll also let you know what math is happening.

Darkening Modes

All of these make white disappear; that is, white is the so-called "neutral color" for these modes. Multiply is the most definitive mode of this group.

Multiply

Multiply is the most useful of the modes in its section. Indeed, it's probably the most frequently used blend mode in Photoshop.

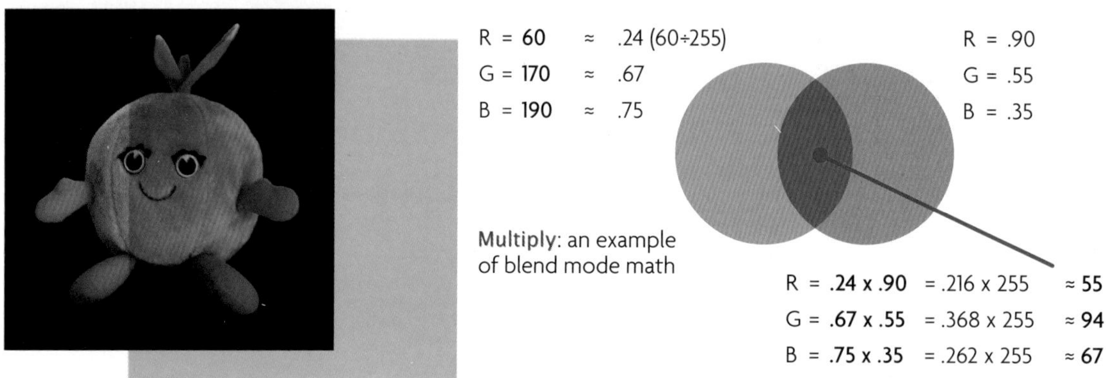

Multiply: an example of blend mode math

Recall that when blending, each pixel's colors use numbers in the range of 0–1 (instead of 0–255). When we choose the Multiply mode, those are the numbers that literally get multiplied. Since each RGB value for white would be exactly 1, white has no impact on the colors below, and essentially disappears. A fine metaphor for this effect is slide (transparency) film. Hopefully some readers will remember this twentieth-century technology. Picture two slides on a light table that's shining light through them.

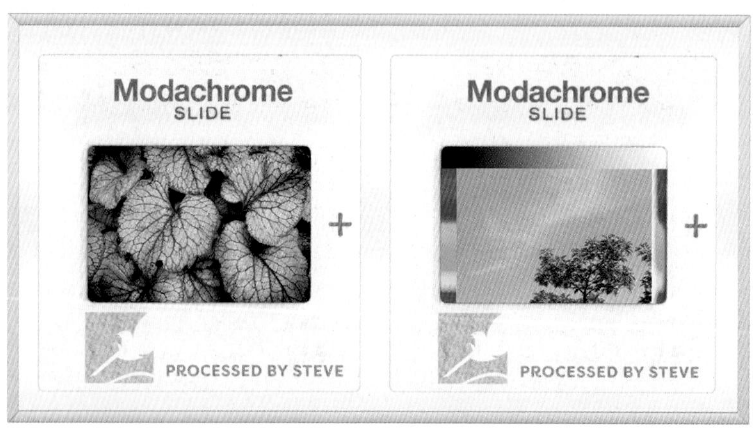

Now imagine overlapping the slides. Wherever the top image is white, it's clear, and we see the image under it. Where it's black, it's completely opaque, obscuring the image below.

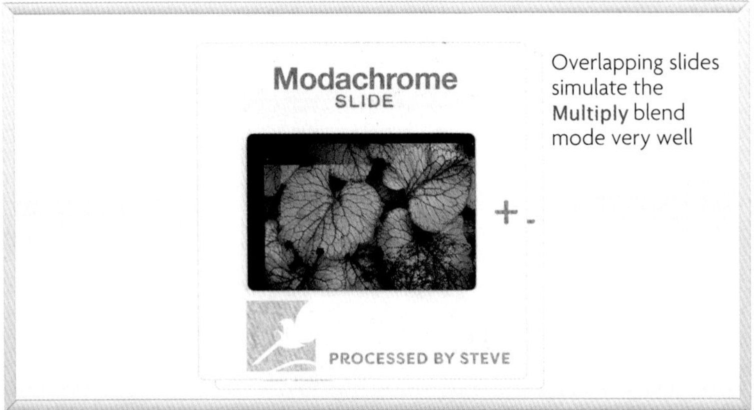

Overlapping slides simulate the Multiply blend mode very well

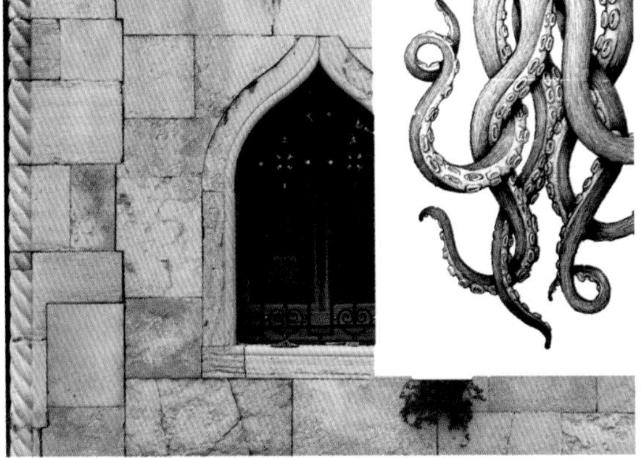
Layer with drawing set to Normal

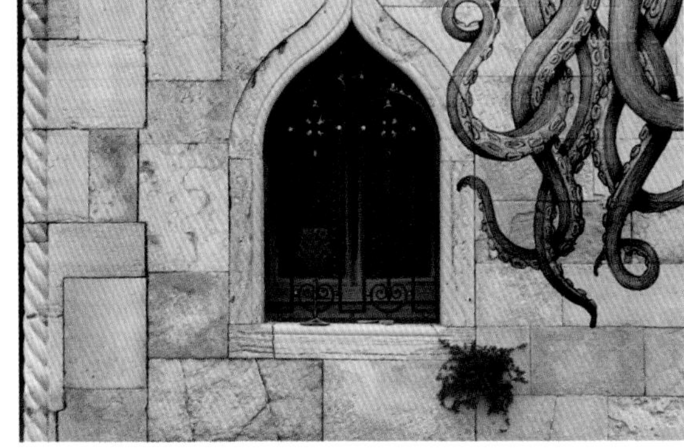
Drawing layer set to Multiply

Darken

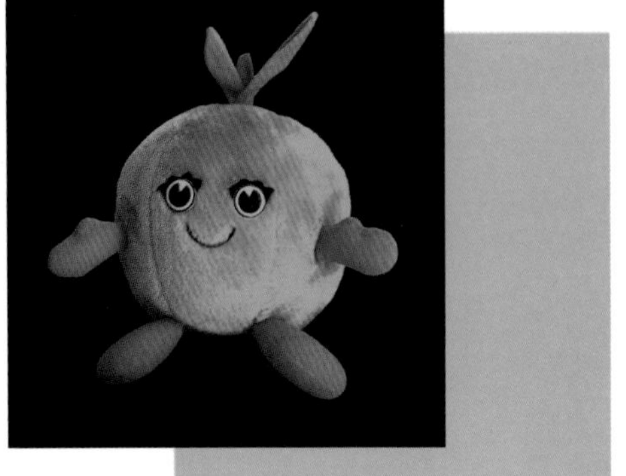

With Darken, Photoshop chooses the lower red, green, and blue values for each pixel.
So if a pixel has color values of 60R, 170G, 190B (▬), and the pixel below it has values of 230R, 140G, 90B (▬), the result will be the lower of each: 60R, 140G, 90B (▬).

Darken often looks similar to Multiply, but because of the way it works, it could look quite different. And sometimes this mode looks nearly identical to Darker Color, but sometimes it's radically different! When I suspect one of those might be appropriate, I always try both in case it's one of those circumstances in which they differ substantially.

Color Burn

Color Burn differs from Multiply in that it gives more intense colors under midtones in the layer to which the mode is applied. More highlight detail is lost or diminished too.

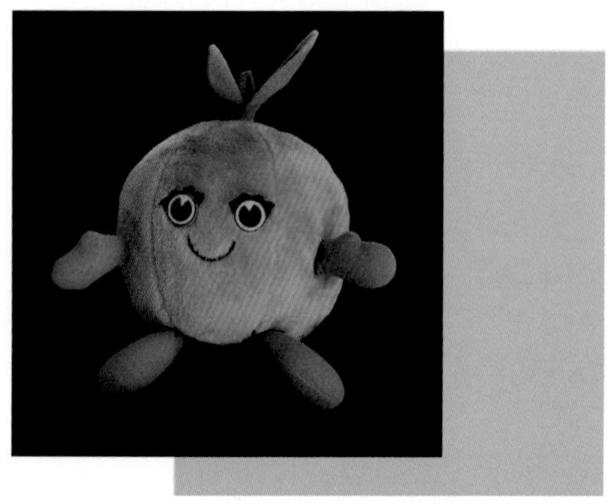

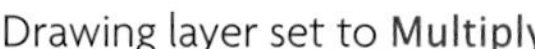

Drawing layer set to Multiply

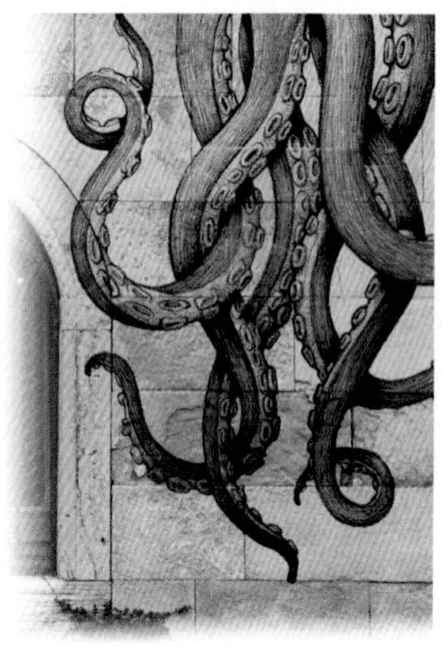

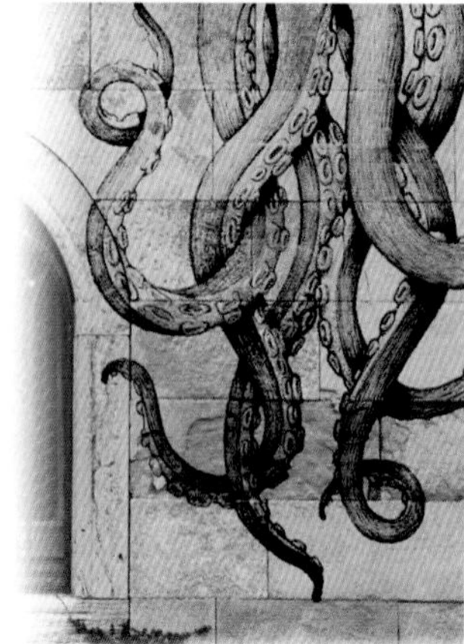

Drawing layer set to Color Burn

Linear Burn

Linear Burn is darker and has more contrast than Multiply. I use this mode when the image ordinarily would demand Multiply but is a little too faint.

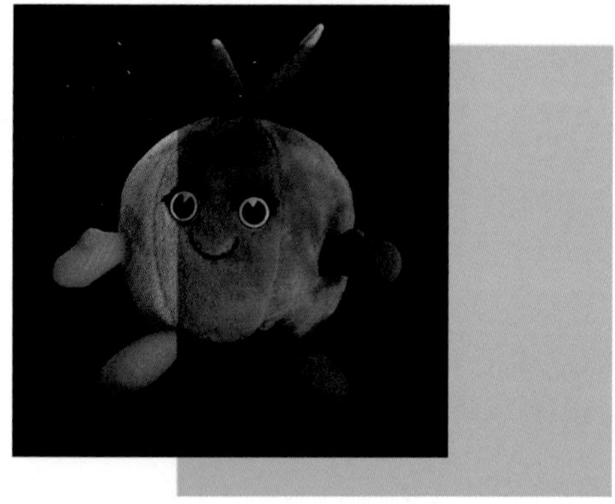

Drawing layer set to Multiply

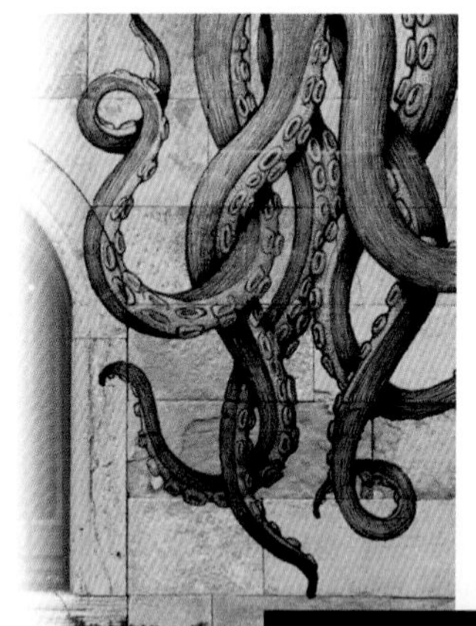

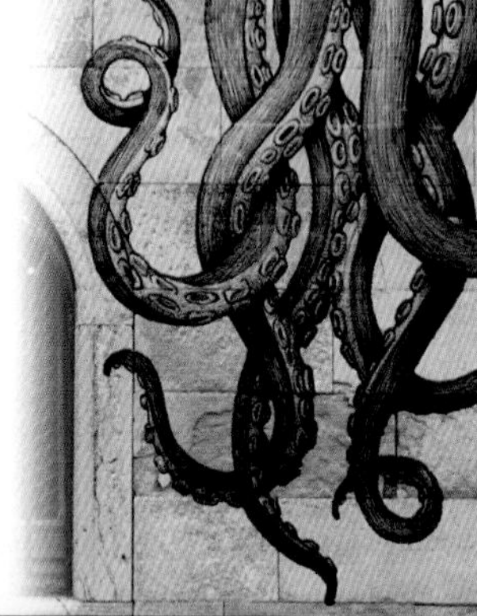

Darker Color

Darker Color not only makes white invisible and gives a dark result like the others in this section, but it does a direct pixel-by-pixel comparison to do so. Imagine that both the layer being blended and the one with which it is blended are completely desaturated (with the

Hue/Saturation adjustment, for example). Each pixel's luminance is then compared, and the darker of the two is shown. Of course, neither layer is *visibly* desaturated, but Photoshop uses that adjustment invisibly to determine the luminance values to compare. For an interesting use case, see the description of the opposite mode, Lighter Color (page 184).

Lightening Modes

Screen

Imagine projecting two images onto the same screen from two different projectors. They would fill in each other's shadows, giving a result lighter than either one by itself. Where either image is black, it has no effect on the other. In this way, Screen is the opposite of Multiply, and black is its neutral color since it disappears. Handy for simulating chalk on a blackboard!

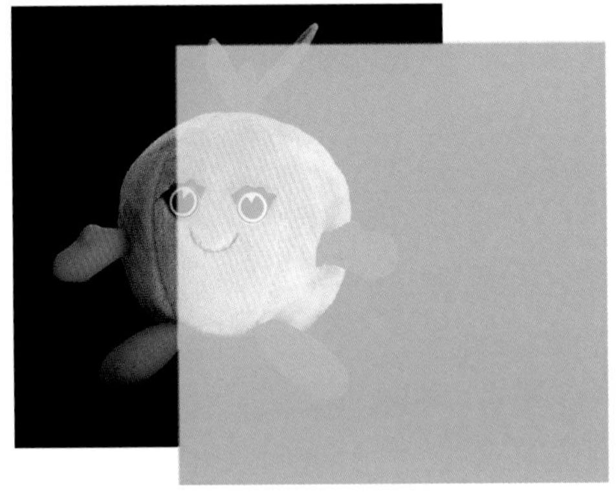

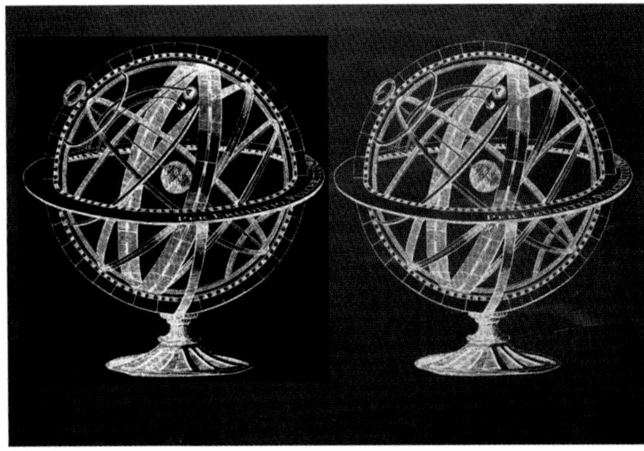

Lighten

Lighten sometimes looks similar to Screen, but because of the way it works, it often looks quite different. For each pixel, Photoshop chooses the higher red, green, and blue values.

So if a pixel has color values of 230R, 140G, 90B, and the pixel below it has values of 60R, 170G, 190B, the result will be the higher of each: 230R, 170G, 190B.

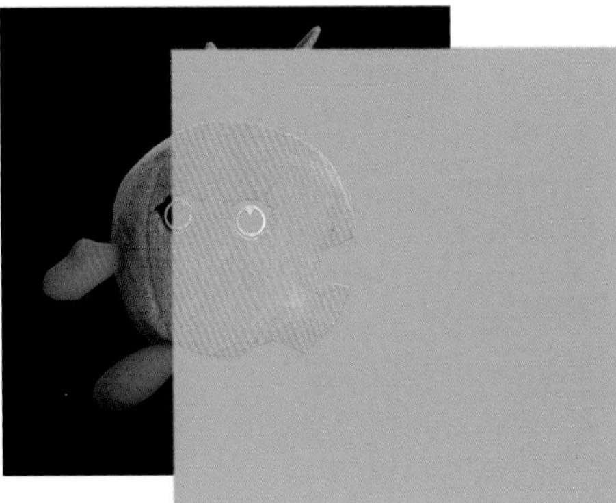

Sometimes this mode looks nearly identical to Lighter Color, but sometimes it's radically different! When I suspect one of those might be appropriate, I always try both in case it's one of those circumstances in which they differ substantially.

Color Dodge

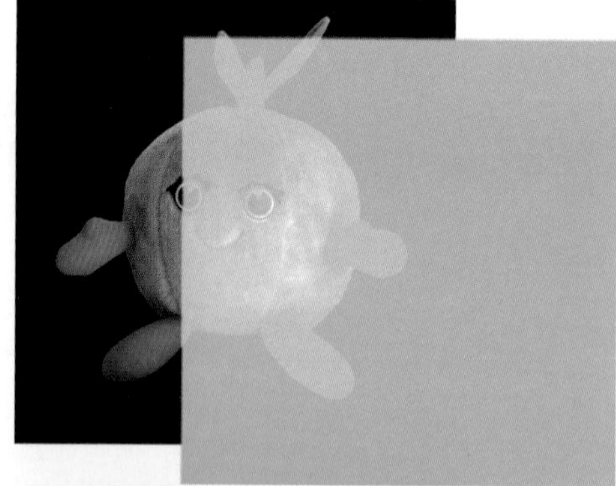

Color Dodge is the opposite of Color Burn: It gives a light result and hides black, as the others in this section do, and it can intensify the color of the layer to which its applied more than the one below it (as Color Burn does).

I use this as the Highlight Mode for the Bevel & Emboss layer effect when I want a strong specular highlight to help simulate chrome or another shiny substance. See "Bevel & Emboss" (page 199) for more on this effect.

Linear Dodge (Add)

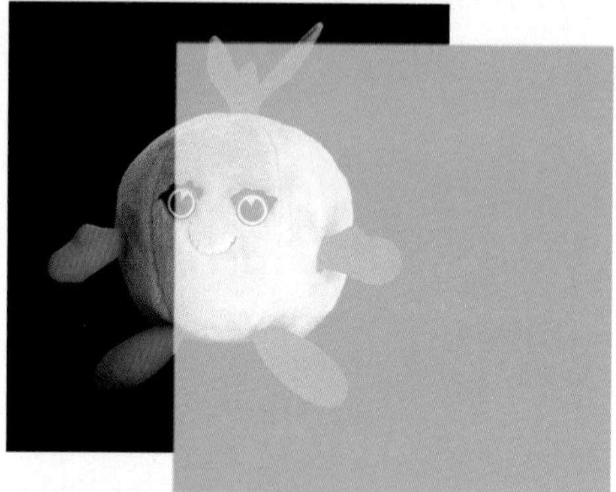

Mathematically, this is one of the simplest blend modes. Linear Dodge literally adds the normalized RGB values (0–1 rather than 0–255) of each pixel. If the result exceeds 1, it's simply set to 1 (white).

Lighter Color

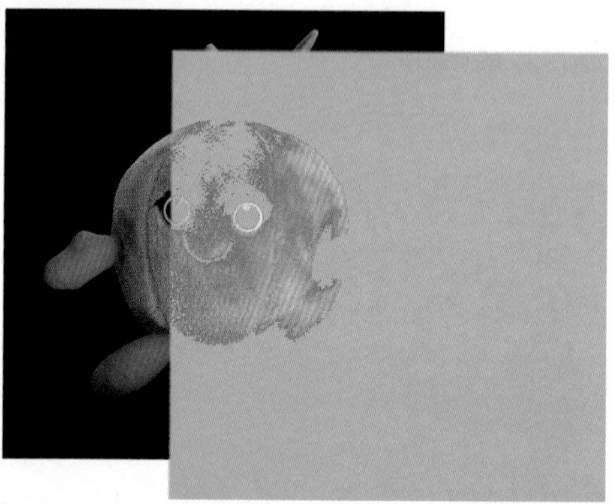

Lighter Color not only makes black invisible and gives a light result like the others in this section, but it is more comparative than the others. Imagine that both the layer being blended and the one with which it is blended are completely desaturated (with the Hue/Saturation adjustment, for example). Each pixel's luminance is then compared and the lighter of the two is shown. Of course, neither layer is visibly desaturated, but Photoshop uses that adjustment invisibly to determine the luminance values to compare.

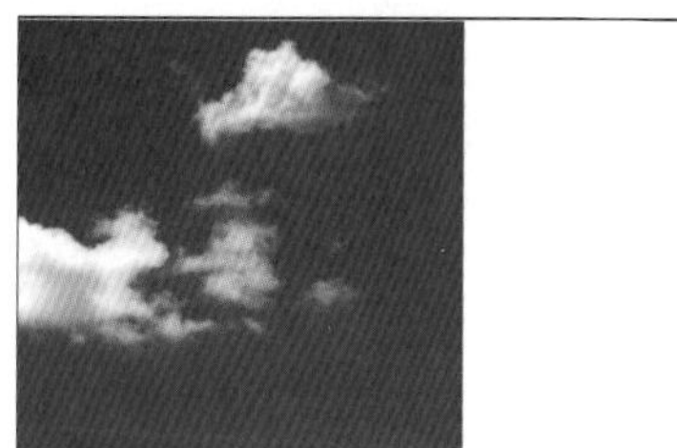

Upper layer set to Lighter Color

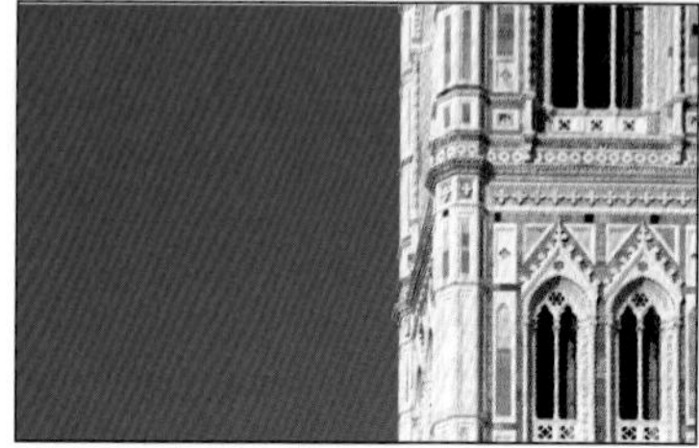

Lower layer

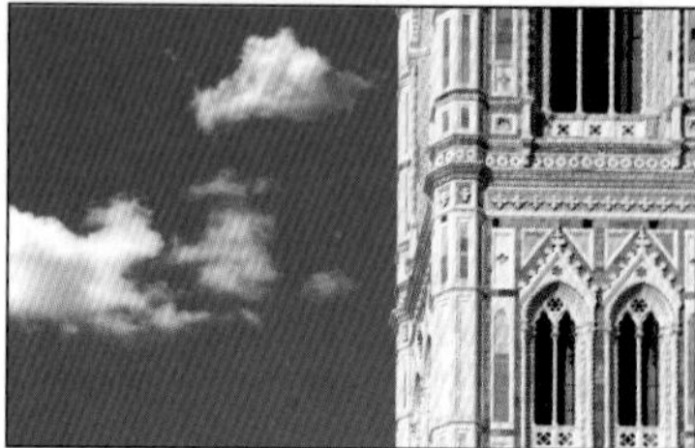

Result

Contrast Modes

Hard Light

Hard Light and Overlay tie for the title of "most definitive" in this section of blend modes.

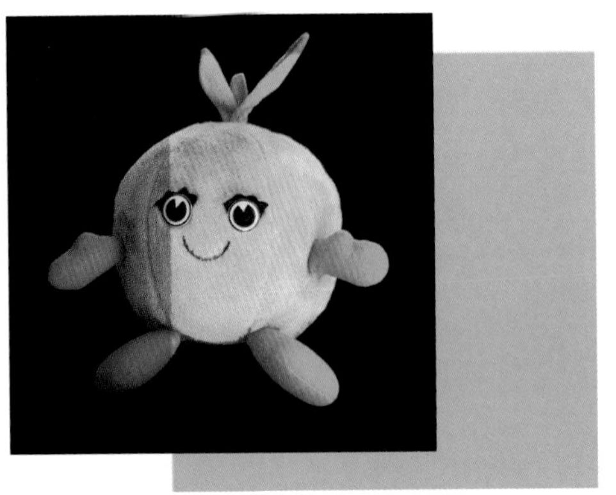

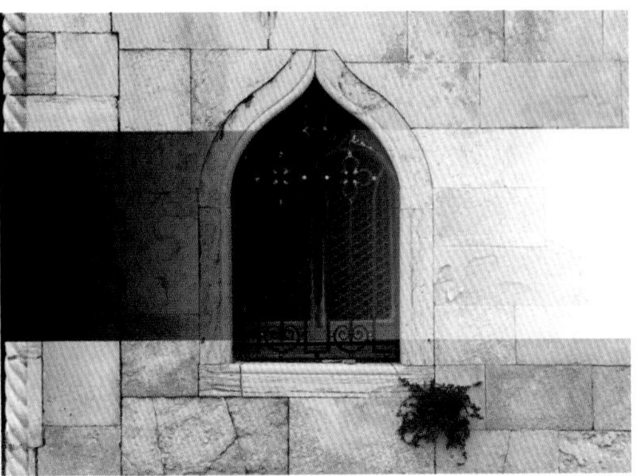

In fact, Hard Light and Overlay are closely related: You can achieve the same visual result as Hard Light by inverting the layer order and using Overlay mode on the layer that's now on top.

Think of Hard Light as a combination of Screen (when lighter than middle gray) and Multiply (when darker). Middle gray vanishes. In the window image above, a black-to-white gradient layer above the window is set to Hard Light. The center of the gradient disappears.

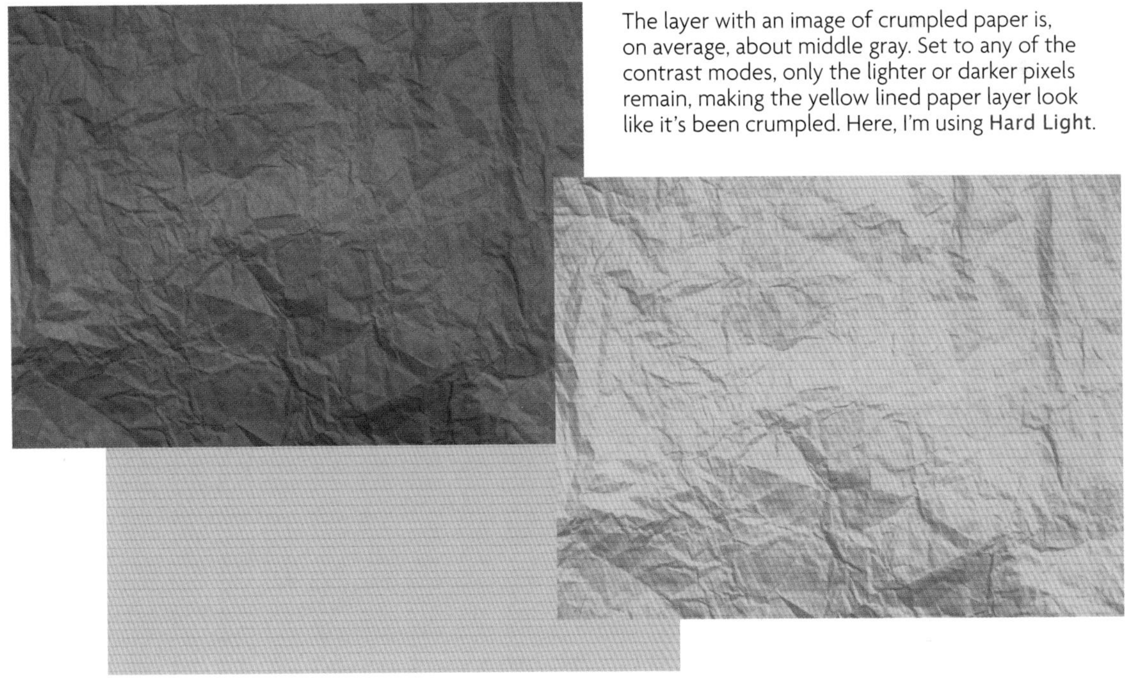

The layer with an image of crumpled paper is, on average, about middle gray. Set to any of the contrast modes, only the lighter or darker pixels remain, making the yellow lined paper layer look like it's been crumpled. Here, I'm using Hard Light.

Overlay

You can think of Overlay as a visually less intense version of Hard Light.

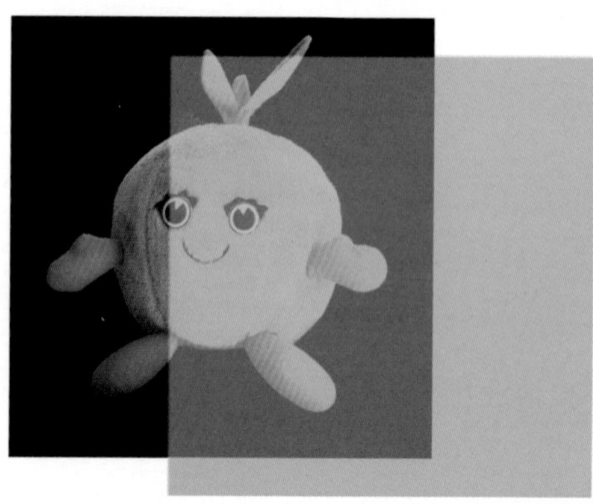

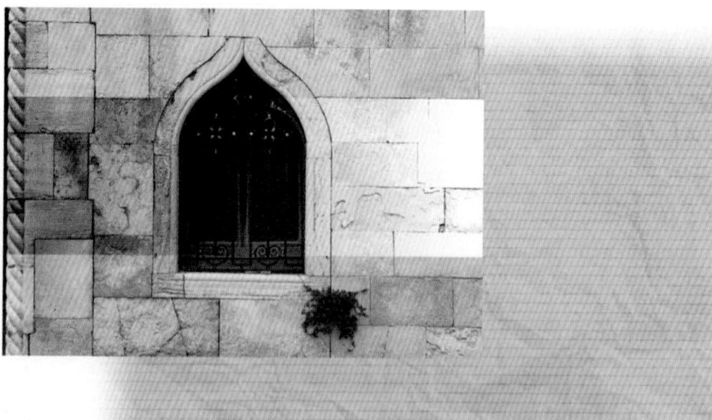

You can see above that neither black nor white are truly opaque; they merely darken or lighten the pixels under them. In the crumpled paper example, the paper looks less violently crumpled. The wall surrounding the window is less obscured than with Hard Light.

Soft Light

As the name implies, this mode is the least intense of this group. Think of it as a softer version of Overlay, to which it is very similar but less intense.

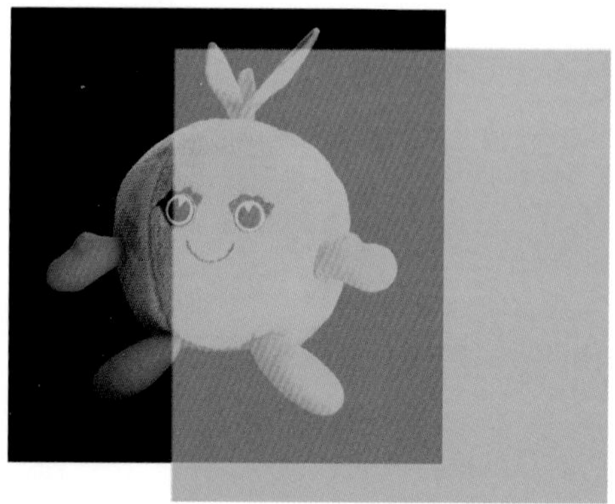

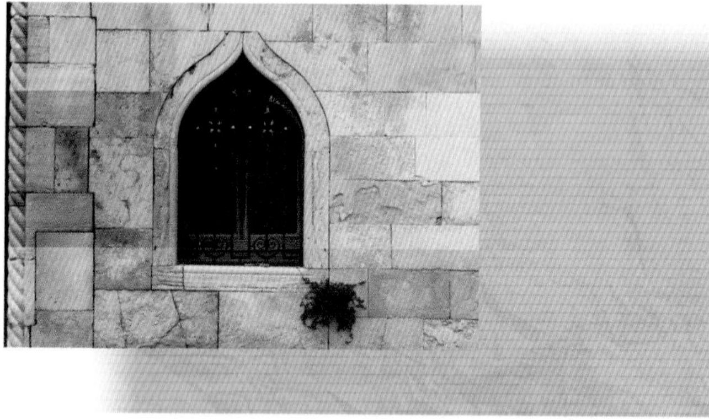

Vivid Light and Linear Light

Think of Vivid Light as a combination of Color Dodge (when lighter than middle gray) and Color Burn (when darker), and Linear Light as a combination of Linear Dodge and Linear Burn. Middle gray vanishes with both.

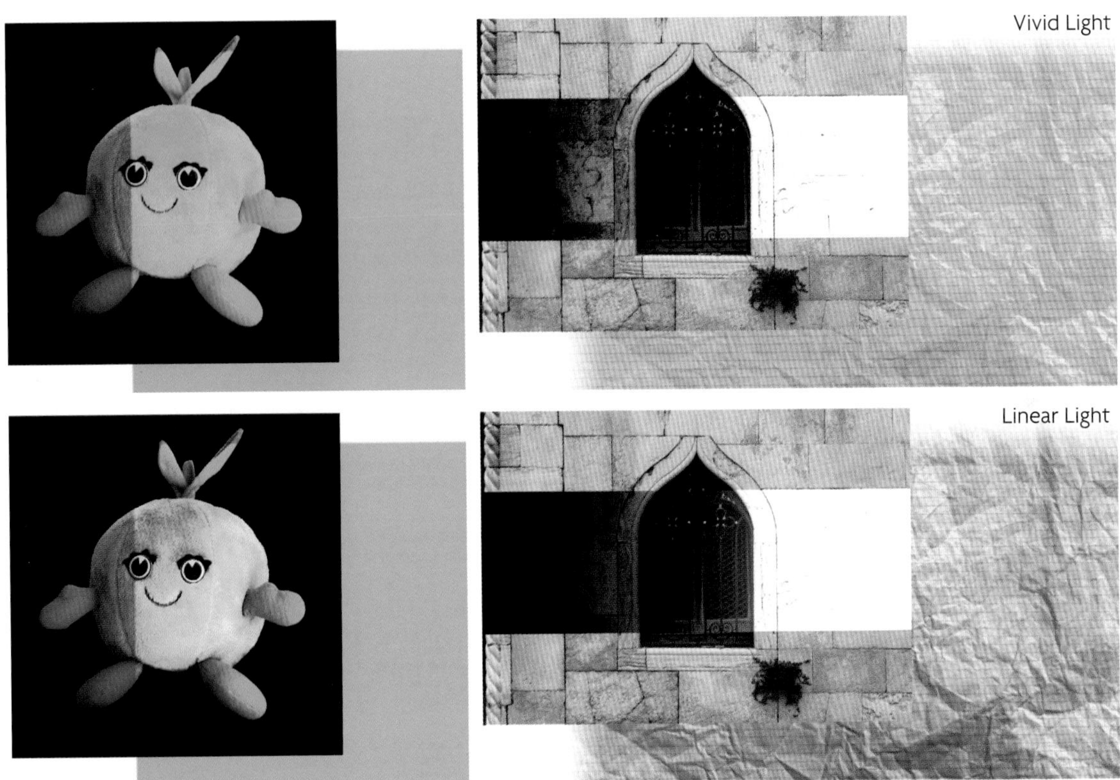

Pin Light

When Pin Light is applied to a color, that color will replace colors below it, depending on which is lighter or darker. If Pin Light is applied to a color lighter than middle gray, it will replace colors below it that are darker than it is. If Pin Light is applied to a color darker than middle gray, it will replace colors below it that are lighter than it is.

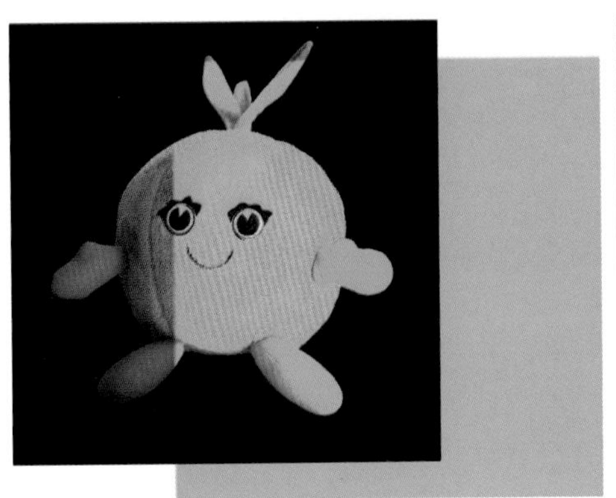

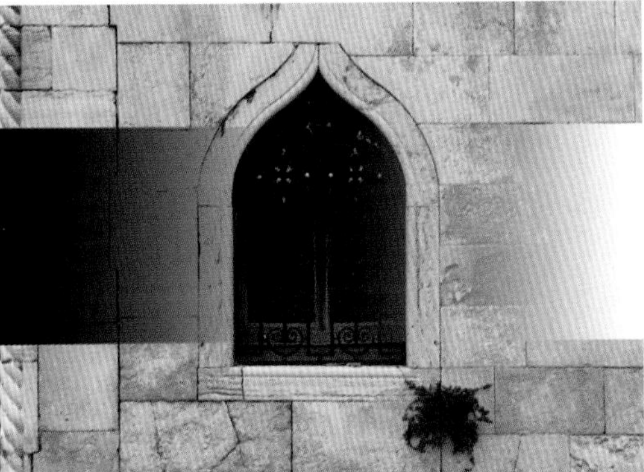

Hard Mix

Hard Mix is brutal. The resulting pixels have red, green, and blue values of either 0 or 255! That means those pixels will be red, green, blue, yellow, cyan, magenta, black, or white. That's it. It does this by simply adding those values for each pixel. If the total is less than 255, it's set to 0. If it's 255 or more, it's set to 255. So if a pixel has color values of 130R, 140G, 45B, and the pixel below it has values of 60R, 170G, 190B, the result will be the higher of each: 0R, 255G, 0B, since both 130+60 and 45+190 are less than 255, and 140+170 is more.

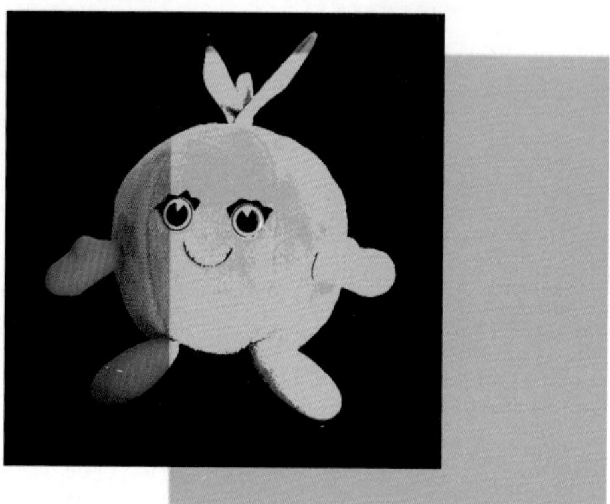

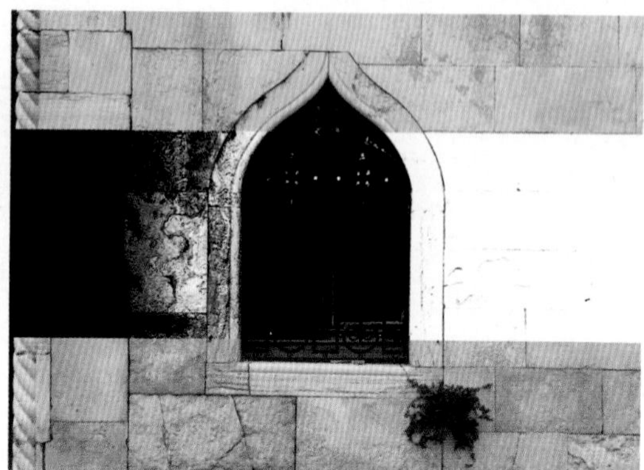

Arithmetic Modes

Subtract

Although Difference is listed first in this section of the menu, the Subtract mode represents the group better. Mathematically, this is one of the simplest blend modes: Subtract literally subtracts the RGB values of each pixel. If the result is negative, it's simply set to 0 (black).

The lighter the pixels to which this mode is applied, the darker the result, since you're subtracting higher values from the underlying layer. If you subtract black (0), you've subtracted nothing and the underlying layer remains the same. The example below gives a hint why these are sometimes called the inversion modes.

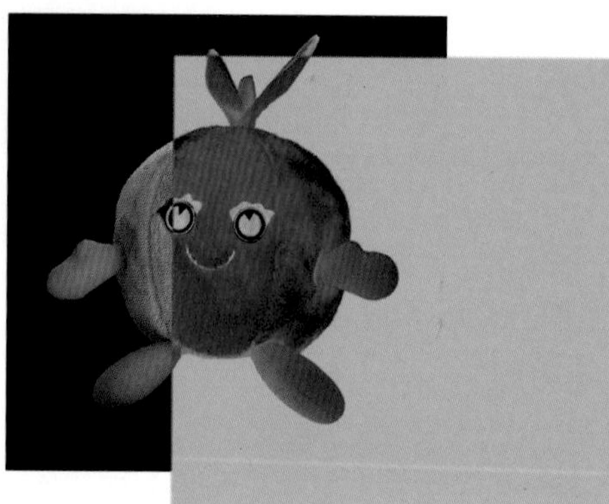

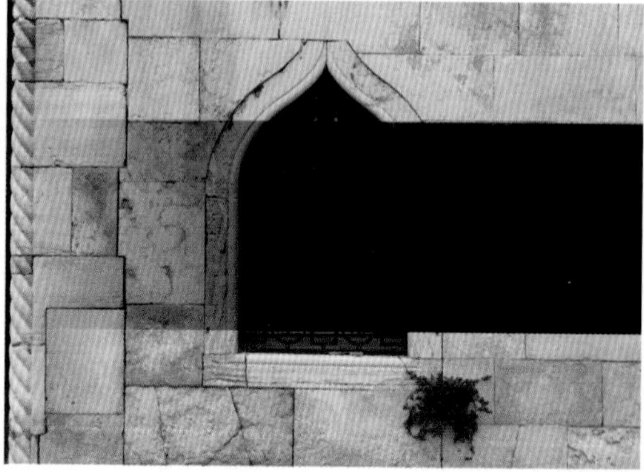

Difference

The word "difference" means the result of a subtraction. And indeed, Difference mode is *very* similar to Subtract. The only difference (I couldn't help it!) between the two is that this mode always subtracts the darker pixel values from the lighter ones. So when the pixels to which Difference is applied are lighter than the ones underneath, the underlying pixels get inverted.

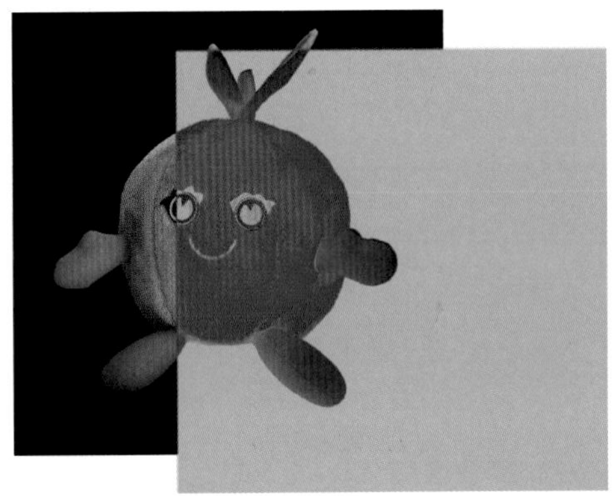

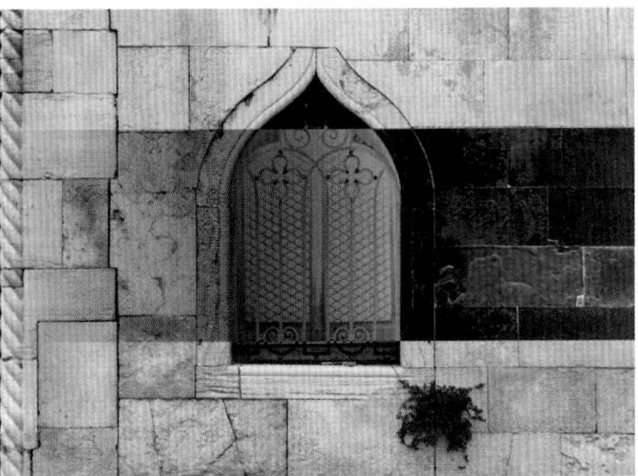

The most common use for the Difference mode is getting two similar layers aligned or registered to each other. Photoshop's Auto-Align Layers feature is great most of the time, but when we need to manually get content lined up, Difference can help.

Consider two identical layers, one atop the other. That is, the difference between them is exactly 0. Thus, if the top one is set to Difference mode, everything turns black.

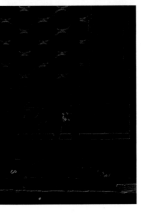

Here, a close-up of the window image we've been using. The window layer has been duplicated then offset 1 pixel up and 1 pixel to the left.

This image would be boringly black if the layers were lined up again.

Exclusion

Think of Exclusion as a weaker form of Difference. It uses the same rules, but produces a lower-contrast result. When two identical images are aligned to one another, the result will not be completely black.

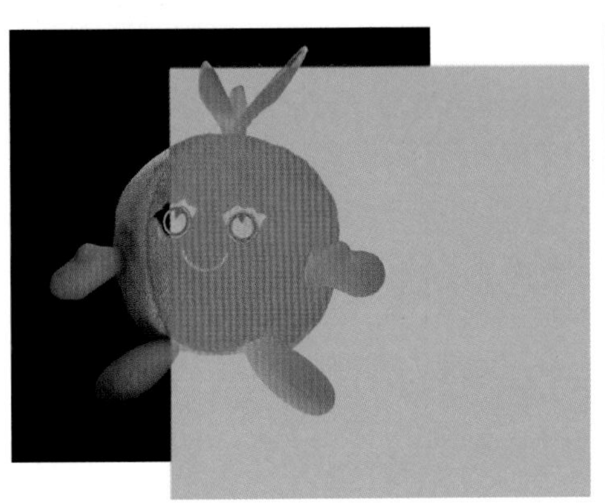

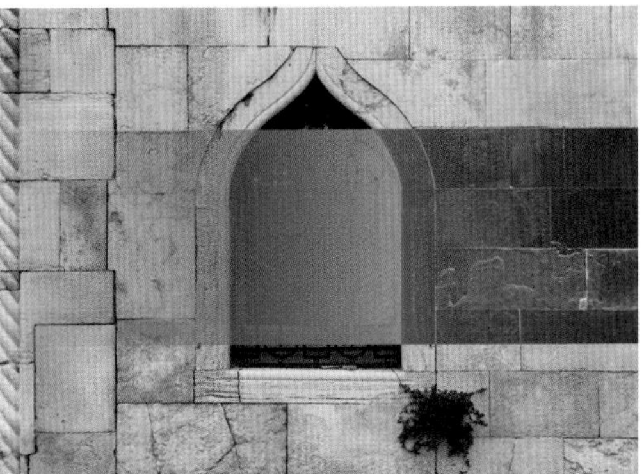

Divide

More math! Divide produces a lightening result by dividing the normalized color numbers (0–1 rather than 1–255). The values of the pixels below are divided by the values of the pixels to which the mode is applied. If you divide by white (1), the underlying layer remains unchanged. Dividing by black, which is dividing by 0, creates a singularity that destroys civilization. Or it produces white. I'll let you find out!

It appears that Photoshop allows dividing by 0. Those tricky engineers!

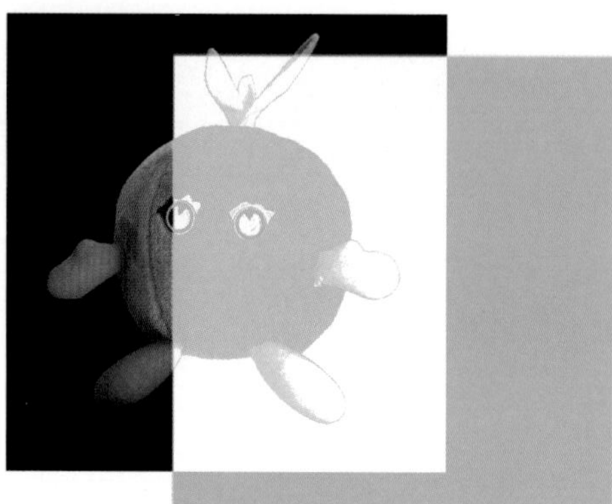

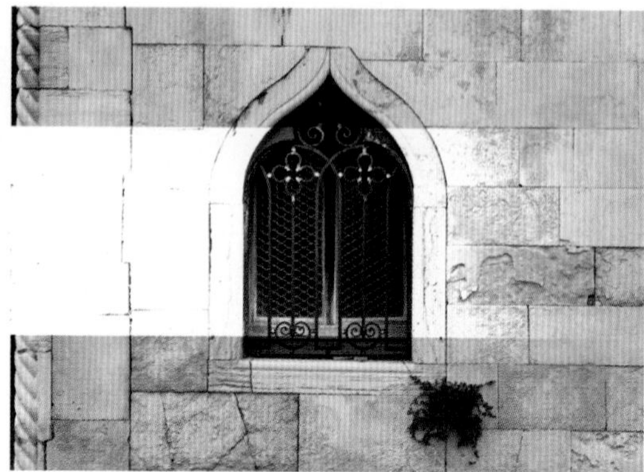

Component Modes

This group can be both very practical and wonderfully creative. To understand these modes, consider separating an image into two parts: its color and its luminosity. A simple black-and-white image is one in which the color is removed, leaving only its luminosity behind. The color is, well, everything else. And that, too, can be thought of as having two components: hue (which part of the color wheel) and saturation (how intense the hue).

I find it easier to explain them in nearly the opposite order than they appear in the menu. We'll use the following images to explore these four modes:

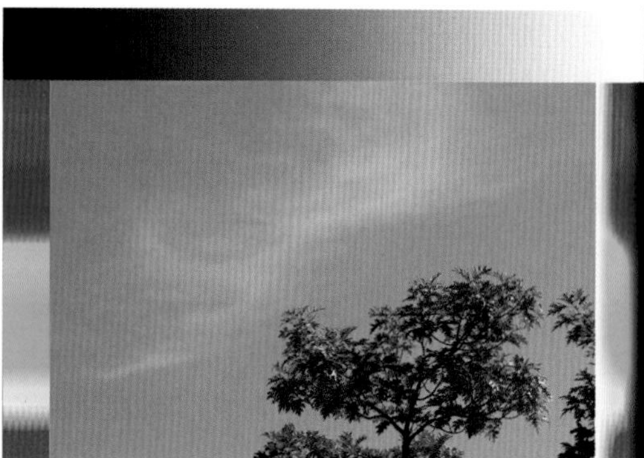

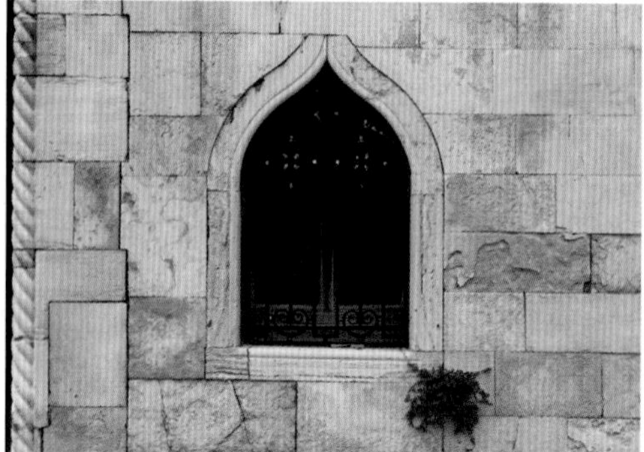

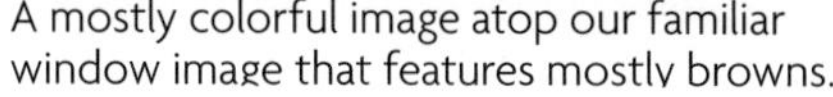

A mostly colorful image atop our familiar window image that features mostly browns.

Note that the image that will be our top layer, the one to which we'll apply these blend modes, is very colorful except for the grayscale across the top. Where there is color, it's quite saturated (except for the clouds and little else).

Luminosity

Luminosity mode essentially removes the color component, leaving only the luminosity (the tonal part) of the image. Any color we see comes from the layer(s) underneath—in this case, the blue-green below Peachy or the beige-and-brown window image below the tree layer. Where the underlying layer is either white or black or otherwise desaturated, the result is desaturated.

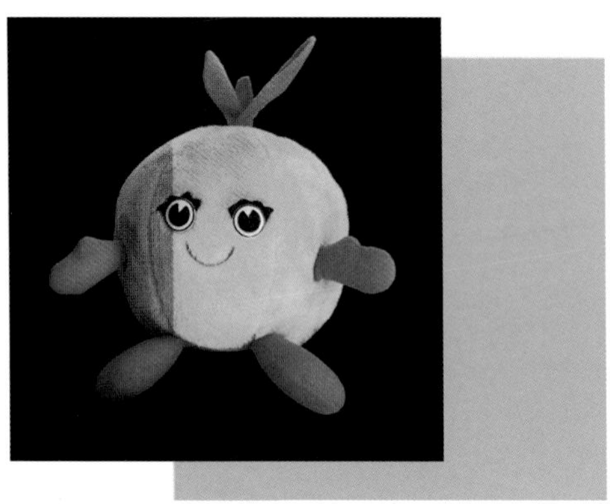

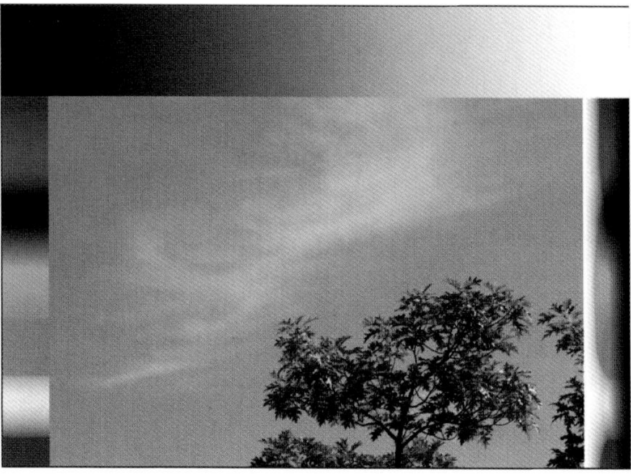

Color

This mode is the exact opposite of Luminosity. Color retains only the color from the layer to which it's applied, and any tonal detail you see comes from below. The grayscale at the top of the tree image has no color, and thus gives a grayscale look to the underlying image (the window). The rich, saturated colors elsewhere get applied to that underlying image.

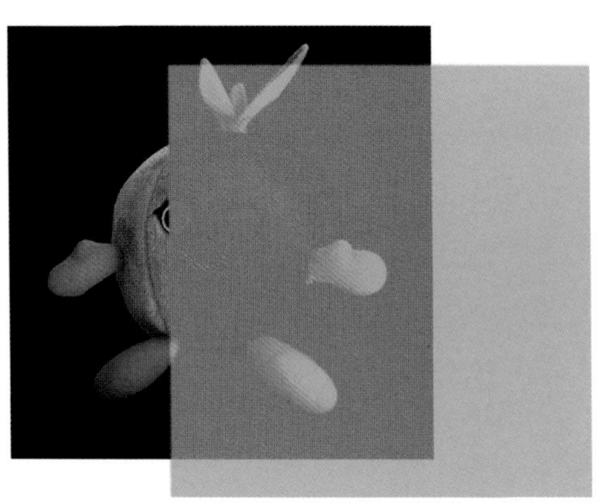

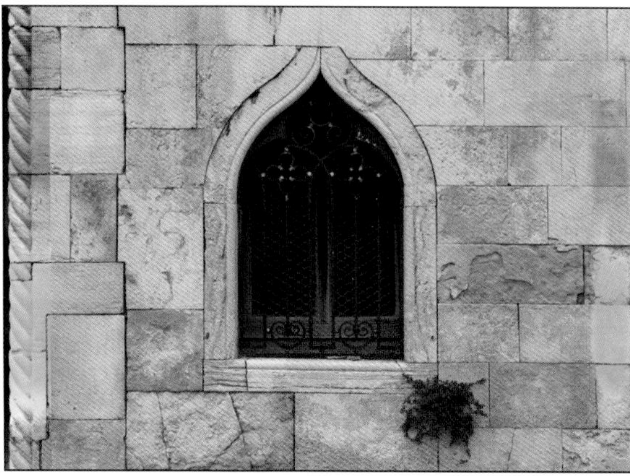

Hue

At first glance, Hue is very similar to Color. The grayscale makes the underlying image colorless, and tonal details come from the layer below. But note that the colors are not that saturated in the tree/window image, but are in the Peachy image. The level of saturation, like the tonal detail, comes from the layer below. Where the browns of the window image are saturated, so is the result. Since the layer below Peachy is very saturated, so is that result.

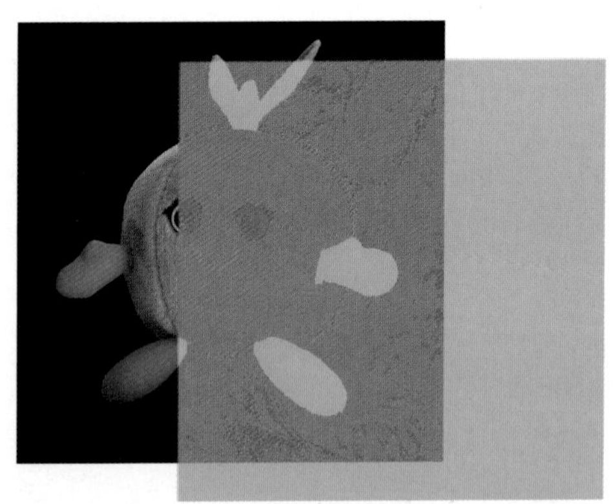

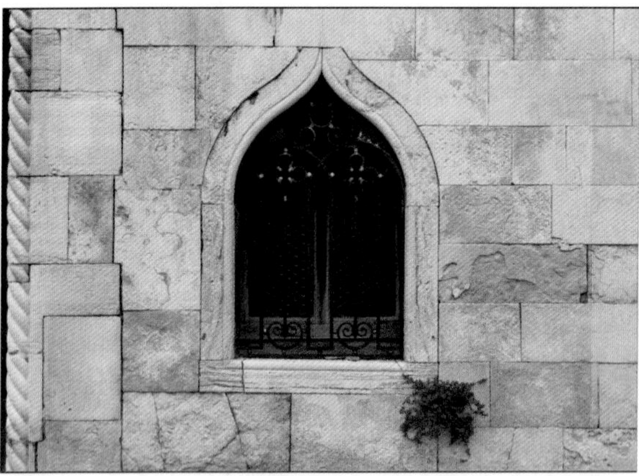

Saturation

I think you're on to me at this point. When we set the top layer to Saturation, the hue and luminosity come from below. However intense (saturated) the bottom layer is, and however light and dark, so is the result.

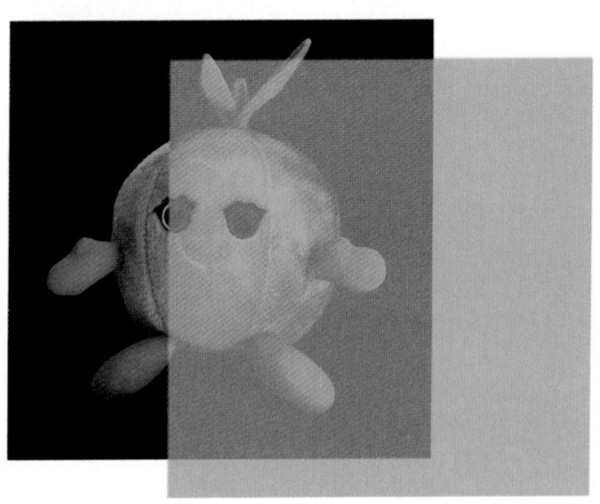

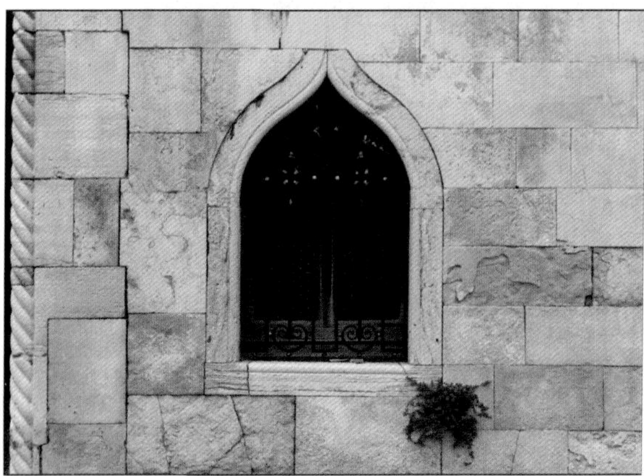

Blend Modes & Smart Filters

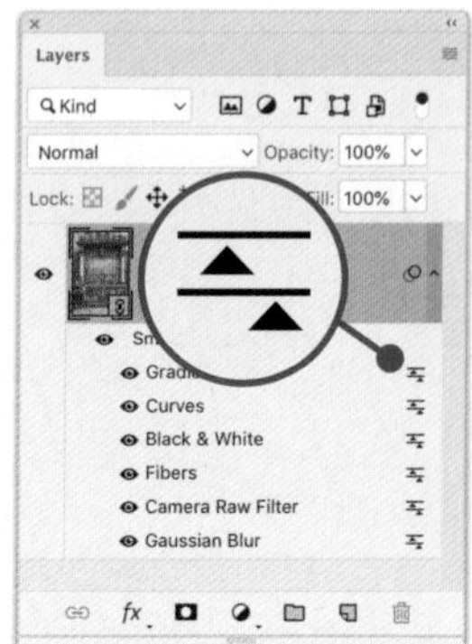

When a filter is applied to a Smart Object, it becomes an editable Smart Filter. Double-clicking the filter's name in the Layers panel opens that filter's dialog so it can be adjusted. However, many Photoshop users don't realize that the small icon to the right of most Smart Filters can be double-clicked as well, resulting in a very different dialog box: the filter's Blending Options.

The details of filters are covered in the "Filters & Transforms" chapter of this Compendium.

In this image, I wanted to simulate the look and feel of the images made by the nineteenth-century photographers Hill and Adamson. My wife, a photo historian, and I visited some of their old haunts in Edinburgh, Scotland, to capture some of the same subjects they did. Speaking of haunts, many of their photos were made in graveyards.

With about five Smart Filters, I was able to achieve a fairly good match. But I wanted the image to look a little bit more spooky than theirs, so I added a blended blur to the image.

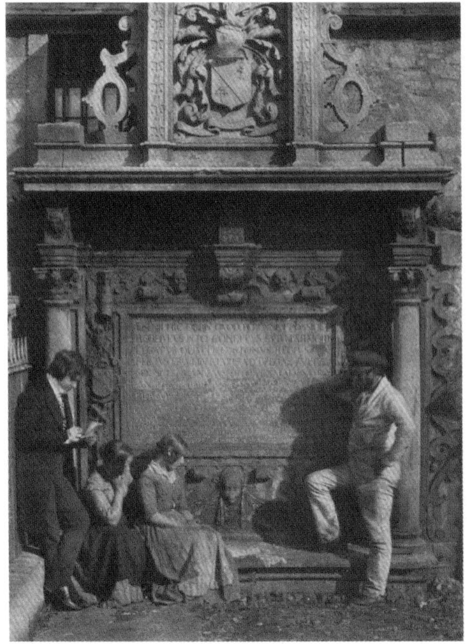

The Artist and the Gravedigger
David Octavius Hill and Robert Adamson
1843–1847

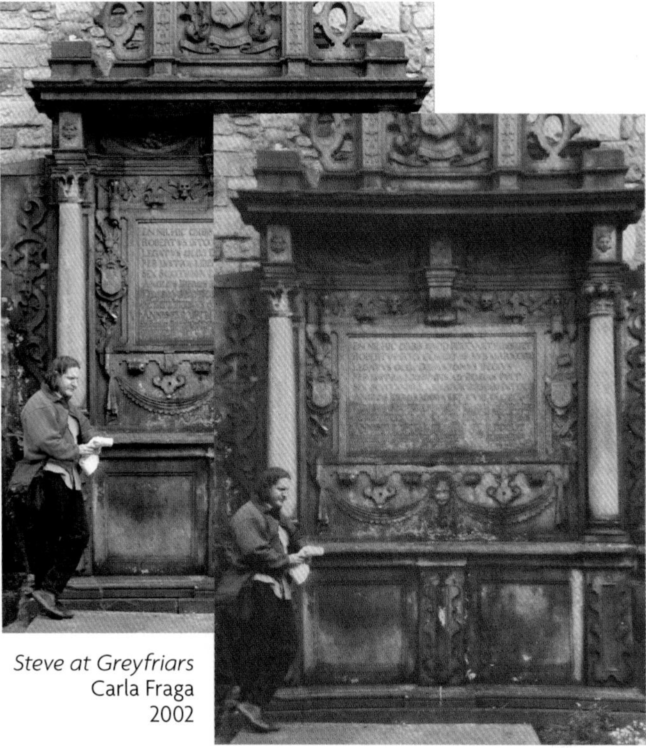

Steve at Greyfriars
Carla Fraga
2002

I applied the Gaussian Blur filter, then opened its Blending Options by double-clicking .

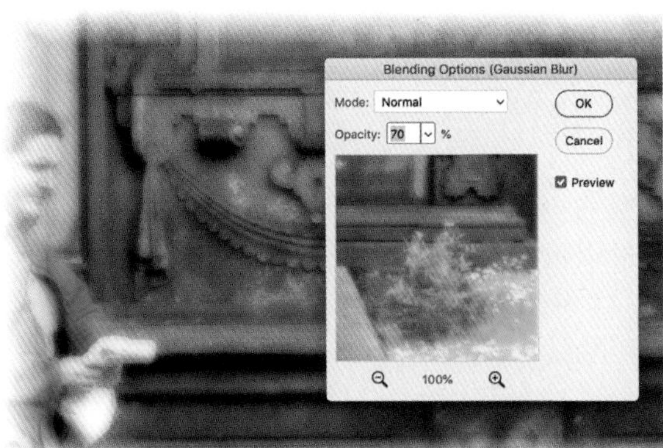

Gaussian Blur filter at 70% Opacity

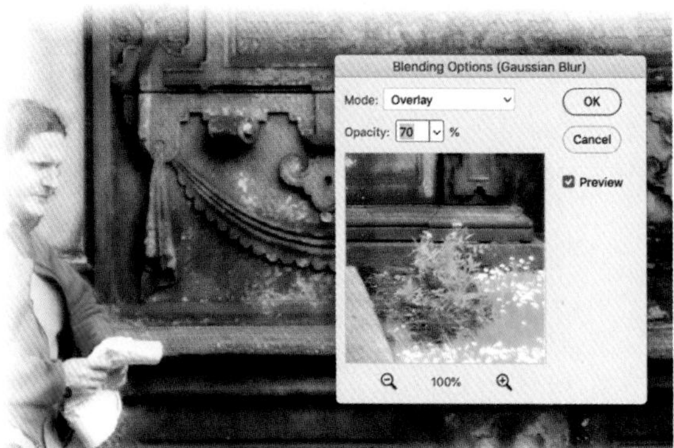

Gaussian Blur filter at 70% Opacity and Overlay blend mode

The effect of the blur is obvious: The image lost all focus. But when using the Smart Filter's Blending Options, something interesting happens. I lowered the Opacity of the blur to 70%. This replicates an effect in which we would duplicate a layer, blur the duplicate, then lower its Opacity. So, essentially, you're seeing a bit of the blurred version and a bit of the sharp version at the same time.

Now imagine changing the blend mode of that duplicate layer. That's what changing the blur's blend mode does—without the duplicate layers! I chose Overlay to give both light and dark elements of the photo a kind of ghostly glow.

I then used several other filters and adjustments to achieve this spookier version of a Hill and Adamson print.

Blend Modes & Adjustment Layers

Sometimes when we apply an adjustment to an image, we get more than we intend. For example, when I increase an image's contrast, I sometimes dislike the increased saturation that comes with it. By changing the blend mode to Luminosity, *only* luminosity, and not color, is affected.

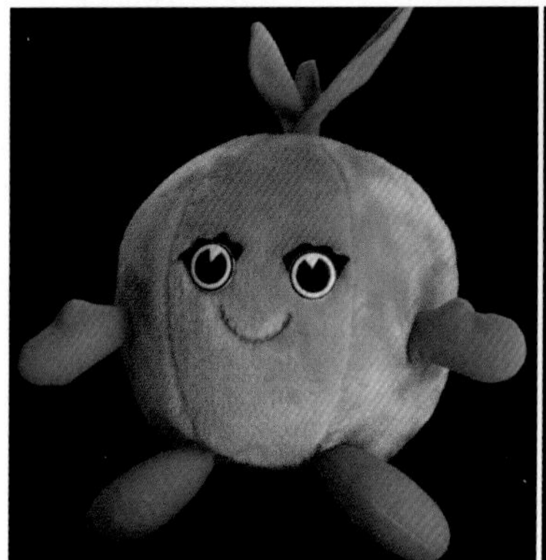

Original image

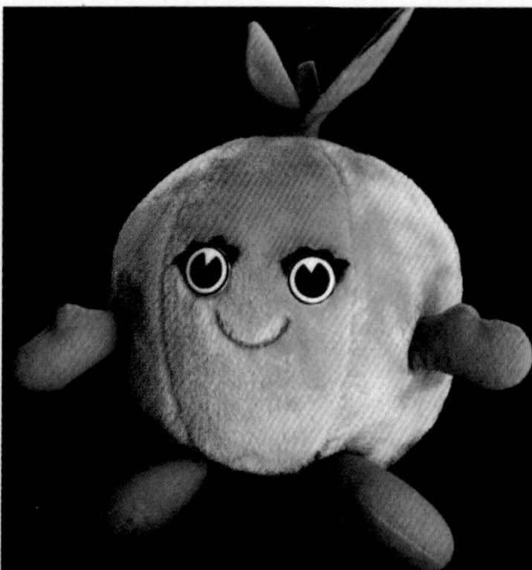

Contrast dramatically increased with Curves adjustment layer

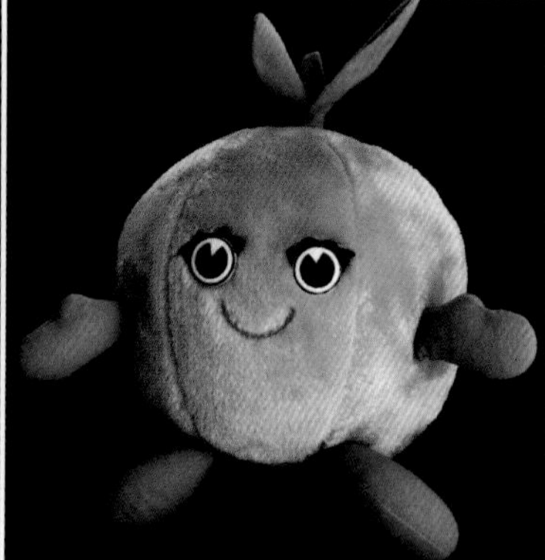

Adjustment layer set to Luminosity blend mode, removing color effect

In Photoshop's earlier days, we would try to lighten an underexposed image by duplicating its layer and setting the blend mode of the duplicate to Screen. If the image was very dark, we might do that a couple of times. Of course, this bloated the file size. Later, we'd create an adjustment layer (it didn't matter which one, as we wouldn't actually make any adjustment per se) and set its mode to Screen (or Multiply for overexposed images). Even with no adjustment, this was identical to a duplicate layer set to Screen, but with little or no effect on file size.

In short, the effect of applying a blend mode to an adjustment layer is the same as adjusting a duplicate layer with that blend mode applied.

Blend Modes & Groups

By default, a group uses a blend mode called Pass Through. With this mode, layers in the group blend with layers outside the group as they would if they were not grouped. That is, those layers' blending *passes through* to the layers outside the group.

Any other blend mode is very different, including Normal. The layers in the group act *as if* they'd been merged, with the result blending with the rest of the document. The effect is similar to converting the layers into a Smart Object and changing its blend mode.

In the following example, a color fill layer is blended with an image of an illustration, and the result, grouped, is blended with the image below it.

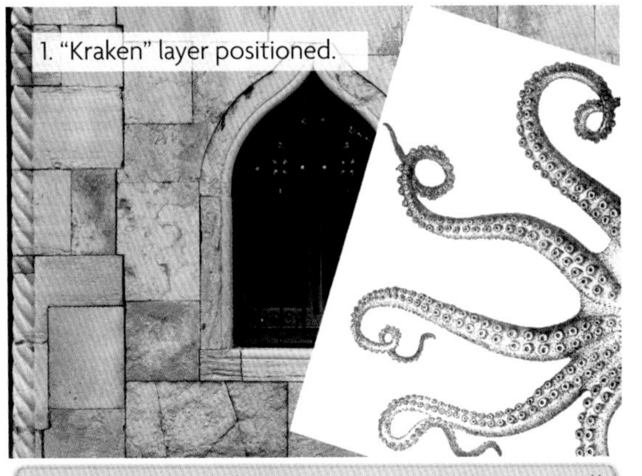
1. "Kraken" layer positioned.

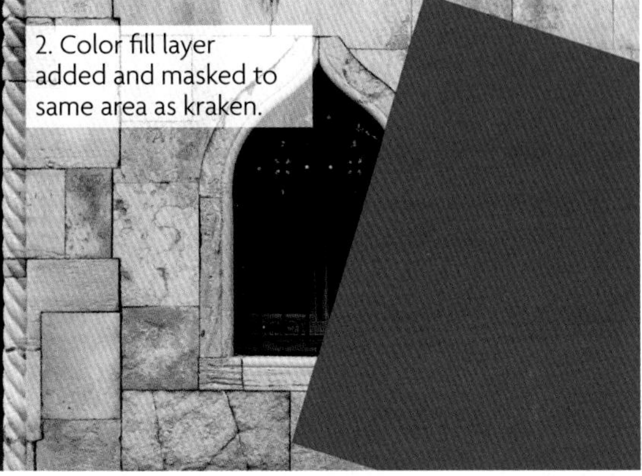
2. Color fill layer added and masked to same area as kraken.

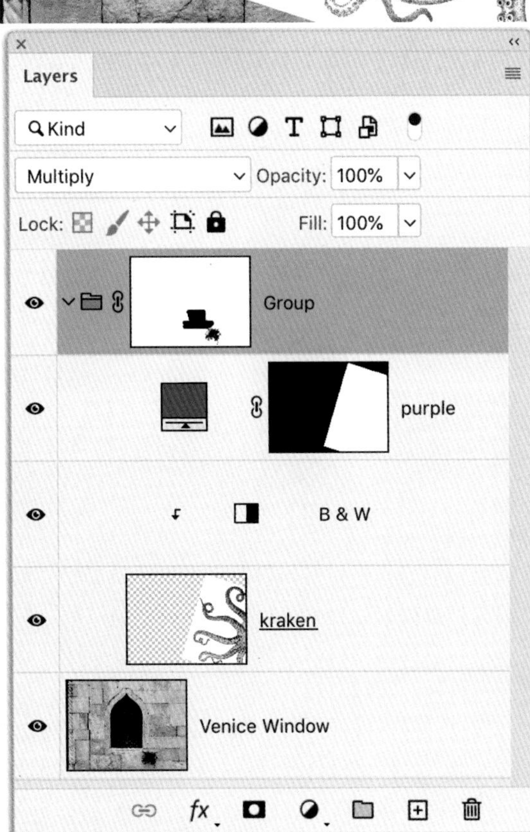

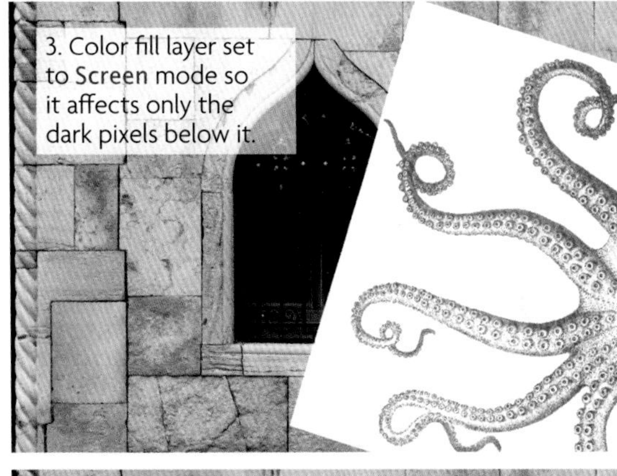
3. Color fill layer set to Screen mode so it affects only the dark pixels below it.

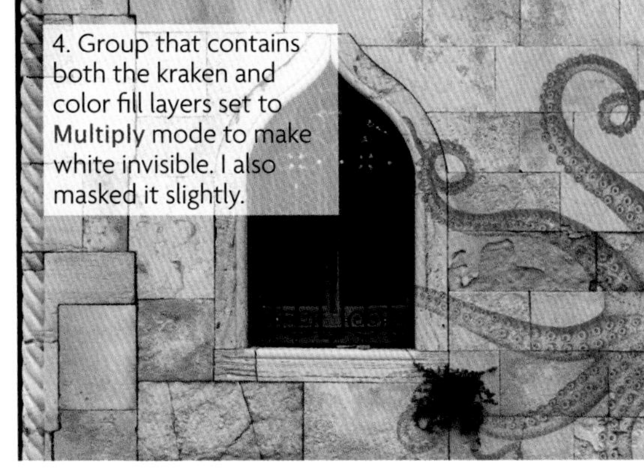
4. Group that contains both the kraken and color fill layers set to Multiply mode to make white invisible. I also masked it slightly.

Layer Styles & Effects

Layer Styles, also known as layer effects, are effective ways to add editable, transferable, high-performance panache to layer content. Some effects (or "fx") can be applied multiple times to the same layer for even more elaborate results.

Applying and Editing Styles

To apply effects to a selected layer, drag a style preset from the Styles panel; use the fx menu at the bottom of the Layers panel; or choose an effect from Layer > Layer Style. To refine a preset's parameters, double-click on the letters fx to the right of the layer's name. The other methods immediately open the same dialog box. In that dialog box, you can add multiple effects, adjust them, disable them, etc. From the same dialog, you can access the layer's blending options and a list of styles you've saved for later access in any document.

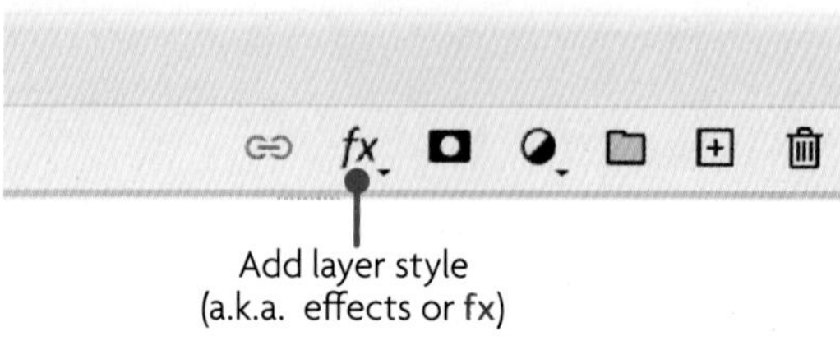

To reveal all presets in the Styles panel, hold down ⌘/Ctrl as you click a disclosure arrow (>) to the left of a style group's name. Doing that again hides them. Use the Styles panel menu to create new style presets or groups. Drag styles into groups to organize them.

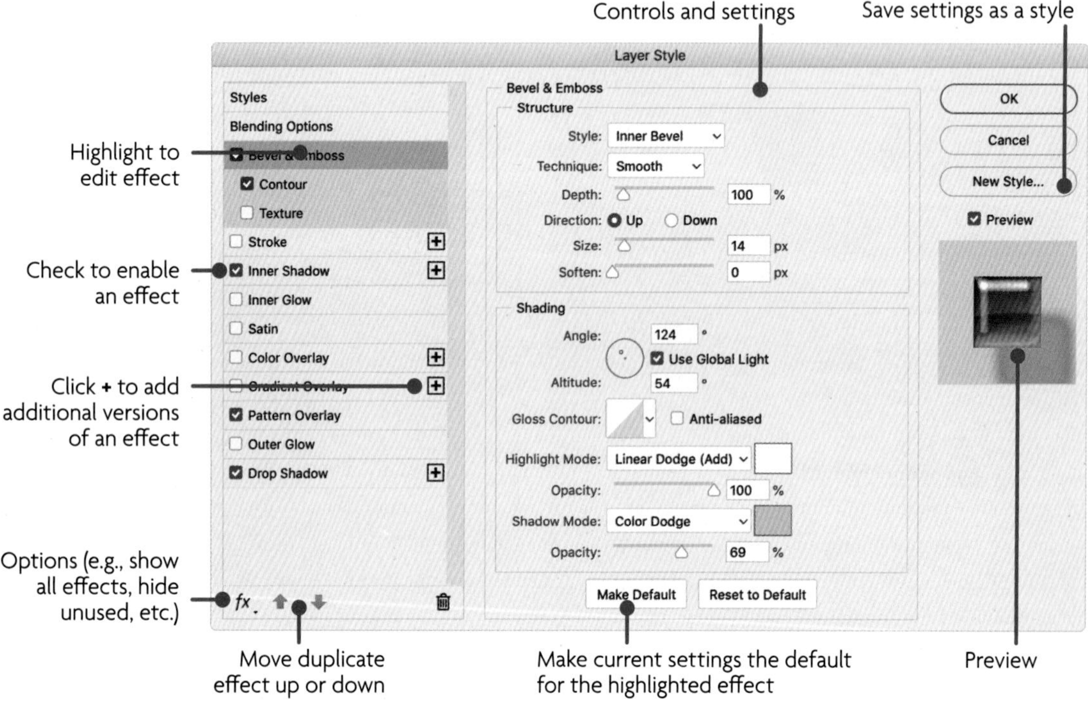

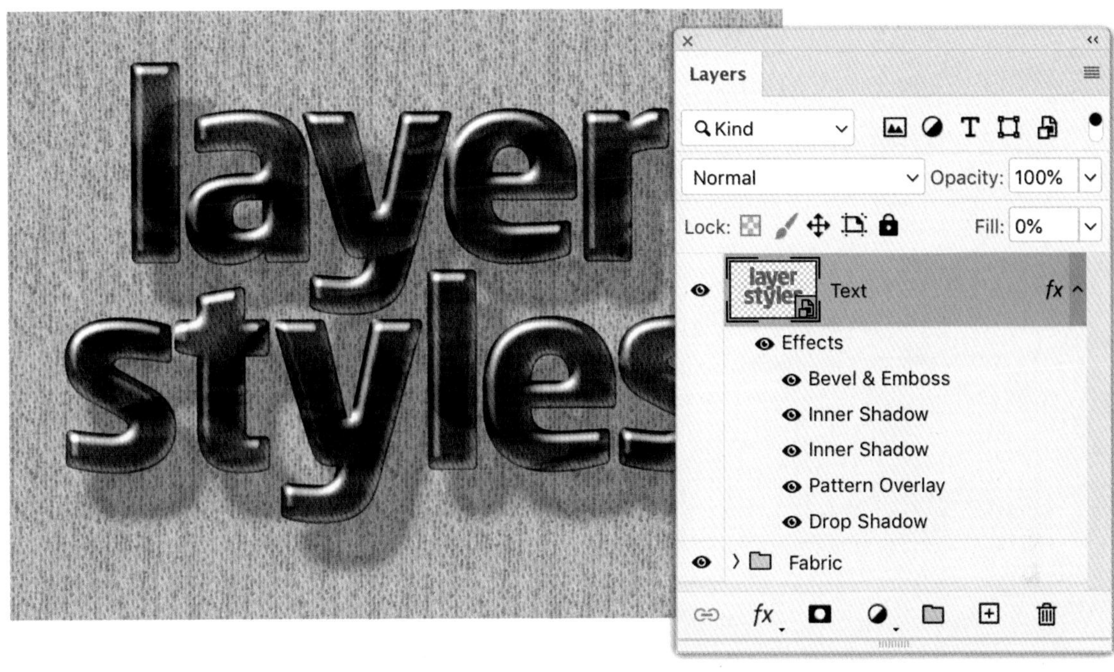

In the Layer Style dialog, be sure to click on the name of an effect to both apply it and see its controls. Merely checking its checkbox will enable that effect, but you'll have no idea how it's configured.

Later, to revisit or edit the style you've previously applied, you can reopen the Layer Style dialog by using any of several methods:

- Double-click the fx icon to the right of the layer's name
- Double-click the specific effect listed under the layer
- Select the layer, then use the fx menu at the bottom of the Layers panel
- Select the layer then use the Layer > Layer Style menu

Be ready and willing to explore and experiment! The number of options is nearly infinite. And just because something is called a "shadow" doesn't mean it can't be used as a glow—or the other way around. There are no inflexible rules in this feature. Have fun!

Saving Styles

If you configure a combination of effects that you like, you may wish to save it as a style that can be applied easily later. I sometimes create styles while I'm experimenting so I can get back to a successful combination if my continued tinkering should lead to a dead end.

From the Layer Style dialog, click the New Style… button. A small dialog box appears in which you can name the style (a good idea) and choose a couple of options. The style illustrated above benefits from a reduced Fill opacity, so I needed to check Include Layer Blending Options so a later application of the style will derive the same benefit. You can also add the style to a Creative Cloud library so it can be accessed from other devices.

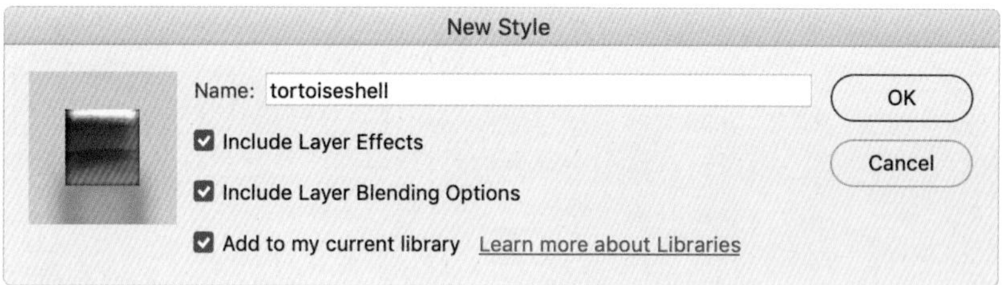

Fill differs from Opacity in one crucial way: where Opacity affects a layer entirely, effects and all, Fill only affects the layer's native content, leaving the effects fully intact. In the tortoiseshell example above, I didn't want to see the purple color of the text at all, so I reduced Fill to 0.

The Effects Listed

To help guide your experiments, I've compiled a brief description of each type of effect, with a couple of examples in most cases. There are several controls that you'll see in multiple effects' controls. For example, every effect in which Global Light is checked uses the same light source angle—throughout the document! That means if you adjust the angle in one effect for one layer, you could be adjusting every effect on every layer.

Drop Shadow

We've all seen many of these. It's a fast way to give a sense of space and separation between elements in an image. By default, the shadow is black and uses the Multiply blend mode to darken whatever is under it. The color and mode are editable. The mode is chosen via the menu near the top of the dialog, and the color by clicking the small color (black) square to the right of the mode.

To adjust the shadow's position, simply move the cursor into the image while the dialog is open. You'll see it become a move tool cursor that moves not the layer but the shadow. As you move the shadow, the Distance and Angle controls will change in the dialog.

The Size slider effectively blurs the shadow. The blurrier it is, the larger the area it covers. To increase the shadow's solidity over that area, use Spread.

The above controls comprise the shadow's Structure. The Quality section has two controls: Contour and Noise. The latter is easy to adjust and see. Why make a shadow grainy in this way? A little noise can help the shadow hold up in its wispiest areas on some printers. Some think it just looks more interesting.

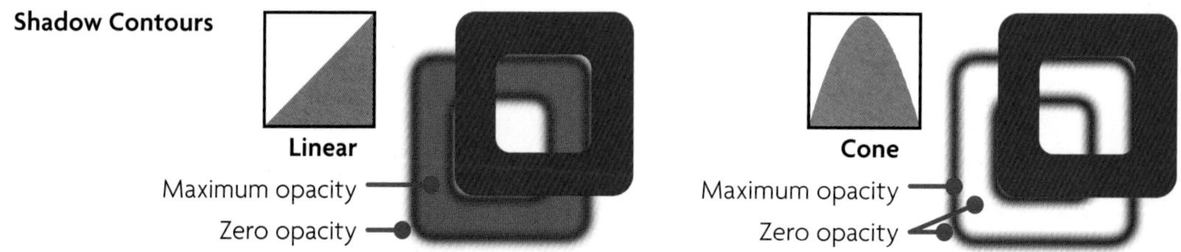

Contour is a more subtle and tricky control. It is a kind of graph of the shadow's opacity as you move from its outer edge to its center. By default, the center of the shadow is exactly as opaque as the Opacity setting indicates. Consider that the maximum opacity. The Linear contour gives the most intuitive result: 0% opacity at the outermost edge to the maximum in the center. Cone goes from 0% opacity at the edge to maximum opacity closer in, then back to 0% in the shadow's center. I used a custom derivative of the cone Contour for the tortoiseshell style earlier. Why? Look at the shadow of a water glass and note how it's denser near the edges.

There are several Contours to choose from that can even be edited. Most users are surprised that there are so many options for something as mundane as a shadow. The deeper one goes, it seems, the more one finds!

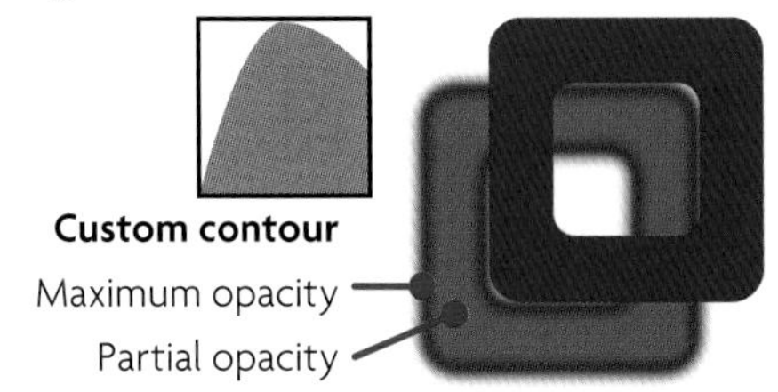

Bevel & Emboss

This effect gives a sense of volume for a two-dimensional layer by letting one edge catch light and the opposite edge fall into shadow (controlled by the Highlight and Shadow parts of the Shading section of the dialog).

Style: Sets whether and how the effect is spread over the layer and/or its surroundings.

Technique: Sets whether the effect is clean-cut. Chisel Soft often looks like something cut with a dull knife (a bit chewed up).

Depth: The strength of the effect. Affects contrast between lit and shadowed sides.

Direction: Sets whether the layer looks like it rises out of or sinks into its surroundings.

Size: The total distance near the layer's edge that's affected.

Soften: Blurs the effect.

Angle/Altitude: Control the location of the light source on a virtual dome over the layer.

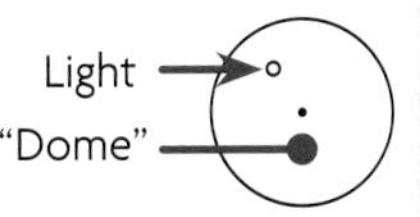

Gloss Contour: Acts like a Curves adjustment applied to the lighting of the effect. *Very* different from the Contour sub-effect.

Highlight/Shadow Modes, color, and Opacity: Control the appearance and intensity of the lighting on the layer.

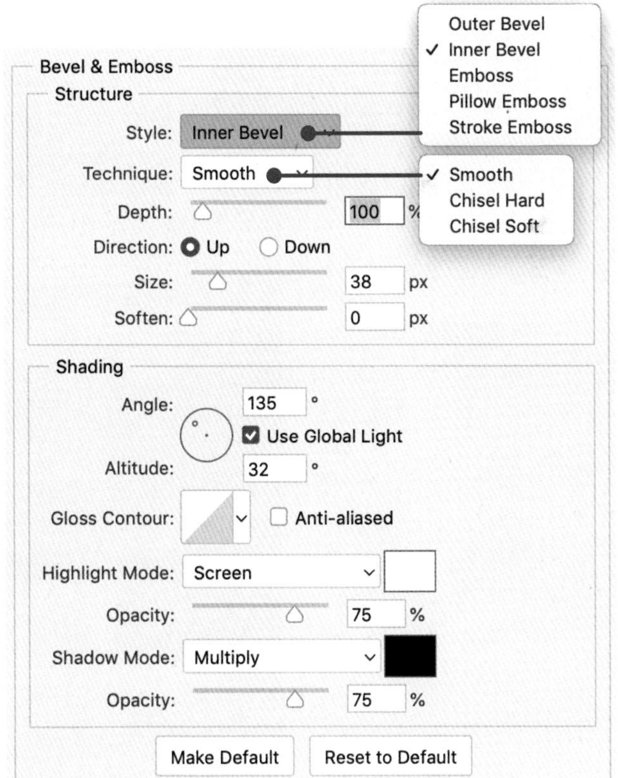

The largest impact comes from the topmost options. The Style menu determines the layer's relationship to its surroundings and how much the light is caught by them. For example, Inner Bevel keeps the effect within the layer's boundaries, giving the impression that the layer is independent of the rest of the document. Outer Bevel keeps the effect outside the layer's boundaries, as if it were a plateau. Emboss and Pillow Emboss split the effect between the layer and its surroundings.

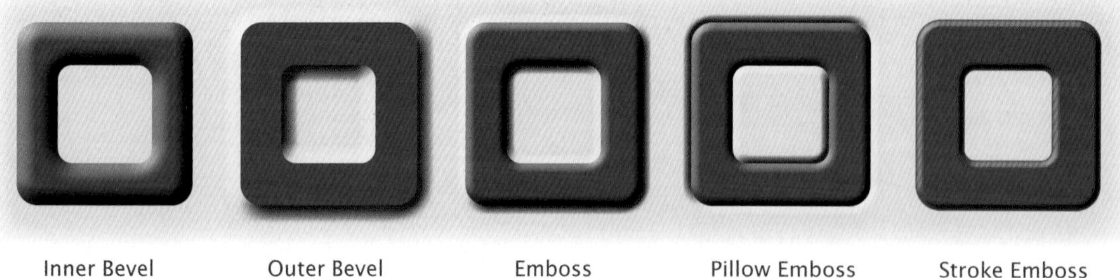

Up and Down determine whether the layer is rising up from its surroundings or is depressed into it. Above, the bevels and embosses are set to Up; below, they're set to Down. Note that the Stroke Emboss *requires* a Stroke effect.

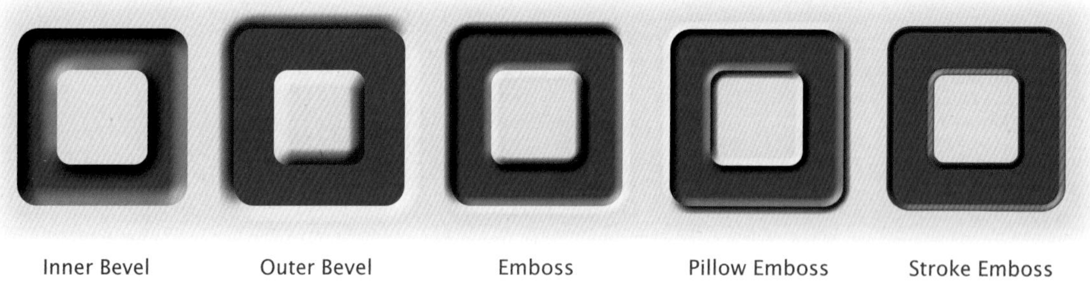

I find that a Down Outer Bevel combines effectively with an Inner Shadow. Below is a simple stencil effect using just those two effects on some text. I did change the bevel's Technique from Smooth to Chisel Hard for cleaner-cut look.

A Chisel Hard Bevel and Inner Shadow

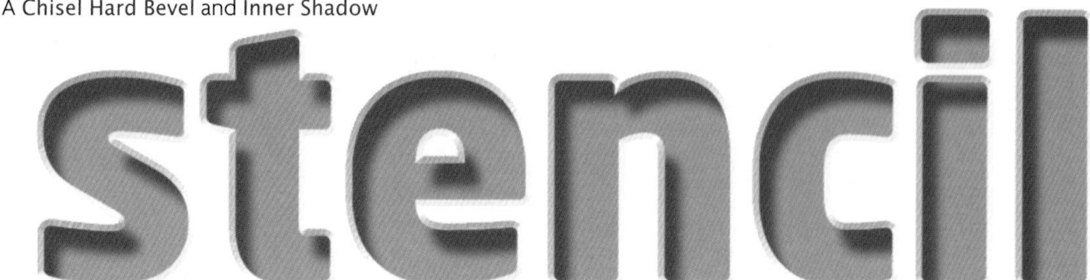

The Highlight and Shadow Modes benefit from experimentation. For example, the tortoise-shell effect that began this section has an unusual setting for the shadow side of its emboss. I changed the color to a yellow (via the color chip to the right of the Shadow Mode menu) and changed the Shadow Mode to Color Dodge, definitely not a mode that darkens.

By default, the Shadow Mode is set to Multiply and black

By changing it to something that lightens, it looks like an inner reflection in the layer

I changed the Highlight Mode, too, so the highlight would be a little stronger and seem more reflective.

Contour

Not an effect unto itself, Contour helps give form and definition to a Bevel effect. If a bevel itself isn't supplying the right edge on your layer, you may try using the various contours in the menu (or make your own, as illustrated below). To achieve more fidelity to some contours, set the bevel's Technique to Chisel Hard.

To smooth rounded corners, check the box for Anti-aliased. This removes a harsh "stair-step" effect. Finally, so that the contour is evenly applied across the width of the bevel, set the Range to 50%. Other settings stretch one end of the contour, crushing the other.

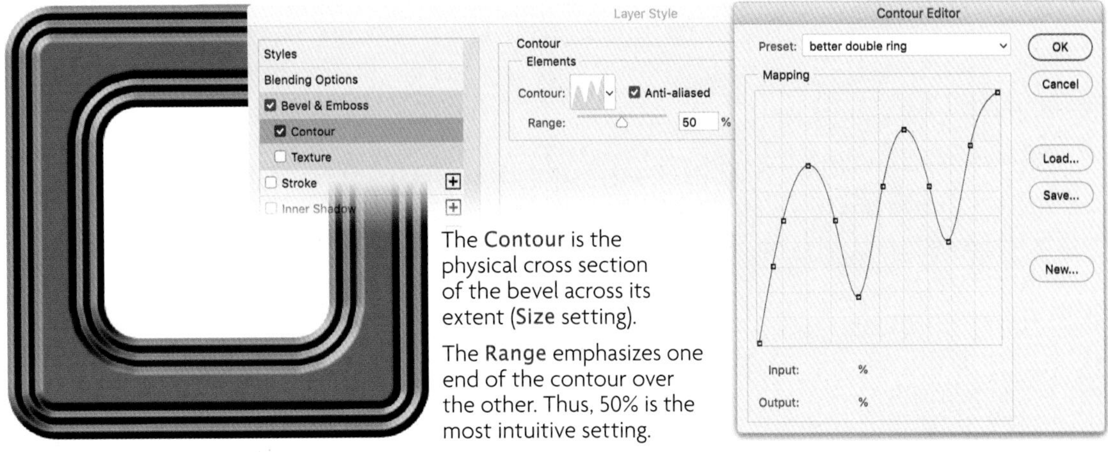

The Contour is the physical cross section of the bevel across its extent (Size setting).

The Range emphasizes one end of the contour over the other. Thus, 50% is the most intuitive setting.

Texture

Texture is another sub-effect of Bevel. With it, a pattern's tone is used to give depth cues to the surface of the layer. Dark and light become up and down, respectively. Unfortunately, this is reversed from other features in Photoshop that use tone as depth. So I almost always check the Invert checkbox to make it more consistent with those other features.

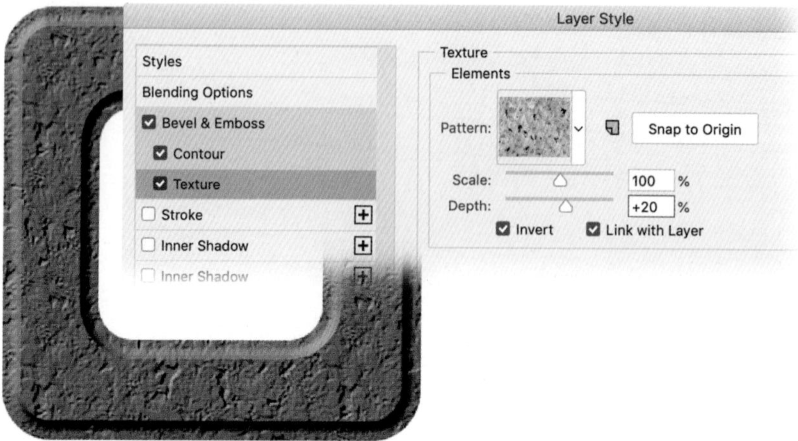

Contrasty patterns almost always look horrible at first: The texture is too intense. Reducing the Depth setting takes care of that. Negative Depth settings are the same as using Invert. Scale simply makes the pattern bigger or smaller. If you need the ups and downs to keep their positions relative to the layer, be sure Link with Layer is checked so the pattern moves with the layer; otherwise, the pattern will be affixed to the document edges. Finally, Snap to Origin is supposed to move the upper-left corner of a pattern tile to the upper left of the layer or the document. I find this button unreliable.

Stroke

At first glance, the options for the Stroke effect seem few and straightforward. One chooses a color to surround the layer's perimeter, how thick it should be, and some blending options.

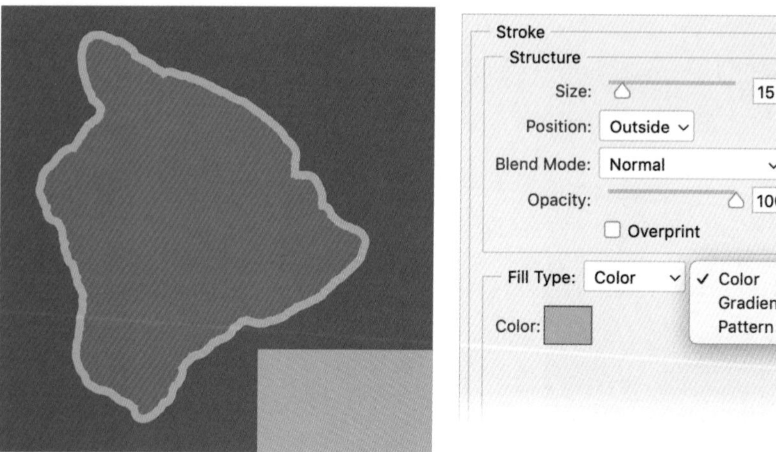

However, a look at the innocuous Fill Type menu reveals that gradients and patterns can be used as strokes as well.

A Pattern stroke is little more complex than a solid color. The only other option to consider is the pattern's Scale and whether, like the patterns used for a bevel's texture, it should be Linked with Layer or not.

Gradient strokes are another animal. You may recall how complex Gradient Fill layers are. Since many options are similar, you may wish to review "Gradient" (page 141).

Gradient strokes have the same types (Linear, Radial, etc.) as any other gradients, plus a striking addition: Shape Burst.

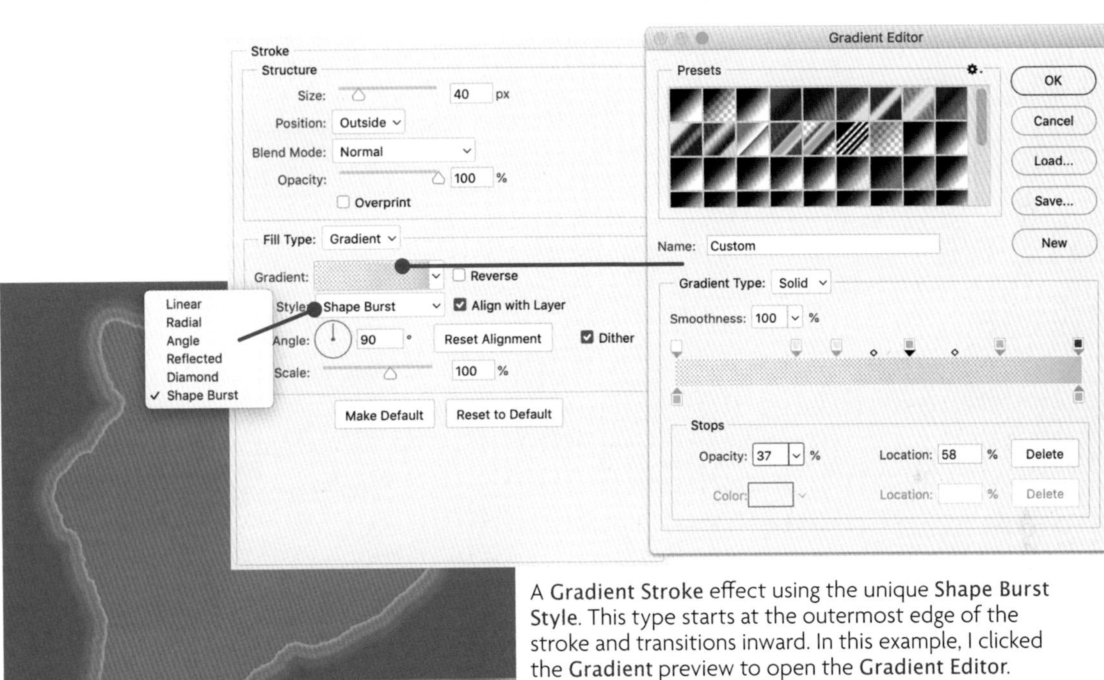

A Gradient Stroke effect using the unique Shape Burst Style. This type starts at the outermost edge of the stroke and transitions inward. In this example, I clicked the Gradient preview to open the Gradient Editor. There, I created a gradient that starts transparent, ends almost opaque, and oscillates in opacity on the way up in a wave-like manner. A linear sample can be seen in the lower-right corner of the image.

All strokes can have their Position set to be completely Inside the layer, Outside (as in the examples above), or Centered on the layer's edge.

Inner Shadow

Nearly everything I wrote about the Drop Shadow is true for the Inner Shadow effect. The difference is that we usually use Inner Shadow to make our layer look like a hole in what's around it. Sometimes I use it with 0 Distance to darken the edges of an object. The earlier stencil (page 200) shows the more common use: to make the layer seem like it's a surface below.

Inner Glow and Outer Glow

Both glow effects have controls that are quite similar to the Drop Shadow effect: Blend Mode, Opacity, color, and Contour. In fact, by changing the color (to something dark) and Blend Mode (to one that darkens), a glow can become another shadow. But unlike a shadow, glows can use more than one color by using a gradient, rather than a color. To understand a glow's Contour, I recommend reading its description in the section "Drop Shadow" (page 198).

As the name implies, an Outer Glow effect resides outside a layer's boundaries. An Inner Glow is on the inside, either emanating from the center or the edge of the layer, depending on which Source is selected. The default Technique is Softer: The glow somewhat loosely approximates the shape of the layer. Precise forces the glow to better conform to the layer's shape.

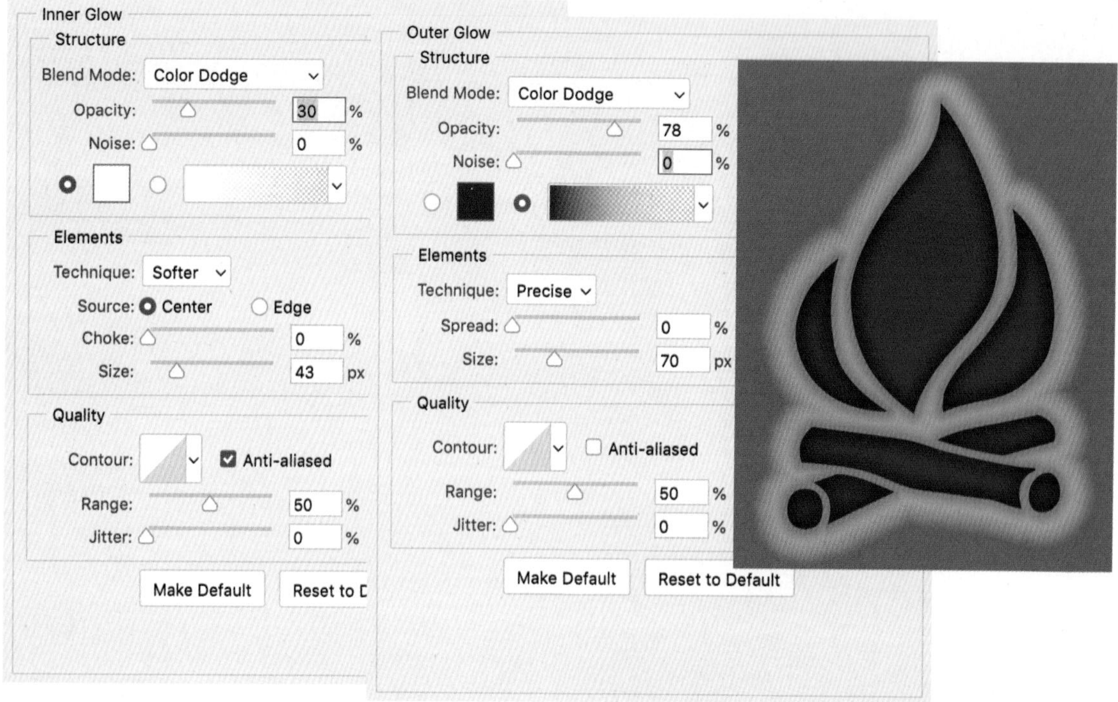

In the example above, I'm using both glows. The Inner Glow is set to use the default color of white, but I chose Color Dodge as the Blend Mode to accentuate the red fill of the layer. I also set its Source to Center. The Outer Glow uses a gradient with a Precise Technique to better fit the layer's shape. You may notice that a Gradient Stroke effect (see previous page) and Outer Glow can be very similar.

If you find that the wispiest parts of a glow cut off abruptly when printed, you can introduce a small amount of Noise. With gradient glows, the Jitter slider can also be used to dither (add noise to) the gradient.

Satin

Most find this effect a little mysterious when first attempted. But if you configure it right, you can begin to see what it's up to. It essentially makes virtual silhouettes of the layer in the chosen Color and Blend Mode. One of these silhouettes is offset from the layer using the Distance and Angle settings. The other is moved the same distance, but in the opposite direction. Where they overlap, they disappear to create a kind of interference pattern similar to moiré pattern. This pattern is clipped to the edges of the layer to conceal the trick.

A shape layer.

Two silhouettes disappearing where they overlap. Both are offset about 20 pixels, one at 45°, the other in the opposite direction.

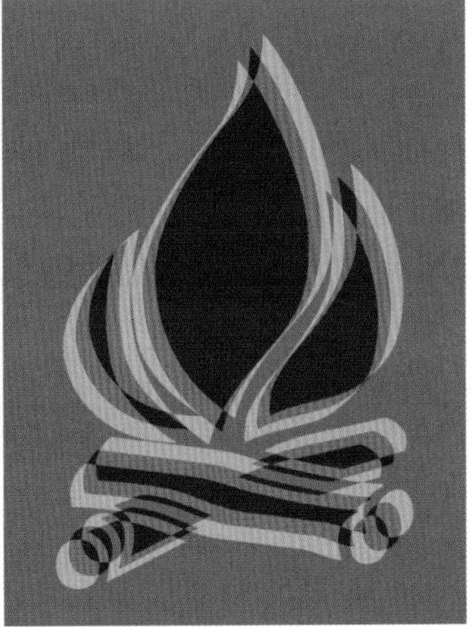

Those silhouettes relative to the layer.

The actual Satin effect with 20 pixels Distance and 45° Angle. The color is set to white and the Blend Mode to Color Dodge. With Size at a minimum value, the silhouettes are sharp-edged.

Size (a form of blur) increased enough to make the effect translucent.

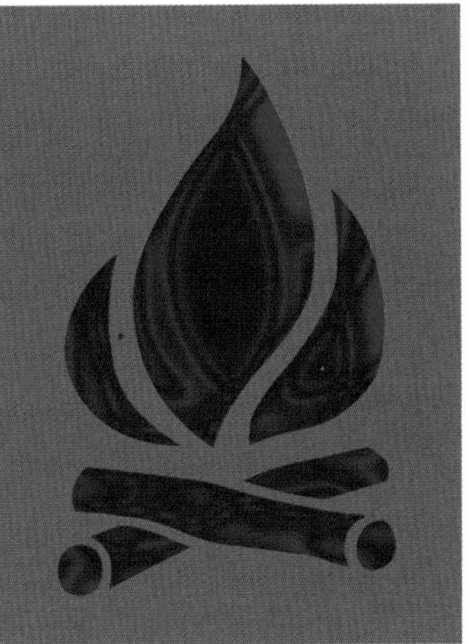

Size and Distance increased and a wavy Contour chosen to create a ripply pattern.

Overlays: Color, Gradient, and Pattern

Imagine duplicating a layer and replacing its nontransparent content with a color, gradient, and/or pattern. This is what the overlay effects do. With Opacity or Blend Mode adjusted, the overlay can interact interestingly with the original content. Below are simple examples of the three overlays (with the original for comparison):

Note that both the Gradient and Pattern Overlay effects can be scaled, and gradients can be angled. Also, as you're editing a Gradient and Pattern Overlay, you can use the cursor to move the overlay by dragging on the image itself.

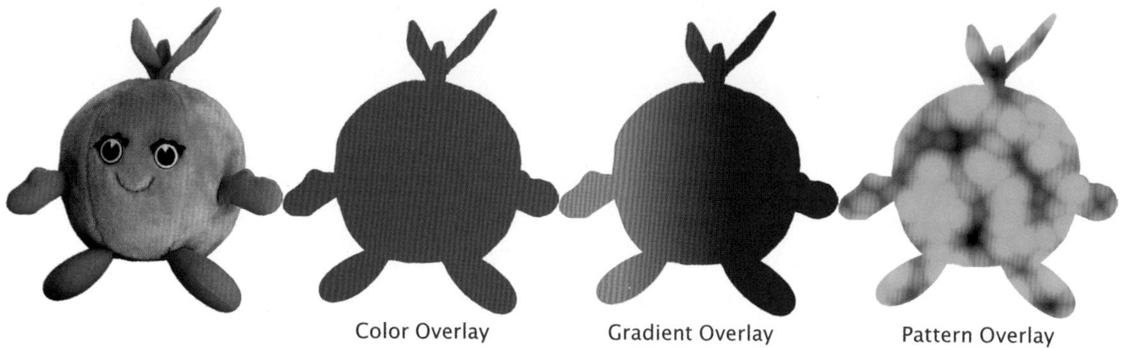

Layer Styles & Groups

Effects can be applied to layer groups as easily as to individual layers. When you do so, those effects impact the group as if its layers had been merged or converted to a Smart Object, but without that level of entanglement.

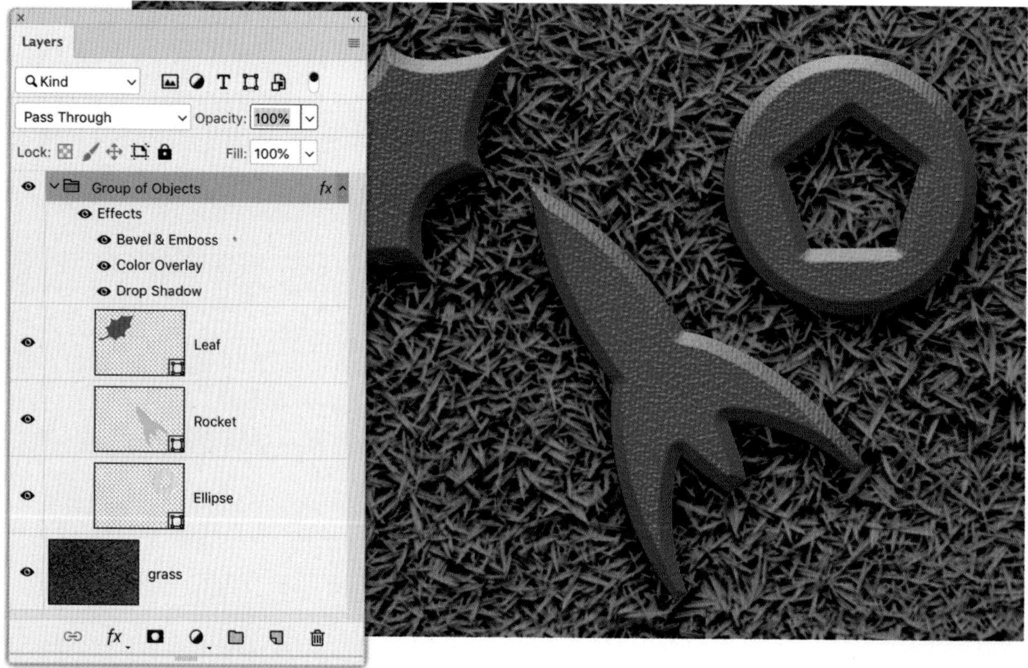

Advanced Blending Options

Hidden in the Layer Style dialog box are several options that are useful both on their own and with "Layer Styles & Effects" (page 196). So, you may wish to return to this topic after using Layer Styles a bit.

To access all the Blending Options, double-click *near* (not on) a layer's name; click on the fx menu at the bottom of the Layers panel and choose Blending Options…; or choose Layer > Layer Style > Blending Options…. After settings from the Advanced Blending section are applied, an icon appears to the right of the layer's name to alert you: .

Fill Opacity

Simply put, Fill Opacity is identical to ordinary Opacity, except Fill does not affect Layer Styles. That is, if the Fill setting is lowered, the layer's "native" content disappears, but any effects do not. So you may have a Drop Shadow (page 198) that seems to be cast by nothing! More usefully, we can create styles without regard to the layer's original appearance and know that the style's appearance will be consistent.

Channels

This is an odd little option! For a layer with no layer under it, disabling a channel here is identical to disabling the visibility of a channel in the Channels panel—but for that layer alone. So, if you uncheck the blue (B) channel, an image will become rather yellow.

Interestingly, if there is a layer below, a disabled channel's data is replaced with the same channel's data from the layer(s) below. If there is a lot of blue data, for example, then the result will look rather blue!

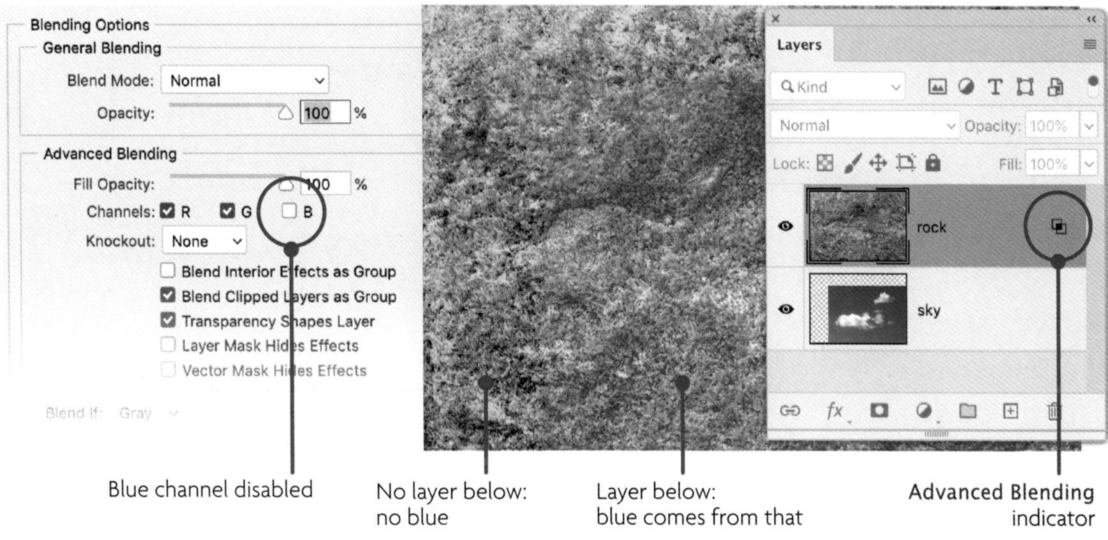

Knockout

Knockout is as much a masking technique as it is a way to blend layers. It's also tricky in that choosing a setting alone does nothing at all. You must choose Shallow or Deep from the Knockout menu, and also adjust the Fill Opacity. If the Fill is set to 0, then the layer's native content disappears and acts as a mask on layers below it. Since it's using Fill Opacity, Layer Styles like overlays and shadows remain.

If Knockout is set to Deep, the layer will knock out all the layers below it except for a Background, if there is one. If it's set to Shallow, then the layer masks, or "knocks out," layers below it in the same layer group. If no groups exist, Shallow and Deep have the same result. Hovering over the Knockout menu summons a reminder tooltip. Knockout is great for masking many layers at once, and can be limited by simply grouping layers.

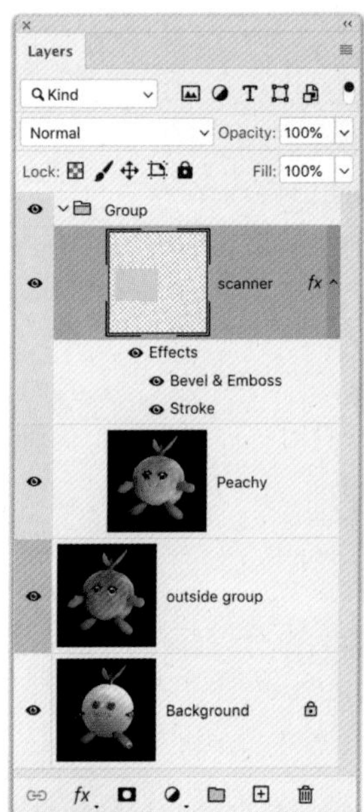

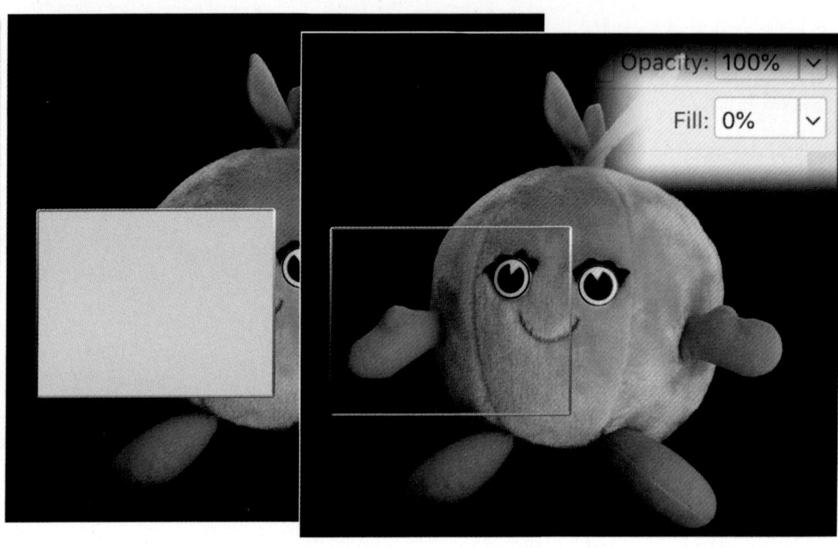

A picture of Peachy is grouped with a green rectangle layer. Below the group are two layers with variations on Peachy, one a disturbing Background. Above right, the rectangle is set to 0% Fill Opacity. Below left, Knockout is set to Shallow, and below right, it's set to Deep, each revealing layers below the group.

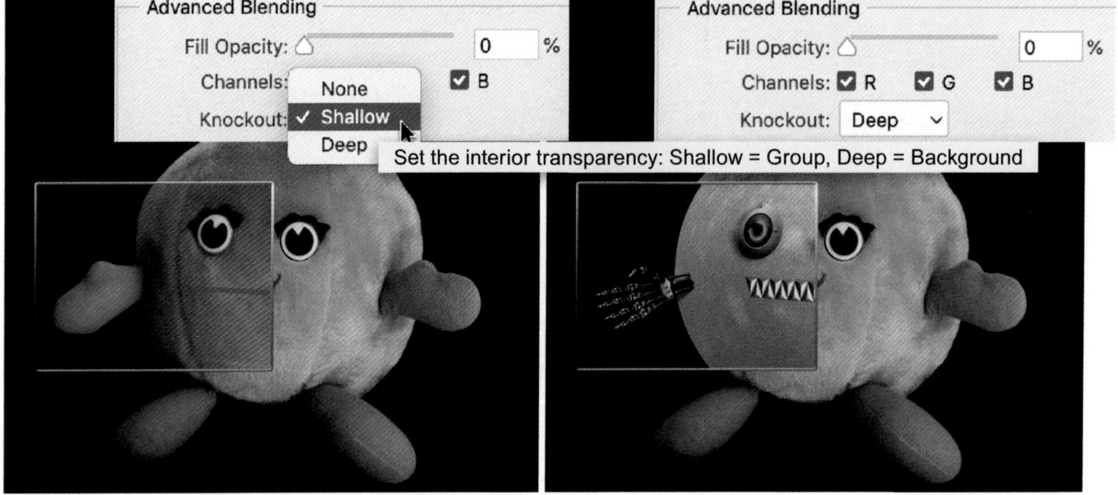

Blend Interior Effects as Group

This option is subtle and difficult to use effectively. It impacts only some of the effects that act within a layer's interior: Inner Glow, Satin, and the Overlay effects. Inner Shadow is *not* included. Enabling this option causes these effects to blend with each other as a unit ("as group"), and to be treated as part of the layer's native content when the layer blends with the rest of the document.

The upshot is that Fill Opacity, which normally has no impact on *any* effects, will impact these "interior" effects when this feature is enabled.

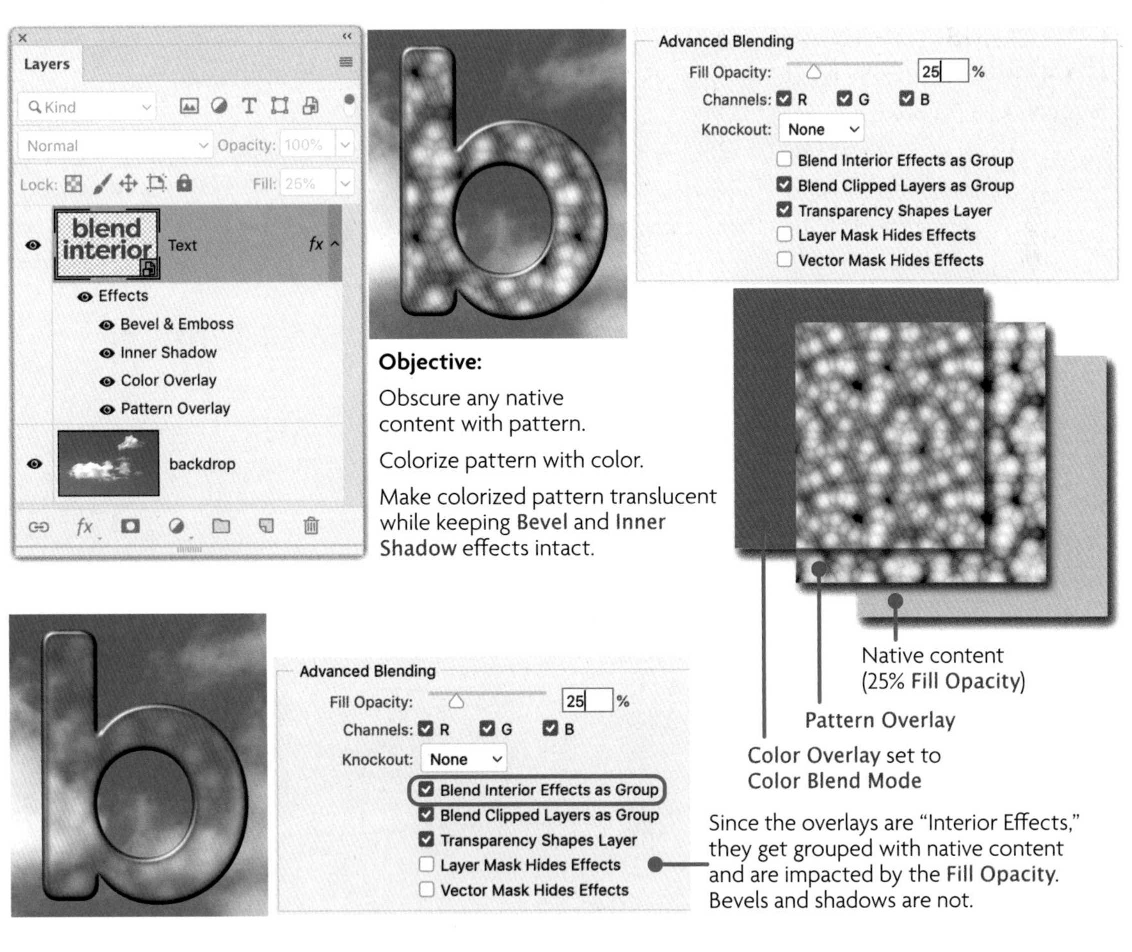

Blend Clipped Layers as Group

This option, enabled by default, treats layers that are clipped to another as part of that other layer's native content. See "Clipping Mask" (page 295) to know how layers are masked in this way. So, those clipped layers will vanish if the base layer of that clipping mask has its Fill Opacity set to 0.

If you want clipped layers to retain their own blending, disable this option in the base layer's Blending Options.

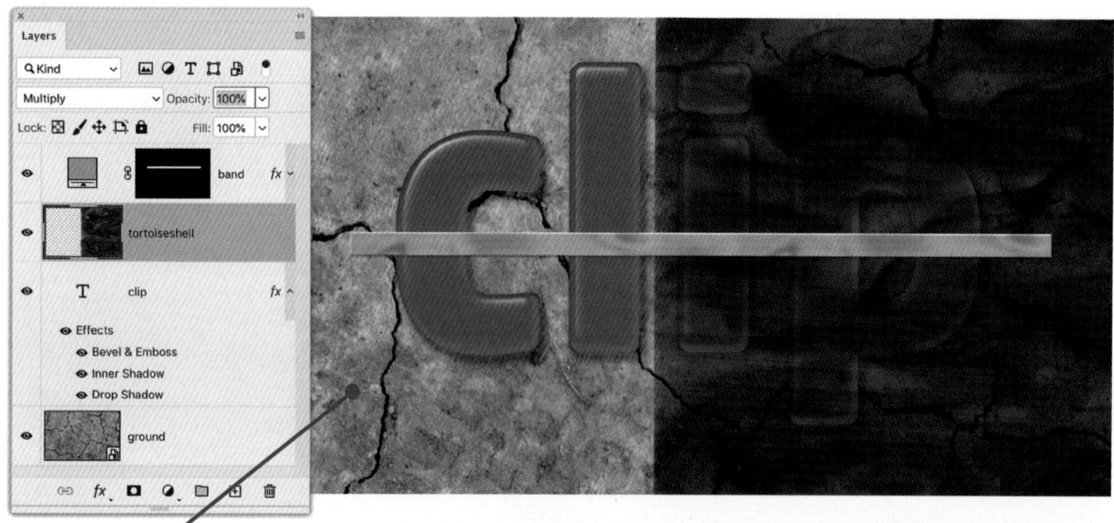

Above: A layer containing a tortoiseshell pattern set to **Multiply** blend mode (to simulate that translucent substance), a thin grayish layer set to **Normal** to look like a metal band, and a type layer with effects to make it look dimensional.

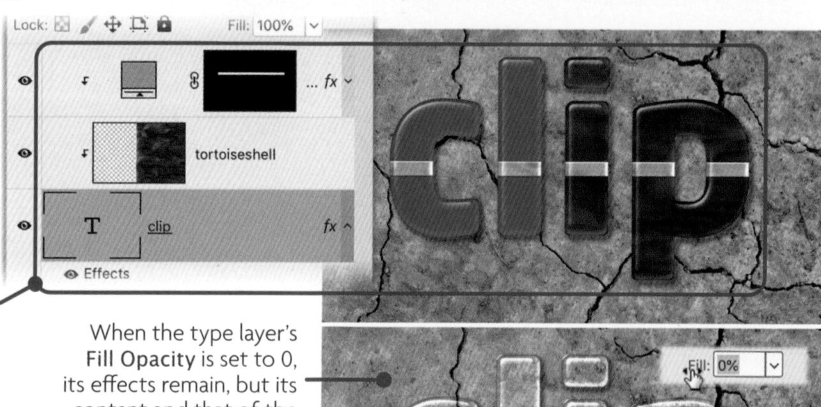

Right: The metal band and tortoiseshell layers clipped to the type layer. The clipped layers act as if they've been merged into the type layer, inheriting its effects.

When the type layer's **Fill Opacity** is set to 0, its effects remain, but its content and that of the clipped layers are lost since they're treated "as group."

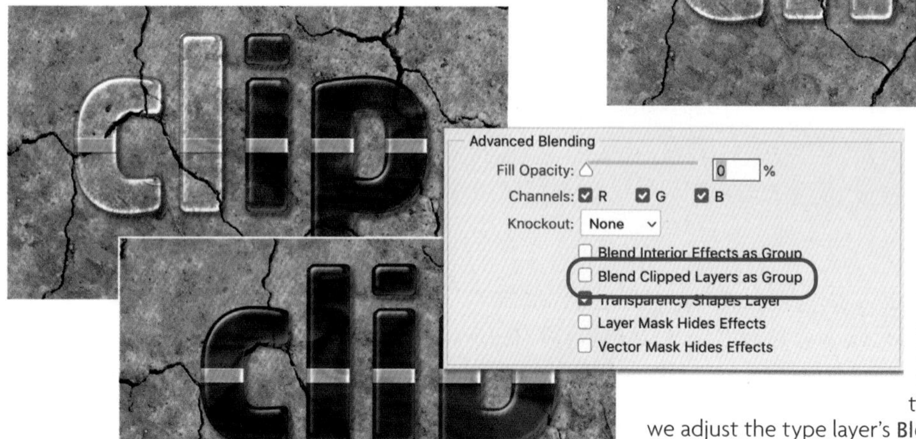

To retain the opaque metal band layer and the translucent tortoiseshell layer, we adjust the type layer's **Blending Options** to disable **Blend Clipped Layers as Group**.

At bottom: Tortoiseshell layer moved into correct position.

Transparency Shapes Layer

Ordinarily, a mask works with layer content to form the shape of a layer to which effects are applied. This Advanced Blending Option, enabled by default, uses the layer's inherently nontransparent content to exhibit effects. This does not take into account transparency produced by masking. When this option is disabled, only a mask's shape forms the layer, and gaps or holes in the layer's content are ignored. Sadly, this option has no effect on vector shape layers.

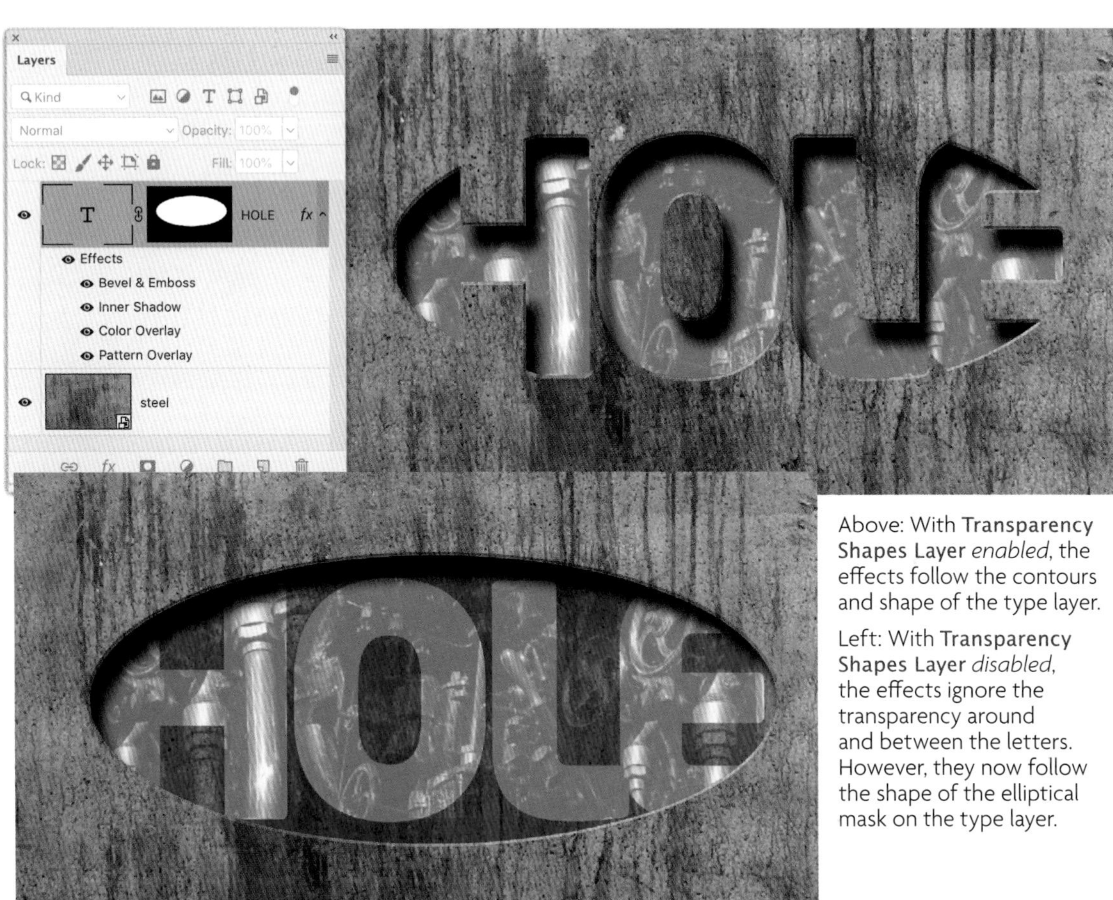

Above: With Transparency Shapes Layer *enabled*, the effects follow the contours and shape of the type layer.

Left: With Transparency Shapes Layer *disabled*, the effects ignore the transparency around and between the letters. However, they now follow the shape of the elliptical mask on the type layer.

Layer/Vector Mask Hides Effects

As mentioned above, a mask usually collaborates with layer content to form the shape of a layer to which effects are applied. When either Layer or Vector Mask Hides Effects is enabled, however, a mask will no longer be a factor in determining where effects are applied, but will instead mask both content and effects.

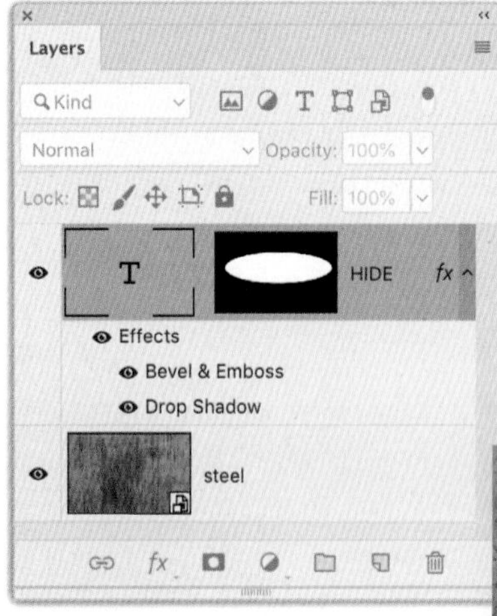

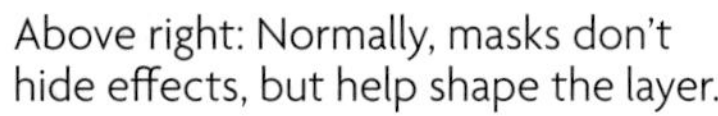

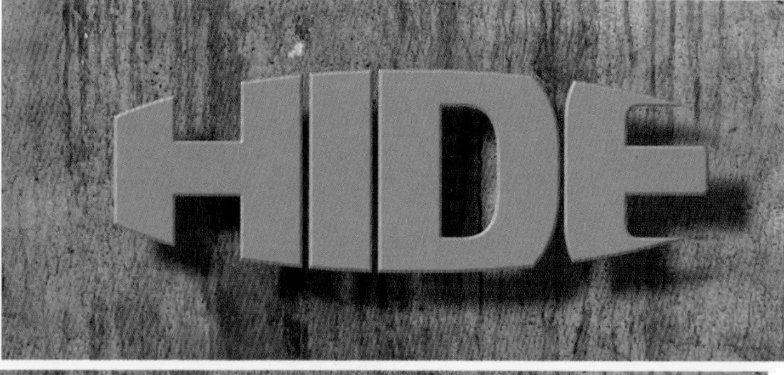

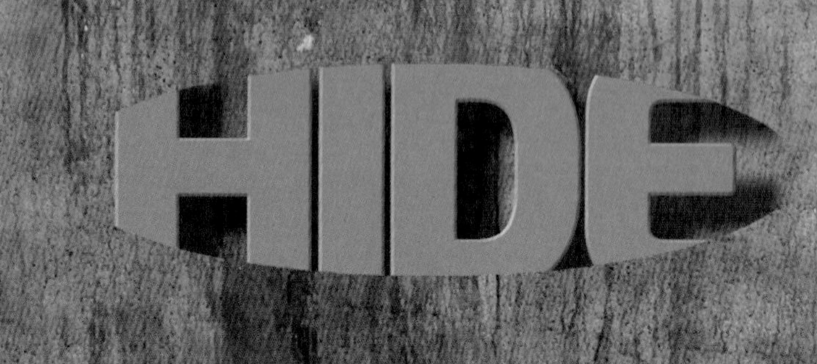

Above right: Normally, masks don't hide effects, but help shape the layer.

Right: With Layer or Vector Mask Hides Effects enabled, a mask hides content and effects.

Blend If

These sliders in a layer's Blending Options control a layer's visibility based on its own tones or the tones of the layer(s) visible below. You can also use the shades of gray of each color channel. That's why, when I teach this feature, I call it "visible if." As usual, you may use the fx menu at the bottom of the Layers panel to access the Blending Options.

These sliders currently indicate that the stone type layer is visible over all of its own tonal range (levels 0–255) and that of the layer below.

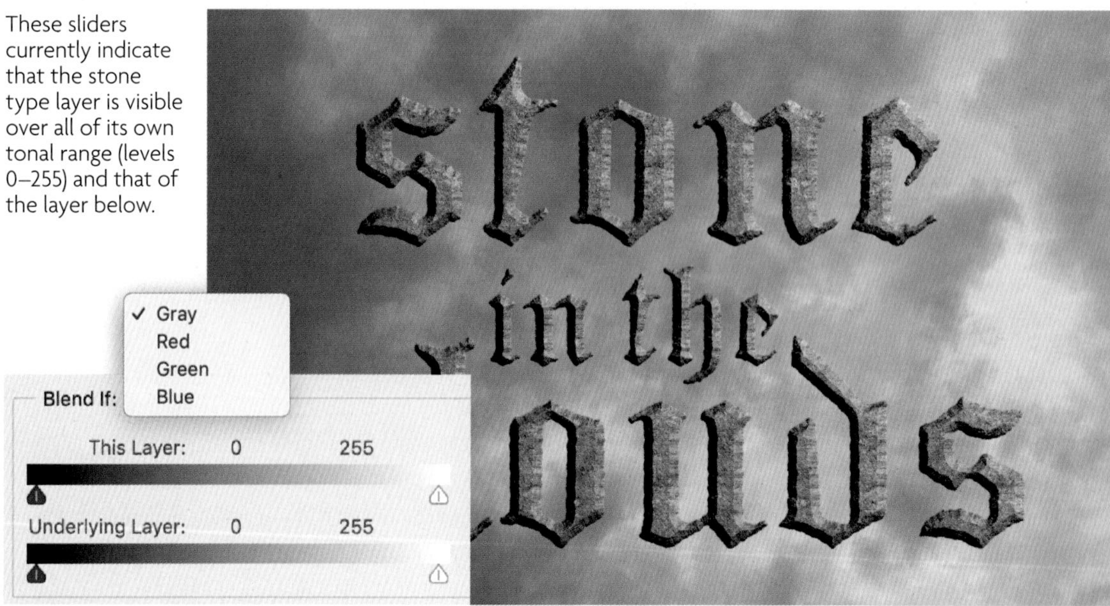

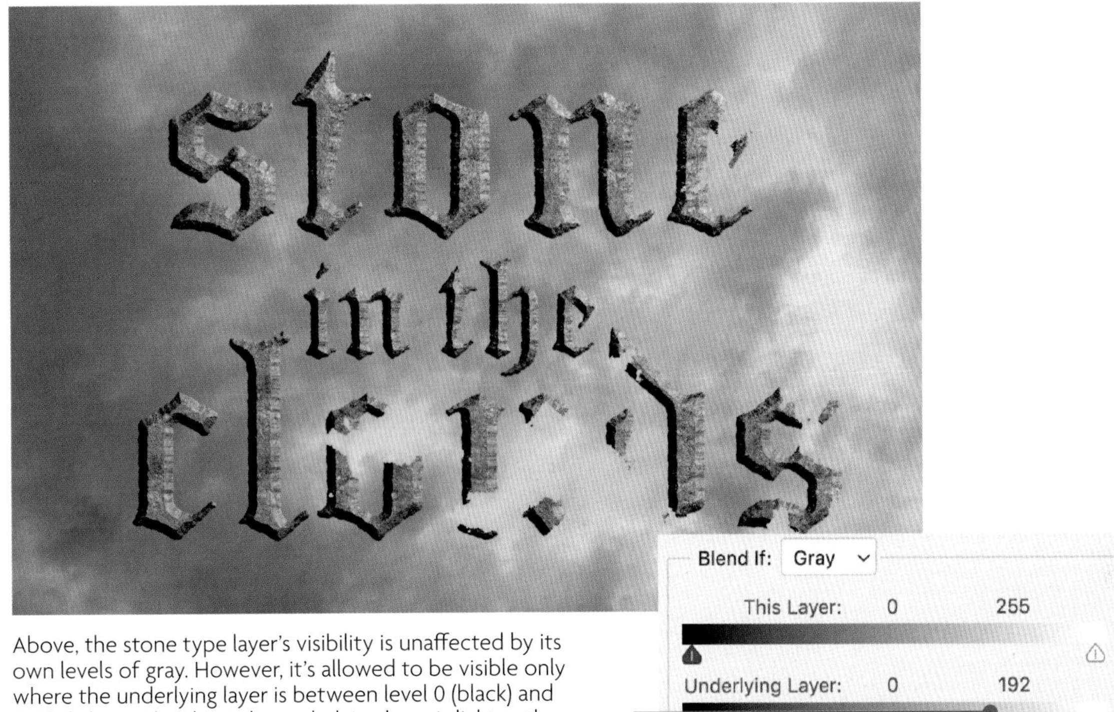

Above, the stone type layer's visibility is unaffected by its own levels of gray. However, it's allowed to be visible only where the underlying layer is between level 0 (black) and 192 (a light gray). Where the underlying layer is lighter, the type is hidden. Unfortunately, the cutoff is rather abrupt.

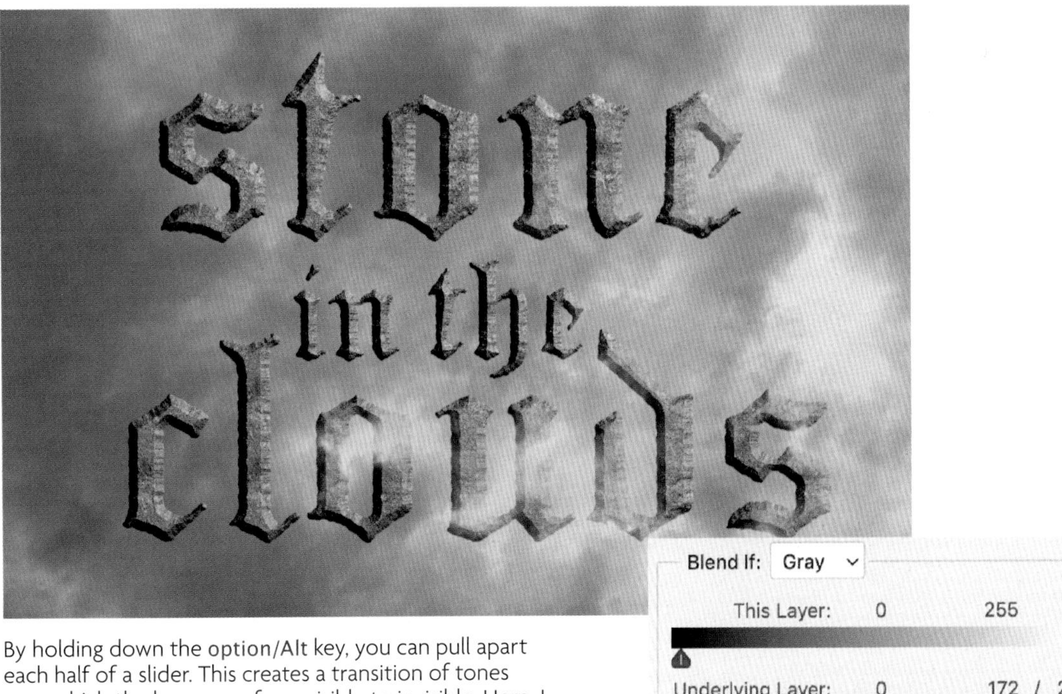

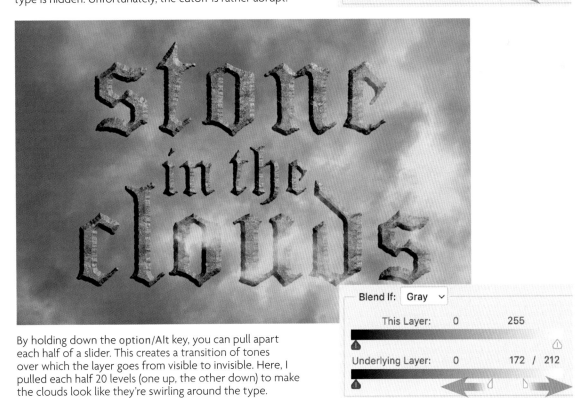

By holding down the option/Alt key, you can pull apart each half of a slider. This creates a transition of tones over which the layer goes from visible to invisible. Here, I pulled each half 20 levels (one up, the other down) to make the clouds look like they're swirling around the type.

2 Adjustments & Color

Even the best photos need at least a tweak. Many need much more.

To acquaint you with Photoshop's adjustment tools, this chapter has several parts:

How Color Works covers color theory and practice as it applies to Photoshop. It may be a bit technical, but it does answer the question about why prints may not match what you see on screen.

Then we discuss ***Sampling and Monitoring Image Colors***, or how to choose or assign a color for painting and other tasks.

In ***Adjustment Methods and Principles***, we'll discuss the three major approaches to adjustments. Because we're all fallible and because many adjustments are interpretive, I'll emphasize the nondestructive methods. These allow you to revisit and readjust later.

Finally, I'll present the ***The Adjustments, Listed***, so you can decide which you need for a given circumstance. Photoshop offers many!

How Color Works

Of course, that could be the title of an entire book or series. I'll attempt to restrict myself to what you need to know to work in Photoshop. Please keep one thing in mind throughout this discussion: A color is what it looks like and not a bunch of numbers! That is, a color "happens" in your brain via the eyes. The trick is supplying your eyes and brain with the stimuli they need to recognize the color you want them to.

Color Modes

There are different ways in which we describe a color in Photoshop, and so Photoshop can operate in several color *modes*: RGB, CMYK, Lab, Grayscale, and a couple of derivatives of these. Each mode attempts to work with color in the way different media or devices do. Grayscale, for example, is useful for images that will be output to devices that use only black ink. Although it may seem intuitive to work in the color mode of an anticipated output device, it is often far more optimal to work in one mode, and then create a copy for output. Which color mode should you use? You should choose one that offers more choices for color accuracy at output and is relatively intuitive. Let's look at the candidates.

RGB and Photo History

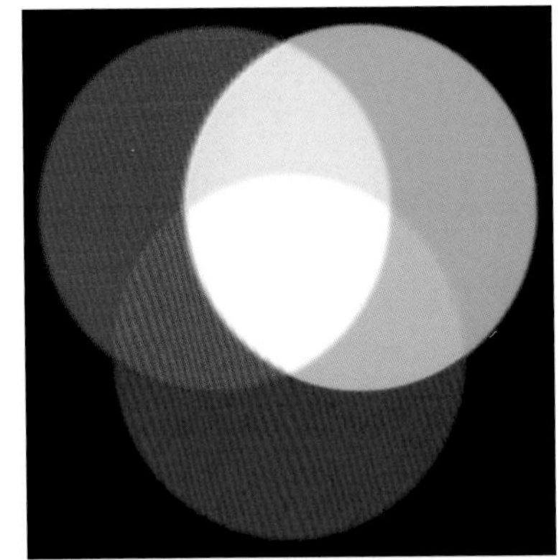

RGB is about light in the darkness. No light: no color. By controlling the ratio of **R**ed, **G**reen, and **B**lue, we can create any color we want! Where both red and green light overlap, we get yellow. Green and blue combine to make cyan light. Magenta is the result of red and blue. All three make white. This is why we call these the *additive primaries.*

Note which color is absent or lacking. For example, cyan is the absence of red. When an image looks too magenta, we add a bit of green.

RGB has a rich and storied history. The theory that these three colors of light could be combined to make any color goes back to the early nineteenth century. In 1855, the physicist James Clerk Maxwell suggested the three-color photographic method that is used in nearly all processes today. A photographer named Thomas Sutton made the first color photograph on Maxwell's behalf using Maxwell's method. Three black-and-white images were made of the same subject (a tartan ribbon). Each was made through a colored filter: red, green, and blue. The resulting negatives were made into positive transparencies ("slides"). Readers familiar with something called film may feel mild nostalgia at reading that sentence.

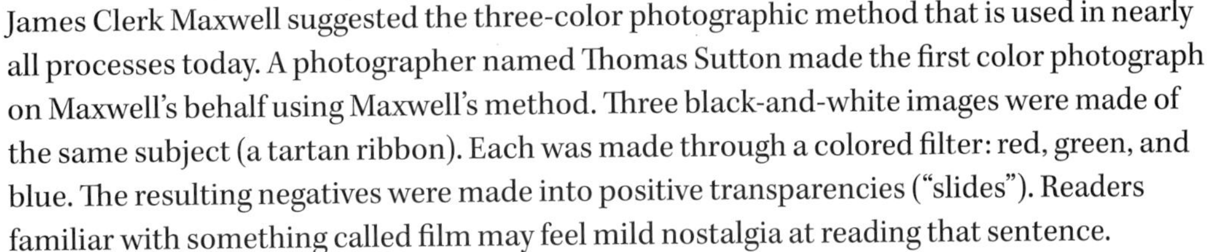

Consider the following historic image. About 110 years ago, the photographer (Sergei Mikhailovich Prokudin-Gorskii) rapidly made three images of the subject on black-and-white film through color filters as Sutton had decades before him.

And, like Sutton, Prokudin-Gorskii also made slides (fanciful reproductions below). You can learn more about his process and images from the Library of Congress website: https://www.loc.gov/collections/prokudin-gorskii/about-this-collection/.

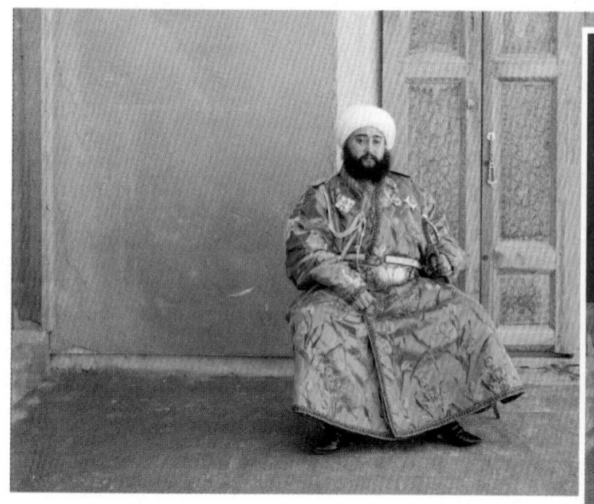

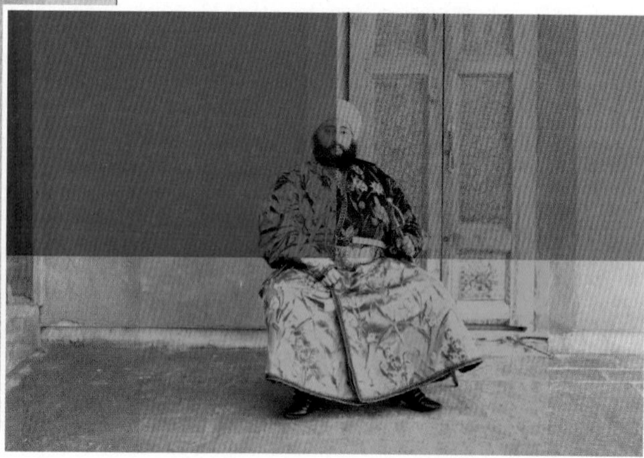

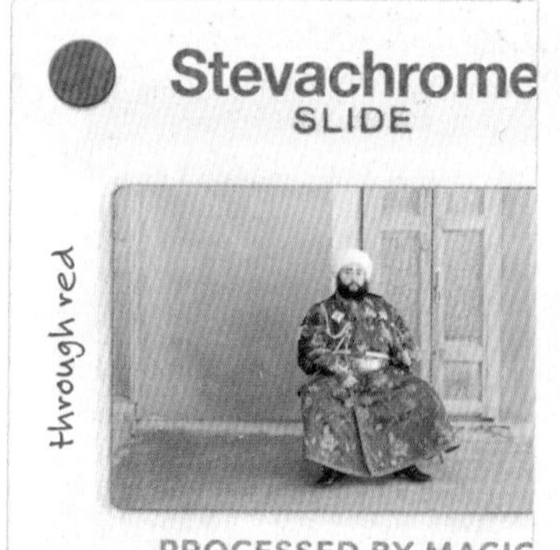

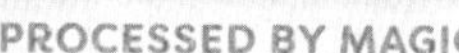

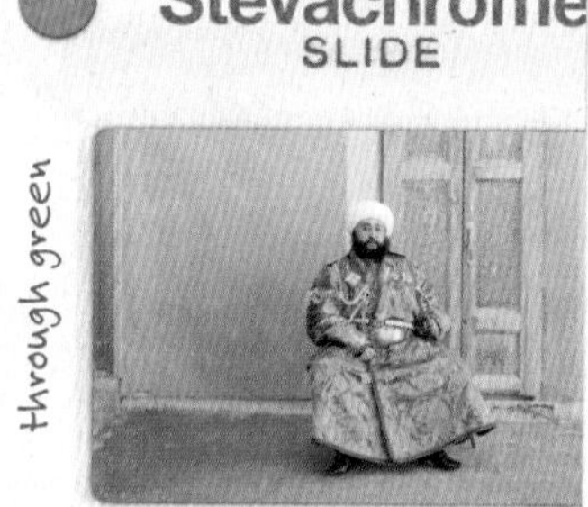

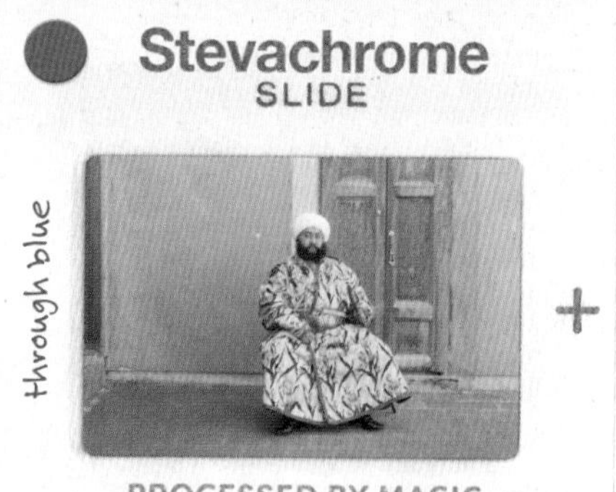

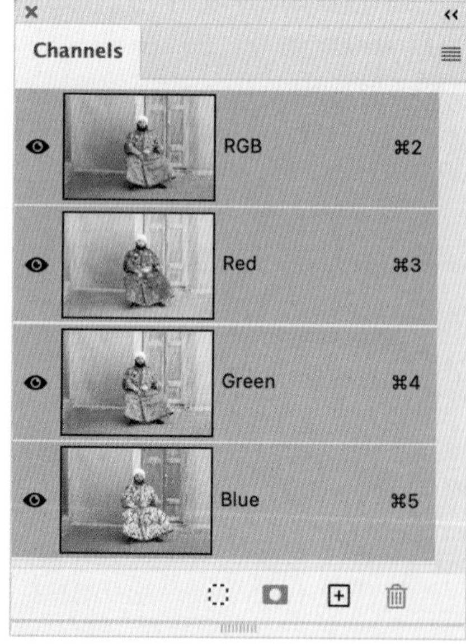

You can see how the blue filter's slide yields a light garment—since it's blue. The slide made through the red filter would have red light projected through it, the "green" slide would use green light, and the "blue" slide, blue light.

When the three projected images are aligned, the result on the screen will recreate the colors in the scene! Color images have been made in much this way for about 170 years! Modern camera sensor arrays typically have millions of microscopic, monochromatic sensors with equally small red, green, and blue filters in front of them. The data from each get combined to give us a color image. Even in Photoshop, we can see this history: Images in Photoshop have three color channels. They are each black-and-white images through which you're to imagine red, green, and blue light projected onto the screen of your retina.

It gets tricky when we try to express how much of each of those colors we want. With most software, we use numbers between **0** (no light) and **255** (the maximum) for each. The RGB value of 0 0 0 is black—all lights out. However, as mentioned earlier, values like maximum red (255 R) on one device may not be as intensely red as on another. That is, 255 R will be a *different color* on different devices; maybe like Santa's suit on one and more neon on another. After all, any device can produce only so great a range of colors. We refer to that range as the device's "gamut," which is described by an important data file called its profile. We'll discuss profiles shortly.

So, we say that RGB values are *device dependent*. To accurately refer to a specific green, we might have to say something like "30 R 190 G 25 B as viewed on an Eizo CX270 monitor." As we will see, a color-managed workflow that uses profiles deals with that for us. That's one reason we call it "color managed."

CMYK and Inks

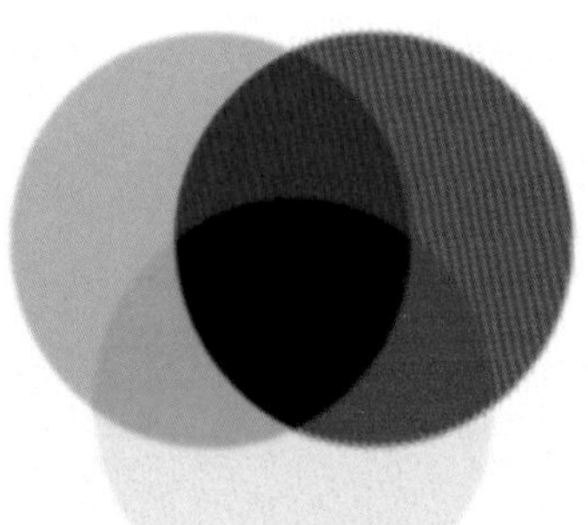

CMYK is about dots of **C**yan, **M**agenta, **Y**ellow, and blac**K** ink on a substrate-like paper. Each ink absorbs a different color of light. Cyan, for example, absorbs red light, subtracting it from what gets to our eyes. This is why we call these the *subtractive primaries*.

Without ink, there's only the white of the paper. By controlling the ratio of those four inks, we can make many colors. We measure the amount of each from 0% (none) to 100% (the full amount). In principle, we could use only cyan, magenta, and yellow, because the combination of all three inks *should* absorb all light, and thus appear black. However, this may be too much ink for many papers, or even if that much ink could be used, it may appear as dark brown instead of black. This is why we need black pigment too. Thus, CMYK is known as the four-color process, or "process color" for short.

Some printers use toner and some use ink. Those from different manufacturers produce somewhat different color. Paper also affects color, of course. Thus, *every CMYK device is different*. So, as with RGB, CMYK devices also have profiles that describe the range of color they can produce. That means that the CMYK numbers (or *build*) for any perceived color will vary from paper to paper, and from printer to printer.

Note: No single CMYK build looks the same on all printers.

Just as with RGB, CMYK numbers are device dependent: That is, they are meaningless without reference to a specific device. But again, the use of profiles in a color-managed workflow helps.

Profiles describe a device's color space. What's a color space? Since you asked...

Color Spaces, Profiles, and Lab

Since these terms are used so often, and often incorrectly, let's be sure we understand what's meant by them.

A color space can be compared to a physical one. Any position in a room can be mapped with the familiar x, y, z coordinates. Colors are mapped in a grand space called Lab, a mathematical model of human vision. **L** stands for "luminance," with the **a** and **b** coordinates together mapping hue and saturation. Colors on the L-axis are gray. Colors farther from the L-axis are more saturated than those closer to it.

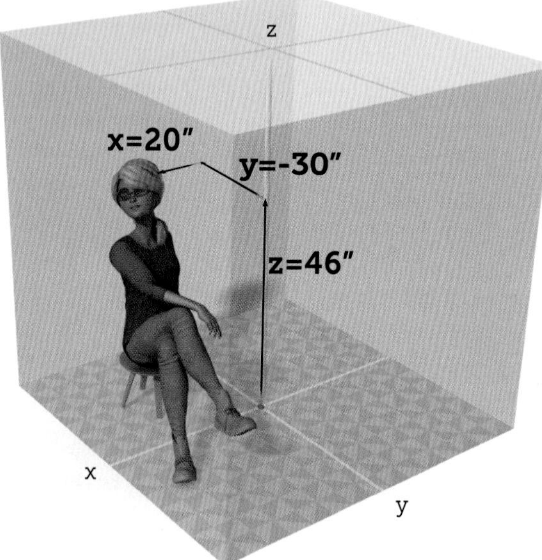

Where It's At!

We usually specify a location in any space by using three numbers.

In a room, that could be the distance to the left or right of a spot on the floor (x), the distance forward or back from that spot (y), and the height above the floor (z).

Mapping Color

Lab color space represents the range of human vision. Any point in that space, like this purple, is a color we see.

Instead of x, y, and z, we use L, a, and b: **L** for luminance, with the **a** and **b** coordinates together mapping hue and saturation. Colors on the L-axis are gray. Colors farther from the L-axis are more saturated than those closer to it.

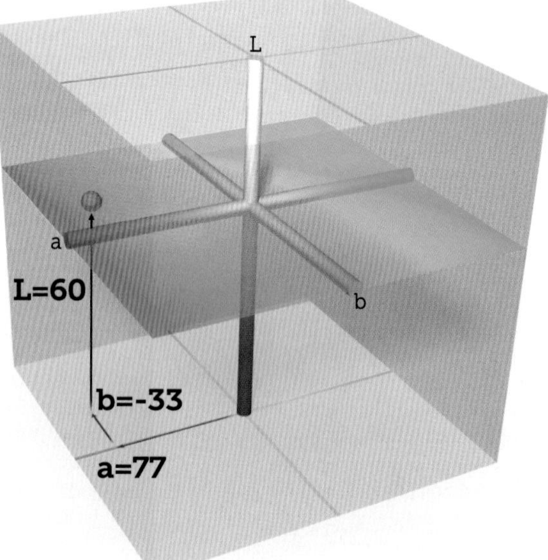

Sitting in a physical space, we can imagine the limited volume described by the points we can reach with our arms. A device (e.g., a printer or monitor) can produce only a limited "volume" of color within Lab space. That volume of colors is the specific device's color space.

Each unique device has its own unique color space. Lab itself is *our* color space: the range we can perceive.

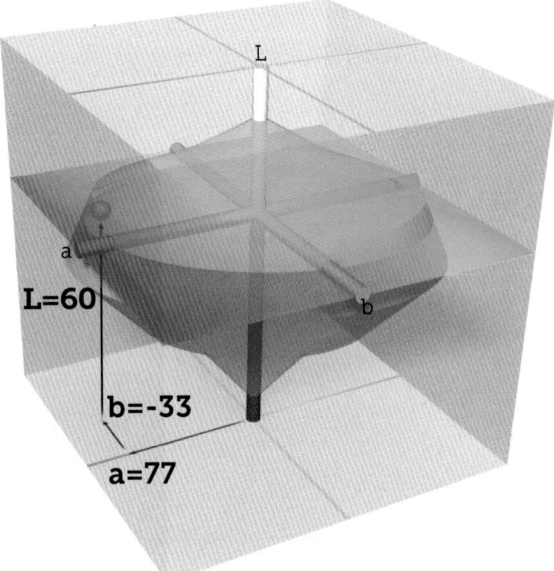

Device Color Space

This volume within Lab space represents the color space of a hypothetical output device (like a printer). The mapped purple appears to be "within **gamut**." That is, we can expect it to output accurately.

All color spaces, and therefore all devices, are compared to Lab (the colors we can see). Some devices produce a greater range of color than others.

A **profile** describes a device's color space and lets us compare it to others and convert from its color space to another's. That is, profiles help us move from an input device, like a scanner or camera, through software like Photoshop, to an output device, while keeping "in-gamut" colors accurate throughout.

In review, a ***color mode*** is the general way color is approached: either by adding three colors of light (RGB) or by subtracting light as it reflects off four colors of ink (CMYK). When I hear or read an instruction like "use the CMYK color space," I cringe. I'm the annoying person who then asks, "which one?" A ***color space*** describes the color capability of a specific real or virtual device.

A ***profile*** is a data file that describes a color space. It is the means by which our software gets to know the color capabilities of a device. When looking at a list of color spaces, we are actually perusing a list of their profiles. Thus, folks often use the words "profile" and "color space" interchangeably, which is understandable.

Setting Working Space Profiles

Photoshop should be considered a device—it's the virtual device we work in! Since it's software, we can decide how large a color space it uses (how broad a range of color we can access). This also means that we are deciding the colors our color numbers refer to. Using Edit > Color Settings…, we choose settings that include this Working Color Space. That decision depends on workflow. We can choose from a number of different spaces ranging from the relatively small sRGB that approximates the color space of typical computer monitors, to the very large ProPhoto RGB space that encompass all the colors cameras can capture. There are two in between those: Adobe RGB, which attempts to closely match the color spaces of high-end printing presses on good paper, and P3, a "wide-gamut" monitor profile based on one used in digital cinema.

Depending on my needs, I may work in any of these, occasionally converting from one to another, changing the color numbers of every pixel. Luckily, computers do this math well and quickly, and can figure out which numbers to use for each color as we switch from one device profile to another.

Go to Edit > Color Settings… to see and configure your settings. I configured mine in both Photoshop and InDesign to help me in the preparation of this book. I began by choosing a preset called "Europe General Purpose 3" because it supplies the appropriate working spaces: sRGB for my illustrations and screenshots, and FOGRA39 since it is the CMYK profile for the press where this book was printed. I made a small adjustment to the RGB policy by choosing "Convert to Working RGB." Many of the images I've used in this book may have used a different profile than sRGB, and I wanted them to all be the same. I chose to convert them to sRGB because if you are reading this as an ebook, sRGB is what the code inside that device expects. For print, those images in sRGB were converted to a CMYK color space profile, namely the working space profile. If I were creating only a printed book, a compelling argument could be made to use Adobe RGB for the RGB working space. But for this project, which targets many media, including e-readers, I decided sRGB was adequate and flexible. Other workflows, however, may require other choices.

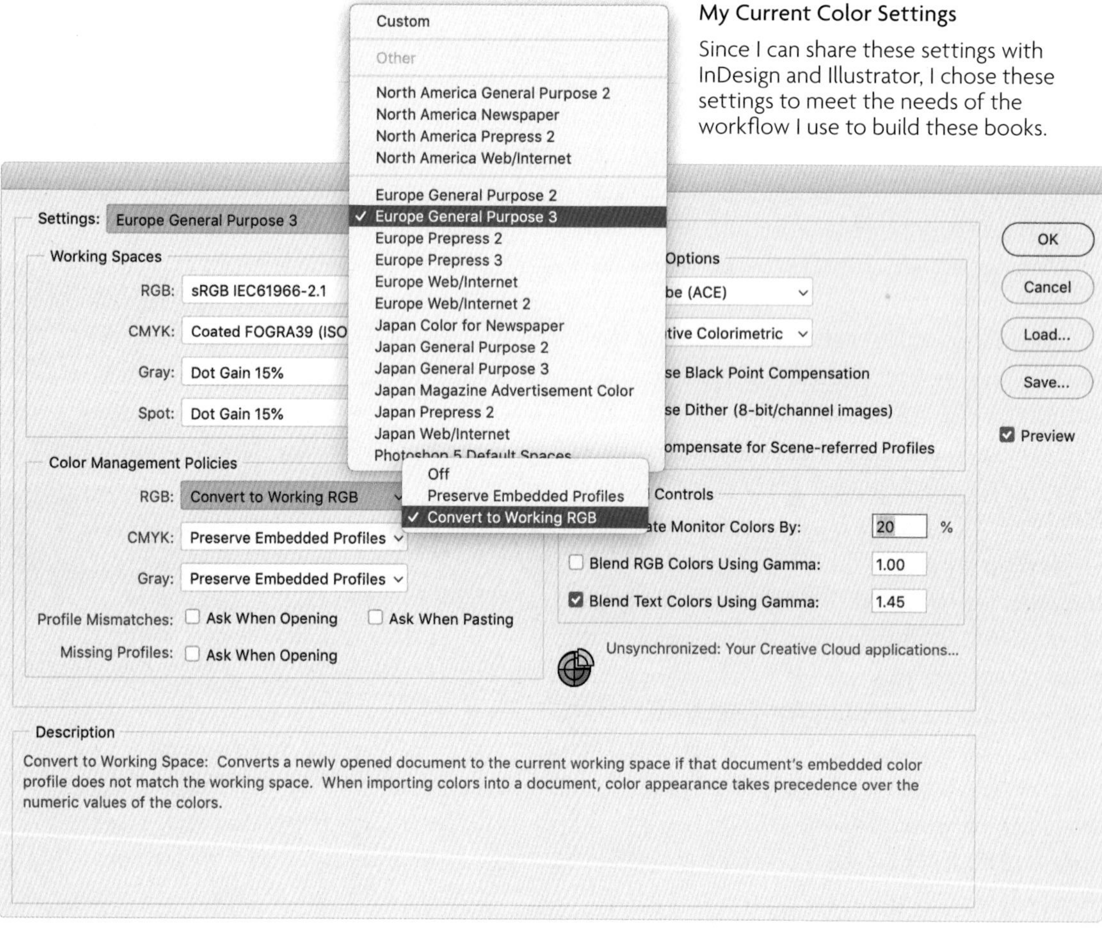

My Current Color Settings

Since I can share these settings with InDesign and Illustrator, I chose these settings to meet the needs of the workflow I use to build these books.

Settings: North America Prepress 2

Working Spaces

RGB: Adobe RGB (1998)

CMYK: U.S. Web Coated (SWOP) v2

Gray: Dot Gain 20%

Spot: Dot Gain 20%

Color Management Policies

RGB: Preserve Embedded Profiles

CMYK: Preserve Embedded Profiles

Gray: Preserve Embedded Profiles

Profile Mismatches: Ask When Opening Ask When Pasting

Missing Profiles: Ask When Opening

For Photoshop users eager to preserve more of their original's color, especially if you will want to do higher-end printing, I'd recommend choosing the preset called "North America Prepress 2." Although it will frequently cause disconcerting dialog boxes to appear when opening images (note the checked boxes for Profile Mismatches), it can provide the flexibility and color fidelity that many photographers, designers, and illustrators desire.

The Color Management Policies for this preset attempt to retain the image's color space profile even if it differs from Adobe RGB, the working color space of this preset. However, those Ask When checkboxes mean that you'll have the option to convert to Adobe RGB when a file you're opening uses something else.

However, most users will benefit from the default, "North America General Purpose 2." To be frank, it's easy. It also avoids the Mismatch and Missing Profile dialogs that are inevitable with "North America Prepress 2." Nonetheless, read on to better understand that choice!

Embedded Profiles

How does an image file "know" what profile it uses? Most of the time, that profile is embedded in the image so Photoshop (and other software) can correctly interpret its color numbers.

Converting vs Assigning Profiles

Two monitors may be sent the same signal to generate an intense red, but one will be more red than the other. This is just like when I turn the volume of an audio device up to 11: Two different loudspeakers may produce different volumes of sound from that same signal.

To get identical results, I'd have to use a different signal for each of those different devices. That is, I may have to lower the volume to 9 for the louder speaker to match the other, or send different color numbers to the more vibrant monitor to match a less vibrant one. This is ***conversion***. When we use Photoshop to convert an image to a printer's profile, for example, it changes the color numbers of every pixel to the numbers required by that printer to achieve the same colors.

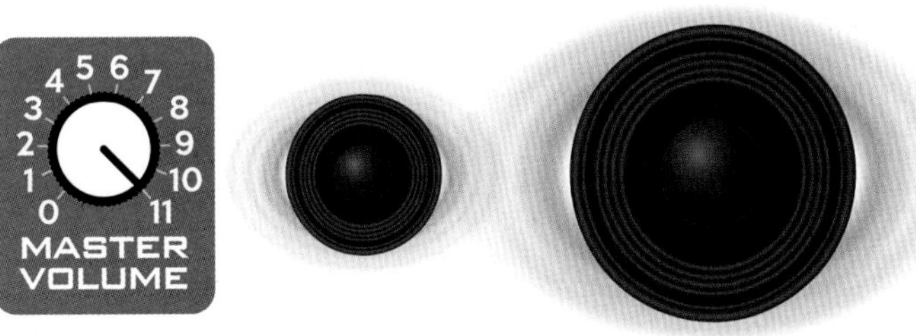

Adjustments & Color
Brushes & Painting
Selections & Masks
Filters & Transforms
Retouching & Reworking
Camera Raw & Lightroom
Extending Photoshop

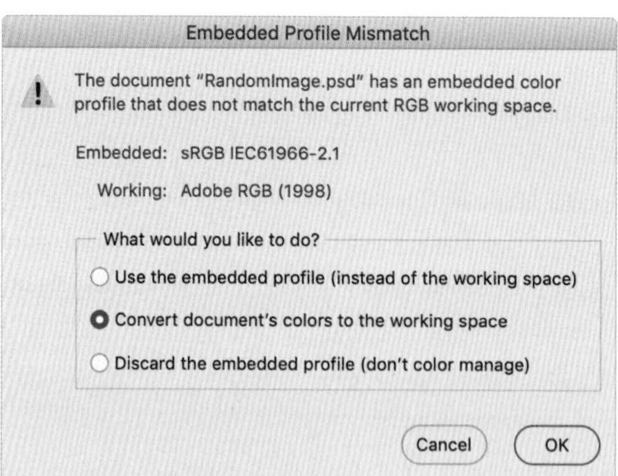

When we open a document that uses a color space profile that differs from our working space, and our Color Management Policies have been set to Ask When Opening, we can choose to convert it to our working space profile. Converting from one space to another changes the numbers to preserve the visual appearance of all the colors in an image.

In the case of an image downloaded from a website, it will likely be in the sRGB color space, whether the image editor who made it embedded that profile in the file or not. If there is an embedded profile, we'll see a dialog like the one above. If the embedded profile differs from our working space, most likely, we should convert it. In this way, if we sample a color from the image, we can use the same color numbers in InDesign or Illustrator (provided they, too, use the same working space), and we will achieve the same visual result.

If we're editing an image provided by a colleague, we may choose to Use the embedded profile so we can return it in the same color space as it had when sent to us.

If we open an image with no embedded profile, we will have to guess which to use. Below, we see the dialog we'd get in that case. Almost always, the image is in the sRGB color space, but the profile wasn't embedded for some reason. So, we choose to assign that profile to inform Photoshop what color each pixel is trying to be. We can also, at the same time, check the box to convert the image to our working space, if we desire.

Missing Profile
The document "RandomImage.psd" does not have an embedded RGB profile.
What would you like to do?
Leave as is (don't color manage)
Assign working RGB: Adobe RGB (1998)
Assign profile: sRGB IEC61966-2.1
and then convert document to working RGB
Cancel
OK

Adjusting in RGB or CMYK or Lab

In which color mode should we work? My simple, if surprisingly controversial answer is RGB.

Readers of this book who have been exposed to prepress technicians (or who *are* prepress technicians) will now be frowning and suspicious. For decades, folks in the print trade have told the rest of us to use CMYK files if the destination for our images is print. Indeed, when a commercial printer, like the one who printed this book, asks for CMYK files, that is what I provide. But I first ask them in which color space they should be. That is, which profile should I choose when I convert my RGB files to CMYK.

Bear in mind that a color *mode* is the general way color is approached: either by adding three colors of light (RGB) or by subtracting light as it reflects off of ink (CMYK). When someone instructs you to "use the CMYK color space," ask, "which one?"

We need to be specific because a CMYK profile does more than describe the color space of the device to which we're printing. There are other attributes included, such as dot gain, the paper's ink limit, and more. So if we were to perform color correction in CMYK, we would need to know at the outset which profile to use. Most of us rarely know on which continent our projects will be printed, let alone on which paper! And in a multimedia world, our images will likely be viewed on screens (RGB devices) as well as in print.

Remaining Healthily Device-Agnostic

Earlier in this chapter, we discussed "Setting Working Space Profiles" (page 219). I mentioned that Adobe RGB was a good choice for those who will likely print their work. Even sRGB can produce decent results and will be consistent with online versions. It surprises prepress people to learn that Adobe RGB was actually designed with them in mind, and that it neatly encompasses most printable colors.

Photographers who use Lightroom find themselves working in a very large color space called ProPhoto RGB because that is what Lightroom usually passes along to Photoshop. This color space is large enough to contain all the colors most cameras can capture and seems a good fit for the photo crowd. However, there is no monitor or printer that can produce even close to this range of color. That means what we see on our displays is a conversion from ProPhoto RGB to our monitor's color space. We may be misled by that view.

Better displays can produce AdobeRGB, and some new, high-end ones can produce the larger P3. Neither is close to ProPhoto. So my considered recommendation for photographers is to use Adobe RGB or sRGB for images edited in Photoshop. Your originals, likely Raw files, are not affected by this decision and remain in the full range of color your camera provided.

I often set Adobe RGB as my Working Space in all my Adobe apps. I make exceptions for some projects like this book, since it is published as an e-book as well as printed. Because there are quirks in the e-book process, it is far easier to work in sRGB, despite its being a slightly smaller color space.

For those whose images will be displayed exclusively on the web, sRGB is for you. Many desktop printers are standardized to this profile. This is why it is Photoshop's default.

In any case, you can later configure an image for any print output by converting to that output's color space profile when you finally know it.

What about Lab?

Over the years, I've found myself in dark corners of the internet where self-proclaimed Photoshop gurus claim that mysterious and wonderful adjustments can be achieved exclusively in Lab mode, a device-independent but difficult mode for the uninitiated. Then they spout smoke and hokum to prove their point.

They usually go on about being able to separate color adjustments from tonal adjustments. It is true that if one is in Lab mode, adjusting the L channel has no impact on color, and only impacts tone or luminosity, the L in Lab. But it is also true that trying to adjust color is very difficult in Lab, since the a and b channels are unintuitive, unlike the red, green, or blue ones of RGB. But these gurus brush that off as grumblings of the ignorant.

I'll be clear: There is no need for us to work in Lab mode. In RGB, there are ways to do any adjustment and affect only tone or color (or both) as we choose!

Don't take my word for it. After we've explored the adjustments covered in the rest of this chapter, open an image, save a copy (just in case), and then go to Image > Mode > Lab Color. Try a few adjustments. It might be fun, but I suspect you will not find it very useful.

Choosing Color

When we paint, add text, or correct color, sometimes we simply want what we want: the color of the shirt our subject is wearing, a Pantone color, or an arbitrary one.

Color Picker

Near the bottom of the Tools panel, you will find several buttons related to choosing color.

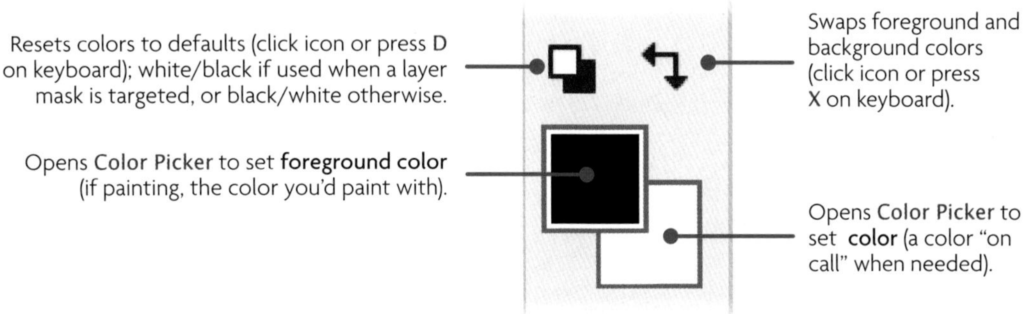
Resets colors to defaults (click icon or press D on keyboard); white/black if used when a layer mask is targeted, or black/white otherwise.
Opens Color Picker to set **foreground color** (if painting, the color you'd paint with).
Swaps foreground and background colors (click icon or press X on keyboard).
Opens Color Picker to set **color** (a color "on call" when needed).

When you click the boxes that display the foreground or background colors, you will open the Color Picker, enabling you to change those colors.

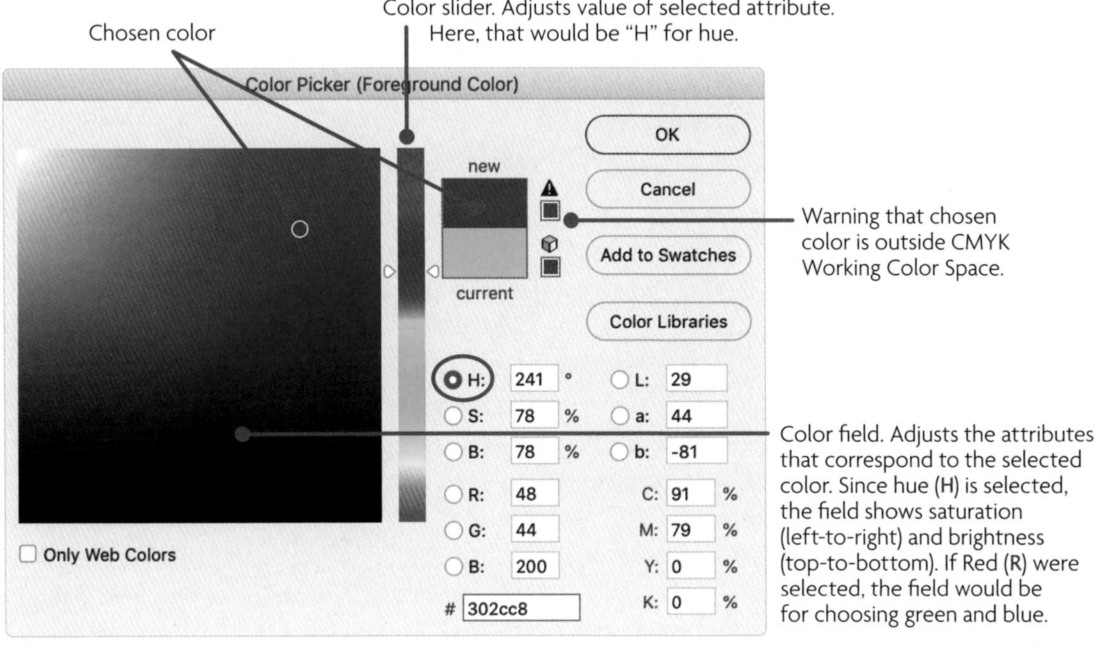
Chosen color
Color slider. Adjusts value of selected attribute. Here, that would be "H" for hue.
Color Picker (Foreground Color)
OK
Cancel
Add to Swatches
Color Libraries
new
current
H: 241 °
S: 78 %
B: 78 %
R: 48
G: 44
B: 200
302cc8
L: 29
a: 44
b: -81
C: 91 %
M: 79 %
Y: 0 %
K: 0 %
Only Web Colors
Warning that chosen color is outside CMYK Working Color Space.
Color field. Adjusts the attributes that correspond to the selected color. Since hue (H) is selected, the field shows saturation (left-to-right) and brightness (top-to-bottom). If Red (R) were selected, the field would be for choosing green and blue.

The Color Picker is a powerful and useful interface for choosing color. You may ignore two small parts of it, however. The checkbox labeled Only Web Colors and the cube-shaped warning icon are vestiges of the early days of the web and have no relevance today.

You usually start by clicking or dragging within the color slider in the middle of the dialog box. By default, this chooses a hue. The large field on the left has the two attributes that correspond to the slider. By default, these are saturation and brightness, but would be red (R) and green if the slider was set to blue by clicking the B button. The second step in choosing a color is either clicking or dragging in this field to adjust the chosen color.

If you move your cursor away from the open Color Picker window, it will look like a small eyedropper. In fact, it will act very much like the Eyedropper tool (discussed shortly). Clicking in an open image "samples" the color from the area where you clicked.

If you know the color numbers of a desired color, you can type those into the numeric fields. If you would like to use a color that exists in standard libraries), click the Color Libraries button and the interface will change:

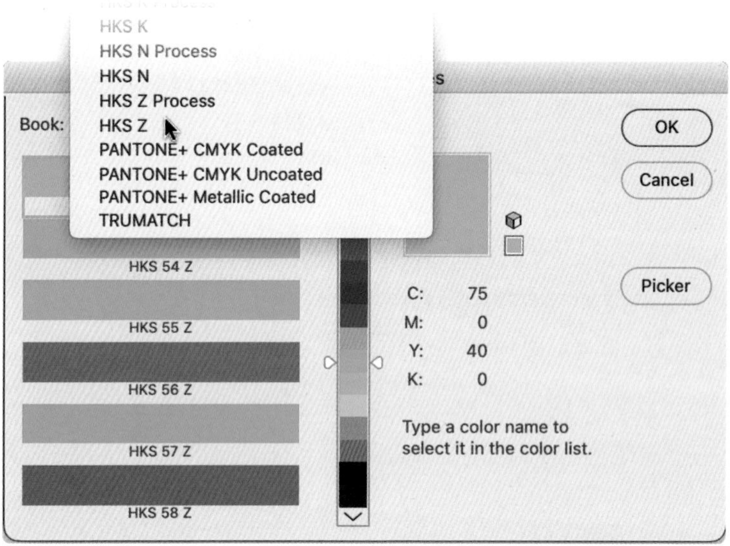

As of this writing, the default library recently became the HKS Z Process "book," a European newsprint standard and so an odd choice for a default. That's why I think it is likely to change again. Also, you may choose from many other libraries via the Book menu in the dialog box. The specific color shown initially will be the one closest visually to the color that was selected in the picker before you clicked Color Libraries. If you know the number ("name") of a color, just start typing it (not too slowly). For example, typing "72" will select HKS 72 Z. Note that although you may choose a color from a spot color library, the color will not generate a separate printing plate, nor will a print shop know you might have desired one. The color will be a process color that will output as close to the desired color as the output device allows. Spot color work is surprisingly difficult in Photoshop alone.

The Picker button returns you to the standard Color Picker. Clicking OK commits your choice. In an application with nearly twenty ways to zoom, you will not be surprised to learn there are other ways to choose a color.

Color Panel

Depending on the workspace, you may see the Color panel in the upper right of the Photoshop interface. If not, you can get it by choosing Window > Color. Using the Color panel menu, you can select from many different interfaces for choosing color in this panel.

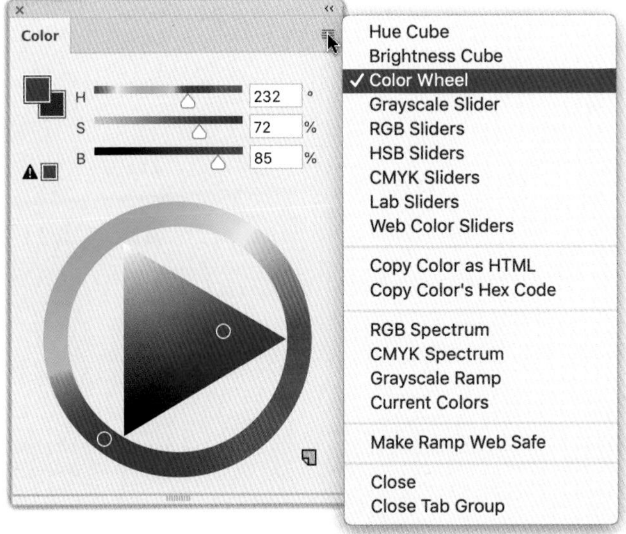

The default is called Hue Cube, which resembles the Color Picker interface. Depending on the task, I rather like the Color Wheel interface (shown above). I can choose a hue from the wheel (fine-tuning with the slider at the top, if needed), then I can choose how light and/or saturated the color is by clicking or dragging in the triangle (or, again, using the sliders).

If you wish to choose a different background color, click its box in the Color panel. Be sure to click the foreground color later or you may forget which is targeted for editing! A second click on either box opens the Color Picker.

Heads-Up Display

While painting or editing a gradient's color stop in Photoshop, you can easily sample colors from the document (discussed in the next section), or you can summon the color HUD (Heads-up Display). The HUD can be triggered on a Mac by holding down control-option-⌘, then holding down the mouse button. On Windows, hold down Shift-Alt, then hold down the *right* mouse button. The HUD will remain until you release the mouse, so don't let go until you've chosen a color! The HUD's interface can be chosen in Preferences > General. Illustrated here is the Hue Wheel (Medium) choice. Much thoughtfulness went into its design.

Sampling and Monitoring Image Colors

There are many times, especially in graphic design, when we want to use a color we find in an image. We have a tool for that: the Eyedropper tool. To have a live, ongoing sample in order to monitor colors as we make adjustments, we have its cousin the Color Sampler tool. Both have more depth than most users realize.

Eyedropper Tool

The Eyedropper tool reads, or "samples," colors displayed on screen—and not just in Photoshop. Access the tool from the Tools panel or by pressing the letter i. The letter i accesses any one of six tools, so if the wrong one appears, press shift-i repeatedly to cycle through them.

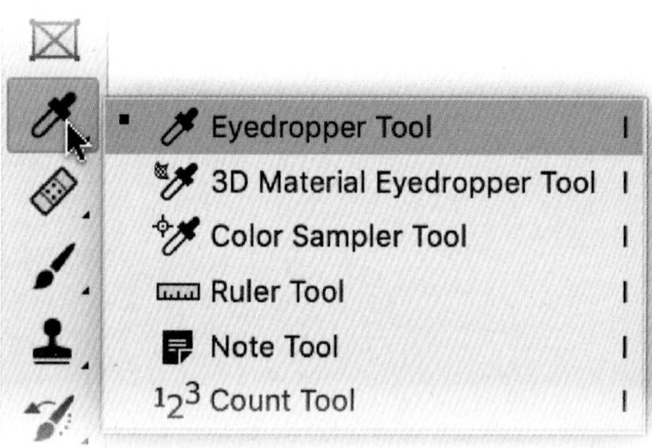

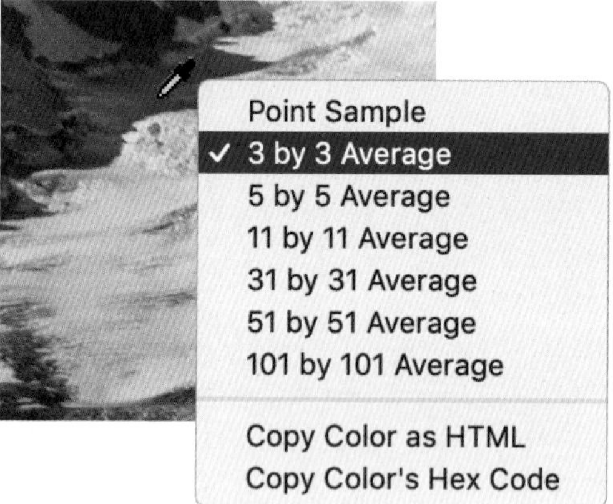

Clicking on an area in an image with the Eyedropper tool changes the foreground color to the color that was below the tip of the cursor (its lower-left end); holding option/Alt while using the tool changes the background color. Some users find the default cursor imprecise. The Eyedropper, like many tools, offers a precise cursor that you enable by turning on your keyboard's caps lock.

Photoshop continuously reads color under the cursor while you hold down the mouse button, committing it only when you release. So if you press down the mouse button within an image, you can then drag the cursor *anywhere* on your screen, in Photoshop or not, and the color under the cursor will be recorded when you release the mouse.

Sometimes, like when an image has a lot of noise, reading the color of one pixel, a "Point Sample," may not be desired. By right-clicking with the Eyedropper tool, you can choose to average between nine (3 by 3) to over ten thousand (101 by 101) pixels. Be aware that this setting is sticky and will be retained until changed again. Also, and more dangerously, this setting affects other tools that sample color: the Color Sampler tool, the Magic Wand tool, and the Eyedropper tool that appears when using the Color Picker. Luckily, in each of these cases, you can see and change this setting in the Options Bar along the top of the screen.

Color Sampler Tool

At any time, and with any tool active, the Info panel will show you, in its upper left, the color numbers under your cursor. But sometimes you need to monitor a particular part of the image (or many parts) while performing an adjustment, for example. This is the job of the Color Sampler tool.

Each time you click in the image with this tool, you create a numbered sampling point. You'll see each one's number in the Info panel. When an adjustment layer is selected, you'll see two sets of numbers: Before the slash are the unadjusted values; after are the adjusted ones.

You can place up to ten sample points.

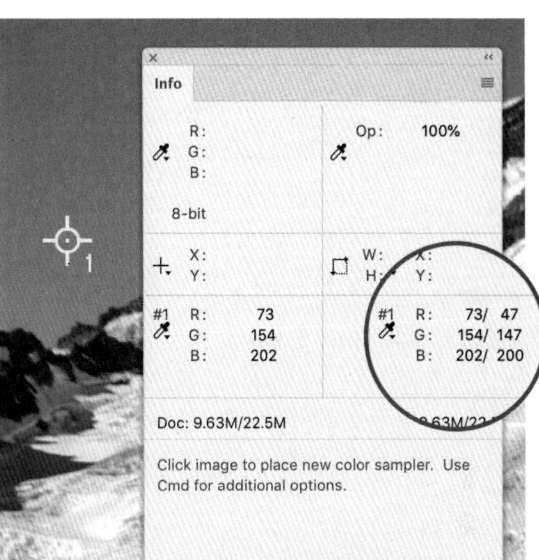

Color Samples & Soft Proofing

An interesting use of this tool is to monitor what potential CMYK values would be if we were to convert our RGB image to a specific CMYK color space. In a way, this allows us to do anticipatory adjustments to an image while it's still in flexible RGB.

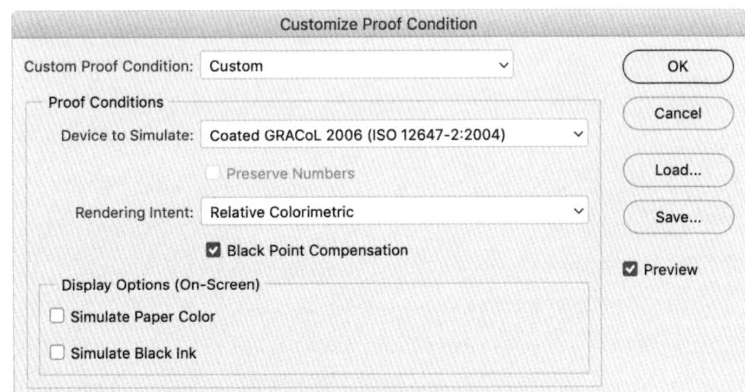

Sometimes we're curious what an image will look like if we were to convert it to a different color space. For that, we perform a "soft proof" (as in "software proof").

From View > Proof Setup > Custom..., we can choose the device we wish to simulate on-screen. The soft proof can be turned on or off with View > Proof Colors or ⌘-Y/Ctrl-Y.

Color Samplers can show you what the CMYK numbers would be if you were to really convert your document to that simulated device, whether you're viewing the soft proof or not. Click on one of the sample dropper icons and choose Proof Color.

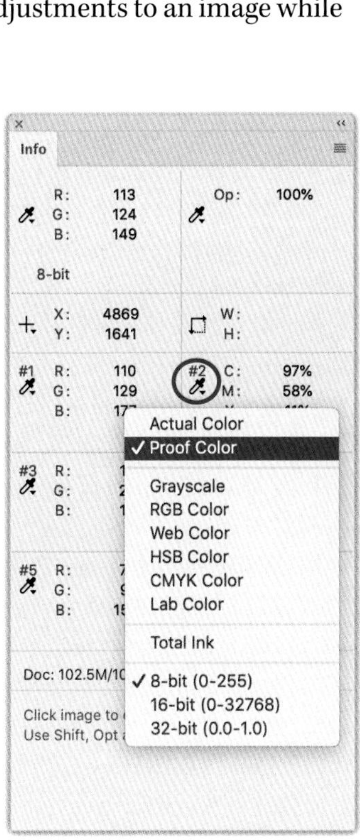

Adjustment Methods and Principles

Over the decades since Photoshop's first release, there have been many approaches to adjusting images with the tools it offers. In the early days, we had only destructive methods, those that truly alter the color numbers of the pixels. We ended up with many copies of images if we were cautious and feared we may need to go back to an earlier version. Currently, Photoshop offers many nondestructive methods for adjusting images or parts of them. We can readjust or unadjust at will. Sadly, many tips and tutorials you might find online continue to suggest techniques that are tedious and unnecessary. Only a very few Photoshop adjustments and functions still require these methods.

Almost all adjustments allow you to create time-saving presets that can be chosen from that adjustment's preset menu. Use either the Properties panel menu (for adjustment layers) or the gear icon (for adjustments from the Image > Adjustments menu).

Best Practices

There are several general adjustment techniques, but some are better than others!

Direct to Pixels

When the active layer is either a Background or pixel layer, an old and usually unnecessary method of performing an adjustment is to go to Image > Adjustments and choose one of the listed adjustment types (outlined later in this chapter).

Unless you immediately undo such an action, there is no way to remove the adjustment or to even see which adjustment you just performed. An old and unnecessary trick was to duplicate the layer that needs such an adjustment. In this way, you can delete the adjusted layer should it prove to be problematic. Read on for newer, better methods.

Adjustment Layers

In the previous chapter, I had a little bit to say about this: see "Adjustment Layers" (page 155). The key takeaway is that these allow us to affect many layers at once, not affect others, and easily mask adjustments so they affect only the areas we wish them to. I will focus on this method since the most important adjustments can be applied this way.

Adjustments as Smart Filters

When we have Smart Objects in our documents, we can use adjustment layers and we can also apply adjustments as filters. There's at least one filter disguised as an adjustment and it hides in the Image > Adjustment menu: Shadows/Highlights. And there are filters, like the Camera Raw filter, that are very useful as adjustments! Both are best applied to Smart Objects, as they then become editable and removable Smart Filters.

Interestingly, nearly all the items in the Image > Adjustment menu can be applied this way. So my advice becomes more nuanced (some might pun, layered): If the layer is a pixel layer, don't use that menu, but if you make it a Smart Object, feel free!

Histograms

Although a great deal of this chapter is about color, I have not forgotten that tone is where the details are. Indeed, I create many grayscale (a.k.a. black-and-white) images. In these, we are careful to maintain gradation where it's important. A picture of someone dressed in white requires us to take pains to maintain highlight detail, whereas a portrait of a friend on a snowy slope may be more dramatic if we allow the snow to lose all detail as a field of white.

To monitor how many pixels may be completely white or black, if any, we can consult an image's *histogram*. Imagine this image, composed of ~10,000 pixels:

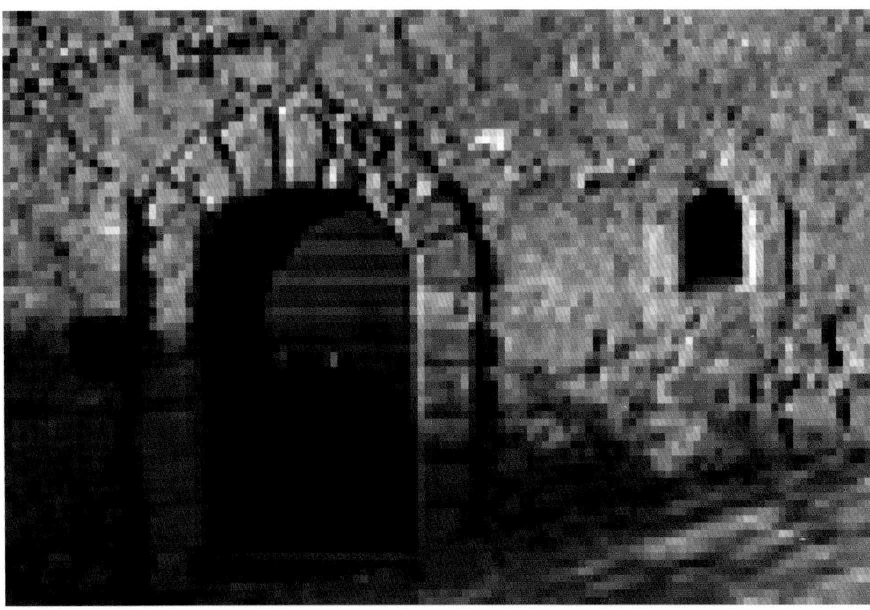

Imagine we take all those pixels and carefully arrange them, each stack containing pixels of the same shade of gray. Since a standard grayscale image has up to 256 levels (shades of gray), we'd have up to that many stacks, with the darkest to the left, and lightest to the right:

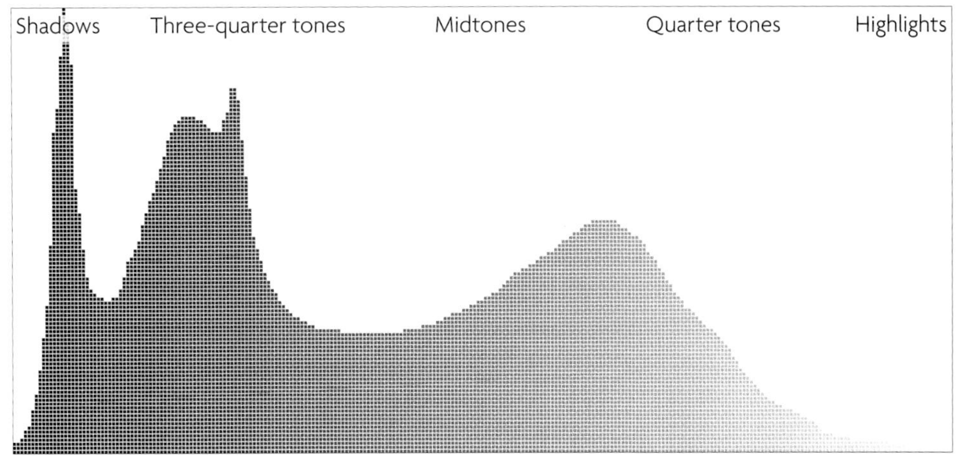

In this histogram, the stacks are very tiny at each end, meaning there are very few pixels that are absolutely white or black with no detail. To use a technical word, few pixels are "clipped."

If we wish to maintain either highlight or shadow detail in an image (or both), we should monitor the image for clipping. If the darkest or lightest pixels are some distance from the ends, our image may be lacking in contrast. Admittedly, in a photo of a foggy Seattle morning, all the pixels would be huddled near the middle of the histogram.

Since each color channel is a grayscale (black-and-white) image, each has a histogram and can be evaluated for contrast and clipping. Some adjustments show us these histograms (e.g., Levels and Curves). But we can see them at any time with the Histogram panel.

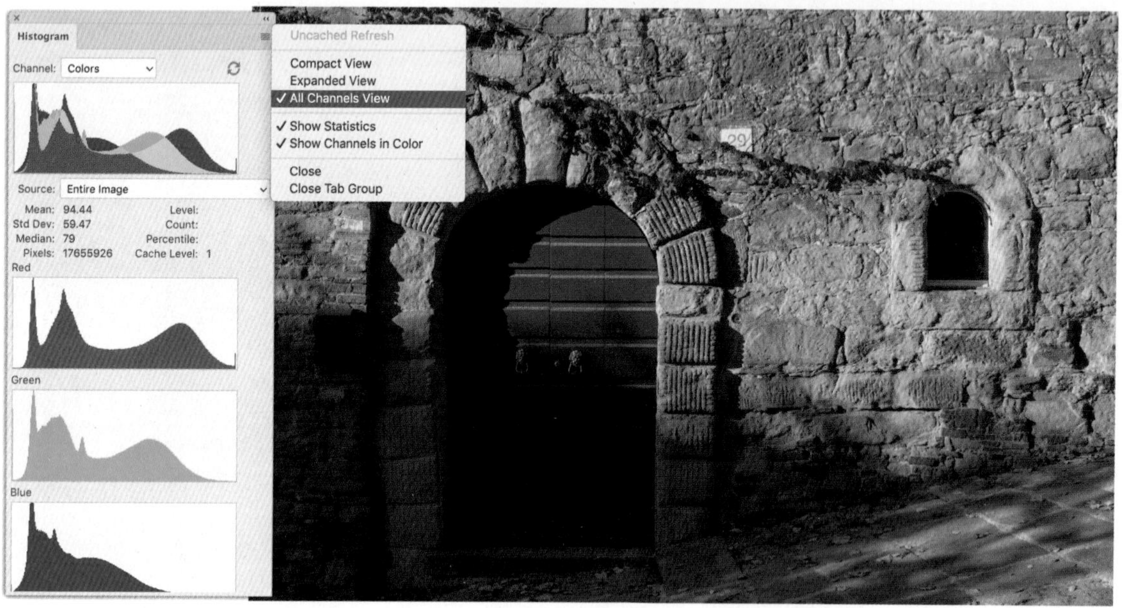

Get that panel by going to Window > Histogram. I like to adjust what it shows me by opening the panel menu and choosing either Expanded View or All Channels View, and selecting Colors from the Channel menu at the top of the panel. Just below the Channel menu, the three color channels are superimposed so we can discern each one. Clicking or dragging in the histogram shows data about those specific levels—not often needed, but you never know.

Bit Depth

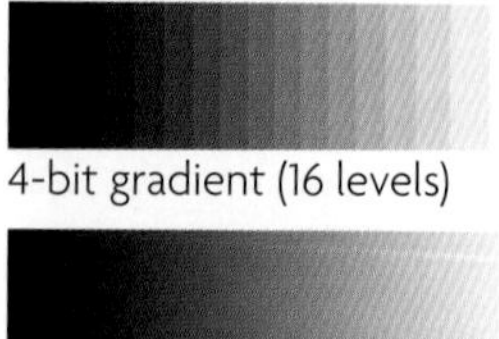

4-bit gradient (16 levels)

8-bit gradient (256 levels)

I wrote earlier that images commonly have up to 256 levels of tone in each channel (0 to 255). Why that many? Because computers calculate with binary digits (zeros and ones, *bits* for short), and 8 bits provide 256 combinations. Photoshop can handle more: 16 bits/channel, for 65,536 levels or 32 bits (used differently), to give us an unlimited tonal range! This is good news, since many camera images use up to 16 bits/channel. This gives us silky transitions by preventing abrupt jumps in tone called "banding" or "posterization." We also gain more latitude when adjusting.

The Adjustments, Listed

Overview

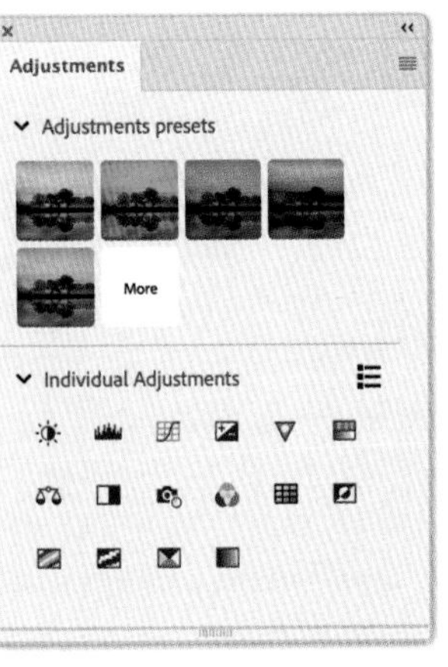

Beta As I write, this panel is undergoing a redesign and has this arrangement in the beta version. The top section creates groups of adjustments to achieve an overall visual effect.

The lower section can display individual adjustments as icons or as a list including their names.

The majority of color and tonal adjustments can be applied nondestructively as adjustment layers or Smart Filters (applied to Smart Objects). The remaining few can be applied only directly to pixels, and thus care should be taken if you might ever wish to reverse their effect later. In the explanations below, where possible, I have used the icons found in the Adjustments panel for easier identification. Also, I've divided adjustments into two main categories: production and creative, since some lend themselves to practical use more than others. Of course, many can be used in either way.

To see the full list of Photoshop adjustments and to apply them directly or as Smart Filters, go to Image > Adjustments. The most important of those can also be applied by clicking one of the following icons in the Adjustments panel:

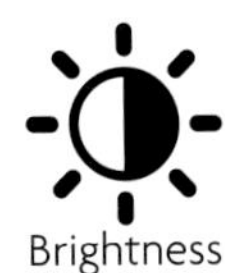
Brightness /Contrast

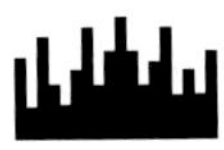
Levels

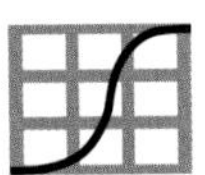
Curves

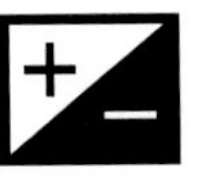
Exposure

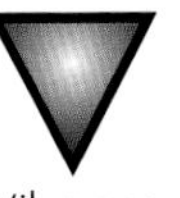
Vibrance

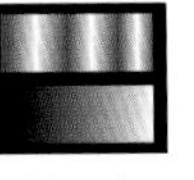
Hue/ Saturation

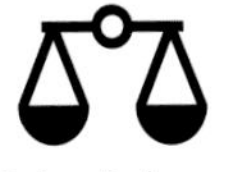
Color Balance

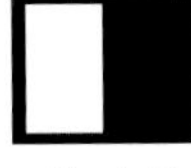
Black & White

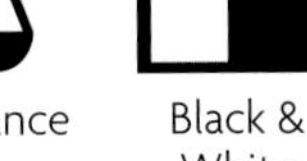

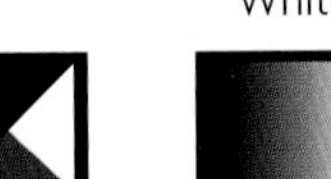

Photo Filter

Channel Mixer

Color Lookup

Invert

Posterize

Threshold

Selective Color

Gradient Map

When using the Adjustments panel to create an adjustment layer, the Properties panel will show the controls for the adjustment (usually sliders) as well as some common elements (below). For most adjustments, double-clicking a slider resets it to its default position.

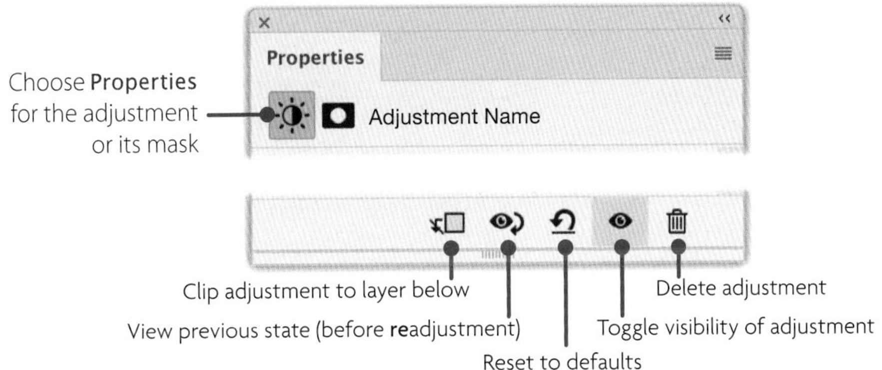

Production Adjustments

The boundary between "Production" and "Creative" adjustments is an amorphous one. You should feel very free to use those listed in each category however you choose. But note, the first set is used in practical, production workflows far more frequently than the latter.

The Properties panel is where we configure adjustment layers, and we'll focus on those. I'll deal with the few adjustments that can be applied only destructively at the end of this section.

Brightness/Contrast

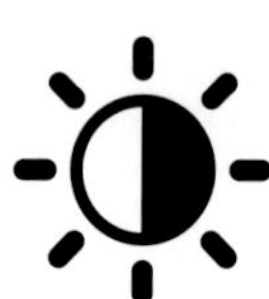

This adjustment offers only two sliders, one for Brightness, which behaves like the Levels adjustment's midtone slider, and one for Contrast, which approximates a Curves adjustment with either an S-shaped curve (for increased contrast) or an inverse S. See "Levels" (page 235) and "Curves" (page 238) for more on those more powerful adjustments.

The Auto button is the simplest way to adjust these two attributes simultaneously; it may at least offer a starting point for your adjustment. Once dismissed as horrible, Brightness/Contrast is now quite useful, though it offers little control. You may find that this tool works great if the color does not need to be adjusted or if you'd like to deal with tonal and color adjustments separately.

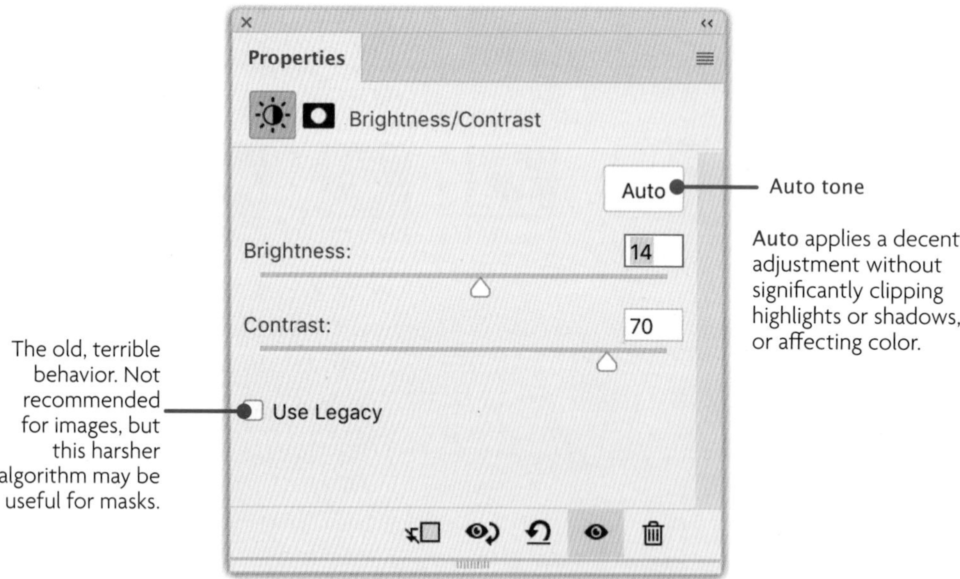
Properties
Brightness/Contrast
Auto
Brightness:
14
Contrast:
70
Use Legacy
Auto tone
Auto applies a decent adjustment without significantly clipping highlights or shadows, or affecting color.
The old, terrible behavior. Not recommended for images, but this harsher algorithm may be useful for masks.

To ensure that you are not clipping highlights or shadows, keep an eye on the Histogram panel. See "Histograms" (page 231).

Levels

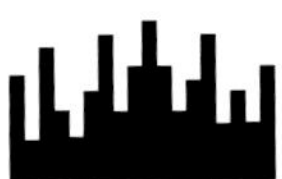

More precise than Brightness/Contrast but less so than Curves, Levels is a great tool for setting black and white points, making the overall image lighter or darker, or doing quick color corrections. More so than with other adjustments, using Levels feels like we're directly interacting with an image's histogram.

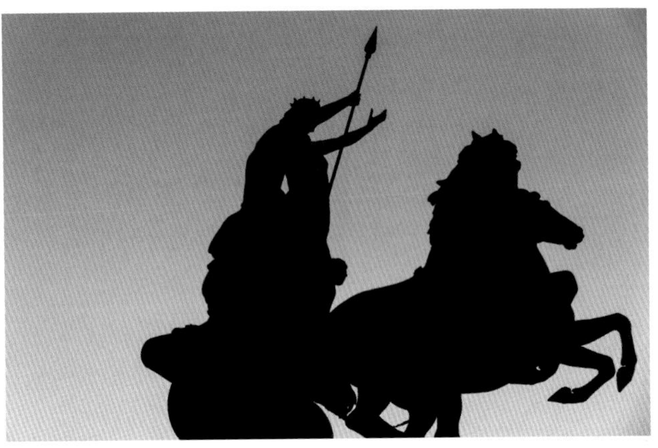

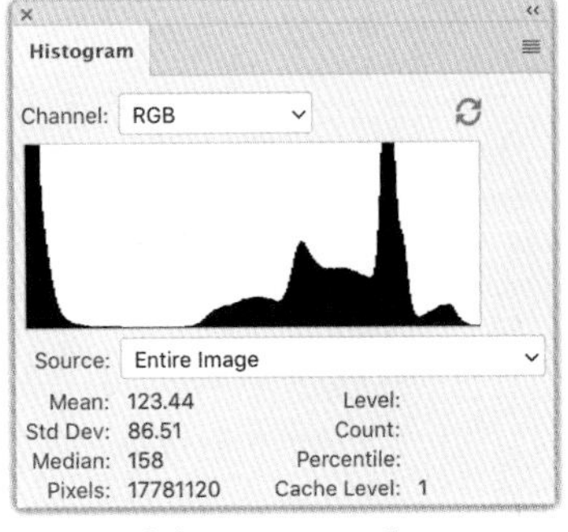

The histogram of this image confirms that its tones (or levels) are distinctly confined to the sky or the sculpture.

The objective for an image like this may be to bring out more shadow detail (in the sculpture) without sacrificing the highlights (sky) too much or muddying the blacks.

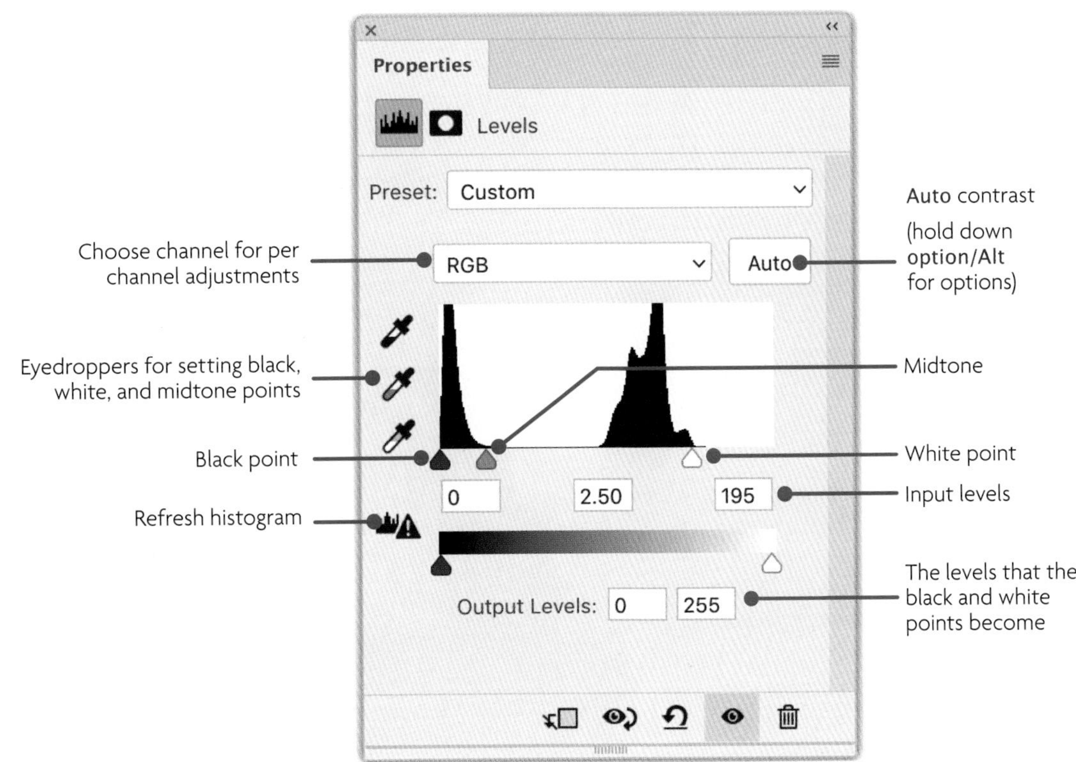

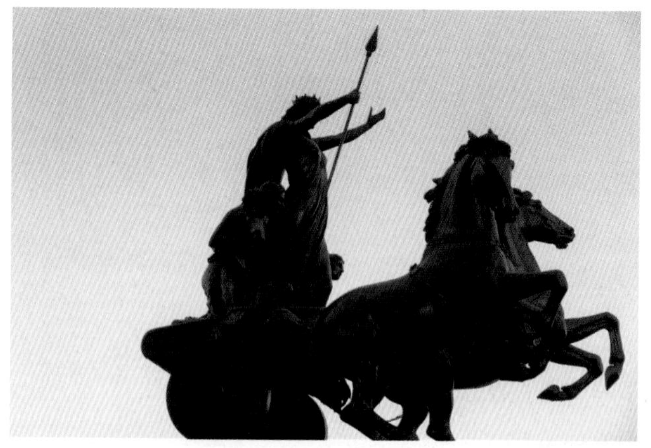

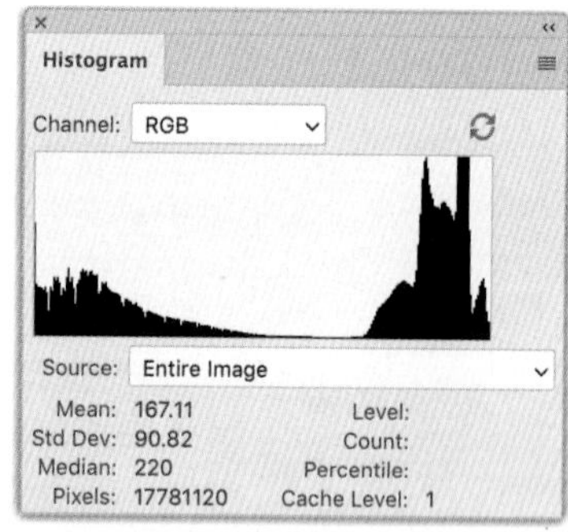

This histogram shows how the shadows have been expanded up to the midtones, and the highlights compressed, but with few pixels clipped.

The illustrated adjustment lightens the image:

- Black remains black: Both input and output black levels are still set to 0.
- White point adjusted: An input level of 195 outputs to white (255).
- Midtones significantly adjusted: There are now 2.50 times as many *original* levels that are lighter than middle gray as there are those that are darker. In the Histogram panel, this has the effect of stretching the levels on the left and compressing those on the right, since the middle gray is still in the middle.

Clipping Preview

To monitor which and how many pixels are getting clipped while adjusting the black and white points, hold down option/Alt. As you option/Alt-drag the black point, the image will turn white except where shadow clipping is occurring. As you option/Alt-drag the white point, the image will turn black except where highlight clipping is occurring.

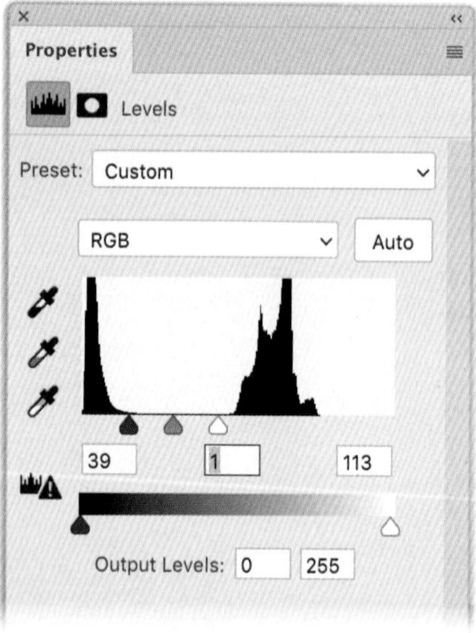

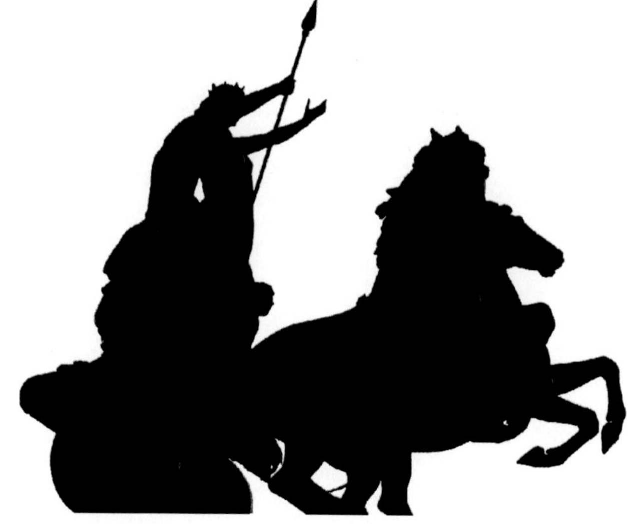

The previous adjustment significantly increases contrast:

- Black input at 39 means that all levels below (left of) that become 0, the output black level.
- White input at 113 means that all levels above (right of) that become 255, the white output level.
- Midtones are still set at 1.
- Since there were few three-quarter-tone pixels, the image has become a silhouette, with its histogram showing spikes at black and white, indicating massive shadow and highlight clipping.

You can perform this contrast enhancement on each channel too. Select the channel whose levels you wish to edit from the Channel menu in the Properties panel. Instead of white or black for a clipping warning, you'll see the color of the channel you're editing.

There are automatic-adjustment algorithms you can access by option/Alt-clicking on the Auto button. See "Auto Tone & Auto Color" (page 240) in the description of the Curves adjustment.

Curves

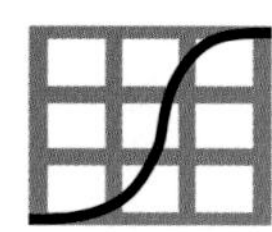

To refine tones with far more precision than Levels, use the Curves adjustment. Curves is commonly used to adjust contrast in the image and to make precise adjustments to individual tonal ranges in the image as a whole or on a per-channel basis. It does everything Levels does and much more. For that reason, you may wish to look over the description of "Levels" (page 235).

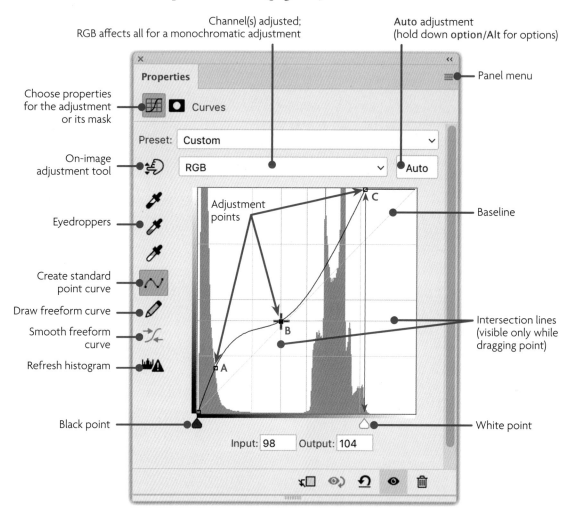

When you first choose a Curves adjustment, the "curve" is a straight line from the lower left to the upper right of the window in which you see a histogram and do your adjusting. As you tweak the curve, a faint baseline indicates where you started.

The curve is essentially a graph where we compare and affect tones coming into the adjustment (input levels) to the tones they become (output levels). By simply dragging the curve up or down, we create a point where we drag, making the image lighter or darker, respectively. If you prefer dragging up to make an image darker (as if you're adding ink to the image rather than light), use the adjustment layer's Properties panel to choose Curves Display Options.

Curves Display Options
Options
Show Amount of: Light (0-255)
Pigment/Ink %
OK
Cancel
Show: Channel Overlays
Histogram
Baseline
Intersection Line

In the Curves Display Options dialog, you can make the graph a more granular 10 x 10 grid, or choose to hide the Baseline, Histogram, or the Intersection Lines you see when you drag a point on the curve. By default, black is at the lower left and white at the upper right. In the screenshot of the Properties panel on the previous page, the active point (B) is being dragged slightly above the baseline position. Its Input reads 98 and its Output is 104, a slight lightening, but the curve is still close to the baseline near the midtones, leaving them almost unaffected by this adjustment.

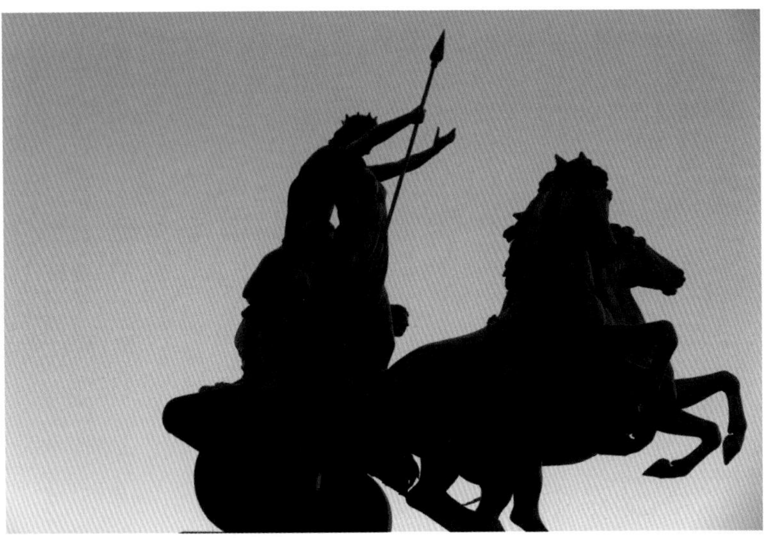

The other point (A) is well above where it started, creating a dramatic lightening of the shadows, represented by the large spike on the left side of the histogram. Since the curve is steep through that part of the histogram, contrast has been increased in that part of the tonal range. In fact, that is what I was attempting to do through both large humps in the histogram. However, when we add contrast to one part of the tonal range, we're borrowing it from adjacent tones. Luckily, in this case, there were few if any pixels in several parts of the histogram (anything lighter than 204, and a sizable range between the shadows and midtones). By allowing those to become flatter, I could give contrast to the parts that are represented.

So I dragged the white-point slider, moving the white point (C) to 204 as Input, so that tone and all lighter tones would Output to 255 (white). I created and then lowered the point near the midtones (B) to create a steeper curve through the new highlights and to keep the image from becoming too light overall.

Summary: The parts of the histogram where the curve is steeper experience increased contrast. Where the curve is flatter, so is the image ("flat" = "lacking contrast"). The Curves adjustment allows us to lighten, darken, and affect contrast differently across the entire tonal range.

Auto Tone & Auto Color

Curves is much more effective than Levels, as it offers everything Levels does, including the automatic settings accessed by option/Alt-clicking on the Auto button. Doing so opens a dialog with four algorithms to choose from, as well as a few other refinements.

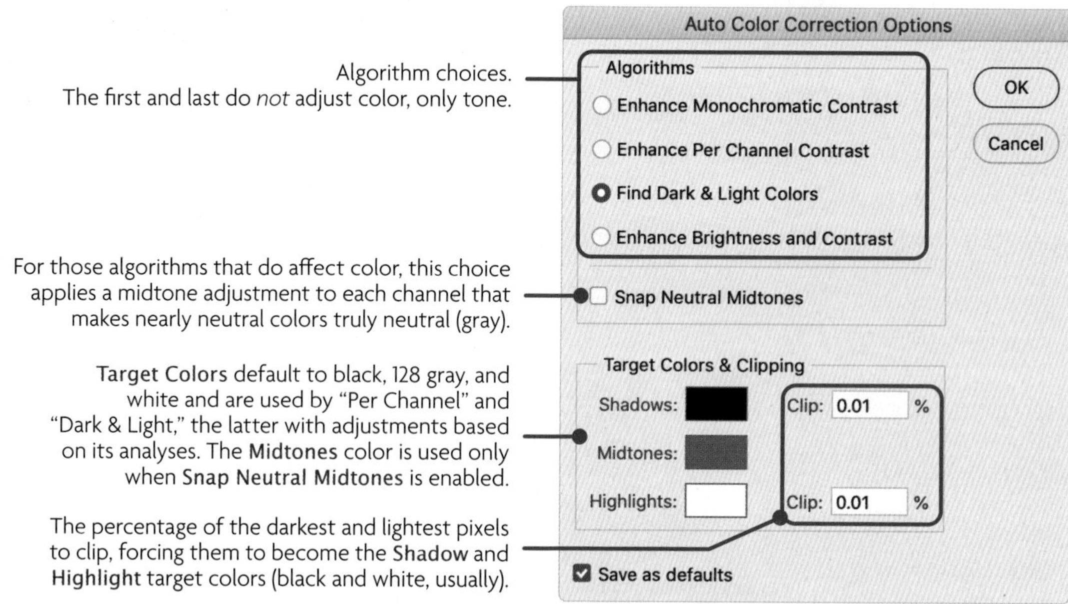
Auto Color Correction Options
Algorithms
Enhance Monochromatic Contrast
Enhance Per Channel Contrast
Find Dark & Light Colors
Enhance Brightness and Contrast
OK
Cancel
Snap Neutral Midtones
Target Colors & Clipping
Shadows:
Midtones:
Highlights:
Clip: 0.01 %
Clip: 0.01 %
Save as defaults
Algorithm choices. The first and last do *not* adjust color, only tone.
For those algorithms that do affect color, this choice applies a midtone adjustment to each channel that makes nearly neutral colors truly neutral (gray).
Target Colors default to black, 128 gray, and white and are used by "Per Channel" and "Dark & Light," the latter with adjustments based on its analyses. The Midtones color is used only when Snap Neutral Midtones is enabled.
The percentage of the darkest and lightest pixels to clip, forcing them to become the Shadow and Highlight target colors (black and white, usually).

When you've used this dialog to apply an adjustment that seems to be a better default than the first algorithm (which is very likely), enable Save as defaults. Then the adjustment you used will be what's applied when you simply click the Auto button in Levels or Curves.

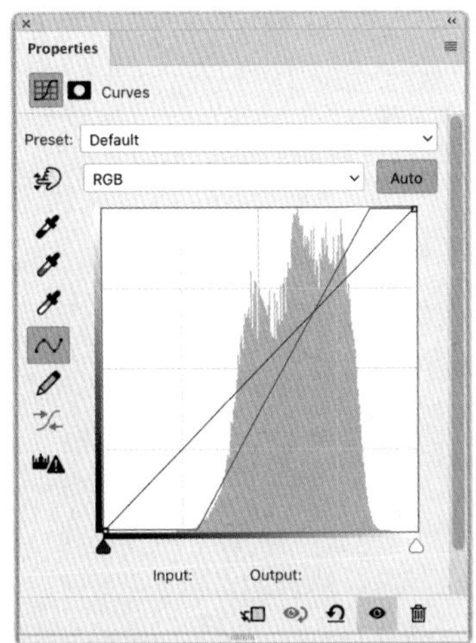

Enhance Monochromatic Contrast simply moves the white and black points inward, clipping the lightest and darkest pixels using the **Clip** percentage settings. Use this only on images that either have no color cast or have one that you'll fix in another way.

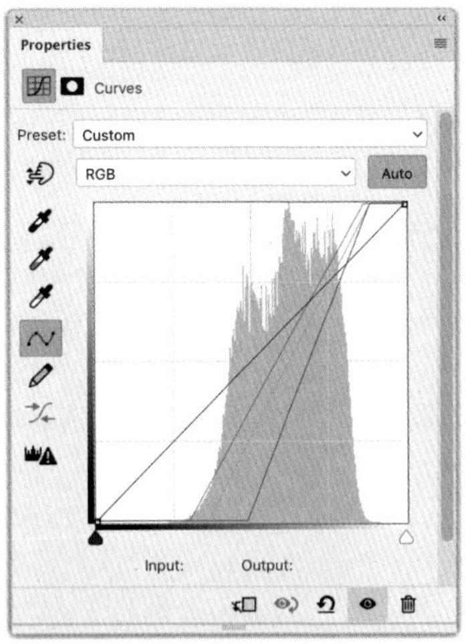

Find Dark & Light Colors analyzes images for desirable shadow and/or highlight color casts and preserves them (**Auto color**). So although the result can often be very similar to **Enhance Per Channel Contrast**, it can sometimes be *very* different.

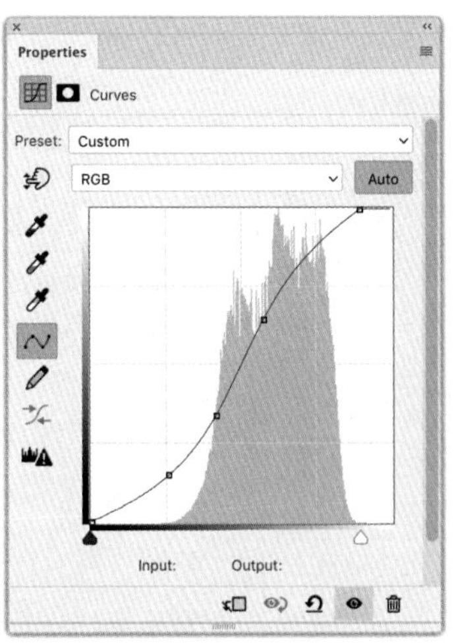

Enhance Brightness and Contrast analyzes the image and applies a monochromatic adjustment (**Auto tone**). Use this only on images that either have no color cast or have one that you'll fix in another way.

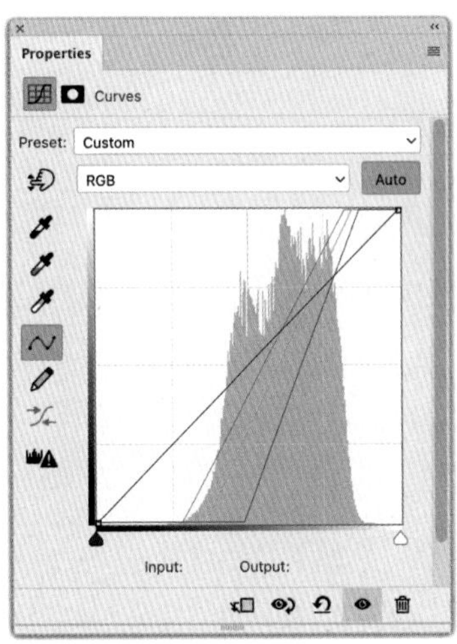

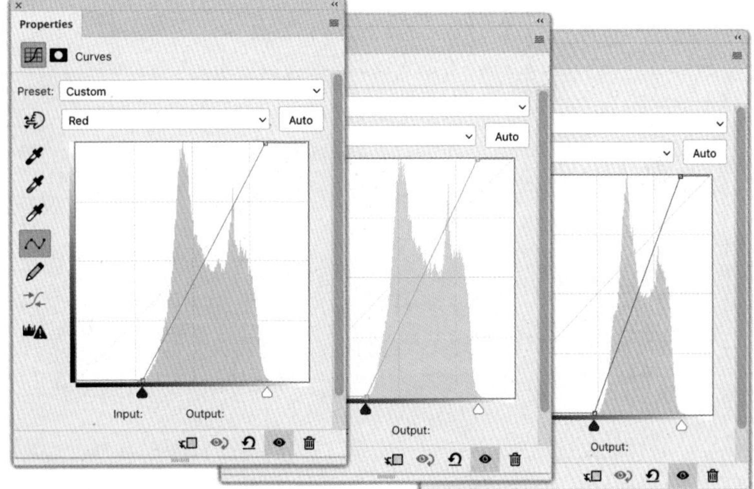

Enhance Per Channel Contrast moves the white and black points inward *on each channel*, clipping the lightest and darkest pixels using the **Clip** percentage settings. This setting is very often either the solution we seek or a promising first step.

Exposure

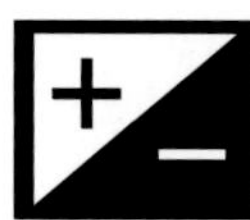

This adjustment is most effective and useful with 32-bit/channel HDR images, allowing you to see details in different parts of that potentially huge range of tones. It is not terribly useful for anything else. It should always be used as an adjustment layer so as not to lose HDR data.

When choosing this adjustment, the Properties panel will offer three sliders. The Exposure slider has the largest impact, but affects shadow areas minimally. The Offset slider affects shadows, often horrifically, but with minimal impact on the highlights. The Gamma slider affects contrast. When editing HDR images, you can access a version of the Exposure slider at any time at the bottom of the image window, as seen below.

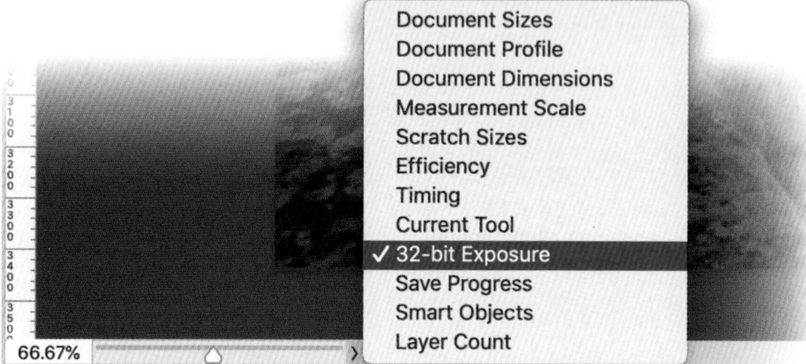

I appreciate this feature when editing 32-bit/channel images, as it lets me see different parts of the tonal range, often hugely greater than that of my monitor, without doing any harm. In 3D programs, they can be used as light sources that surround a 3D model.

Vibrance

Vibrance is a simple and effective choice for adjusting saturation. Its two sliders differ only in degree and scope. Both are restrained compared to the Saturation slider in Hue/Saturation (despite having the same name).

In this adjustment, Vibrance increases saturation mostly in less-saturated areas to avoid color clipping. It also avoids affecting skin tones more than the Saturation sliders in either adjustment, especially the one in Hue/Saturation. In short, the Vibrance slider is my favorite way to adjust saturation safely.

Since these sliders affect different hues differently, reducing each to -100 produces different results too. Vibrance leaves some color lurking in what had been the most-saturated areas. The Saturation sliders in both the Vibrance and Hue/Saturation adjustments yield a colorless result, the former looking very similar to a conversion to grayscale mode, and the latter like a default Black & White adjustment.

Hue/Saturation

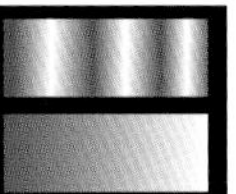

Despite its name, this adjustment actually affects three attributes: hue, saturation, and lightness (HSL). Unlike the Vibrance adjustment, you can choose to affect these three attributes differently for different hues. It often surprises users how precisely one can target hues for adjustment. You may have seen garments or other product photos in catalogs that differ from one another only in their color. Hue/Saturation very likely played a major roll in that.

When you first create a Hue/Saturation adjustment layer, the Properties panel shows that you're adjusting all hues at once: The hue menu (Preset) is set to Master.

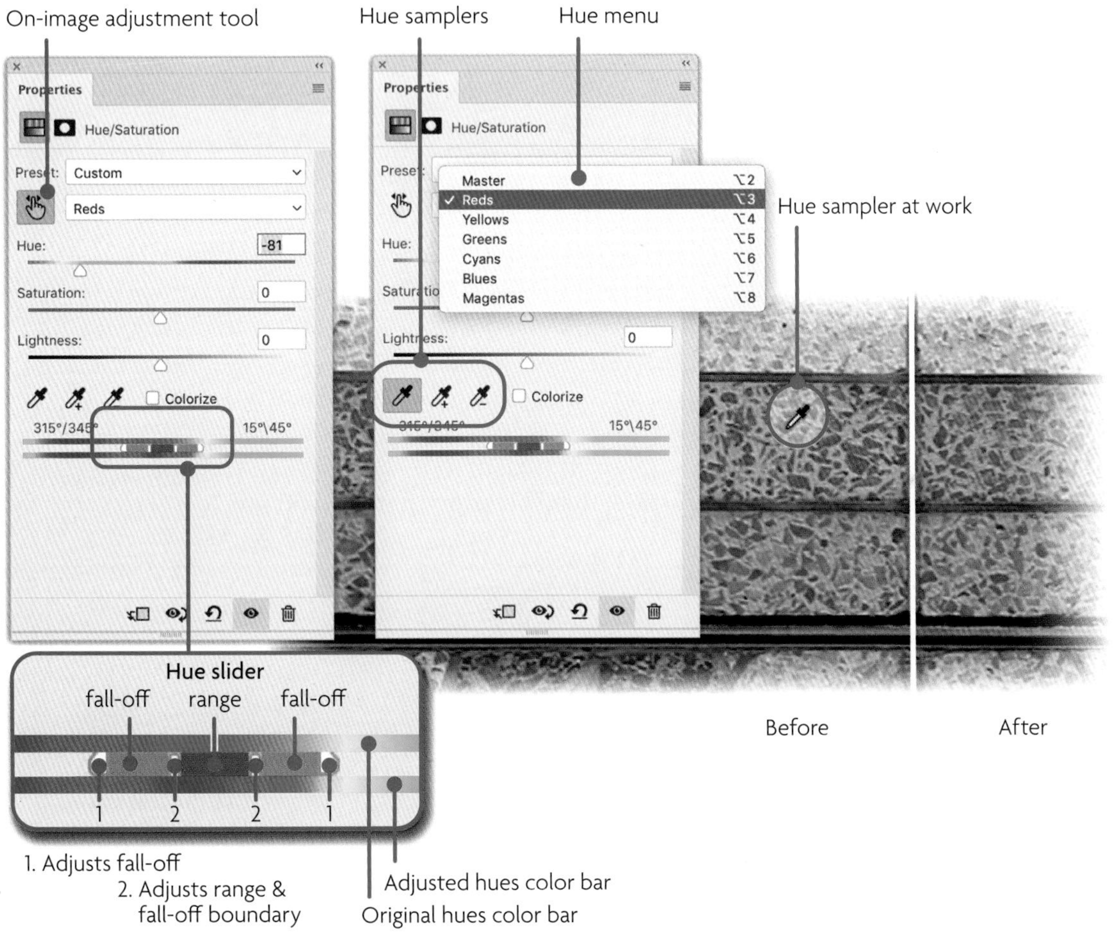

On-image adjustment tool
Hue samplers
Hue menu
Hue sampler at work
Before
After
Hue slider
fall-off range fall-off
1 2 2 1
1. Adjusts fall-off
2. Adjusts range & fall-off boundary
Adjusted hues color bar
Original hues color bar

Note: There are two UI elements called the "hue slider!" The obvious one labeled Hue is above the Saturation slider and is used to alter hue in the image. The other appears between the color bars near the bottom of the panel when adjusting an individual hue and is used to fine-tune the hue being altered. For this conversation, I'll refer to the upper one as the "Hue slider" and the lower one as the "hue slider."

When you adjust the Hue, you offset colors' positions on the color wheel. Thus, dragging the Hue slider all the way to the left or right changes the value in the field to +/- 180, as in 180°

(the opposite hue). The color bars at the bottom of the panel offset to one another to indicate what each original hue (top color bar) has become (lower color bar). Double-click the word Hue or its slider to reset.

The Saturation slider can completely desaturate an image (-100%), much like converting to grayscale. It can also radically increase saturation to sickening levels (+100%). For more tolerable saturation adjustments, when that's all you need, I recommend using the Vibrance adjustment.

The Lightness slider is rather blunt and horrible when the hue menu is set to Master. When adjusting a single hue, however, it is quite useful.

There are two ways to adjust one hue at a time. The more methodical way is to choose a hue like Reds or Blues from the hue menu. The multi-sectioned hue slider appears between the color bars at the bottom of the adjustment, centered under Photoshop's definition of that hue. To ensure that Photoshop is adjusting the hue you want it to, select the first hue sampler (eyedropper), then click on pixels containing that hue. (The active part of the cursor is its lower-left corner. For a precise crosshair cursor, enable your keyboard's caps lock.) You'll see that the hue slider has probably moved under the exact hues on which you clicked.

A faster way to get to the right hue is to use the On-image adjustment tool: . Choose it, then move the cursor over the image. It will look like the hue-sampler eyedropper (or crosshair if caps lock is on). When you click on a color, the hue menu will automatically change. Use the hue-sampler dropper to center on the precise hue you want to adjust. If the hue slider is too close to one end, ⌘/Ctrl-drag the color bars to see all of it again.

Now, when you move the three adjustment sliders, only that hue will change. In the illustration on the previous page, we can see that not only reds are changing, but also oranges and yellows, since they are in the fall-off zone of the hue slider.

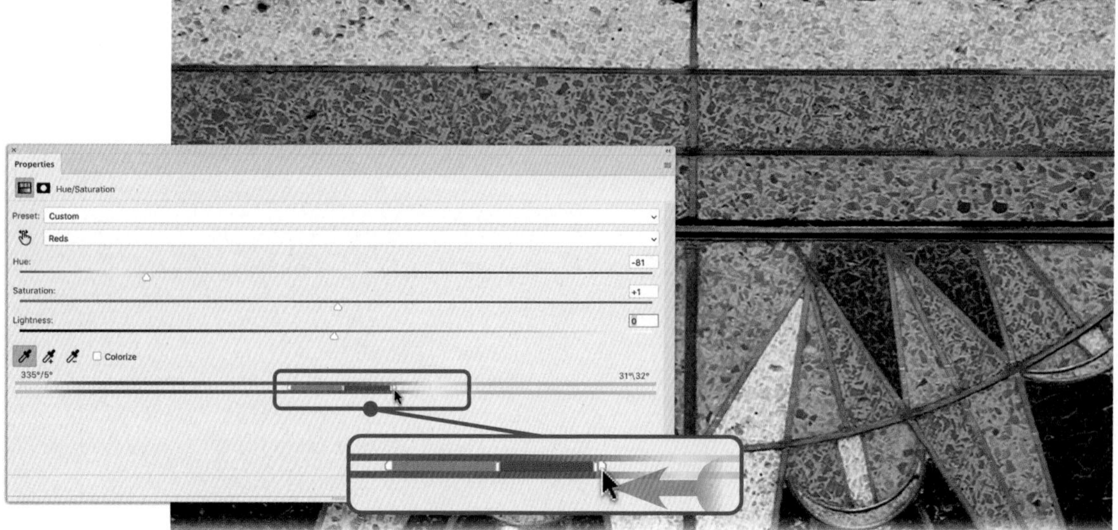

You can drag different parts of the hue slider to control the range of hues being affected. In this case, I dragged the rightmost piece (labeled 1 in the previous illustration) to the left to prevent the oranges and yellows from being affected. To gain precision, I first made the Properties panel wider.

Color Balance

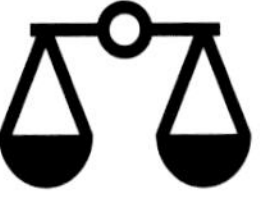

With this adjustment, you can adjust hues in different parts of the tonal range. It's not as precise as Curves, but it is fast. I sometimes use it to remove blue from shadows by choosing Shadows from the Tone menu and then adjusting the balance toward Yellows from Blues.

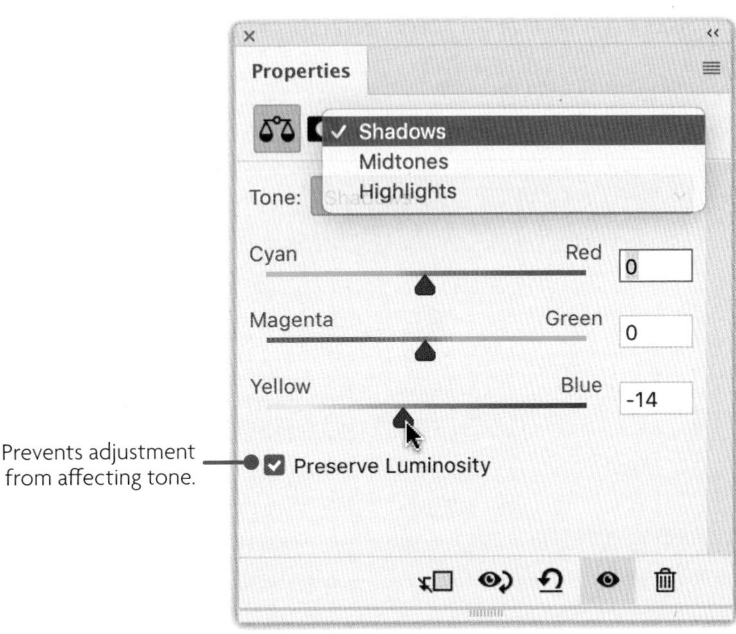

Preserve Luminosity keeps the image from getting lighter or darker as you make adjustments. If those shadows are really blue, for example, they could get much darker if I remove blue without that option enabled.

Photo Filter

I love this adjustment! It's simple and very effective. If an image has a color cast, you can use Photo Filter to create a counteracting color cast. Or if you feel an image would benefit from an overall hint of color (e.g., warmth), you can apply that as subtly or aggressively as you'd like.

In this example, I masked the sky to warm up only the buildings, and I disabled Preserve Luminosity, allowing the buildings to get darker and more richly colored.

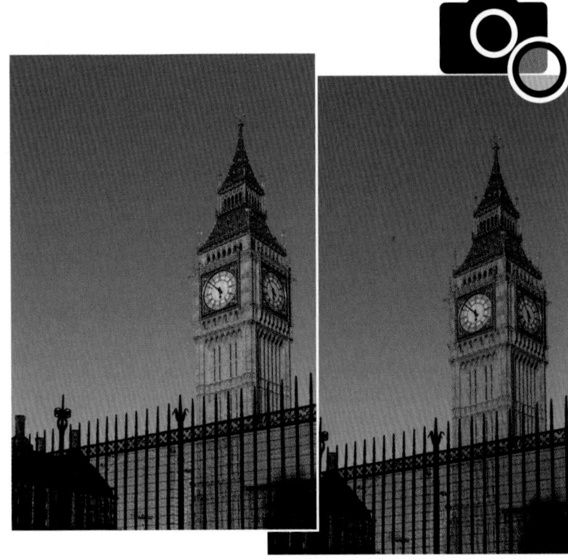

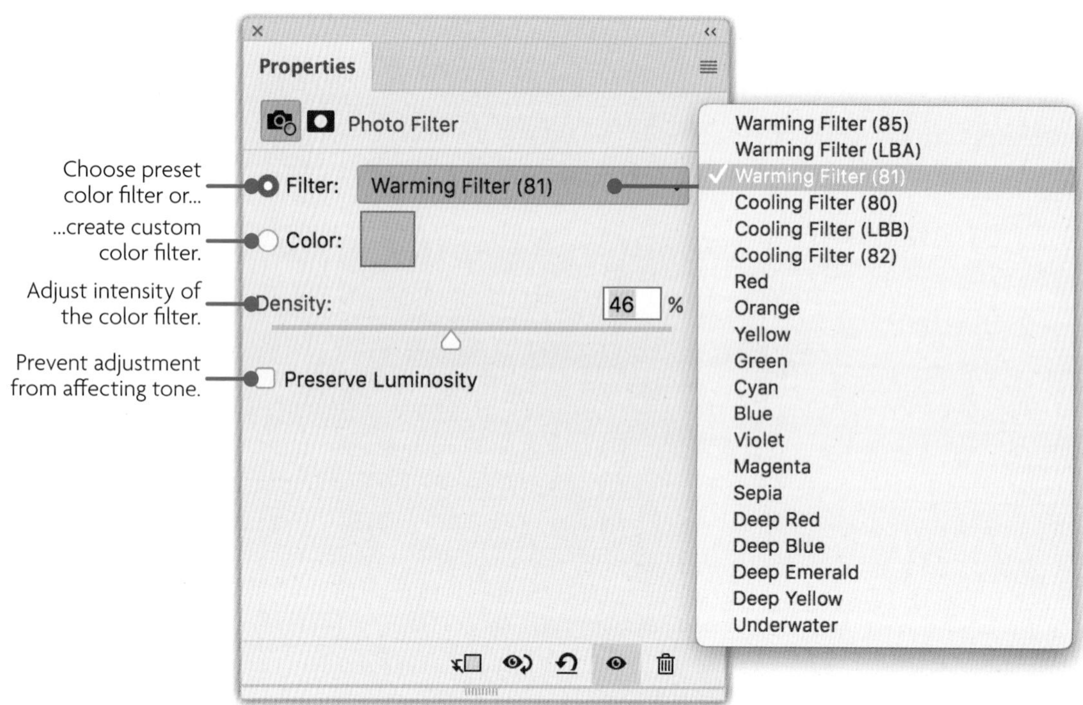

I sometimes use this adjustment to figure out just what color permeates my image. If I suspect the color cast is greenish, I'll try a Magenta filter and play with its Density. Double-clicking the Density slider resets it back to its default value of 25%.

Selective Color

This is yet another adjustment that allows you to alter the color of individual hues. It is built to be friendly to those accustomed to thinking in CMYK, whether they're in CMYK mode or not.

You start by choosing a color (including non-colors like white, black, and neutrals) from the Colors menu. Then you can use the four sliders to adjust that color. Each slider affects (or simulates affecting) a process color (Cyan, Magenta, Yellow, or blacK) by adding or removing ink from that plate. In RGB, it acts the same way without having to commit to a specific CMYK color space. For more on why that's wise, see "Adjusting in RGB or CMYK or Lab" (page 223).

For example, if you want greens in an image to be brighter green, you can remove Magenta. The buttons at the bottom of the adjustment, Relative and Absolute, affect how the addition or subtraction of "ink" is calculated. Remember that process colors are controlled by percentages: all set to 0% is just white paper; 100% is the maximum for each. Absolute will alter the amount of that ink exactly as the slider indicates. So if an area used 50% magenta, an adjustment of -20% will change it to 30%. Relative is proportional to what's already there. So that -20% will remove 20% of 50, or 10%, resulting in that area using 40% magenta.

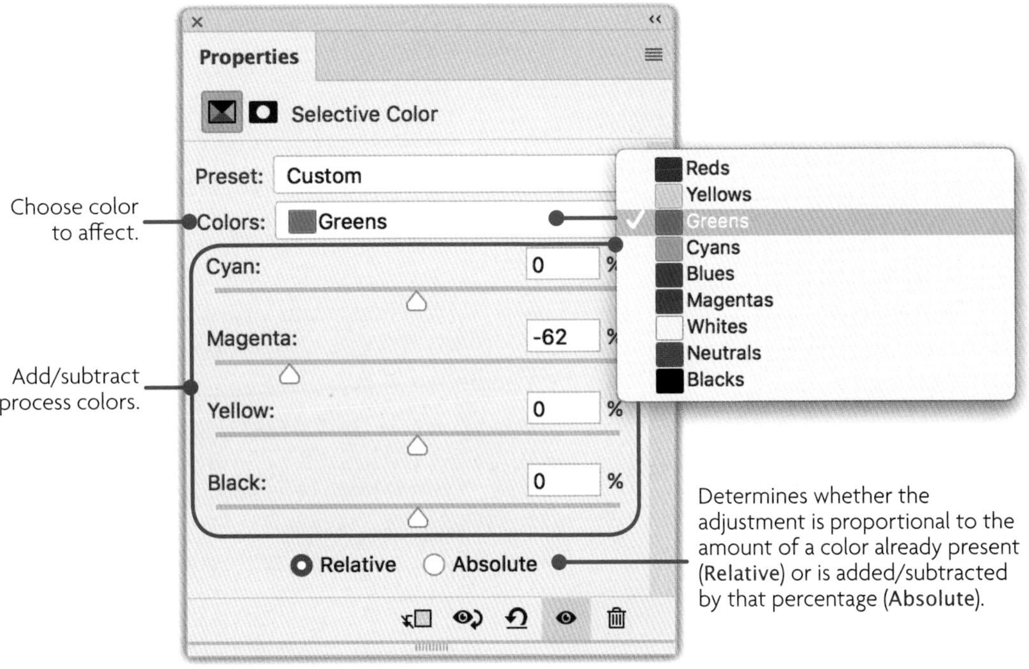

Choose color to affect.

Add/subtract process colors.

Determines whether the adjustment is proportional to the amount of a color already present (**Relative**) or is added/subtracted by that percentage (**Absolute**).

Channel Mixer

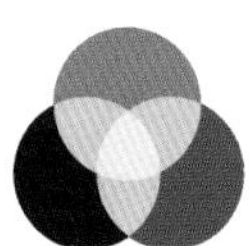

Because people are often given the bad advice of converting to CMYK before they know which color space they really need, the resulting file often needs work. Although Channel Mixer can be used in RGB, it seldom is. Most often, it's used in CMYK by prepress professionals to rehabilitate a document, giving one process color plate more substance by borrowing from another, for example:

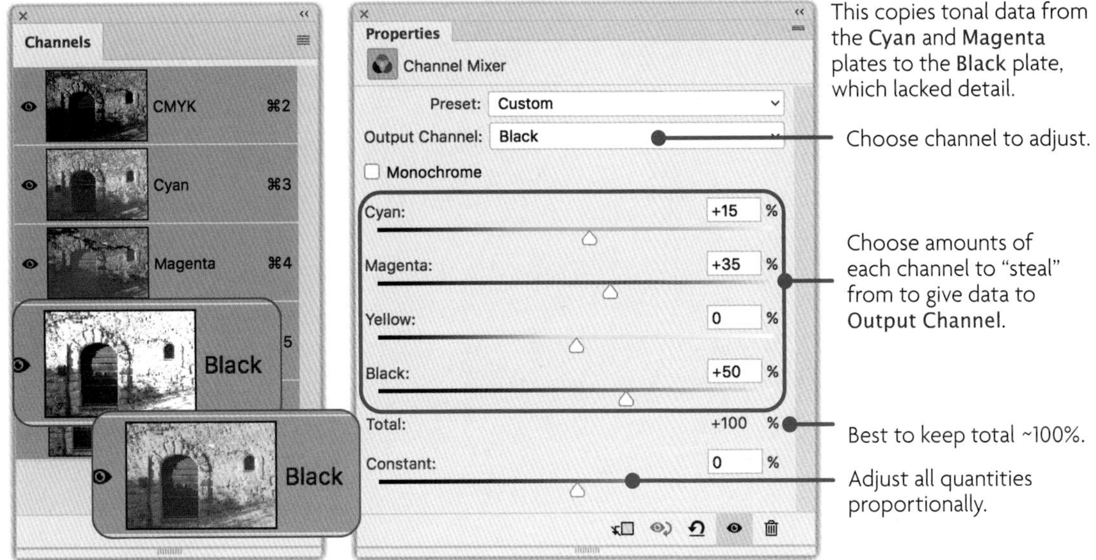

This copies tonal data from the **Cyan** and **Magenta** plates to the **Black** plate, which lacked detail.

Choose channel to adjust.

Choose amounts of each channel to "steal" from to give data to **Output Channel**.

Best to keep total ~100%.

Adjust all quantities proportionally.

Camera Raw Filter

Several "adjustments" can be applied only like filters, including this one. I *strongly* recommend converting the layer(s) to be adjusted to a Smart Object first to perform these adjustments nondestructively.

This filter can be applied using Filter > Camera Raw Filter…. It's prodigious capabilities are covered in chapter 7, "Camera Raw & Lightroom" (page 354).

Shadows/Highlights

This adjustment attempts to recover nearly lost highlight and/or shadow detail with minimal effect on the other or on midtones. It is actually a filter in disguise, hidden in the Image > Adjustments menu. Thus, you should convert the layer(s) to be adjusted to a Smart Object to perform this adjustment nondestructively. When the Shadows/Highlights dialog is open, be sure to check Show More Options to access the adjustment's full capability.

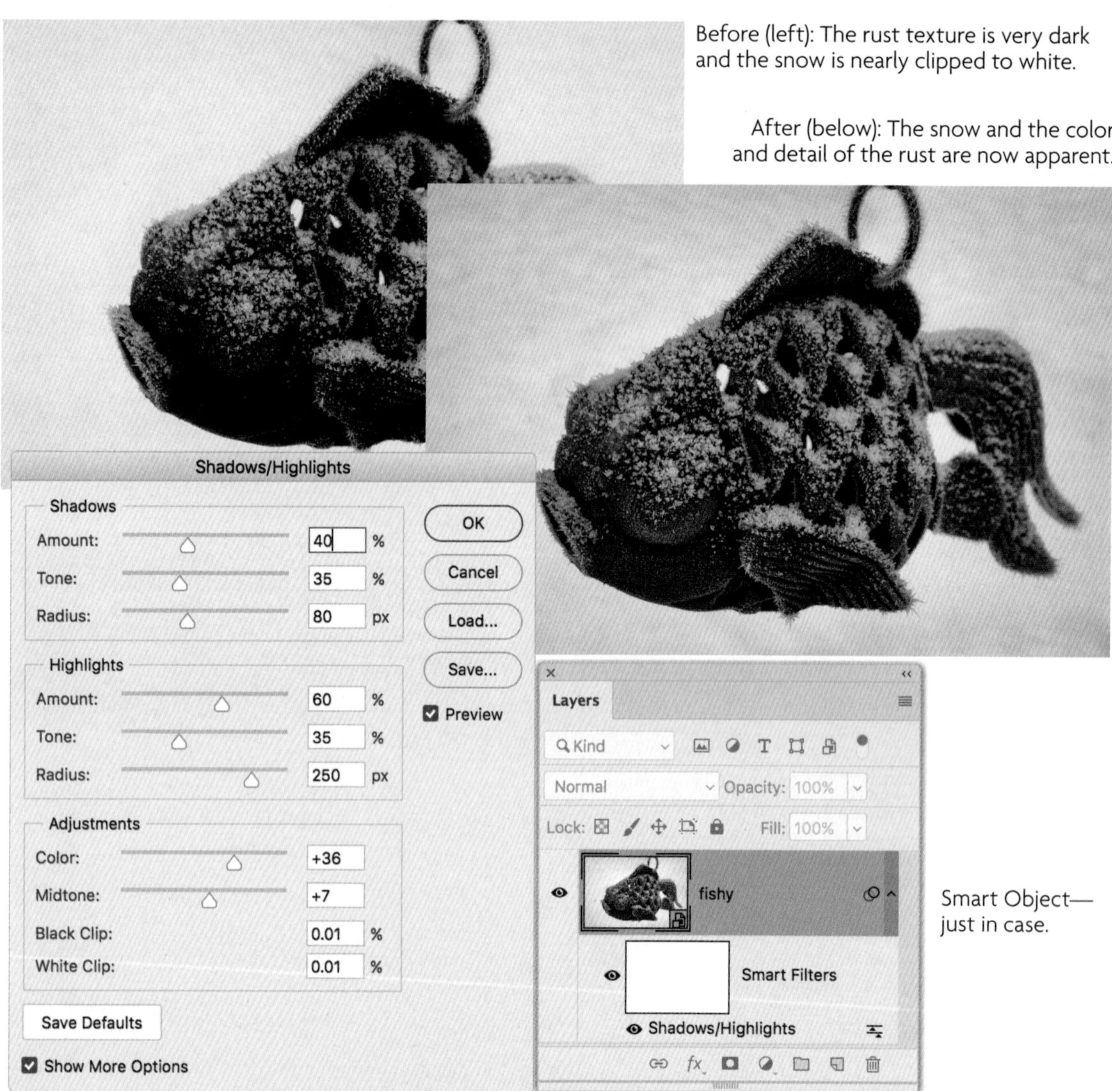

Before (left): The rust texture is very dark and the snow is nearly clipped to white.

After (below): The snow and the color and detail of the rust are now apparent.

Smart Object—just in case.

The dialog has three sections: Shadows, Highlights, and Adjustments. The first, Shadows, lightens tones just barely lighter than black, while Highlights darkens tones just barely darker than white. Within each of those first two are three sliders:

- Intuitively, the Amount sliders control how much each adjustment lightens or darkens.
- The Tone sliders control how far into the tonal range each adjustment extends. Thus, if Tone is set to 35%, the effect covers about a third of the full tonal range. I find that particular value a better starting point than the default of 50%.
- Finally, the tricky Radius sliders. These define the tonal "regions" affected. Large expanses of shadows, for example, may require a Radius in the hundreds of pixels. Thin, narrow areas may be happier with a setting in the tens of pixels. I like the advice of the wise Dr. Russell Brown (russellbrown.com): "Move the Radius slider up and down until the image looks better—then stop!" This simple advice works because when the Radius value is too high or low, there is either too little effect to notice or obvious halos around objects.

Since shadows and highlights lack saturation, the Color slider in the Adjustments section adds some. Midtone adds contrast to the middle of the tonal range, which may have been lost in this adjustment. It may cause you to lose some of your gains, however. A small number of pixels should likely be allowed to clip, so the 0.01% values are good defaults.

HDR Toning

HDR Toning is not actually an adjustment. Like Shadows/Highlights, it is a filter. Be warned that ***it is extraordinarily destructive***. Not only can it not be applied to a Smart Object, the document to which it's applied must be flattened to a single Background layer!

It *can* be used to recover nearly lost shadow or highlight detail and give those areas pleasing saturation, but it can also make an image obnoxiously surreal.

Use this filter with discretion and only on a copy of your original files.

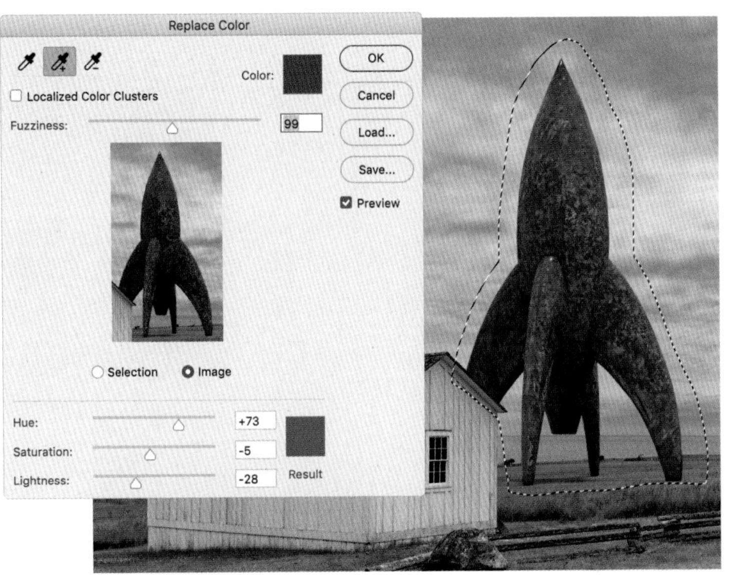

Replace Color

This adjustment cannot be applied as an adjustment layer nor as a Smart Filter. It may have some appeal, as it combines the interface of a Color Range selection to choose a color and the three sliders of a Hue/Saturation adjustment to change that color. But since it can be used only directly on pixels, I'd prefer to use those other tools individually and nondestructively.

Equalize

Recall that a histogram shows the relative number of pixels each level (shade of gray) has on each channel. Typically, some levels have fewer pixels to represent them, and others have more. Equalize tries to give each level, on each color channel, the same number of pixels, resulting in a rather level histogram. The darkest tone is made black and the lightest, white.

If there are already many black or white pixels, you may still see a spike at one end of the histogram or the other.

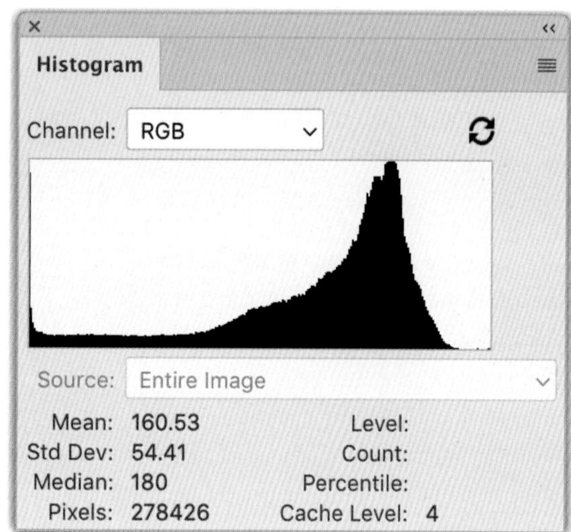

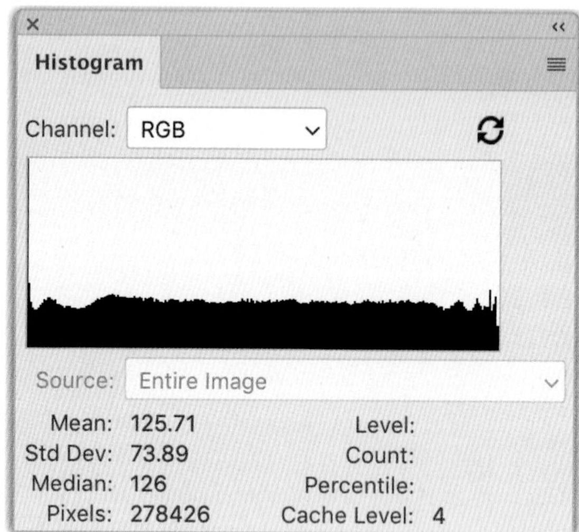

An image's histogram before (left) and after (right) applying the Equalize adjustment.

If the image started off rather light, the result will be darker, or if it started dark, the image will be lightened. To force a result, you may start with a selection. If there's an active selection, a dialog box opens asking whether to apply Equalize to only that area, or to use the tones in that area as the basis of the adjustment that affects the whole image.

I rarely use this adjustment because its uses are limited and it cannot be applied as an adjustment layer or Smart Filter. I sometimes find it useful on a copy of a document before using the Threshold adjustment (see page 253).

Creative Adjustments

Again, I'm listing the following adjustments here because they're most often used for more creative, interpretive results. Of course, if that's what you do day-to-day, then they're wonderfully practical production tools too.

Black & White

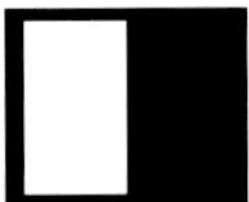

The name nearly says it all. With this adjustment, especially as an adjustment layer, we seemingly discard color but translate the image's existing hues into lighter or darker tones as we choose.

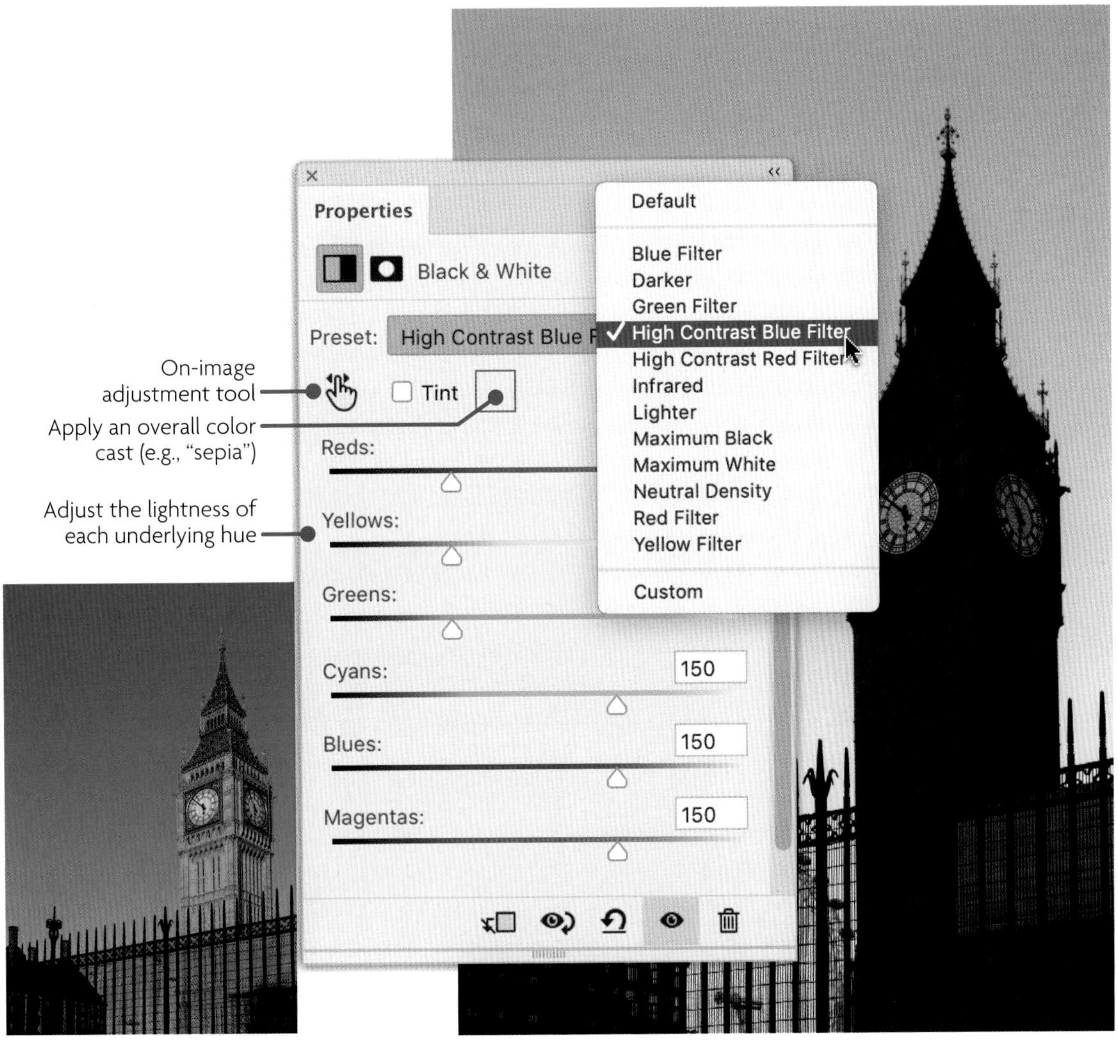

On-image adjustment tool

Apply an overall color cast (e.g., "sepia")

Adjust the lightness of each underlying hue

Invert

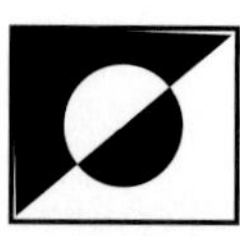

This adjustment is very simple: It creates a "negative" version of the image. All colors and tones become their opposites. Using a blend mode like Color or Luminosity, you can restrict the effect to those attributes.

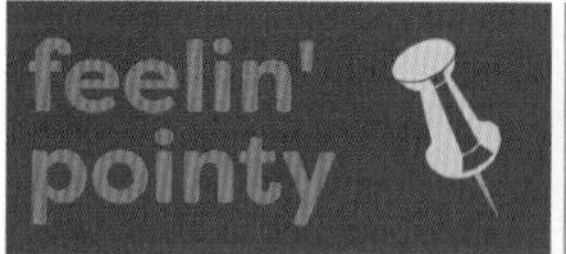

The original graphic

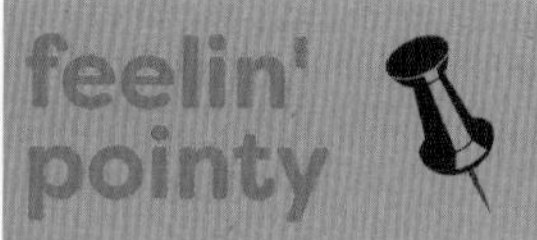

An Invert adjustment added normally

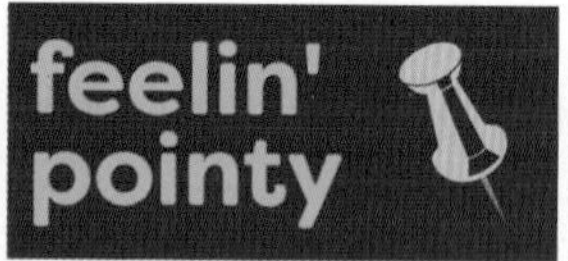

An Invert adjustment added using the Color blend mode, leaving tone unaffected

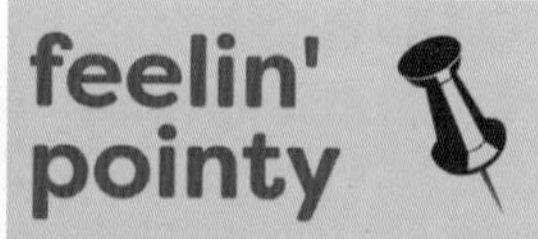

An Invert adjustment added using the Luminosity blend mode, leaving color unaffected

Posterize

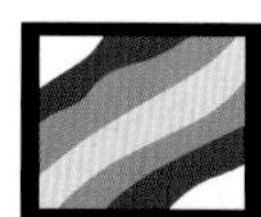

Posterize reduces the number of levels or tones in an image. If the image is grayscale, the number set for Levels is exactly how many shades will be left. In color images, each channel is a grayscale image and is reduced to the specified number of levels. In either case, gradations become visibly "banded."

Often, using another adjustment first (or an adjustment layer below) can yield a more pleasing or seemingly detailed result. I often use the Equalize adjustment on a copy of the layer my image occupies before creating a Posterize adjustment layer.

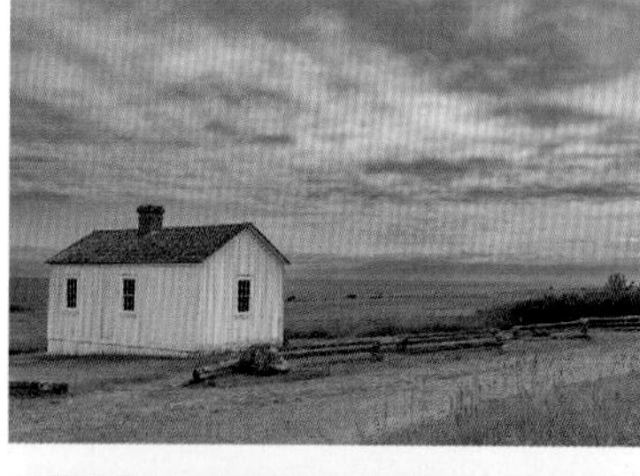
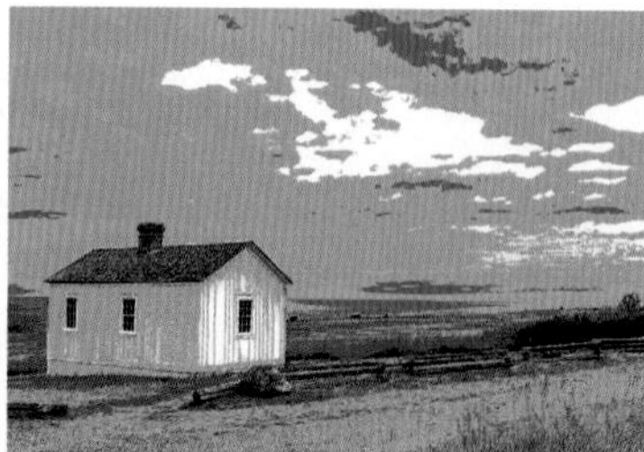
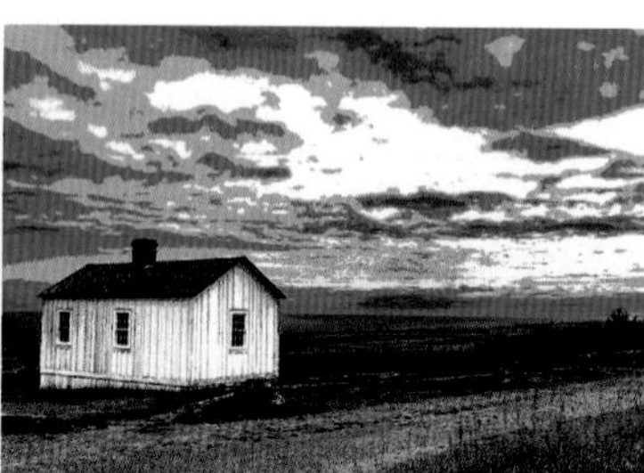
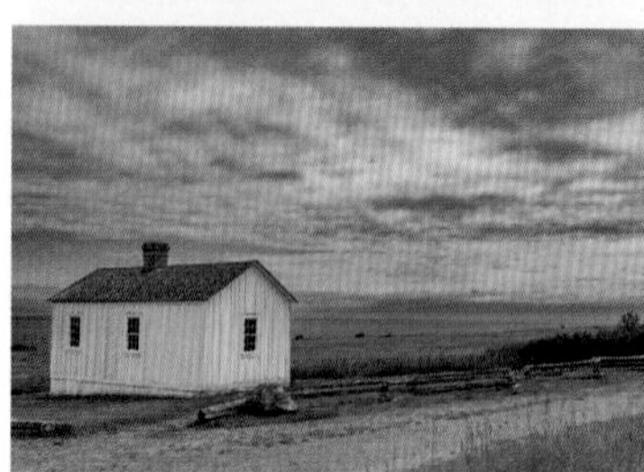
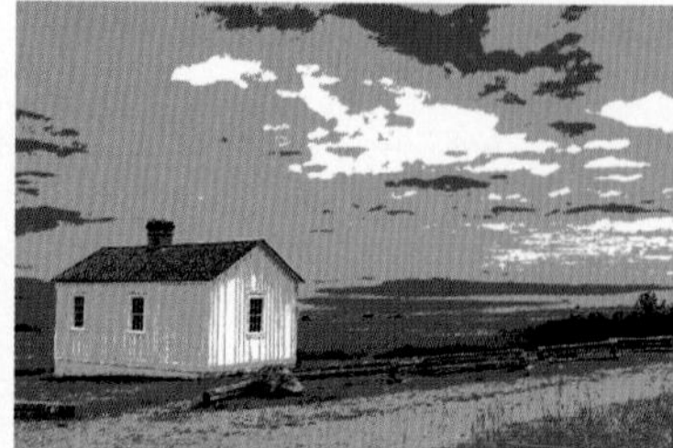
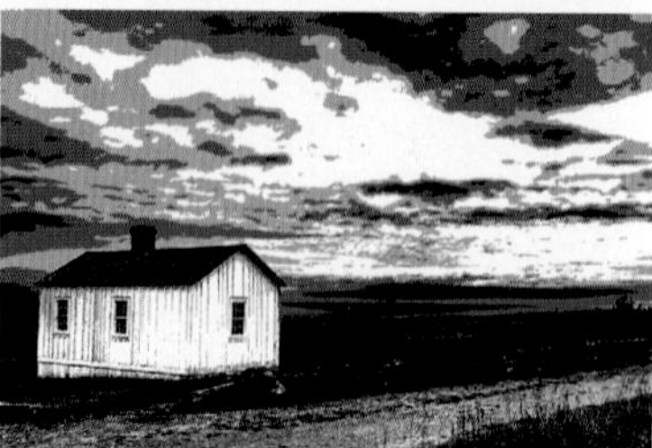

Original in color and grayscale

With Posterize (Levels set to 4)

With Posterize (Levels set to 4) *after* Equalize adjustment

Threshold

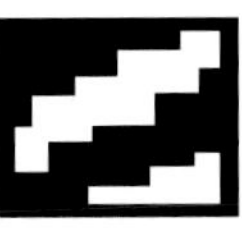

The result of Threshold is initially very similar to applying a Posterize adjustment to a grayscale version of your image with Levels set to 2. That is, you're left with two shades of gray: black and white—nothing else. This is often done to create a stenciled look. Unlike Posterize, Threshold allows you to choose the Level below which becomes black and above which becomes white.

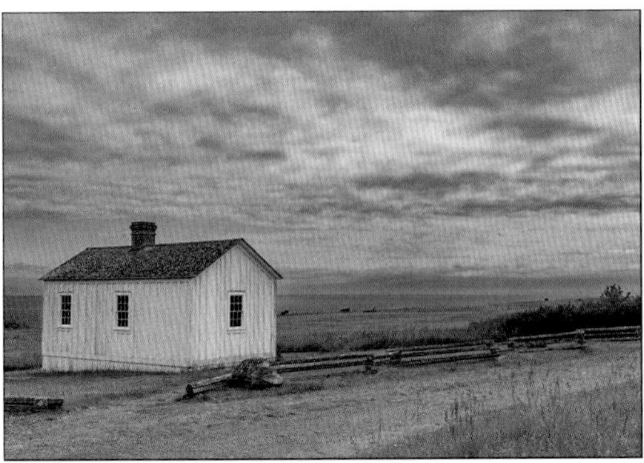

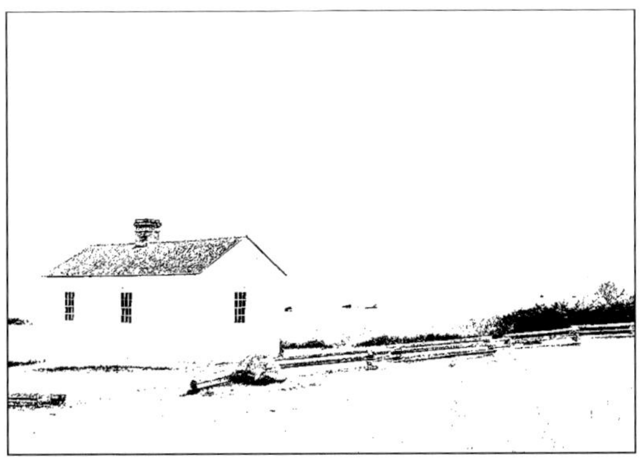

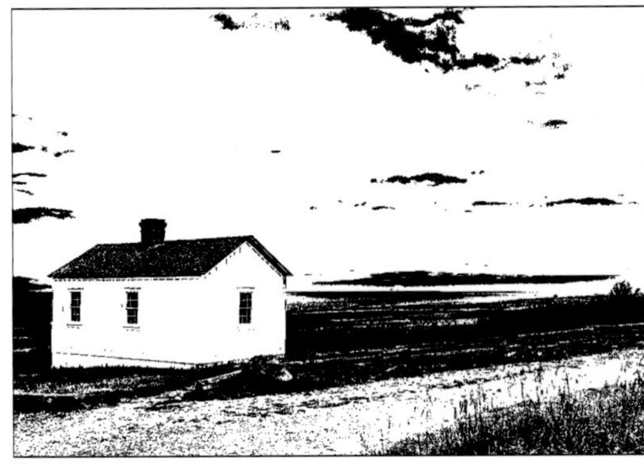

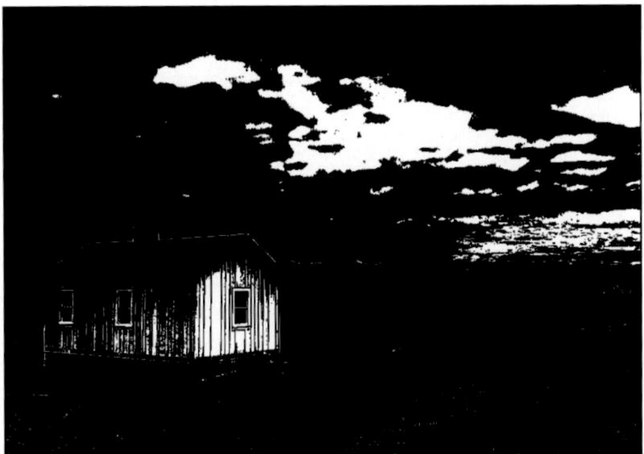

Clockwise from top left: the original image; Threshold Level at 64; Threshold Level at 127 (middle gray); and Threshold Level at 200

Gradient Map

This is a powerful adjustment for "toning" images in way that is reminiscent of darkroom processes. Of course, as this is Photoshop, we can go much further. With this adjustment we apply a gradient whose colors "map" to levels (shades of gray) in the image. The color at the left edge of the gradient preview replaces black in the image; the color at the right edge replaces white; and, as you'd guess, any color in between those replaces tones in between. Look at the following silly example:

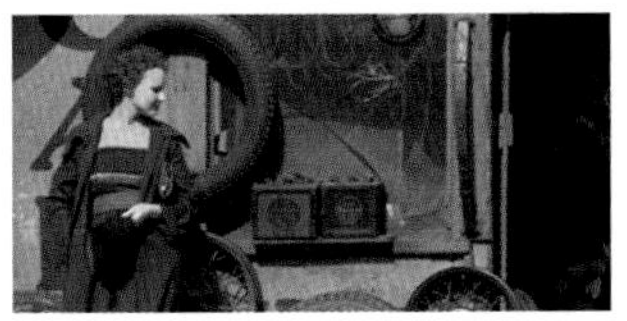

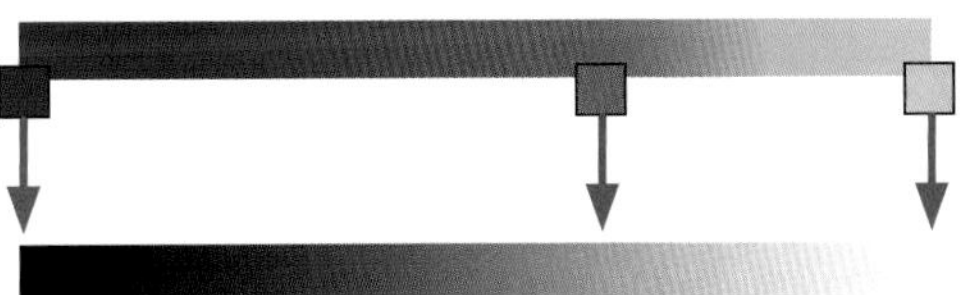

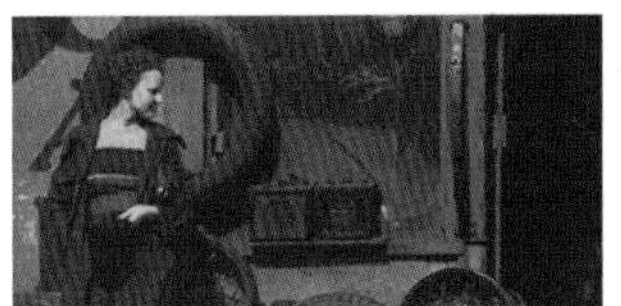

In this case, a purple has been mapped to black; orange is mapped to tones a little lighter than midtones; and cyan is mapped to white. Below are more plausible examples. One emulates a cold-toned image on warm (yellowish) paper, and the other a more typical "sepia" look.

Clicking on the gradient in the Properties panel opens the Gradient Editor, which allows us to control its colors in a way similar to other gradients. See "Gradient" (page 141).

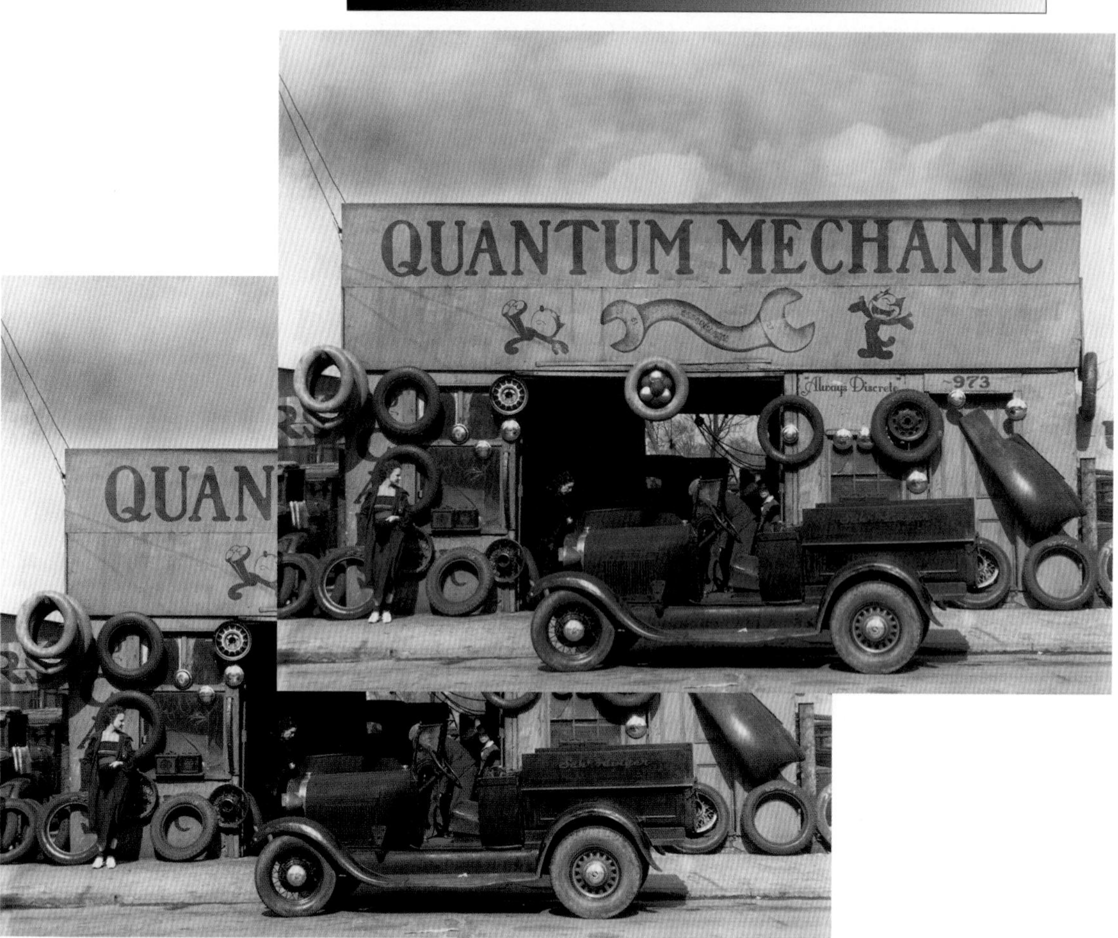

Color Lookup

Color Lookup is another "mapping" adjustment. Unlike Gradient Map, which maps colors only to tones, Color Lookup can map colors to colors, to quickly achieve a consistent look and feel, even one that is complex.

This type of adjustment was created by the film industry, which has to deal with imagery from many sources in many different formats. By applying a color lookup table, or "LUT," they can match raw footage from various sources to achieve the desired look.

However, the main purpose of LUTs is *not* color correction, but creative color alteration. In the world of cinema, this is called "grading," and using LUTs is part of it.

Using a LUT

To achieve reliable results, an image should start well-exposed (neither too light nor too dark) and have proper White Balance (page 358). Then a LUT can help us achieve consistent appearances, whether that's a film-stock emulation, a special effect (like night from day), or a gentle color/tonal shift. Note that I said it "can."

LUTs come in several basic flavors: 3DLUT, where the "3D" refers to the three color channels (RGB); DeviceLink, which are RGB or CMYK color profiles, the latter having four dimensions but still confusingly called 3DLUTs; and, finally, Abstract profiles, the only ones that are color calibrated, but which few software applications use. The first two kinds will look different in different color spaces so will generally need a tweak to match when images come from different sources. The last is wonderfully consistent since it adapts to the current color space to match actual color.

So, if you're working exclusively within Photoshop, try to use Abstract LUTs. If you use other applications, too, then you may have to use 3DLUTs since they're more widely used. Because of their near ubiquity, you'll likely find more 3DLUTs to use.

Choose the Color Lookup adjustment from the Adjustments panel, then choose one of the many LUTs that come with Photoshop. You may use one you've made or downloaded, too, by choosing to Load it from the appropriate menu (.cube, .look, and .3dl are 3DLUTs, for example, but DeviceLink and Abstract are ICC profiles with .icc extensions and may be hard to distinguish from one another).

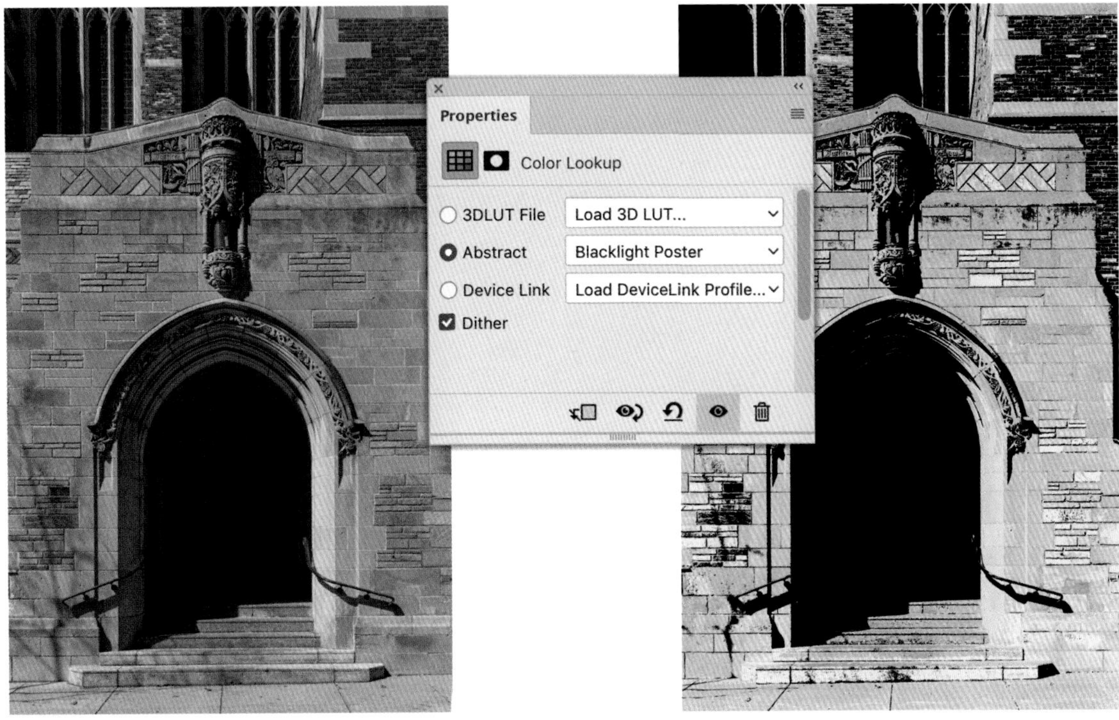

Creating a LUT

Creating your own color lookup table (LUT) is not hard. It does benefit from foresight, however. For any kind of LUT, you need to start with a simple Background layer and no others. Then use adjustment layers to create the look you want to achieve with the LUT. Although you may use color Fill layers with blend modes as well, that is less reliable.

If your objective is to create LUTs for use in Photoshop alone, you should create Abstract profile LUTs to ensure color accuracy and consistency. To do so, the document not only needs to start with a Background layer, but it also needs to be in Lab Color mode (Image > Mode > Lab Color). In fact, this is the only reason most of us will ever have to use Lab mode! Not all adjustment layers are available in Lab, and those that are will behave slightly differently than they do in RGB mode. Abstract profile LUTs can be used in all color modes too!

If you're in prepress and are compelled to work in CMYK, you'll need the exported DeviceLink profile (the only one exported that doesn't have "RGB" appended to its name). To use a LUT in video applications, it's most likely you'll need a 3DLUT.

- Consider using a duplicate of your original image.
- Start with a Background layer.
- For color-accurate Abstract profile LUTs, convert to Lab Color mode. The exported LUT without "RGB" appended to its name is the Abstract profile. Otherwise, working in RGB is fine.
- Create adjustment layers with intact (but unused) masks.
- Choose File > Export > Color Lookup Tables....
- Provide a Description and, if desired, copyright attribution ("© Copyright" and the year are automatically prepended to this).
- Choose the Quality (accuracy) and Formats you want. For the former, 64 is considered a good accuracy/file size compromise, and I check all of the latter and weed them out later.
- Click OK to choose a location and base name for the exported LUT files.

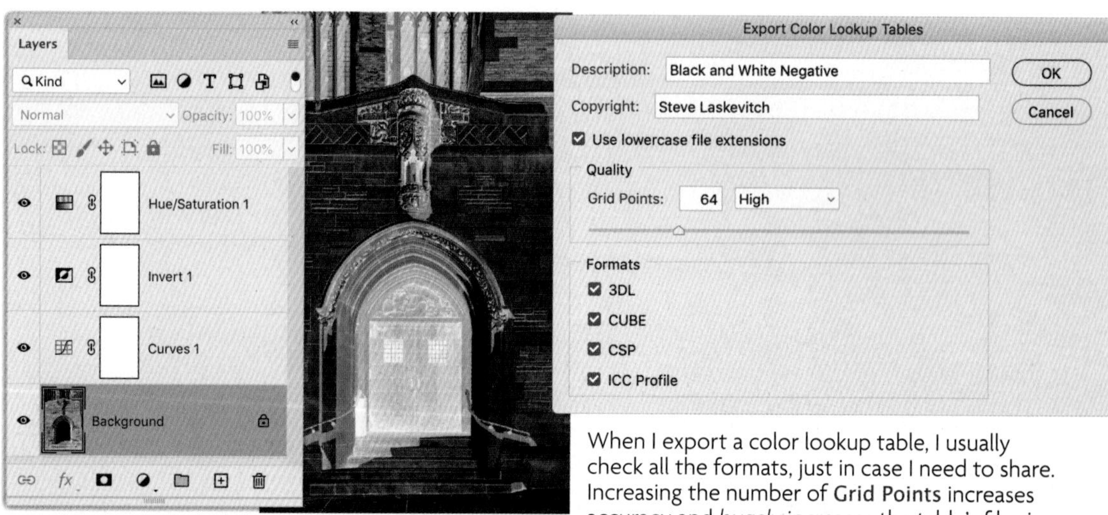

When I export a color lookup table, I usually check all the formats, just in case I need to share. Increasing the number of Grid Points increases accuracy and *hugely* increases the table's file size.

3 Brushes & Painting

Many tools in Photoshop use brushes. With some, we paint in an expected and intuitive way, adding color to our digital canvas. With other tools, we find ourselves "painting" with imagery, past versions of our documents, or image adjustments. Almost every mask we make requires at least a little touch-up—by painting.

That's why dabblers, designers, and photographers—not just painters and illustrators—need to understand how painting works in Photoshop, and how to configure the brushes we use to do so.

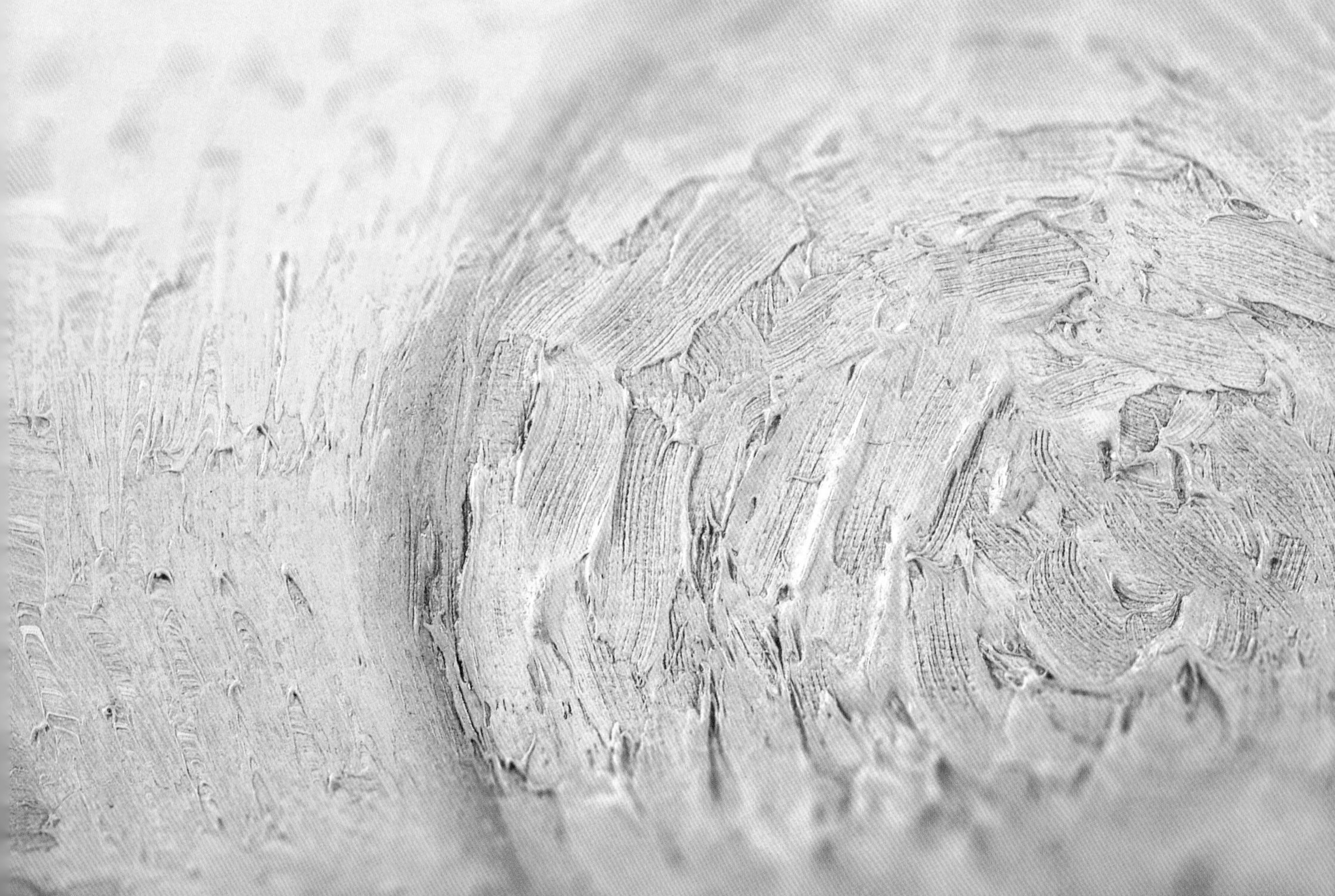

Layers & Smart Objects

Adjustments & Color

Brushes & Painting

Brushes and Brush Settings

Almost every tool that uses a brush cursor can be elaborately configured using the Brush Settings panel. Those configurations can be saved in the Brushes panel (formerly called Brush Presets). Configuration means choosing (or creating) a brush tip and adding behaviors to it. Note that some settings leverage stylus and tablet input devices, especially those that are pressure-sensitive. Also, when creating Brushes (a.k.a. presets), these can be designated as tool-specific or can be used by any brush-using tool. There is also a vibrant marketplace of Brushes from and for illustrators and artists.

This section examines brush settings usable by any of those tools, although I usually illustrate their use with the intuitive Brush tool. Many of the desktop settings discussed here can be applied to use on an iPad, and are especially aided by use of an Apple Pencil. In following sections of this chapter, we'll look at the Brush tool and others individually.

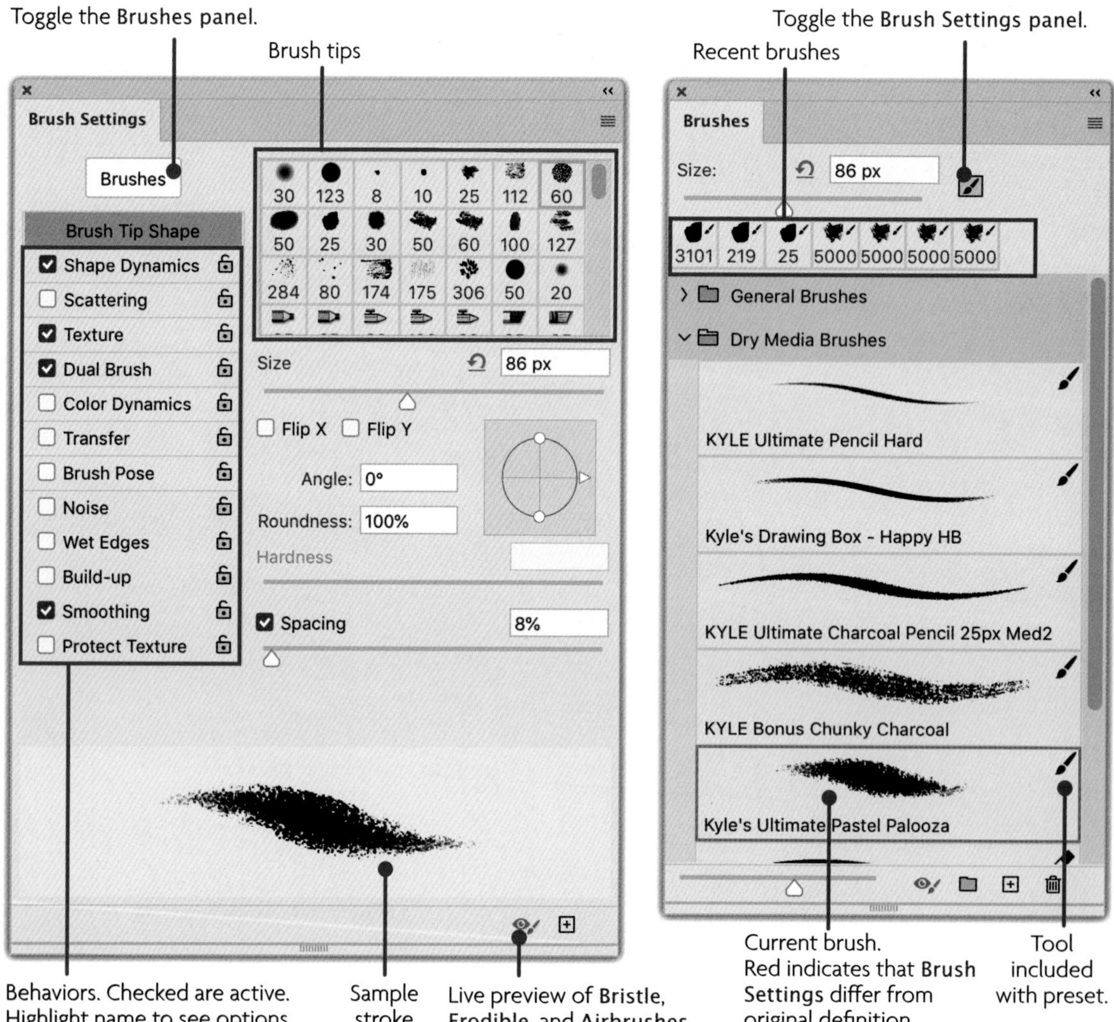

Brush Tips

Brush tips are the algorithms or bits of raster artwork that describe what comes into contact with our canvas. Some brush tips are generated by the software (the algorithmic ones) and have parameters like Size, Roundness, and Hardness. Others are actual pixel-based images, which can also be scaled and skewed, but, like any image, need to be of sufficient resolution if they're to be used at large sizes.

The list shown in the Brush Settings panel (when Brush Tip Shape is highlighted) comes from all those tips used by presets in the Brushes panel, making this discussion a bit circular. For any tool that can use Brush Settings, there's a button in the Options Bar ( ) to toggle the Brush Settings panel. That panel has a Brushes button to toggle the Brushes panel. Both panels are, of course, listed in the Window menu.

To have all types of tips, open the Brushes panel menu and choose Converted Legacy Tool Presets. Many work best with tablets and pens that sense the tilt and rotation of the pen and the pressure applied to the tablet (a Wacom Intuos Pro tablet with an Art pen, for example).

Brush Tip Parameters

Depending on what kind of tip you select, you will see different parameters. The choices are derived from the brush presets that are currently loaded.

Standard: Round and Raster Image–Based Tips

These two types of brushes share almost all the same parameters. The only exception is Hardness. Bear in mind that raster image–based brushes have an original sample size, and if exceeded, it can cause a brush stroke's edges to look blurry or pixelated.

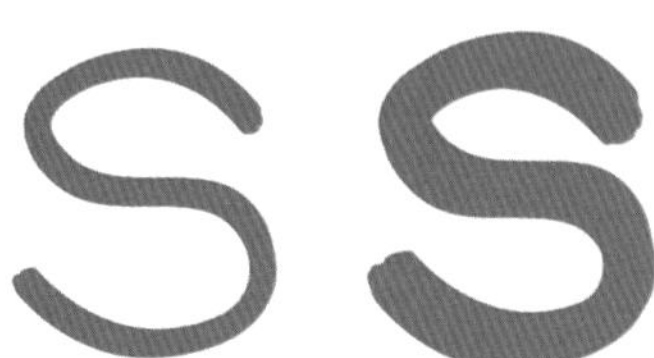

Size From one pixel to 5000 pixels across. For image-based tips, there's a button to the left of the **Size** field that resets the size to its original sampled size. Size can be changed by tapping the bracket keys (the left bracket [for smaller, right] for larger).

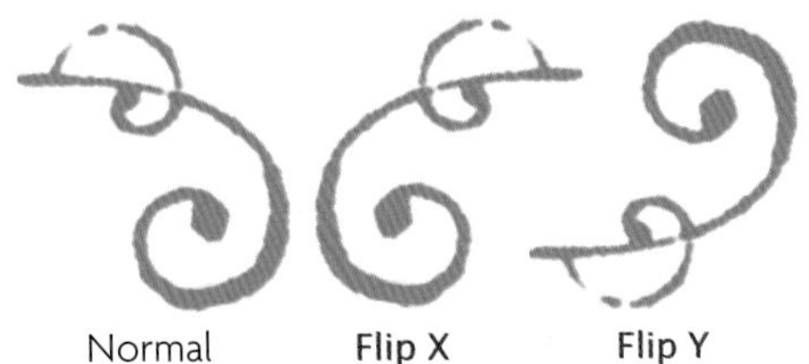

Flip X and Flip Y Flips (mirrors) a brush tip horizontally (**X**) or vertically (**Y**).

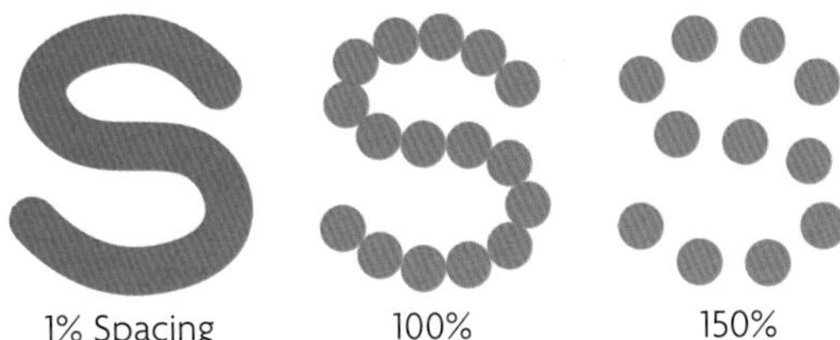

Spacing A brush stroke is not a continuous flow of color, but is a series of (usually) overlapping dabs of the brush tip. A stroke looks smooth and continuous with tighter **Spacing** (low values). A value of 100% produces a stroke in which each dab is laid down perfectly adjacent to the ones on either side.

Angle: 171°
Roundness: 31%

Roundness and Angle The **Roundness** setting squishes a brush tip. The **Angle** control rotates the tip. With harder round brushes, these controls yield nice calligraphic brush tips that produce strokes that naturally alternate from thick to thin. **Angle** can be changed by tapping the left or right arrow keys (← or →). Add **Shift** to change angle 15° at a time.

Hardness For standard round brushes only, this controls the sharpness or fade of the edges of the brush tip, and therefore strokes made with it. Change the **Hardness** in 25% increments by holding down **Shift** and tapping the left or right bracket keys ([or]).

To visually change the Hardness or Size, summon the HUD: control-option-drag (Mac)/ Ctrl-Alt-right-click-drag (Windows) vertically to adjust hardness, or horizontally for size.

Loading and Saving Brushes

New Brush
Name: round
Capture Brush Size in Preset
Include Tool Settings
Include Color
10
OK
Cancel

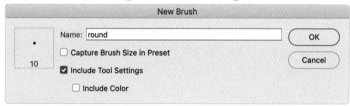

If the preset is optimized for a particular size, enable **Capture Brush Size in Preset**. If it makes sense with only one tool (e.g., **Brush tool**, **Clone Stamp tool**, etc.), enable **Include Tool Settings**. Likewise, if the current color choice is critical, enable **Include Color**.

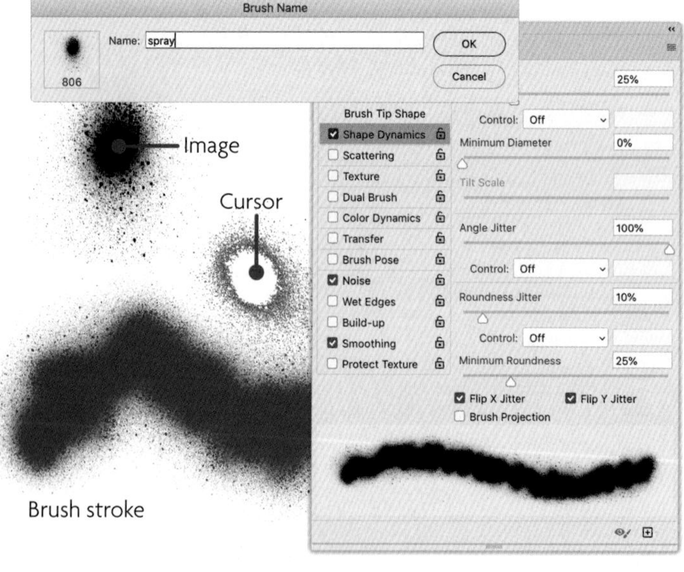

Brushes are presets that capture brush tips (discussed above) and behaviors configured in the Brush Settings panel. Of course, you can and will make your own brushes, but a good way to get some brushes that are close to what you would build is to load some that Adobe provides.

Use the Brushes panel menu and choose Get More Brushes…. This will take you to a web page from which you can download brushes whose behaviors you can study and customize. This has the additional benefit of adding their brush tips to the list in the Brush Settings panel.

To create your own brush, choose Edit > Define Brush Preset…; or go to either the Brush Settings panel or the Brushes panel and click the Create new brush button (⊞); or use the panel menu and choose New Brush Preset… to name your preset and set a few options.

Image to Brush

If you want to use an image up to 5000 pixels across as a brush tip, be aware that Photoshop will use only its tonal (grayscale) values. Black will be the opaque parts of the brush tip, white will make no mark at all. Open such an image and then choose Edit > Define Brush Preset.... The initial preset will have no behaviors. Set those behaviors with the Brush Settings panel, then create another more useful preset as described above.

Brush Behavior

The Brush Settings panel is where you choose brush tips and imbue them with behavior—that is, how the tip interacts with the canvas. Most of the behavior options have many settings to choose from and configure, while others are just toggles.

The iPad app Adobe Fresco enjoys many of these features too. If you master them on the desktop, you can take them on the road as well!

Common Settings

Many of the settings (Dynamics and Transfer, for example) have a Jitter setting to randomly alter the behavior. Fade is an option that causes the behavior being edited to diminish over the duration of a brush stroke. It requires you enter a distance (in multiples of the brush tip width) over which the fade occurs.

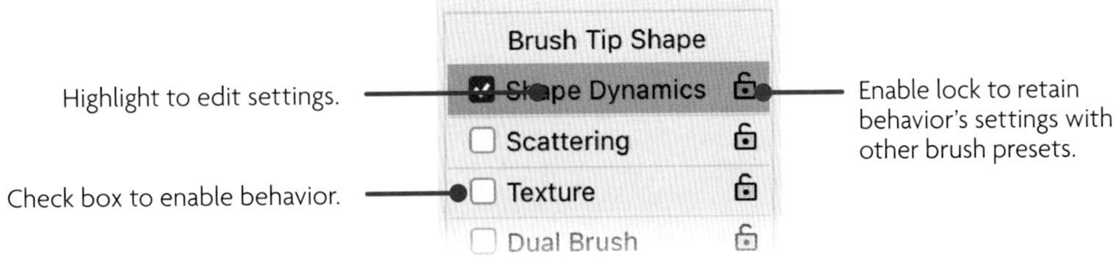
Brush Tip Shape
Highlight to edit settings.
Shape Dynamics
Enable lock to retain behavior's settings with other brush presets.
Scattering
Check box to enable behavior.
Texture
Dual Brush

Many behaviors can be controlled with a tablet's pen/stylus. You can decide whether the pressure applied with the pen, its angle to the tablet, its rotation in the hand, or other attribute is what controls the behavior. Note that not all tablets and pens support all of those options—higher-end versions are usually required. But since many tablets support pressure control, the Brush tool, the Pencil tool, and a few others have shortcut buttons in the Options Bar that let you quickly allow a pen's pressure to control the tool's size and/or opacity.

Brush behavior buttons in the Options Bar:

 Use pen pressure to control opacity.

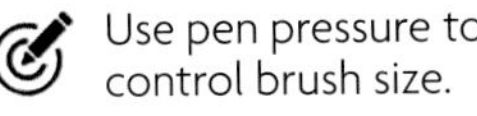 Use pen pressure to control brush size.

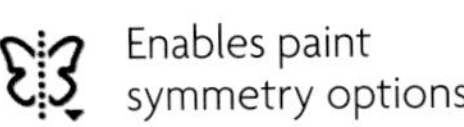 Enables paint symmetry options.

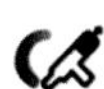 Enables paint build-up. Holding the mouse button will cause the tool's effect to accumulate.

Shape Dynamics and Scattering

These two are often used together to cause a brush tip to become art that is sprayed playfully across the canvas as you paint. The Shape Dynamics illustrated here make heavy use of randomness, or "jitter." Size, Angle, and Roundness are all being randomized here to some extent, as well as an occasional mirroring of the tip (Flip X and Flip Y). To prevent it from being too random, I also set values for Minimum Diameter and Minimum Roundness.

If I intended to use a stylus that supports tilt controls, I may have used Brush Projection too. This distorts the tip in a way that mimics a flexible object being pressed to the canvas, giving a kind of perspective skew to it. Each attribute (Size, Angle, and Roundness) has a Control menu. From these, you can choose to have your stylus's pressure or rotation, for example, control attributes like tip size or angle.

Scattering is exactly what it sounds like: the sprinkling of the brush tip to either side of the brush's path (and forward and back if Both Axes is enabled). A broad scatter may make the brush tips too spread out, so we have a Count control to multiply their number.

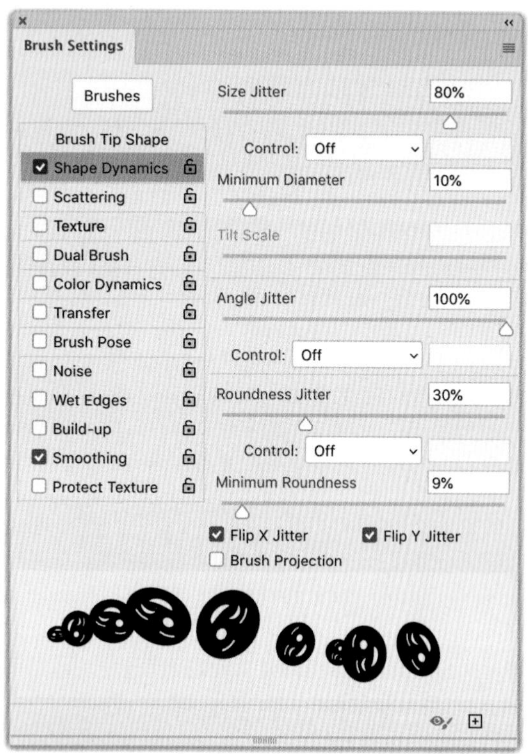

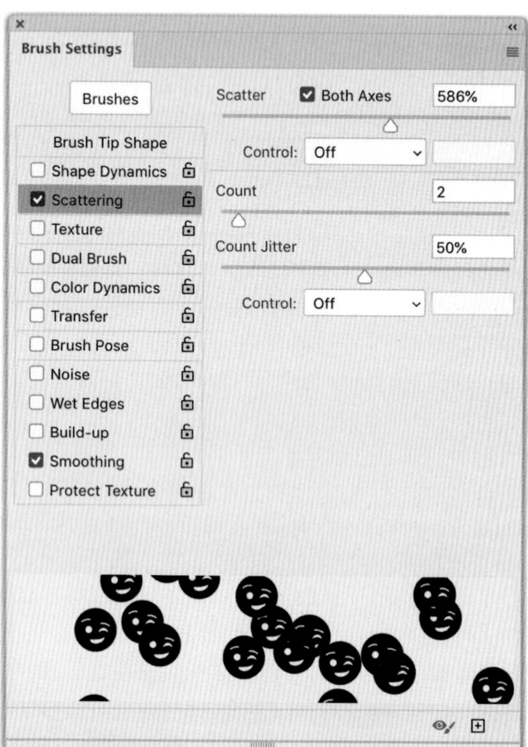

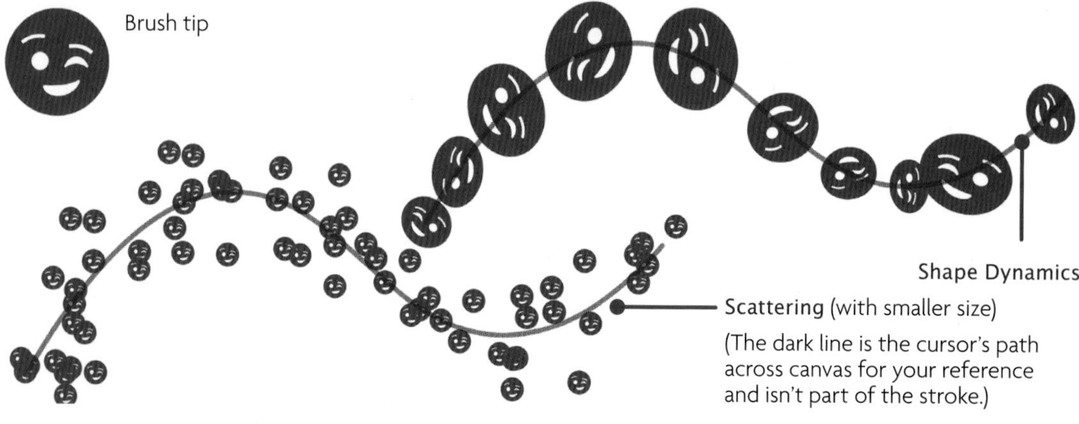

Texture and Dual Brush

These settings allow either a pattern (Texture) or another brush tip (Dual Brush) to blend with your brush stroke. The biggest factor in how these blend with your brush tip is the selected Mode (as in blend mode: see "Blend Modes" on page 176).

The Texture pattern can be made bigger or smaller, brighter or darker, and more or less contrasty to better interact with the brush tip. The Depth slider controls how strong the interaction is. The tip chosen in Dual Brush can have its own dynamics and scattering.

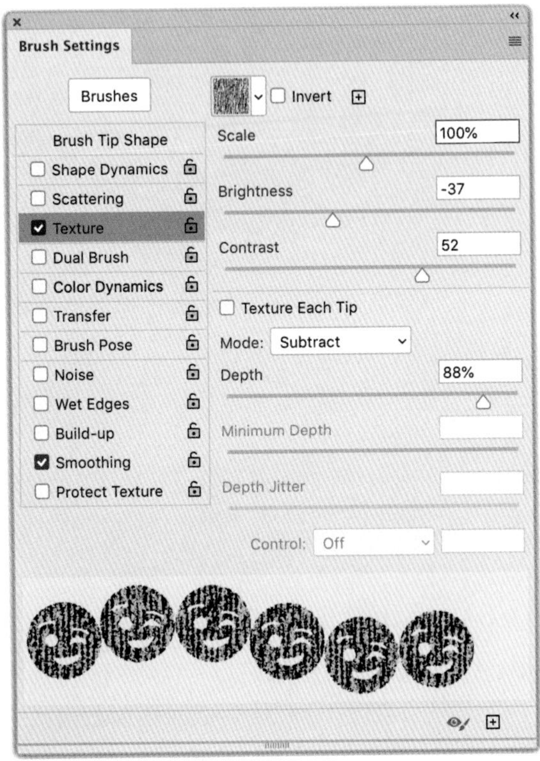

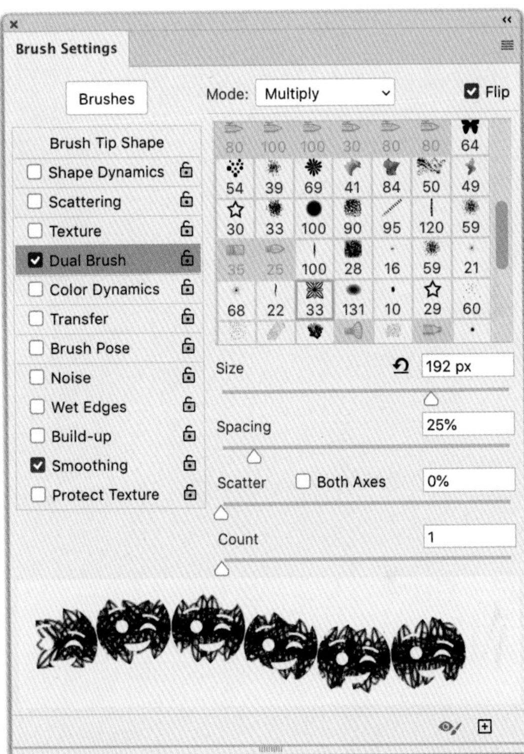

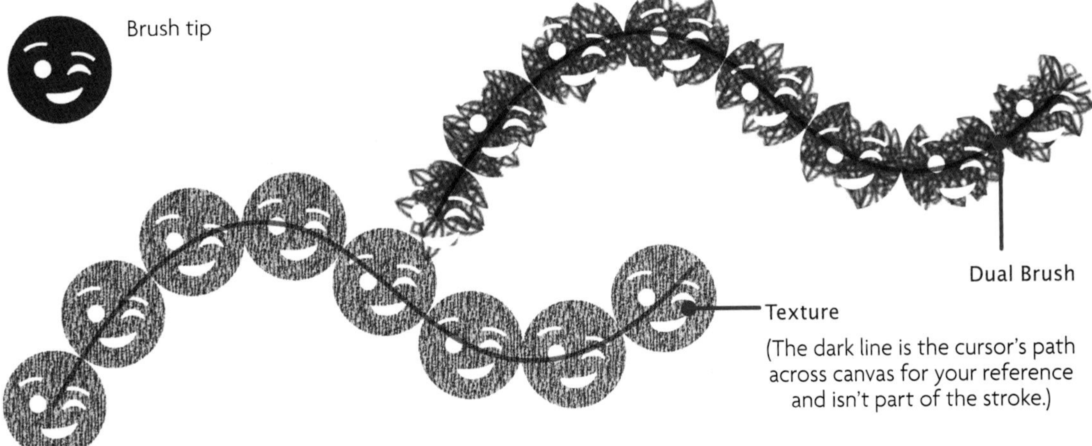

Color Dynamics

This one is straightforward: The color with which you paint varies, either stroke-by-stroke or tip-by-tip (if Apply Per Tip is enabled). When painting with the Brush tool, the foreground color is used. Using Foreground/Background Jitter, this is alternated with the background color. How much so is controlled by the percentage you choose. Similarly, the other jitter sliders alter the hue, saturation, and/or brightness of the stroke or tips. Purity is another word for saturation, and the slider affects the saturation of the entire affair.

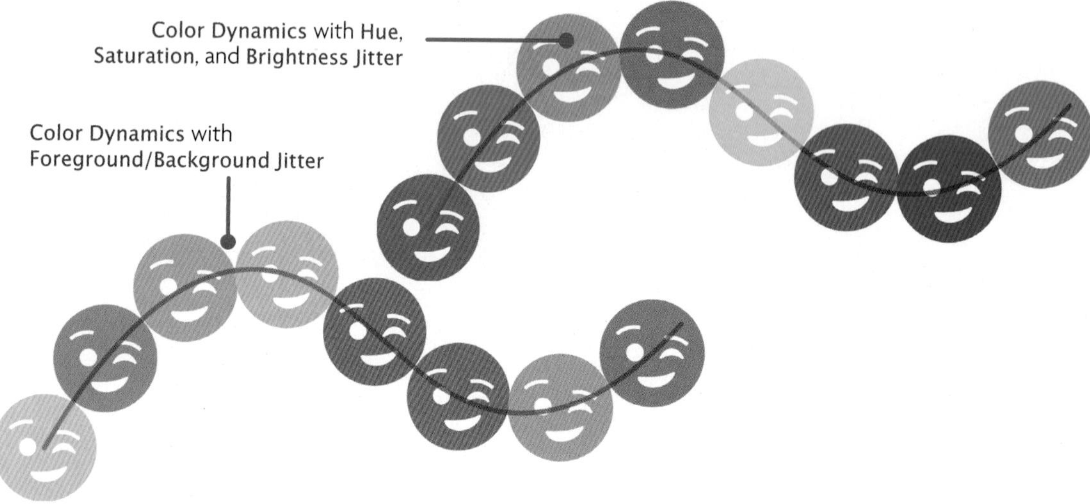

Controlling Transfer: Opacity and Flow

The most common use of the Transfer controls is to assign a brush's opacity to the pressure one exerts with a stylus. I can't emphasize strongly enough how useful this is when masking adjustment layers, gradually painting in (or out) adjustments to areas of an image.

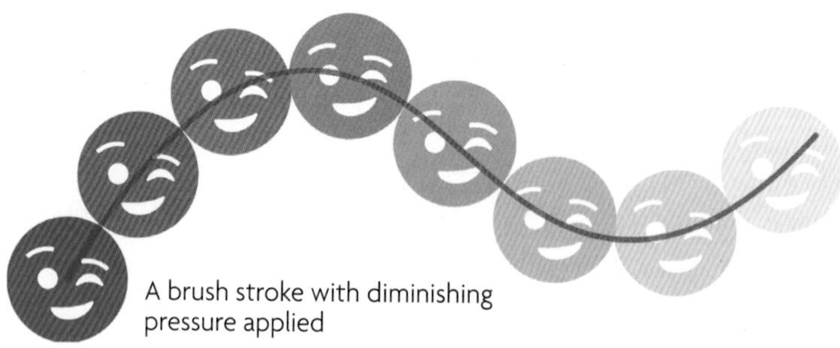

If you'd like to build up paint (effect) density by brushing over the same area during the same brush stroke, use Flow rather than Opacity. Otherwise, they're pretty much the same.

If you don't have a stylus, buy one! Or you can choose Fade from the Control menu to have a stroke change its opacity over the distance covered by a specified number of tips. Tighter spacing means a more rapid fade. Wetness is for use with the Mixer Brush tool only.

Brush Pose

When a brush could benefit from a tilted stylus, but you don't have a stylus that supports tilt, you can use this setting to impose a tilt. Of course, it'll be static. This is also useful if you don't want your stylus's tilt to play a role and you do want a static Tilt (or Pressure or Rotation).

Tilt X is side-to-side tilt, and Tilt Y is fore and aft tilt.

Noise, Wet Edges, and Build-up

Noise adds a slight random texture to a brush stroke. This can be helpful when printing to devices that don't preserve a brush's wispiest edges.

The Wet Edges setting causes the center of the stroke to be translucent, with the edges holding more of the effect.

Build-up, when enabled, will cause a stationary brush tip to continuously add more paint in the manner of an airbrush continuously spraying onto the same spot.

Smoothing

Smoothing: 31%

Smoothing Options
- Pulled String Mode
- Stroke Catch-up
- Catch-up on Stroke End
- Adjust for Zoom

Smoothing can help produce silky strokes from even the most jittery mouse use. In the Options Bar, you'll find a setting for the amount of Smoothing to apply. Next to that setting is a gear icon that reveals Smoothing Options, which are methods that can be employed to do the smoothing. Some work together. For example, Adjust for Zoom allows less smoothing when zoomed in, enhancing precision work.

Pulled String Mode

Imagine the brush tip is a load at the end of a string you're pulling. A longer string (higher Smoothing setting) will produce a smoother curve when you make a tight turn. If you "back up," you have to take up the slack before the brush moves again. I find this a clever way to get really elegant brush strokes.

Stroke Catch-up

Imagine chasing a dog who knows it's being chased. It will run a serpentine path to avoid you, but your path will be less volatile as you try to catch up. Unlike when I chase a dog, the brush does a better job of catching up to the cursor. Releasing the mouse (or lifting the stylus) stops the stroke before it catches up—unless the next setting is enabled.

Catch-up on Stroke End

When the mouse is released (or the stylus is lifted), the brush stroke, which had lagged somewhat behind the cursor, will *suddenly* catch up to the cursor's location. Higher Smoothing settings mean more lag and a greater catch-up distance.

Protect Texture

When locked (the padlock icon to the right enabled), this will ensure that settings that use a pattern for texture (Texture and Dual Brush) retain their patterns when you choose another brush preset.

Tools with Brush Settings

Almost all you need to know about the following tools is covered earlier in this chapter. What differs from one tool to another can be found in the Options Bar when you choose each tool. Those options are discussed below.

Brush

The quintessential painting tool. This paints with the foreground color. To erase, hold down the grave accent (`) key for an eraser with the same brush characteristics as the Brush tool, or hold down the E key to access the Eraser tool with its own previously set options.

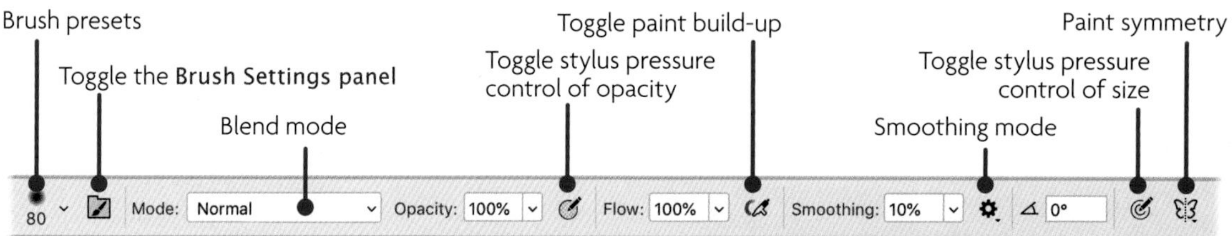

Symmetry

The Symmetry options create axes around which your brush strokes reflect to create (hopefully) interesting forms. Here, I created a 7-axis Radial Symmetry and painted just four strokes with a highly elliptical brush tip.

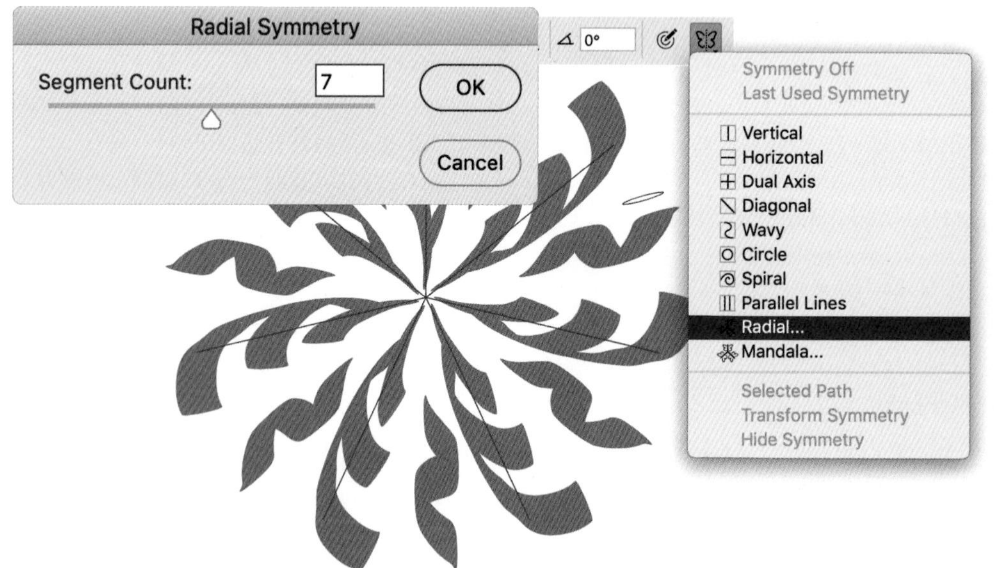

Pencil

This is essentially a hard, aliased-edged brush. The edges of a stroke with the Pencil tool are crisp with no fade-off whatsoever. I use this primarily when I need to paint literally one pixel at a time with no slop.

The Pencil tool has an odd option: Auto Erase. When enabled, starting a pencil stroke with the cursor's center over pixels that match the current foreground color actually paints with the background color.

Mixer Brush

As the name implies, this tool samples color from the image as it paints, mixing colors. You can control the process, as you might with real paint and brushes, by adding more fresh paint to the brush ("loading"), cleaning the brush, or painting when previous paint is dry.

If you find this function appealing, you will likely adore Adobe Fresco, the iPad app that leverages traditional media even more powerfully and intuitively.

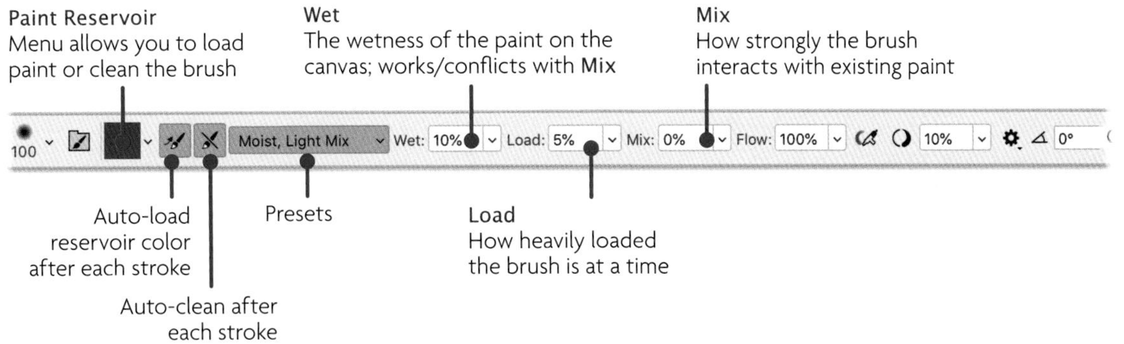
Paint Reservoir
Menu allows you to load paint or clean the brush
Wet
The wetness of the paint on the canvas; works/conflicts with Mix
Mix
How strongly the brush interacts with existing paint
100
Moist, Light Mix
Wet: 10%
Load: 5%
Mix: 0%
Flow: 100%
10%
0°
Auto-load reservoir color after each stroke
Presets
Load
How heavily loaded the brush is at a time
Auto-clean after each stroke

Retouching Tools

See the "Retouching & Repair" chapter of this Compendium for details on using these tools.

Color Replacement

This rather destructive tool is like painting with the Brush tool set to a blend mode of Color (or Hue, Saturation, or Luminosity). But unlike that, it cannot affect colors on a separate layer.

Pattern Stamp

Similar to, but less flexible than painting the mask of a layer filled with a pattern. You choose a pattern from the Options Bar, as well as brush attributes, and the pattern appears as you paint.

History and Art History Brushes

These tools leverage the History panel, which contains a list of document states created after each act you perform. Those states are named after the tool or action performed that created that state. Clicking a history state's name restores the document to that state, typically graying out the states listed below. If you perform another action, the grayed-out states vanish and the new action's resulting state takes their place. Just like in science fiction, if you travel back in time and do something, it will create a new timeline.

To the left of each history state is a space in which you can click. This sets that state as the source of data with which the History Brush tool paints. As long as the layer or element existed when that state was made, you'll be able to paint on it, restoring the areas where you paint to the condition they had when that state was made. It's like painting with undo.

The Art History Brush tool uses the same method as the History Brush tool, but it paints an interpreted, impressionistic version of the history state. I think it is preferable to use the Mixer Brush tool or the Oil Paint filter on an image to achieve a painterly interpretation.

Erasers

The Eraser tool uses a brush whose settings you can configure in the Brush Settings panel. On layers that support transparency, it truly erases; otherwise, it paints with the background color. In almost all circumstances, it is better to mask images rather than erase them. There are a few exceptions. I will erase retouching I later discover to be inadequate, or brush strokes that I didn't execute well.

Background and Magic Erasers

These old tools were introduced before we had marvelous nondestructive ways of masking (hiding) pixels we didn't want to see. Far better results can be more quickly achieved with the Select Subject command or the Object Selection tool and the Select and Mask workspace.

Tone and Focus Tools

As with the erasure tools, there are tools for tone and focus for which there are superior workflows and functions.

Dodge/Burn/Sponge

These three tools lighten, darken, and desaturate, respectively. However, once done, there is no going back. In other words, they are destructive techniques, unlike adjustment layers on whose masks we can paint to achieve precise adjustments to areas of images. The Dodge, Burn, and Sponge tools are coarse and amateurish by comparison. They do, however, use Brush Settings to apply their result.

Blur/Sharpen/Smudge

These tools also use painterly methods to affect focus in images, but again, we can achieve better, more controlled results with filters applied to Smart Objects. The Smudge tool can be useful to artists in conjunction with other brushes when literally painting in Photoshop.

4 Selections & Masks

An electronic stencil is one way to understand a selection or mask. We craft selections to prepare a section of our document for whatever next step awaits it. Masks, with simple shades of gray, allow us to hide images or visual effects where they shouldn't be seen. Most often, we create masks from selections. In this chapter, we examine the reasons and methods to create both.

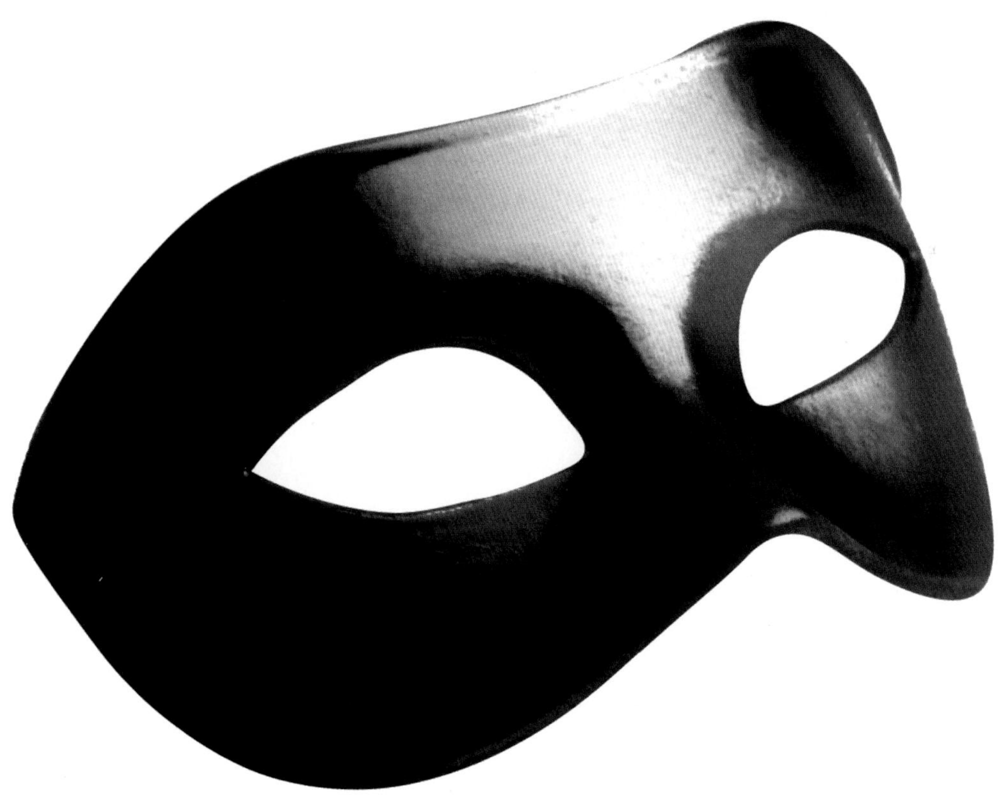

Selections: Limiting the Damage

Photoshop possesses many tools for designating which pixels in a document are affected by the next action performed. Since pixels can be partially selected, selections can also designate how affected those pixels will be.

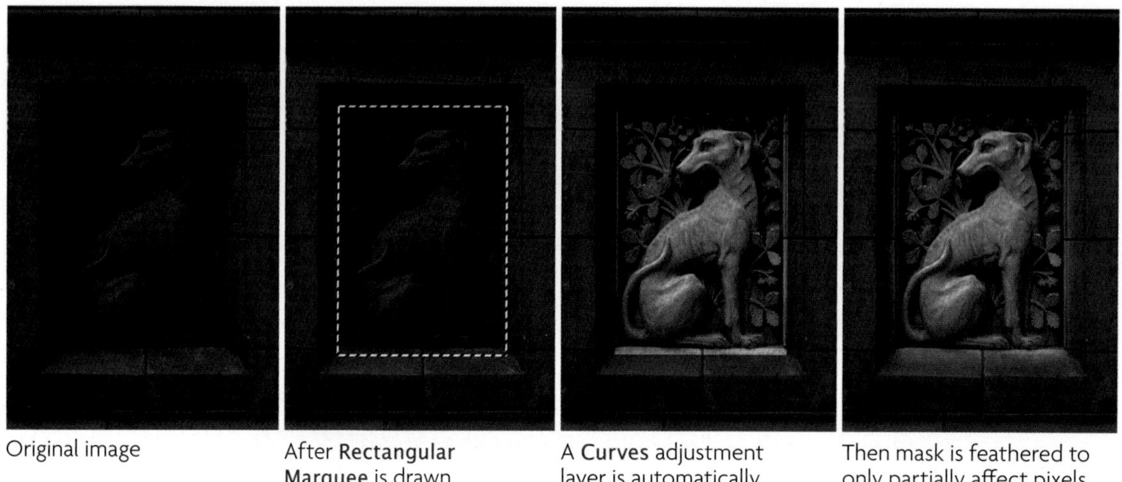

Original image

After **Rectangular Marquee** is drawn

A **Curves** adjustment layer is automatically masked to selected area

Then mask is feathered to only partially affect pixels at the selection's edge

The steps are almost always the same:

- Make a selection with one of the tools discussed on the following pages.
- Refine that selection, if necessary.
- Perform some task, often resulting in a mask that reveals the result where desired and hides it elsewhere.
- Refine the mask, if necessary.

Selection Tools

Picture or recall a stencil. It could be made of cardboard or plastic and has carefully shaped holes in it. When used with an imprecise tool (a can of spray paint, for example), it creates a result as precise as the holes cut into the stencil. Our selections are very similar. We designate one or more areas (corresponding to the stencil's holes) that will be affected when we apply a potentially imprecise tool, such as the Brush tool.

With software, we can have shockingly intricate selections that push the stencil metaphor to the edge of usefulness. When areas are partially selected, that metaphor is undone. (A porous stencil?)

Let's have a look at the different tools and methods available to isolate parts of images and our actions on them. The next section then covers modifying and combining selection tools by adding to and subtracting from selections and more.

Marquees

There are four tools in this set: Rectangular, Elliptical, Single Row, and Single Column Marquee tools. The first two of these get regular use and are accessed by the letter M (use Shift-M to toggle between them). With either, drag diagonally to create a selection (upward or downward, left or right). Use Shift to constrain the shape to a square or circle. Modifying with the option/Alt key causes the selection to grow from its center. You can use both modifier keys to both constrain and center the selection.

Single Row or Single Column marquees are created with a single click and will span the entire canvas in one direction, but will be only one pixel high or wide, depending on which tool you're using.

Lassos

There are three tools in this set, but only two are worth using. The Lasso tool allows you to draw the shape of your selection in a freehand manner. If you don't complete a closed shape while drawing, Photoshop will close it with a straight line between where you release and where you began.

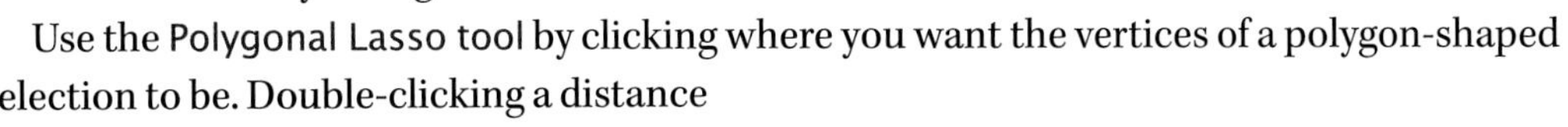

Use the Polygonal Lasso tool by clicking where you want the vertices of a polygon-shaped selection to be. Double-clicking a distance from your starting point will close the selection with a straight line.

The maddening Magnetic Lasso tool attempts to conform the growing selection to edges it detects near the cursor as you drag. It finds the edges you'd like it to and many others as well. The newer Quick Selection tool (discussed below) is far faster and more reliably finds edges.

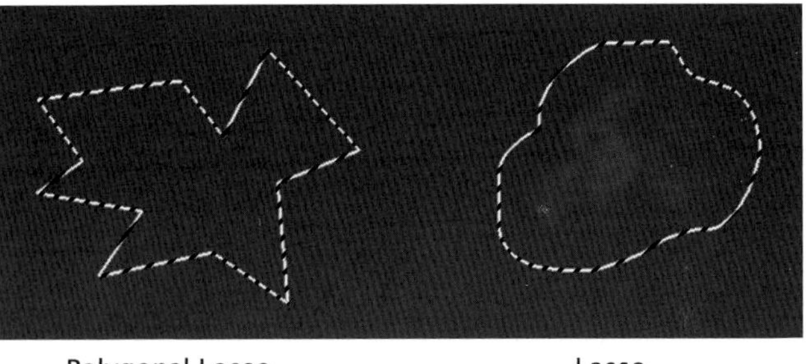

Polygonal Lasso Lasso

Magic Wand

Part of Photoshop since its beginning, this venerable tool is now hidden by newer ones: the Object and Quick Selection tools. Right-click on whichever is shown in the Tools panel to get to the others. You might call this the "elder wand." This tool utilizes a Tolerance setting you choose in the Options Bar. When you click a pixel in the image, the Magic Wand tool reads, or "samples," its color, then grows a selection of similar colors from that point outward. The Tolerance determines what constitutes "similar." The algorithm is interestingly complicated. In some contexts, the Tolerance number is simply the range of levels (shades of gray) on each channel around the levels of the pixel clicked. In other contexts, it's more sophisticated. With use, it becomes more intuitive and you'll learn to adjust this setting in small increments.

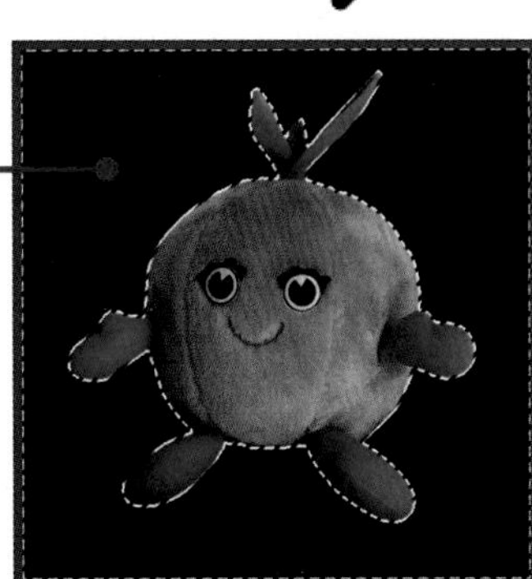

Clicking here with a Tolerance setting high enough to include variations in the black backdrop (~40) selects everything except Peachy quite well.

You can also adjust the precision of the sampled color. In the Options Bar or by right-clicking on the image, you can choose the area sampled (Sample Size). The default is a single pixel. I like to enable caps lock on my keyboard to engage Photoshop's precise cursors when I choose that setting. It shows a crosshair that helps me click on exactly the right pixel. Other settings average areas of nine pixels (3 by 3) up to over ten thousand pixels (101 by 101). The standard wand cursor is fine for those. **Warning:** Almost all tools that sample color (including various eyedroppers throughout the program) will be affected by the Sample Size choice.

Also by default, the Magic Wand tool selects contiguous pixels, ignoring similar ones that are separated from the sample by an area of dissimilar color or tone. In the Peachy example, selecting the black velvet left the black parts of the eyes unselected. Uncheck the Contiguous checkbox in the Options Bar to change this behavior.

Quick Selection

This tool is a smarter, edge-detecting version of the Magic Wand tool. You sample an area with its brushlike cursor. From this, Photoshop learns the color, texture, tone, and proximity you're trying to select. From your initial brush stroke, the selection grows to include pixels that share those attributes, stopping at detected edges.

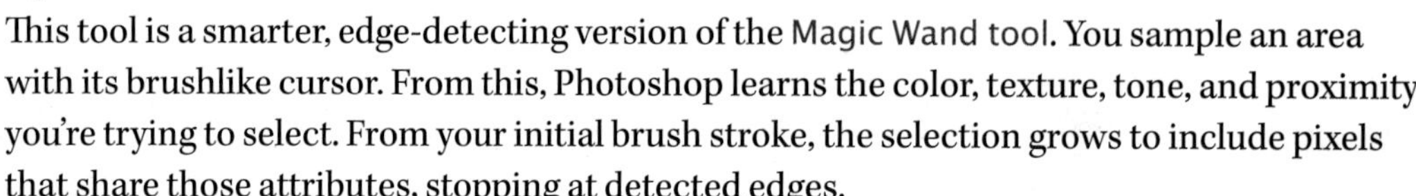

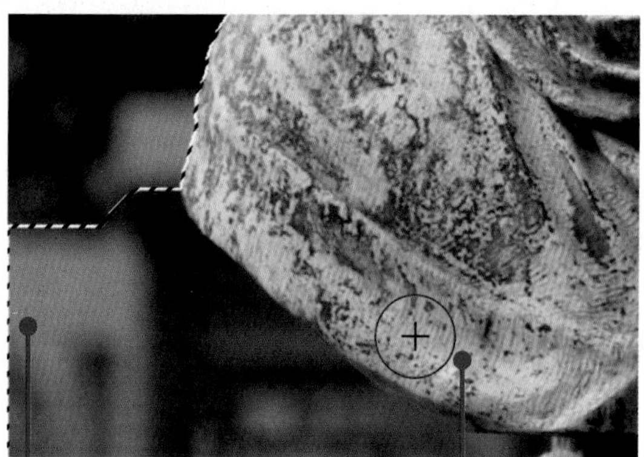

Initial selection attempt. Despite keeping the cursor *inside* the bronze sculpture's boundaries, Photoshop extended the selection beyond it.

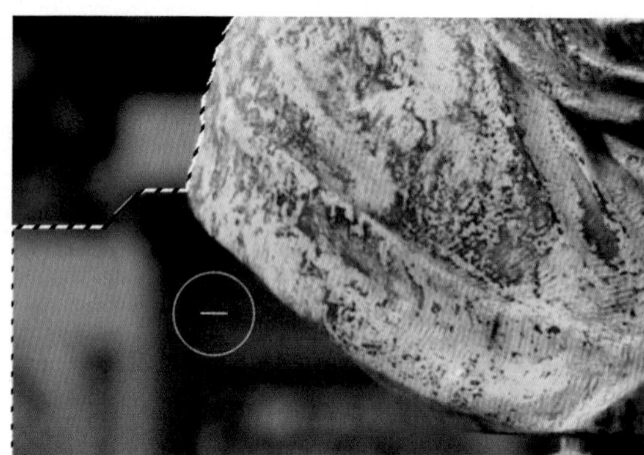

Before starting to brush, I hold down the option/Alt key to remove pixels from selection. I'll be careful to keep the cursor *outside* the sculpture's bounds when I start to "paint."

You can increase the sample area by using a larger brush size (adjusted with the [and] keys) and/or making a larger brush stroke. Be wary, however, since this also makes Photoshop a little more aggressive in its selection making. I recommend smaller brush sizes and more numerous short brush strokes. After the first stroke, this tool is automatically in an additive mode *without* needing to use the Shift key.

Also, since the program is learning from you, prevent the edges of the brush from crossing the edges of what you're trying to select. If this happens, undo that step rather than trying to remove those pixels from the errant selection.

If *Photoshop* overshoots those edges on its own, correct it by holding down option/Alt and carefully brushing over the undesired areas to subtract them from the selection. This improves its learning. In other words, undo *your* mistakes, and gently correct Photoshop's.

Object Selection

Continually updated, this AI-trained tool can allow rapid selection of objects it recognizes as such in an image. When you first choose this tool, its Object Finder begins its work. (You'll see the Refresh button churning in the Options Bar.)

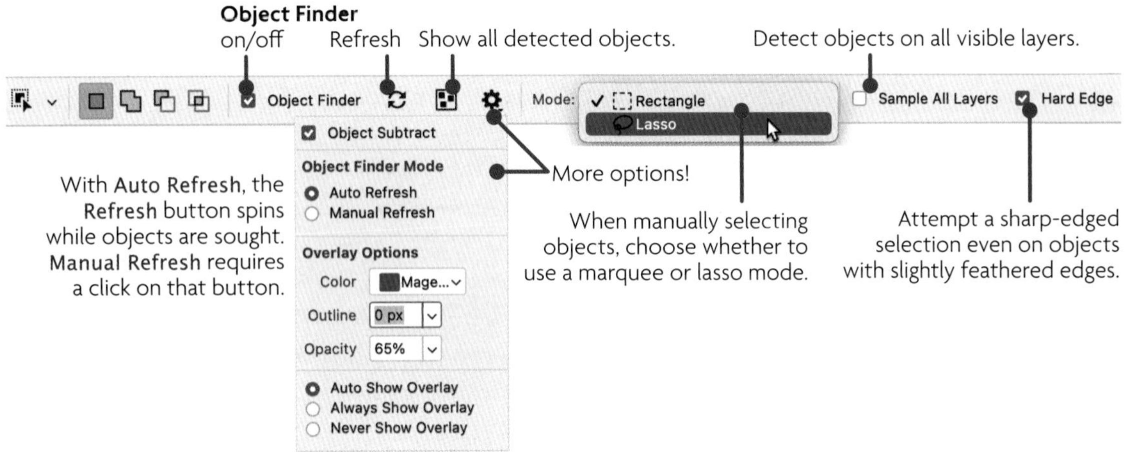

Moving the cursor over objects the tool has had time to detect, you'll see the object highlighted in magenta (or color of your choice). A simple click selects it. If an object in the image isn't recognized as such, use the Object Selection tool as you would the Rectangular Marquee tool (drag a box around it) or as the Lasso tool (freehand draw around it). Photoshop will likely select that object or close to it. You can then refine with any of the tools and functions discussed in this chapter.

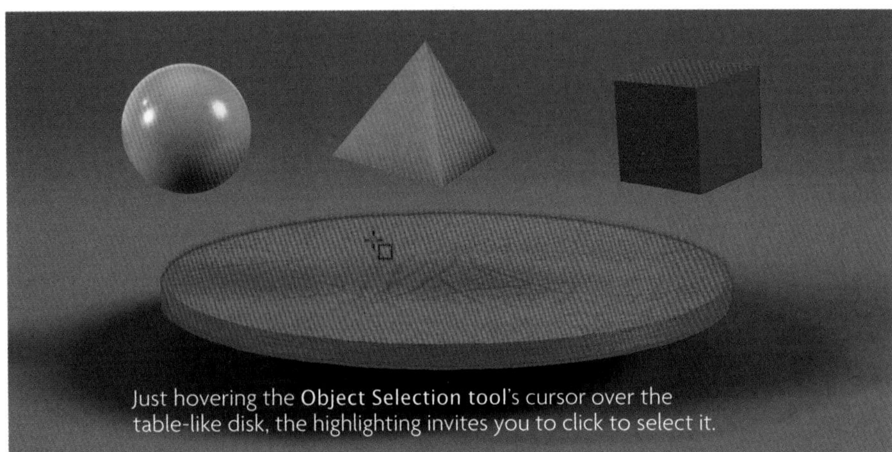

Just hovering the Object Selection tool's cursor over the table-like disk, the highlighting invites you to click to select it.

To avoid the suspense, you can have Photoshop show you all the objects it's located by clicking the Show All Objects button in the Options Bar, or engage that function by holding down the N key.

A novel function geared toward new users or longtime users in a hurry (and/or wanting to live dangerously) is to select an unwanted object with this tool and then use the shortcut Shift-delete/Shift-Backspace. Essentially, this does a quick but destructive Content-Aware Fill (page 343). I prefer the latter since it allows me to revisit the result later.

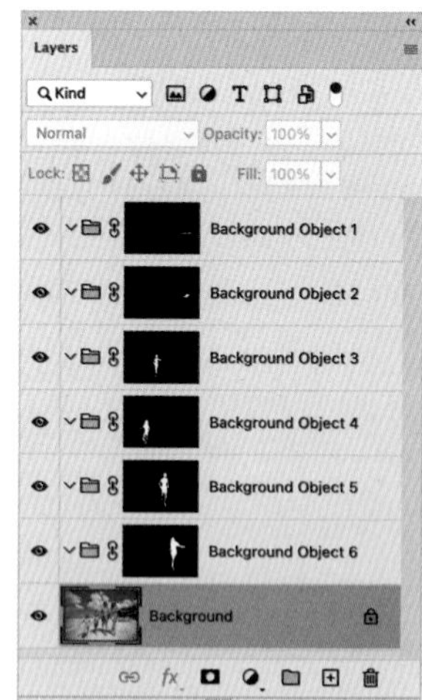

Object selection is also behind the Mask All Objects feature found in the Layers menu or the Layers panel menu. This finds all objects in an active layer, then makes a masked empty layer group for each one (right). By moving/copying the layer to one of those Groups (page 158), the corresponding object will be visible and nothing else.

Select Subject

Available from Select > Subject or a button in the Options Bar when the Magic Wand, Quick Selection, or Object Selection tool is active, this function uses AI to analyze the image for a likely subject and selects it!

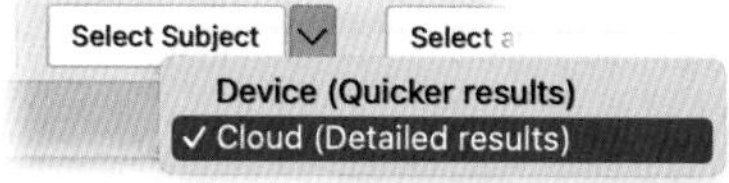

This function is also available in the Select and Mask interface. For more on that feature, see "Select and Mask" (page 278). Wherever it appears, it presents a choice to use your computer or iPad ("Device") to process the selection, or Adobe's computers ("Cloud"). Although uploading and downloading large images takes time on slower internet connections, the cloud result is noticeably better. To choose a processing default, visit the Image Processing preferences.

If Select Subject still fails, you still have all the other selection methods in this chapter to make or refine the selection. But be sure to try this method again whenever Photoshop updates, as it may then do a better job.

Select Sky

You will never guess what *this* AI-augmented function does! If you need to isolate the sky in an image, just choose Select > Sky. **Beware**: Although the "marching ants" may imply a crisp selection edge, it will actually be a bit amorphous around the edges. That is, non-sky pixels near the sky will be partially selected and sky pixels near the non-sky areas will not be fully selected. This is usually beneficial for adjustments of the sky, giving a hazy horizon a touch of that adjustment as well.

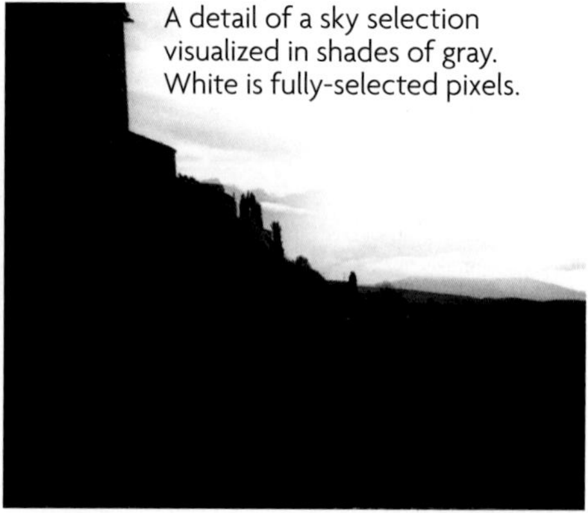
A detail of a sky selection visualized in shades of gray. White is fully-selected pixels.

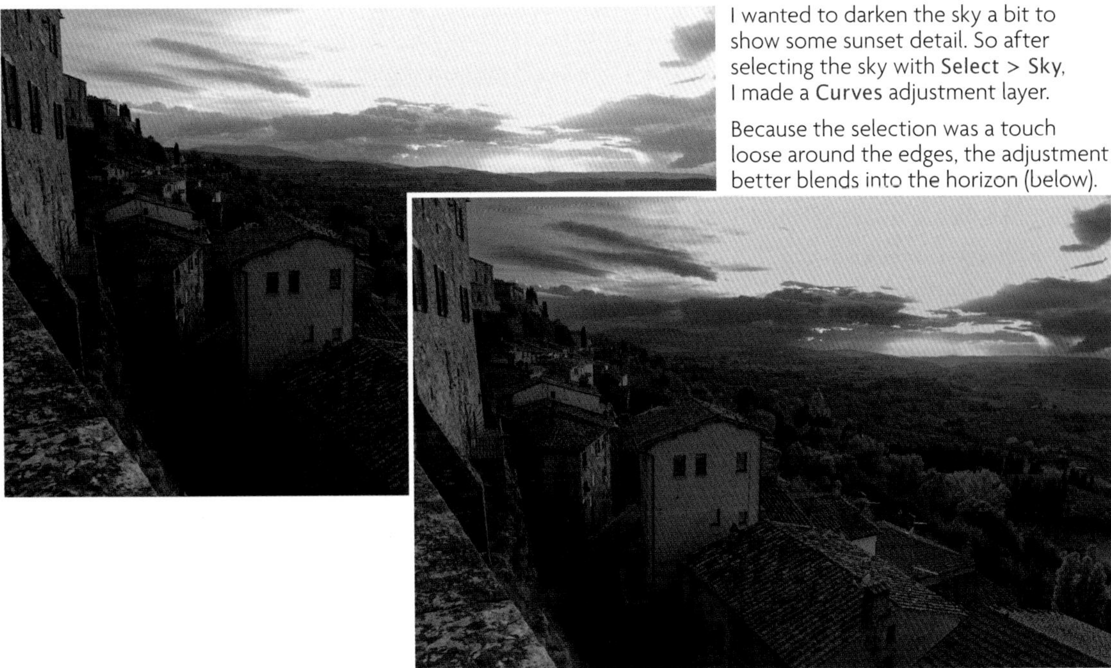

I wanted to darken the sky a bit to show some sunset detail. So after selecting the sky with **Select > Sky**, I made a **Curves** adjustment layer.

Because the selection was a touch loose around the edges, the adjustment better blends into the horizon (below).

Quick Mask: Previewer & Helper

Quick Mask is an old method of previewing and, less often these days, adjusting selections. When I have an especially intricate or convoluted selection, Quick Mask helps me see just what is and isn't selected. You enter this mode by tapping the letter Q on the keyboard, clicking the Quick Mask button near the bottom of the Tools panel ( ), or choosing Select > Edit in Quick Mask Mode. When you do any of these things, the Quick Mask button inverts ( ); the active layer's highlight color changes; and, if there's an active selection, the "marching ants" disappear, leaving a color overlay over the unselected areas of the image:

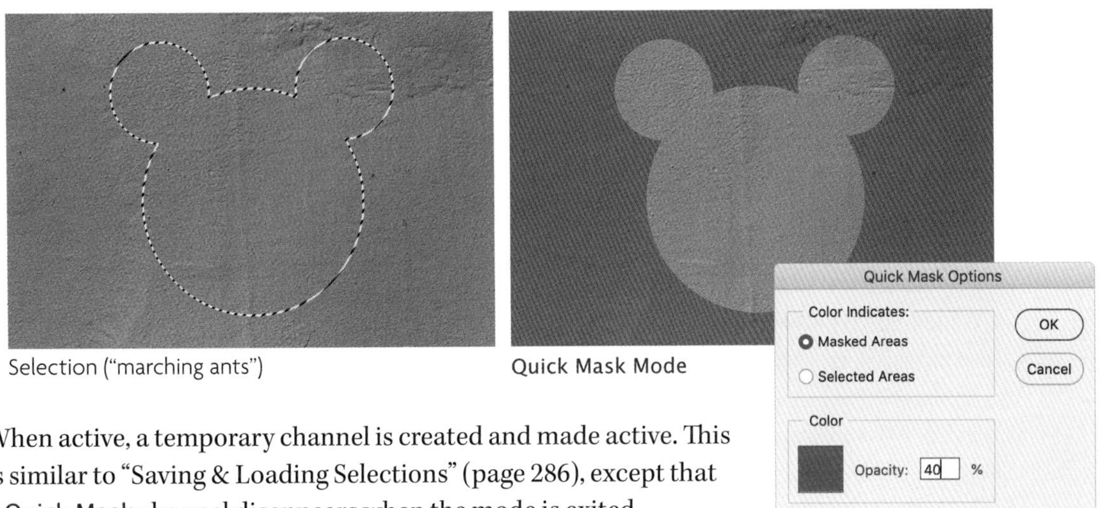

Selection ("marching ants")

Quick Mask Mode

When active, a temporary channel is created and made active. This is similar to "Saving & Loading Selections" (page 286), except that a Quick Mask channel disappears when the mode is exited.

All channels are grayscale images and can be edited as such:

You can paint or perform tonal adjustments on them, for example. When viewed alone, a channel indeed looks grayscale. But when you simultaneously view both the standard color channels (RGB) *and* one of these extra channels, like Quick Mask's, the black of that channel is replaced with a translucent color so you can see it overlaid on the image. In this case, that color is usually red, but it can be changed by double-clicking the Quick Mask button. You can also choose to change its opacity and whether the color overlays the selected area or the unselected, or "masked," area.

When you paint on a Quick Mask with white, you are effectively adding to what's selected. Black adds to what is masked. Blurring a Quick Mask makes the edges semi-selected like the Select > Feather... command. Painting with a soft brush or with shades of gray will also make areas partially selected.

Some users who regularly need painterly selections set their Quick Mask Options to have color indicate Selected Areas. When they need to paint a selection, they tap Q (with no preliminary selection), then start painting. When they hit Q again, they have a selection with the qualities of their paint strokes.

This ability to paint a selection has found its way into "Select and Mask" (page 278). Using a Quick Mask-like preview can be found there and with the other selection methods that follow. Readers interested in the historical analogs to Quick Mask should search for information on "rubylith" in the fields of graphic design and lithography.

Color Range

Color Range is a dialog box with several tools and selection previews that help us to isolate areas based on their color. As the name implies, our objective is to define the *range* of color we want to select.

Choose Select > Color Range to start the process. Ignore the dialog's initial preview, as it assumes, usually incorrectly, that we're trying to select Foreground Color pixels. Luckily, we can use the already-active eyedropper sampler to click in the image to specify a starting point for the color range's definition. If you want to exclude a range of color from your selection (like a blue sky behind a subject you want to select), check the Invert checkbox.

The Add to Sample tool (eyedropper with a plus sign in the Color Range dialog) extends the range to include more colors. The Subtract from Sample tool is not as good at its job as its companion, however. Thus I try to avoid needing it!

At the top is a menu (Select) of predefined hues and tones. These achieve mixed results. In that menu is Skin Tones, which activates the Detect Faces checkbox. For quickly selecting different parts of the tonal range (rather than a color range), you can choose Highlights, Midtones, or Shadows, which can be fine-tuned with the Range slider.

You can use the Fuzziness slider to narrow or expand the range of Sampled Colors, which is the most useful choice. I usually set this to a low value, use the Add to Sample tool, and then adjust Fuzziness as needed.

To keep the selection closer to where you clicked to sample colors, check Localized Color Clusters. The Range slider then becomes active so you can control just how close to your samples the selection will be.

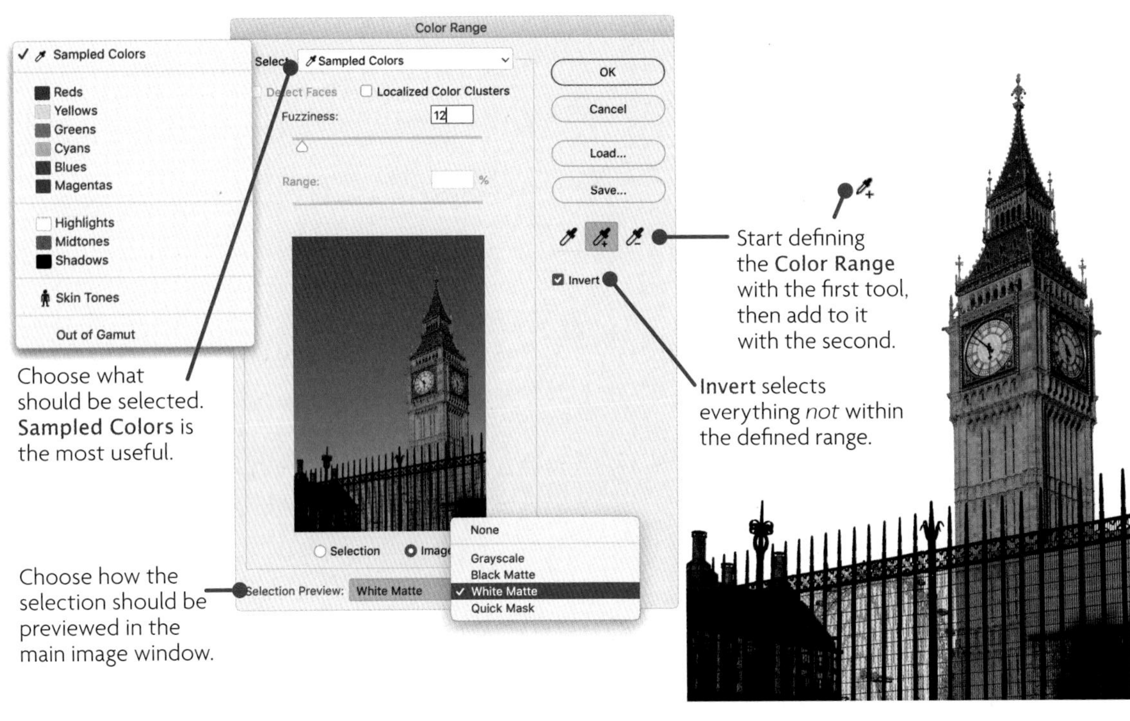

While monitoring your progress, the preview in the dialog will become frustratingly small. Use the Selection Preview menu to choose different ways of using the main image window as your preview. Grayscale will show the selected areas in white (or gray for partially selected areas), and the excluded areas in black. White or Black Matte cover the excluded pixels in white or black, leaving the selected areas in their own color. Quick Mask is a translucent, matte red by default. See "Quick Mask: Previewer & Helper" (page 275) for more about this selection-viewing aid. To recall what the image actually looks like while working, hold down command/Ctrl or choose Image below the preview in the dialog box.

Finally, if you anticipate needing to select similar ranges of colors in other images, you can use the Save… button to create a file that can later be loaded via the Load… button.

Focus Area

This function analyzes the image to select what's "sharp," or in-focus. To access this function, choose Select > Focus Area. At first, Photoshop automatically tries to determine a range of sharpness (the In-Focus Range), but you can adjust this parameter to tighten or loosen its constraints. If areas are either overlooked or mistakenly included, you can use the Focus Area Add and Subtract tools. These are just versions of the Quick Selection tool embedded in this dialog box. Since noise in an image can influence the analysis of what is sharp or blurry, the so-called Advanced section has an Image Noise Level slider. Raise this if noisy but blurry areas are being included in the selection.

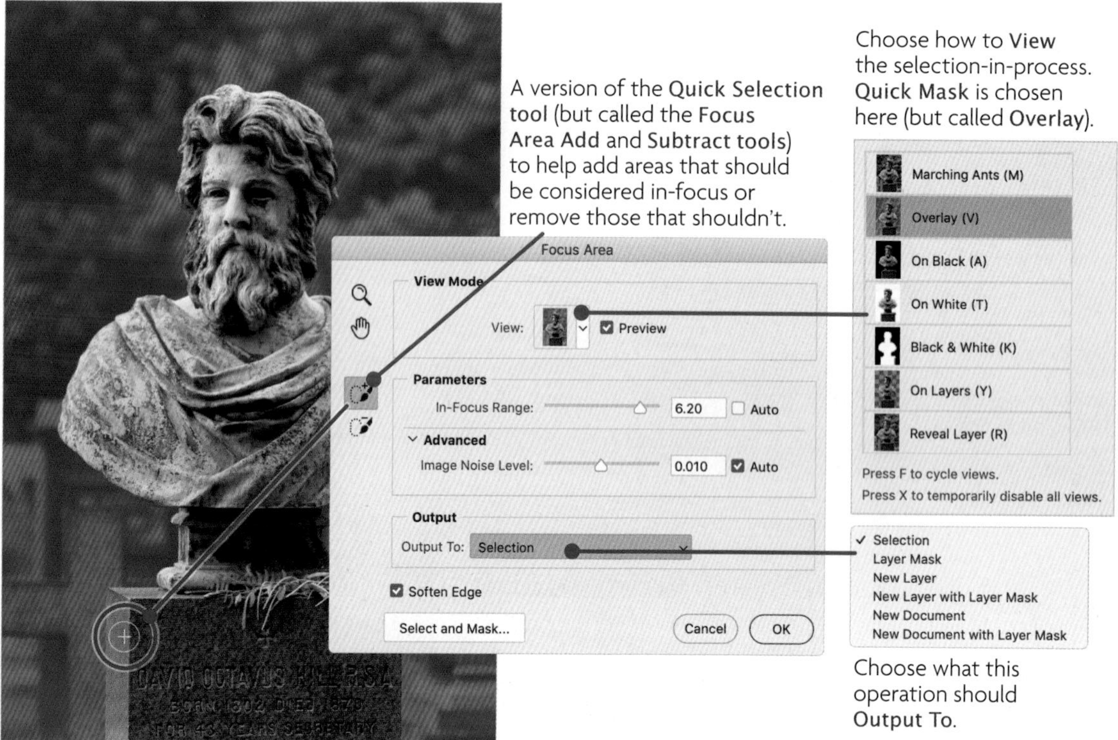

The View and Output To choices that are included in this dialog are also in the Select and Mask workspace (discussed next). In fact, there's a button to make the hand-off to that workspace easier if it's needed. The choices in the View menu help you to differentiate the selected area from masked areas. Output To can save you a later step, especially if that was to make a layer mask from the selection you're making with this dialog.

Select and Mask

This is an entire workspace dedicated to the task of making selections. For that reason, you sometimes hear it referred to as a "task space." Access it by using the shortcut ⌘-option-R/Ctrl-Alt-R or by pressing the Select and Mask... button in the Options Bar when any selection tool (and a layer) is active.

In the Select and Mask workspace, you'll find several of the tools discussed on the previous pages: the Lasso and Polygonal Lasso tools, the Quick Selection tool, and the Object Selection tool, as well as a simple Brush tool that paints a selection much like it would in Quick Mask mode. When using any of these, holding down option/Alt will remove areas from the selection as you'd expect.

This environment used to be called Refine Edge, and I still use it most often to refine rather than create selections. It seems that with each version of Photoshop, the differences between Quick Selection tools inside Select and Mask and outside are diminishing. But be aware that small differences remain, so if you are displeased with the result of the one inside, you may wish to try the other, and then only refine in Select and Mask.

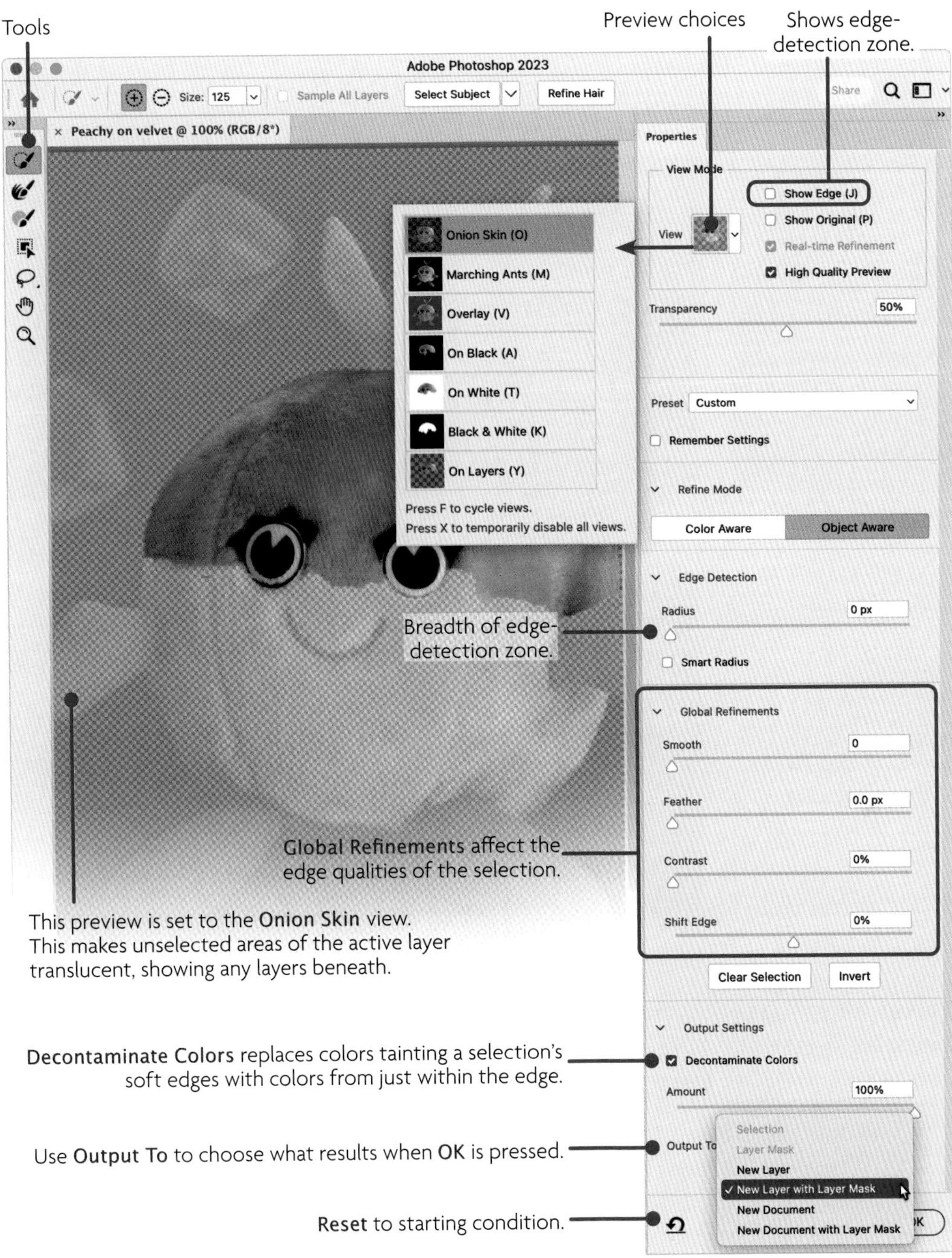

Select and Mask Views

With some selections, especially complex ones or those with soft, delicate edges, it can be hard to tell how good of a job you're doing. Luckily, we can choose from seven different views. Each can be accessed from the View menu or via a shortcut key. Be aware that dialog boxes and task workspaces like **Select and Mask** often have shortcuts for their specific functions, but those same shortcuts will do other things in the rest of the program. So, to access the default View called Onion Skin, you can tap the O key. (In case you're curious, the tools this shortcut accesses outside this workspace are very nearly useless: the Dodge, Burn, and Sponge tools.)

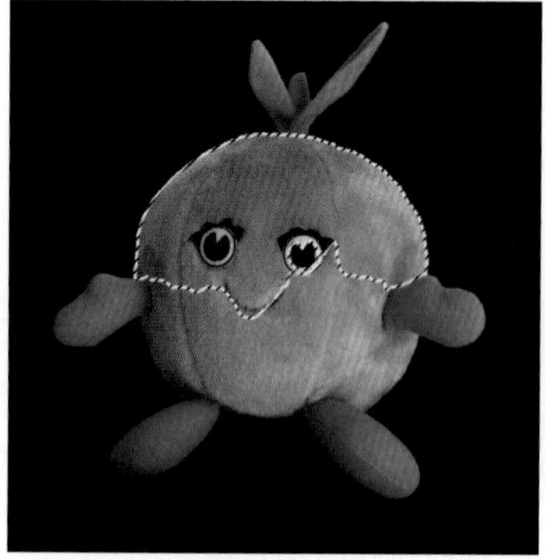

Marching Ants

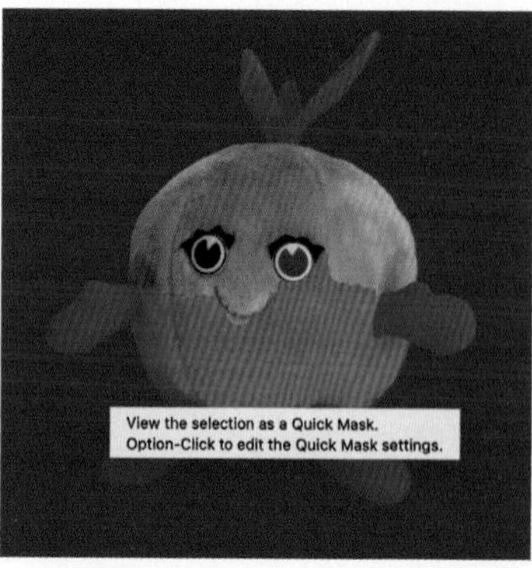

Overlay with 50% Opacity

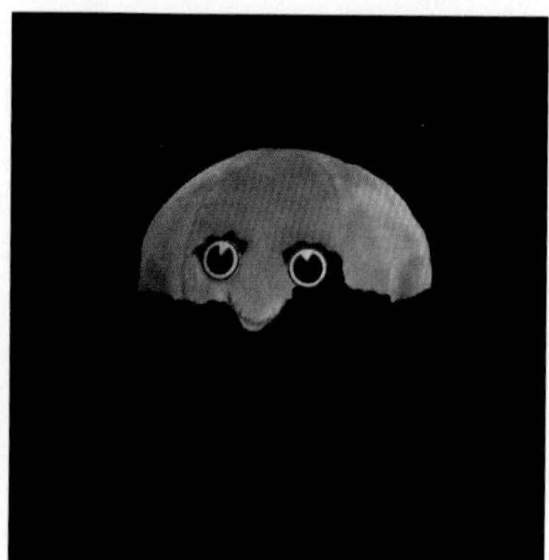

On Black with 100% Opacity

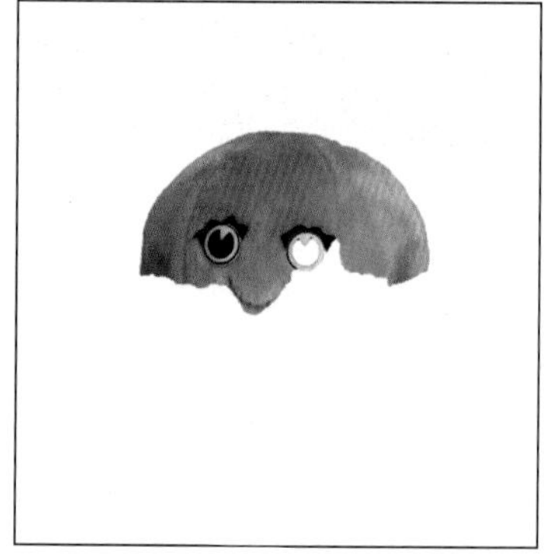

On White with 100% Opacity

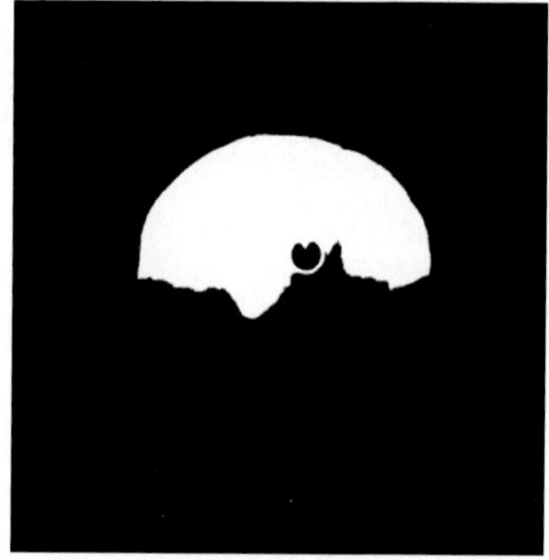

Black & White

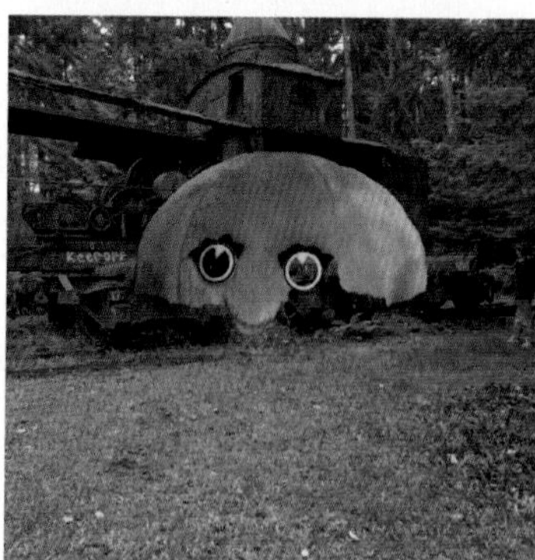

On Layers

Onion Skin (O) Makes unselected areas of the active layer translucent, showing any layers below the active one. This is the default View. Adjust the Transparency slider for greater contrast between selected and masked (unselected) areas.

Marching Ants (M) Just the regular marquee. It's nice to have the old nickname for it made official. This offers no way to tell if areas are less than half selected, as the marquee is not drawn for them.

Overlay (V) This is Quick Mask with another name. You can adjust its opacity, color, and where it's displayed (selected or masked areas). See "Quick Mask: Previewer & Helper" (page 275) for more.

On Black (A) This mode is good when your subject was originally surrounded by light pixels. You can adjust the Opacity of this black matte.

On White (T) This mode is good when your subject was originally surrounded by dark pixels. You can adjust the Opacity of this white matte.

Black & White (K) Shows the selection as a mask with shades of gray indicating levels of selectedness. White is used for fully selected areas, and black for areas not selected at all. If the goal for your selection is a layer mask (as most are), this shows you exactly what that mask will look like. I like the clarity of this View when my image is visually busy and the selection is complex.

On Layers (Y) This View is especially useful when your objective is making a layer mask. You can develop your selection seeing exactly what the result will be.

Select and Mask Global Refinements

These four sliders change the character of the selection's edge. Note that the last one, Shift Edge, is dramatically affected by other settings, and thus should be tweaked after all else.

In these examples, I chose the Black & White View to better show the character of the edges.

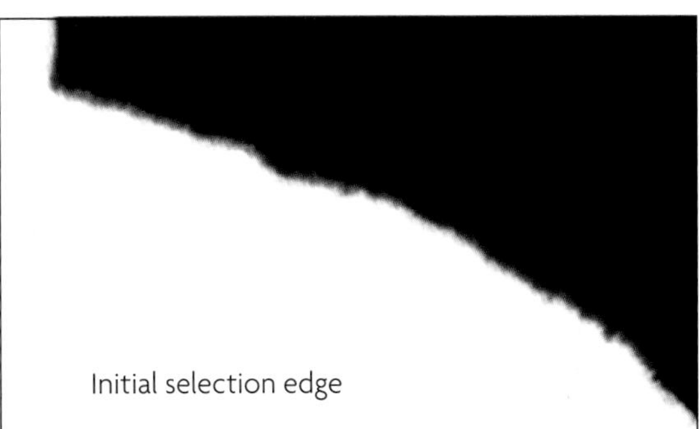
Initial selection edge

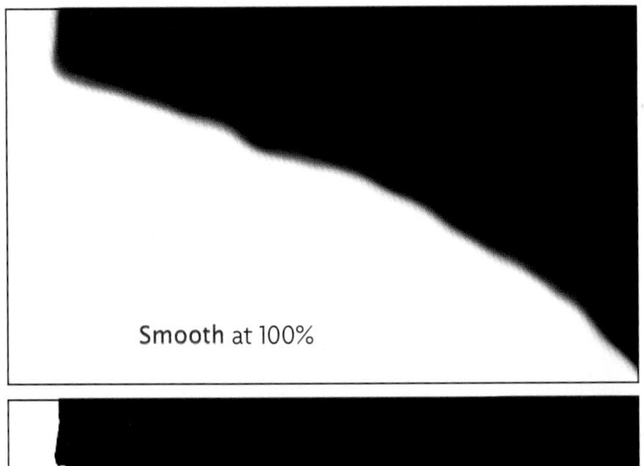
Smooth at 100%

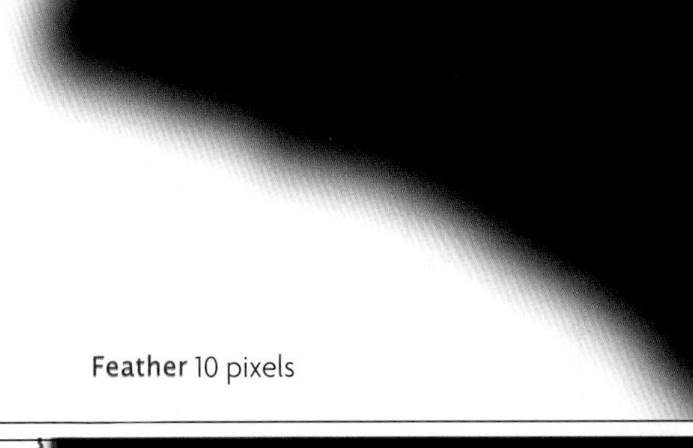
Feather 10 pixels

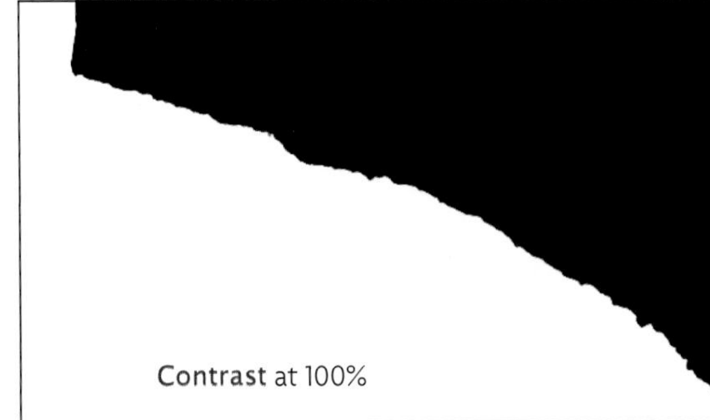
Contrast at 100%

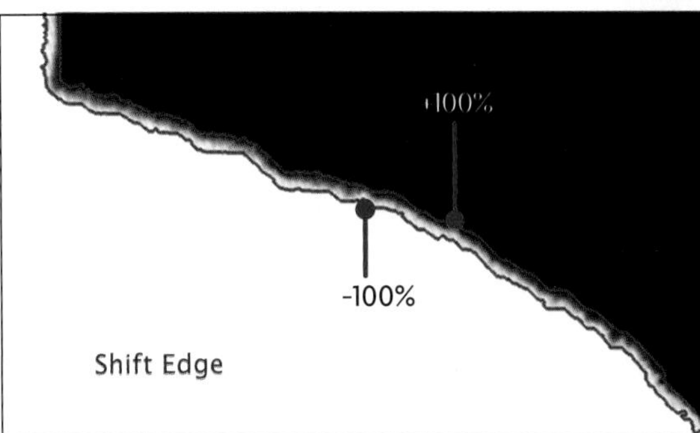

Shift Edge

Smooth I suggest thinking of smooth as sanding. The selection edge will be less rough, but may retain some of its softness (blurriness or ambiguity).

Feather This refinement literally blurs the selection.

Contrast This is the opposite of Feather, in a way. Rather than add shades of selectedness at the edges, as Feather does, Contrast reduces those shades. At 100%, areas are either selected fully or not at all.

Shift Edge This refinement is the trickiest. The distance the selection edge is "shifted" depends on its softness: +100% extends the selection to its wispiest outer edges, whereas –100% pulls it in to its most solidly selected areas. With a sharp-edged selection, a –30% Shift Edge will be imperceptible, but if you use a high Feather value, that amount may be significant. The Edge Detection Radius can also amplify this refinement's effect. That is why I recommend saving this refinement for last.

Edge Detection and Refinement

The real power of this workspace is Edge Detection. This powerful refinement relies on your defining a zone where Photoshop looks for edges more carefully. That zone can be defined in several ways and can be based on color contrasts or object detection.

If the area being selected differs from the rest of the image by its color, try setting the Refine Mode to Color Aware. If color contrasts aren't strong enough, Object Aware is best.

If the subject has a fairly uniform amount of ambiguity at the edges (torn paper, fleece or wool jackets, buzz cuts, plush fruit), use the Radius slider. It uses that value to define a (usually) narrow band straddling the selection's edge. Below, a Radius setting of 23 px causes Photoshop to scrutinize an area 56 pixels wide, centered on the edge of the current selection.

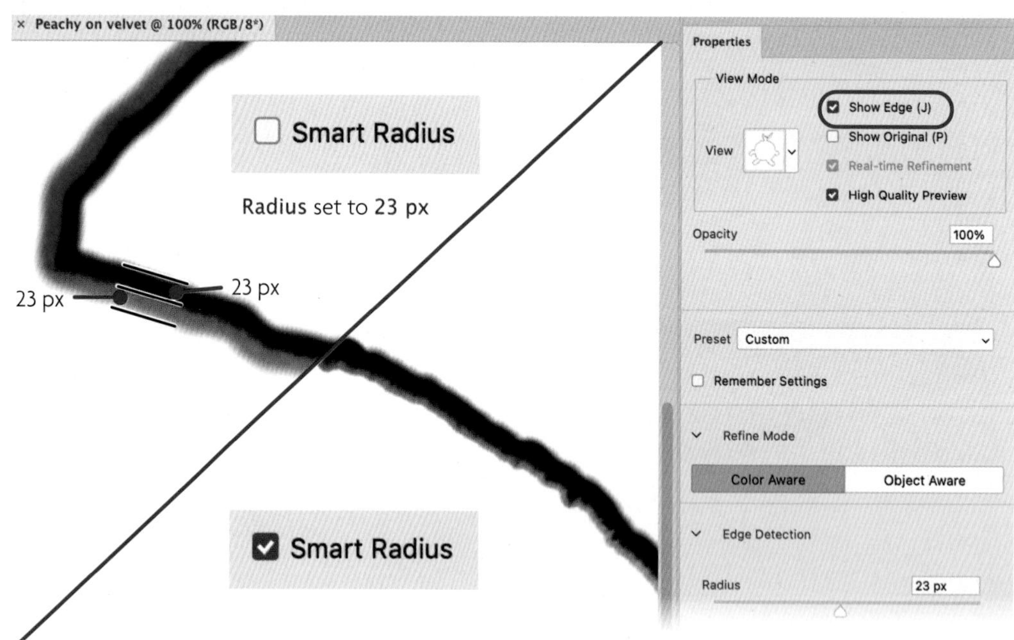

When you check the box for Smart Radius, the area under scrutiny narrows a bit as Photoshop works even harder to discern finer edge details in the image. If you're curious about just where Edge Detection is taking place, check the Show Edges checkbox at the top of the View Mode section, as I did for the image above. Remember to disable this again so you can see the actual selection edge.

When wispy or amorphous details like long hair are present, especially in some areas but not others, you can to use the Refine Edge Brush tool. Paint with it to indicate where

Photoshop should do its Edge Detection. Its remove mode is useful if you make a mistake.

If the area is specifically hair rather than sheer fabric, for example, try the Refine Hair button at the top. It may save you a good deal of time painting over stray hairs. If not, read on!

The Refine Edge Brush tool is best used by brushing outward from fully selected areas to include parts of the image where delicate details are entangled with unwanted pixels. When hair is involved, my motion is similar to actually brushing hair. Remove areas from edge detection by option/Alt-painting. This is an amazing function, but residue is sometimes left behind.

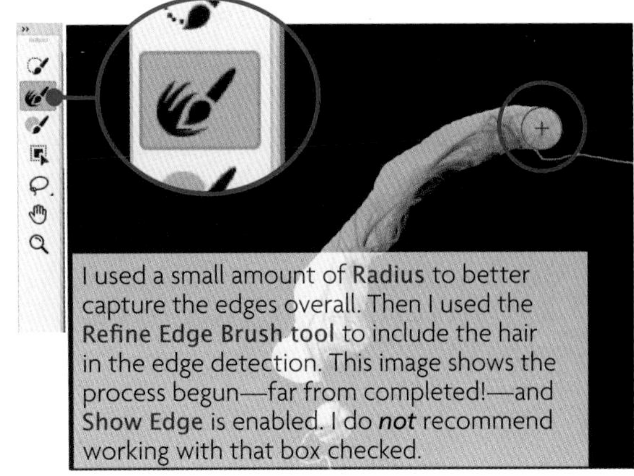
I used a small amount of **Radius** to better capture the edges overall. Then I used the **Refine Edge Brush tool** to include the hair in the edge detection. This image shows the process begun—far from completed!—and **Show Edge** is enabled. I do ***not*** recommend working with that box checked.

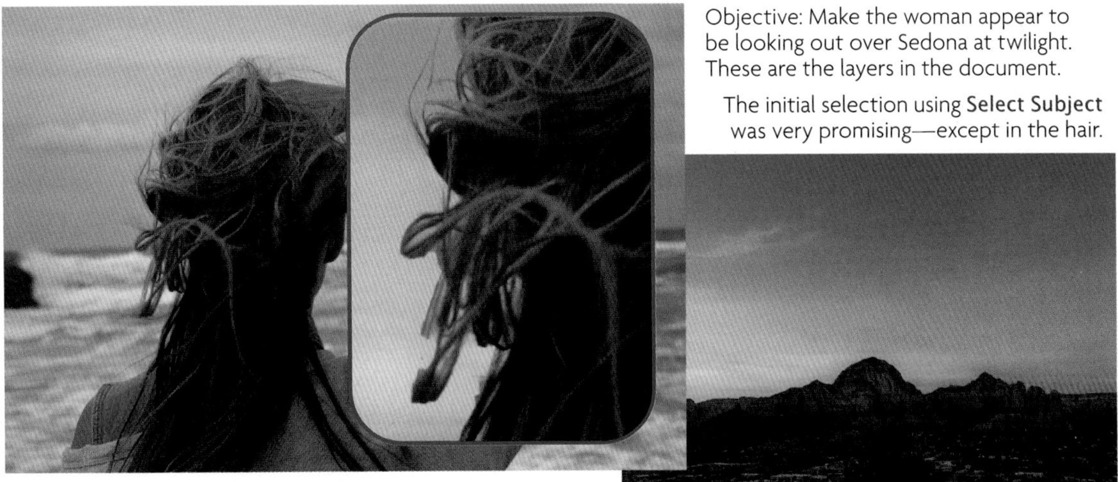
Objective: Make the woman appear to be looking out over Sedona at twilight. These are the layers in the document.

The initial selection using **Select Subject** was very promising—except in the hair.

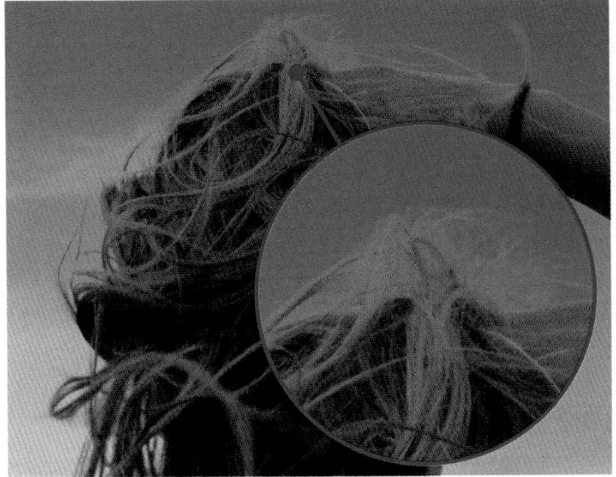

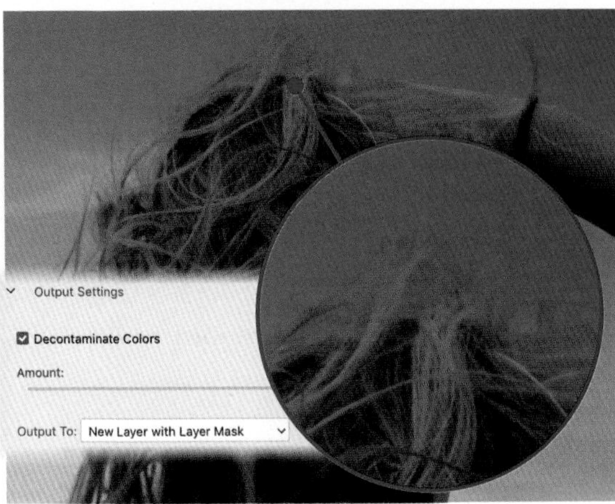

Some original gray sky still clings to the hair—until we **Decontaminate Colors**! This pushes color outward from parts of the image just inside the **Edge Detection** region onto those edge pixels.

Any colors that were originally behind the selected subject will likely be entangled in the pixels at the edges—that is, right where we are doing edge detection. In this example, some gray still contaminates the hair. In the Select and Mask Output Settings section, we can check Decontaminate Colors. This finds the colors within the selected subject nearest our edge-detection zone (set by the Radius slider and our Refine Edge Brush tool brush strokes). With those colors, this checkbox essentially recontaminates those edges with subject colors so those edges can be placed in front of any backdrop.

Since colorizing pixels in an image can be considered destructive, choosing to Decontaminate Colors changes the setting of the Output To menu too. Photoshop creates a duplicate layer with a layer mask that hides the effects of adding colors to the edges. The original layer is still present, but its visibility is turned off.

To finish such a composite, we usually need to add adjustments or other effects to better match lighting between the elements. For this image, I added one adjustment to the image of the woman to increase its contrast and warm it to match the Arizona scene. The Neural Filter called Harmonization (page 299) works well in these situations too. I also blurred the backdrop to have the composite better match the depth of field in the photo of the woman. Finally, as always, I did a little touch-up on the layer mask made by the Select and Mask process, trimming a few hairs here and there.

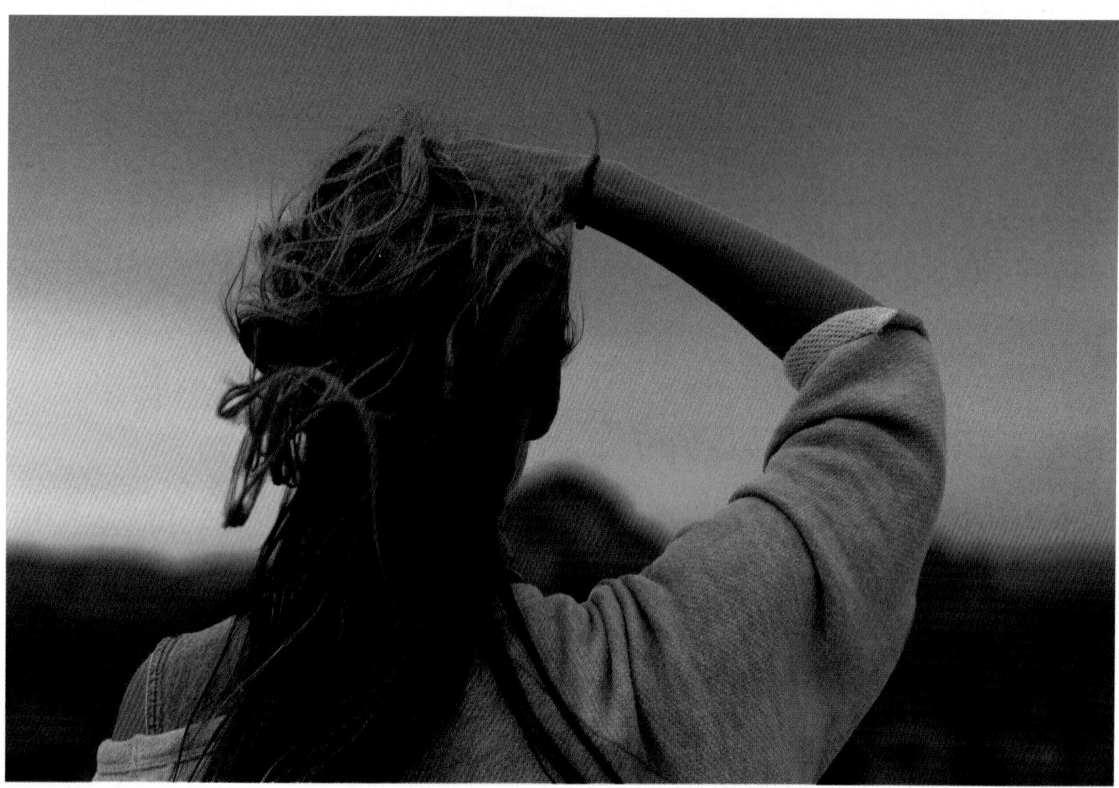

Other Selection Modifiers

While most modifications to a selection can be achieved through the Select and Mask task space, there are a few menu-driven methods to mention.

To invert a selection (selecting what's not selected and deselecting what is), use Select > Inverse.

The Select > Modify menu has a few choices too. Border... transforms an area selection into a narrow band of selection as wide as you designate in its dialog box. Expand... and Contract... grow or shrink a selection by precisely the number of pixels you specify. Both of those as well as Feather... and Smooth... can be accomplished more visually in Select and Mask.

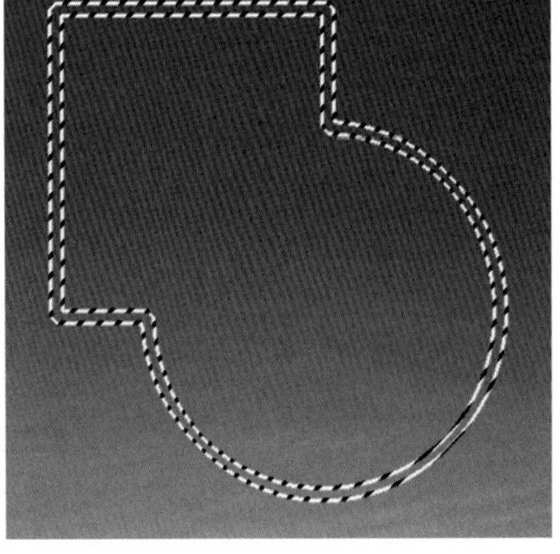

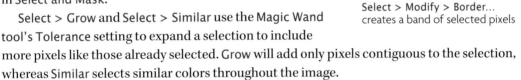

Select > Modify > Border... creates a band of selected pixels

Select > Grow and Select > Similar use the Magic Wand tool's Tolerance setting to expand a selection to include more pixels like those already selected. Grow will add only pixels contiguous to the selection, whereas Similar selects similar colors throughout the image.

Finally, you can use Select > Transform Selection to manipulate a selection in a way similar to "Free Transform" (page 335).

Combining Selection Tools

Once you've created a selection (and there's a marquee in your image), you can alter it with any of the tools you'd use to create a selection. Holding down the Shift key will cause a plus sign (+) to appear next to the cursor, indicating that you're adding to the existing selection.

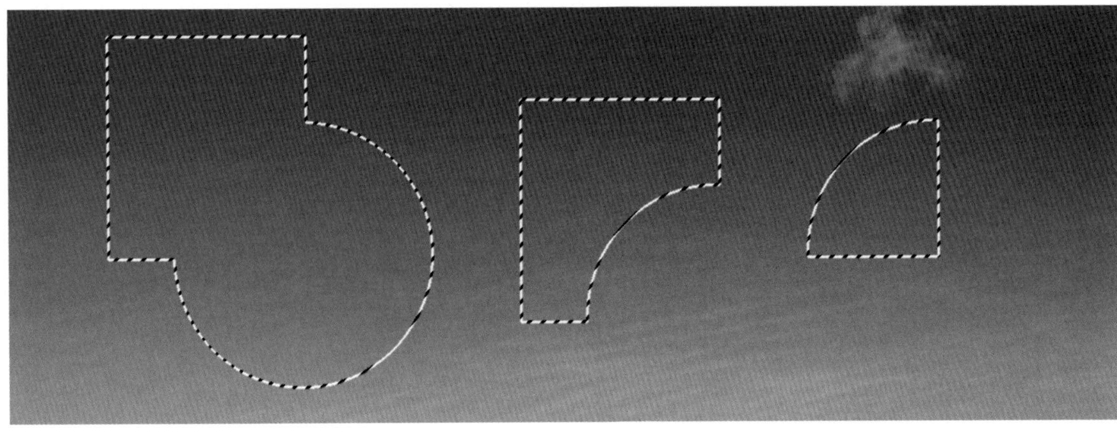

Elliptical selection added to square one

Elliptical selection subtracted from square one

Elliptical selection intersected with square one

Holding the option/Alt key reveals a minus sign (−) so you can remove pixels from the current selection.

Holding both those keys (shift-option/Shift-Alt) will leave selected the intersection (overlap) of the existing selection and the one made while holding those keys.

Earlier, I mentioned what these keys do when you're first making a selection (constraining or centering the selection). Achieving both results with these keys is slightly difficult. For example, to add a perfectly circular area to an existing selection, you must be holding down the Shift key *as you begin dragging* with the Elliptical Marquee tool. *While still dragging*, you must temporarily release and then again hold down the Shift key to indicate you want a circle (constrained ellipse), and then keep the Shift key depressed as you complete the selection.

The Quick Selection tool automatically enters a mode that adds to an existing selection once you start a selection with it. The Options Bar for each tool also contains buttons for adding, subtracting, and (for most) intersecting with an existing selection.

Color Range intersects its result with an existing selection.

Saving & Loading Selections

The Quick Mask feature uses a temporary channel to help us visualize and even edit a selection as a grayscale image. We can create a more enduring version of this by saving a selection. When an active selection is saved, a new channel, called an "alpha channel," is made below the channels that control color (RGB or CMYK, etc.). Usually, white is used for the selected areas, black for masked, and shades of gray for soft selection edges. Later, that alpha channel can be loaded as a selection again or used by certain filters (e.g., Lens Blur) to affect specific areas of an image.

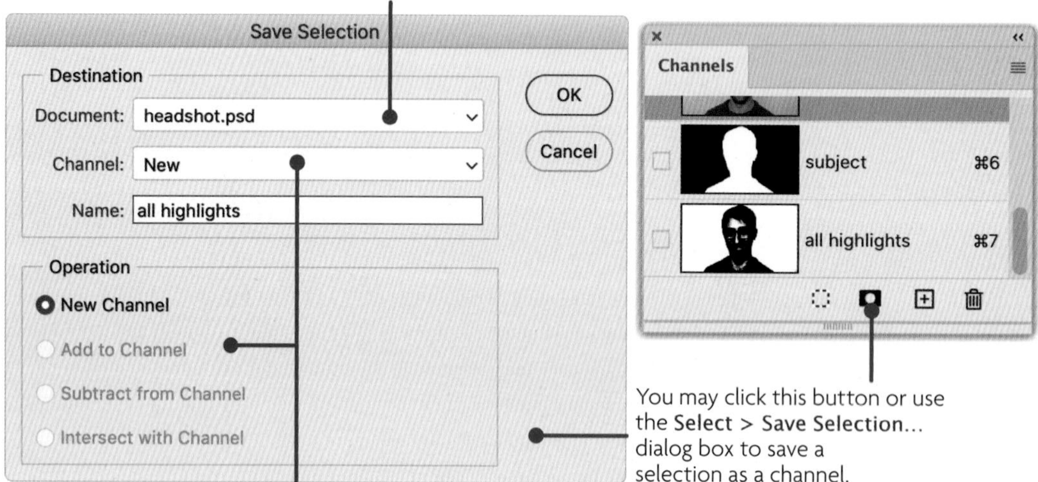

Choosing an existing Channel activates the choices of Operations.

To save a selection, you can choose Select > Save Selection..., after which a dialog box with options appears, or you can click the Save selection as channel button (◘) at the bottom of the Channels panel. In the latter case, the channels will be automatically named "Alpha 1," "Alpha 2," etc. Hold down option/Alt when clicking the Save selection as channel button to choose a name for the channel.

With the Select menu method, you can choose a name, the document in which the channel is added, and how/whether the selection affects other alpha channels. In the Save Selection dialog, you may choose to save the selection to another document with the same pixel dimensions or create a new document. The latter will contain no channels other than the alpha channel, in essence making it a grayscale document. This procedure is useful for features that use such documents as "maps." Photoshop's 3D features, for example, can use these documents' shades of gray to show where a texture is metallic, rough, or transparent.

If the Destination Document has alpha channels already, you can choose one from the Channel menu. If you do, all four choices in the Operation section of the dialog become available. The default is to create a New Channel, but when you choose an existing channel, this becomes Replace Channel. The other operations are similar to those discussed in the previous section, "Combining Selection Tools" (page 285). These operations can also be performed when loading a selection.

To load a saved selection, you can choose Select > Load Selection…. The Load Selection dialog box has similar choices as saving: From which document and channel should the selection come, and how should it interact with a live, existing selection if one exists?

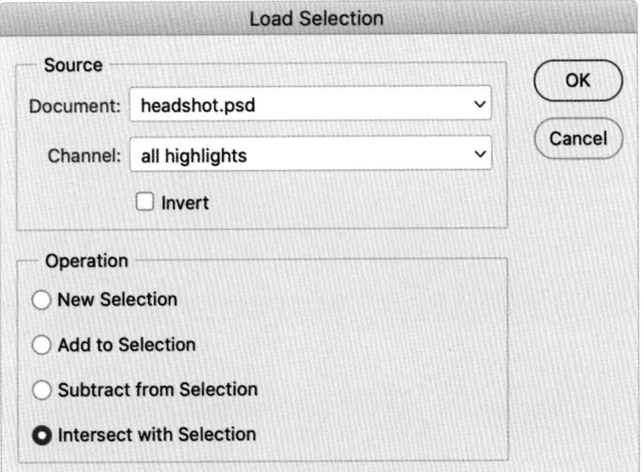

In this example, I had already loaded the channel called "subject" as a selection. With those marching ants active, I then chose to load a channel called "all highlights" (dialog above).

Since I wanted to select only the highlights on the subject, I chose to **Intersect with Selection**. I saved the result as a new channel called "subject highlights."

I repeated the process but checked the **Invert** checkbox so I would load a selection of everything *except* the highlights, intersecting that with the already loaded subject selection. This resulted in a selection of non-highlight pixels on the subject only. I saved this too.

It's in loading selections that I usually leverage the choices of Operation. When I save selections, I sometimes have a look at them to do a little cleanup by painting with white or black. In retouching and color correction workflows that involve teams, some individuals are tasked with creating these channels so experts at color correction can follow them without having to make the selections.

A faster way to load a channel as a selection is to click on the channel while holding down the ⌘/Ctrl key. As you hover over a channel with that key held, you'll see a hand cursor with a small marquee on it (like the one at right). If you have an existing selection and hold down ⌘-shift/Ctrl-Shift, a plus-sign appears in that cursor, confirming that you'll add that channel to the selection. ⌘-option/Ctrl-Alt removes the channel from the selection (minus sign appears in cursor), and ⌘-option-shift/Ctrl-Alt-Shift intersects the channel and selection (an "X" appears in the cursor).

You'll find this works for layer content too! Use this method on a layer's thumbnail to select a layer's nontransparent content or a layer mask to load it just like any other channel.

Another advantage to this method is that you can load *any* channel as a selection, including the color channels. By ⌘/Ctrl-clicking the RGB composite channel, you are making a selection proportional to the luminosity in the image. That is, the lighter an area is, the more selected it will be. In the lingo of Photoshop old-timers, this is making a "luminosity mask." Inverting such a selection favors the shadows. Either way, these are excellent selections from which to make adjustments that impact one end of the tonal range more than the other. See "Luminosity Masks" (page 291) for more.

Masks

Masks are grayscale images whose grays control visibility of a layer, group, or Smart Object.

A Metaphor and Example

Although Photoshop thinks of masks as alpha channels, that's not so easy for humans.

Slides

Some users who find the concept of masking challenging find this metaphor useful—if they're familiar with slides (photographic transparencies). Images recording onto slide film are most opaque where they're darkest. Whites in a scene (snow, clouds, etc.) are rendered as clear film. So, the dark parts of a slide hold back the projector's light while the more transparent parts that represent the lighter part of the image allow the light to reach the screen.

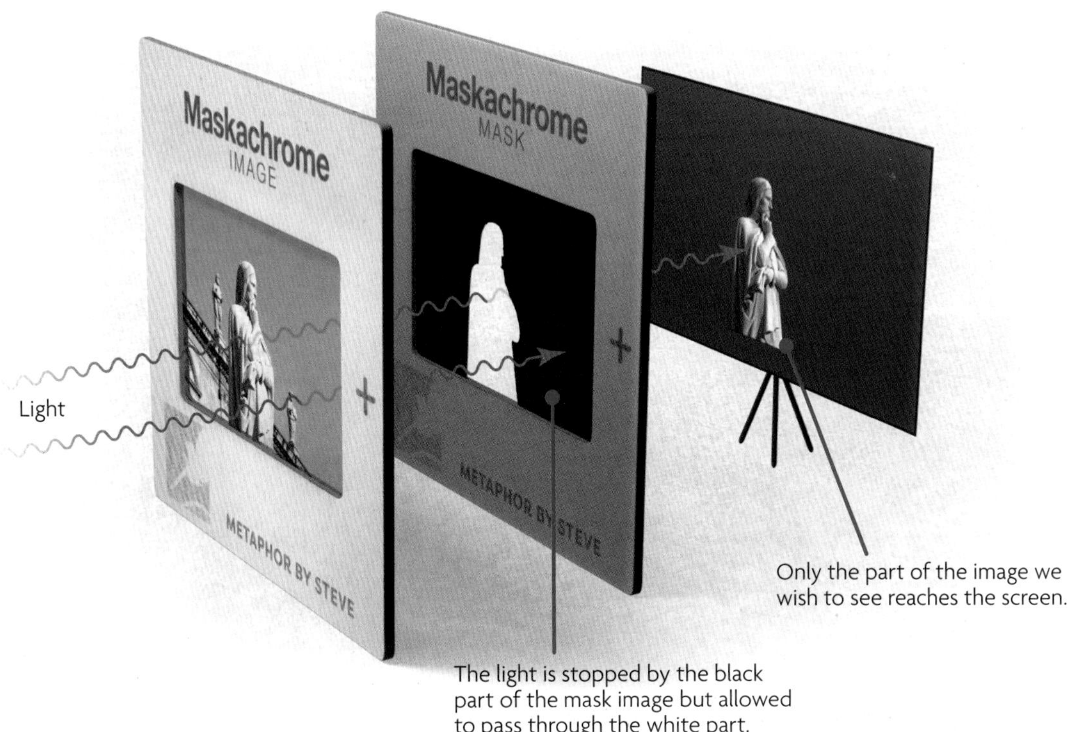
Maskachrome
IMAGE
METAPHOR BY STEVE
Maskachrome
MASK
METAPHOR BY STEVE
Light
Only the part of the image we wish to see reaches the screen.
The light is stopped by the black part of the mask image but allowed to pass through the white part.

Now imagine sandwiching two slides together and projecting the result onto a screen. One slide is just a photo. The other slide is completely clear in parts (as white would make it) and black elsewhere. The black prevents the light from reaching the screen, thus hiding parts of the photo.

That's the metaphor. In Photoshop, we access the image or its mask primarily through the Layers panel.

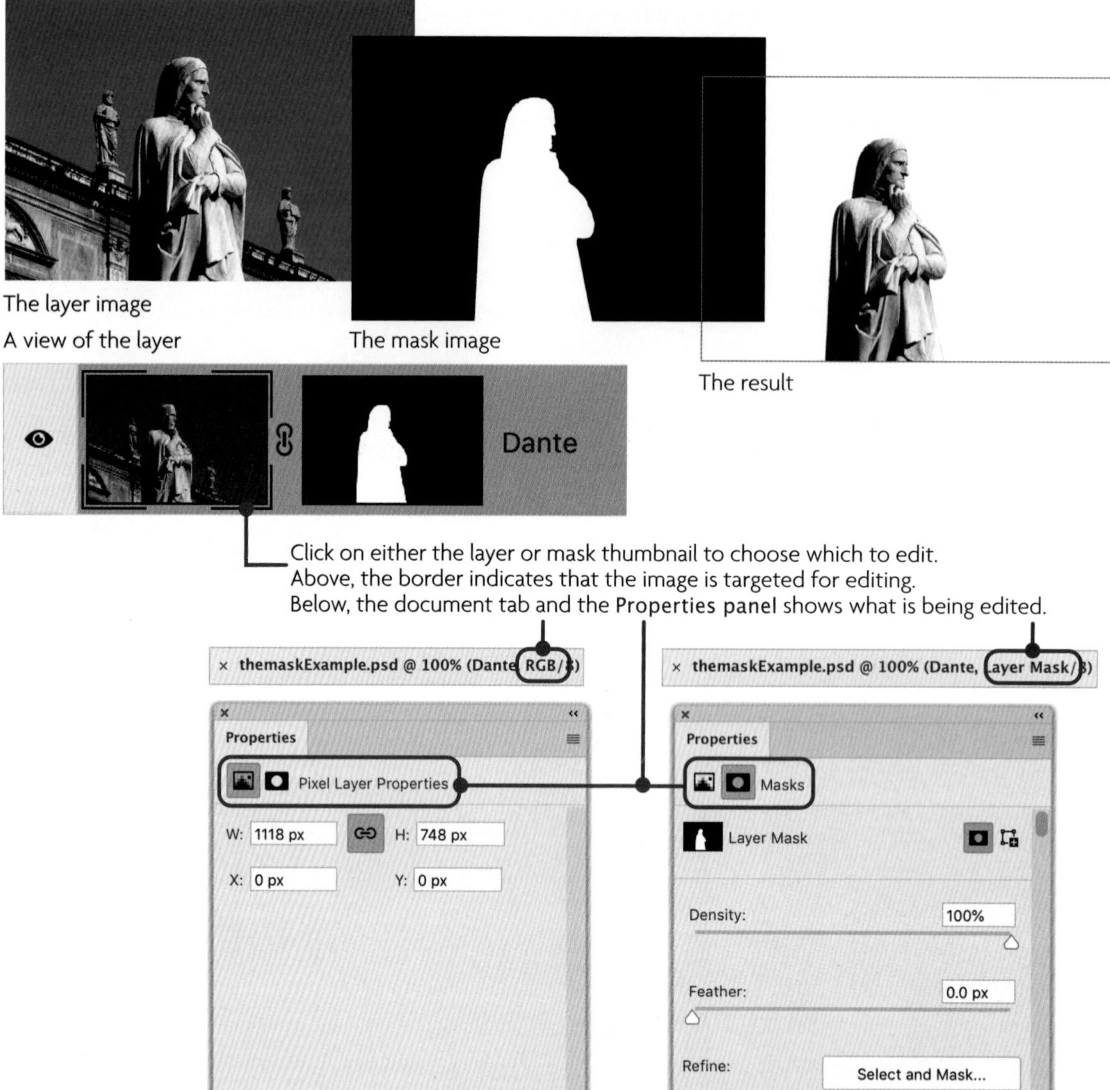

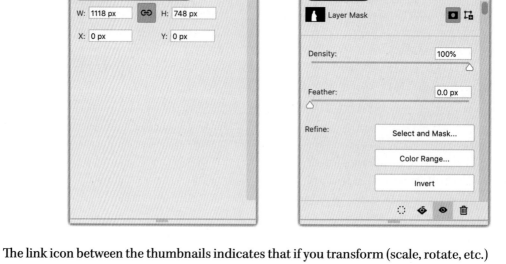

The link icon between the thumbnails indicates that if you transform (scale, rotate, etc.) either the mask or the image, the other transforms too. When either thumbnail is clicked, it is given a small border (easily missed) that indicates that it's the thing being edited. There are also indications of which is under examination in the Properties panel and the tab identifying the document (just under the Options Bar). If you click on the link icon, it will disappear, indicating that edits to either the mask image or the layer image won't affect the other. Clicking between the thumbnails reestablishes the link.

Interestingly, not all edits flow through that link in both directions like transformations do. Filters applied to the mask affect only the mask, whether the chain is present or not. When *some* filters (those that blur or distort) are applied to the layer image, both layer and mask are affected. Filters that change only the appearance of the layer image will not affect the mask. This inconsistency sounds confusing, but works well in practice.

Creation

There are two primary ways masks are made: from selections or by painting. The vast majority of masks are made from selections, then undergo painted refinements. Masks can also be made via the Select and Mask workspace or the Focus Area selection dialog box, by choosing Layer Mask in the Output menu of either. Select and Mask combines methods by offering ways to refine and make selections as well as paint them, and then output them to a mask.

Masks from Selection

With an active selection of the area you'd like to keep visible, highlight the appropriate layer, group, or Smart Object, then either click the Add layer mask button ( ) at the bottom of the Layers panel or choose Layer > Layer Mask > Reveal Selection. If your selection was actually of the area that you'd like to hide, you could choose Hide Selection from the Layer Mask menu or option/Alt-click the Add layer mask button.

If your selection is precise, your mask will be too.

Luminosity Masks

As mentioned earlier, by ⌘/Ctrl-clicking the RGB composite channel, you are making a selection proportional to the luminosity in the image. That is, the lighter an area is, the more selected it will be. When you create a layer mask with such a selection active, it will be a grayscale version of the image, "hiding" the darkest parts of the image. Want it the other way? Click Invert in the Properties panel.

Painting Masks

Sometimes you want to hide (or show) very arbitrary areas of a layer, group, or Smart Object. With one of those items highlighted in the Layers panel, click the Add layer mask button ( ) at the bottom of the Layers panel to make a white-filled mask (which hides nothing), or option/Alt-click the Add layer mask button to hide everything initially. You can also use the Layer > Layer Mask menu and choose Reveal All or Hide All.

With the mask targeted (look for the little border around its thumbnail), use the Brush tool or the Gradient tool to apply white, black, or shades of gray. You can apply filters to the mask you've painted (e.g., apply the Gaussian Blur filter to create fades from visible to invisible). When I use gradients, I configure them to transition from black (or white) to transparent, so they hide (or reveal) what I want, without overwriting other parts of the mask.

Masks from Transparency

Sometimes I'd like to mask a file I've received as a PNG that already has transparent regions in it. I could create a mask and simply paint with white or black. However, there are times when I'd like the mask to become the cause of the transparency so I can finesse its edges.

By choosing Layer > Layer Mask > From Transparency, a mask is made with white where the original layer was fully opaque, black where it was fully transparent, and grays for translucent areas. The layer image itself will no longer have any transparency, but the areas that are hidden will be black (for dark subjects), white (for light ones), or image pixels that had been masked previously. See "Applying Masks" on the following page.

Properties

There are properties and tasks that we often need to access. Look to the Properties panel.

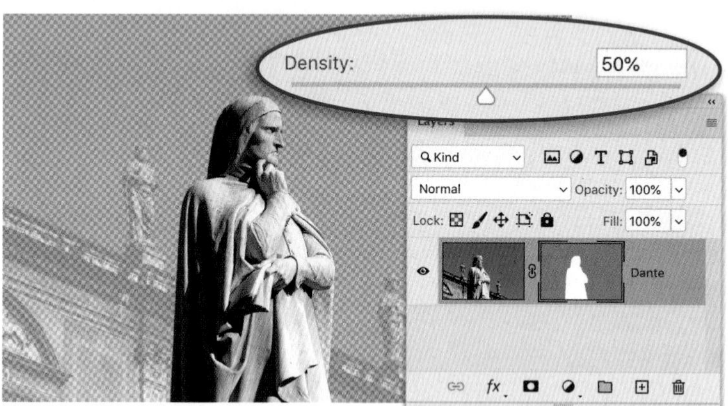

Density

Density is a slider that allows us to nondestructively alter how dark a mask's blacks are. Densities less that 100% permit hidden areas to be partially visible.

Feather

Feather is a slider that allows us to nondestructively blur a mask to create zones of transition from visible to hidden. The result is similar to using the Gaussian Blur filter with values up to 1000 pixels.

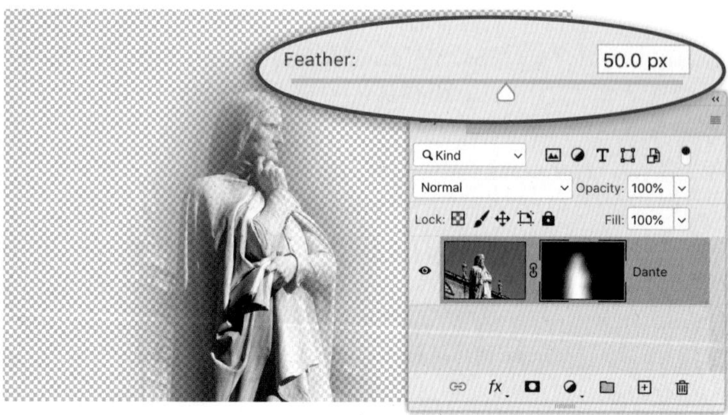

Refine

There are three "refinements" we can apply to masks from the Properties panel.

Select and Mask

This is the same workspace discussed earlier; see "Select and Mask" (page 278). The only difference is that the default Output is a new, improved mask.

Color Range

Clicking the Color Range button opens the same dialog box discussed earlier in this chapter; see "Color Range" (page 276). It will behave as if the masked area is selected and the color range you create will intersect with it. That is, you'll end up with less visible than before.

Invert

The Invert button reverses white and black. Hidden areas become visible, and visible areas are hidden.

Applying Masks

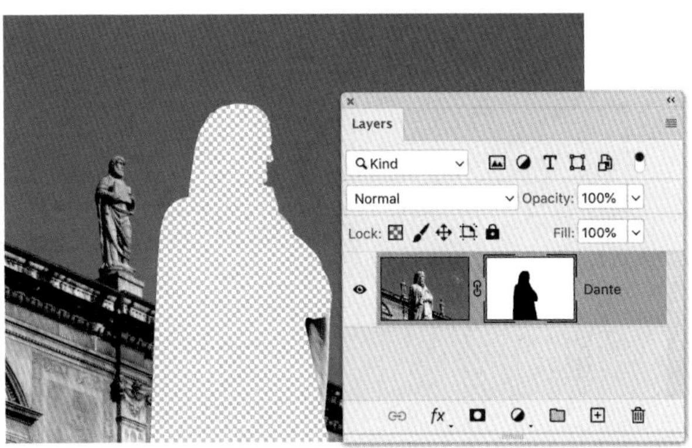

This action, accessed by right-clicking a mask thumbnail, or by choosing Layer > Layer Mask > Apply, deletes areas of the layer hidden by the mask and removes the mask itself, leaving transparent areas on the layer. It is rare to ever need this function. Unexpectedly, the areas that are deleted (or at least those close to what had been visible) are retained invisibly in the document data. So if you subsequently use the command Layer > Layer Mask > From Transparency, much of what was deleted may return!

Selections *from* Masks

There will be times when you need a selection from an existing mask. If the layer with the mask is highlighted, you can use the Select > Load Selection... command. The mask will appear in the list of channels from which a selection can be made.

It is usually faster to hold down the ⌘/Ctrl key and click the mask's thumbnail.

Masks on Groups

Masks can be applied to layer groups as readily as to individual layers. Layers in the group can have their own masks too. This implies a workaround to the limitation in Photoshop that a layer can have only one mask. If that layer is the sole occupant of a group, you can mask the group, and two masks will be active on that layer. Want more? Groups can contain groups!

Masks on Smart Objects or within Them?

Among the many advantages of a Smart Object are that it can be transformed repeatedly and filters can be applied without the SO's contents being adversely affected. Those contents can include layers with masks, of course.

But a mask applied to a Smart Object isn't protected from harm. If the SO and its mask are subjected to filters or repeated transformations, the mask will be a bit battered. The one advantage to a mask applied to the SO rather than its content is that you can more easily see it in the Layers panel. If that is unnecessary, I prefer to make a group inside the SO and mask it.

Vector Masks

If you've created a vector shape using one of the pen or shape tools, you can use it as a mask on any selected layer, group, or Smart Object. The tools we use to create such shapes are the same ones we use to create vector shape layers. See "Vector Shape Layers" (page 146) for more on those tools. There is one key difference, however: In the Options Bar, choose Path as the tool mode, otherwise you'll be making shape layers.

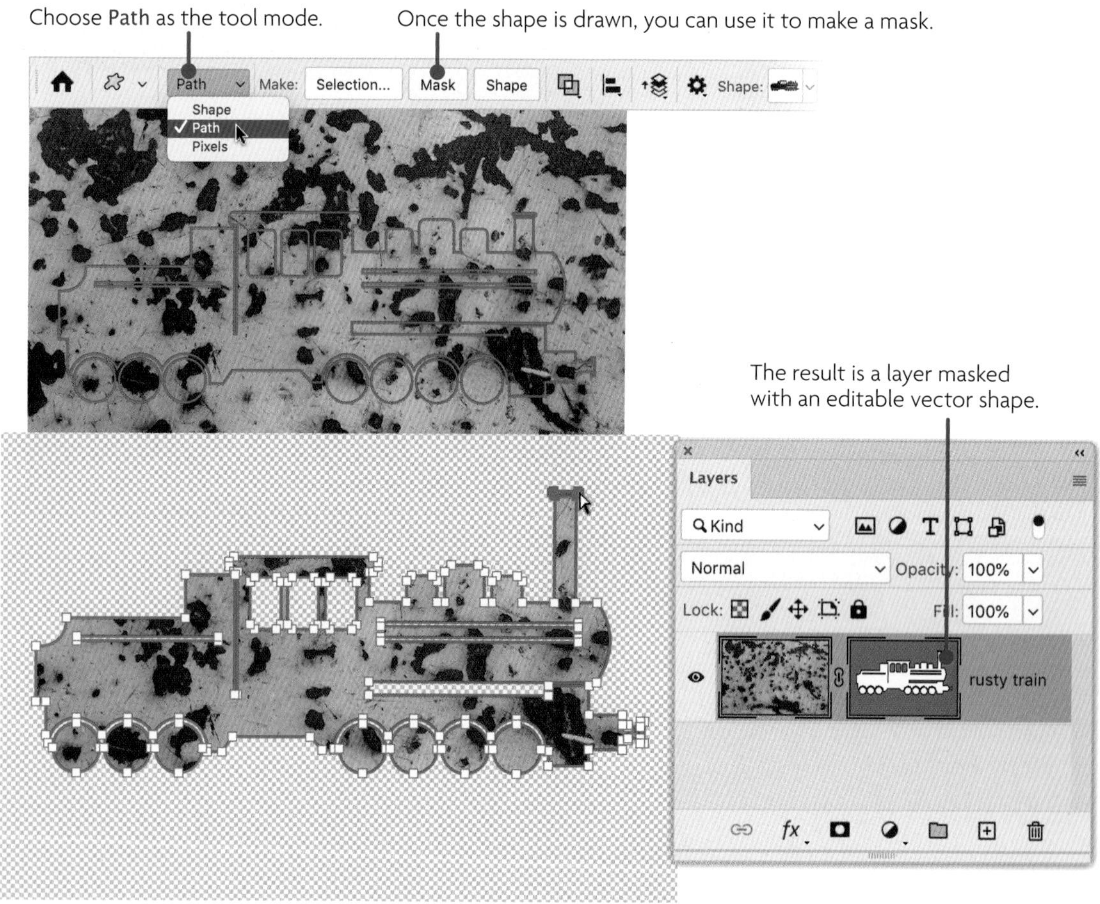

Other Masking Features

Frame Tool

Useful in limited circumstances, the Frame tool creates a Frame layer. If a document has only a Background and no other layer, this Frame layer will be empty. Otherwise, the topmost layer, whether selected or not, will be masked to the rectangle or ellipse drawn. You can also convert a vector shape into a frame with the same limitations. With a Frame layer highlighted, you may drag an asset from the Library panel, or choose File > Place Embedded… or Place Linked… to give the frame content or replace the content it had.

In each of those cases, the frame's content is a Smart Object. If your document has a number of layers, the Frame tool can be aggravating, as it may mask layers you'd wish it didn't. If you need to mask a layer with an editable shape, use a vector mask.

Clipping Mask

This technique uses the visible extent of a layer, group, or Smart Object to control the visibility of layers above it. So if a photo is clipped to a type layer below it, the photo is visible only where the type (the base layer) is.

Simply option/Alt-click on the line between two layers to create a clipping mask or to add more. Each layer remains independently editable, so if the base layer changes, the visibility of what's clipped keeps up! There is a bit more entanglement: The base layer controls the blending of all the layers in the clipping mask. So if the base layer's opacity is lowered, the entire arrangement diminishes. See "Blend Clipped Layers as Group" (page 209) for more on that. A group can be used as the base "layer," but cannot be clipped.

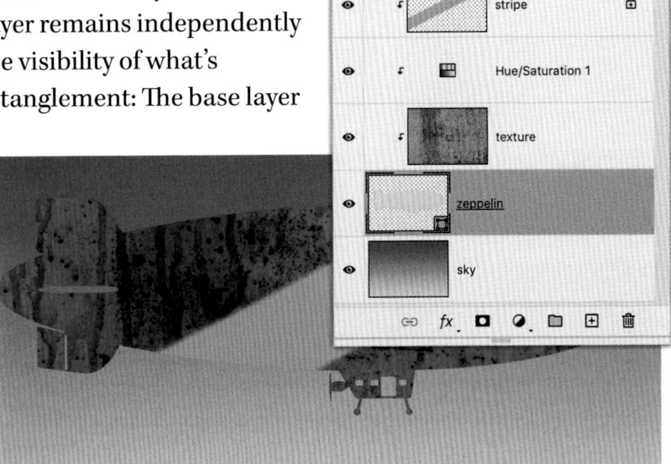

I'm using a shape layer as the base layer for this clipping mask. Three layers are clipped: a photo of a texture, a Hue/Saturation adjustment (affecting only the clipped texture layer under it), and a painted stripe. Note the base layer's name is underlined, and the clipped layers are indented with arrows pointing down to the base layer.

Knockout

This Advanced Blending Option allows the content of a layer, group, or Smart Object to act as a drill through layers below it. See "Knockout" (page 208) for an explanation.

Blend If

Another Advanced Blending Option. This one hides content based on the tone of the layer or those below it. See "Blend If" (page 212) to learn how this works.

5 Filters & Transforms

Clothes often fit better when altered. Some might say that for images too. Two major categories of alteration for images are filters and transforms.

Most filters can be applied nondestructively to Smart Objects, and all filters can be applied to ordinary layers. Some filters are elaborate software and may require preparation, whereas others are super-simple. I will attempt to list many of them by general intention. That said, wonderful creative opportunities come from using features in unintended ways.

To scale, rotate, twist, bend, or distort images, we have an array of transformative tools, commands, and filters. Most of them are worthy of mention too.

Filters

Filters are like small software applications within Photoshop that enact sometimes dramatic changes to our images. Some are very simple, almost trivial; some are like full-featured image-editing applications. Most are controlled via a dialog box with a few sliders and usually a preview. Some take over the screen with their own workspace.

There are 70 stand-alone filters plus 3 *galleries*: the Filter Gallery with its 47 filters, the Blur Gallery featuring 5 of the ways to blur (out of nearly 20 in total), and the Neural Filters. You can mix each gallery's filters to create a combination effect, and then add other filters too. It's dizzying!

Significantly, most filters can (and *should*) be applied to Smart Objects to become "Smart Filters." This allows you to experiment more freely, trying combinations of filters with different settings to achieve a desired effect.

Below, I'll describe many filters, but not all 134! I'll discuss approaches and strategies and show some examples. I strongly recommend setting aside time to experiment, guided by this text. An additional resource is provide by Adobe itself: their *Photoshop filter effects reference* (do a web search for that phrase and you'll find it immediately). Nothing beats experience, however. Play with filters as often as you can to build a visual vocabulary. The most elaborate is the Camera Raw filter. Its sharpening power is covered in this chapter, but a comprehensive look can be had in the "Camera Raw & Lightroom" chapter.

Neural Filters

This is the name for a developing filter "gallery" that utilizes Adobe's artificial intelligence (AI) algorithms to process our images or infiltrate pixels into them to change their mood or form. Photoshop users have seen combo filters before: Blur Gallery and the original Filter Gallery (which can be independent filters via a preference setting).

Go to Filter > Neural Filters to see them. Much of what's on offer is experimental (as shown by a Beta label). There's even a teaser section called Wait List, which solicits votes for filters to be developed. If one of the filters in the All Filters list intrigues you, download it by clicking the cloud icon and/or activate it via its switch. Like the other filter galleries, you can activate multiple filters to combine their effects. Some processing takes place on your computer and some filters need the power of Adobe's cloud processing. Don't expect them to be very fast: Watch for the processing note to complete near the bottom of your image before judging the result.

At the bottom of the filter list is a menu with Output choices. To preserve your original, choose New Layer or Smart Filter (which will convert the active layer to a Smart Object automatically).

Portraits

Skin Smoothing goes beyond other tools we've used and attempts to use Adobe's huge database of skin images to achieve its results.

Smart Portrait can be disturbing. Its Happiness slider is already notorious for generating toothy grins on even pursed-lipped subjects.

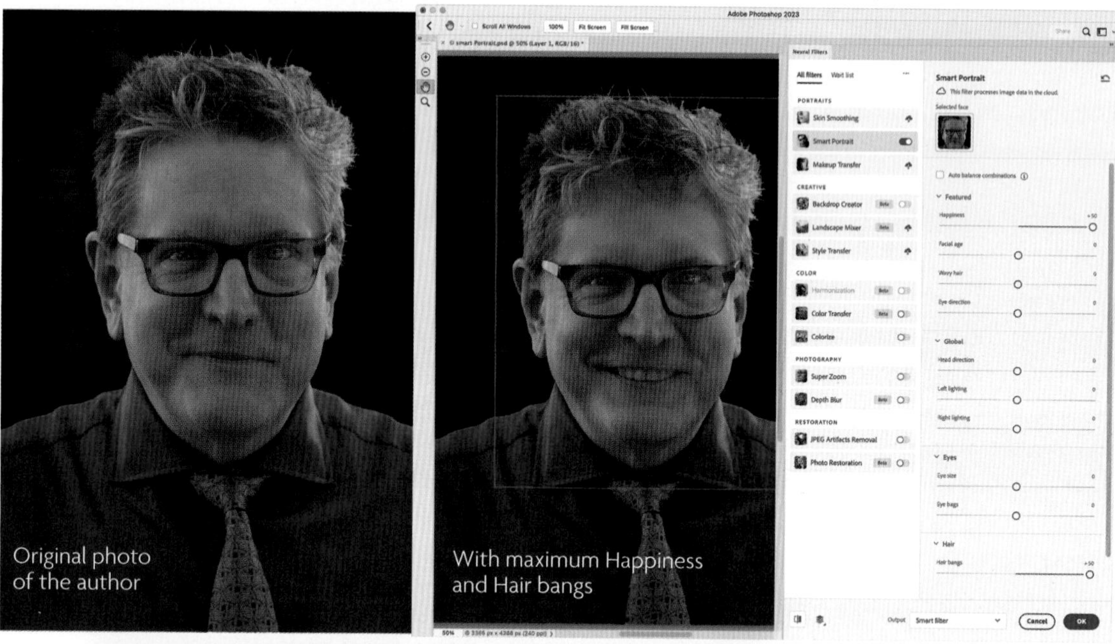

Original photo of the author

With maximum Happiness and Hair bangs

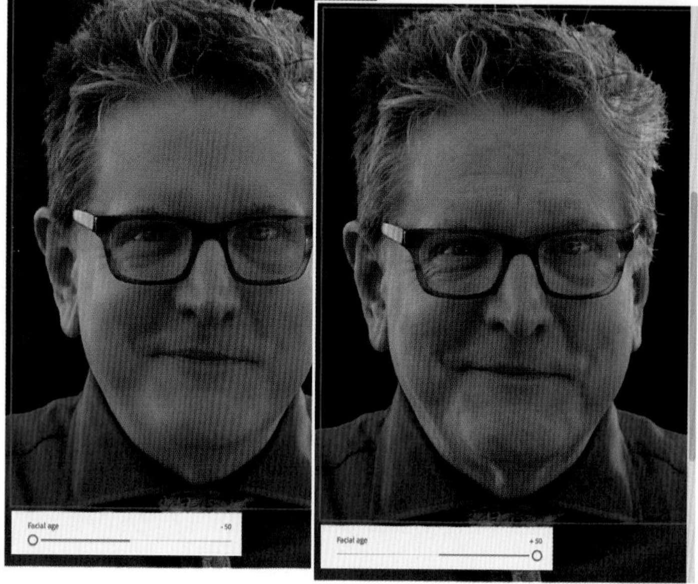

Facial age -50, left, and +50. The numbers clearly do not correspond to years!

Makeup Transfer is one of several that uses another image to affect yours. The makeup applied to a model in a chosen image finds its way to one in your photo. I've found that eye makeup has trouble working its way around my glasses.

Creative

Backdrop Creator generates a more-or-less abstract image from text prompts you type into a text field. Very much in beta as of this writing.

Landscape Mixer may use one of several included ("Preset") images or one of your own to alter the time of day, season, or terrain of a landscape image.

Style Transfer also uses other images to alter your own, giving color, texture, and the feel of the source image. Although some choices of Artist Styles or Image Styles will disappoint, this may still prove a fast way to make a photo look as though it were painted.

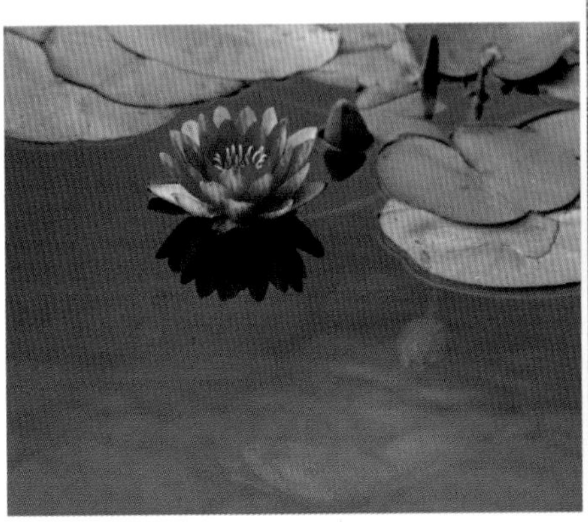

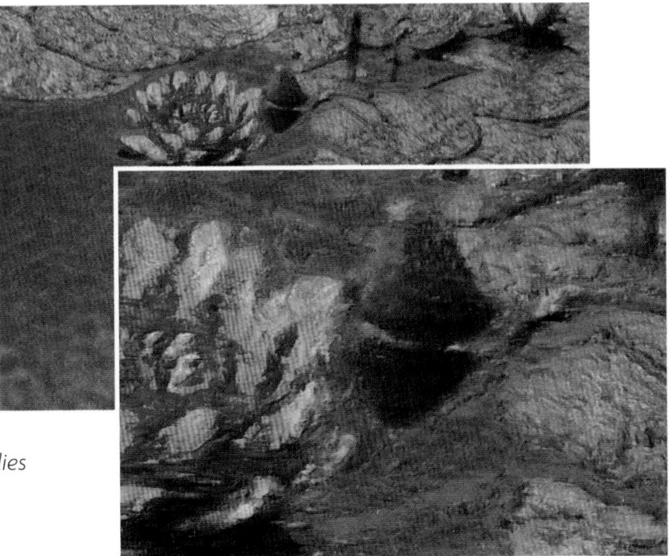

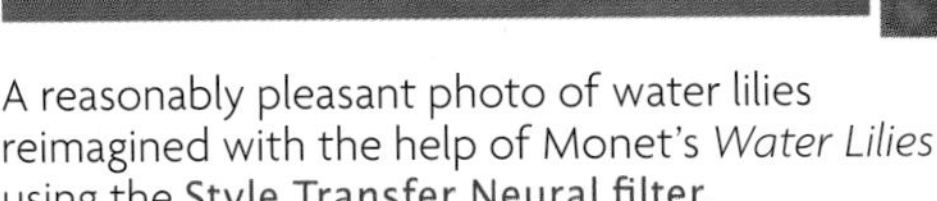

A reasonably pleasant photo of water lilies reimagined with the help of Monet's *Water Lilies* using the Style Transfer Neural filter.

Color

Harmonization adjusts the color and contrast of a layer that's been added to a document to match the lighting of its new setting (a layer visible below it, for example).

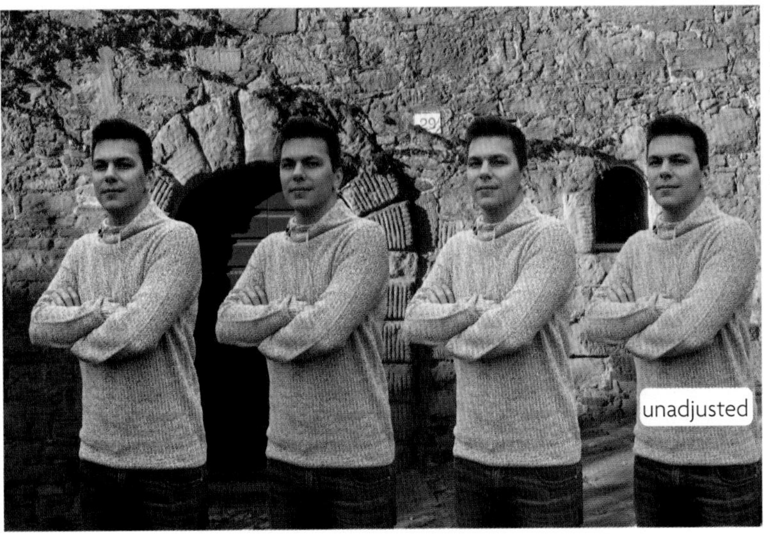

Harmonization attempts to allow a composite's ingredients to match the setting in which they've been placed.

I put this fellow in three different places and the Harmonization feature picked up on the lighting behind him in each case. An unadjusted copy is at the right for comparison.

Color Transfer at first seems like Style Transfer, but far gentler. No textures are transfered, just color. If the Preserve Luminance option is enabled, it is very much like creating a gradient of the colors in a source image from dark to light and applying it as a Gradient Map adjustment.

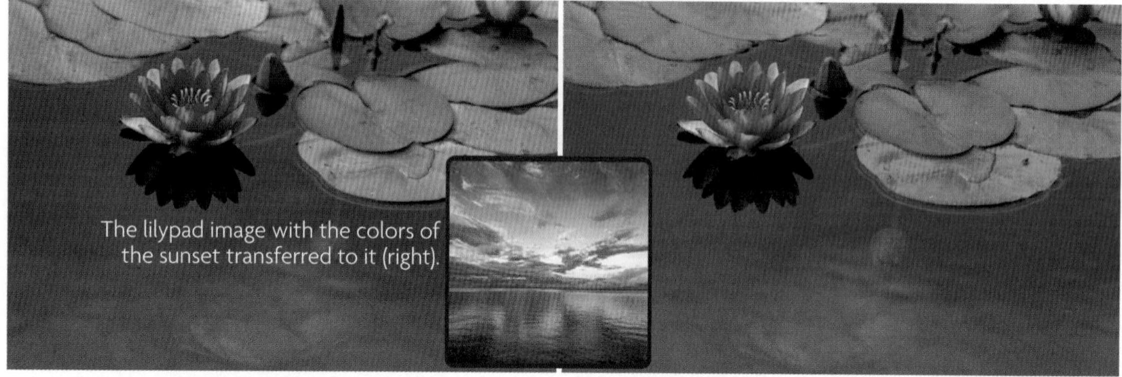

The lilypad image with the colors of the sunset transferred to it (right).

Colorize attempts to apply plausible colors to a black-and-white image. Although I (and others who've dabbled in colorization) can do a far, far better job *in time*, this filter takes only seconds and its results can be edited.

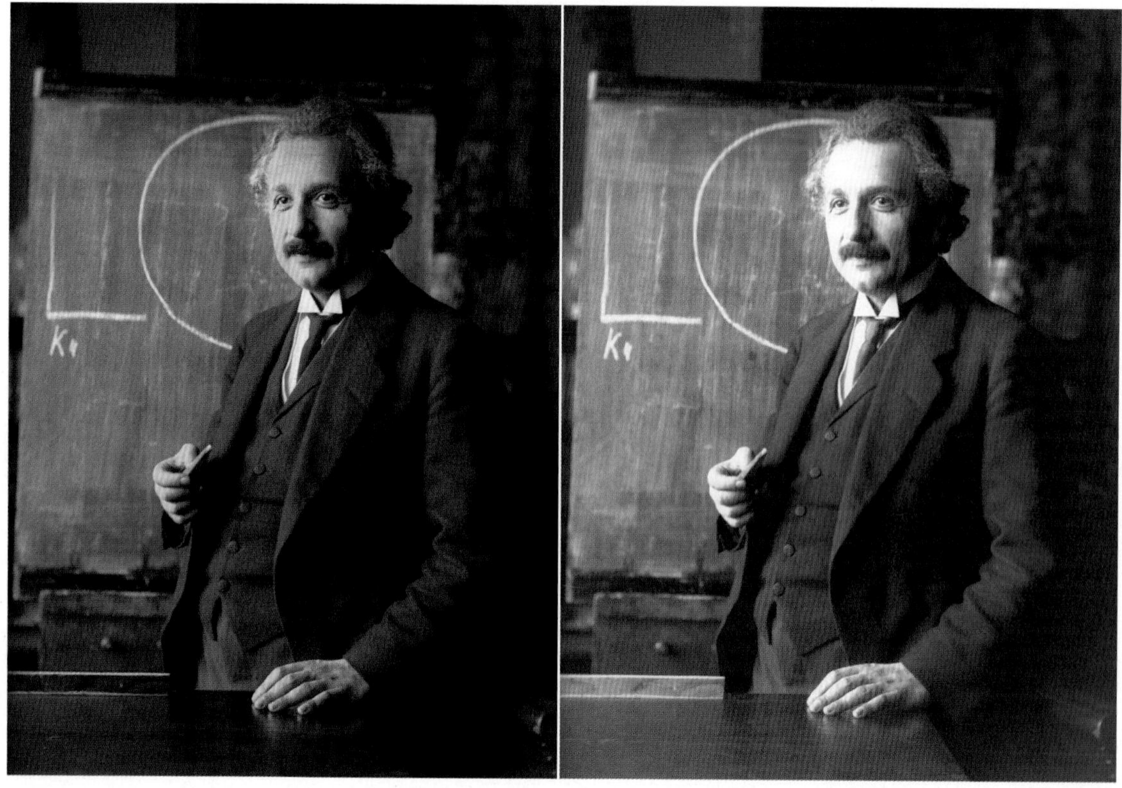

Black-and-white photo colorized by the author (left) and with the **Colorize** neural filter (right).

Photography

Super Zoom yields synthesized detail for even extreme enlargements. Its Enhance image details is what helps make most edges sharp, and Enhance face details is used specifically to provide face details (skin texture, eyelashes, etc). They thoughtfully provide JPEG artifact removal, as those artifacts become quite noticeable upon enlargement. Below are small sections of images. The first is a full-resolution image I downsampled to 20% so I could compare Super Zoom to the old Preserve Details 2.0 upsampling.

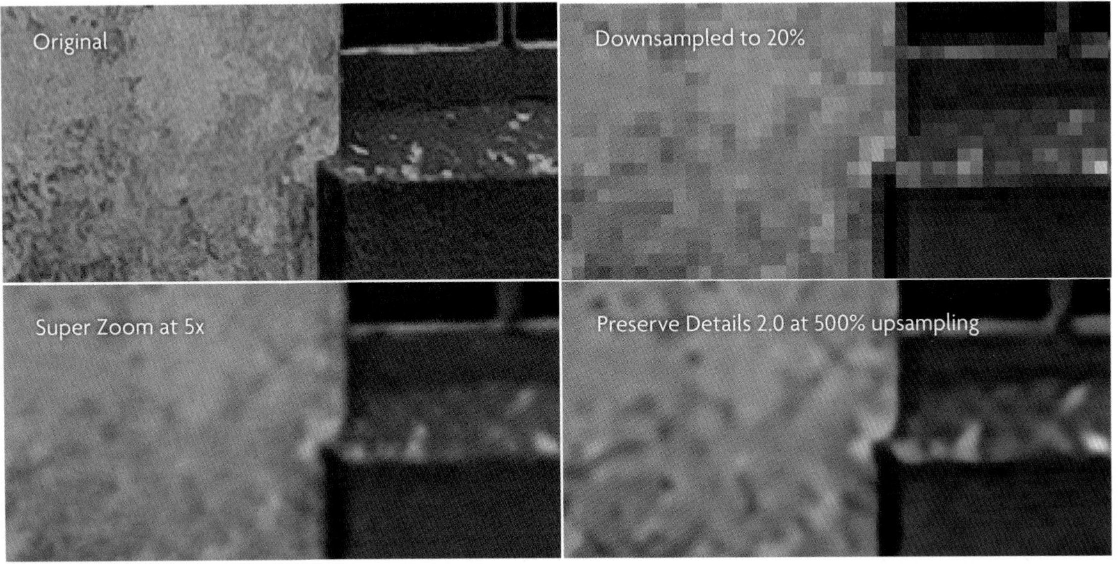

Restoration

JPEG Artifacts Removal minimizes the visual residue of a JPEG's lossy compression, especially if done at a lower "quality" setting.

Photo Restoration looks for likely scratches, dust, cracks, etc., and fills them in rather like Content Aware Fill. Color is also evened out and details enhanced in a way like Super Zoom performs. Although it shows impressive promise, there is much work to be done to make this a bigger part of a retouching workflow. It will be interesting to see how this function evolves.

Depth Blur

Photoshop has many filters to blur images or parts thereof; in fact, the next section of this chapter is dedicated to them. But we can harness a bit of artificial intelligence to blur images in a way to simulate shallow depth of field, choosing whether which distance from the lens is in focus and how blurred the rest should be.

Depth Blur analyzes an image to determine proximity of elements in it to the photographer. A click in a preview image sets the distance that should be in sharp focus, and the rest is blurred per the various sliders below. You can even add haze to the blurred distance, colorize the image, and add grain to the out-of-focus parts to enhance the reality of the illusion.

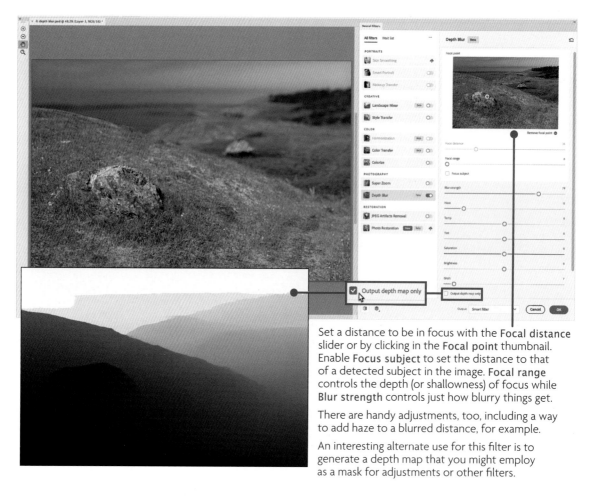

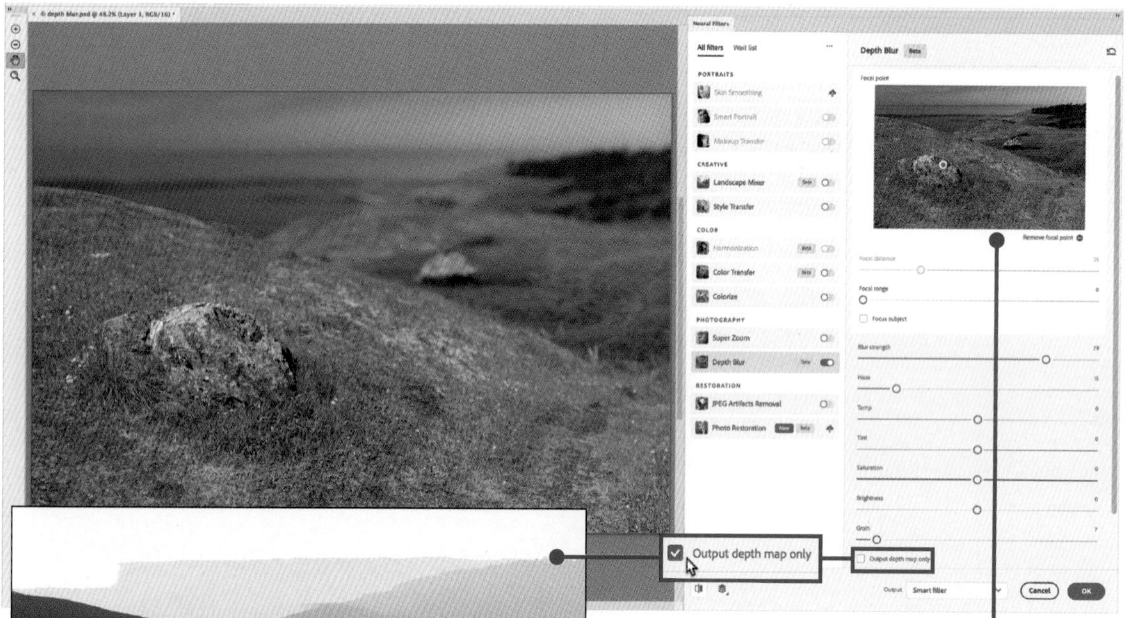

Set a distance to be in focus with the **Focal distance** slider or by clicking in the **Focal point** thumbnail. Enable **Focus subject** to set the distance to that of a detected subject in the image. **Focal range** controls the depth (or shallowness) of focus while **Blur strength** controls just how blurry things get.

There are handy adjustments, too, including a way to add haze to a blurred distance, for example.

An interesting alternate use for this filter is to generate a depth map that you might employ as a mask for adjustments or other filters.

Focus (Blurring and Sharpening)

Blur Filters

Blurring is an effective way to draw attention to the parts of an image that aren't blurred or reduce noise or other artifacts in an image.

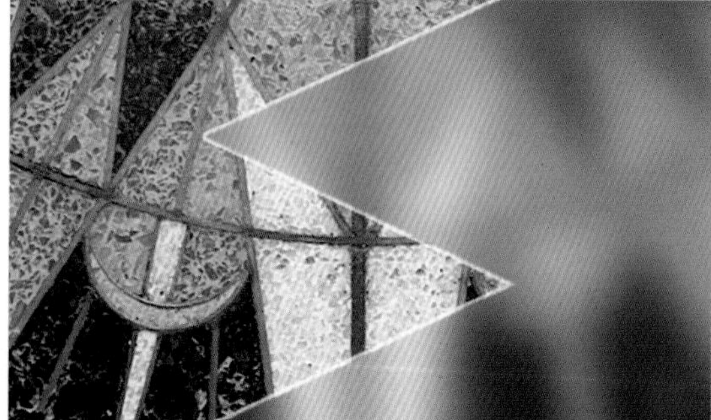

Gaussian Blur: The simplest and most intuitive, this removes "high-frequency" details. It has one control, the **Radius** slider. to determine its amount.

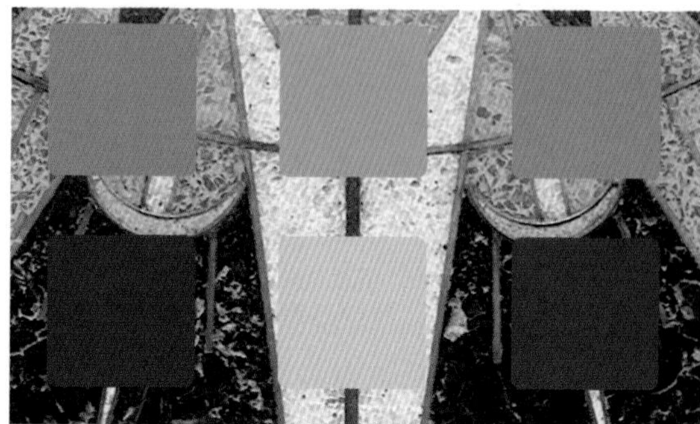

Average: This yields the average color of the area selected. Here, six regions were averaged, one at a time. There are no controls for this filter.

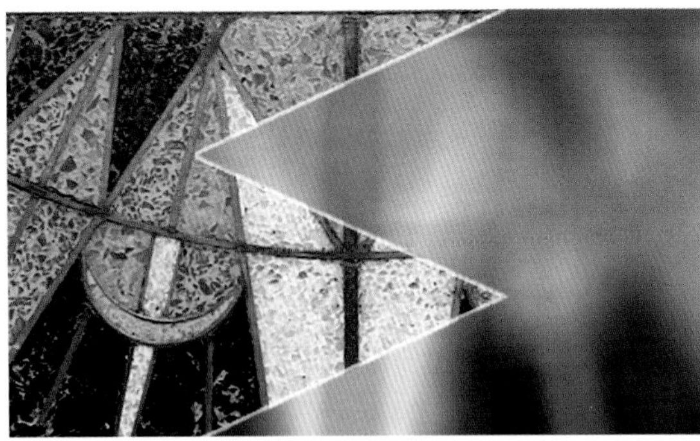

Box Blur: Although this uses an average of colors surrounding each pixel blurred, the result resembles an unfocused image projected through a square aperture. **Radius** controls the amount of blur.

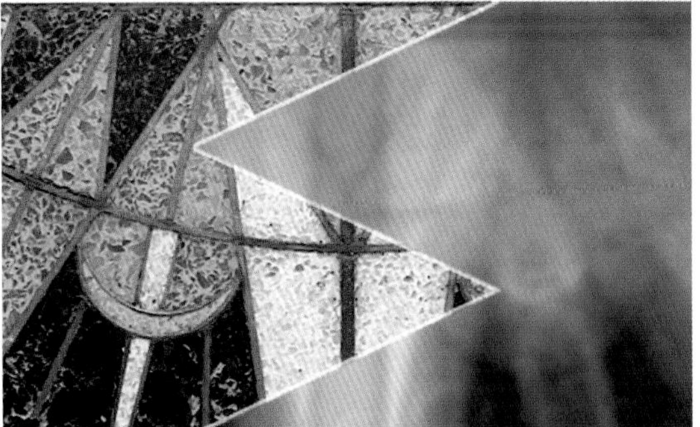

Shape Blur: This is similar to **Box Blur** but with many choices. The result resembles an unfocused image projected through an aperture (hole) of the chosen shape (in this example, a ring).

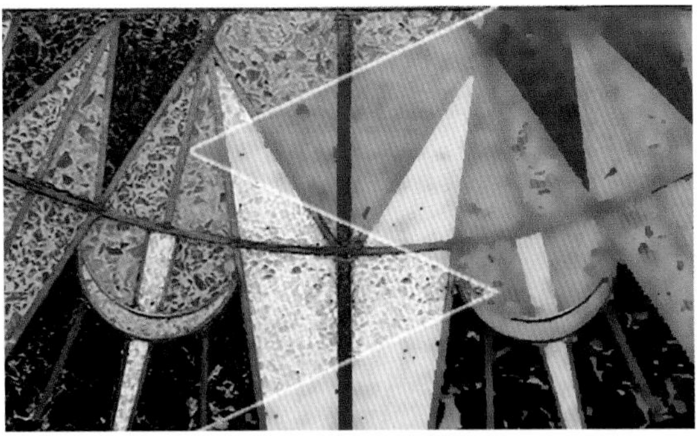

Smart Blur: Unlike most of the others, this can keep edges sharp while reducing noise and details in other areas. It searches a **Radius** around each pixel and blurs it and those similar to it. Similarity is determined by the **Threshold** value. Choose **High Quality** and **Normal Mode**.

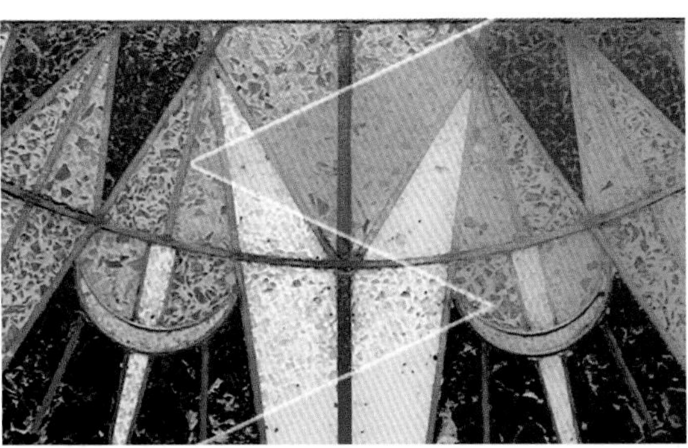

Surface Blur: This is like **Smart Blur**, but is better at removing only noise while leaving other details. For this purpose, lower settings for **Radius** and **Threshold** are recommended.

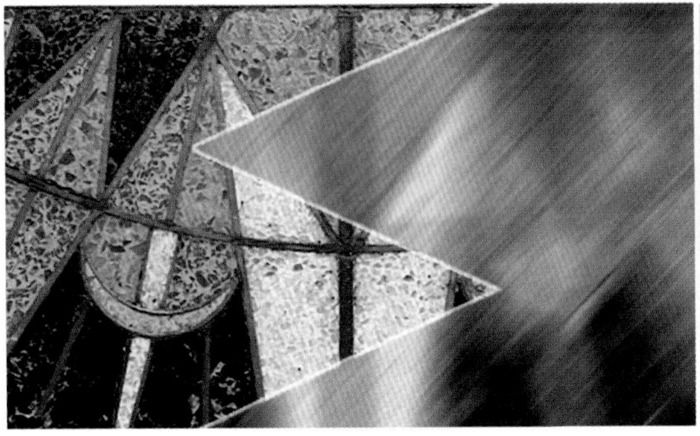

Motion Blur (45°)

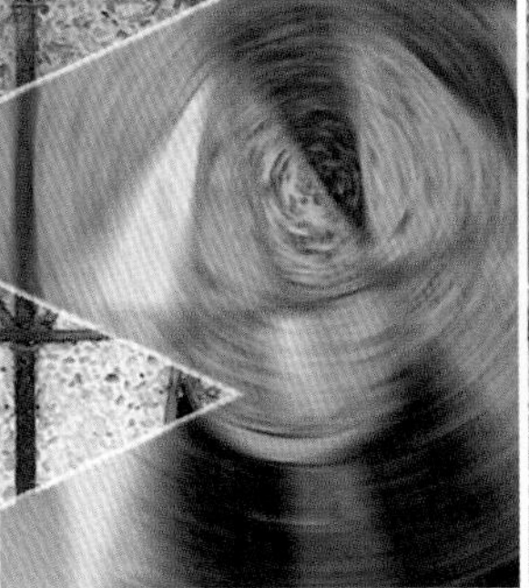

Radial Blur (Spin)

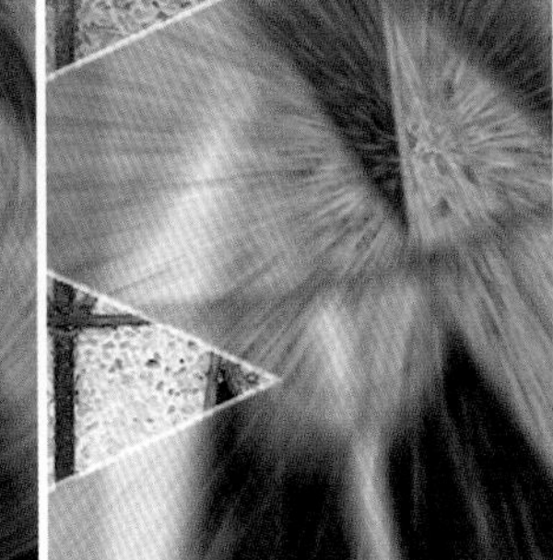

Radial Blur (Zoom)

Both **Motion Blur** and **Radial Blur** simulate blurring caused by motion. **Motion Blur** is linear, and you set the **Angle** and **Distance**. **Radial** can simulate a spinning subject (or camera) by choosing **Spin**.

By choosing **Zoom**, you simulate an approaching/receding subject or changing lens zoom.
For **Quality**, always choose the best!
Adjust the **Amount** to taste.

Blur Gallery

When you choose any of the filters in Filter > Blur Gallery, you enter a new workspace that will let you switch from one of those filters to the others, adding one to another or using one to keep an area sharp that another was blurring.

Each uses Pins, points from which an amount of blur emanates. Some have additional interface elements as well. To complete the illusion, you can use that workspace to add noise or motion effects to the blurred areas, and bokeh affects to blurred light sources. Finally, you can choose to have an alpha channel made that serves as a map of which areas were blurred and, by its shades of gray, how much.

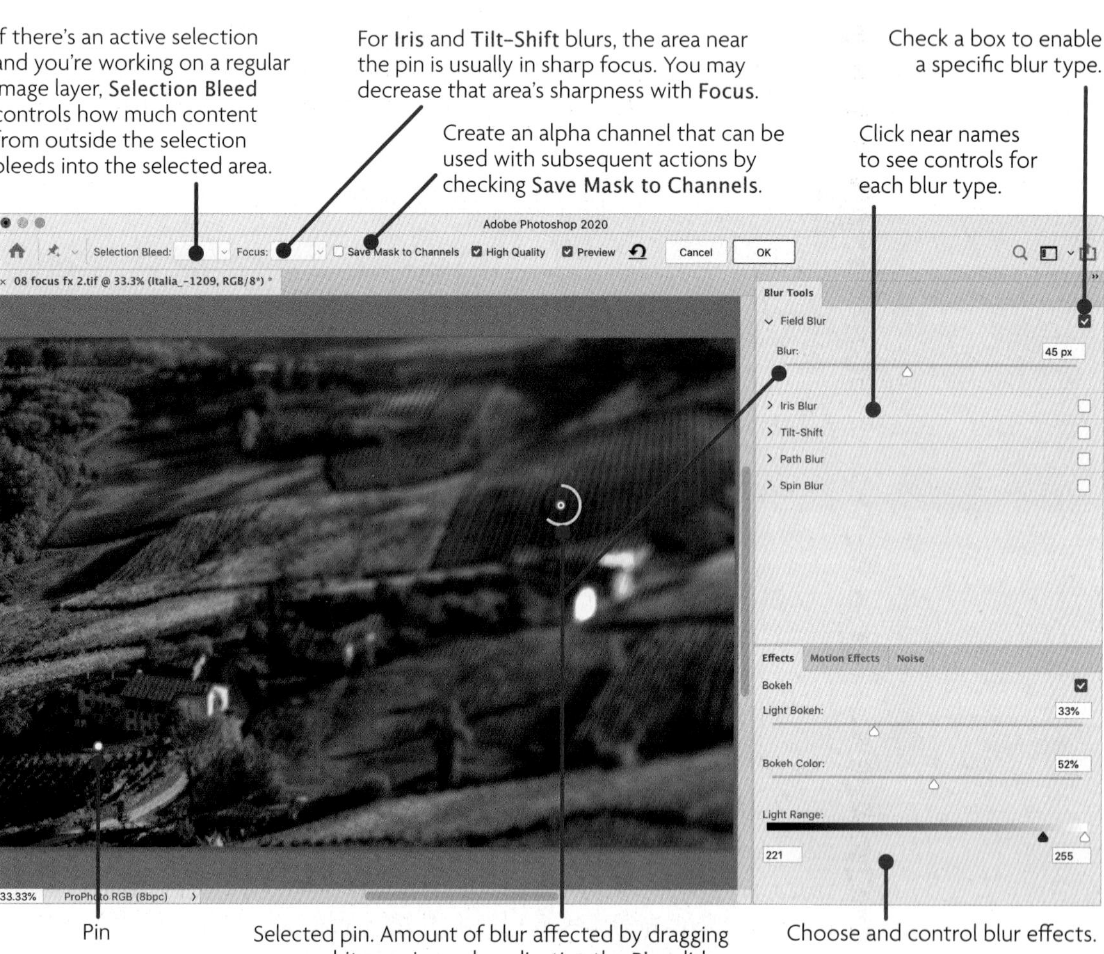

This example shows a two-pin Field Blur. The lower-left pin emits very little blur, but the upper-right one emits significantly more. The amount is shown by both the extent of the white in the ring surrounding the pin and by the Blur slider in the panel at right. You can actually drag the white part of the ring to change the amount of blur! Dragging the pin moves the source of blurriness.

To see where (and relatively how much) blur is being applied, you can hold down the M key (for "Mask"). This shows the area of maximum blur with white, and unblurred areas with black. If you check the Save Mask to Channels box, this is what the resultant alpha channel will look like too.

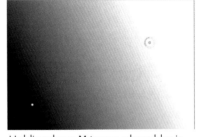

Holding down M to see where blur is and isn't.

There are other imaging consequences to blurry images that may be desirable. For these, you need the panels at the lower right of the Blur Gallery workspace.

Bokeh is the blooming of light around bright reflections or light sources in a blurred area. Light Bokeh controls the amount of blooming that occurs. Bokeh Color allows those blooms to adopt color from around them. The Light Range is the range of tones that exhibit bokeh (in the example, all tones lighter than 221). You can see the result on the brightly lit bits of those buildings on the right.

Motion Effects are for Path Blur only. This simulates illumination of the blurred subject by strobe (flash), creating sharp versions of the subject within the blurred one.

When parts of a noisy image are blurred, the noise from that area is removed too. However, it can be restored (simulated, actually) with the Noise controls.

Add more pins by clicking where you want one. The cursor will look like this: .

Remove a pin by selecting it and tapping backspace/delete.

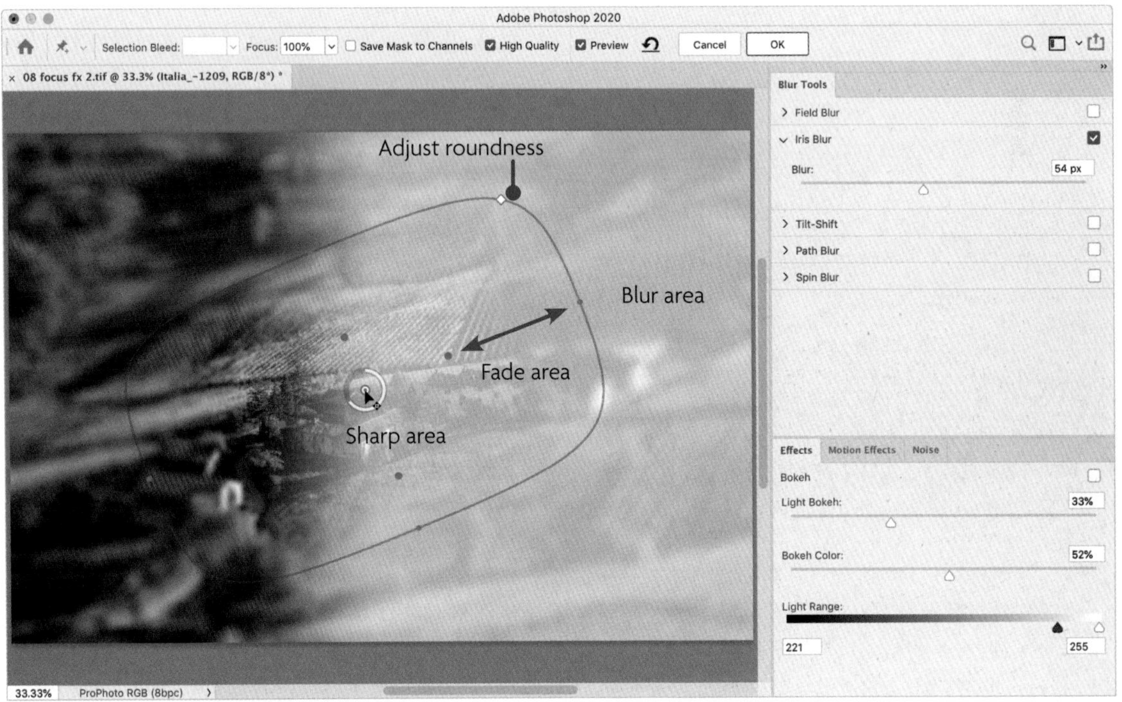

Iris Blur creates a sharp central area surrounding the default pin up to four blue circles. From those outward to a faint gray line is the fade area in which sharpness gives way to blur. By dragging the circles, you can adjust the size of the sharp area. Dragging the gray line adjusts the extent of the whole affair. However, modifier keys are powerful here:

- Holding Shift while dragging the outer gray circle forces it to be a circle.
- Option/Alt-dragging the gray circle resizes only the fade area, leaving the inner sharp area as is.
- Option/Alt-dragging one of the blue circles moves only it, creating an asymmetrical sharp iris.

There are also points along the outer gray circle that are special. Dragging the tiny blue circles on it inward or outward allows you to resize the whole interface in one dimension (width or height). Dragging them along the circle rotates the whole iris. Finally, the small square on the gray circle is for changing the iris from elliptical to rectangular.

I use this filter to simulate old or cheap plastic lenses, which have poor edge sharpness.

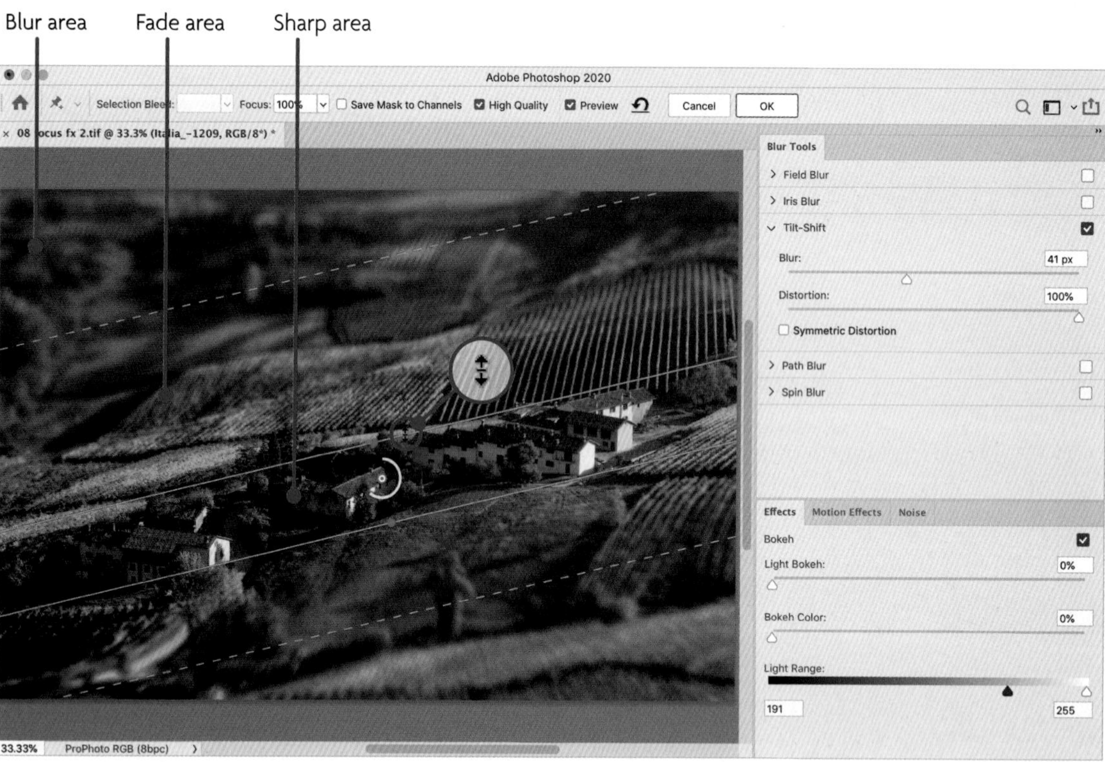

Tilt-Shift Blur attempts to simulate the focus control of a tilt-shift lens or an old-school camera with a bellows between the lens board and the film plane. With those, one can have a narrow zone of focus with relatively abrupt blurriness in both the foreground and background.

When you choose this blur in the gallery, an initially horizontal zone of sharpness appears around the pin. The fade area, in which focus falls off to the amount of Blur you choose, runs between the solid gray lines and the dashed ones. Beyond the dashes is the blur area. You can drag any of the lines to change those zones. If you carefully drag the blue circles on the solid line, you will rotate the whole effect. Since those are often close to the pin, which is the axis of rotation, it can be a bit tricky. The Distortion slider distorts the area that started at the bottom (before any rotation). Negative values distort parallel to the sharp zone, and positive values distort perpendicular to it. You can see foreground objects getting pushed around one way or the other if the Blur and Distortion values are high enough. If you want that effect on both sides of the sharp area, then check Symmetric Distortion.

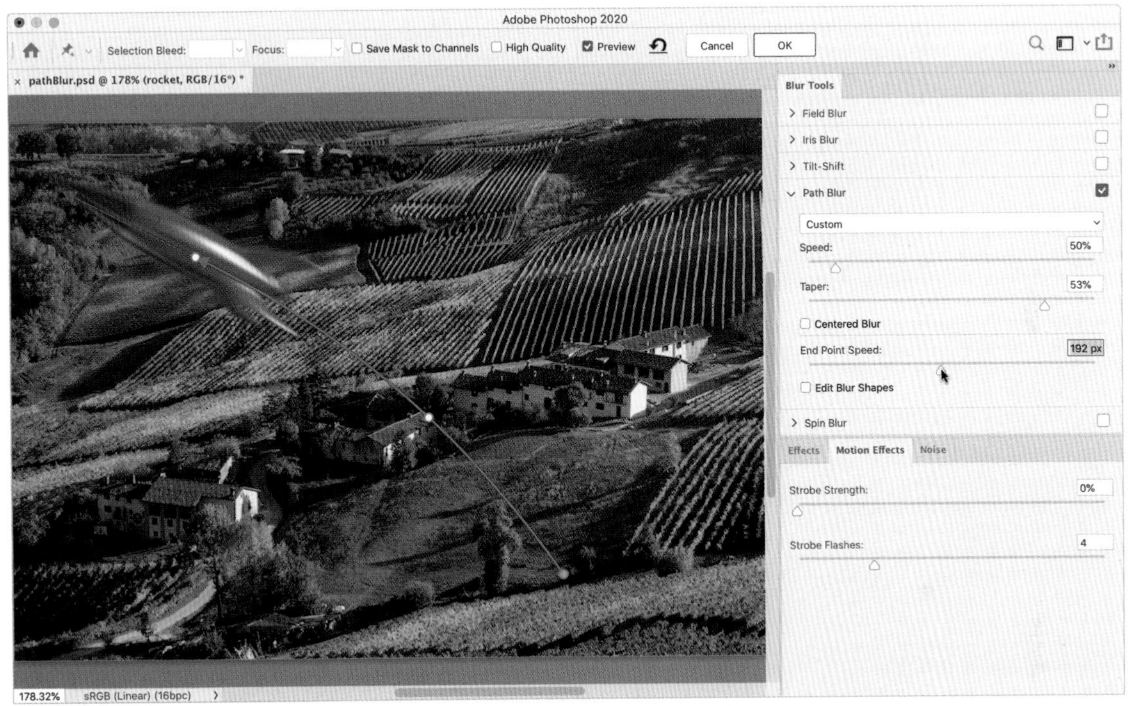

Path Blur simulates motion blur. It creates an editable path you use to indicate the direction and magnitude of motion. I often use this to give life to an object I've introduced to a scene.

The idea is that the object moved during the exposure. By default, this filter assumes uniform speed and direction. However, you can click on either end point and alter the End Point Speed, as I did above. When you do, a red arrow appears to indicate the direction of motion. The longer the arrow, the faster the motion. I set the starting point to zero, and the point nearest the rocket to nearly 200 pixels of blur to simulate an accelerating object. I pushed the center point, too, to give a slight arc to the motion. I also introduced a little bit of Taper to recover some of the edges that were a little too blurry perpendicular to the motion.

Each end point can have a bit of its own motion, too, if you check Edit Blur Shapes. So you can simulate an object (or the camera making the photo) that wiggled a little at one end of the exposure.

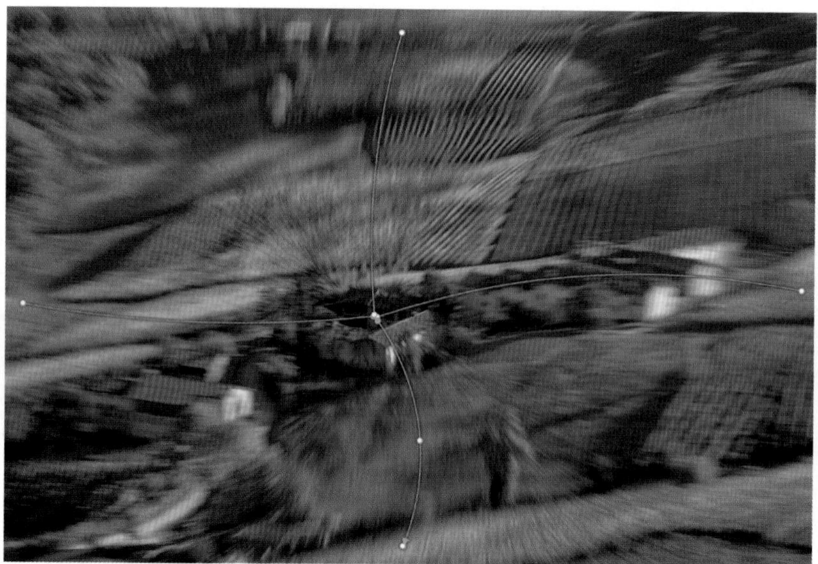

Four paths with no blur at the central ends and lots at the outer ends can give a twisted radial blur effect.

Spin Blur can make wheels or windmills turn. With Spin Blur, we indicate how many degrees of rotation has happened during the exposure. The circular blur area can be made elliptical by dragging the blue circles at its edge, so things that are not directly facing us can be spun too.

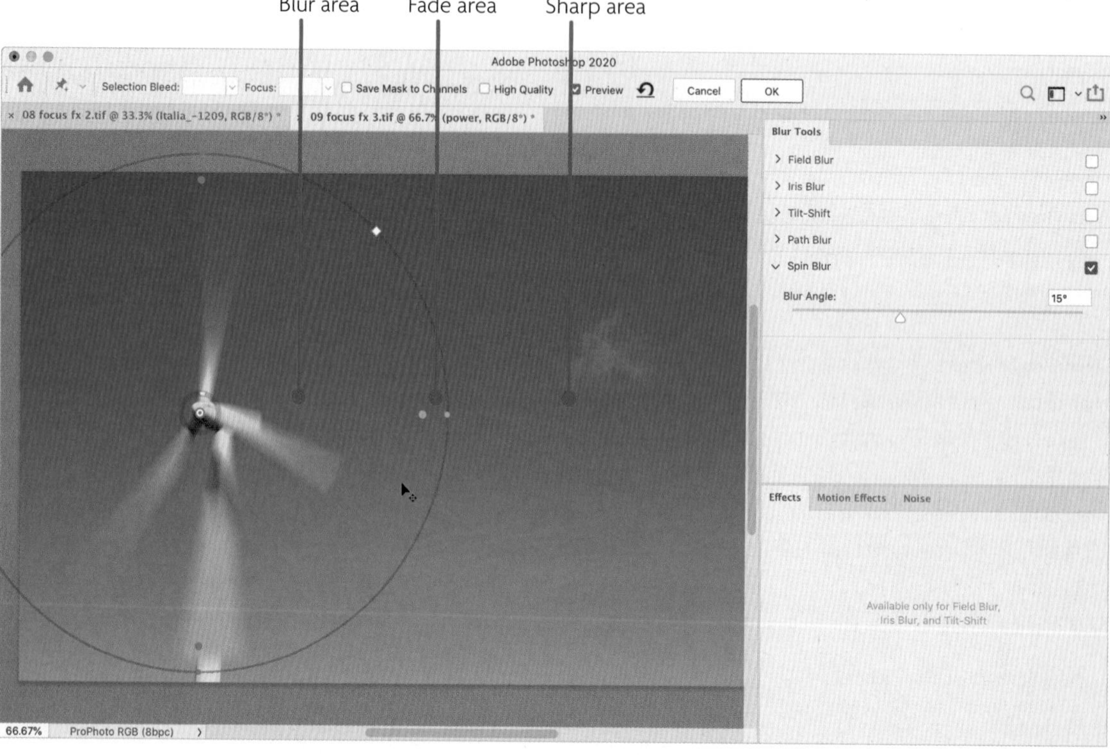

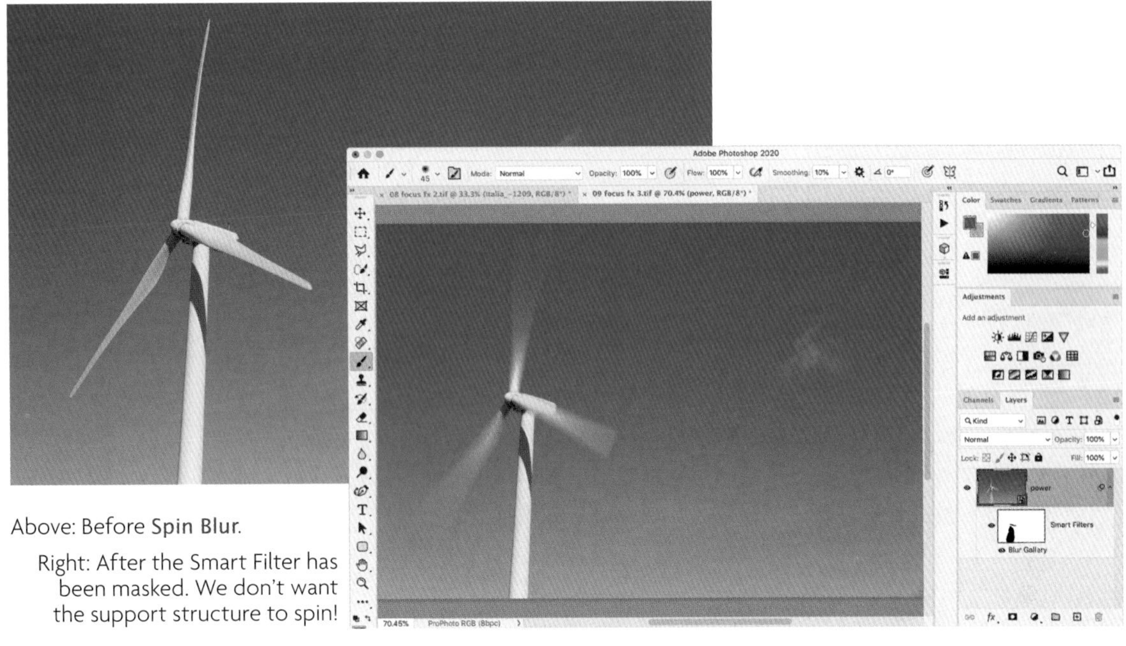

Above: Before Spin Blur.

Right: After the Smart Filter has been masked. We don't want the support structure to spin!

Lens Blur

Related to the Blur Gallery in that different parts of an image can be blurred differently, Lens Blur also differs in two ways. Since it is more tightly wed to the physics of optics, and is therefore more demanding of our computer hardware, it cannot be applied to a Smart Object. So we have to duplicate the layer to which we want to apply this filter.

The other difference is that, rather than *generating* a channel to indicate what's been blurred and by how much, Lens Blur *uses* an existing alpha channel to indicate depth or distance and then uses that information to simulate a lens's depth of field.

Recall that alpha channels (like all channels) are grayscale images—see "Saving & Loading Selections" (page 286) for information on how to create these from selections. You can also duplicate one of the color channels to create an alpha channel that looks just like it.

The following rocket image was made with the help of Adobe Dimension. Substance Stager would also have been a good choice. Each image element (the rocket, planet, moon, and background) are different virtual distances from the viewer. In the rendered Photoshop Document that Dimension produces, there's a group of layers that can be handy for post-render adjustments. One of those layers is a grayscale image called "Depth Information." In it, white represents the closest element (the rocket), and black the farthest (the backdrop of stars). This is similar to (but reversed from) the Depth Map that the Depth blur neural filter can produce. To use this information in the Lens Blur filter, I needed this image as a channel.

I hid the layers above "Depth Information," so it was the only one visible. Since it was grayscale, the Red, Green, and Blue channels were all identical to it. So I highlighted one of those, right-clicked it, and chose Duplicate Channel…. naming that duplicate "depth info."

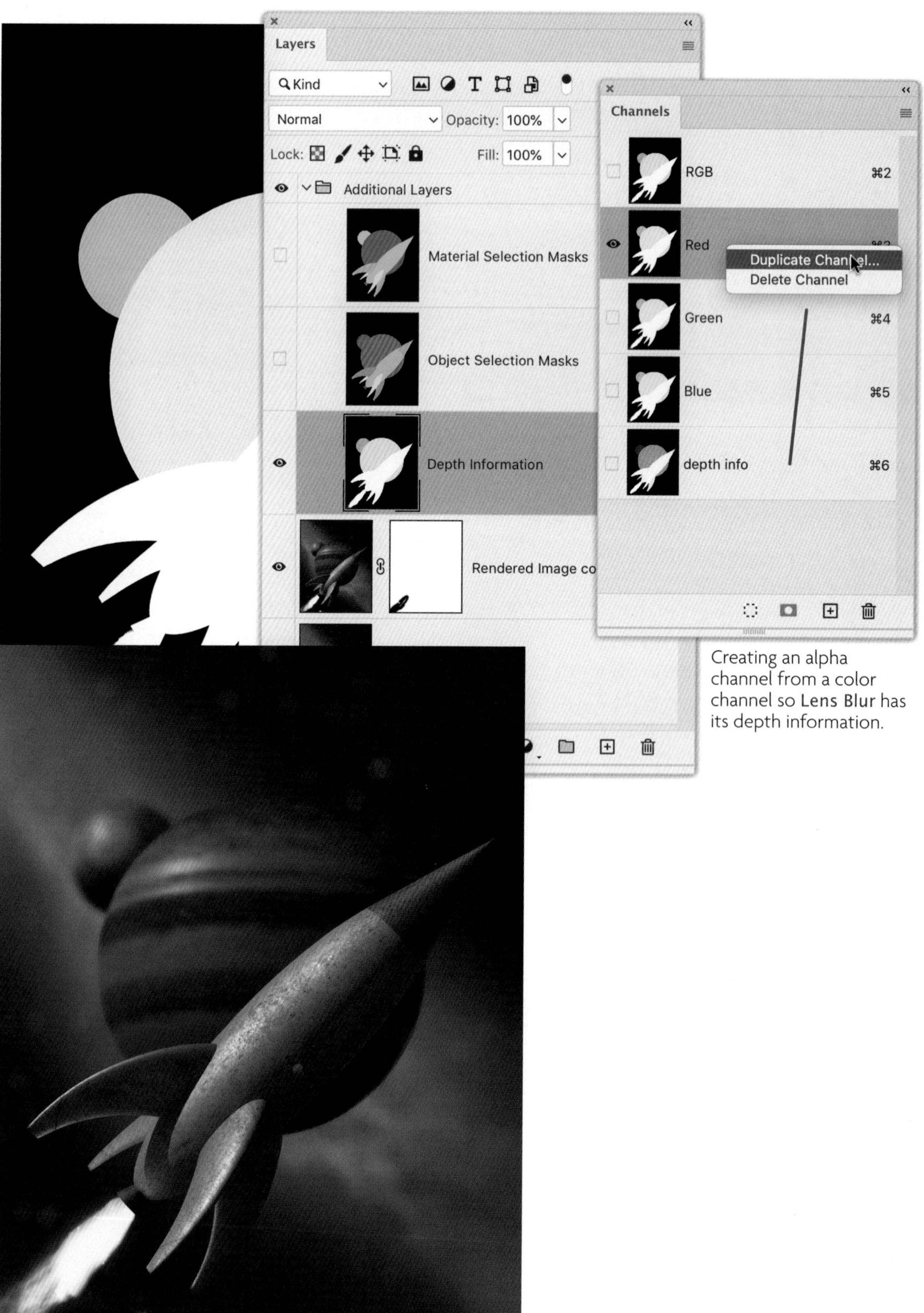

Creating an alpha channel from a color channel so **Lens Blur** has its depth information.

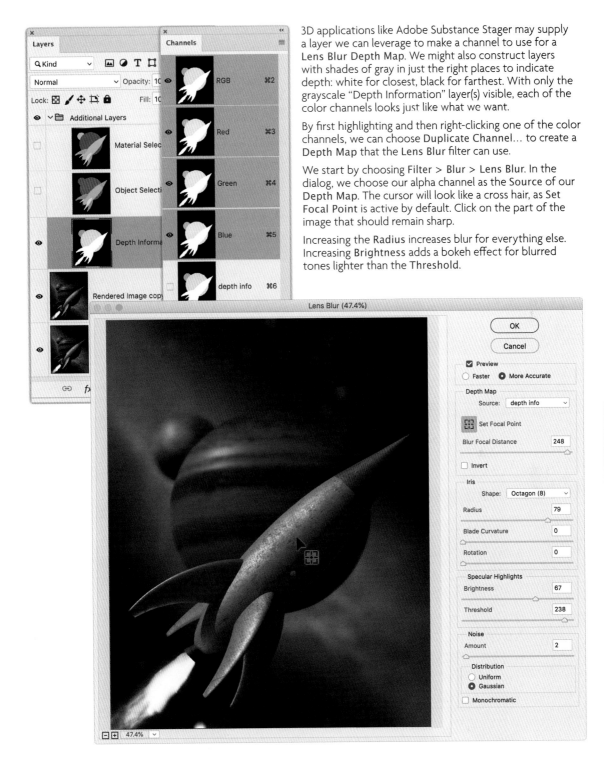

3D applications like Adobe Substance Stager may supply a layer we can leverage to make a channel to use for a Lens Blur Depth Map. We might also construct layers with shades of gray in just the right places to indicate depth: white for closest, black for farthest. With only the grayscale "Depth Information" layer(s) visible, each of the color channels looks just like what we want.

By first highlighting and then right-clicking one of the color channels, we can choose Duplicate Channel… to create a Depth Map that the Lens Blur filter can use.

We start by choosing Filter > Blur > Lens Blur. In the dialog, we choose our alpha channel as the Source of our Depth Map. The cursor will look like a cross hair, as Set Focal Point is active by default. Click on the part of the image that should remain sharp.

Increasing the Radius increases blur for everything else. Increasing Brightness adds a bokeh effect for blurred tones lighter than the Threshold.

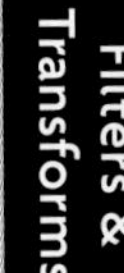

Apple's iOS devices and some cameras can capture images in a format called HEIC (High Efficiency Image Coding). These may contain a depth channel you can use. For documents without such a useful layer or channel, you will have to construct one or use the Depth blur neural filter to do so. You can select an object to be the subject, then save that selection as a channel.

Access the filter via Filter > Blur > Lens Blur. Within the filter's interface, direct your attention to the Depth Map section. Choose the alpha channel you created as the Source. Then use the Set Focal Point tool to choose which part of the image should be sharp. The level (shade of gray) at that location in the alpha channel will be used. Anywhere that value is used in the Depth Map, the image will be sharp. That level is displayed as the Blur Focal Distance.

The Iris section is where the physics simulation kicks in. This filter tries to simulate a real lens's behavior and properties. The lens properties that affect a blur's properties are the size, shape, and orientation of the aperture. Typically, the iris of a lens is formed by a number of blades—we choose how many with Shape. The larger the Radius, the more narrow a lens's depth of field, and thus the blurrier things are if they're not at the focal distance.

The shape of the iris also affects the shape of bokeh, or the blooming of highlights in out-of-focus areas. Bokeh is controlled in the Specular Highlights section.

Finally, Noise can be applied to the blurred areas so their noise level matches that of the areas that remain sharp.

I find this filter works best when sharp subjects are in front of blurred backdrops. Edges of blurred objects in front of sharp ones don't always blur correctly, as seen below:

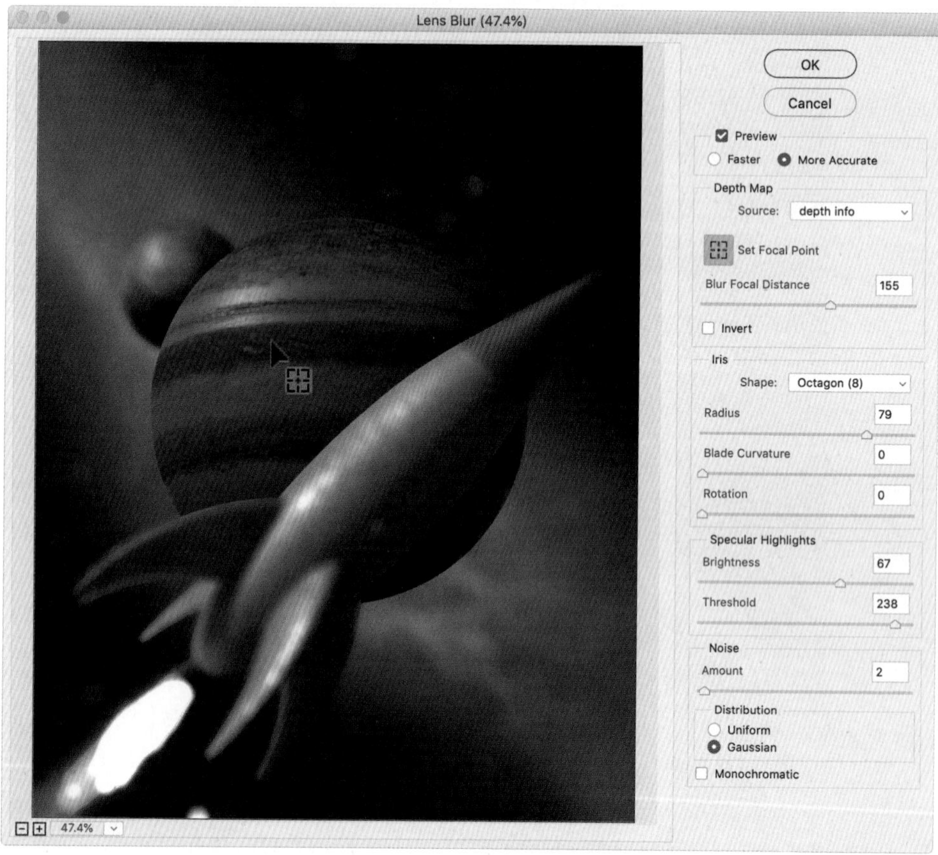

Sharpen Filters

Sharpening has fewer methods, especially those that are effective. Do not look to Photoshop to "refocus" the lens that made a blurry photo. No doubt, spy agencies have software for that, but it isn't Photoshop. However, images that have a bit of softness can be made to *appear* sharper by enhancing contrast at edges. One filter, Shake Reduction, attempts to be the exception. It analyzes motion in an image and attempts to cancel its effects. In extremely limited cases, it helps.

Smart Sharpen

This filter is one of the two best ways to sharpen an image. All images need a touch of sharpening (at least), but the image in the following examples needs more than that.

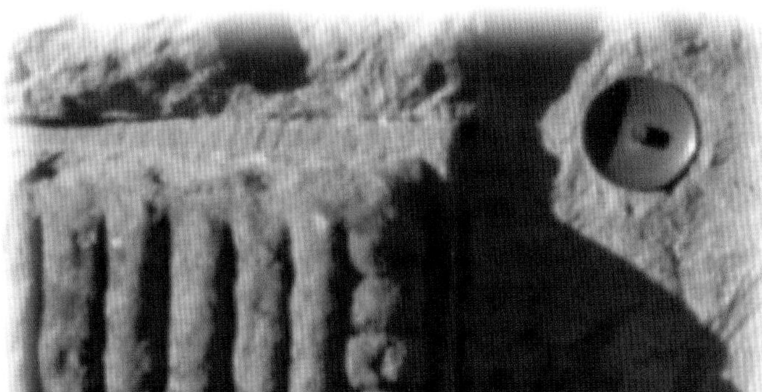

At left is the original, unsharpened image. It was made with a defective lens, so the inherent softness is somewhat greater than usual.

Below are the unusually high settings to compensate for this image. It's remarkable how excellent this filter is!

I very strongly recommend applying this filter to a Smart Object so it can be revisited or masked if necessary. Once the dialog box opens, I drag one of its corners to make it larger, then I disable Preview. In this way, the original image acts as a large "before" view. A click somewhere in the document window centers the filter's preview window on that location.

I find the following procedure works very well when approaching this filter:

- After choosing Filter > Sharpen > Smart Sharpen…, start with the Remove menu. Almost always, I choose Lens Blur, as that does active edge and detail detection. Gaussian approximates the imprecise Unsharp Mask filter, but sometimes I simply like the way it looks. Motion Blur requires us to specify the angle of motion that we're trying to cancel out, but it is rarely effective.
- I set Reduce Noise to 0—for now. If the sharpening I achieve is satisfactory but accentuates noise in the image, I'll return to this slider and raise it minimally.
- I *temporarily* set the Amount to its maximum so I can more clearly gauge how much Radius I need. This is the distance from the detected edges that the sharpening effect extends. It should be subliminally small. To see it accurately, zoom both the document window and the preview window to 100% magnification. If you have a high-definition display, you may need to use 200%. In the example, I'm using 300% in the hope that you'll be able to see the effects of the filter in this book. A typical Radius value is about 1 pixel. This image's softness was so extreme that I've set it to 1.8.
- I then set a more appropriate Amount. For images with large, relatively smooth expanses, you will likely use a lower value (or a higher one with a bit of noise reduction). With highly textural images like this one, you can use higher values, especially when an image is as soft as this one. I find for this image, I leave Amount at the maximum, but with a small amount of Reduce Noise. This is unusual!
- Finally, if either the shadows or highlights exhibit artifacts that the other controls don't address without compromising the sharpening, you can fade the sharpening from them. For these controls, the Radius is that of an area that should be averaged and judged to be a shadow or highlight area. Tonal Width is how much of the tonal range should be considered a shadow or highlight. Fade Amount is how much to reduce the sharpening in that part of the tonal range.

Unsharp Mask

Some longtime Photoshop users are familiar with, and might recommend, this filter. However, unlike Smart Sharpen, it does *not* do active edge or detail detection. Instead, it relies on the user to indicate what an edge is by specifying how brightness differs from one side of the edge to the other using a Threshold slider.

The algorithm used by the Unsharp Mask filter resides in Smart Sharpen too. If you'd like to compare algorithms, simply choose Gaussian rather than Lens Blur from the Remove menu in the Smart Sharpen dialog.

Some use Unsharp Mask with low Amount and high Radius settings to add local contrast to an image. I think there are also better ways to do that: Clarity or Texture in the Camera Raw filter, for example.

Curious about the name? It's derived from a clever and very old film technique that literally masked (hid) the unsharp areas of an image. I used that technique a few times when I had access to lots of film and darkroom time.

Camera Raw Sharpening

When processing a raw image in Adobe Camera Raw or Lightroom, we find what is likely the best is to sharpen in the Detail panel. We can also access this fabulous tool with Photoshop's Camera Raw filter. In the ACR interface, tapping the Q key presents a before-and-after view (the letter is Y in Lightroom).

Go to the Detail panel to sharpen and control noise. Also click the disclosure arrow next to Sharpening to see all its controls.

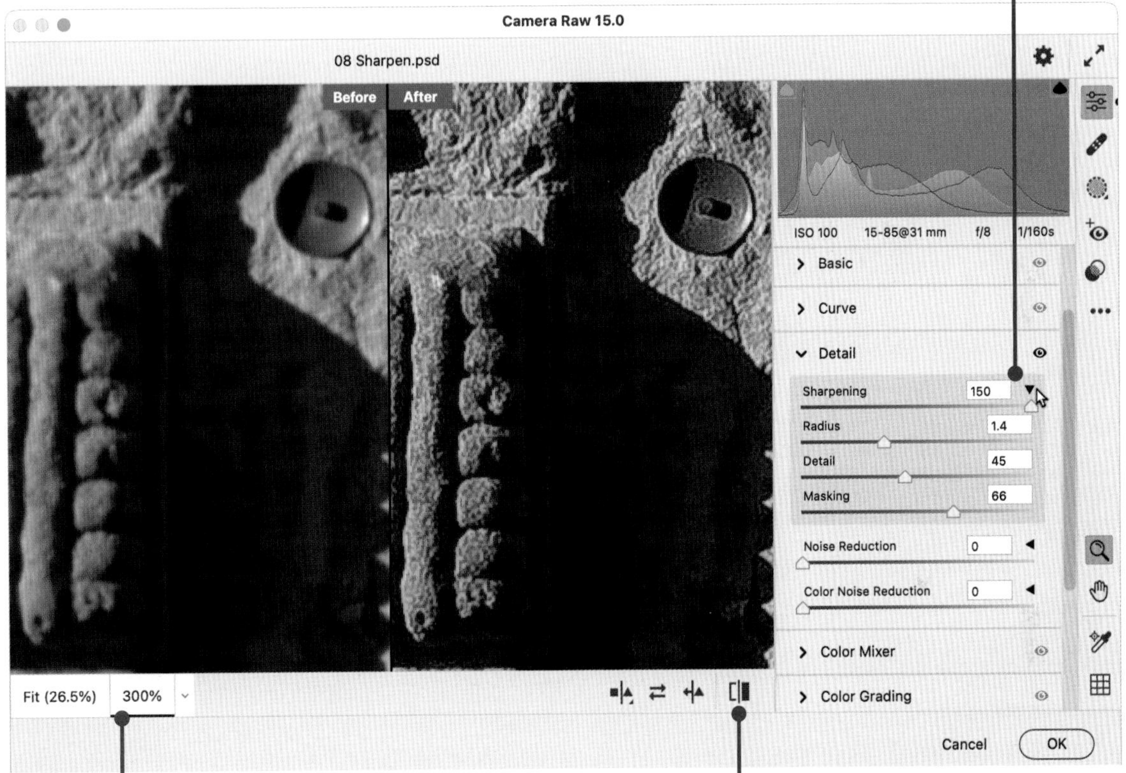

Magnification

Access the Before/After view. You can tap Q (or Y in Lightroom) to do so.

Two of the four sliders are very similar to those in Smart Sharpen: Amount and Radius. Just like in Smart Sharpen, Amount controls the amount of contrast enhancement at the edges, and Radius defines how broad those edges are. Remember that sharpening is just careful contrast enhancement at edges in our images.

There are two additional sliders as well: Detail and Masking. Some edges are around extremely tiny elements in an image, like noise. Some are around larger objects. Detail is a way to indicate the scale of those details that are sharpened. A value of 100 means that all details, no matter how small, will be sharpened equally. This can accentuate noise. Interestingly, 0 still allows sharpening, but *most strongly* of the largest edges. Detail shifts sharpening's *emphasis*.

The Masking slider is a work of inspired genius. This one control embodies a clever multi-step workflow developed by the late Photoshop master Bruce Fraser that sharpens only strong edges and allows no sharpening at all in some areas. Higher values protect areas like skin tones (so pores don't get sharpened), but the strong contrast edges of eyelashes will ensure that they are sharpened nicely. To see exactly which areas will be masked, hold down option/Alt while dragging the Masking slider. Areas shown in white will be sharpened, areas in black won't. **Note**: While holding down that key, you'll see the word "Reset" in many places. Clicking Reset Detail, for example, will restart the sharpening process.

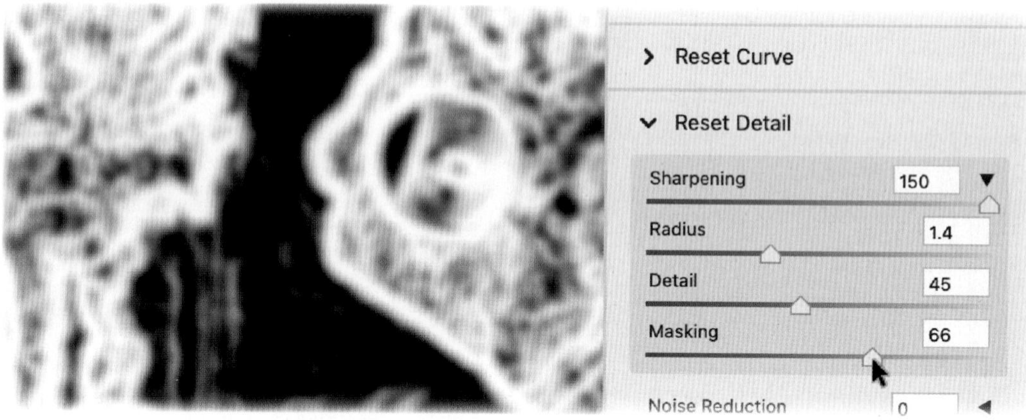

In fact, each of those sliders offers a different view if you hold down the option/Alt key as you drag them. Amount will show you a grayscale version of the image so you can focus on the tonal details (like edge contrast). With Detail, option/Alt gives you a better idea of which edges are being emphasized by sharpening.

If sharpening makes an image's noise more apparent, there are elaborate controls for Noise Reduction below those for Sharpening in the same Detail panel.

Texture

Although the Filter menu is divided into categories, I categorize them a little differently. Many filters can fall into multiple categories. Of course, Photoshop users find unintended uses for filters too. Not for the last time, I encourage you to explore and play!

Add Noise & Grain

Whether I'm trying to simulate film grain (or sensor noise) or add texture to a surface, Filter > Noise > Add Noise… and the Grain filter within the Filter Gallery are useful. Note that only 8-bit/channel images are compatible with the Filter Gallery.

Reduce Noise

It's always best to deal with noise in images as close to capture as possible: That's why my camera is set to capture raw files, and I deal with noise in either Lightroom or Adobe Camera Raw. However, we are sometimes given images that retain noise that is distracting or unpleasant.

Choose Filter > Noise > Reduce Noise…. Note that there are two kinds of noise: luminance (managed with the Strength slider) and color (managed with the Reduce Color Noise slider). Reducing luminance noise risks blurring away actual details, so the dialog offers a slider that forces the filter to find and Preserve Details. If in the course of reducing noise the overall effect still looks soft, use the Sharpen Details slider. You will likely find yourself cycling through the sliders as you compromise the settings of one with the others. If you determine that most of the noise is on one color channel (often, that's the Blue channel), you can enable Advanced mode. This simply lets you control noise reduction on each channel individually.

Median

As the name implies, this filter performs a kind of average. With a minute Radius setting (like 1), this filter will look at the color values of the pixels surrounding each pixel in the image. It then assigns the middle values to the pixel under examination. Larger Radius values mean more pixels are being averaged.

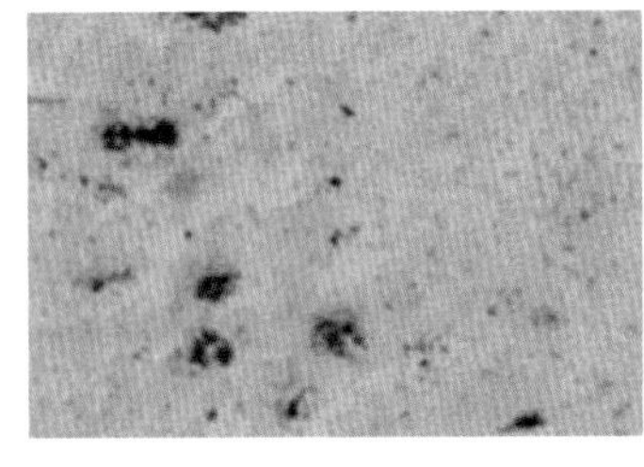

Original

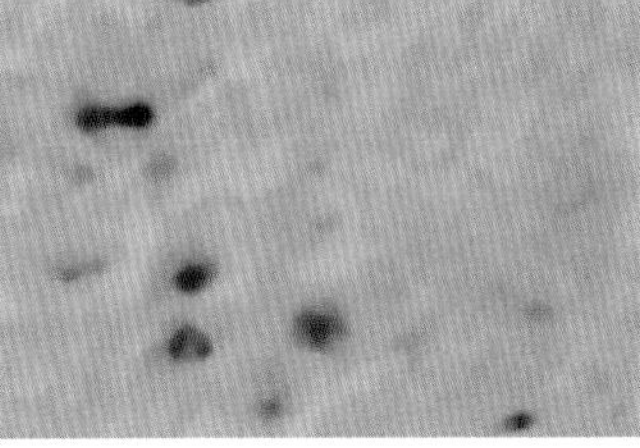

With 4 pixel Median
(that's a high value, usually)

The benefit is that tiny blemishes or damage in an image can be eliminated, while still preserving edges. Get to this filter by choosing Filter > Noise Median....

Creation

Something from nothing! That's what these filters provide. Well, most of the filters in Filter > Render can be applied to an empty layer (or Smart Object). There are two exceptions: Flame and Lens Flare. Those need a little preparation.

Clouds & Fibers

Many creative recipes require multiple ingredients. This is why I often use filters in combination to achieve the results I seek. When I need a random starting texture, these two filters can provide that.

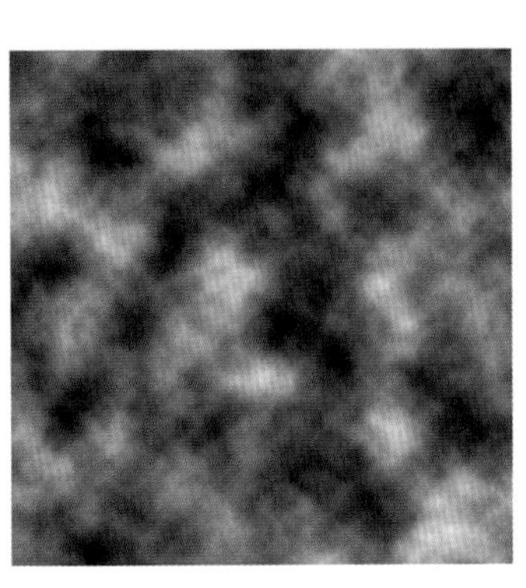

Clouds

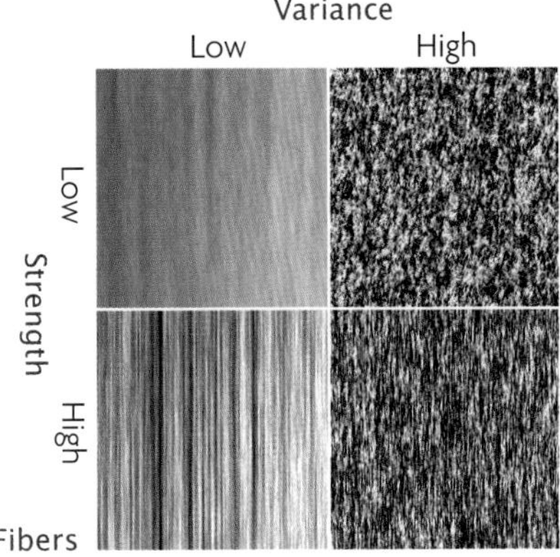

Fibers

Sadly, the Clouds filter doesn't make nice clouds that you'd use in a sky. And what results from the Fibers filter does not resemble fabric. Both create a random image using the current foreground and background colors, so you may wish to set those before applying either filter.

Clouds is completely random. Fibers, however, is guided randomness. It has two properties you can adjust: Variance (higher values yield shorter "fibers") and Strength (higher values yield a more stretched or well-combed look).

Tree

Although there are many controls (menus and sliders) in this filter's dialog, there is a random element to it too. Algorithms that generate random results are often said to start with a "seed," which I find pleasantly punny with this filter.

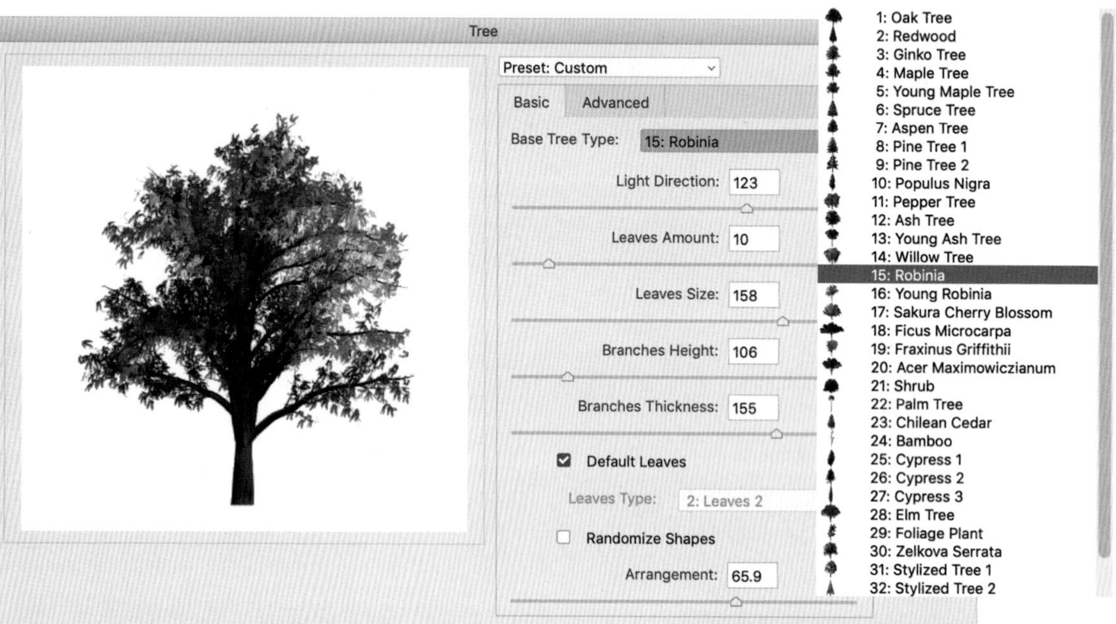

Choose the species (even fanciful Stylized Trees) with either matching Default Leaves or leaves from a different species. Light Direction can be from any angle, from the left to the right of the tree. The other sliders control the density of branches and foliage. The Advanced tab allows you to control the color and contrast of the leaves and branches. When you choose Flat Shading, Photoshop creates a more cartoon-like result. Camera Tilt changes the altitude of the viewer: At 0, the viewer is assumed to be at the tree's base gazing upward, with higher values elevating the camera and tilting it down. Finally, Leaves Rotation Lock gives a better sense of the leaves' shapes with a face-on view of them.

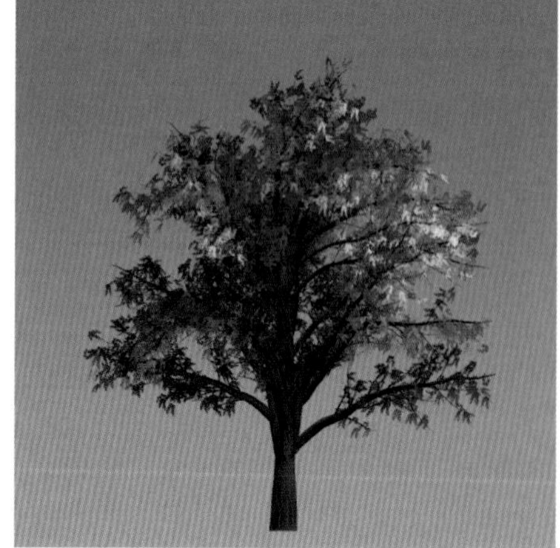

Flame

This filter needs a path no longer than 3000 pixels to indicate the base or source of the flames. Use one of the Pen tools or other vector shape tools, configuring the tool to draw a Path (rather than Shape) in the Options Bar. Once drawn, create an empty layer to hold the flame, then choose Filter > Render > Flame….

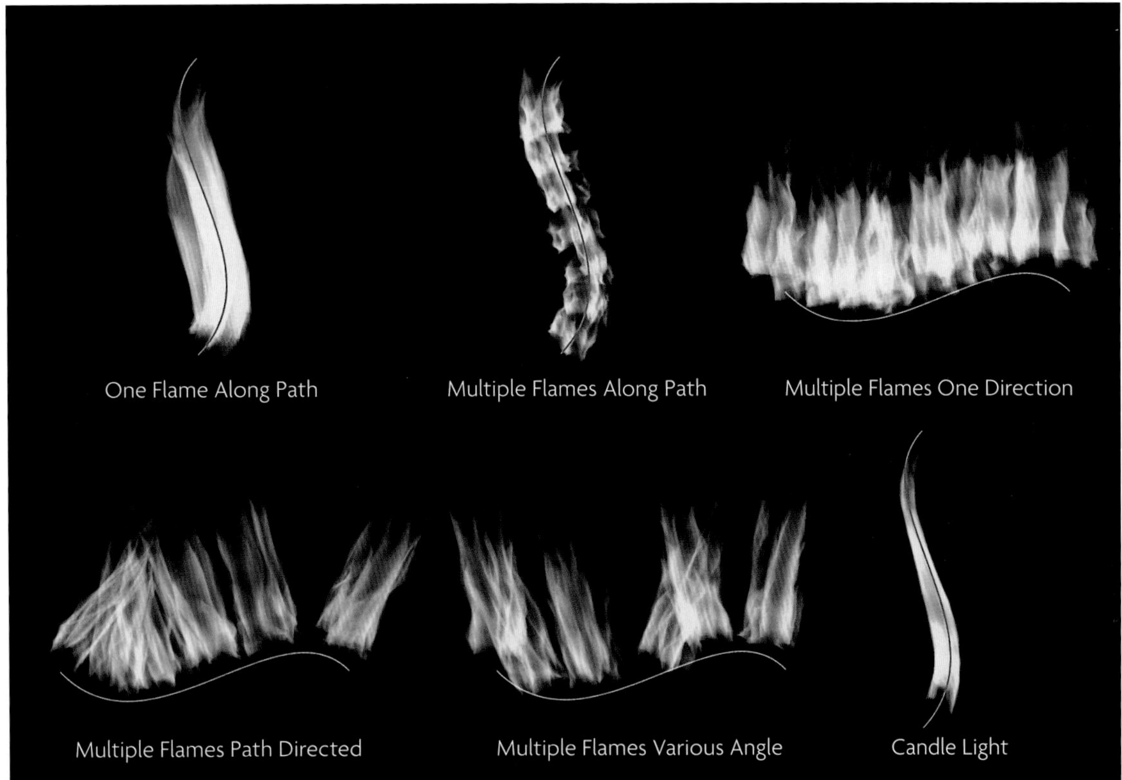

This filter has an extraordinary number of parameters to configure. Whether you desire a single candle flame or a raging inferno, you should be able to get it configured. Note that not all parameters are available for all Flame Types (illustrated above). For example, Angle rotates the flames from their default for two types: that would be vertical with Multiple Flames One Direction, and perpendicular to the path you drew for Multiple Flames Path Directed. For Multiple Flames Various Angle, Angle sets the range for random rotations for each flame.

The Length and Width of each flame are easily controlled, as is the Interval, or space between multiples. If you put the flame along a closed path (a "loop"), ensure that Adjust Interval for Loops is checked to have even spacing. The best-looking flames are attained with Quality set to Fine, but expect to wait some time for them to render. All of the illustrated examples use Medium quality. Each path is also shown here for your reference, but the path won't be part of the resulting flame normally.

The Advanced tab has even more options. The Turbulent and Jag sliders control the undulations of the flames in a coarse or fine way, respectively. To make the bottom of each flame more aligned with each other and your path, use a low number for Flame Bottom Alignment. If you wish to be able to consistently repeat a specific look, disable Randomize Shapes, then use the Arrangement slider. If all the other settings are the same, you'll get the same results.

The flame's shape and style can also be chosen, as illustrated below. In all of these examples, the paths were drawn either from the bottom up or from left to right. You may get inverted results otherwise.

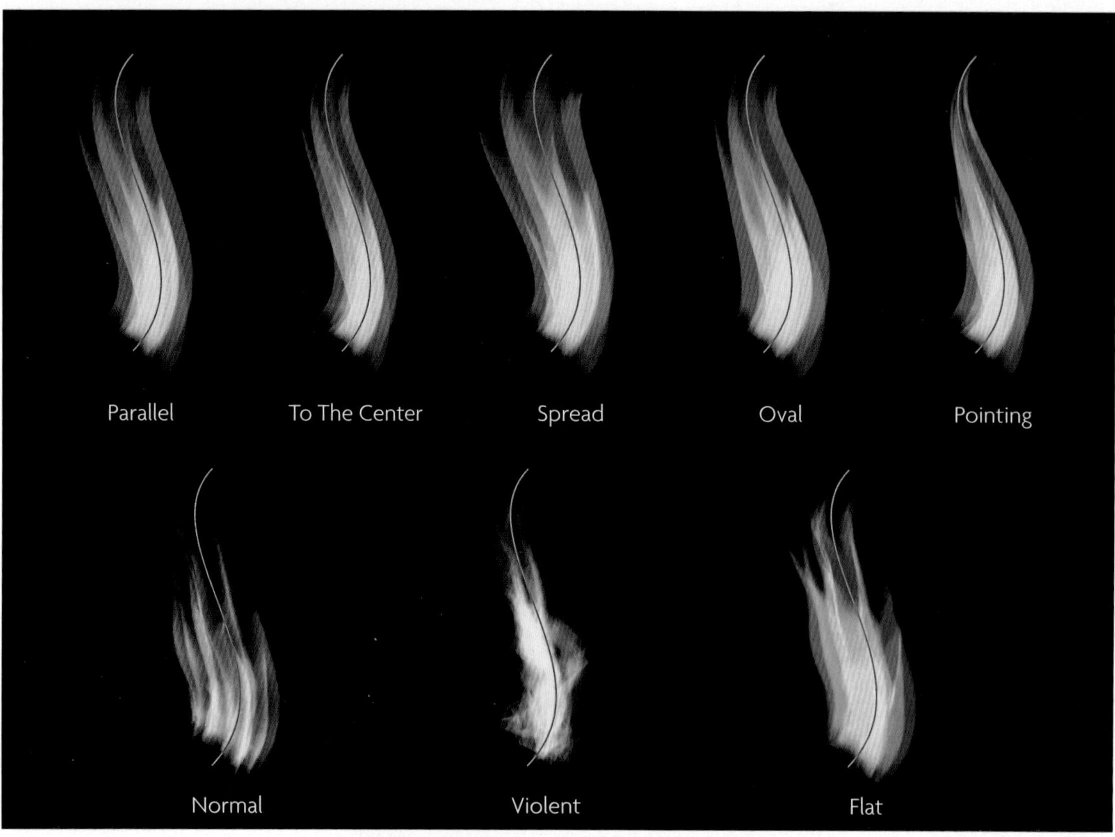

We can set a tree alight with the Flame filter. Here, I changed the background behind a tree created with the Tree filter to black (for a nighttime look), and added a red spotlight on the tree with the Lighting Effects filter to create a fiery glow.

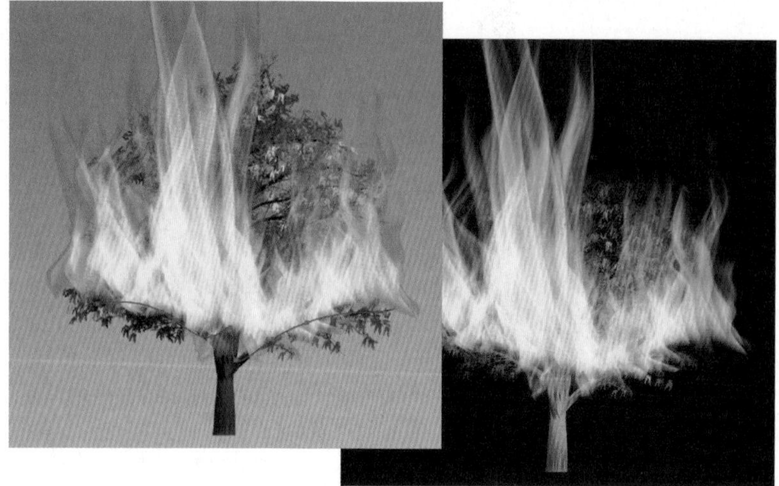

Lens Flare

This filter simulates the flare that sometimes occurs when making a photograph with a strong light source in the frame. Although you can apply this filter to an image layer directly, or more wisely to a Smart Object, I almost always use a layer filled with black. To revisit my settings later, I make that black-filled layer a Smart Object. This makes it easier to colorize the flare to better match the color of the light source in the image.

I also use the Info panel to note the light source's position; that is, its distance (in pixels) from the image's left and top edges.

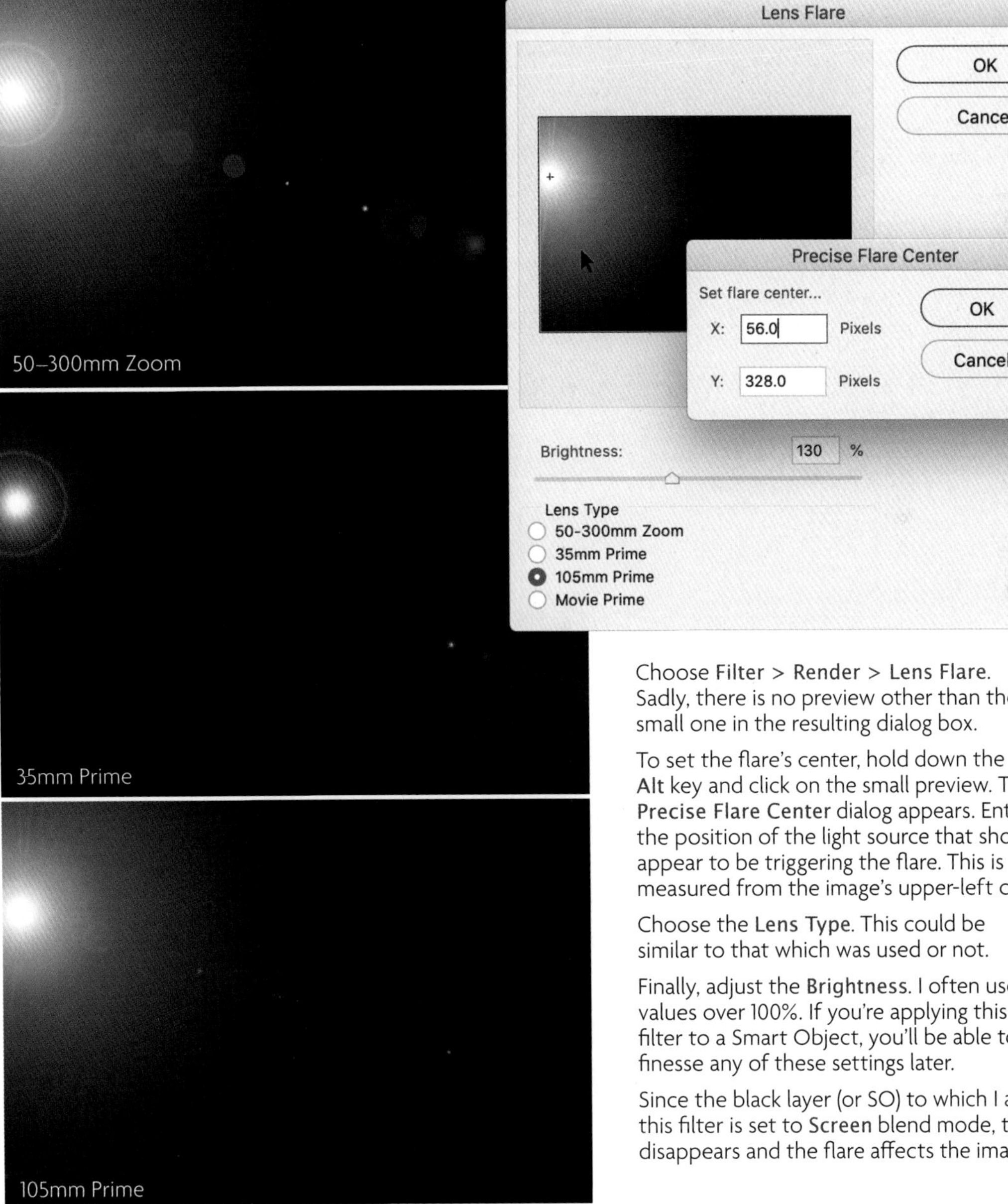

Choose **Filter > Render > Lens Flare**. Sadly, there is no preview other than the small one in the resulting dialog box.

To set the flare's center, hold down the **option/Alt** key and click on the small preview. The **Precise Flare Center** dialog appears. Enter the position of the light source that should appear to be triggering the flare. This is measured from the image's upper-left corner.

Choose the **Lens Type**. This could be similar to that which was used or not.

Finally, adjust the **Brightness**. I often use values over 100%. If you're applying this filter to a Smart Object, you'll be able to finesse any of these settings later.

Since the black layer (or SO) to which I apply this filter is set to **Screen** blend mode, the black disappears and the flare affects the image below.

I create a black fill layer and convert it to a Smart Object. I set the black SO layer's blend mode to Screen (the black vanishes, but the flare will remain).

After the Lens Flare filter is applied, and if the light in the image has a notable color, I apply an adjustment (like Photo Filter) to the Smart Object.

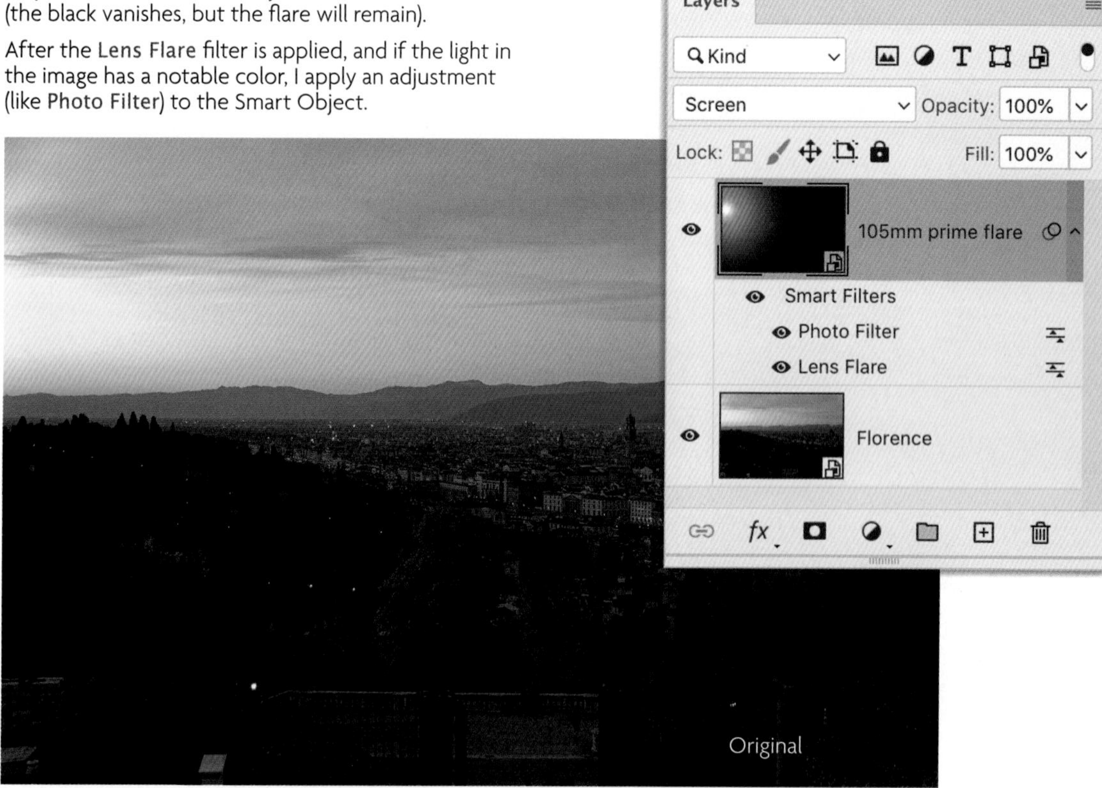

Original

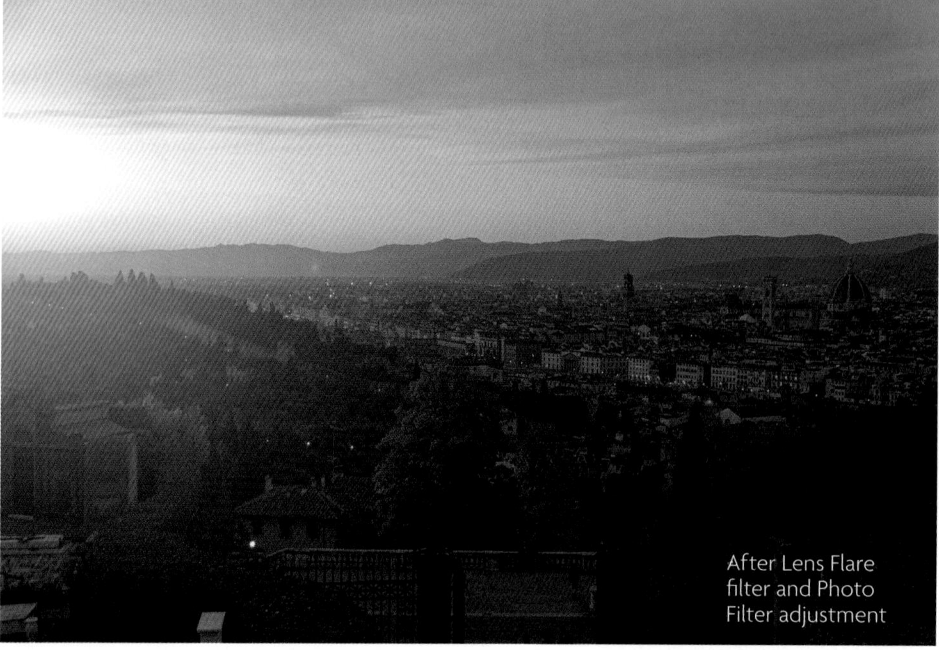
After Lens Flare filter and Photo Filter adjustment

Artifying

The majority of the filters that I put in this category attempt to make one medium (photography, usually) appear to be made in another. Be sure to look at the neural filters as well (see "Creative" on page 299).

Oil Paint

I've heard heated conversations about this filter and whether or not it can make a photo look like an oil painting. On a couple of occasions, I've used it to create a usable interpretation of a photo that was decently composed but either lacked sharpness or had some other flaw. Perhaps I'm not as critical of this filter as some folks because I'm not a painter!

The dialog that appears when you choose Filter > Stylize > Oil Paint offers several parameters to adjust to get the look you desire.

The greatest impact is had with first two, Stylization and Cleanliness, which control stroke smoothness and length. High Stylization and low Cleanliness yield a more Van Gogh–like look, while reversing those sliders yields a more subtle result. Scale controls the paint's thickness, and Bristle Detail controls the depth of the ruts left by the bristles in each stroke. Control how light interacts with the paint by adjusting the Angle and Shine sliders.

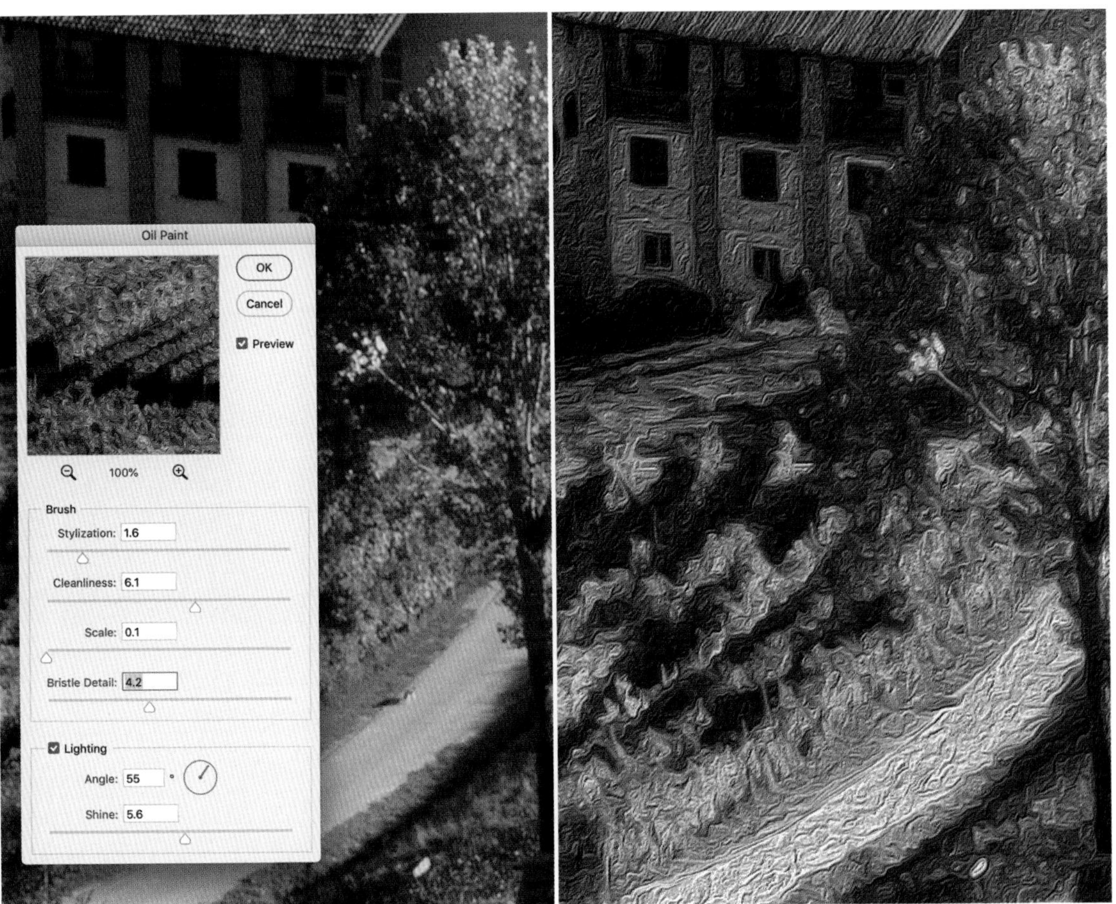

Halftones

A halftone is the dot pattern you see when a printed image is magnified. Of course, this is typically a necessity of making a printed piece, but many like it as an aesthetic.

There are at least three ways to create a halftone effect in Photoshop. There are two filters, discussed below, which simulate true halftones. The process that generates a true halftone, but only with black dots, involves converting an image to Grayscale mode, and then to a mode called Bitmap, choosing a halftone dot pattern and resolution along the way. The filters are easier and less of a commitment but are just effects, not true halftones. But for creative ends, that is just fine!

Color Halftone

This filter is accessed by choosing Filter > Pixelate > Color Halftone.... It generates a fairly good simulation of CMYK dots. In fact, I use its result to explain the four-color process to my students. In the filter dialog, you choose the dot size (Max. Radius) and the Screen Angle for each ink color. The defaults represent typical values used by printers, but they can be changed, of course. Unfortunately, there is no preview. You have to commit it to see the result. That's why it's always good to use a Smart Object.

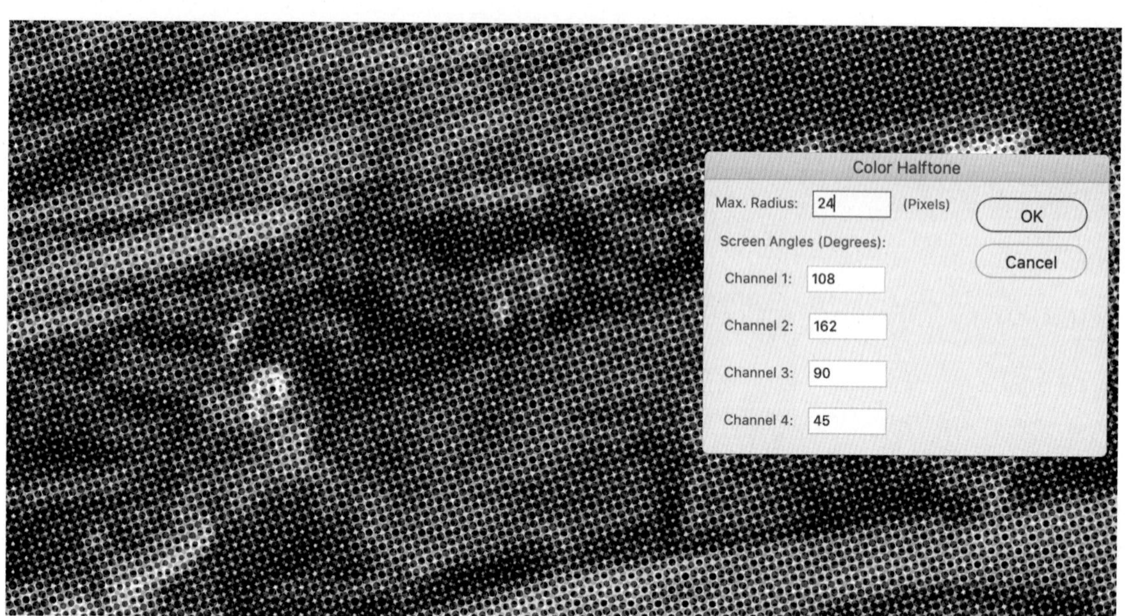

When the image is grayscale, we need only worry about the settings for the black dots. In either color or grayscale, the dots are opaque and vary in size: larger for dark areas, and smaller for light ones.

Filter Gallery Halftone

This filter creates a monochromatic halftone effect from color or grayscale images (but only in 8-bit/channel mode) using the current foreground color. It can be accessed from Filter > Filter Gallery.... Once there, you'll find Halftone in the Sketch section.

Its dots are more uniform in size, unlike a true halftone, but it does create light dots on black for dark areas, and dark dots on white for light ones, like a halftone should. It also makes rather muddy dots, unless you increase its Contrast setting. Finally, it can produce circles or lines instead of dots, if you prefer.

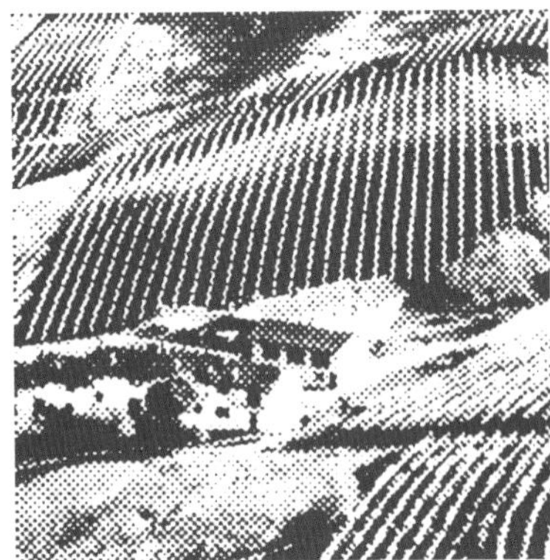
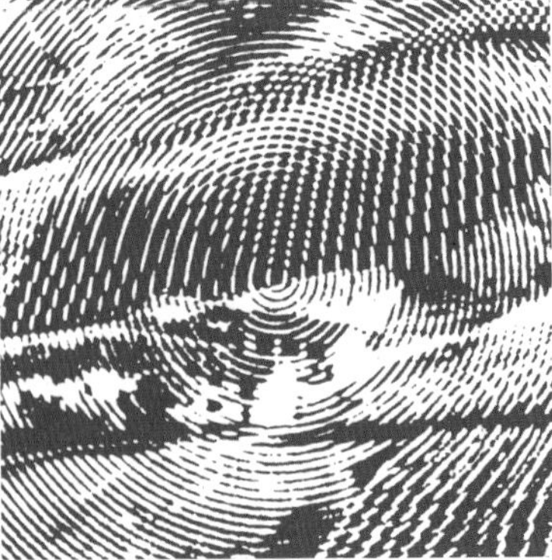
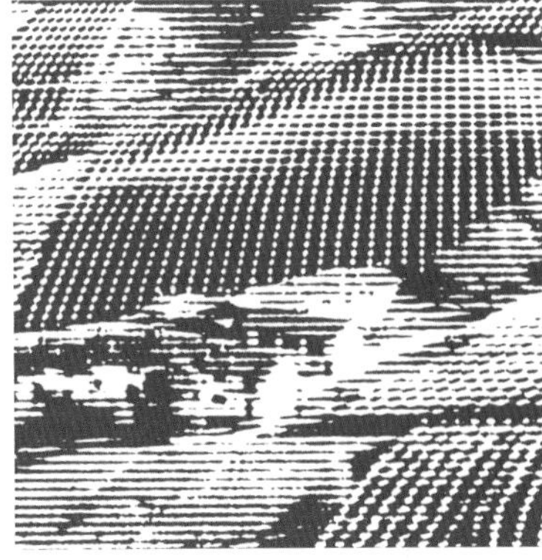

Other Filter Gallery Examples

Note that Filter Gallery filters do not work in 16- or 32-bit/channel modes. But if you create a Smart Object of one or more layers while in those modes, you can then convert the containing document to 8 bits/channel, retaining the greater bit depth inside the SO.

But the name "Gallery" should be a small hint of the good news: The many filters in the Filter Gallery can be combined in a way similar to applying multiple filters to a Smart Object. Go to Filter > Filter Gallery... and plan to experiment with the nearly 50 effects you find there.

For quicker access to these filters in the Filter menu, enable Show all Filter Gallery groups and names in Preferences > Plugins.

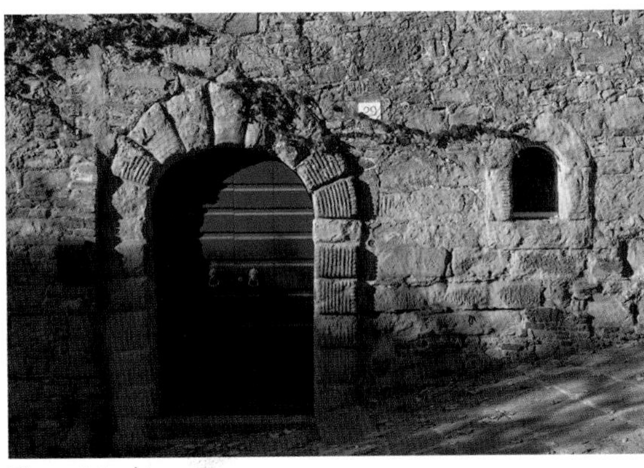
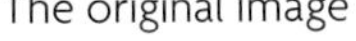
The original image

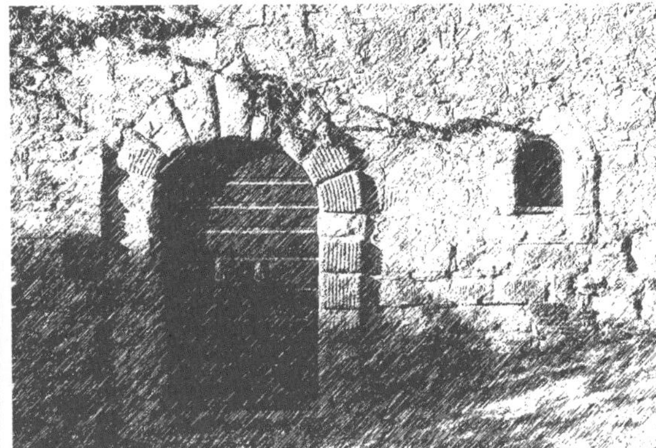
Filter Gallery: Sketch > Graphic Pen

Many of the filters in the Sketch and Artistic sections create strokes like those created by a brush, pen, etc. Their length, width, intensity, and resulting contrast are often the parameters you can adjust. Some, like the Graphic Pen filter, will use the current foreground color.

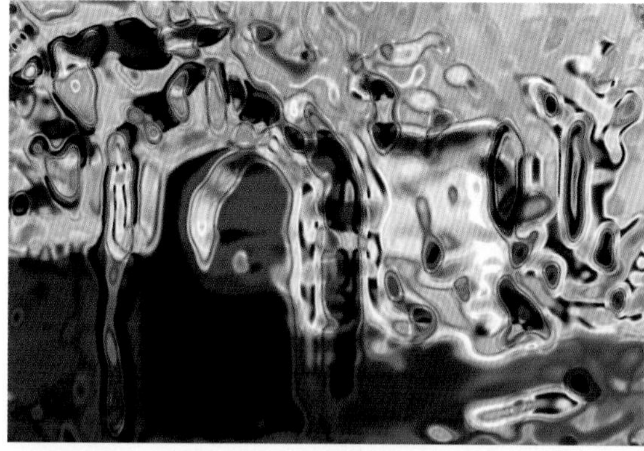

Filter Gallery: Sketch > Chrome
It's best if a Gaussian Blur is applied before, and some contrast enhancement is performed after (using Curves, Levels, or Brightness/Contrast).

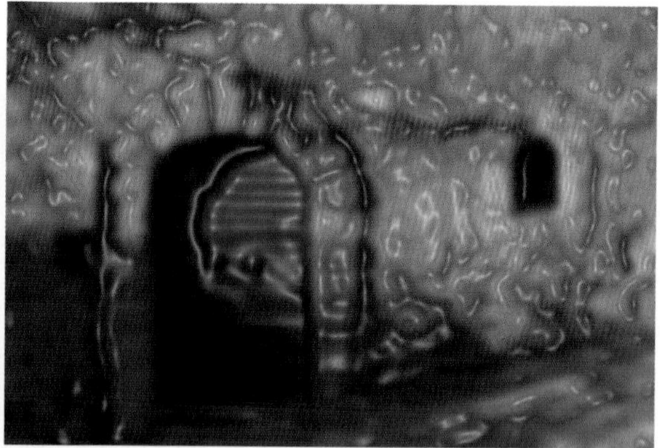

Filter Gallery: Artistic > Plastic Wrap
This one benefits from a Gaussian Blur first.

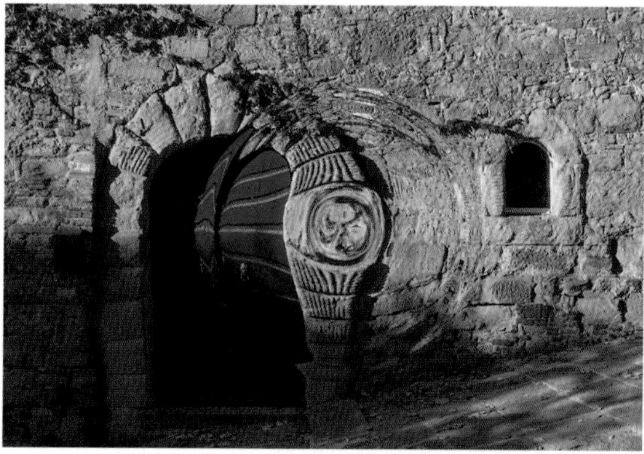

Filter Gallery: Distort > Glass
To be truly useful, you need to create a grayscale image to map how the glass's thickness varies.

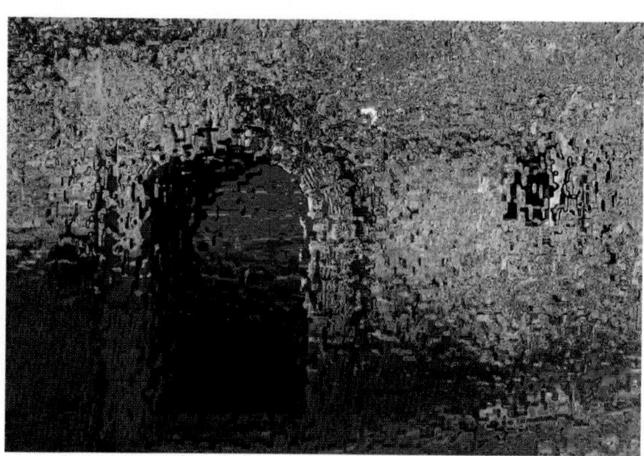

Filter Gallery: Distort > Ocean Ripple

I use Chrome and Plastic Wrap to create indistinct reflections. It helps to blur the image first.

Some filters use grayscale images as "maps" to control distortion or shading. A Glass filter texture map shows how the glass's thickness changes with gradation. Areas with no transitions are flat glass and don't distort. The center of the map used here acts a bit like a lens.

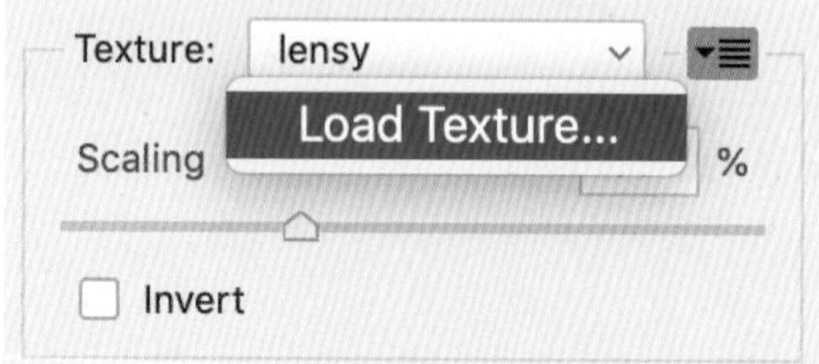

The default choices for Texture in the Glass filter are a bit cheesy. It's almost always worth loading a custom one. See the text above for more on that.

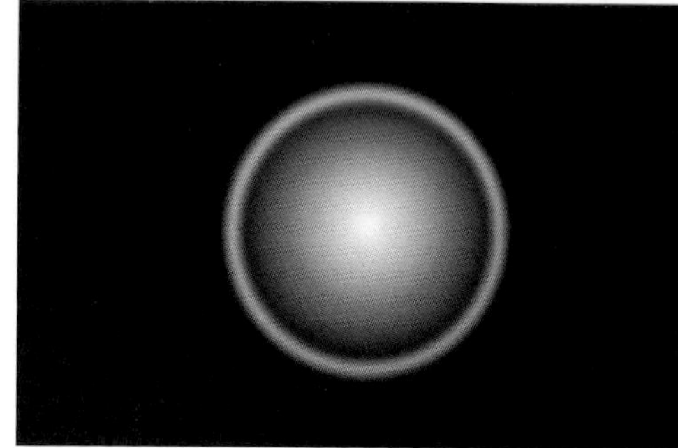

Distortion

Time for some bending and twisting! When you visit the Filter > Distort menu, try to keep in mind that not all the names should be taken at face value. For example, the Pinch filter can bloat things if you use a negative Amount. Some of these filters are quite simple, others require preparation, and some are as deep as small software applications.

There are also several filters in the Filter Gallery that distort. Examples of Glass and Ocean Ripple are shown in the previous section.

Pinch versus Spherize

Neither of these filters previews in the document window, but they do have their own small preview panes. Spherize bloats and Pinch pinches, with positive Amount values, and the opposite is true with negative values. I would describe the distortion produced by Pinch as looser, and that produced by Spherize as better delineated at its elliptical edge. Both distort elliptical areas (circular if the image is square).

When applying these filters to a selected area, the results differ depending on whether the layer is a Smart Object or just a pixel layer. If it's an SO, the entire image is distorted, but a filter mask is created to hide the parts outside the original selection. If the layer is an ordinary pixel layer, then the distortion will take place only within the selection, blending in with the undistorted pixels at the edge—*but the selection needs to be elliptical.*

Liquify

The Liquify filter (Filter > Liquify) was another program that Adobe bought and re-engineered. With it, we can sculpt an image, pushing pixels to and fro. It's powerful and fun. You have certainly seen its use in fashion photography to augment or diminish subjects' attributes.

This filter has face detection, noting the presence of faces and letting you target each one so you can add a smile or frown or adjust other parts of the face's structure with sliders or the Face tool. The effect of these sliders is less dramatic than it is with the Smart Portrait neural filter (page 298). But Liquify's other tools offer manual (and possibly extreme) manipulation. Each uses a "brush" that can be resized with sliders, or more quickly with the bracket keys ([or]). Most notable is the Forward Warp tool, used to sculpt an image.

I use the Twirl Clockwise tool to curl hair or flip paper corners. Holding option/Alt twirls counterclockwise. Pucker and Bloat shrink or enlarge what's within the brush perimeter.

The Mask tools are used to protect areas of the image (Freeze Mask tool) or allow editing (Thaw Mask tool). To correct distortion that is too abrupt, use the Smooth tool. To restore parts of the image either completely or partially to their original state, use the Reconstruct tool. Light dabs are best to gently nudge the image back to its pristine state. The Reconstruct... button provides a complete or partial undo of the whole adventure. It allows you to input how much of the total distortion remains. Dragging the slider triggers a preview so you needn't guess what value is right.

Finally, the Push Left tool creates a rather messy and uncontrollable distortion.

Tools

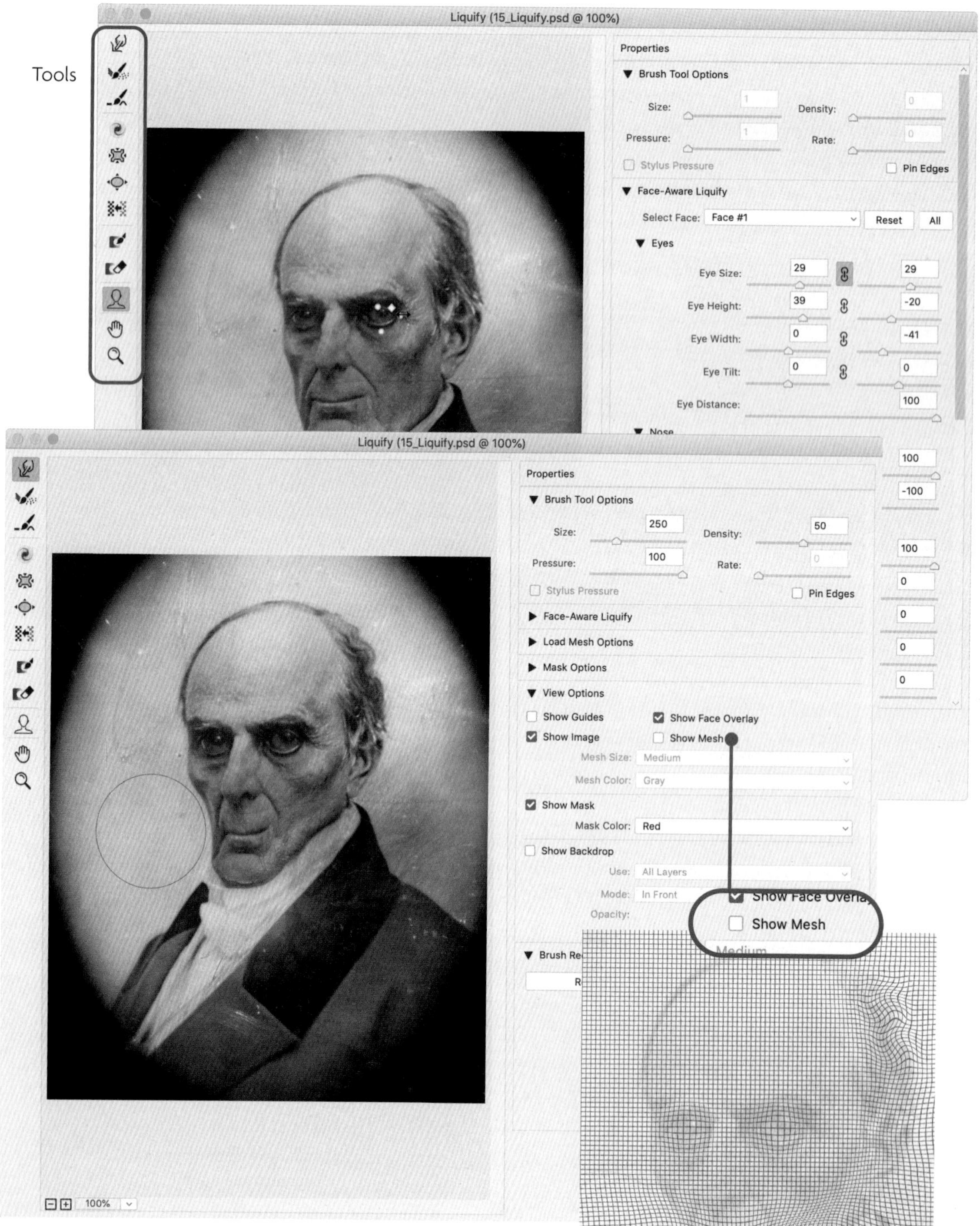

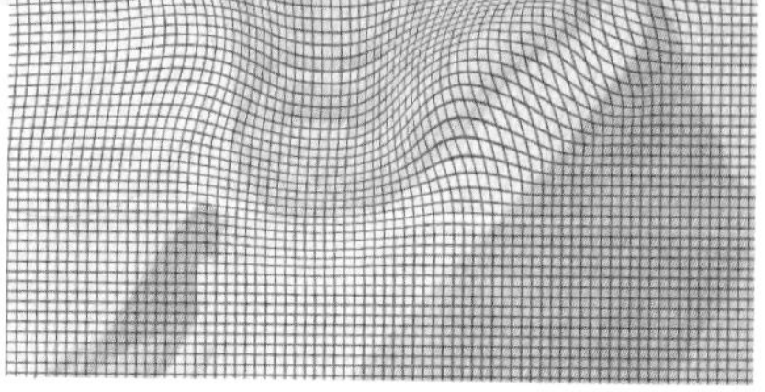

Top: Using Face-Aware Liquify with the Face tool and feature-adjusting sliders. Any face detected in the image can be edited separately.

Bottom: Using the Forward Warp tool for more dramatic image sculpting.

To evaluate the amount of distortion, enable Show Mesh (right).

Adaptive Wide Angle

When dealing with an image captured with a wide-angle lens, especially a fish-eye lens, lines that were straight in the world may be curved in the image. This is also true when creating a panoramic image with File > Automate > Photomerge…. The Adaptive Wide Angle filter allows you to choose lines in the image that you would like to straighten, likely at the cost of more distortion elsewhere.

Although this filter purports to help with correcting converging perspective lines common in photos of buildings, the Camera Raw filter has a better solution: see "Geometry Panel & Upright Perspective Correction" (page 365).

With panoramic images, however, this filter does a lovely job of straightening horizon lines that are curved if not composed in the image's center, for example. Simply drag the Constraint tool from one end of the horizon to the other.

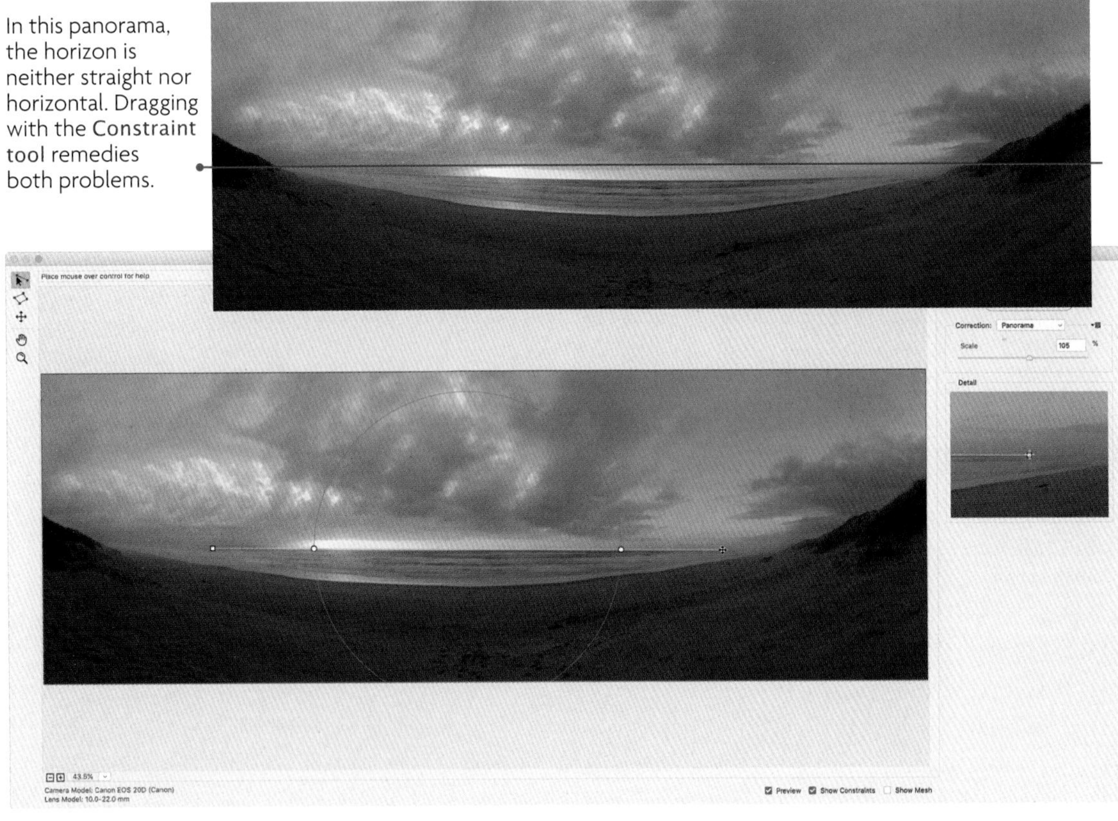

In this panorama, the horizon is neither straight nor horizontal. Dragging with the Constraint tool remedies both problems.

Wave & Ripple

These two filters, both of which are found by going to Filter > Distort, create undulations. The result of the Ripple filter is more uniform and geometric. The Wave filter provides from 1 to 999 wave generators, creating undulations of random wavelength and amplitude within ranges you specify. Imagine several people of various sizes bobbing in a pool, and the resulting wave action.

This guided randomness yields a more "natural" distortion. Sadly, neither filter has more than a small preview in its dialog box.

The Wave filter offers two other wave types besides the smooth Sine wave. Triangle yields a sawtooth distortion, and Square creates an offset block pattern.

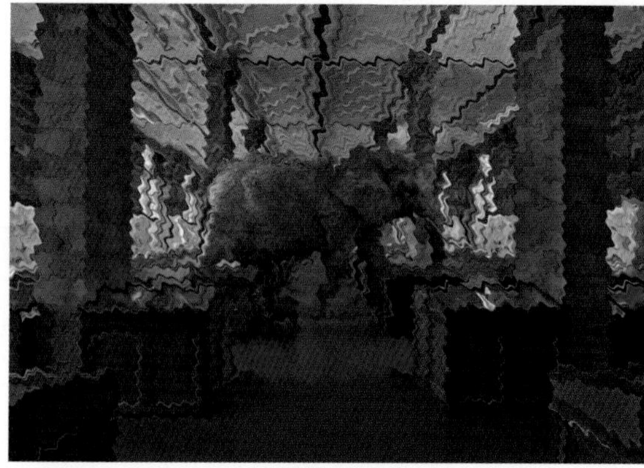

The **Ripple** filter creates relatively small and uniform undulations.

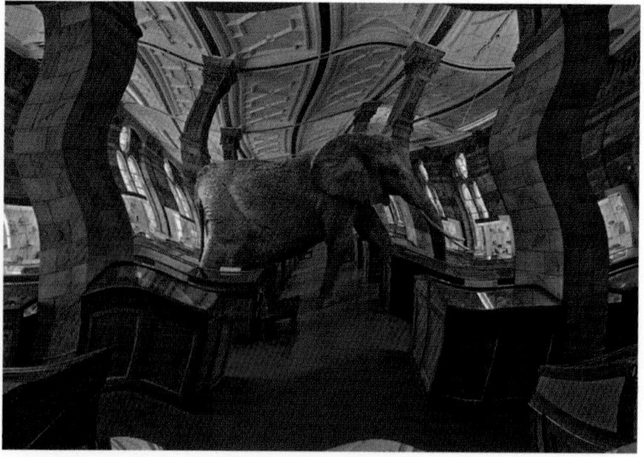

The **Wave** filter, using three "generators," creating **Sine**-wave distortions.

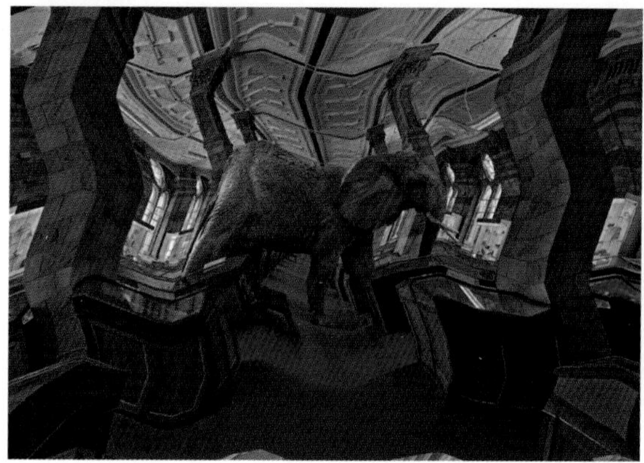

The **Wave** filter, using three "generators," creating **Triangle**-wave distortions.

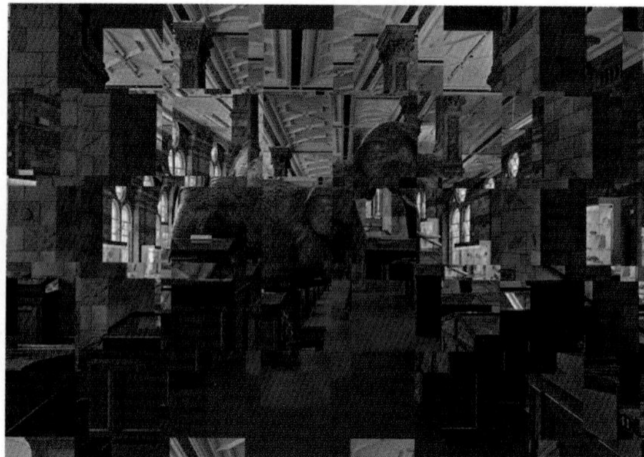

The **Wave** filter, using two "generators," creating **Square**-wave distortions.

Displace

With work, this filter can be an effective way to have an image appear to follow the convolutions of a dimensional subject. For example, I've used it to warp type around the curving pages of an open book. The difficult part is creating the required displacement "map."

This map needs to be a separate document whose channels' tones (shades of gray) control the horizontal and/or vertical displacement of the image to which the filter is applied. **Note:** The map document must be a PSD and, for ease, should have the same pixel dimensions as the one you're distorting.

If the displacement map is grayscale (has one channel), then its tonal values control both horizontal and vertical displacement; otherwise, the first two channels deal with horizontal and vertical displacement respectively. A displacement map filled with 50% gray causes no displacement at all. Lighter shades move the distorted image's pixels left and/or up; darker shades move the pixels right and/or down. If the map pixels are white, 127 levels above middle gray, then the image is shifted 127 pixels. If that's too much (or too little), the filter's dialog offers fields to enter a percentage by which to adjust the movement both horizontally and vertically. Since there is no preview, a lot of trial and error is required, so allot time for your experiments with this filter!

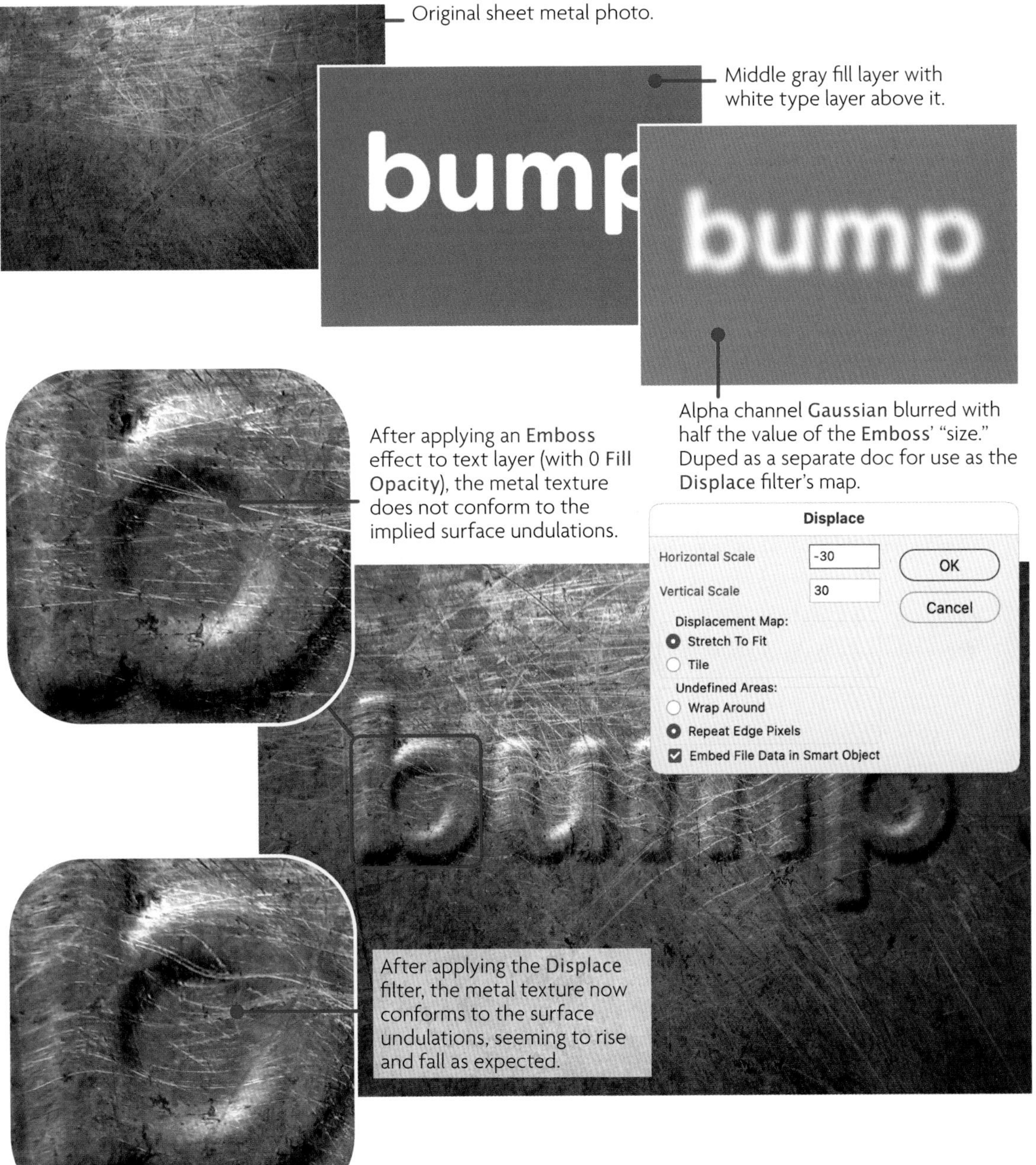

Original sheet metal photo.

Middle gray fill layer with white type layer above it.

Alpha channel Gaussian blurred with half the value of the Emboss' "size." Duped as a separate doc for use as the Displace filter's map.

After applying an Emboss effect to text layer (with 0 Fill Opacity), the metal texture does not conform to the implied surface undulations.

After applying the Displace filter, the metal texture now conforms to the surface undulations, seeming to rise and fall as expected.

I most often use the Displace filter to enhance the realism of other effects. In the example above, I created a type layer with the word "bump" in white. I applied an Emboss effect to that type layer and set its Fill Opacity to 0 to create the illusion that the sheet metal layer below was embossed. Sadly, the linear scratches in the metal image continued to run straight, weakening the illusion. So, I turned to the Displace filter.

To make the Displace filter's displacement map, I used the same type layer with normal opacity and the emboss disabled, and created a middle-gray color fill layer below the type. I simply duplicated one of the color channels (Red, Green, or Blue) by right-clicking it, creating an alpha channel. This I blurred with the Gaussian Blur filter set to a value half that of the Emboss effect's Size setting.

Unfortunately, the Displace filter requires that its map be a separate document. So I right-clicked the alpha channel, chose Duplicate Channel..., and specified New as the document where the dupe should go. This generates a new document, which I saved in a convenient place.

Now, all was ready—finally! I made the sheet metal image a Smart Object since I knew the first attempts would not be quite right. After a few attempts, I decided that the image pixels should be displaced up and right about 35–40 pixels, about 30% of what the Displace filter would do if Horizontal Scale and Vertical Scale were set to 100. So I used a value of 30 in both those fields in the filter's dialog box. However, the white parts of the displacement map image would move image pixels to the left, so I entered –30 into the Horizontal Scale field.

I was not concerned about whether the Displacement Map was stretched or tiled, as it was the same size as the image. Also, since the map was gray at the edges, I knew there would be no displacement there, and thus no Undefined Areas would result.

Polar Coordinates

In your favorite web browser, search for the phrase "cylinder mirror anamorphosis," and you'll see the premise behind this filter. My friend Blake Garner applies this filter, performs other distortions (the Wind filter, I believe), and then applies the Polar Coordinates filter again to convert back to rectangular coordinates. Fun!

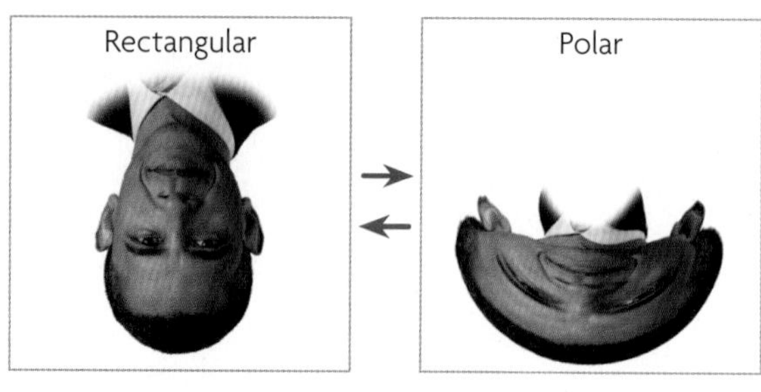

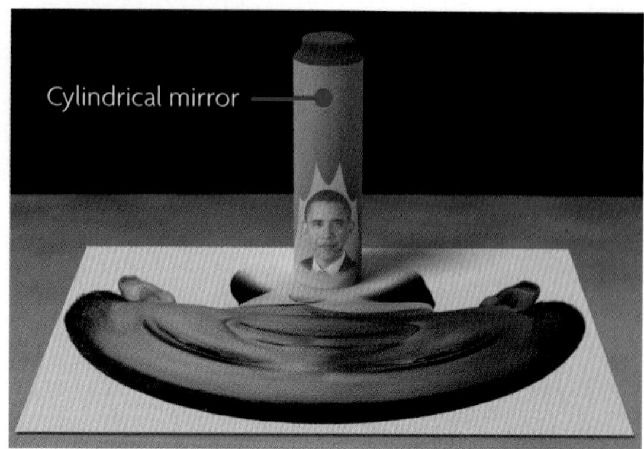

Historically, this "projection" allowed viewing hard-to-decipher anamorphic images with cylindrical mirrors.

If you should come upon a historic image distorted in this way, you can use this filter to convert it to rectangular coordinates, since it can convert in either direction.

Technical

The filters in Filter > Other tend to be for very special purposes. Here are the most commonly used of these hard-to-categorize filters.

Offset

Most practically, this filter is used to aid the creation of patterns. With it, we literally move, or "offset," the edges of an image. For example, if I were using an image that's 3000 pixels wide and 2000 pixels high, I might move the top edge down about 500 pixels and the left edge rightward about 700 pixels (I like to avoid moving the edges to the center).

Rather than leave a void at the top or left, the default behavior is to wrap the bottom of the image around to the top, and the right side around the left. When an image is made into a pattern, this is its behavior: it tiles. To ensure that obvious seams don't appear when the pattern is made, I retouch the offset image to make its former top and bottom edges transition more seamlessly into each other. The same with the left and right. I then repeat the Offset filter to see if my retouching introduced any new seams, which I remove. When repeated application of the Offset filter reveals no more odd transitions, I can use Edit > Define Pattern....

When set to Wrap Around, the Offset filter causes the former top and bottom edges of the image, as well as the former left and right edges, to abut.

When making a pattern, this can be useful: Use retouching tools to make the "seam" less obvious. Then reapply the filter, and retouch more. You can repeat these steps until there are no seams or obvious repeats, then use Edit > Define Pattern....

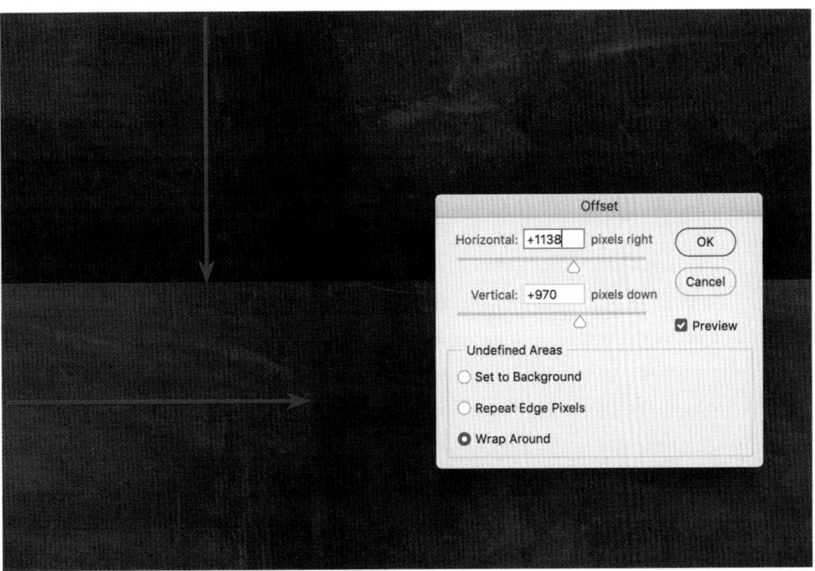

Maximum/Minimum

Useful almost exclusively for masks (or other occasional high-contrast grayscale images), the Maximum and Minimum filters make white areas larger or smaller, respectively, by the number of pixels you specify. If there are sharp turns (corners), you can choose Squareness from the Preserve menu to keep them corners. If you'd prefer to round them off, choose Roundness.

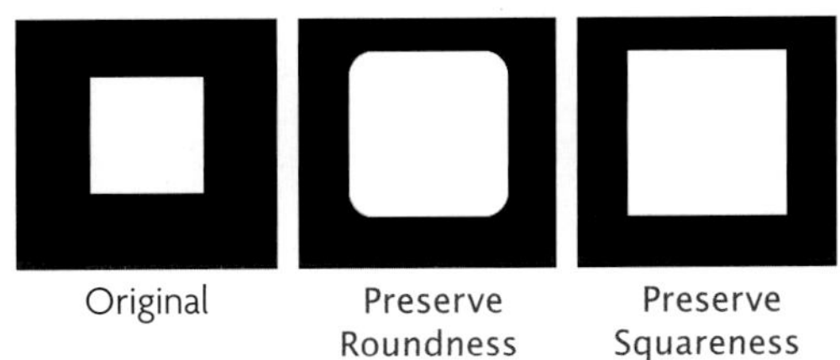

Original | Preserve Roundness | Preserve Squareness

High Pass

The Gaussian Blur filter is sometimes referred to as a low-pass filter because it keeps only low-frequency content. Fine details (high-frequency content) are lost when blurred. The High Pass filter is the opposite. Only fine details remain, and soft textures and blurriness are removed. The result is mostly middle gray with fine edges throughout.

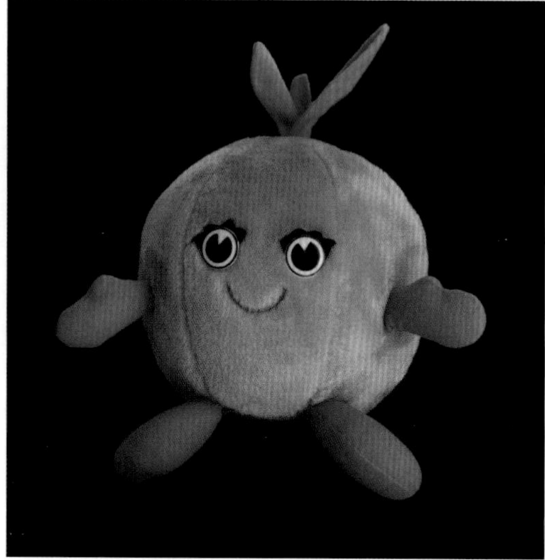

The original image

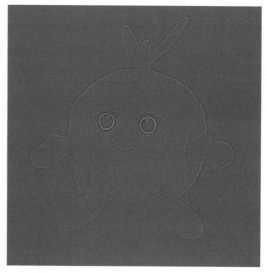

After the High Pass filter is applied
(I enhanced its contrast for this illustration)

When a blend mode that hides middle ray (Hard Light, Overlay, etc.) is applied to the result, only the edge details remain. When blended with the original image, the result is a sharper image. Some Photoshop old-timers claim this method has virtues. However, there are many new ways to sharpen that are superior and more direct. That said, there are a few multi-filter processes in which I've needed this filter to provide the stronger edge contrast I needed.

Transforms

Simply put, transforms are the ways in which we change the geometry (size, shape, and orientation) in our images. Note that you may not transform a Background layer at all, and it's best to transform Smart Objects whenever possible.

Free Transform

This function is the most widely used because it includes most of the other transformations. In fact, if you choose any of the transformations in the Edit > Transform menu, you're actually just activating Free Transform. So, for speed and ease, just use the shortcut ⌘-T/Ctrl-T.

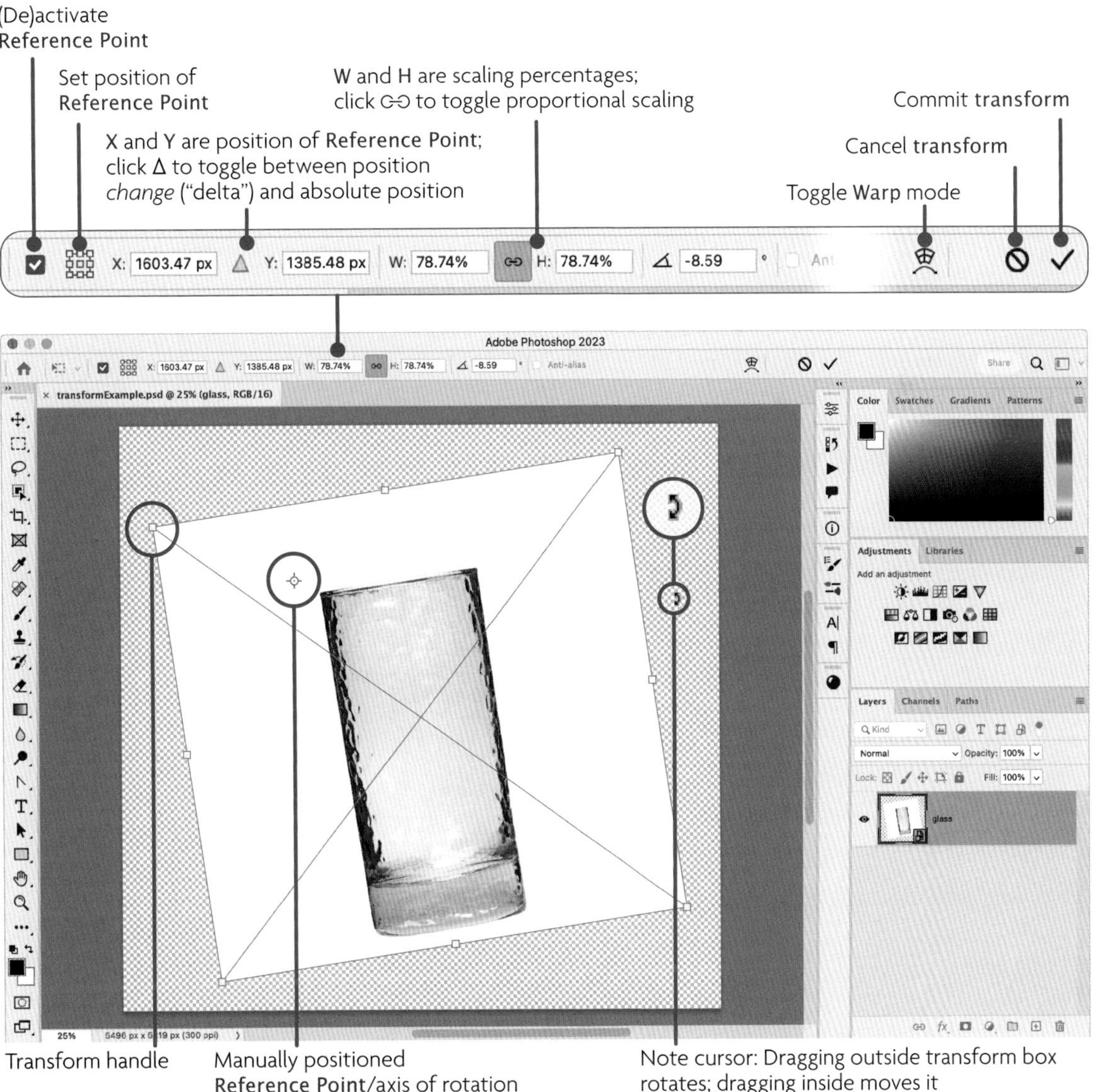
(De)activate Reference Point
Set position of Reference Point
X and Y are position of Reference Point; click Δ to toggle between position *change* ("delta") and absolute position
W and H are scaling percentages; click ⚯ to toggle proportional scaling
Toggle Warp mode
Cancel transform
Commit transform
X: 1603.47 px
Y: 1385.48 px
W: 78.74%
H: 78.74%
-8.59
Adobe Photoshop 2023
transformExample.psd @ 25% (glass, RGB/16)
Transform handle
Manually positioned Reference Point/axis of rotation
Note cursor: Dragging outside transform box rotates; dragging inside moves it

Filters & Transforms
Retouching & Reworking
Camera Raw & Lightroom
Extending Photoshop

Once activated, a box with transform handles appears and the Options Bar shows your transform's status and controls. I recommend activating the Reference Point so you can change the axis of rotation (if you need to rotate) and the point from which "centered" scaling happens. You'll also be able to monitor the absolute or relative position of each control handle—useful for precision transformations.

Note that by default, scaling is proportional. That is, the layer(s) or areas being scaled won't distort. If you want to allow disproportionate scaling (to affect the "aspect ratio"), either hold down shift as you scale, or click the chain (⊖) between the width and height scaling fields. Holding shift is an ad hoc toggle, whereas the chain button will remain in the state you choose until you click it again.

To commit a transform, click the check-mark button (✓) or press the return/Enter key. To cancel, either click the cancel button (⊘) or press the escape key. Just to the left of these two buttons is the Warp mode toggle. With this, you can go from geometric transforms to more fluid, freeform ones, and back.

Translation, Scaling, and Rotation

To scale in Free Transform, simply drag a control handle on the edge of the box. If the aspect ratio is being maintained (the chain is active between the W and H fields), hold shift to alter the shape of what's being transformed. Otherwise, shift will hold the aspect ratio.

To move ("translate") what's being transformed, just drag the box from anywhere within its interior. To rotate, drag outside the box. If you've activated the Reference Point, you'll see a small crosshair in the middle of the box. That is the axis of rotation. You can reposition it freely by dragging it to anywhere in the document window, or by clicking the small widget in the Options Bar to set it to one of the box's handles. Rotation will then act around that point.

A numeric position, scaling percentage, and rotation angle can be entered in the fields in the Options Bar.

Perspective Adjustment

If you ⌘/Ctrl-drag a corner, it moves alone. ⌘/Ctrl-dragging a side handle moves the corners on either side of it together. This is handy for creating quick perspective transforms. To correct perspective distortion, use the Camera Raw filter: see "Geometry Panel & Upright Perspective Correction" (page 365) to learn how.

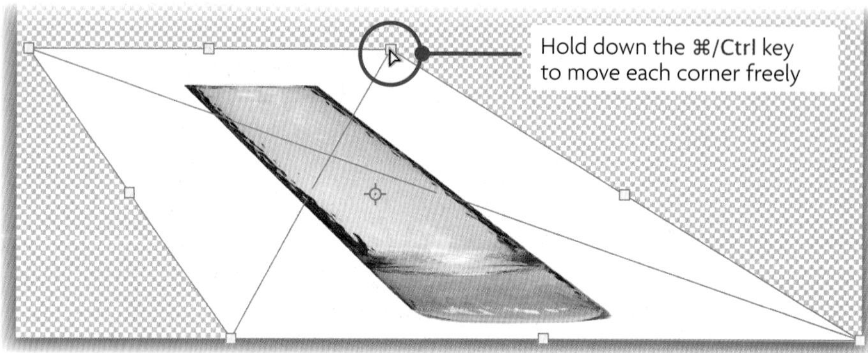
Hold down the ⌘/Ctrl key
to move each corner freely

Warping and Sculpting

For a less geometric and constraining transform, click the Warp button (⛫). I liken this to printing the image on a rubber sheet, then stretching and shrinking it in various ways across its extent.

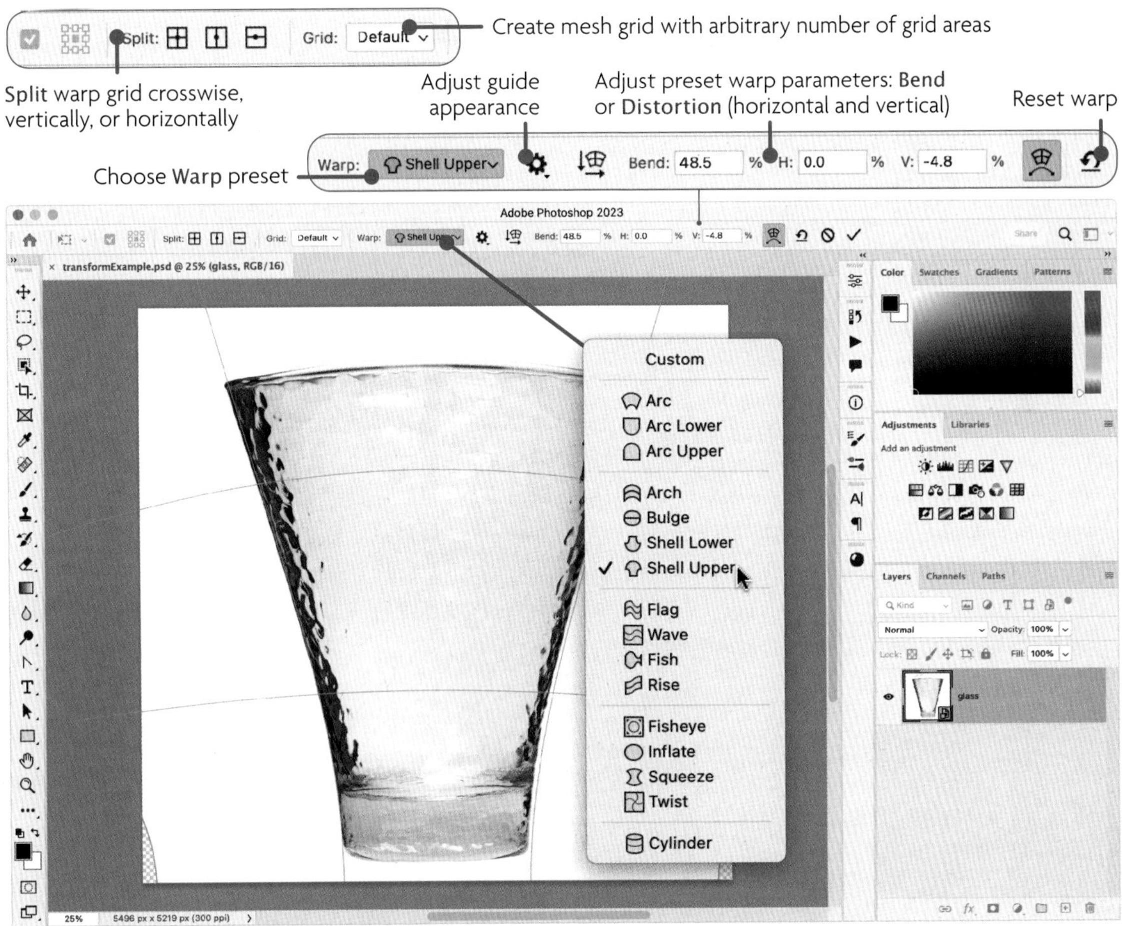

There are two fundamental ways to approach Warp transforms: with presets that can be adjusted or by using a warp grid. The 15 presets are found in a menu in the Options Bar labeled Warp. Each can be customized by adjusting the parameters to the right of that menu or manipulating the controls (small white squares) inside or along the edge of the transformation grid. The Options Bar controls can be "scrubbed": that is, dragging their names left or right changes their values.

The left side of the Options Bar (while in Warp mode) holds the means to create your own grid lines. Even with none, the canvas is considered a grid that can be dragged to distort the image upon it. The more grid lines there are, the more you can limit the scope of any distortion. You can drag any grid line, area, point, or handle on a point to distort the image up to the parts controlled by other grid lines.

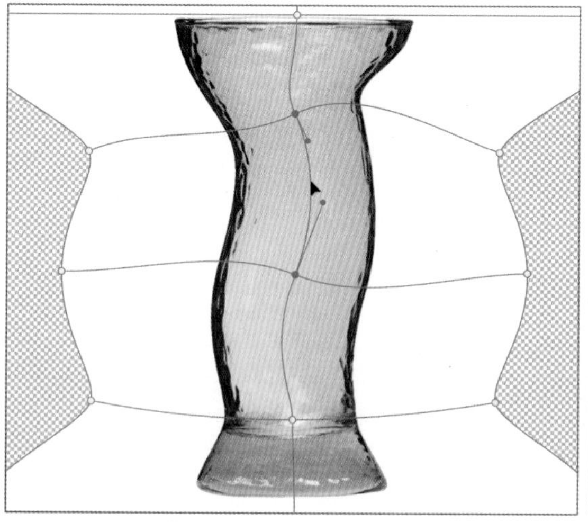

Dragging a **Warp** grid line to affect the areas on either side and the handles on the points at each end of that segment.

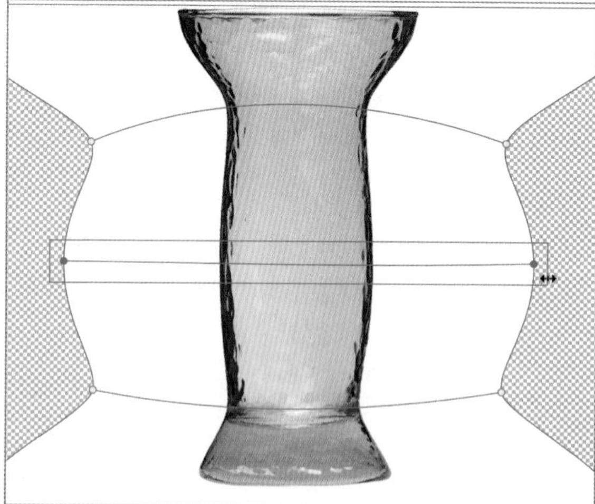

If you select multiple points (click to select one, **shift**-click to select others), a transform box surrounds them so they can be moved closer to or farther away from each other.

To create evenly spaced grid lines (and therefore areas and points) in whatever number you desire, use the Grid menu. To place lines one or two at a time, use the Split buttons. When you click a button, a grid line gets attached to your cursor. To place it, just move the cursor somewhere in the image then click to set it. The Crosswise Split button creates one horizontal and one vertical line intersecting where you click.

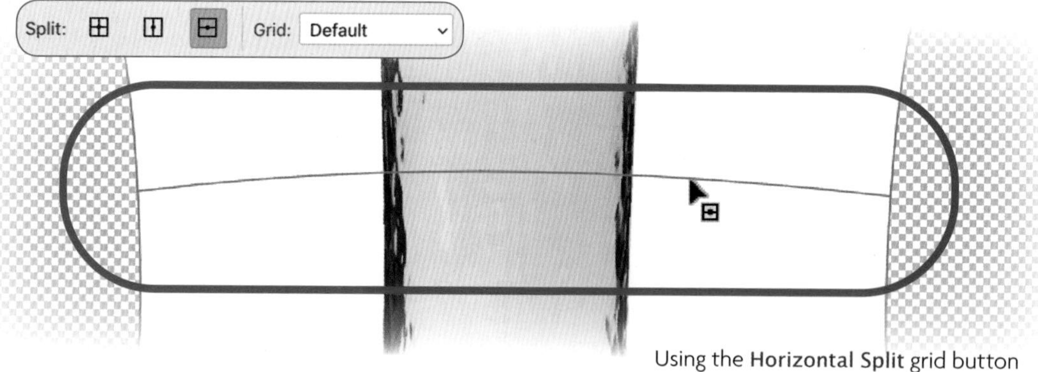

Using the **Horizontal Split** grid button

For symmetrical distortion, select the points on either side of the grid or area to be adjusted, then resize the box that appears around them. It appears just for this purpose whenever multiple points are selected. It's like free transforming a free transform!

Mirroring

To quickly flip one or more layers, access Free Transform (⌘-T/Ctrl-T), right-click, then choose Flip Horizontal (or Flip Vertical). Right-clicking within a Free Transform is also a fast way to rotate 90° or 180°.

Content-Aware Scale

Select Content-Aware Scale from the Edit menu. The control handles on this transformation tool resemble those of Free Transform, but it behaves very differently. Sadly, Content-Aware Scale cannot be applied to a Smart Object, so we must duplicate the layer to which we want to apply it. Very early-2000s. If the subject is surrounded by what the engineers call "low-frequency" areas (lacking sharp, fine detail), the subject will remain amazingly intact while the rest of the image is discarded.

Beware if faces are present! Cheeks and foreheads are often "low frequency" and may suffer. If people are present, click the small stick figure in the Options Bar once this tool is active to protect skin tones.

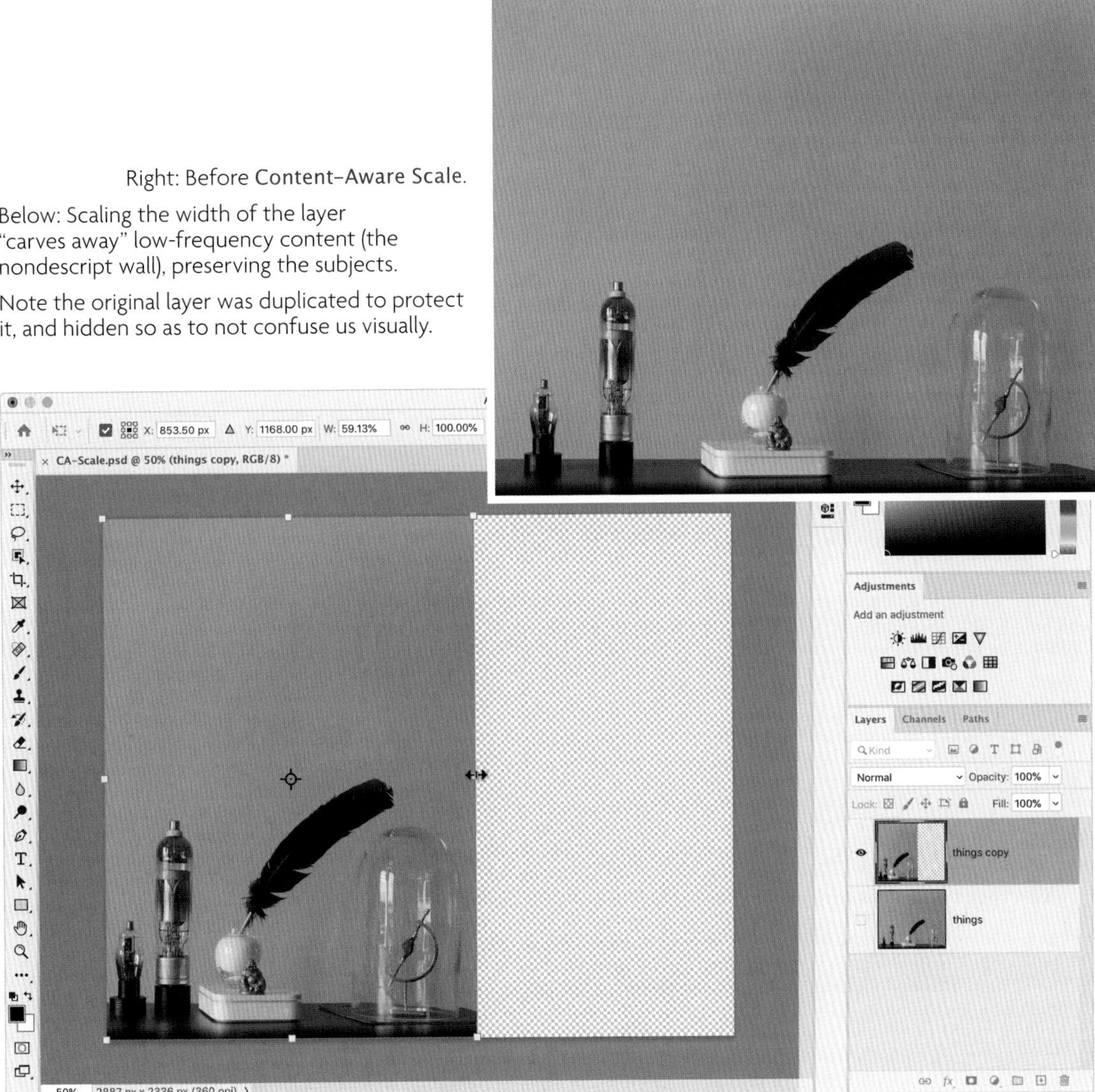

Right: Before Content-Aware Scale.

Below: Scaling the width of the layer "carves away" low-frequency content (the nondescript wall), preserving the subjects.

Note the original layer was duplicated to protect it, and hidden so as to not confuse us visually.

6 Retouching & Reworking

We should try to leave the world better than we found it. I apply that reasoning to images too. With Photoshop's retouching tools, we use good pixels to hide the flaws. We do this nondestructively in case they really weren't so bad after all.

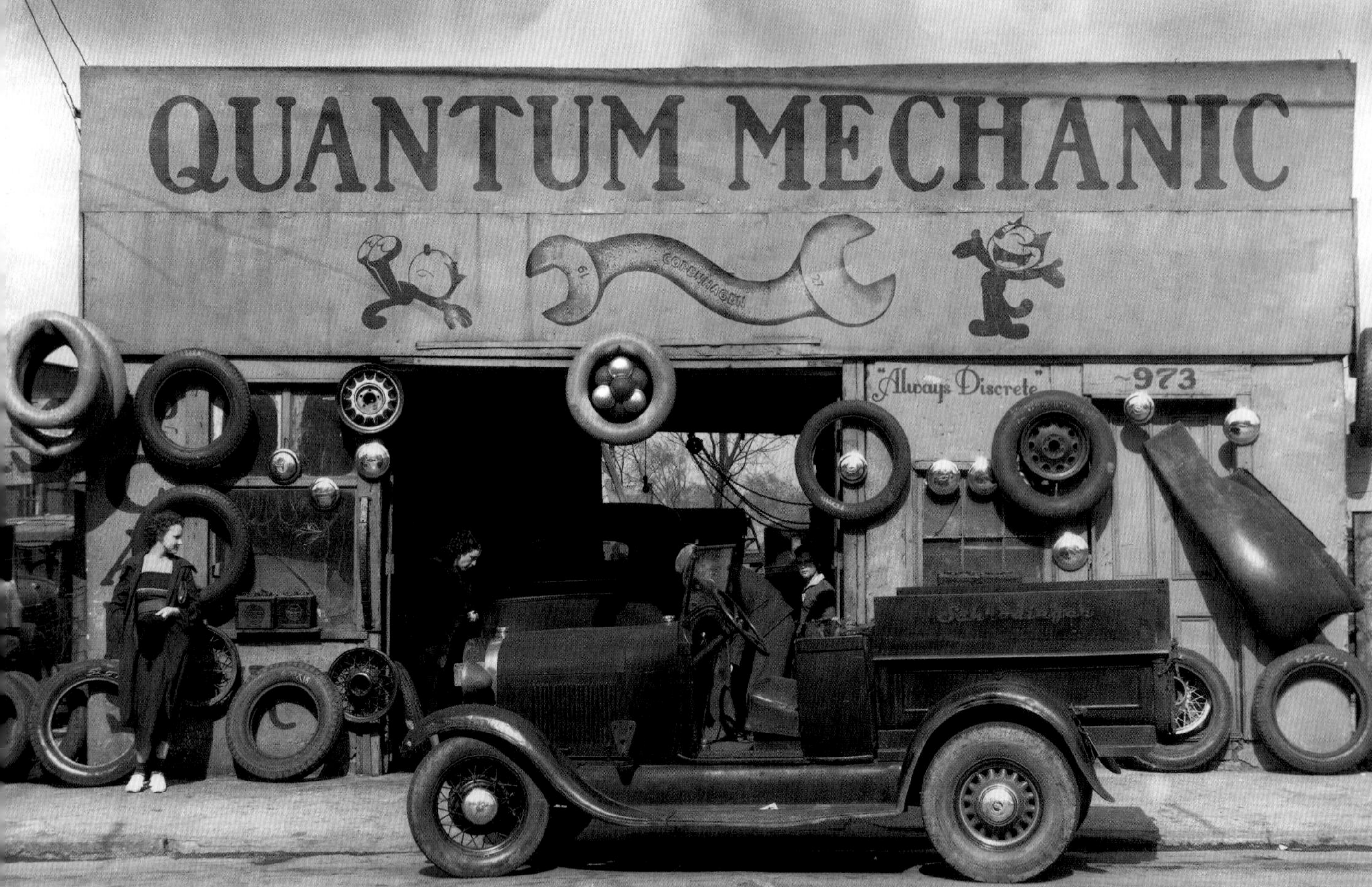

Tools & Methods

As we focus on the tools in Photoshop proper, know that there are tools in Adobe Camera Raw and Lightroom as well. See "Spot Removal Tool: Removing Blemishes" (page 368) for more on those.

All methods involve using "good" bits of imagery to replace or, better, obscure the bad. I say "better" because we sometimes change our minds or catch mistakes late in the game. Working nondestructively, we can remove the imagery we used to cover what we deemed flaws. To do so usually means creating a layer to hold the good stuff, and configuring each tool to sample from all the layers we see, rather than just the active one. Content-Aware Fill can create a layer on the fly. Some methods, sadly, can't use empty layers, and so we have to find alternatives.

Clone Stamp

The eldest of the retouching tools, the Clone Stamp tool uses a brush, usually soft (in that it fades off at the edges), to paint over blemishes with parts of an image we designated earlier.

It's usually best to use a brush that is about as big as the blemishes we're facing. If the problem is a stray hair, a brush that's slightly wider would be appropriate.

- Create a new, empty layer (it's best to give it a name—"Retouching" sounds good).
- Choose the Clone Stamp tool. In the Options Bar, set its Sample option to Current & Below so it can sample from anything you see, without being influenced by layers above (like adjustments).
- Set the size of the brush. You can use the bracket keys: [for smaller,] for larger.
- Hold down option/Alt and click on a patch of good material approximately one brush-width away from the first flaw. You will now see that material in the cursor.
- With no keys held, paint with the Clone Stamp tool on the first blemish. Cover it over completely. Notice that only while you're painting, a crosshair appears where you option/Alt-clicked. That's the source point. The source can be in a different open image!
- There is now an alignment between source and cursor. If your first source point was down and to the left of the cursor, it will be below and to the left of anywhere you paint, until you perform a new sampling by option/Alt-clicking. In this way, it will pick up material that is likely to be similar to that around the blemish.

Healing Brush

This tool is used in a manner very similar to that of the Clone Stamp tool. You option/Alt-click to set a source, then you paint elsewhere to apply that material over a blemish. However, there are two major differences. When you apply the repair, it contextualizes: That is, it adjusts to the tone and color around where you apply it, painting only the texture of the source.

Since it blends into its surroundings, the source doesn't need to follow the cursor like it does with the Clone Stamp tool. The Healing Brush tool will continue to pick up the same material until you sample a new source. So, if you're retouching skin, it is necessary only to sample other skin texture whether it's in shadow or light.

- Create a new, empty layer (it's best to give it a name—"Retouching" sounds good).
- Choose the Healing Brush tool. In the Options Bar, set its Sample option to Current & Below so it can sample from anything you see, without being influenced by layers above (like adjustments).
- Set the size of the brush. You can use the bracket keys: [for smaller,] for larger.
- Hold down option/Alt and click on a patch of good material that matches the texture of the area around the blemishes. It needn't match color or tone. You will now see that material in the cursor.
- With no keys held, paint on blemishes, covering them completely in one stroke, if possible. Notice that only while you're painting, a crosshair appears where you option/Alt-clicked. That's the source point. The source can be in a different open image!

With both the Clone Stamp tool and the Healing Brush tool, the source can be set from another image. Just option/Alt-click in one image, return to the image needing that material, and apply the fix.

Clone Source Panel

There are times when either you need precision in how the source is selected relative to the repair, or you need the source transformed in some way to be an effective patch. The Clone Source panel can provide these. With it, you can specify the exact spacial relationship between source and cursor, and how the source should be scaled, rotated, or reflected.

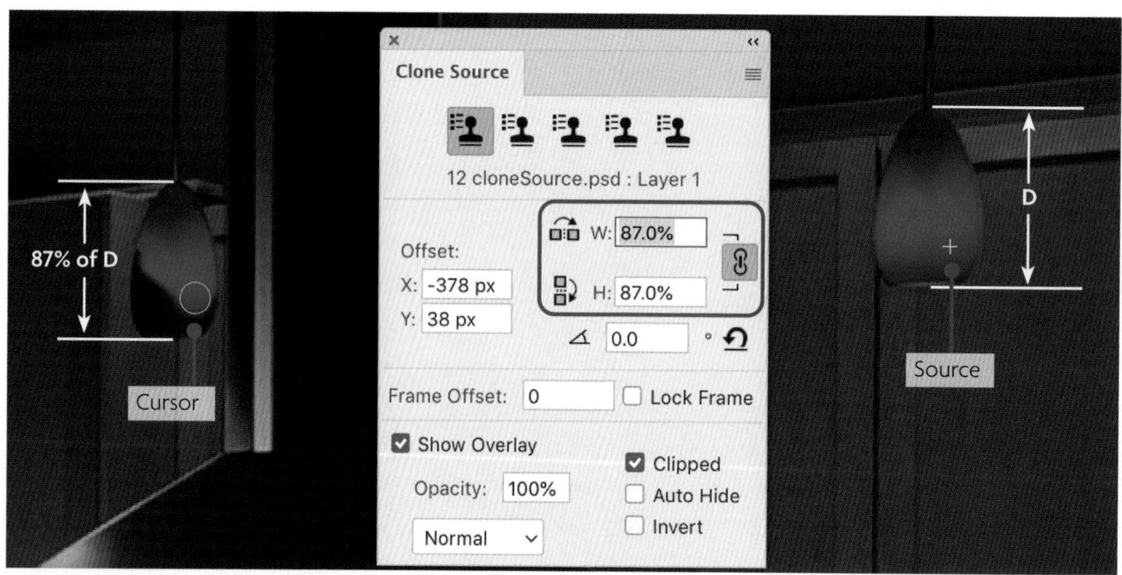

In the previous example, one of the lights wasn't lit, but a slightly closer one was. After creating a retouching layer and setting the Clone Stamp tool to Sample Current & Below, I did a preliminary sample (option/Alt-click) at the top edge of the illuminated lamp, followed by a unmodified click at the top of the dark lamp. That sets the Offset you see in the Clone Source panel. Since the source is too big, I undid that (⌘-Z/Ctrl-Z), but the offset values remain.

To determine the correct scaling, I scrubbed the W and H fields (just dragging their labels). As I did so, a translucent overlay appeared with the lit lamp over the dark one. I continued to reduce the size until the lamps were the same size. Now the scaling was set.

With a small brush size, I then painted with the Clone Stamp tool until I had what I needed. I used even smaller sizes near the edge.

Spot Healing Brush

The tool I use the most! We don't set a source for this one—it figures that out. In the Options Bar, we still set sampling, but in this case it's just a checkbox to Sample All Layers, and it can handle adjustment layers wherever they are. As always, you should create a retouch layer in case you or the tool make a bad decision.

It's easy to use too:

- Size the brush to that of the blemishes.
- Just paint on a blemish, covering it completely in one pass. Photoshop then finds something that fills that area, blending it into the surrounding content.

The algorithm it uses is drawn from the powerful Content-Aware Fill command.

Remove Tool

Beta Still in development as I write, this newest retouching tool is wielded precisely like the Spot Healing Brush tool: painting to cover a flaw then allowing the algorithm to repair it. It offers an additional option via the Options Bar to use multiple brush strokes to cover the flaw then activate the repair by pressing Enter.

Content-Aware Fill

Useful for large areas needing replacement, Content-Aware Fill is a process that uses whatever material you or Photoshop deems appropriate to fill an area. It will even create a new layer for you for what it outputs.

- Select the area to be filled.
- Choose Edit > Content-Aware Fill....

A large dialog box appears. On the right side of the box are your options. The topmost options are for choosing what gets used to fill in your selection.

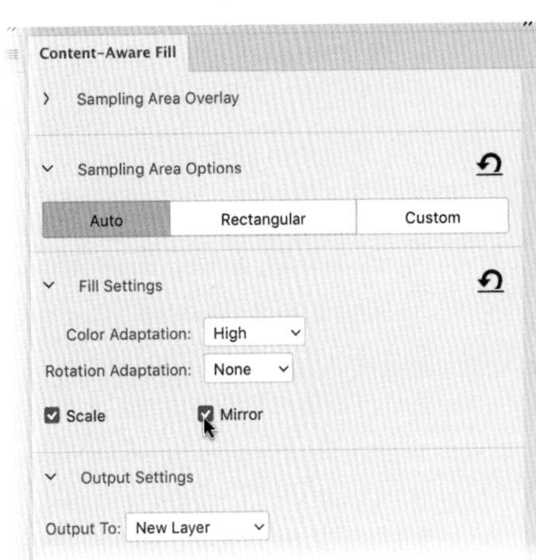

Auto is what the Spot Healing Brush tool uses and is usually effective. In the image window, a translucent overlay indicates what material may be enlisted in the fill.

Rectangular will force that area to be rectangular. This is useful when straight lines are present, like in the following example. However, I found Auto to work at least as well.

Custom requires the use of the Sampling Brush tool. Use it to literally paint on the areas that should be used to fill your area. Sometimes you really do know best.

After each choice, an indicator spins below the Preview panel. Wait for it to complete before judging the result.

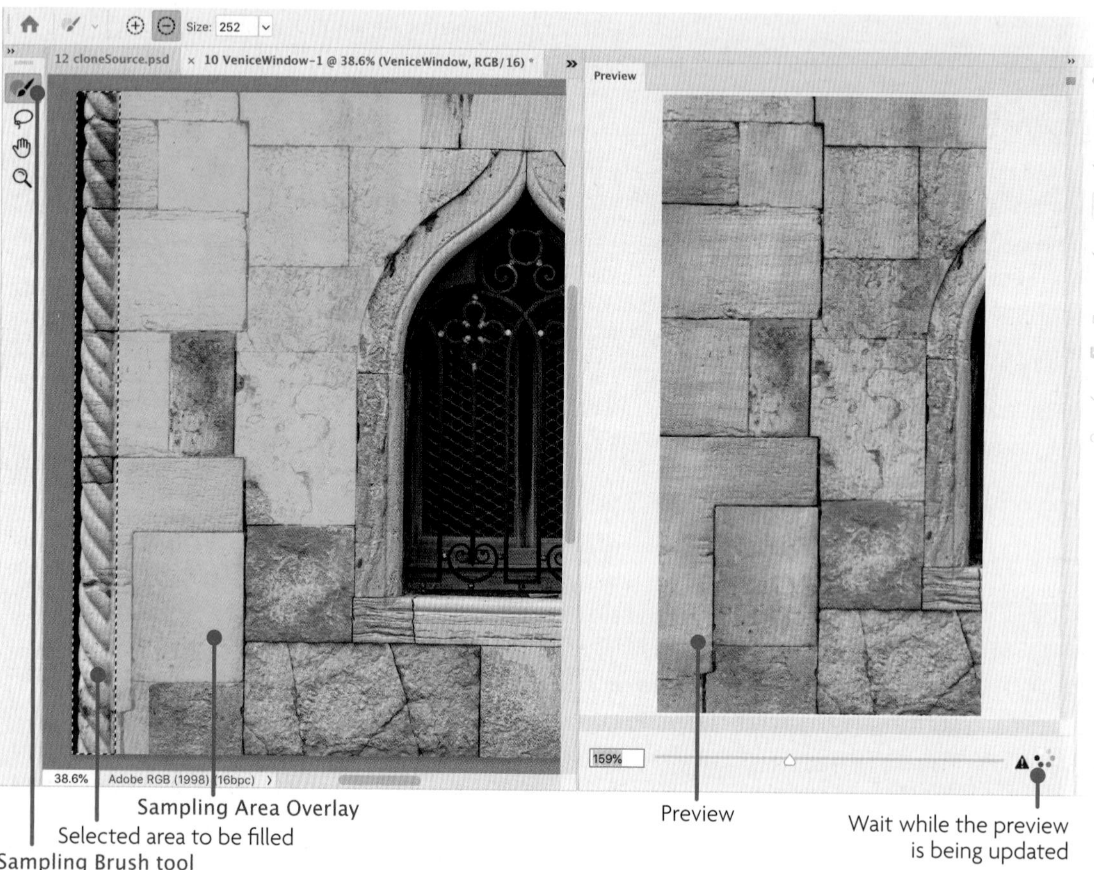

Note the Fill Settings too. Higher settings for Color Adaptation allow Photoshop to alter the color of your repair to better match its new surroundings, somewhat like the Healing Brush tool. The rest allow the source material to be transformed: rotated, scaled, or mirrored. Rotation Adaptation is great when you're repairing an area on the edge of a curve. Another part of the curve could be rotated into place! That plus Scale and Mirror can help immensely when there's a large-scale texture (like brickwork or skyscraper windows). As the warning messages will tell you, these transformation allowances work best with Custom sampling, but I still attempt them with the others.

Wonderfully, it can (and should) Output To a New Layer.

Patch

The Patch tool is a combo function. You *could* use it like the Lasso tool to make a selection of what should be "patched" (or, if you like, the area to be used as a patch). You may use a selection made with any selection tool too. Dragging a selection with the Patch tool provides an animated preview within the selected area of the texture of where you're dragging. When you release, the result will contextualize by default, in the manner of the Healing Brush tool.

The fatal flaw with this tool is that it cannot sample any layer other than the active one. Thus, it can't be used nondestructively like the other tools we've seen. Content-Aware Fill is far superior for contexts where the Patch tool may once have been useful.

Content-Aware Move

Like a combination of Content-Aware Fill and a perfected Patch tool (in that this tool can Sample All Layers), this tool allows you to move a selected sample to another part of the image, transform it, and fill the area where it had been—all in one step.

Below, with an empty layer active, I made a selection of a tree I wanted to move. Using the Content-Aware Move tool, I dragged the tree elsewhere, made it smaller, then pressed Enter.

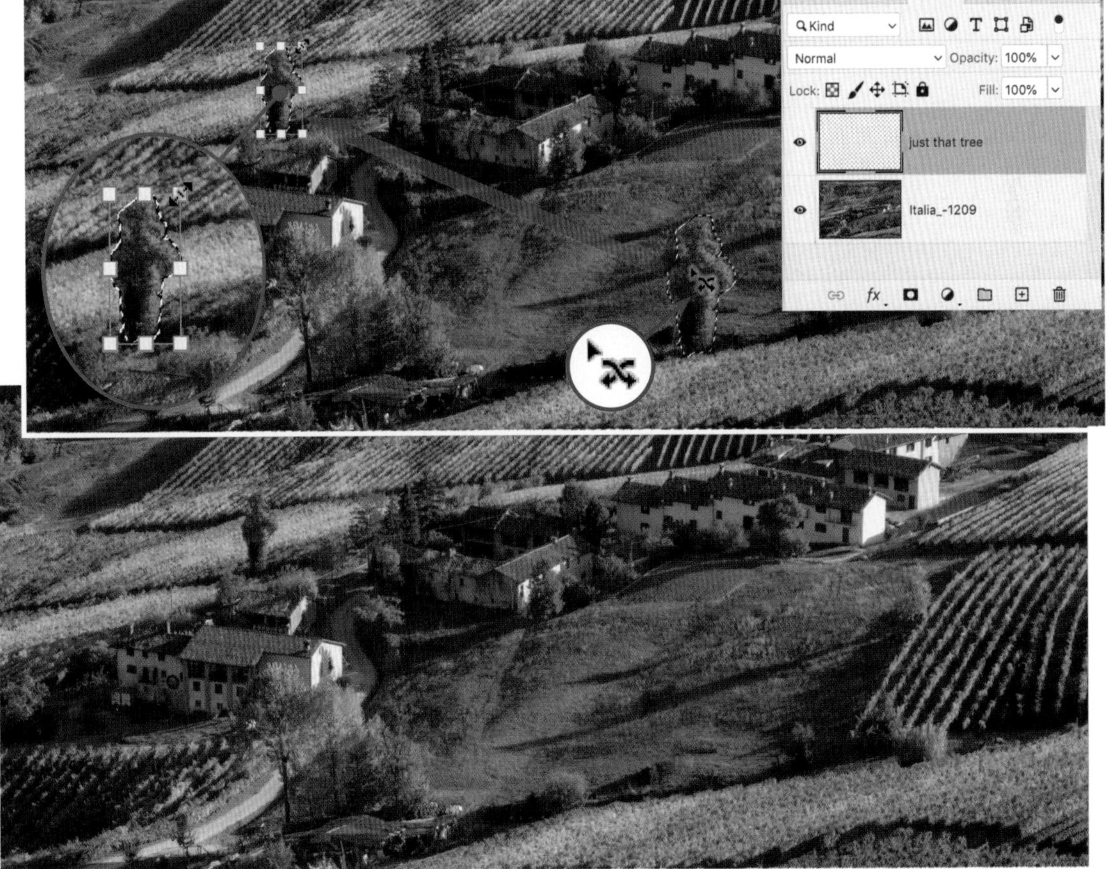

Vanishing Point Filter

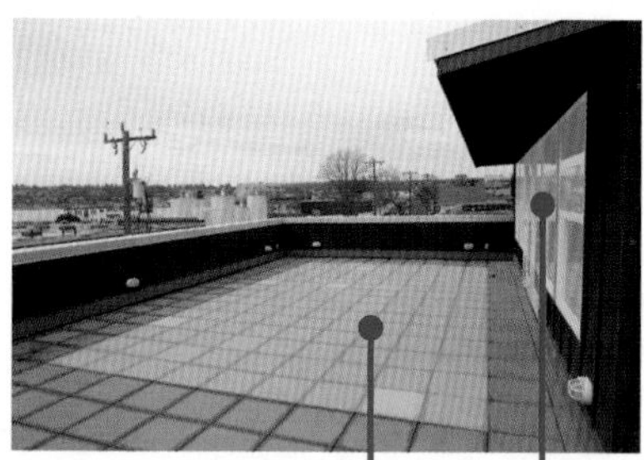

The windows would have served as a perspective plane if the patio didn't have such convenient tiles.

The user interface of this filter is an entire workspace with its own tools, including a hybrid Clone Stamp/Healing Brush tool. Within this workspace, we can indicate perspective in the image by tracing out planes in it. Then we can do retouching that uses that perspective, using material in the foreground to hide flaws farther away.

Start by creating an empty layer, just as we do with most of our retouching techniques. Look over the image to find clear rectangular areas. Well, they'd be rectangles were they not in perspective.

With the empty layer highlighted, choose Filter > Vanishing Point…. Note that instructions appear along the top. As they tell us to, we click at the corners of the chosen portion of the plane. We extend it by dragging the handles in the center of each edge.

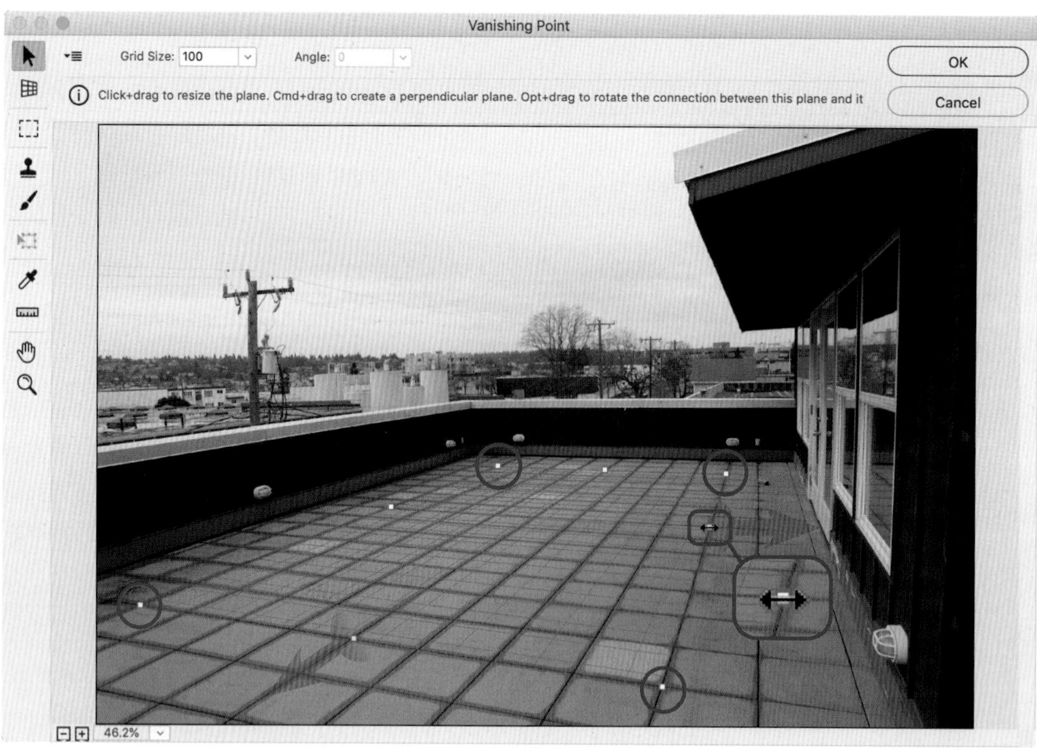

We create places perpendicular to that one by ⌘/Ctrl-dragging. In this way, we can perform retouching by pulling material from any plane and bringing it to any other.

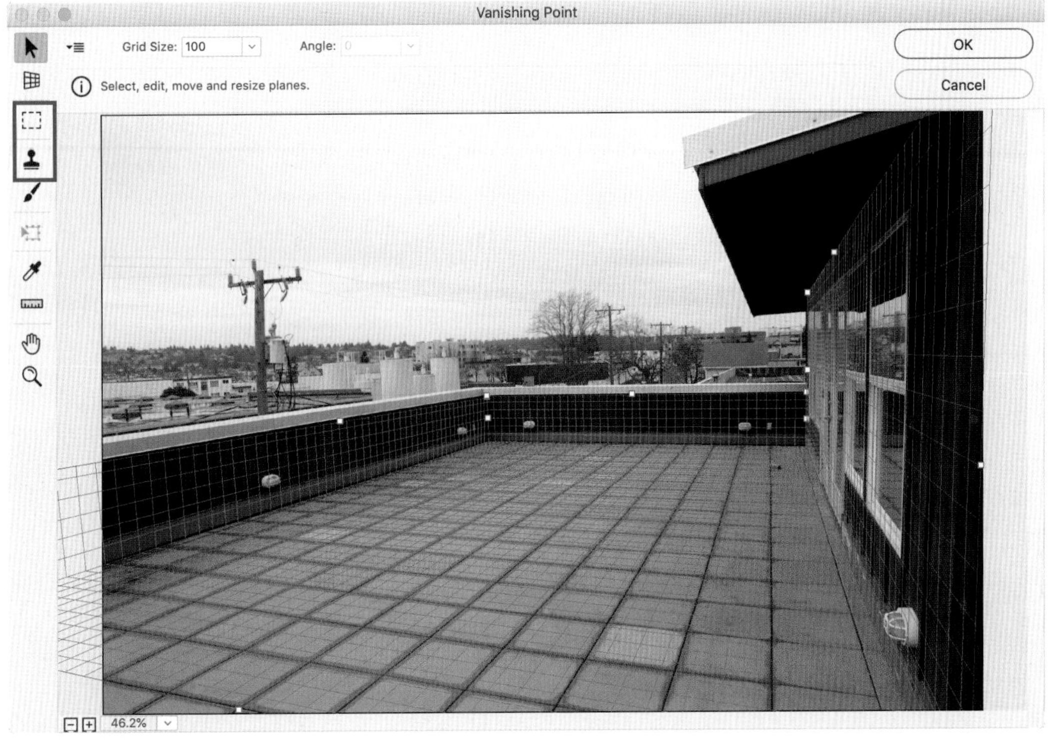

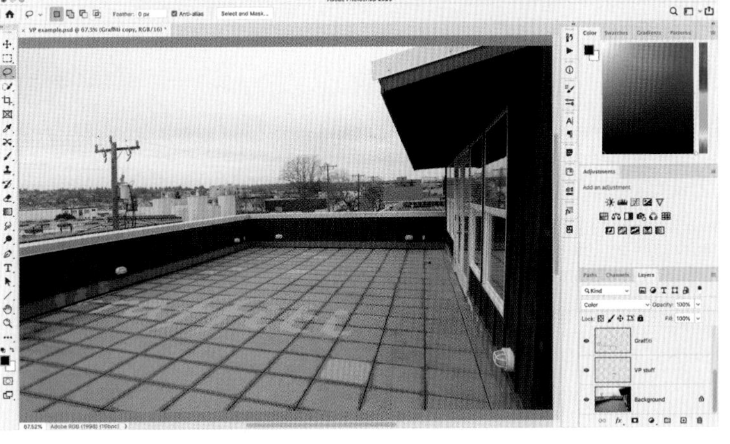

Use the Stamp tool as a Clone Stamp or Healing Brush by changing its settings at the top of the dialog. The Marquee tool makes selections in perspective! After you've drawn one, you can use it as a Patch tool by option/Alt-dragging the selection.

In my case, I copied some "graffiti" I painted on an empty layer. Then I entered Vanishing Point, pasted, and dragged the art onto one or more planes.

Those are the very basics. If you're intrigued, I strongly recommend a particular video tutorial by my friend Matt Warren. This video has the unique attributes of being informative without wasting your time, *and* it's very entertaining. Search the web for "docbadwrench vanishing point video," and prepare to be impressed.

Sky Replacement

Flexible & Customizable New Skies

A perfectly legitimate way to replace a sky in a photo would be to add a new sky as a layer masked to the undesired sky. One might also add adjustment layers to ensure that the foreground and new sky get along visually.

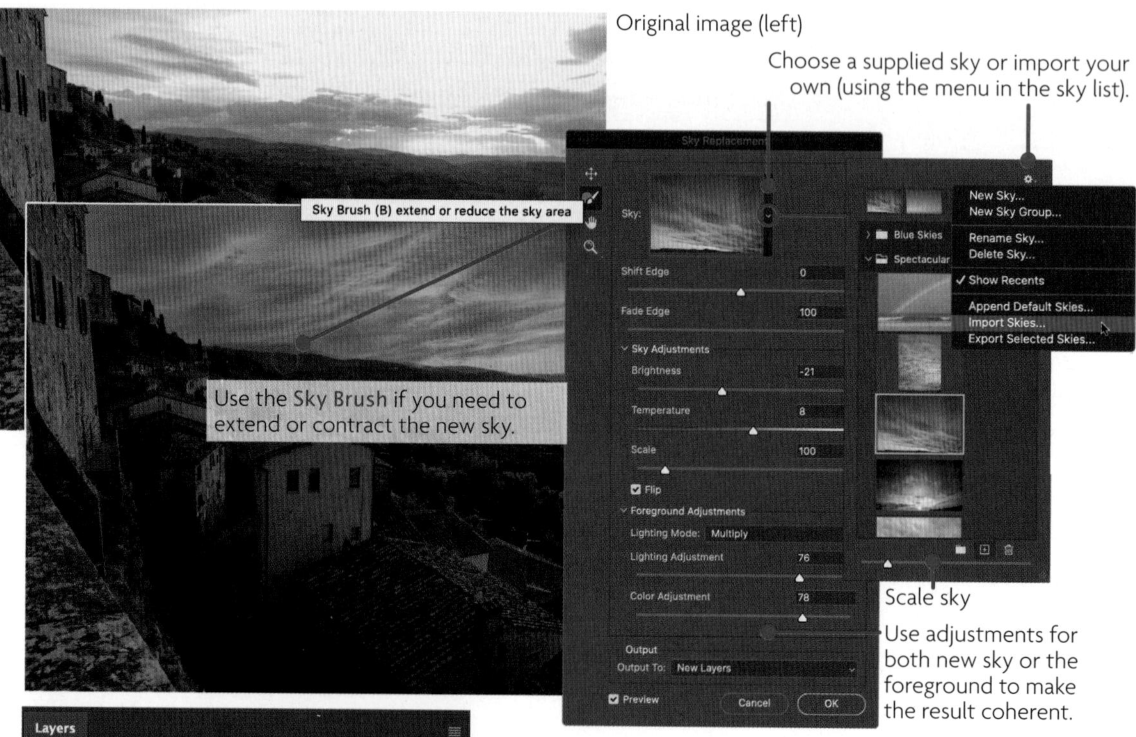

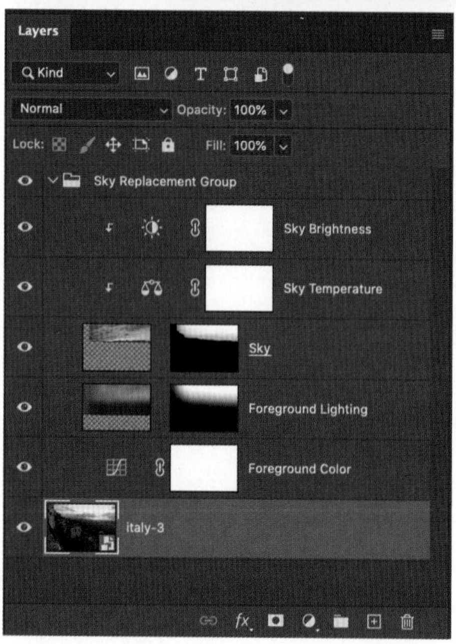

Photoshop's new Sky Replacement feature does those things. Access it by choosing Edit > Sky Replacement…. Choose a sky (or add your own, see above for how) and adjust the result in the dialog box. When you commit, you'll get layers much like we might have created, and can later tweak to taste.

Cosmetic Retouching

There are Photoshop workers who specialize in areas known as glamour, beauty, and fashion retouching. Each of those is considered distinct because the goals vary, but often there are techniques that are shared among them. Some advanced practitioners have even made their own Photoshop plugins and scripts to achieve their look.

I am not one of these specialists. I certainly understand the tools and techniques they use, but not always their objectives. Luckily, from what I've seen, there is less artificiality than some time ago. Rarely do we see utterly featureless skin that resembles plastic more than living tissue, or grotesquely exaggerated body alteration. If what you want to achieve is a gently flattering adjustment, the exercise that follows should be helpful. If you want to do retouching work in Hollywood, you will have to do some additional research and study, perhaps with one of the specialists.

You may have heard some chatter about "frequency separation" in the world of retouching. Removing abrupt blemishes like acne, scars, lines, etc., would fall under "high frequency" concerns. Broader, more global concerns, like uneven color, are thought of as "low frequency." Although I don't subscribe to the convoluted techniques marketed as "frequency separation," I do tend to start with small, abrupt issues and get more general as I go.

Keep Your Options Open

This kind of retouching is all about judgment calls. If you and your client/boss judge differently, it's best to avoid the need to begin again. So, of course, we start by creating one or more retouching layers and using the array of tools discussed in this chapter to remove "high frequency" blemishes. But we will also need to apply filters and adjustments, some with blending options. The layers will need to be packed inside a Smart Object to apply those filters so they're editable. Using `Image > Adjustments` applies adjustments as Smart Filters.

This may also include the several Neural Filters that are geared for Portraits (page 298) like Skin Smoothing and Smart Portrait.

Blemish Removal

When I approach this kind of work, I'll create at least two layers on which to retouch. One is for those details (acne, stray hair, etc.) to be completely *removed*. Even though these may seem obvious, and therefore tempting to remove on the original layer, you may be surprised. A small scar you remove may prove to be a beloved, signature feature.

Another layer, which will have partial opacity, is for those details that need to be *reduced* (furrowed brow wrinkles, for example).

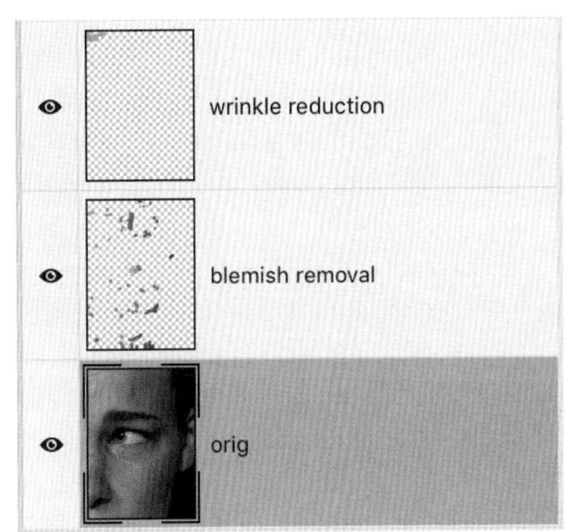

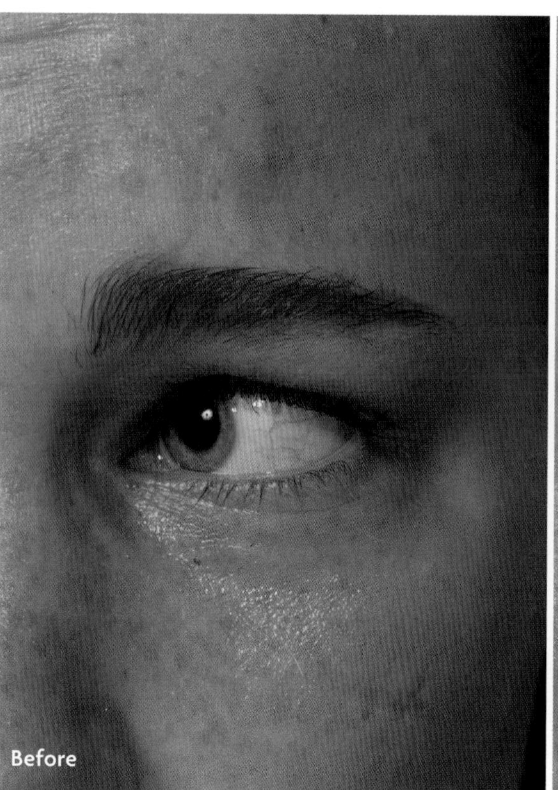
Before

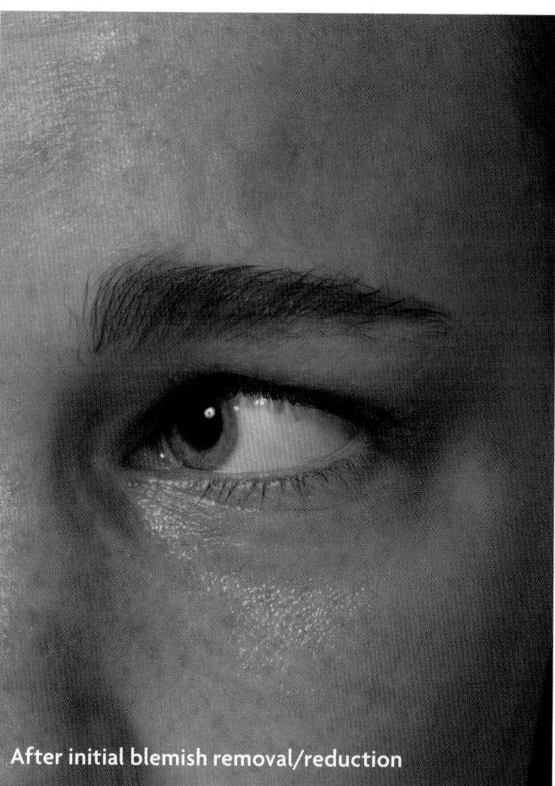
After initial blemish removal/reduction

For many images, this stage may be perfectly adequate. But for those who need to go farther, we have ways. If that's the case, I select all my current layers, right-click near the name of one, and choose Convert to Smart Object.

To remove numerous, tiny annoyances, like the light speckles under the eyes, I will sometimes try the Dust & Scratches filter. Here, I applied it to the Smart Object (so it becomes a Smart Filter). My rule is to use the smallest Radius and largest Threshold possible to avoid affecting desirable details. This filter works by impinging on a small defect with surrounding color. In this case, the filter does impinge on the light speckles with darker color from around them, but also impinges on the delicate dark lashes with the lighter color around those.

A blend mode can help. I double-clicked on the Blending Options icon to the right of the filter's entry under the Smart Object so I could set it to Darker Color. Now only light defects get swamped by darker colors.

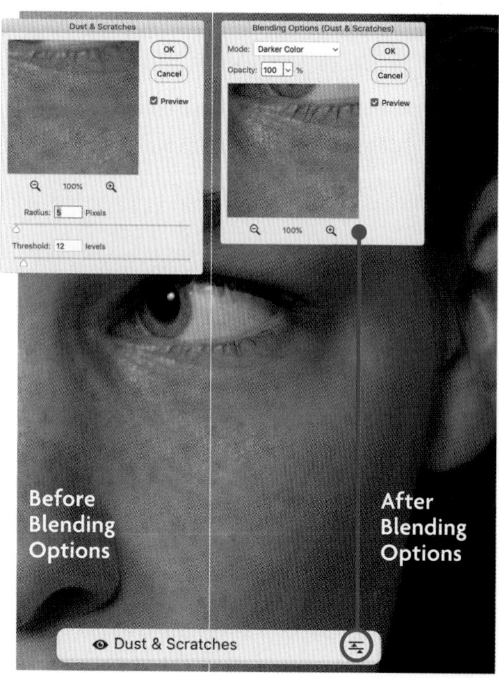

Other Helpful Features

Not all of these are necessary for every portrait, but I've included what I deem likely suspects from Photoshop's filter and adjustment line-up. Blend modes help limit their impact.

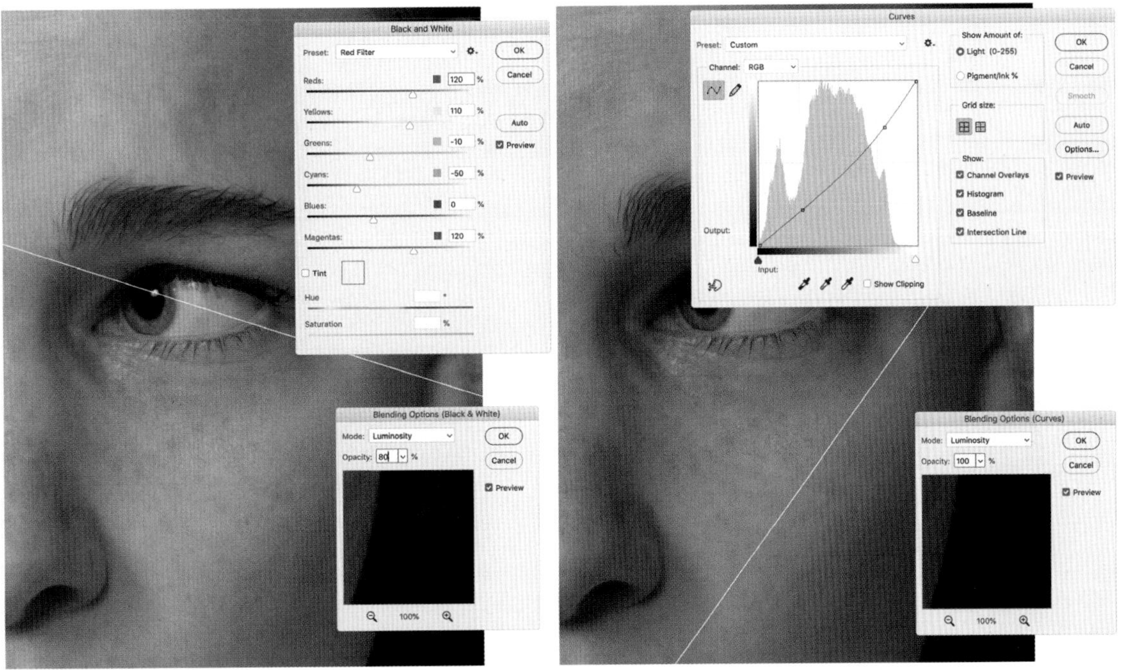

A Black & White adjustment with its Red Filter preset flatters many skin tones, but it's too light. So follow up with a gentle Curve. Set both to Luminosity so color is unaffected.

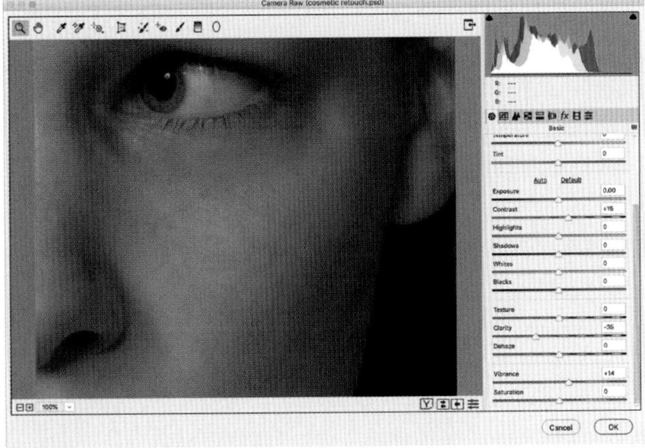

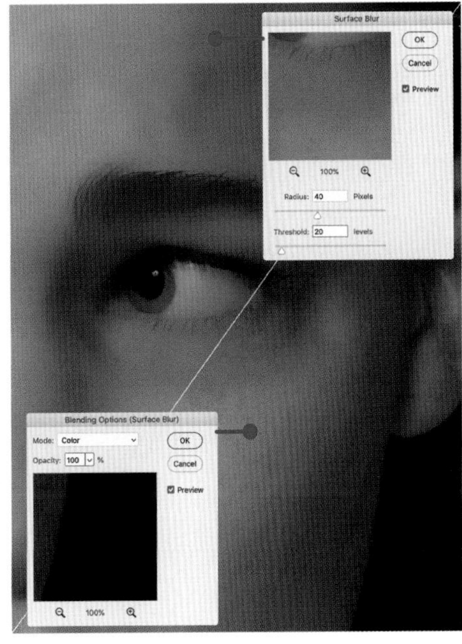

Above: Using the **Clarity** slider of the **Camera Raw** filter to soften the complexion.

Right: The **Surface Blur** filter, infamous for destroying credible skin texture, can be used to smooth only coloration by setting its blend mode to **Color** in its **Blending Options**.

It's OK to apply more adjustments to gently compensate for the things you've done, if necessary. You may also use the Smart Filters mask to hide what you've done if there are areas that suffered more than were helped. I added one more Curve as a Smart Filter with the Luminosity blend mode. I painted on the mask to hide all of these effects from the eyes, which lost their shine.

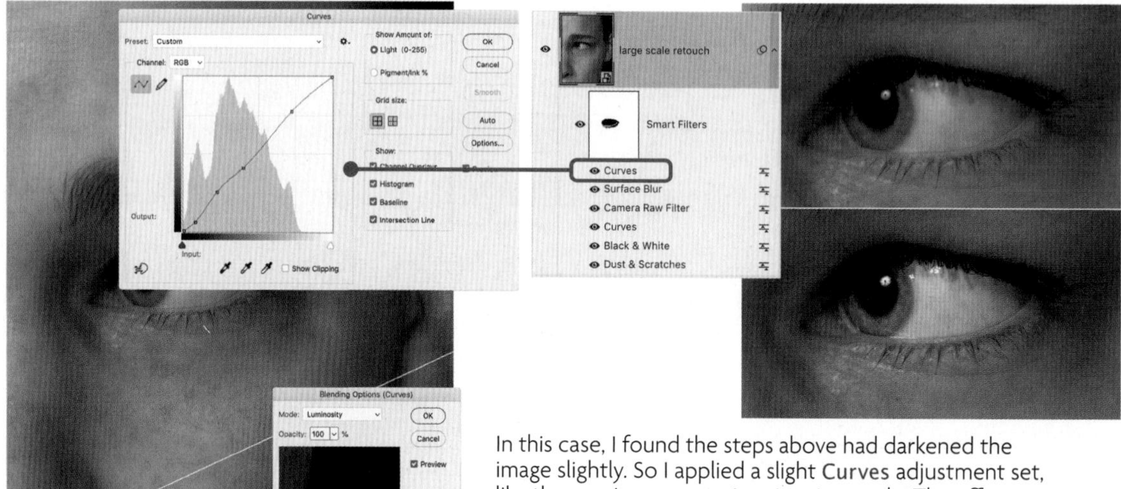

In this case, I found the steps above had darkened the image slightly. So I applied a slight Curves adjustment set, like the previous one, to Luminosity mode. The effect is subtle, but the color was too pink once lightened.

Above right, I painted on the Smart Filters mask to hide all of what was done on the eyes. They had become muddied.

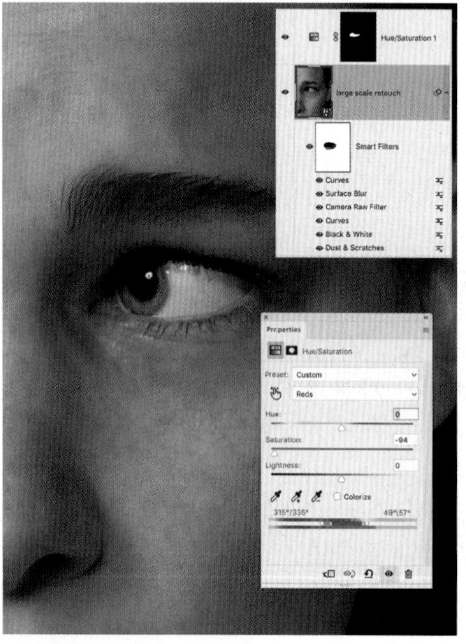

I also added one more adjustment, this time as an adjustment layer with its own mask to affect *only* the eyes. This was a Hue/Saturation adjustment to desaturate the whites of the eyes, getting the last bit of red out.

Any of the stages above could've been the last. Just removing blemishes is often perfectly sufficient. The Black & White adjustment with Curves chaser is a fine trick to even a subject's complexion gently. Remember, you can adjust the opacity as well as blend mode of these in the Blending Options dialog.

When processing raw files, we can use Adobe Camera Raw's Spot Removal tool and Clarity slider early on, and may need no other retouching later.

In short, there are many options you can employ at any stage. Just try to keep them editable so you can return to any and adjust at will.

The images in this section have been a bit small, so here's a larger version of the same portion of the portrait. I've inserted a small island showing "before" so you can evaluate the result.

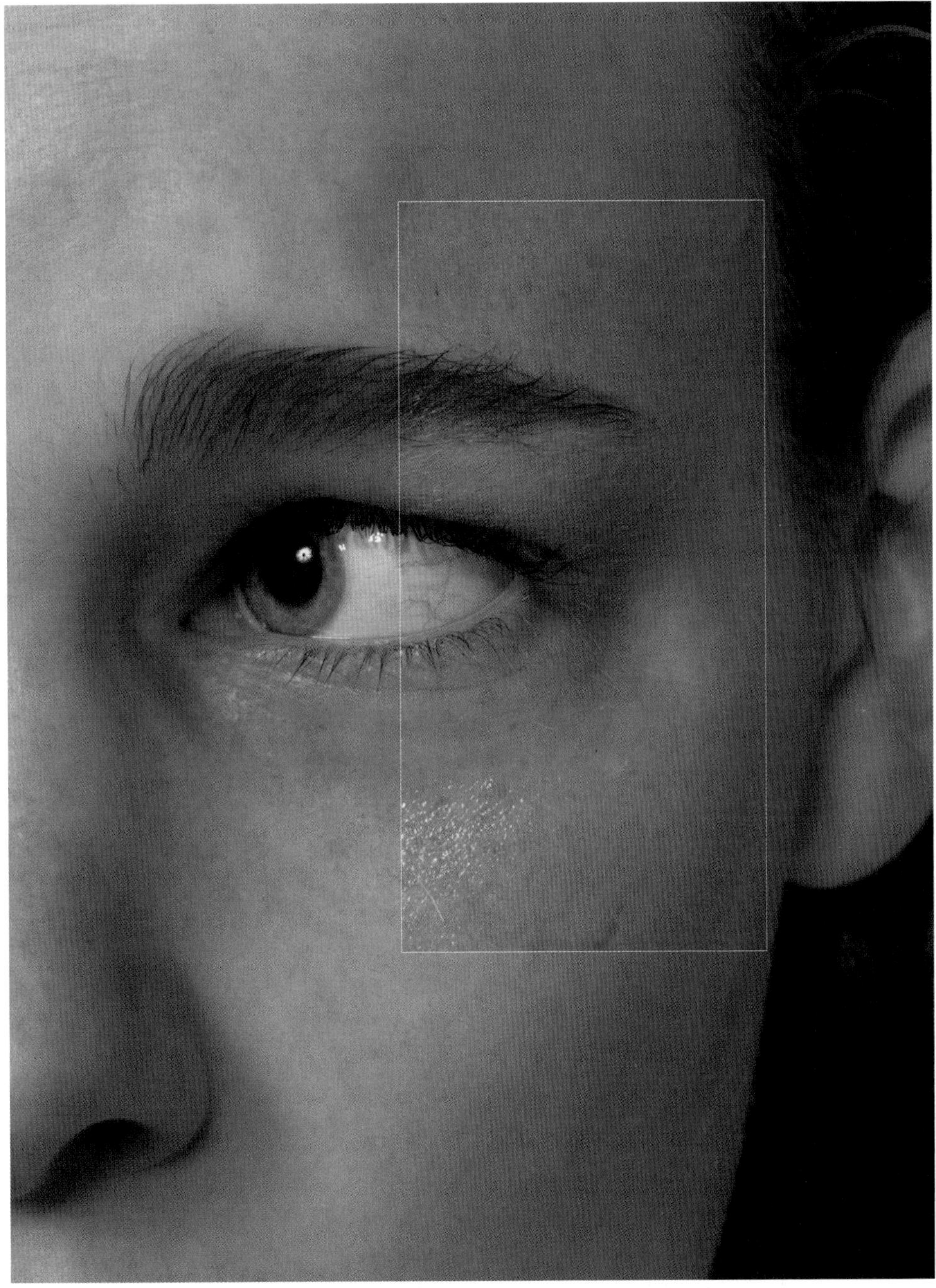

7 Camera Raw & Lightroom

All professional cameras and many others can provide us with more than common JPEGs or TIFFs. We can access the camera's raw capture data. Although Photoshop cannot directly edit this raw data, we can do so with Adobe Camera Raw, a companion to Photoshop, or with Lightroom, Photoshop's photo asset–managing cousin.

You'll soon see that shooting raw is the very best of best practices.

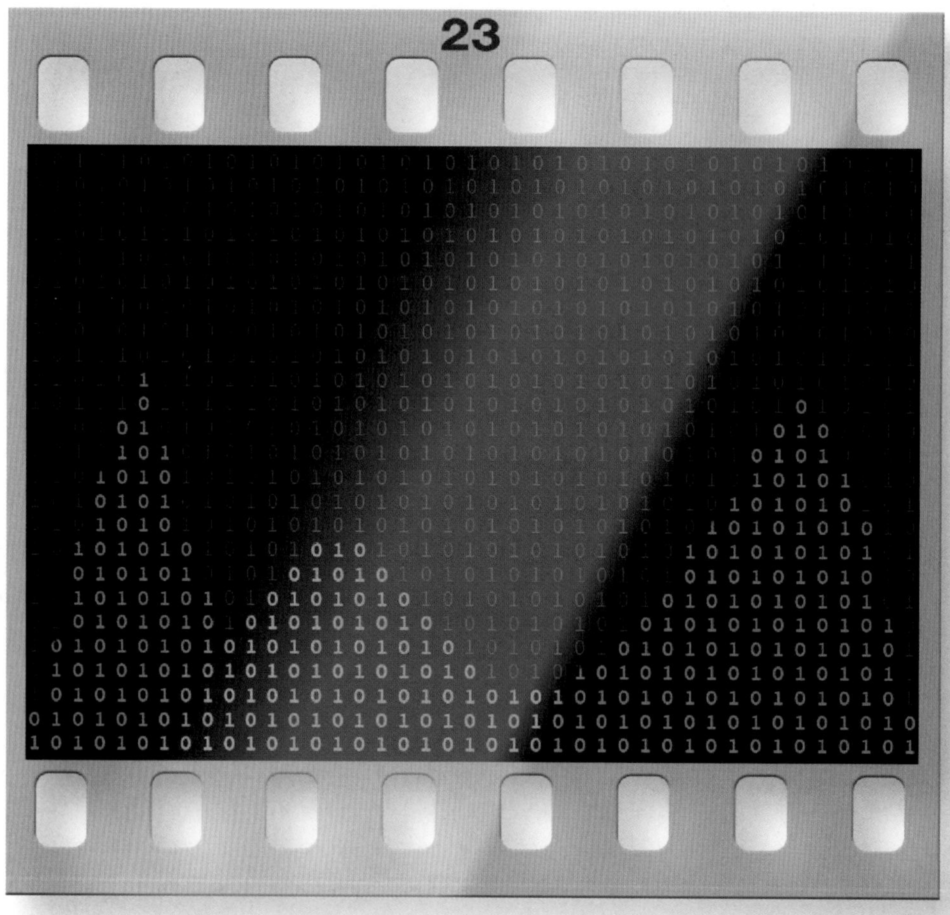

For Raw Files and Beyond

Why We Need Them

The millions of microscopic sensors that collect light in our cameras' photosensor arrays don't actually record an image. Those sensors experience a bump in electric current when light hits them. The camera records the current passed along by every one of those millions of sensors. That doesn't sound like an image, does it? It takes special software to interpret that electrical data and make pixels from it. So, Adobe has created that software.

When we ask our cameras to produce JPEGs or TIFFs, which are made of pixels, the software that creates the image files is in the camera. However, we can often set our cameras to supply the raw data to us for other software (Lightroom or Adobe Camera Raw) to interpret. In turn, these pieces of software can either hand off that data to Photoshop as pixels interpreted from that raw data, or they can put that data inside a Smart Object.

Lightroom and Adobe Camera Raw (ACR) use the same software base to do adjustments. The user interface may look a bit different, but they do the same thing when processing raw data. The difference is that Lightroom has other jobs too. In fact, it's primary use is as an asset manager to help us find, sort, and deliver our many images. I hear from many Lightroom users that they use Lightroom *only* for its great asset-management features. However, I want to be clear that the most efficient workflows tend to be those that *maximize* use of these raw "development" tools. Only after I've done all the adjustments that ACR or Lightroom offer do I move an image to Photoshop—if at all.

Why? As we go through what ACR (and therefore Lightroom) allows us to do, try to keep in mind that it is all nondestructive. No matter how we interpret the raw data, the data itself, the changes in electrical current in those sensors, isn't altered. We can revisit our processing as often as we wish with no ill effect.

When I need a feature that neither ACR nor Lightroom possesses, or one that is much easier to use in Photoshop, that is when I move a copy of that raw data to Photoshop encased in a Smart Object. This is not a book about Lightroom and its fine image-management functions. However, as we discuss ACR, you'll learn a great deal about those same functions in Lightroom.

ACR: Adobe Camera Raw

Adobe Camera Raw (ACR) is an unusual piece of software in that it needs to be "hosted" by either Adobe Bridge or Photoshop. That is, one of those programs must be running for us to be able to use (or even see) ACR.

Photoshop does not directly edit raw data. When you try to open one or more raw files in Photoshop, it will launch (if it isn't running already) and then, when it realizes that you're opening raw data, Photoshop will launch ACR and open the images there. If you are browsing raw files with Bridge, you highlight one or more of them, then, if you prefer to not launch

Photoshop, use the shortcut ⌘-R/Ctrl-R. This forces Bridge to host ACR and Photoshop isn't troubled. Standard techniques to open files, like double-clicking or ⌘-O/Ctrl-O launch Photoshop, and Photoshop hosts Adobe Camera Raw.

The ACR User Interface

You can exercise some control over the look and feel as well as some behavior of ACR. Clicking the small gear icon in the upper right opens ACR's Preferences. For example, near the top of ACR's General preferences, cure the potential annoyance of seeing only one panel at a time by abandoning the default panel behavior and choosing Multiple. If you're tight on space, Responsive may be a better choice. The interface has many options in one view:

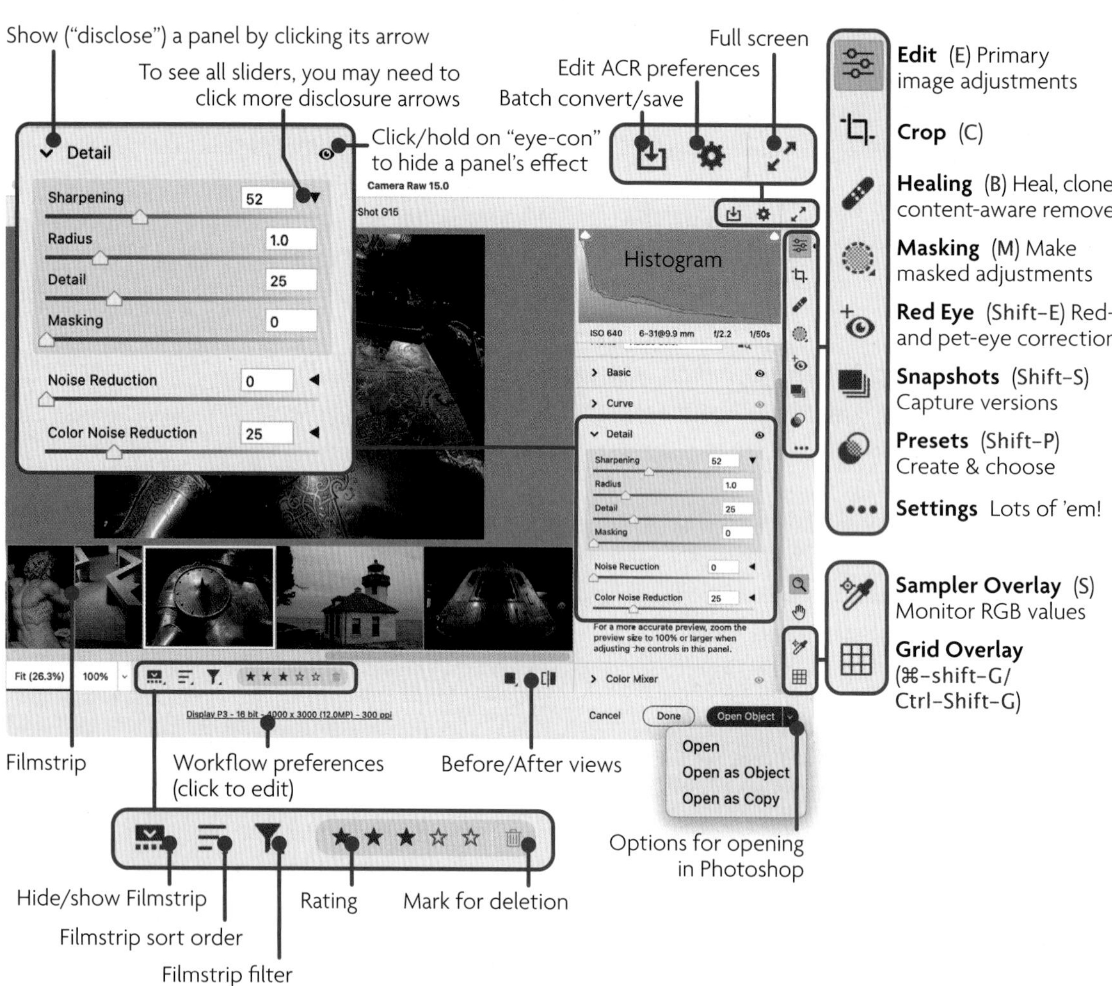

I've chosen to Use Lightroom style zoom and pan as well, since I use Lightroom often and find that comfortably familiar. Holding down ⌘/Ctrl engages a marquee zoom.
Be sure to check out the other pages of the Preferences dialog to see if there other changes you'd like made.

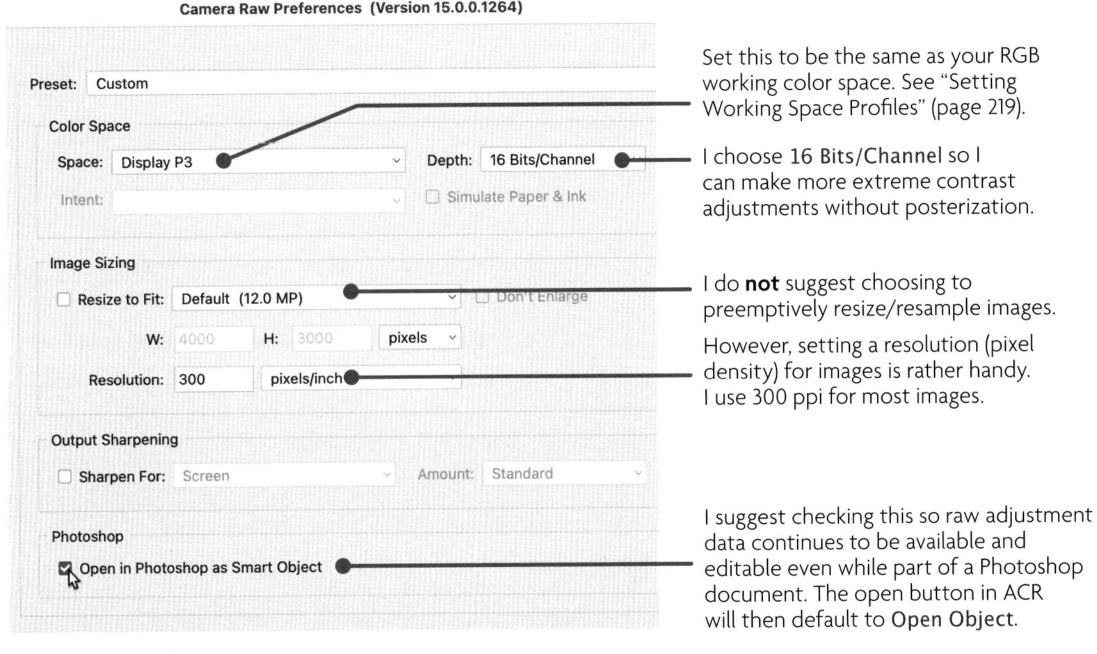
Camera Raw Preferences (Version 15.0.0.1264)
Preset: Custom
Color Space
Space: Display P3
Depth: 16 Bits/Channel
Intent:
Simulate Paper & Ink
Image Sizing
Resize to Fit: Default (12.0 MP)
Don't Enlarge
W: 4000 H: 3000 pixels
Resolution: 300 pixels/inch
Output Sharpening
Sharpen For: Screen
Amount: Standard
Photoshop
Open in Photoshop as Smart Object
Set this to be the same as your RGB working color space. See "Setting Working Space Profiles" (page 219).
I choose 16 Bits/Channel so I can make more extreme contrast adjustments without posterization.
I do not suggest choosing to preemptively resize/resample images.
However, setting a resolution (pixel density) for images is rather handy. I use 300 ppi for most images.
I suggest checking this so raw adjustment data continues to be available and editable even while part of a Photoshop document. The open button in ACR will then default to Open Object.

A special page of those preferences, the Workflow Options, can be accessed by the gear icon or by clicking on their synopsis at the bottom of the user interface. These preferences control what gets passed along should you wish to take an image from ACR to Photoshop.

See the figure above to interpret your choices, the most important of which is to open processed raw files in Photoshop as Smart Objects (bottom checkbox).

Many more settings are accessed by the ellipsis on the right side of the ACR interface. They're surprisingly useful for something so hidden!

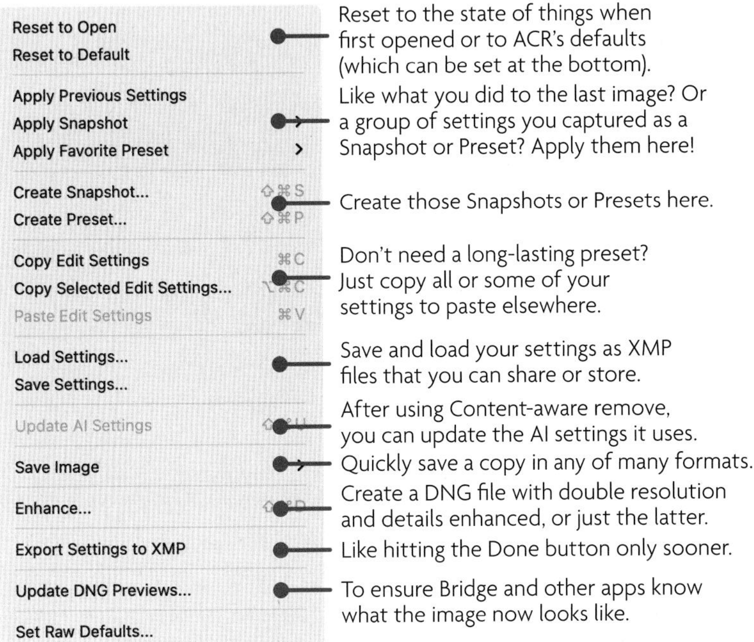
Reset to Open
Reset to Default
Apply Previous Settings
Apply Snapshot
Apply Favorite Preset
Create Snapshot...
Create Preset...
Copy Edit Settings
Copy Selected Edit Settings...
Paste Edit Settings
Load Settings...
Save Settings...
Update AI Settings
Save Image
Enhance...
Export Settings to XMP
Update DNG Previews...
Set Raw Defaults...
Reset to the state of things when first opened or to ACR's defaults (which can be set at the bottom).
Like what you did to the last image? Or a group of settings you captured as a Snapshot or Preset? Apply them here!
Create those Snapshots or Presets here.
Don't need a long-lasting preset? Just copy all or some of your settings to paste elsewhere.
Save and load your settings as XMP files that you can share or store.
After using Content-aware remove, you can update the AI settings it uses.
Quickly save a copy in any of many formats.
Create a DNG file with double resolution and details enhanced, or just the latter.
Like hitting the Done button only sooner.
To ensure Bridge and other apps know what the image now looks like.

Global Adjustments

The vast majority of edits you'll need to perform can be done with the tools and adjustments you see initially: The Edit panels have the most significant controls, and the tools along the right stay with you from panel to panel. The first adjustment to be done, white balance, is usually as easy as it is important.

Although many of ACR's adjustments are similar to those in Photoshop, there are a few that are unique. In the rest of this chapter, I'll go over most of the features of ACR (and therefore Lightroom), making reference, when appropriate, to the Photoshop features from which they're derived.

Much of ACR's capability is available as a Photoshop filter, too—making the Camera Raw filter one of the most powerful. Using that filter, of course, doesn't convert a layer or Smart Object into raw data.

When we're done making adjustments (interpreting the raw data), we simply click the Done button! This creates metadata for the raw file that records our settings. All digital captures already have some metadata in the file: camera and lens data, such as make and model; exposure; date and time; and sometimes GPS coordinates. If we ever create a JPEG or TIFF of this image to share with others, the metadata serves as a recipe for how the raw data and our adjustments in ACR should be baked together to make ordinary pixels. The final image is the sum of all this data.

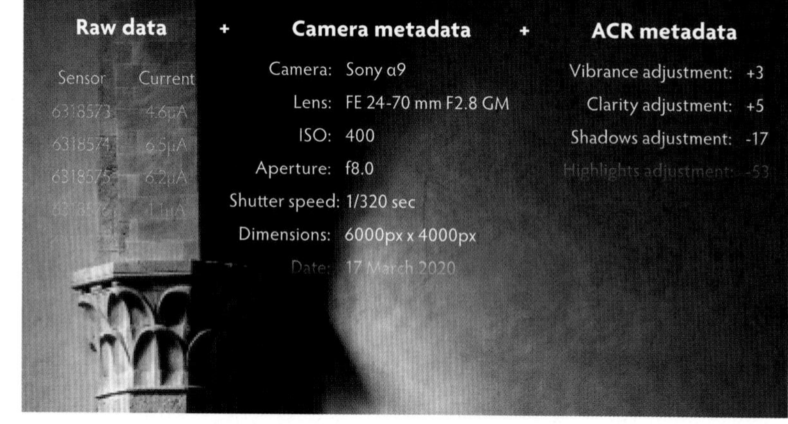

Along the bottom of the ACR interface is the Filmstrip. If you select multiple images there, every edit you make is performed on them all. That is both extremely cool and a bit dangerous. Most of the edits we make are achieved with the panels on the right and the tools on the right.

Basic Panel

On the right side of the ACR interface are the panels we use to adjust our image (interpret the raw data). The first of these, and the most vital, is Basic. This is where we make the biggest adjustments to color and tone.

White Balance

When adjusting our images in Camera Raw or Lightroom, one of the first things we do is set the white balance, specifying the color of the light in the scene so the software can compensate for it. So if the light was very yellow indoor lighting, the Tungsten preset may add the right amount of blue to compensate.

If you choose that preset, the Temperature slider will have a value of 2850, as in 2850 kelvin, the literal temperature at which a tungsten filament in an incandescent bulb glows. The sun is hotter than that, as you'd expect, so its temperature is around 5500K, which is what you get when you choose the Daylight preset. As we go from candlelight, a rather low temperature and a deep yellow light, through tungsten to daylight, the light gets progressively less yellow (more blue). At color temperatures higher than daylight, we need yellow to compensate for the bluishness of the light. Some camera flashes require this correction.

A graph of the color of light from candlelight to strobe is not a perfect line from yellow to blue; a bit of magenta or green may be needed to compensate more perfectly. That's the job of the Tint slider, which also changes a bit when presets are chosen.

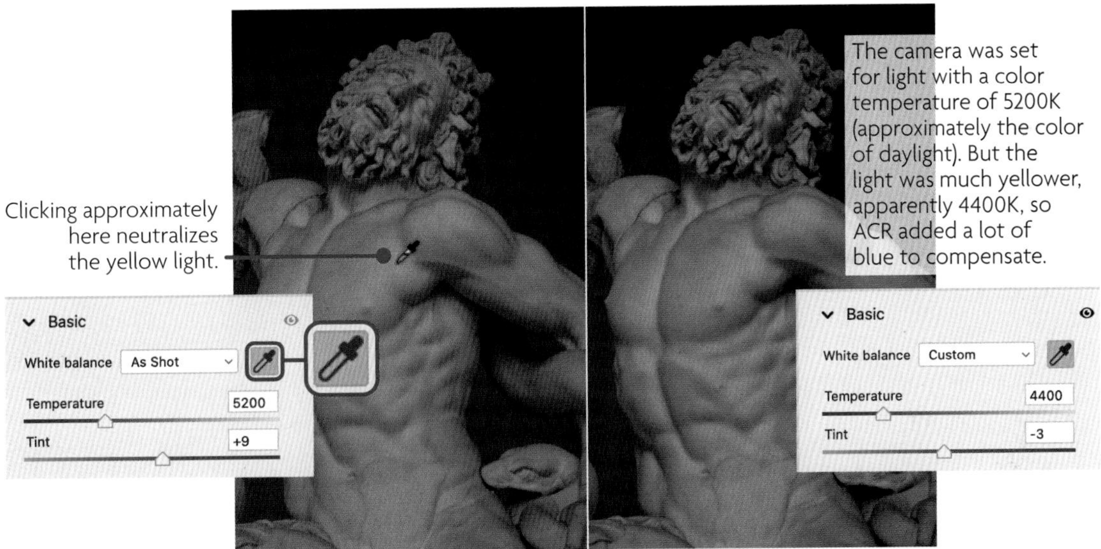
Clicking approximately here neutralizes the yellow light.
Basic
White balance As Shot
Temperature 5200
Tint +9
The camera was set for light with a color temperature of 5200K (approximately the color of daylight). But the light was much yellower, apparently 4400K, so ACR added a lot of blue to compensate.
Basic
White balance Custom
Temperature 4400
Tint -3

To make this process easier, look in your image for something that ought to be a nice neutral gray (a light gray is best). The eyedropper-like tool in the Basic panel is called the White Balance tool. Click on what should be neutral, and the Temperature and Tint sliders will move to make it so!

Remember, if you have multiple images highlighted in the filmstrip, you can click a gray in one image to adjust all of the images at once. This is why I usually carry a light gray object (my camera bag!) with me when I do photography. I also have a smaller gray card I can use when I'm photographing smaller subjects or I don't want to ask my subject to pose with my bag.

Tone and Presence

The sliders below those for white balance (Temperature and Tint) are for what Lightroom calls tone (light and dark) and presence (local contrast, saturation). The expectation is that we'll start at the top and work our way down, and that is good advice. However, I find myself returning to earlier sliders when I've made strong adjustments to later ones. The largest contributor to light and dark in the image is the Exposure slider. It simulates increasing or decreasing the exposure in 1 EV, or stop, increments. If there are clipped highlights or shadows, decreasing global Contrast may help. Looking for spikes on either end of the histogram is one way to know if there's clipping. Another is to look at the small triangles in the top corners of the histogram window. Black means no clipping, colors mean that only one or two channels are clipping, and white means all three are. Clicking those triangles enables a clipping preview in the image: Blue covers shadow pixels that are clipped to black, and red covers blown highlights.

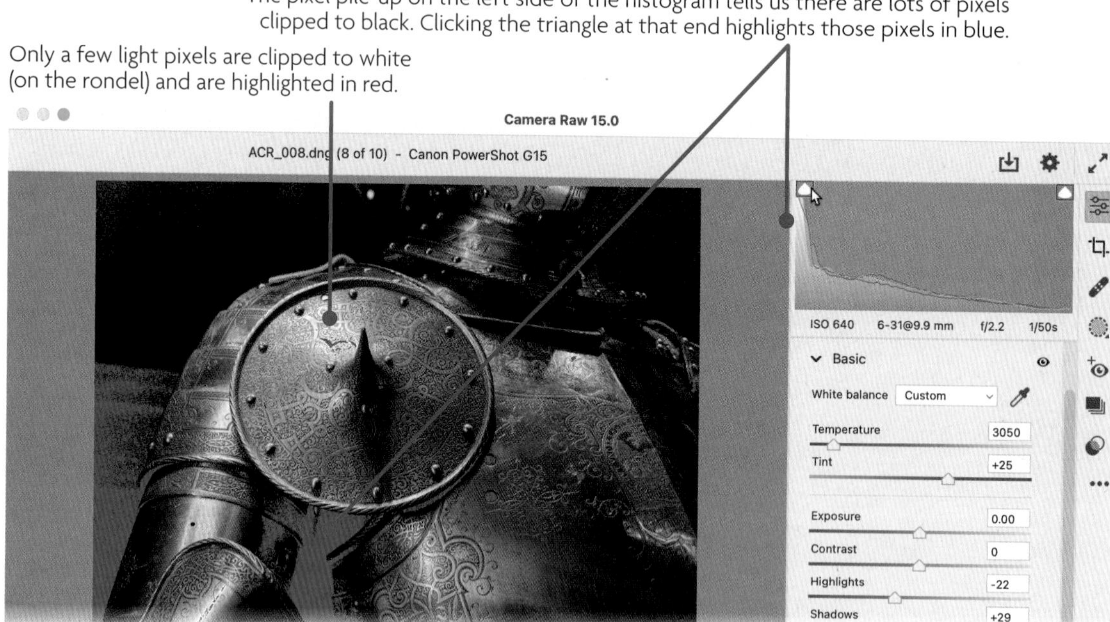

The pixel pile-up on the left side of the histogram tells us there are lots of pixels clipped to black. Clicking the triangle at that end highlights those pixels in blue.

Only a few light pixels are clipped to white (on the rondel) and are highlighted in red.

I will allow the intuitive reader to figure out what parts of the tonal range the Highlights and Shadows sliders most affect. Both also impact the midtones somewhat. The Whites and Blacks sliders set the white point and black point and can most readily incur (or cure) clipping at either end of the tonal range. So, if I'm pleased with my Exposure setting but have clipped highlights, for example, I may be able to recover them with the Whites slider.

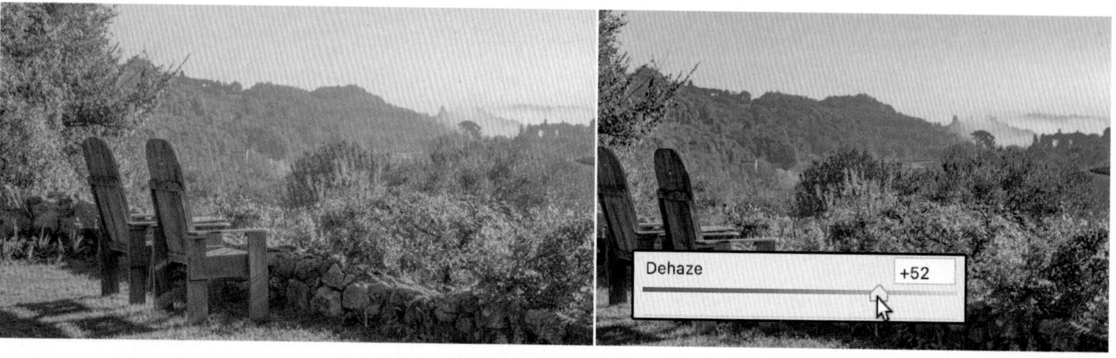

The last five sliders are for affecting "presence." Texture and Clarity affect local contrast and can make an image look gently sharper or softer. Texture is more fine-grained and is intended for enhancing (or concealing) texture in hair or skin. Dehaze attempts to help us with images that would have been aided by the use of a polarizing filter on the lens. It tries to enhance details in atmospheric haze, like in the image below.

Finally, Vibrance and Saturation both affect saturation (color intensity) in an image. However, the Saturation slider is more aggressive and can clip colors, causing a loss of gradation and details in the most vibrant areas. I strongly suggest trying to limit yourself to the Vibrance slider, except when working with those images that are nearly monochromatic at the start.

Black & White Treatment

Just below the histogram, we find two buttons: Auto and B&W.

When choosing B&W (Black & White), we may make very different decisions about contrast than we would in color. Also, ACR's Color Mixer panel adapts to become B&W Mixer, which is very similar to Photoshop's adjustment called "Black & White" (page 251). With either, we can decide which hues in the original image become dark or light shades of gray.

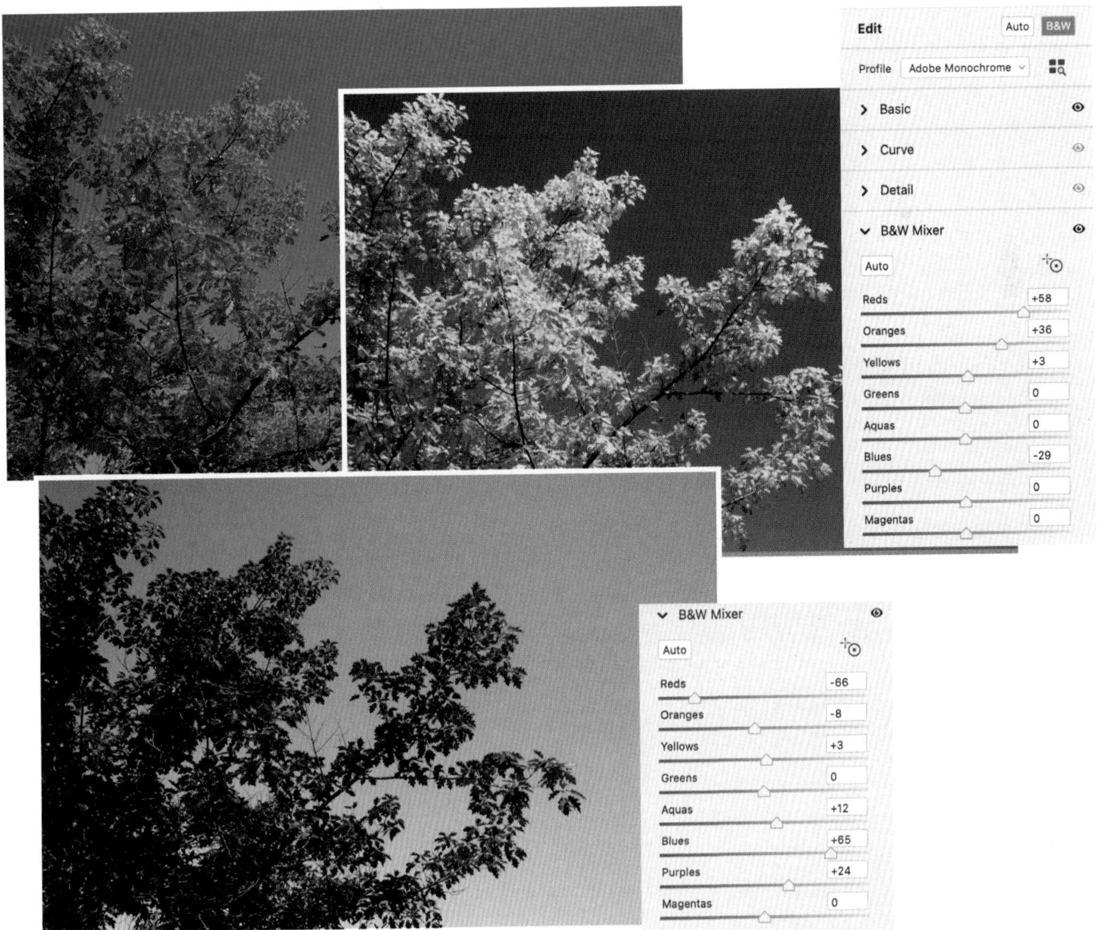

Tone Curve Panel

Since this panel is derived from (and extremely similar to) Photohop's Curves adjustment, see "Curves" (page 238).

Detail Panel: Sharpening & Noise Reduction

For a variety of reasons, many images from digital cameras have a small amount of inherent softness (blurriness). This is why Camera Raw and Lightroom add a small amount of sharpening to every image. You can, of course, control just how much sharpening is applied with the Detail panel. For much more on sharpening, see "Camera Raw Sharpening" (page 315) in the "Filters & Transforms" chapter of this Compendium.

The Detail panel also helps us manage noise in images. Using either high ISO or long exposures can cause speckles to appear in images, especially in dark areas. By default, a small amount of color noise reduction is applied to all images. As with sharpening, you can adjust this to taste. Luckily, the software is very good at knowing the difference between noise and small, colorful elements in our photos.

When the noise is variations of light and dark (luminance noise), we have to be more careful. In reducing that noise, we may also be losing fine details. So, I find I often have to adjust the Luminance Detail and Luminance Contrast to maintain those details, or at least strike a balance between noise and detail. We have similar controls for color noise, but we need them less often.

Color Mixer Panel

This is rather like "Hue/Saturation" (page 243) or "Black & White" (page 251) if in B&W treatment. There are two modes: Adjust HSL or Adjust Color. In the first, you choose whether to adjust Hue, Saturation, or Luminance, then do so hue-by-hue. With Adjust Color mode, you choose the hue to adjust then affect its Hue, Saturation, or Luminance.

Color Grading

The lovely feature in ACR for lending mood to an image is Color Grading. It maps color to different parts of the tonal range. Like in cinema, you can add cool tones to enhance a sense of cold in a snowy scene. Or mix warm and cool to enliven a too-gray image like this armor.

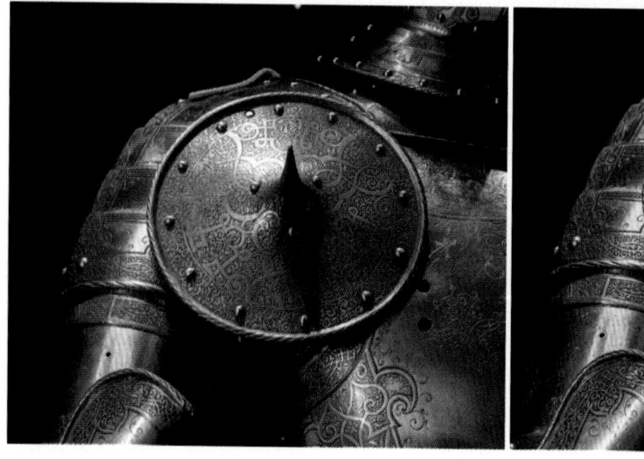
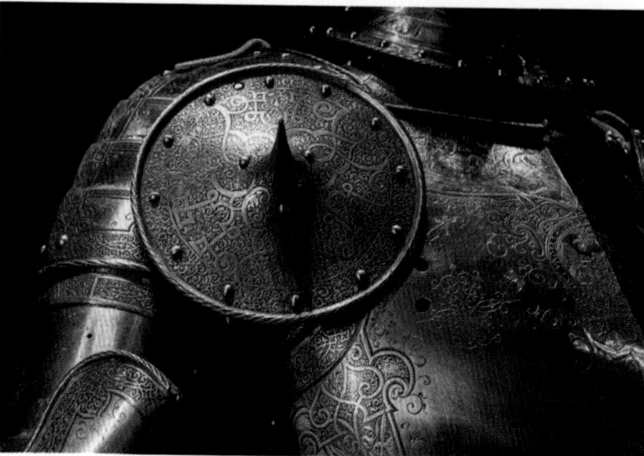

Color Grading applies colors to three parts of the tonal range: highlights, midtones, and shadows, each of which it can also lighten or darken a bit. It also has a global adjustment interface for giving all tonal values a bit of a color bump.

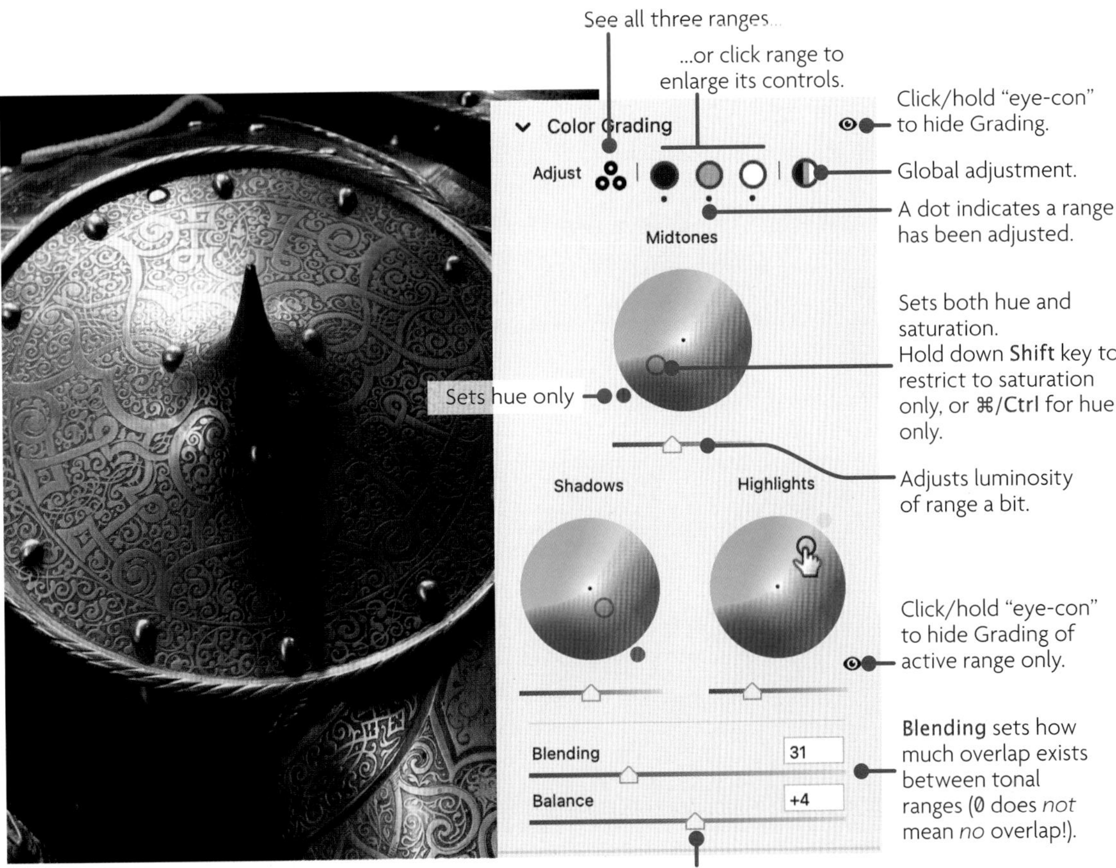
See all three ranges...
...or click range to enlarge its controls.
Click/hold "eye-con" to hide Grading.
Color Grading
Adjust
Global adjustment.
A dot indicates a range has been adjusted.
Midtones
Sets both hue and saturation.
Hold down **Shift** key to restrict to saturation only, or ⌘/**Ctrl** for hue only.
Sets hue only
Shadows
Highlights
Adjusts luminosity of range a bit.
Click/hold "eye-con" to hide Grading of active range only.
Blending
31
Balance
+4
Blending sets how much overlap exists between tonal ranges (0 does *not* mean *no* overlap!).
Balance broadens either the highlight range or the shadow range, effectively extending the hue of each. Extend the highlights by dragging right or the shadows by dragging left.

If you open an image from an old version of ACR with a Split Toning adjustment, ACR will maintain the look you previously achieved. Color Grading can also let you achieve more.

See the figure above to get a grasp on the user interface. However, the best way to master this adjustment is to experiment. I rather like the way I was able to warm up the light on the armor in the photo above while making the steel look cold and more, well, steely. I'm sure you'll find nice uses to give a chill to winter images and some swelter to summer ones.

Optics Panel: For Distortions and More

Many lenses, especially wide-angle lenses, produce images that exhibit overall distortions of the image (barrel and pincushion distortions are the most familiar) and chromatic aberration, which is noticeable as color fringing at high-contrast edges.

Any lens will produce distortions nearly identical to that of every other lens of the same make and model. So, Adobe acquires every lens made and creates a profile for it that describes that lens model's distortions, including any vignetting (darkening at the edges). At the top of the Optics panel are two checkboxes: Remove chromatic aberration and Use profile corrections. I enthusiastically recommend enabling both for *all* images unless you see a problem caused by doing so (*very* unlikely).

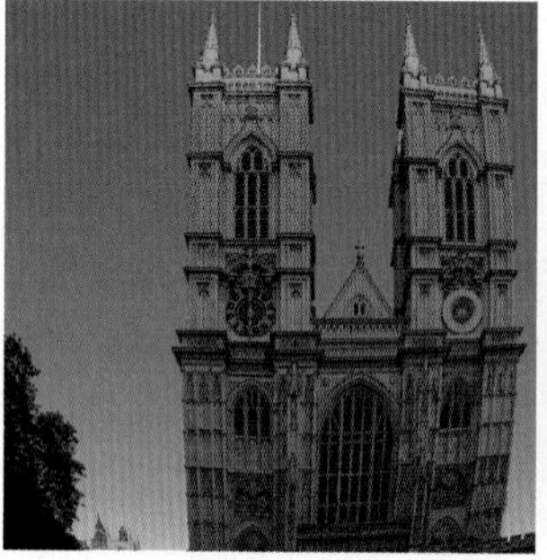

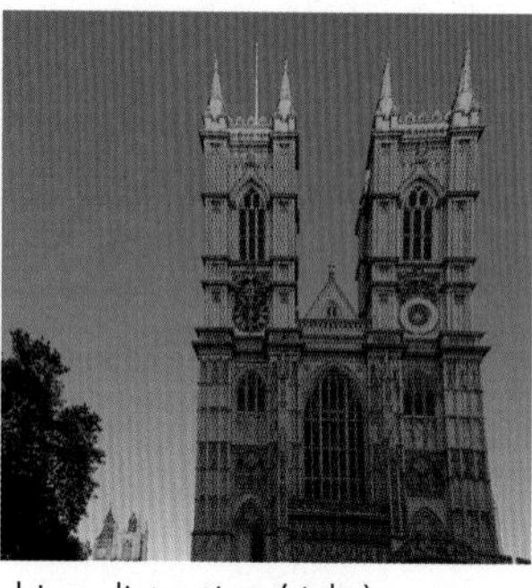

Barrel distortion (left) and pincushion distortion (right).

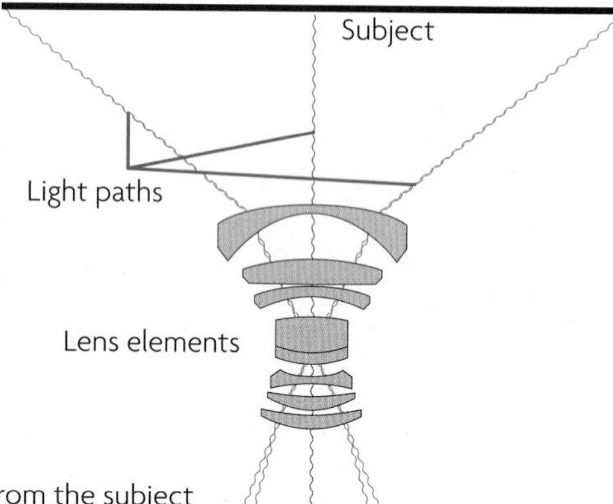

Lateral (or transverse) chromatic aberration: Rays of light from the subject get diffracted in the lens to produce fringing on either side of an edge.

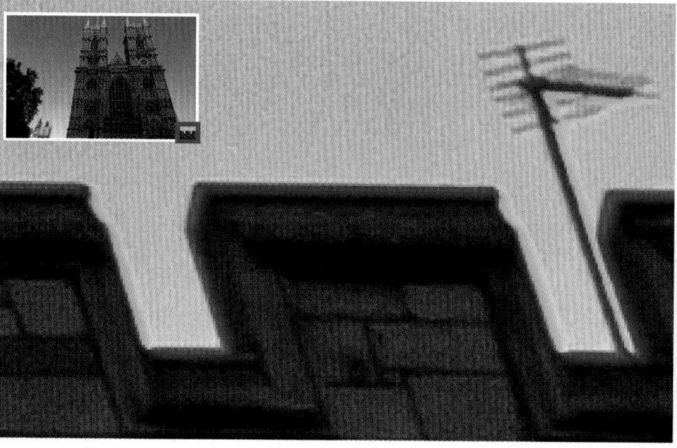

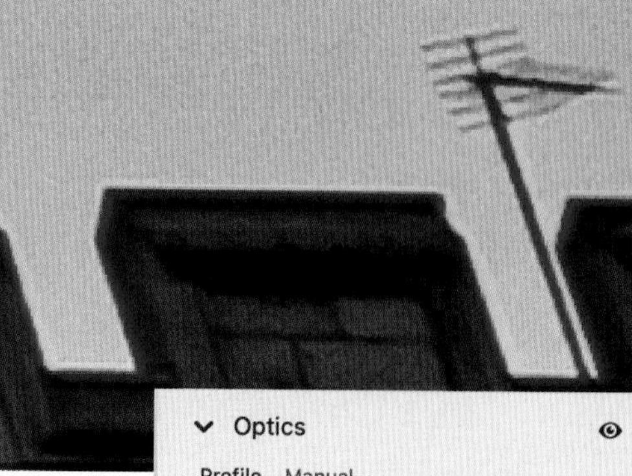

The color fringing you see at left is caused primarily by lateral chromatic aberration: The colors of the fringing are opposite hues on each side of edges in the image, especially those near the perimeter of this wide-angle shot.

In the Optics panel, Remove chromatic aberration deals with this well!

Although those checkboxes do extraordinarily well, you may still detect some remaining purple or green fringing caused by axial (sometimes called longitudinal) chromatic aberration. Usually seen in backlit subjects, this kind requires the use of the Defringe section of the Optics panel. Choose the appropriate color's sliders (purple or green), and increase the Amount until the fringe is reduced or removed. To adjust the color's Hue slider to better restrict the fringe reduction to warmer or cooler versions of the green or purple fringe, there's a dropper with which you can sample the fringe in the image. You may also fine-tune the hue as well with the sliders for each hue. This will help protect desirable elements in the photo that are green or purple because Defringe could affect them too. Adjust the amount to taste.

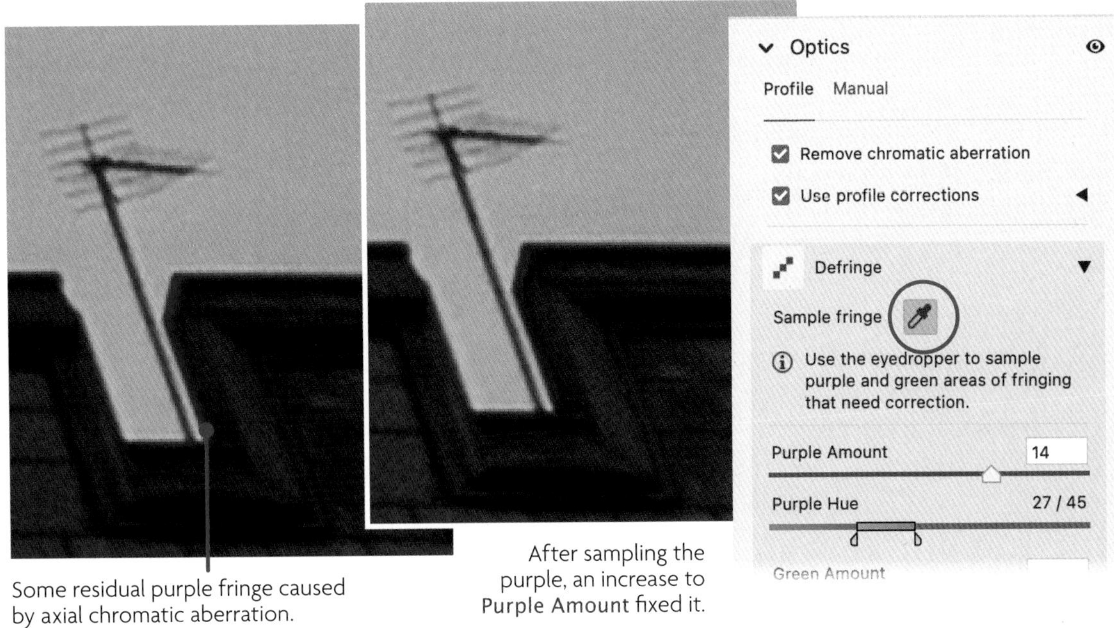

Some residual purple fringe caused by axial chromatic aberration.

After sampling the purple, an increase to Purple Amount fixed it.

Geometry Panel & Upright Perspective Correction

The Geometry panel contains manual and automatic options for perspective correction. A "semiautomatic" option called Guided is also available. Always try the various auto buttons of the Upright feature before working with the guided or manual sliders: You may save yourself a lot of time! Each button next to the word Upright does something a bit different.

Upright

Off

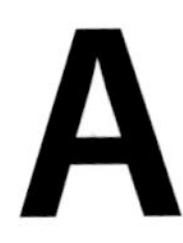
Auto

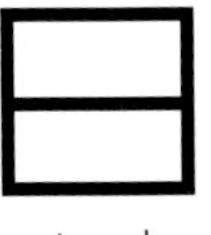
Level

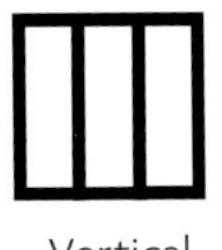
Vertical

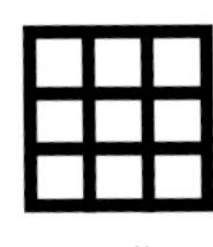
Full

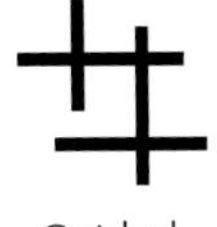
Guided

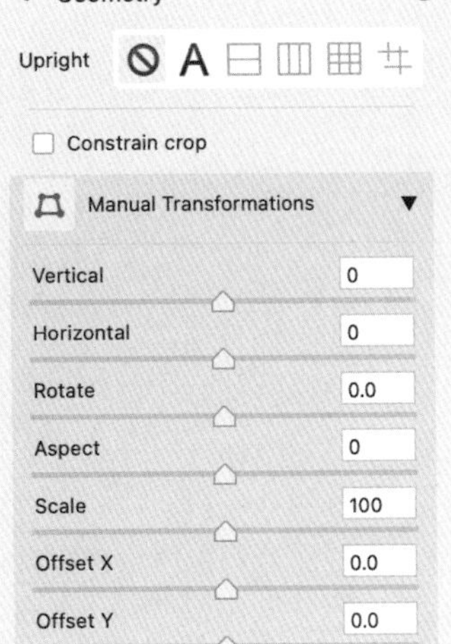

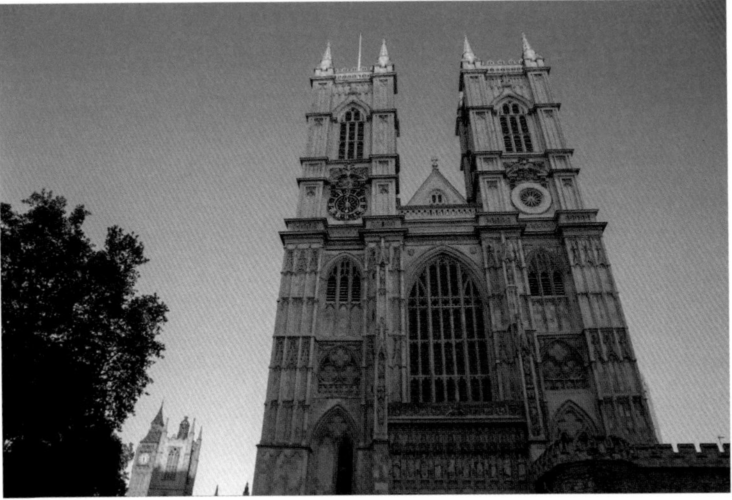

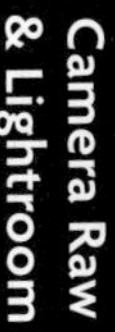

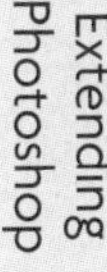

The A is for auto, which tries to apply a pleasing amount of both vertical and horizontal adjustment. The next two are Level and Vertical, which straighten prominent horizontal and vertical lines in the image, respectively, making them parallel to the edges of the image. Level favors horizontals lower in an image, assuming them to be a horizon. The Full button does both at once, and often does an excellent job. When these buttons fall short, there is the last one, Guided. With this, you draw one or two guides along elements in the image that should be perfectly level, and one or two lines along hoped-for verticals. Check the box for a Loupe (magnifier) near the cursor to aid precision. The lines you make can be moved or their angle adjusted by the small circular handles at each end.

Once more than two guides are made, ACR transforms the image. This can be further modified with more guides or the sliders under Manual Transformations. I often adjust Aspect to correct for any stretching, and Offset X and Y to fine-tune the composition.

The Scale slider can be handy to be rid of blank regions introduced during the transformation. If those are significant, I follow up with the Crop tool.

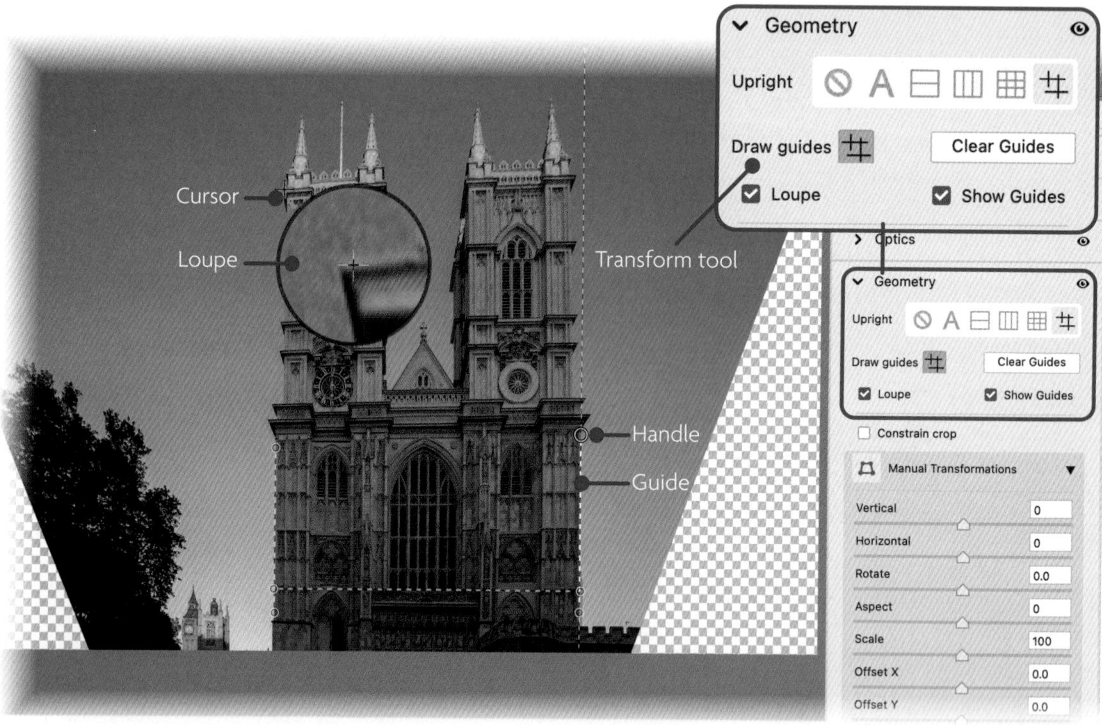

The **Guided Upright** feature allows you to draw up to four guides along lines in the image that you'd like to be either horizontal or vertical (ACR will know which should be which). Here, you can see the fourth (and final) line being finished. The **Loupe** (magnified view near the cursor) helps us line up with landmarks in the image, like this ledge.

Crop Tool: It's Nondestructive Too!

When choosing the Crop tool, first press and hold on it so you can see a few options. If the image possesses transparent areas like the one shown in the previous example, you can ensure they are not part of the final image by choosing Constrain to Image. I sometimes disable that so I can retouch those later. You may also choose an aspect ratio (shape) for the final crop, including Custom... to set your own.

Draw the crop overlay (box), then adjust it by dragging its handles. I usually commit it by choosing another tool, although tapping the Enter key works too.

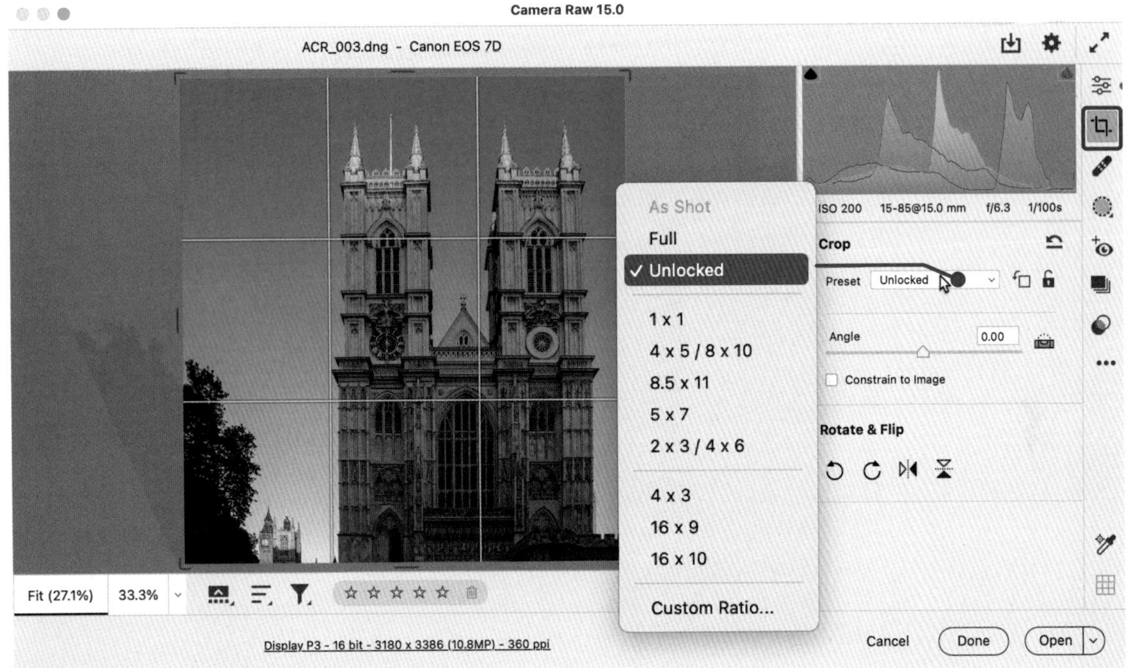

Effects: Film Grain & Vignetting

In the Effects panel, you can simulate old-style film grain and add lightness or darkness around the current, possibly cropped edges of your image. Three sliders let you control the Grain: Amount, Size, and Roughness, and they're as intuitive as they sound.

Vignetting has more options and subtlety. Once you adjust the Amount at all, to the left for darker edges or to the right for lighter ones, both the Style menu and the other sliders become available. The easiest Style to understand is Paint Overlay, as it simply covers the underlying image with black or white, with increasing opacity the farther you drag the Amount slider from the center.

The Midpoint slider moves the vignette inward or outward, and refers to the point midway between the most and least opaque parts of the vignette. To see the vignette farther from the corners of the crop, use a higher value.

Lower Roundness values make the vignette conform to the aspect ratio of the current crop. Higher values make it more circular.

Feather controls the blurriness of the vignette's edge.

The Highlight slider is active only with the Styles Highlight Priority and Color Priority, and when the Amount is negative (the vignette is dark). If you want some highlights in the darkened areas to shine through, choose Highlight Priority, then use the Highlights slider to control how much. To better preserve highlight color rather than its detail, use Color Priority.

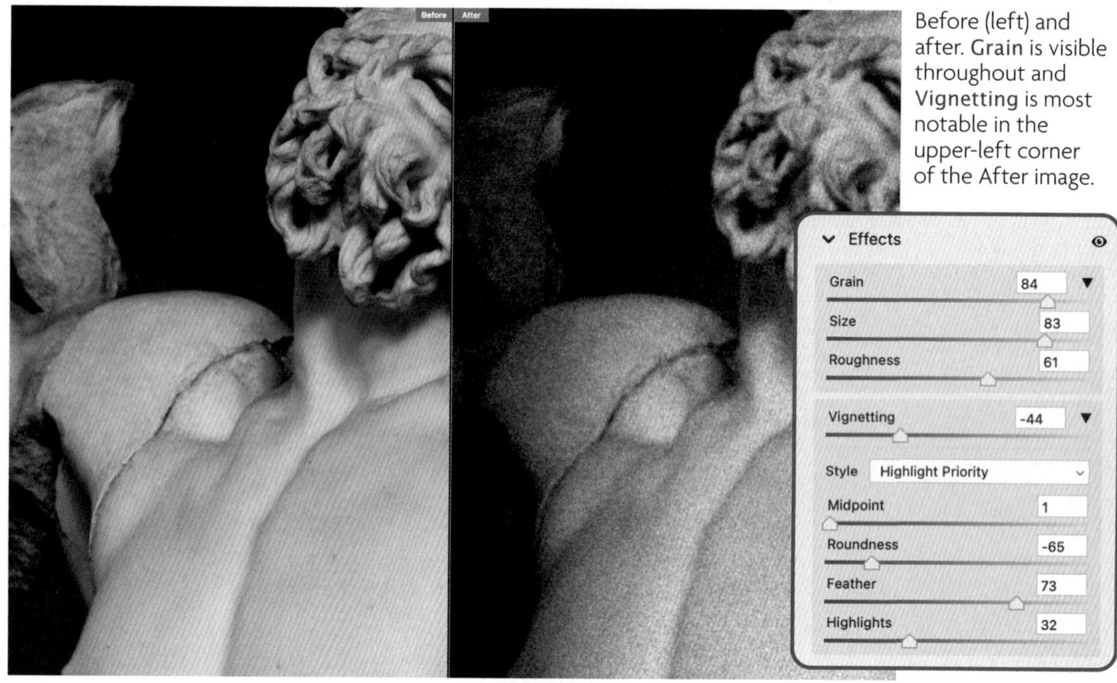

Before (left) and after. **Grain** is visible throughout and **Vignetting** is most notable in the upper-left corner of the After image.

Spot Removal Tool: Removing Blemishes

The **Healing** tools in ACR and Lightroom are interesting interpretations of Photoshop's **Spot Healing Brush**, **Healing Brush**, and **Clone Stamp**. Read more about those in the "Retouching & Repair" chapter, under "Tools & Methods" (page 341). Once in the **Healing** mode, you can choose what type of repair you wish to make, **Content-Aware Remove**, **Heal**, or **Clone**.

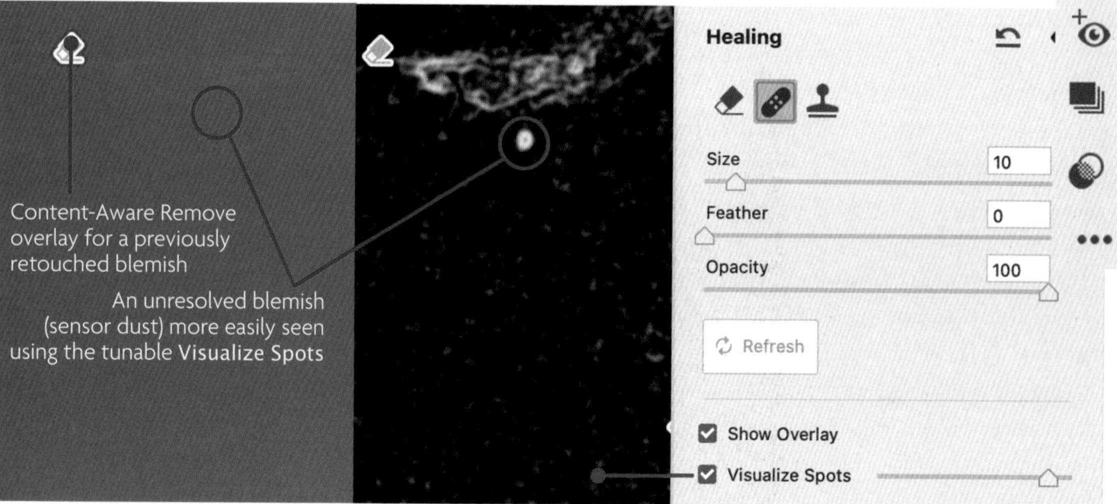

Content-Aware Remove overlay for a previously retouched blemish

An unresolved blemish (sensor dust) more easily seen using the tunable **Visualize Spots**

When editing raw images, every edit has to be writable to the file's metadata, and thus be editable and nondestructive. So, when we click on a blemish with these tools, one or two circular overlays appear: one surrounding the blemish, and, with the Heal and Clone tools, a second designating the source of the repair—that is, the area used to "patch" the blemish. The sizes and locations of all pairs of circles created this way are recorded in metadata. As you work, you may change the size, edge softness ("Feather"), or opacity of the brush.

You may return to a raw file weeks later, choose Healing mode, and you'll see the overlays that are obscuring the blemishes. Select one and you'll see its size, and can move, feather, resize, or delete it, along with its associated source, and even change what type it is!

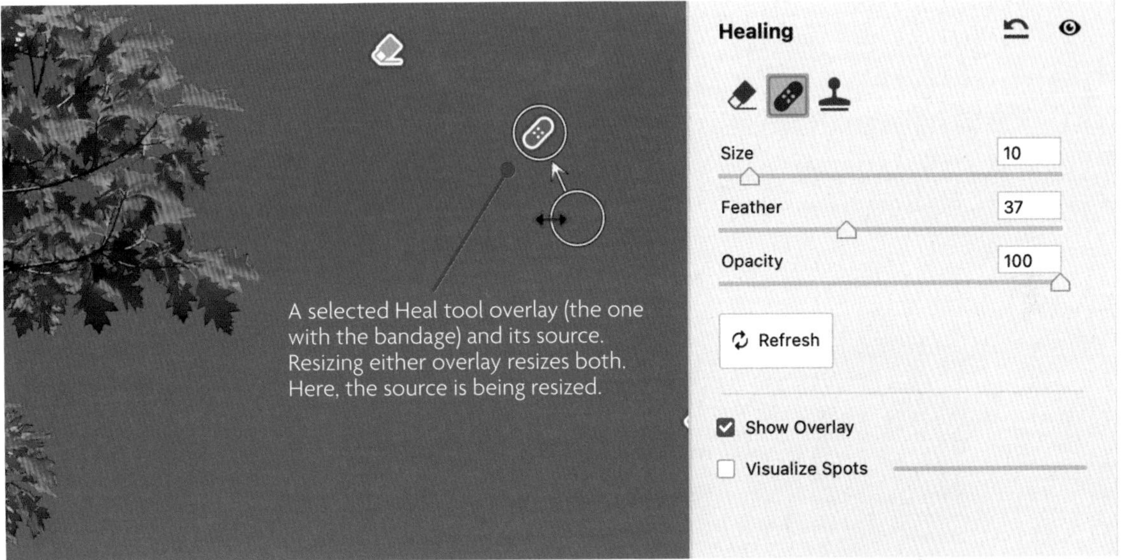

A selected Heal tool overlay (the one with the bandage) and its source. Resizing either overlay resizes both. Here, the source is being resized.

Instead of clicking to create a circular repair, you may drag to create irregular shapes to cover irregularly shaped blemishes. For healing and cloning, this will automatically create a nearby source in the same shape. These may be moved or deleted, their Type or Feather changed, but they may not be resized or amended. Content-Aware Remove is more interesting!

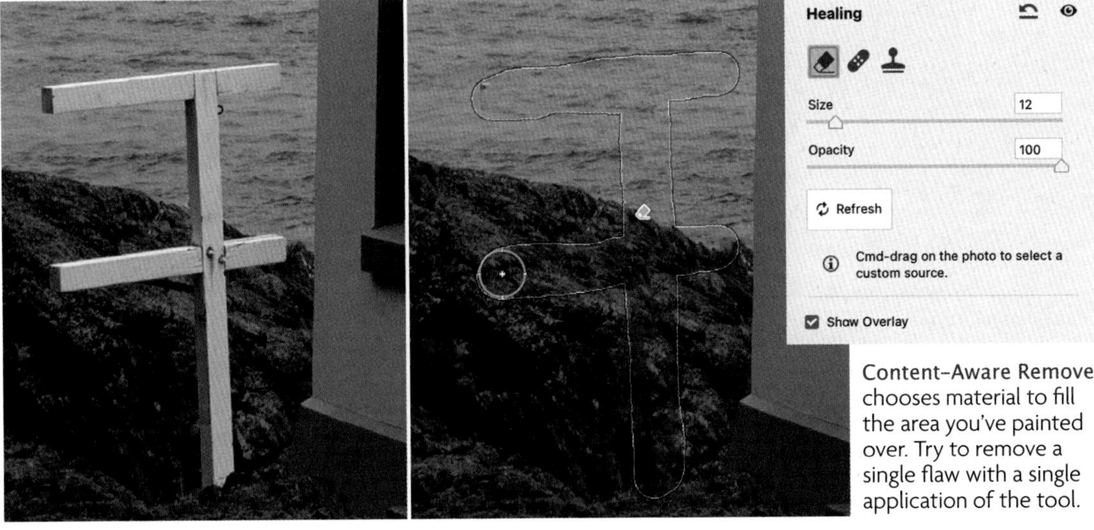

Content-Aware Remove chooses material to fill the area you've painted over. Try to remove a single flaw with a single application of the tool.

Similar to the Spot Healing Brush tool, this tool chooses content from which to fill in the designated area. However, if you don't like its source material, simply hold down ⌘/Ctrl and draw a rectangular marquee around a more suitable source. With Heal or Clone, simply move the source overlay to choose a different source area.

When creating a Clone repair, I often use some amount of Feather to help the repair blend into its surroundings. That is usually unnecessary when healing.

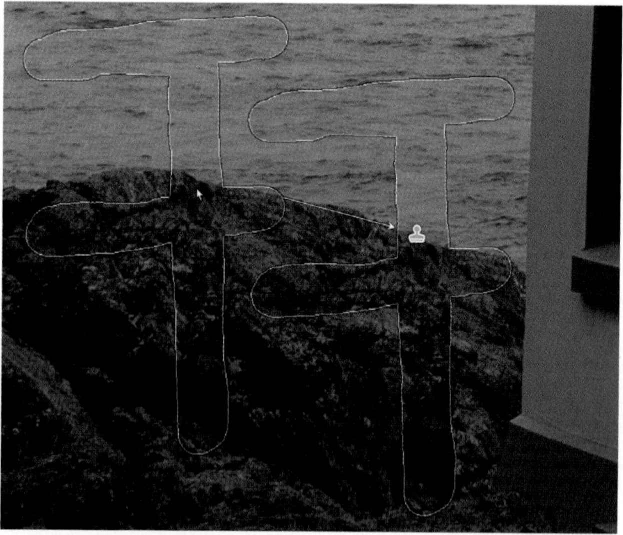

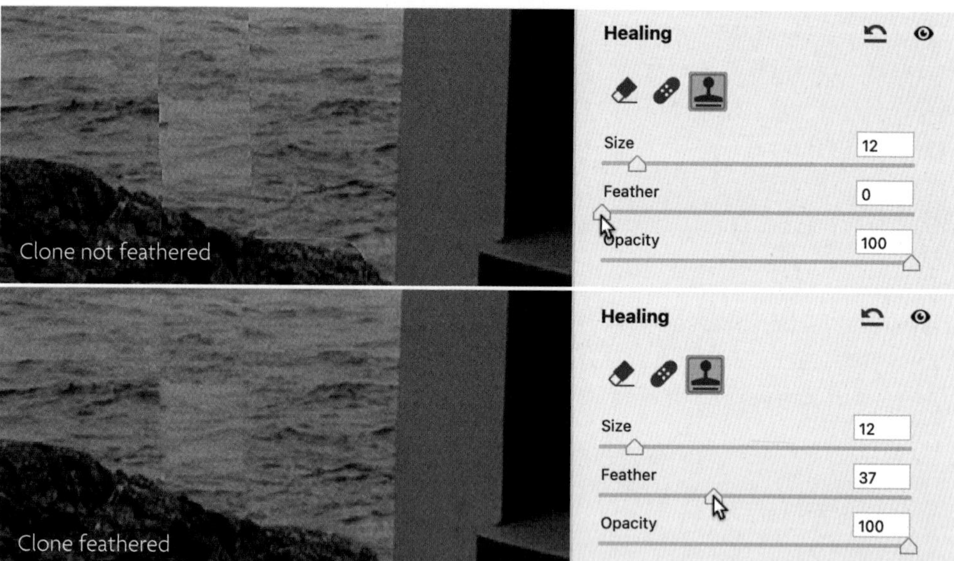

For those blemishes that are hard to see, like sensor dust, you should enable Visualize Spots and adjust its slider. Edges are accentuated in a black-and-white view of the image. Sensor dust, in particular, often appears as roughly circular blobs. You may use the Spot Removal tool in this mode, then disable it to see the image in color again.

Masked Adjustments

ACR and Lightroom refer to these simply as "masks," but that's a touch confusing for us Photoshop users. When we create masks in ACR, we also choose an adjustment or effect to go with it—a package deal. We don't have *layer* masks in these applications, nor can we create composite images. But it is possible to create complex, editable masks to better control where our adjustments take place. The list of possible adjustments that appears after creating a mask is nearly as large as it is in the Edit mode!

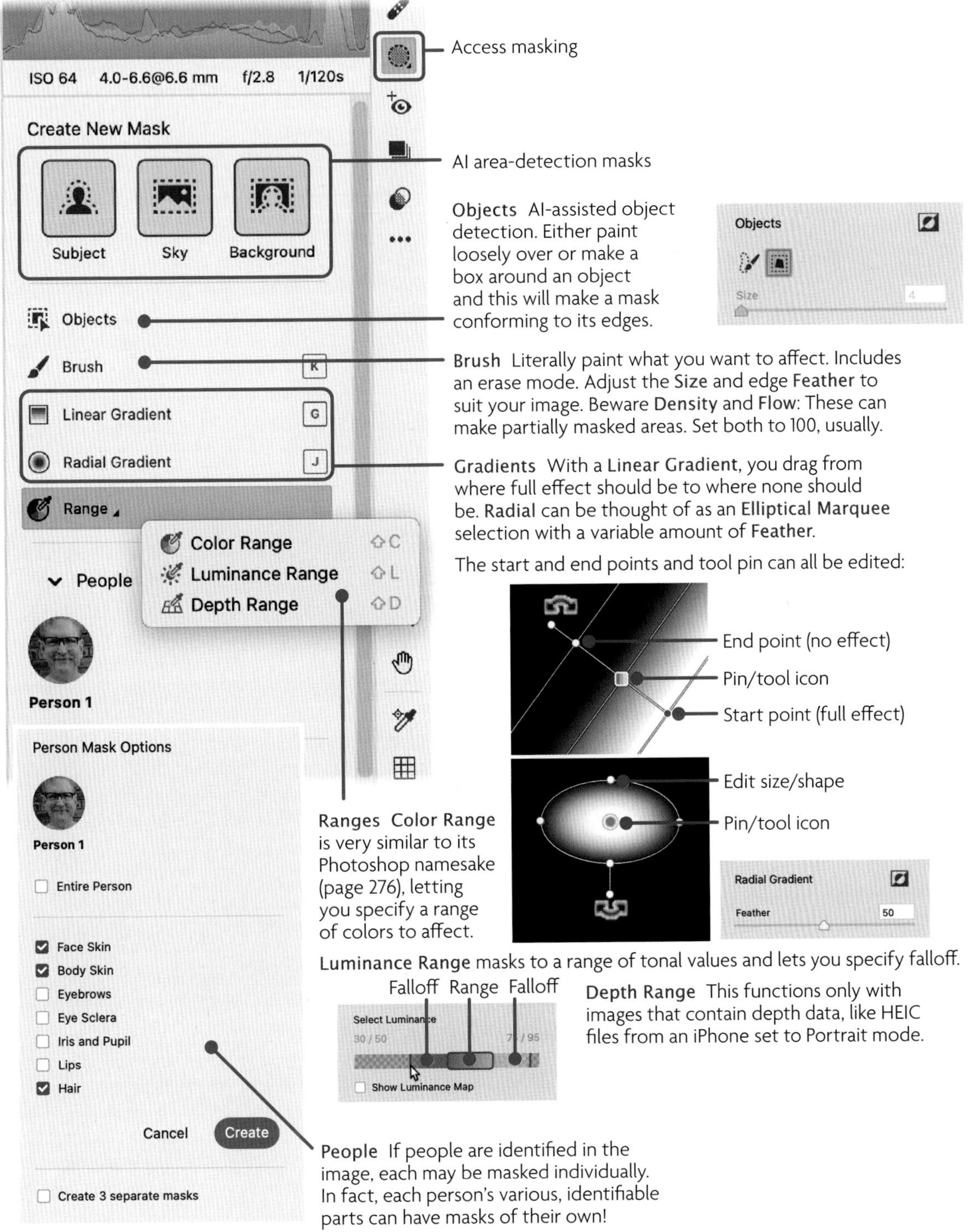

ISO 64 4.0-6.6@6.6 mm f/2.8 1/120s
Create New Mask
Subject
Sky
Background
Objects
Brush
K
Linear Gradient
G
Radial Gradient
J
Range
Color Range
Luminance Range
Depth Range
People
Person 1
Person Mask Options
Person 1
Entire Person
Face Skin
Body Skin
Eyebrows
Eye Sclera
Iris and Pupil
Lips
Hair
Cancel
Create
Create 3 separate masks
Access masking
AI area-detection masks
Objects AI-assisted object detection. Either paint loosely over or make a box around an object and this will make a mask conforming to its edges.
Objects
Size
Brush Literally paint what you want to affect. Includes an erase mode. Adjust the **Size** and edge **Feather** to suit your image. Beware **Density** and **Flow**: These can make partially masked areas. Set both to 100, usually.
Gradients With a **Linear Gradient**, you drag from where full effect should be to where none should be. **Radial** can be thought of as an **Elliptical Marquee** selection with a variable amount of **Feather**.
The start and end points and tool pin can all be edited:
End point (no effect)
Pin/tool icon
Start point (full effect)
Edit size/shape
Pin/tool icon
Radial Gradient
Feather
50
Ranges **Color Range** is very similar to its Photoshop namesake (page 276), letting you specify a range of colors to affect.
Luminance Range masks to a range of tonal values and lets you specify falloff.
Falloff Range Falloff
Select Luminance
Show Luminance Map
Depth Range This functions only with images that contain depth data, like HEIC files from an iPhone set to Portrait mode.
People If people are identified in the image, each may be masked individually. In fact, each person's various, identifiable parts can have masks of their own!

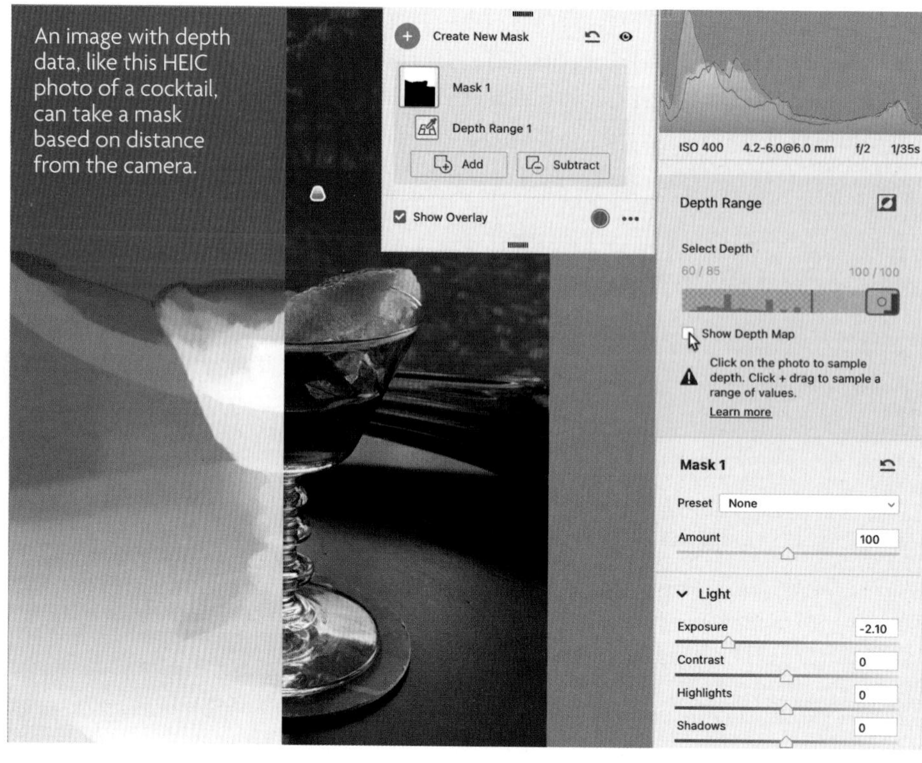

One of the best parts of masking in ACR and Lightroom is that a mask can be a combination of all these types. That is, I can start with a Subject mask, add to it with a brush where it initially missed material, and subtract where there was too much. Below, I did just those things, and I subtracted a Sky selection from the subject so the sky in the upper tier of the lighthouse wouldn't be affected.

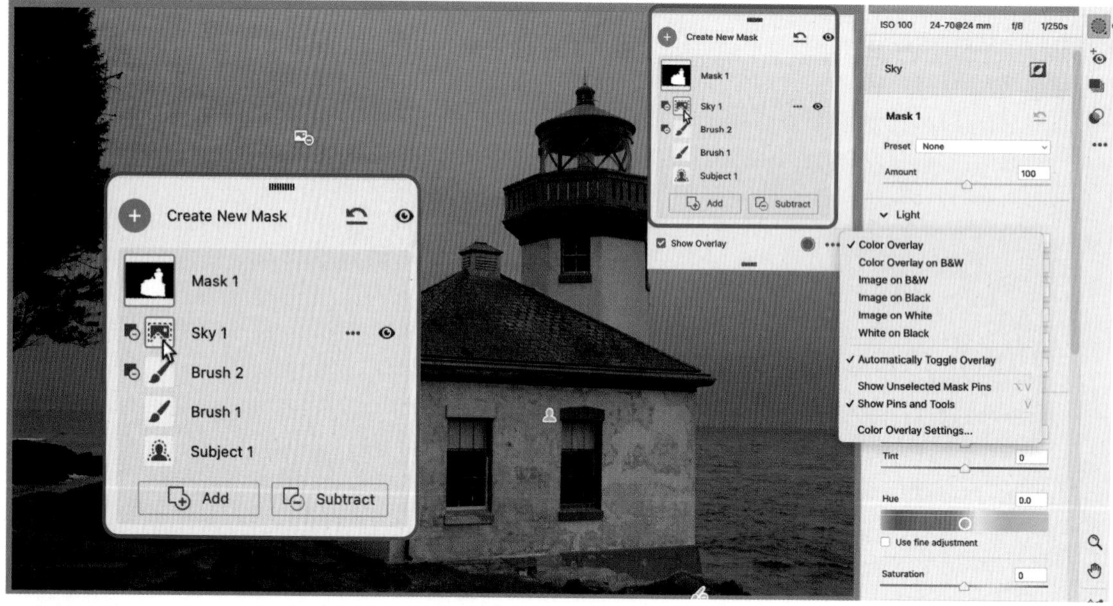

Lightroom to Photoshop

Many photographers manage raw captures and other images with Lightroom, and perform with it the same development tasks that can be done in ACR. I use Lightroom Classic, currently the more full-featured version. If and when you've done all that you can do in Lightroom and find you need the power of Photoshop to do more, I recommend a particular workflow.

The most common way to push an image to Photoshop from Lightroom is to right-click its thumbnail and choose Edit In, a menu with several choices. Since you cannot directly edit raw files in Photoshop, Lightroom generates a TIFF file. If you simply choose Edit in Adobe Photoshop from that Edit In menu, the image will open as a Background layer in that TIFF. However, I recommend going farther down that list to Open as Smart Object in Photoshop.

With the raw data passed as a Smart Object in that TIFF, you can still perform all the tasks you likely wanted to do, with an added benefit. If partway through those tasks you realize that you should have done something more to the raw data, you can do so by editing the Smart Object's contents (double-clicking its thumbnail). You won't be editing the original capture managed by Lightroom, but rather a copy ensconced in the SO. So you'll have all of Photoshop's tools *and* all of Adobe Camera Raw *and* rich raw data to perform it on.

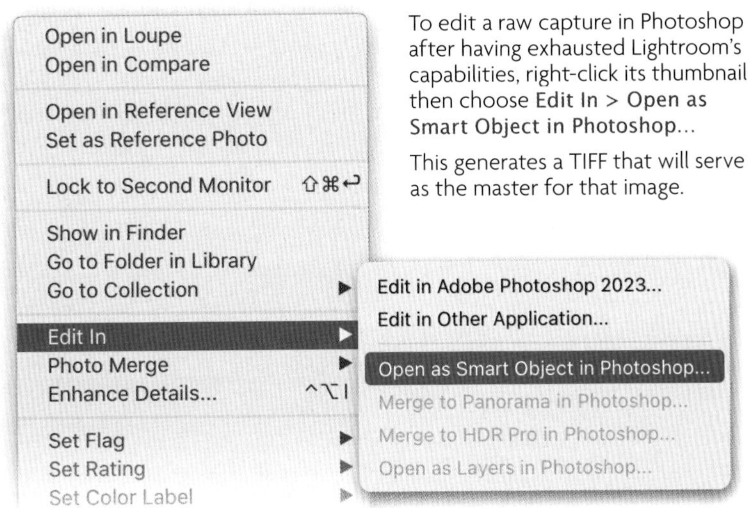

To edit a raw capture in Photoshop after having exhausted Lightroom's capabilities, right-click its thumbnail, then choose Edit In > Open as Smart Object in Photoshop...

This generates a TIFF that will serve as the master for that image.

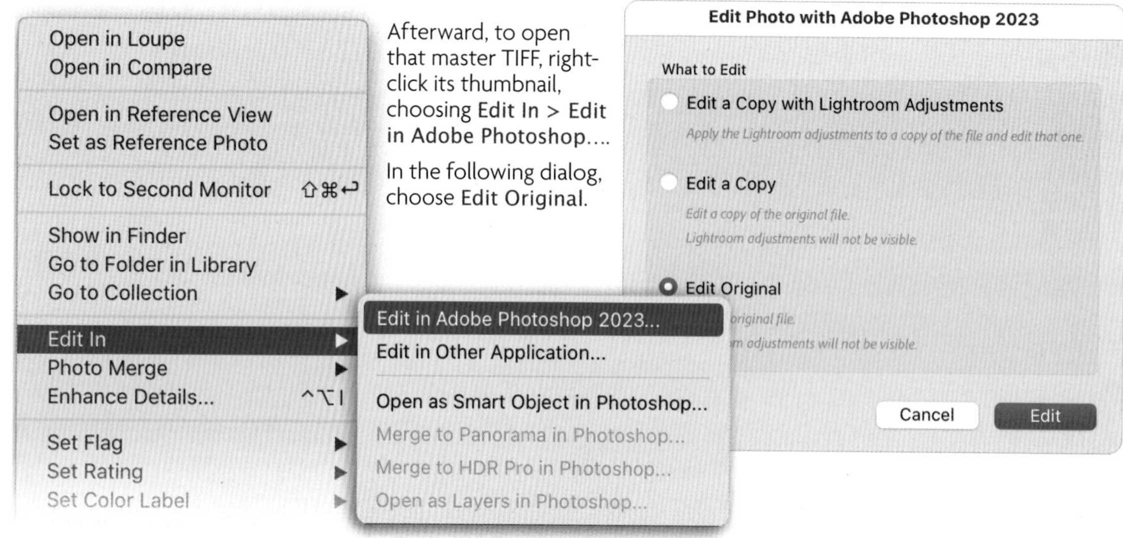

Afterward, to open that master TIFF, right-click its thumbnail, choosing Edit In > Edit in Adobe Photoshop.... In the following dialog, choose Edit Original.

When (and if) you save that TIFF with a simple ⌘-S/Ctrl-S, it gets saved to the same folder as the original capture, and is another file that Lightroom manages. You'll recognize it by its name: There will be "-Edit" appended to it and the extension will be ".tif." For me, that file wouldn't exist if I hadn't exhausted Lightroom's capabilities. So that TIFF becomes my master version of that image, and all future edits should be performed in Photoshop—not in Lightroom!

That means to edit it again, I'd click on its Lightroom thumbnail, but from now on choose Edit In > Edit in Adobe Photoshop. I don't need to create another file with all my previous edits embedded in another Smart Object. I want to open the same TIFF Lightroom made last time. When I choose Edit in Adobe Photoshop, Lightroom will show a dialog box offering choices that can be confusing. You should choose Edit Original, which does *not* mean the original capture, but the file you right-clicked on! The other choices create yet more copies. I am willing to have as many copies as I need, but absolutely no more than that.

8 Extending Photoshop

Photoshop is huge, magnificent, and under continual development. But, as with all software, users discover shortcomings. The engineers of this application have given us ways to extend Photoshop ourselves.

With Actions and Scripts, we can perform operations that Photoshop doesn't have, or we can perform included operations more efficiently.

The recent and rapid development of AI/ML (artificial intelligence/machine learning) tools from Adobe and others will provide even greater power—and raise some difficult questions.

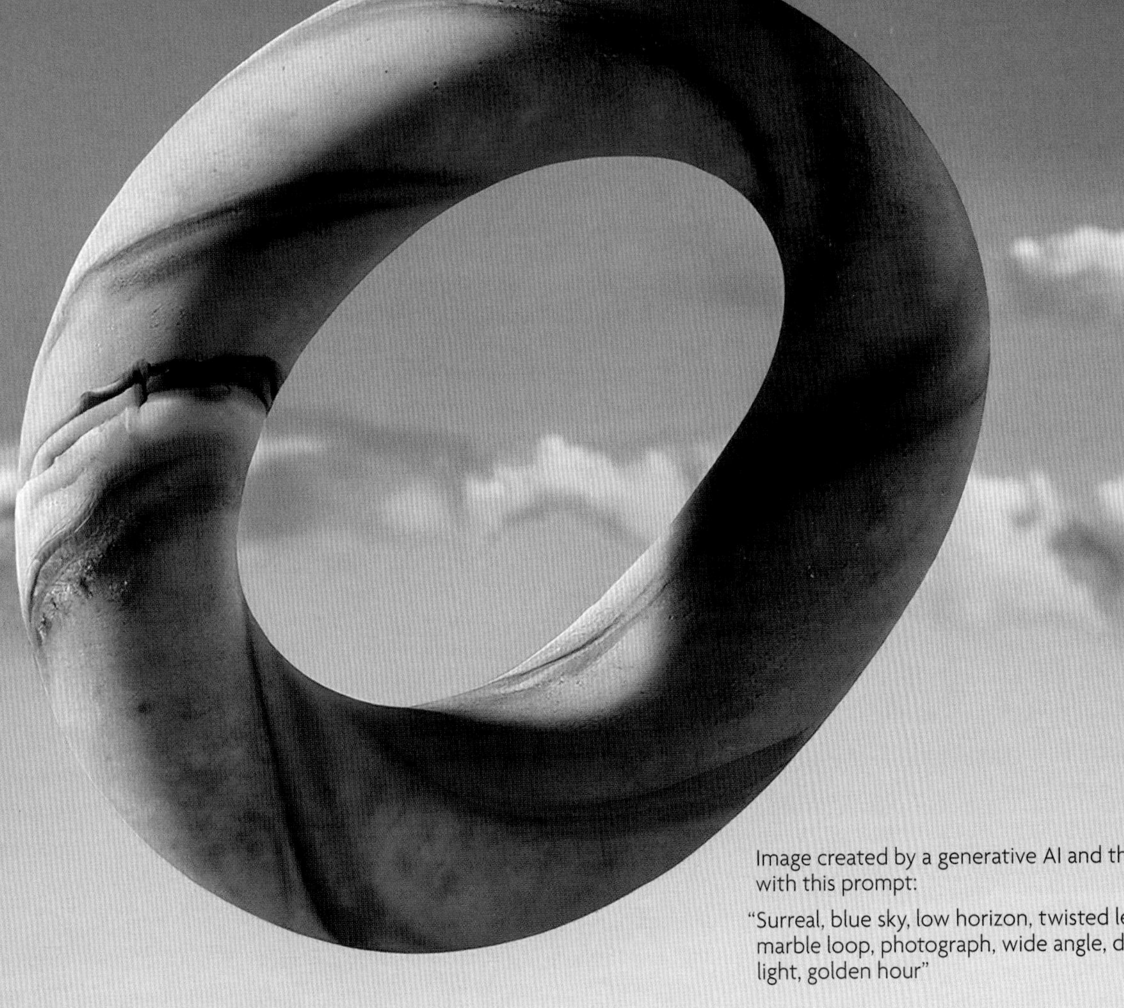

Image created by a generative AI and the author with this prompt:

"Surreal, blue sky, low horizon, twisted levitating marble loop, photograph, wide angle, dramatic light, golden hour"

Actions, Scripts, and Plugins!

Actions

The Photoshop user community is large and it includes some very capable and generous people who have created clever automations that extend Photoshop beyond what the team has created. These automations can take a couple of forms: actions, which most users can make, or scripts, which require real programming knowledge to create, but not to use.

To create or run an action, you'll need the Actions panel. There you'll see a default Set (folder), unsurprisingly called Default Actions. Sadly, they're not very useful. The most practical actions are those that reliably and quickly perform a series of tedious tasks so you don't have to.

Consider this scenario: You're faced with a few hundred images that all need the same multi-step treatment. Perhaps they all need to be cropped to a square format, have their vibrance increased by the same amount, and have a vignette added so they are darker at the edges. The first step may need intervention to choose which square area is retained.

The process of "recording" would go something like this:

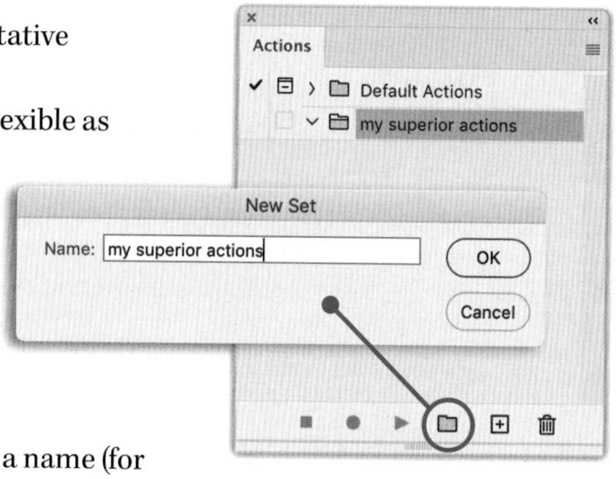

- Open an image that is a good representative of the rest.
- Set the ruler units to percent to be as flexible as possible, especially if images can be vertical or horizontal.
- In the Actions panel, create a New Set (see figure) to separate your useful actions from the less useful defaults.
- Create a new action by clicking the New Action button (⊞). Give the action a name (for the task above, I'd go with "vignetted squares").
- When you commit the name, your new action is being recorded. Almost everything you do will become part of the action, so try not to do anything extraneous. While the action is recording, the small circular icon at the bottom of the Actions panel will be red. Click the square stop button to its left to stop recording. Click the circle again to resume.
- Where user interaction or judgment is required, you can allow that. After you complete recording, click the square to the left of the step in the action that needs a human touch. When played back, the action will pause until the user commits the function. Cropping, transforms, and filter dialog boxes are good examples.

What's Recordable?

Actual edits. That means zooming (including the Fit on Screen command) is *not* recorded. Using the Actions panel menu, however, you can insert menu commands and more.

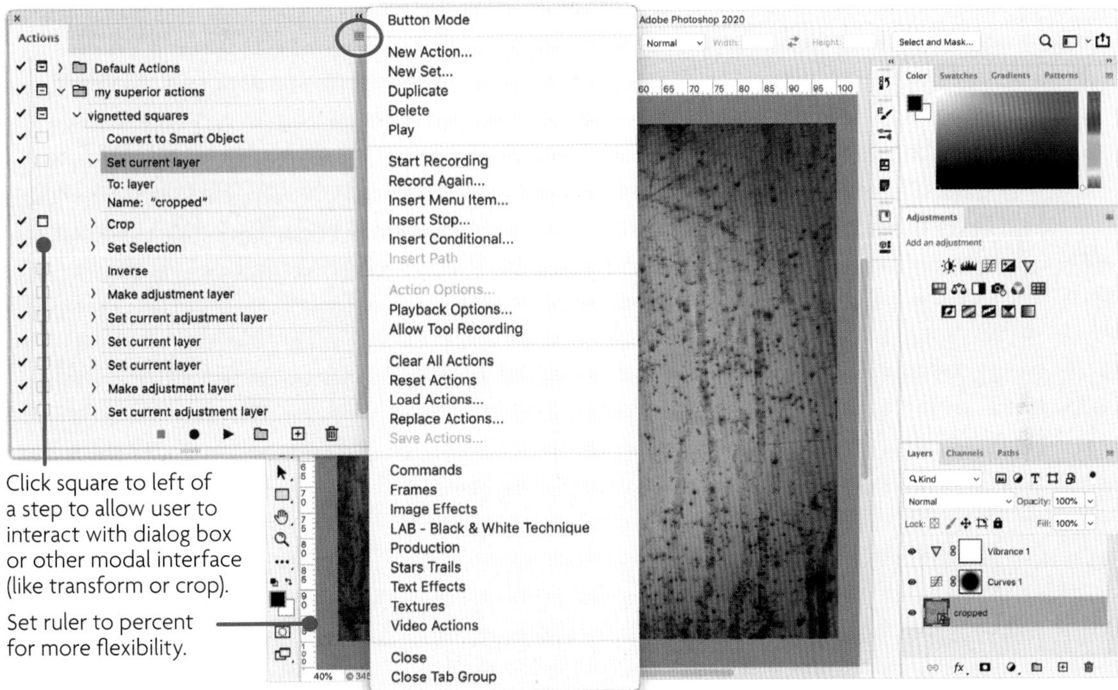

Click square to left of a step to allow user to interact with dialog box or other modal interface (like transform or crop).

Set ruler to percent for more flexibility.

There are many items in the Actions panel menu. Insert Menu Item… gives you a moment to choose one. When an action does resizing, for example, I often like it to end with the image at a viewable size, so I'll use Insert Menu Item… to insert View > Fit on Screen.

Insert Stop… inserts a dialog box of your own to notify the user that they're expected to do something in the next step, perhaps, and to give brief instruction. The Allow Continue checkbox will cause a Continue button to appear in the dialog box so the action can continue after the user sees the dialog box. Otherwise, the action stops at the next step and can be resumed only by pressing the play button.

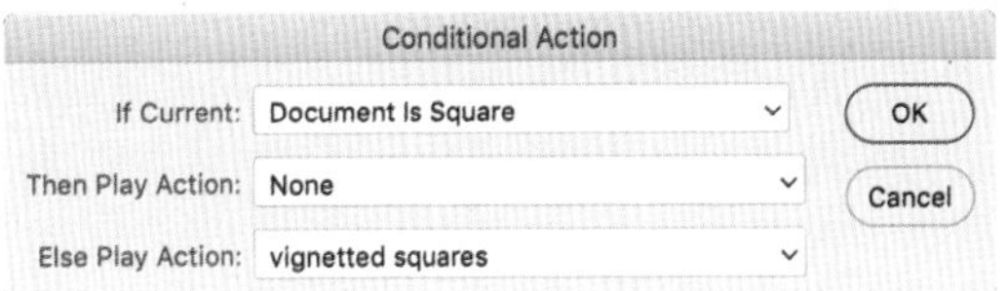

A classic benefit of programming is "if—then—else." That is, ***if*** a certain condition is true, ***then*** perform a certain action, ***else*** (otherwise) perform a different action. Insert Conditional… provides that programming nicety with its own list of conditions to evaluate. You choose a condition to evaluate, and then add other actions you've recorded that can be played if the condition is true or not. To this end, many users like me record many short actions that do only one or two things. We can then call upon them via a conditional in another action.

Playback Options… are useful too. When testing your action (yes, you very certainly should test your action with several images of varying size and shape), you can set playback to be slow enough to see each step. That way, if something goes wrong, you are likely to see at which step it happens. Return playback speed to Accelerated when it's ready for production.

The last items in the Actions panel menu are other sets of actions. Some of these may actually be useful, although most use older techniques that may no longer be considered best practices.

I used actions extensively in the preparation of the screenshots that appear in this book. They clean up extraneous layers that my screenshot software introduces, convert to the appropriate color space, set resolution, trim excess image from beyond the useful parts, and more.

It takes every user many attempts to become adept with actions. The mistakes you make will be learning opportunities, however, so try to relish them. If I'm any good at recording actions, it's because I've made literally thousands of mistakes along the way.

Scripts

These bits of code are "proper" programming with "if—thens" and much more. A number of scripts are to be found within Photoshop itself, or are used to move images from Adobe Bridge to Photoshop with some processing along the way.

Supplied Scripts

In Photoshop's File menu, you'll find scripts in the Scripts submenu, of course, and also in the Automate submenu. For example, the Photomerge script is what we use to create panoramic images. It automates the process by performing many separate Photoshop tasks in a way beyond what an action can achieve.

And that's the point: Scripts are telling the application to do things it already does, but in an order and with settings such that it feels like a wholly new feature.

Scripting Guide

Adobe provides scripting guides at:
https://helpx.adobe.com/photoshop/using/scripting.html
If you have experience with scripting languages, you might try your hand at crafting your own, and these resources will help.

Bridge Scripts

When we use Adobe Bridge to gather a number of images together, we can use scripts we find there to batch process them. From Photoshop, choose File > Browse in Bridge.... Once in Bridge, you can get to scripts by choosing Tools > Photoshop. Yes, they're mainly the same scripts we see in Photoshop. But it's often easier to select the images we want to process in Bridge rather than try to pull them into Photoshop or have dozens open at once. With Bridge, we can select hundreds of images and have Photoshop process them.

Plugins

Plugins are additional software that tie in to Photoshop in many different ways. They can act like filters, give us access to specialized file formats, provide new ways to perform adjustments, and more.

To the Marketplace!

There are hundreds of plugins available. Many of them are free, but not all. Peruse them all in Adobe's Plugin Marketplace. Along the top of the Creative Cloud app, find and click Stock & Marketplace. Then, of the items available, choose Plugins. On the left, first choose to show All Plugins, then check the boxes for the ones you want to see (for example, the checkbox for "Photoshop").

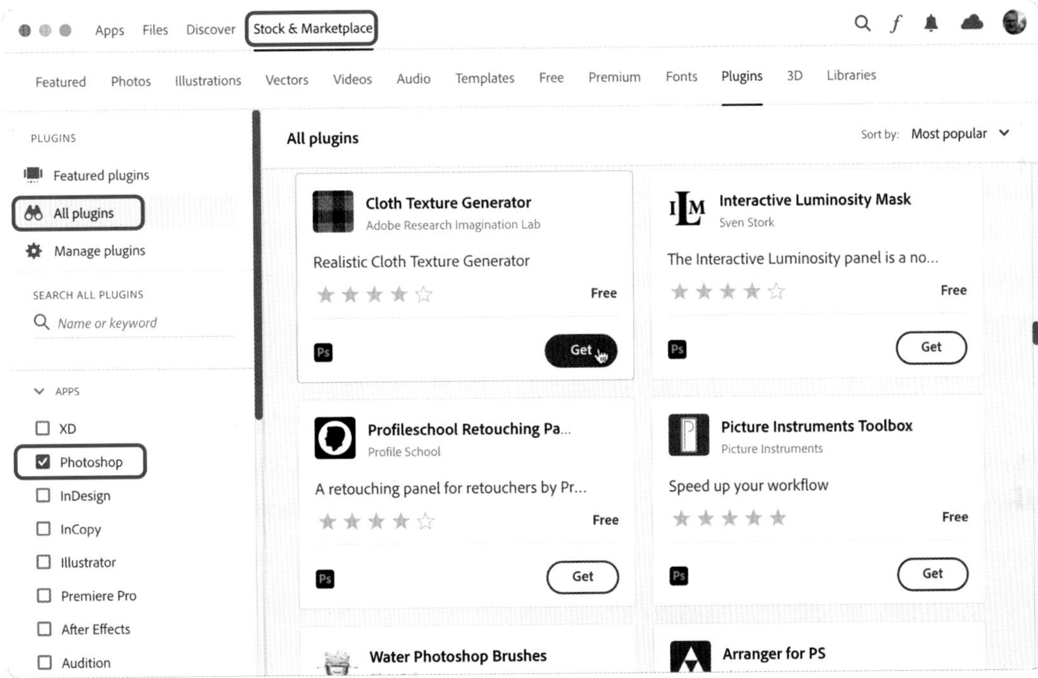

Be aware that you should pay attention to any alerts regarding where to find the plugin once it's installed. You can also click on the plugin in the Creative Cloud app to see its description. There, you can click on Where to Find It.

The Future

Like many, I've been having fun playing with *generative AI*: Images, like the one opening this chapter, generated by artificial intelligence algorithms based on text descriptions ("prompts"). During the time I've prepared this book, I've watched the rapid development of DALL-E 2 from OpenAI, Stable Diffusion by Stability AI, and Midjourney. Just days before I wrote these words, Adobe released its own, Firefly, parts of which will find their way into Photoshop and other applications.

We'll be able to use Firefly's generative power to extend images ("outpainting"), fix flaws within images ("inpainting"), and much more. Do check it out.

I will not write much more about it, as it will certainly be different and more powerful even by the time this book reaches your hands!

The future of image making and Photoshop? Will poets have an advantage creating images from verbal prompts?

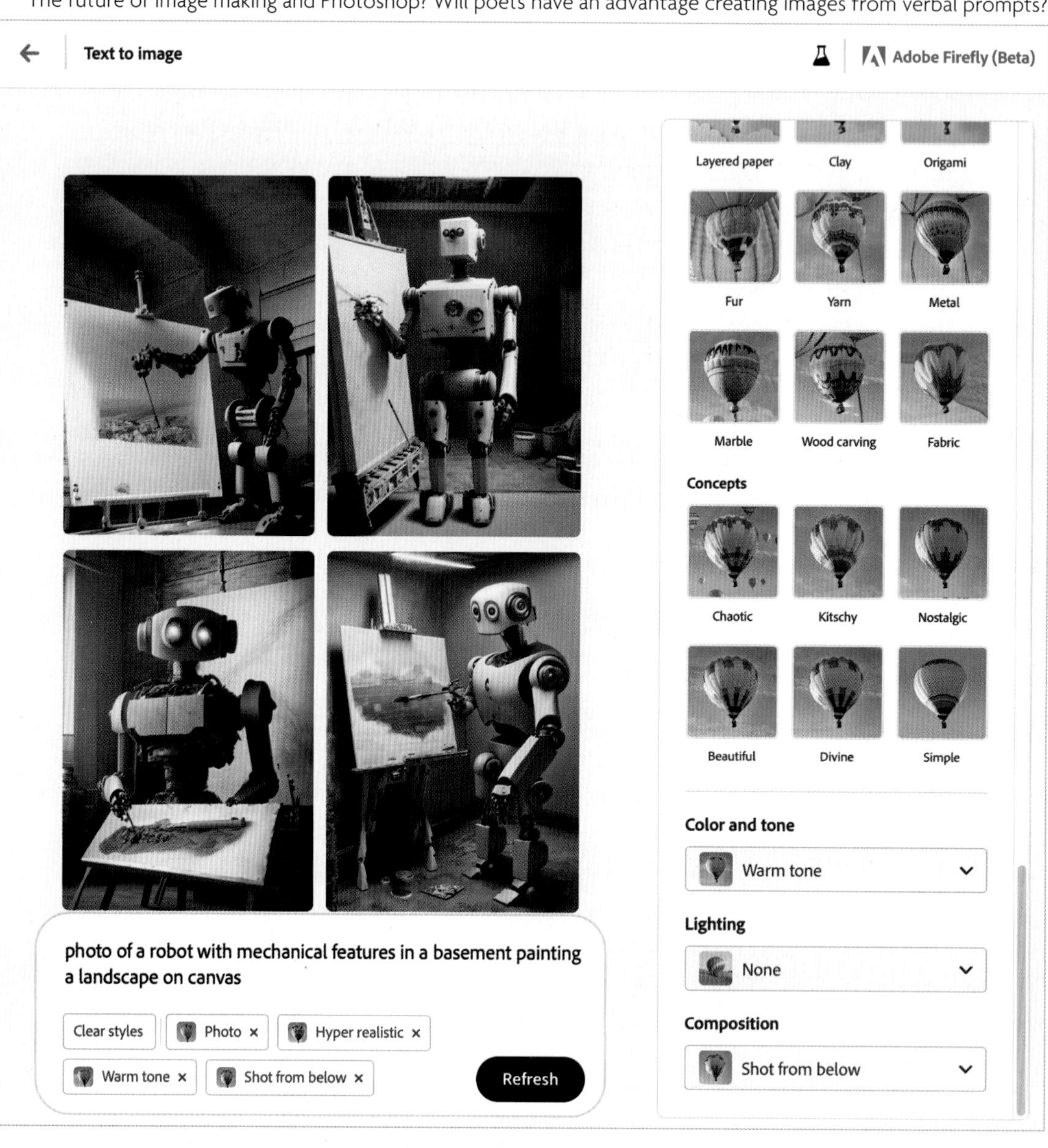

Explore

As actions, scripts, and plugins expand Photoshop's capabilities, I hope this book has expanded yours. Be sure to use the techniques within only as starting points for your own explorations—have fun!

Keyboard Shortcuts

The Adobe applications allow us to customize keyboard shortcuts. Use **Edit > Keyboard Shortcuts...**, create a new **Set** based on the defaults, and you can tweak or invent shortcuts for the commands you use most. What follows are many of Photoshop's default shortcuts. I'm using this convention, as I have throughout the book: **Mac version/Windows version**.

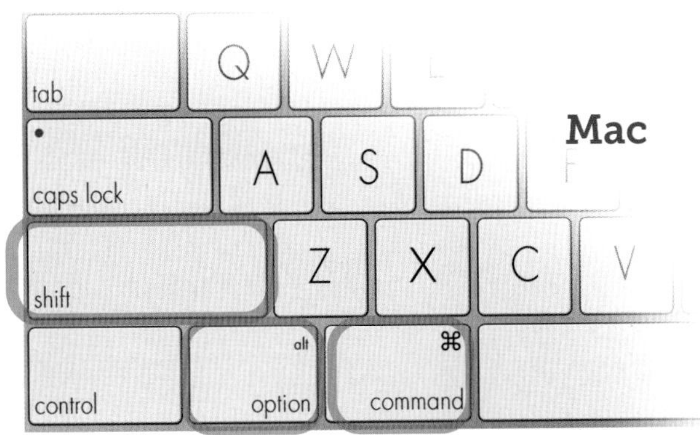

Mac

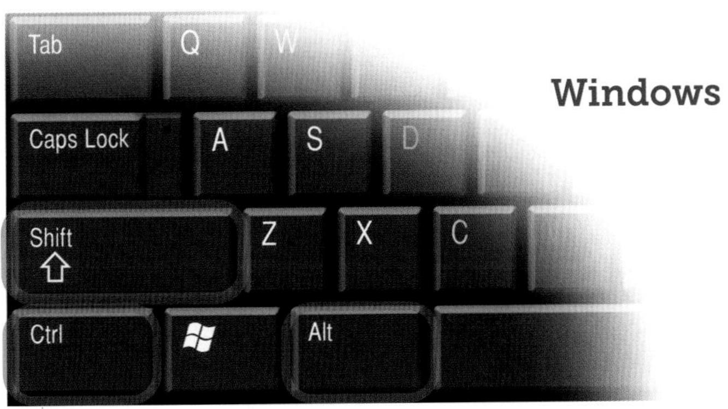

Windows

Preferences		
Preferences General...	**⌘-K**	**Ctrl-K**
Quit Photoshop	**⌘-Q**	**Ctrl-Q**
File Menu		
New...	**⌘-N**	**Ctrl-N**
Open...	**⌘-O**	**Ctrl-O**
Browse in Bridge...	**option-⌘-O**	**Alt-Ctrl-O**
Close	**⌘-W**	**Ctrl-W**
Close All	**option-⌘-W**	**Alt-Ctrl-W**
Close and Go to Bridge...	**shift-⌘-W**	**Shift-Ctrl-W**
Save	**⌘-S**	**Ctrl-S**
Save As...	**shift-⌘-S**	**Shift-Ctrl-S**
Revert	**F12**	
Export		
Export As...	**option-shift-⌘-W**	**Alt-Shift-Ctrl-W**
Save for Web (Legacy)...	**option-shift-⌘-S**	**Alt-Shift-Ctrl-S**
File Info...	**option-shift-⌘-I**	**Alt-Shift-Ctrl-I**
Print...	**⌘-P**	**Ctrl-P**
Print One Copy	**option-shift-⌘-P**	**Alt-Shift-Ctrl-P**
Edit Menu		
Undo	**⌘-Z**	**Ctrl-Z**
Redo	**shift-⌘-Z**	**Shift-Ctrl-Z**
Toggle Last State	**option-⌘-Z**	**Alt-Ctrl-Z**
Fade...	**shift-⌘-F**	**Shift-Ctrl-F**
Cut	**⌘-X**	**Ctrl-X**
Copy	**⌘-C**	**Ctrl-C**
Copy Merged	**shift-⌘-C**	**Shift-Ctrl-C**
Paste	**⌘-V**	**Ctrl-V**

Paste in Place	**shift-⌘-V**	**Shift-Ctrl-V**
Paste Into	**option-shift-⌘-V**	**Alt-Shift-Ctrl-V**
Search	**⌘-F**	**Ctrl-F**
Fill...	**Shift+F5**	
Content-Aware Scale	**option-shift-⌘-C**	**Alt-Shift-Ctrl-C**
Free Transform	**⌘-T**	**Ctrl-T**
Transform Again	**shift-⌘-T**	**Shift-Ctrl-T**
Color Settings...	**shift-⌘-K**	**Shift-Ctrl-K**
Keyboard Shortcuts...	**option-shift-⌘-K**	**Alt-Shift-Ctrl-K**
Menus...	**option-shift-⌘-M**	**Alt-Shift-Ctrl-M**

Image Menu

Levels...	**⌘-L**	**Ctrl-L**
Curves...	**⌘-M**	**Ctrl-M**
Hue/Saturation...	**⌘-U**	**Ctrl-U**
Color Balance...	**⌘-B**	**Ctrl-B**
Black & White...	**option-shift-⌘-B**	**Alt-Shift-Ctrl-B**
Invert	**⌘-I**	**Ctrl-I**
Desaturate	**shift-⌘-U**	**Shift-Ctrl-U**
Auto Tone	**shift-⌘-L**	**Shift-Ctrl-L**
Auto Contrast	**option-shift-⌘-L**	**Alt-Shift-Ctrl-L**
Auto Color	**shift-⌘-B**	**Shift-Ctrl-B**
Image Size...	**option-⌘-I**	**Alt-Ctrl-I**
Canvas Size...	**option-⌘-C**	**Alt-Ctrl-C**

Layer Menu

New Layer...	**shift-⌘-N**	**Shift-Ctrl-N**
Layer via Copy	**⌘-J**	**Ctrl-J**
Layer via Cut	**shift-⌘-J**	**Shift-Ctrl-J**
Quick Export as PNG	**shift-⌘-'**	**Shift-Ctrl-'**
Export As...	**option-shift-⌘-'**	**Alt-Shift-Ctrl-'**

Create/Release Clipping Mask	**option-⌘-G**	**Alt-Ctrl-G**
Group Layers	**⌘-G**	**Ctrl-G**
Ungroup Layers	**shift-⌘-G**	**Shift-Ctrl-G**
Hide Layers	**⌘-,**	**Ctrl-,**
Bring to Front	**shift-⌘-]**	**Shift-Ctrl-]**
Bring Forward	**⌘-]**	**Ctrl-]**
Send Backward	**⌘-[**	**Ctrl-[**
Send to Back	**shift-⌘-[**	**Shift-Ctrl-[**
Lock Layers...	**⌘-/**	**Ctrl-/**
Merge Layers	**⌘-E**	**Ctrl-E**
Merge Visible	**shift-⌘-E**	**Shift-Ctrl-E**

Select Menu

All	**⌘-A**	**Ctrl-A**
Deselect	**⌘-D**	**Ctrl-D**
Reselect	**shift-⌘-D**	**Shift-Ctrl-D**
Inverse	**shift-⌘-I**	**Shift-Ctrl-I**
All Layers	**option-⌘-A**	**Alt-Ctrl-A**
Find Layers	**option-shift-⌘-F**	**Alt-Shift-Ctrl-F**
Select and Mask...	**option-⌘-R**	**Alt-Ctrl-R**
Feather...	**Shift+F6**	

Filter Menu

Last Filter	**control-⌘-F**	**Ctrl-F**
Adaptive Wide Angle...	**option-shift-⌘-A**	**Alt-Shift-Ctrl-A**
Camera Raw Filter...	**shift-⌘-A**	**Shift-Ctrl-A**
Lens Correction...	**shift-⌘-R**	**Shift-Ctrl-R**
Liquify...	**shift-⌘-X**	**Shift-Ctrl-X**
Vanishing Point...	**option-⌘-V**	**Alt-Ctrl-V**

View Menu		
Proof Colors	**⌘-Y**	**Ctrl-Y**
Gamut Warning	**shift-⌘-Y**	**Shift-Ctrl-Y**
Zoom In	**⌘-+**	**Ctrl-+**
Zoom Out	**⌘--**	**Ctrl--**
Fit on Screen	**⌘-0**	**Ctrl-0**
100%	**⌘-1**	**Ctrl-1**
Show/Hide Extras	**⌘-H**	**Ctrl-H**
Show/Hide Target Path	**shift-⌘-H**	**Shift-Ctrl-H**
Show/Hide Grid	**⌘-'**	**Ctrl-'**
Show/Hide Guides	**⌘-;**	**Ctrl-;**
Show/Hide Rulers	**⌘-R**	**Ctrl-R**
Snap	**shift-⌘-;**	**Shift-Ctrl-;**
Lock Guides	**option-⌘-;**	**Alt-Ctrl-;**

Window Menu		
Minimize	**control-⌘-M**	**Ctrl-M**
Actions	**option-F9**	**Alt-F9**
Brush Settings	**F5**	
Color	**F6**	
Info	**F8**	
Layers	**F7**	
Photoshop Help...	**shift-⌘-/**	**Shift-Ctrl-/**

Layers Panel Menu		
New Layer...	**shift-⌘-N**	**Shift-Ctrl-N**
Quick Export as PNG	**shift-⌘-'**	**Shift-Ctrl-'**
Export As...	**option-shift-⌘-'**	**Alt-Shift-Ctrl-'**
Lock Layers...	**⌘-/**	**Ctrl-/**
Create/Release Clipping Mask	**option-⌘-G**	**Alt-Ctrl-G**
Merge Layers	**⌘-E**	**Ctrl-E**
Merge Visible	**shift-⌘-E**	**Shift-Ctrl-E**

Tools

Hold **Shift** to cycle through tools with the same shortcut.

Move Tool	**V**
Artboard Tool	**V**
Rectangular Marquee Tool	**M**
Elliptical Marquee Tool	**M**
Lasso Tool	**L**
Polygonal Lasso Tool	**L**
Magnetic Lasso Tool	**L**
Quick Selection Tool	**W**
Magic Wand Tool	**W**
Crop Tool	**C**
Perspective Crop Tool	**C**
Slice Tool	**C**
Slice Select Tool	**C**
Frame Tool	**K**
Eyedropper Tool	**I**
Color Sampler Tool	**I**
Ruler Tool	**I**
Note Tool	**I**
Count Tool	**I**
Spot Healing Brush Tool	**J**
Healing Brush Tool	**J**
Patch Tool	**J**
Content-Aware Move Tool	**J**
Red Eye Tool	**J**
Brush Tool	**B**
Pencil Tool	**B**
Color Replacement Tool	**B**
Mixer Brush Tool	**B**
Clone Stamp Tool	**S**
Pattern Stamp Tool	**S**
History Brush Tool	**Y**
Art History Brush Tool	**Y**
Eraser Tool	**E**
Background Eraser Tool	**E**
Magic Eraser Tool	**E**
Gradient Tool	**G**
Paint Bucket Tool	**G**
Dodge Tool	**O**
Burn Tool	**O**
Sponge Tool	**O**
Pen Tool	**P**
Freeform Pen Tool	**P**
Horizontal Type Tool	**T**
Vertical Type Tool	**T**
Vertical Type Mask Tool	**T**
Horizontal Type Mask Tool	**T**
Path Selection Tool	**A**
Direct Selection Tool	**A**
Rectangle Tool	**U**
Rounded Rectangle Tool	**U**
Ellipse Tool	**U**
Polygon Tool	**U**
Line Tool	**U**
Custom Shape Tool	**U**
Hand Tool	**H**
Rotate View Tool	**R**
Zoom Tool	**Z**
Default Colors	**D**
Switch Colors	**X**
Toggle Quick Mask Mode	**Q**
Toggle Screen Modes	**F**
Toggle Preserve Transparency	**/**
Decrease Brush Size	**[**
Increase Brush Size	**]**
Decrease Brush Hardness	**{**
Increase Brush Hardness	**}**
Previous Brush	**,**
Next Brush	**.**
First Brush	**<**

Select and Mask Tools

Quick Selection Tool	**W**
Refine Edge Brush Tool	**R**
Brush Tool	**B**
Lasso Tool	**L**
Polygonal Lasso Tool	**L**
Hand Tool	**H**
Zoom Tool	**Z**
Cycle Tool Mode	**E**
Show Edge	**J**
Show Original	**P**
Cycle View Mode	**F**
Disable Views	**X**
Marching Ants	**M**
Overlay	**V**
On Black	**A**
On White	**T**
Black & White	**K**
On Layers	**Y**
Onion Skin	**O**

Content-Aware Fill Tools

Sampling Brush Tool	**B**
Lasso Tool	**L**
Polygonal Lasso Tool	**L**
Hand Tool	**H**
Zoom Tool	**Z**
Cycle Tool Mode	**E**

Index

C

J

K

L

T

U

V

W

Z